ANCIENT STATES AND EMPIRES.

BY THE SAME AUTHOR.

THE OLD ROMAN WORLD:

THE GRANDEUR AND FAILURE OF ITS CIVILIZATION.

1 *vol. crown* 8*vo, with map, uniform with* "*Ancient States and Empires.*"

PRICE $3.00.

ANCIENT STATES AND EMPIRES

FOR

COLLEGES AND SCHOOLS

BY

JOHN LORD LL.D.

AUTHOR OF THE "OLD ROMAN WORLD"

"MODERN HISTORY" &c.

NEW YORK

CHARLES SCRIBNER & COMPANY

1869

ALVORD, PRINTER.

PREFACE.

This work is designed chiefly for educational purposes, since there is still felt the need of some book, which, within moderate limits, shall give a connected history of the ancient world.

The author lays no claim to original investigation in so broad a field. He simply has aimed to present the salient points—the most important events and characters of four thousand years, in a connected narrative, without theories or comments, and without encumbering the book with details of comparatively little interest. Most of the ancient histories for schools, have omitted to notice those great movements to which the Scriptures refer; but these are here briefly presented, since their connection with the Oriental world is intimate and impressive, and ought not to be omitted, even on secular grounds. What is history without a Divine Providence?

In the preparation of this work, the author has been contented with the last standard authorities, which he has merely simplified, abridged, and condensed, being most indebted to Rawlinson, Grote, Thirlwall, Niebuhr, Mommsen, and Merivale,—following out the general plan of Philip Smith, whose admirable digest, in three large octavos, is too extensive for schools.

Although the author has felt warranted in making a free use of his materials, it will be seen that the style, arrangement, and reflections are his own. If the book prove useful, his object will be attained.

STAMFORD *October*, 1869.

CONTENTS.

BOOK I.

THE ANCIENT ORIENTAL NATIONS.

CHAPTER I.

THE ANTEDILUVIAN WORLD.

PAGE

Creation — The Garden of Eden — Fall of Adam — Cain and Abel — The Deluge — Its Traditions, ... 13

CHAPTER II.

POST-DILUVIAN HISTORY TO THE CALL OF ABRAHAM.

Noah and his Sons — The Tower of Babel — Dispersion of the Descendants of Noah — Patriarchal Constitution, ... 19

CHAPTER III.

THE HEBREW RACE TO THE FALL OF JOSEPH.

Abraham — Lot — Covenant with Abraham — Sodom — Isaac — Jacob — Esau — Laban — Joseph, ... 24

CHAPTER IV.

EGYPT AND THE PHARAOHS.

Geography of Ancient Egypt — Wonders — Dynasties — Ramesis II. — Thebes — Religion and Manners of the Old Egyptians, ... 34

CHAPTER V.

THE JEWS TO THE CONQUEST OF CANAAN.

Elevation of Joseph — The Famine — Settlement of the Israelites in Egypt — Moses — The Exodus — The Jewish Code — The Wilderness, ... 43

CHAPTER VI.

THE CONQUEST OF CANAAN TO THE ESTABLISHMENT OF THE KINGDOM OF DAVID.

PAGE

Joshua — The Canaanites — The Judges — Samuel — The Philistines — Saul, ... 56

CHAPTER VII.

THE JEWISH MONARCHY.

David — Solomon — Jerusalem — The Rebellion of the Ten Tribes — The Princes of the House of David — The Princes who reigned at Samaria — The Jewish Captivity, ... 62

CHAPTER VIII.

THE OLD CHALDÆAN AND ASSYRIAN MONARCHIES.

Nineveh -- Assyrian Kings — The Chaldæans — Babylon, ... 80

CHAPTER IX.

THE EMPIRE OF THE MEDES AND PERSIANS.

Media — Median Princes — Lydian Monarchs — The Persians — Zoroaster — Cyrus — Cambyses — Xerxes — Fall of the Monarchy, .. 88

CHAPTER X.

ASIA MINOR AND PHŒNICIA.

The various nations of Asia Minor — Lydians — Crœsus — Phœnicians — Voyages and Colonies — Carthage, ... 100

CHAPTER XI.

THE RULE OF THE HIGH PRIESTS, AND OF THE ASMONEAN AND IDUMEAN KINGS.

Return of the Jews — Esther — Rebuilding of Jerusalem — Alexandria — The High Priests — The Asmonean Princes — Herod and the Idumean Kings, ... 108

CHAPTER XII.

THE ROMAN GOVERNMENT.

Pontius Pilate — Herod Antipas — Agrippa — The Pharisees — The Saducees — The Essenes — Revolt of Jerusalem — Siege and Fall of Jerusalem, ... 128

BOOK II.

THE GRECIAN STATES.

CHAPTER XIII.

THE GEOGRAPHY OF ANCIENT GREECE AND ITS EARLY INHABITANTS.

PAGE
Mountains —Rivers —National Productions — States — Cities — Early Inhabitants, ... 143

CHAPTER XIV.

THE LEGENDS OF ANCIENT GREECE.

The Heroic Ages — Ancient Deities — Legends of Heroes — The Danaides — Hercules — The Argonauts — Pelope — Theseus — Cadmus — Œdipus — Priam — Helen — The Heraclidæ — Early Kings, ... 155

CHAPTER XV.

STATES AND COLONIES TO THE PERSIAN WARS.

Lycurgus and Sparta — The Helots — Constitution of Sparta — Messenia — Corinth — Megara — Athens — Solon — His Legislation — Pisistratus — Bœotia — Phocis — Epirus — Ionian Cities, ... 177

CHAPTER XVI.

GRECIAN CIVILIZATION BEFORE THE PERSIAN WARS.

Legislature — Amphyctionic Council — Delphic Oracle — Olympian Games — Pythian Games — Nemean and Isthmian Games — Temples — Political Rights — Commerce — Art, ... 196

CHAPTER XVII.

THE PERSIAN WAR.

Revolt of Ionian Cities — Their Conquest by the Persians — Darius — Invasion of Greece — Miltiades — Themistocles — Aristides — Marathon —Xerxes — His enormous Army — Thermopylæ —Leonidas — Salamis — Effects of the Battle — Mardonius — Battle of Platæa — Battle of Mycali — Rivalry between Athens and Sparta, 205

CHAPTER XVIII.

THE AGE OF PERICLES.

PAGE

Rivalry between Athens and Sparta — Confederacy of Delos — Sparta — Rebellion of Helots — Cimon — Pericles — The Piræus — The Long Walls of Athens — Aggrandizement of Athens — Democratic Power — Improvements of Athens — Literature and Art, .. 233

CHAPTER XIX.

THE PELOPONNESIAN WAR.

The Causes of the War — Influence of Pericles — Warlike Preparations — Invasion of Attica — The various Campaigns — Plague of Athens — Athens solicits Aid from Persia — Revolt of Mitylene — Nicias — Alcibiades — Cleon — Attack of Megara — Battle of Delium — Brasidas — Loss of Amphipolis — Peace of Nicias — Battle of Mantinæa — Invasion of Sicily — Syracuse — Gels — Mismanagement of Nicias — Treason of Alcibiades — Lysander — Capture of the Athenian Fleet — Annihilation of Athenian Power — Triumph of Sparta — Consequences of the War, ... 250

CHAPTER XX.

MARCH OF CYRUS AND RETREAT OF THE TEN THOUSAND.

Cyrus — Xenophon — Cyrus in Asia — Battle of Cunaxa — Retreat of the Greeks — Their Hardships and Success — Moral effect of the Retreat, ... 294

CHAPTER XXI.

THE LACEDEMONIAN EMPIRE.

Great Power of Sparta — Jealousy of Greece — Tyranny of Sparta — Agesilaus — Alienation of Allies — Conspiracies against Sparta — Revolt of Thebes — Battle of Coroneia — Decline of Sparta, ... 304

CHAPTER XXII.

THE REPUBLIC OF THEBES.

Thebes — Revolt from Sparta — Alliance with Athens — Epaminondas — Pelopidas — Attack of Thebes — Humiliation of Sparta — The Invasion by Epaminondas — Dismemberment of Sparta — Theban Supremacy — Fate of Orchomenes — Battle of Mantinæa — Philip of Macedon, ... 315

CHAPTER XXIII.

DIONYSIUS OF SICILY.

PAGE

Carthagenian War — Dionysius — His great Successes — Imalcar — Invasion of Italy — Fate of Croton — Dion — Dionysius II.— Plato in Sicily — Dion Master of Syracuse — Timoleon — His Noble Character,........ 333

CHAPTER XXIV.

PHILIP OF MACEDON.

Philip and Thebes — His Duplicity and Ambition — Social War — Demosthenes — Phocion — Conquest of Thessaly — Encroachments on Grecian Liberties — Siege of Perinthus — Alliance of Thebes and Athens — Fall of Thebes — Humiliation of Athens,........ 356

CHAPTER XXV.

ALEXANDER THE GREAT.

The Persian Empire — Alexander — Conquest of Greece — Alexander in Asia — Battle of the Granicus — Conquest of Asia Minor — Battle of Issus — Siege of Tyre — Founding of Alexandria — Darius — Battle of Arbela — Conquest of Persia — Death of Clitus — Invasion of India — Hephæstion and his funeral — Death of Alexander — Effects of his Conquests,........ 373

BOOK III.

THE ROMAN EMPIRE.

CHAPTER XXVI.

THE INFANCY OF ROME.

Foundation of Rome — Romulus — Numa — Successive Kings — Early Struggles of Plebeians — The Servian Constitution — Expulsion of the Kings — Early Civilization of Rome,........ 398

CHAPTER XXVII.

THE ROMAN REPUBLIC TO THE INVASION OF THE GAULS.

Legends of Early Rome — The Heroic Age — Conflict between Patricians and Plebeians — Change in the Constitution — Republican Laws — Cincinnatus — The Decemvirs — Siege of Veii — The Gauls — Sack of Rome,........ 410

CHAPTER XXVIII.

THE CONQUEST OF ITALY.

PAGE

The Samnite War — Subjection of Latium — Tarenteum — Pyrrhus —Subjection of Italy, ... 422

CHAPTER XXIX.

THE FIRST PUNIC WAR.

Causes of the War — Sicily — Hiero — Carthage — Creation of a Roman Fleet — Battle of Mylæ — Regulus — Hamilcar — Hasdrubal — Acquisition of Sicily, ... 429

CHAPTER XXX.

THE SECOND PUNIC WAR.

Hannibal — Fall of Saguntum — Invasion of Italy — Battle of the Thrasimene Lake — Scipio — Fabius — Battle of Cannæ — Revolt of Allies — Wisdom and Talent of Hannibal — Victories of Scipio — Siege of Syracuse — Scipio in Africa — Battle of Zama, ... 439

CHAPTER XXXI.

MACEDONIAN AND ASIATIC WARS.

Macedonia — Philip — Achæan League — Independence of Greece — Antiochus — Protectorate of Rome in Asia — Battle of Pydna — Æmilius Paulus, ... 455

CHAPTER XXXII.

THE THIRD PUNIC WAR.

Massinassa — War against Carthage — Scipio — Siege of Carthage — Fall of Carthage — Effect of The Punic Wars — Great accession of Roman Territories, ... 464

CHAPTER XXXIII.

ROMAN CONQUESTS TO THE TIME OF THE GRACCHI.

The Spanish Peninsula — War with the Spaniards — Scipio — War with Macedonia — War in Achaia — War in Asia, ... 473

CHAPTER XXXIV.

ROMAN CIVILIZATION AT THE CLOSE OF THE THIRD PUNIC WAR.

The Aristocracy — The Provincial Governors — Festivals and Games — Cato — Change in the Constitution — Agriculture — Commerce — Slavery — Small Farmers — Great Fortunes — Literature — Art, .. 478

CHAPTER XXXV.

PAGE

THE REFORM MOVEMENT OF THE GRACCHI.

Evils of the Government — Tiberius Gracchus — His Reforms, and Death — Caius Gracchus — Attack on the Aristocracy — Success of Gracchus and Death, ... 488

CHAPTER XXXVI.

THE WAR WITH JUGURTHA AND THE CIMBRI.

The Numidian War — Jugurtha — Mileteus — Marius — The Cimbri — Invasion of Italy — The Victories of Marius, ... 499

CHAPTER XXXVII.

THE SOCIAL WAR.

The Servile Classes — Insurrection — Sulla — His Legislation, ... 507

CHAPTER XXXVIII.

THE MITHRIDATIC AND CIVIL WARS. MARIUS AND SULLA.

Mithridates — Pontus — Sulla; Battle of — Chœronica — Rising of Asia — Cinna — Civil War — Dictatorship of Sulla — Abdication of Sulla, ... 512

CHAPTER XXXIX.

ROME TO THE CIVIL WARS OF POMPEY AND CÆSAR.

Reaction in favor of the Aristocracy — Pompey — The Servile War — War with the Pirates — Second Mithridatic War — Lucullus — Pompey in the East — Cicero — Catiline — Cæsar, ... 520

CHAPTER XL.

THE CIVIL WARS BETWEEN POMPEY AND CÆSAR.

Rivalship between Cæsar and Pompey — Military Preparations — War — Defeat of Pompey — Flight and Death of Pompey — Consequences of the Battle of Pharsalia — Cæsar in the East and West — His Dictatorship — Triumphs — Death — Character, ... 534

CHAPTER XLI.

THE CIVIL WARS FOLLOWING THE DEATH OF CÆSAR.

Antonius — Octavius — Lepidus — Brutus — Cassius — Cicero — The Triumvirate — Civil War — Battle of Philippi — Battle of Actium — Supremacy of Octavius, ... 546

CHAPTER XLII.

THE ROMAN EMPIRE ON THE ACCESSION OF AUGUSTUS.

PAGE

Extent the of Empire — Cities — Rome — Government — Army — Commerce — Literature — Art, ... 558

CHAPTER XLIII.

THE SIX CÆSARS OF THE JULIAN LINE.

Augustus — Ministers — Campaign — Tiberius—Wars with the Germans — Germanicus — Caligula — Claudius — The Conquest of Britain — Messalina — Agrippina — Nero, ... 567

CHAPTER XLIV.

THE CLIMAX OF THE EMPIRE.

Galba — Vespasian — Titus — Domitian — Nerva — Trajan — Hadrian — Antonius Pius — Marcus Aurelius — Commodus, ... 595

CHAPTER XLV.

THE DECLINE OF THE EMPIRE.

Moral Corruption — Pertinax — Septimius Severus — Caracalla — Elagabulus — Alexander Severus — Maximin — Decius — Gallienus — Invasion of the Barbarians — Warlike Emperors — Arrest of Ruin — Diocletian — Constantine — Division of the Empire, ... 605

CHAPTER XLVI.

THE FALL OF THE EMPIRE.

Successors of Constantine — Theodosius — Irruption of Barbarians — The Goths — Alaric — Capture of Rome — The Vandals—Second Siege and Sack of Rome — The Huns — Fall of the Western Empire — Conclusion, ... 628

BOOK I.

ANCIENT ORIENTAL NATIONS.

CHAPTER I.

THE ANTEDILUVIAN WORLD.

The history of this world begins, according to the chronology of Archbishop Ussher, which is generally received as convenient rather than probable, in the year 4004 before Christ. In six days God created light and darkness, day and night, the firmament and the continents in the midst of the waters, fruits, grain, and herbs, moon and stars, fowl and fish, living creatures upon the face of the earth, and finally man, with dominion "over the fish of the sea, and the fowls of the air, and cattle, and all the earth, and every creeping thing that creepeth upon the earth." He created man in his own image, and blessed him with universal dominion. He formed him from the dust of the ground, and breathed into his nostrils the breath of life. On the seventh day, God rested from this vast work of creation, and blessed the seventh day and sanctified it, as we suppose, for a day of solemn observance for all generations.

The Creation.

He there planted a garden eastward in Eden, with every tree pleasant to the sight and good for food, and there placed man to dress and keep it. The original occupation of man, and his destined happiness, were thus centered in agricultural labor.

The garden of Eden.

But man was alone; so God caused a deep sleep to fall upon him, and took one of his ribs and made a woman. And Adam said, "this woman," which the Lord had brought unto him, "is bone of my bone, and flesh of my flesh; therefore shall a man leave his father and mother, and shall cleave unto his wife: and they shall be one flesh." Thus marriage was instituted. We observe three divine institutions while man yet remained in a state of innocence and bliss—the Sabbath; agricultural employment; and marriage.

Adam and Eve.

Adam and his wife lived, we know not how long, in the garden of Eden, with perfect innocence, bliss, and dominion. They did not even know what sin was. There were no other conditions imposed upon them than they were not to eat of the fruit of the tree of knowledge of good and evil, which was in the midst of the garden—a pre-eminently goodly tree, "pleasant to the eyes, and one to be desired."

Primeval Paradise.

Where was this garden—this paradise—located? This is a mooted question—difficult to be answered. It lay, thus far we know, at the head waters of four rivers, two of which were the Euphrates and the Tigris. We infer thence, that it was situated among the mountains of Armenia, south of the Caucasus, subsequently the cradle of the noblest races of men,—a temperate region, in the latitude of Greece and Italy.

Situation of Eden.

We suppose that the garden was beautiful and fruitful, beyond all subsequent experience—watered by mists from the earth, and not by rains from the clouds, ever fresh and green, while its two noble occupants lived upon its produce, directly communing with God, in whose image they were made, moral and spiritual—free from all sin and misery, and, as we may conjecture, conversant with truth in its loftiest forms.

Glory of Eden.

But sin entered into the beautiful world that was made, and death by sin. This is the first recorded fact in human history, next to primeval innocence and happiness.

The progenitors of the race were tempted, and did not resist the temptation. The form of it may have been allegorical and symbolic; but, as recorded by Moses, was yet a stupendous reality, especially in view of its consequences.

The temptation.

The tempter was the devil—the antagonist of God—the evil power of the world—the principle of evil—a Satanic agency which Scripture, and all nations, in some form, have recognized. When rebellion against God began, we do not know; but it certainly existed when Adam was placed in Eden.

The Devil.

The form which Satanic power assumed was a serpent—then the most subtle of the beasts of the field, and we may reasonably suppose, not merely subtle, but attractive, graceful, beautiful, bewitching.

His assumption of the form of a serpent.

The first to feel its evil fascination was the woman, and she was induced to disobey what she knew to be a direct command, by the desire of knowledge as well as enjoyment of the appetite. She put trust in the serpent. She believed a lie. She was beguiled.

The disobedience of Eve.

The man was not directly beguiled by the serpent. Why the serpent assailed woman rather than man, the Scriptures do not say. The man yielded to his wife. "She gave him the fruit, and he did eat."

The Fall of Adam.

Immediately a great change came over both. Their eyes were opened. They felt shame and remorse, for they had sinned. They hid themselves from the presence of the Lord, and were afraid.

The effect.

God pronounced the penalty—unto the woman, the pains and sorrows attending childbirth, and subserviency to her husband; unto the man labor, toil, sorrow—the curse of the ground which he was to till—thorns and thistles—no rest, and food obtained only by the sweat of the brow; and all these pains and labors were inflicted upon both until they should return to the dust from whence they were taken—an eternal decree, never abrogated, to last as long as man should till the earth, or woman bring forth children.

The penalty.

Thus came sin into the world, through the temptations of Satan and the weakness of man, with the penalty of labor, pain, sorrow, and death.

Introduction of sin.

Man was expelled from Paradise, and precluded from re-entering it by the flaming sword of cherubim, until the locality of Eden, by thorns and briars, and the deluge, was obliterated forever. And man and woman were sent out into the world to reap the fruit of their folly and sin, and to gain their subsistence in severe toil, and amid the accumulated evils which sin introduced.

Expulsion from paradise.

The only mitigation of the sentence was the eternal enmity between the seed of the woman and the seed of the Serpent, in which the final victory should be given to the former. The rite of sacrifice was introduced as a type of the satisfaction for sin by the death of a substitute for the sinner; and thus a hope of final forgiveness held out for sin. Meanwhile the miseries of life were alleviated by the fruits of labor, by industry.

The mitigation of the punishment.

Industry, then, became, on the expulsion from Eden, one of the final laws of human happiness on earth, while the sacrifice held out hopes of eternal life by the substitution which the sacrifice typified—the Saviour who was in due time to appear.

Industry—one of the fundamental conditions of life.

With the expulsion from Eden came the sad conflicts of the race—conflicts with external wickedness—conflicts with the earth—conflicts with evil passions in a man's own soul.

The first conflict was between Cain, the husbandman, and Abel, the shepherd; the representatives of two great divisions of the human family in the early ages. Cain killed Abel because the offering of the latter was preferred to that of the former. The virtue of Abel was faith: the sin of Cain was jealousy, pride, resentment, and despair. The punishment of Cain was expulsion from his father's house, the further curse of the land for *him*, and the hatred of the human family. He relinquished his occupation, became a wanderer, and gained a precarious support, while his descendants invented arts and built cities.

Cain and Abel.

Eve bear another son—Seth, among whose descendants the worship of God was preserved for a long time; but the descendants of Seth intermarried finally with the descendants of Cain, from whom sprung a race of lawless men, so that the earth was filled with violence. The material civilization which the descendants of Cain introduced did not preserve them from moral degeneracy. So great was the increasing wickedness, with the growth of the race, that "it repented the Lord that he had made man," and he resolved to destroy the whole race, with the exception of one religious family, and change the whole surface of the earth by a mighty flood, which should involve in destruction all animals and fowls of the air—all the antediluvian works of man.

The descendants of Cain.

It is of no consequence to inquire whether the Deluge was universal or partial—whether it covered the whole earth or the existing habitations of men. All were destroyed by it, except Noah, and his wife, and his three sons, with their wives. The authenticity of the fact rests with Moses, and with him we are willing to leave it.

The deluge.

This dreadful catastrophe took place in the 600th year of Noah's life, and 2349 years before Christ, when the world was 1655 years old, according to Usshur, but much older according to Hale and other authorities—when more time had elapsed than from the Deluge to the reign of Solomon. And hence there more people destroyed, in all probability, than existed on the earth in the time of Solomon. And as men lived longer in those primeval times than subsequently, and were larger and stronger, "for there were giants in those days," and early invented tents, the harp, the organ, and were artificers in brass and iron, and built cities—as they were full of inventions as well as imaginations, it is not unreasonable to infer, though we can not know with certainty, that the antediluvian world was more splendid and luxurious than the world in the time of Solomon and Homer—the era of the Pyramids of Egypt.

The probable condition of the antediluvian world.

2

The art of building was certainly then carried to considerable perfection, for the ark, which Noah built, was four hundred and fifty feet long, seventy-five wide, and forty-five deep; and was constructed so curiously as to hold specimens of all known animals and birds, with provisions for them for more than ten months.

The ark.

This sacred ark or ship, built of gopher wood, floated on the world's waves, until, in the seventh month, it rested upon the mountains of Ararat. It was nearly a year before Noah ventured from the ark. His first act, after he issued forth, was to build an altar and offer sacrifice to the God who had preserved him and his family alone, of the human race. And the Lord was well pleased, and made a covenant with him that he would never again send a like destruction upon the earth, and as a sign and seal of the covenant which he made with all flesh, he set his bow in the cloud. We hence infer that the primeval world was watered by mists from the earth, like the garden of Eden, and not by rains.

The Divine covenant with Noah.

"The memory of the Deluge is preserved in the traditions of nearly all nations, as well as in the narrative of Moses; and most heathen mythologies have some kind of sacred ark." Moreover, there are various geological phenomena in all parts of the world, which can not be accounted for on any other ground than some violent disruption produced by a universal Deluge. The Deluge itself can not be explained, although there are many ingenious theories to show it might be in accordance with natural causes. The Scriptures allude to it as a supernatural event, for an express end. When the supernatural power of God can be disproved, then it will be time to explain the Deluge by natural causes, or deny it altogether. The Christian world now accepts it as Moses narrates it.

The tradition of the deluge.

CHAPTER II.

POSTDILUVIAN HISTORY TO THE CALL OF ABRAHAM.—THE PATRIARCHAL CONSTITUTION, AND THE DIVISION OF NATIONS.

WHEN Noah and his family issued from the ark, they were blessed by God. They were promised a vast posterity, dominion over nature, and all animals for food, as well as the fruits of the earth. But new laws were imposed, against murder, and against the eating of blood. An authority was given to the magistrate to punish murder. "Whosoever sheddeth man's blood, by man shall *his* blood be shed." This was not merely a penalty, but a prediction. The sacredness of life, and the punishment for murder are equally asserted, and asserted with peculiar emphasis. This may be said to be the Noachic Code, afterward extended by Moses. From that day to this, murder has been accounted the greatest human crime, and has been the most severely punished. On the whole, this crime has been the rarest in the subsequent history of the world, although committed with awful frequency, but seldom till other crimes are exhausted. The sacredness of life is the greatest of human privileges.

The Noachic Code.

The government was patriarchal. The head of a family had almost unlimited power. And this government was religious as well as civil. The head of the family was both priest and king. He erected altars and divided inheritances. He ruled his sons, even if they had wives and children. And as the old patriarchs lived to a great age, their authority extended over several generations and great numbers of people.

Patriarchal constitutions.

Noah pursued the life of a husbandman, and planted vines, probably like the antediluvians. Nor did he escape the shame of drunkenness, though we have no evidence it was an habitual sin.

From this sin and shame great consequences followed. Noah was indecently exposed. The second son made light of it; the two others covered up the nakedness of their father. For this levity Ham was cursed in his children. Canaan, his son, was decreed to be a servant of servants—the ancestor of the races afterward exterminated by the Jews. To Shem, for his piety, was given a special religious blessing. Through him all the nations of the earth were blessed. To Japhet was promised especial temporal prosperity, and a participation of the blessing of Shem. The European races are now reaping this prosperity, and the religious privileges of Christianity.

Consequences of the sin of Noah.

Four generations passed without any signal event. They all spoke the same language, and pursued the same avocations. They lived in Armenia, but gradually spread over the surrounding countries and especially toward the west and south. They journeyed to the land of Shinar, and dwelt on its fertile plains. This was the great level of Lower Mesopotamia, or Chaldea, watered by the Euphrates.

Settlements of his descendants.

Here they built a city, and aspired to build a tower which should reach unto the heavens. It was vanity and pride which incited them,—also fear lest they should be scattered.

The Tower of Babel.

We read that Nimrod—one of the descendants of Ham—a mighty hunter, had migrated to this plain, and set up a kingdom at Babel—perhaps a revolt against patriarchal authority. Here was a great settlement—perhaps the central seat of the descendants of Noah, where Nimrod—the strongest man of his times—usurped dominion. Under his auspices the city was built—a stronghold from which he would defy all other powers. Perhaps here he

Nimrod.

instituted idolatry, since a tower was also a temple. But, whether fear or ambition or idolatry prompted the building of Babel, it displeased the Lord.

The punishment which he inflicted upon the builders was confusion of tongues. The people could not understand each other, and were obliged to disperse. The tower was left unfinished. The Lord "scattered the people abroad upon the face of all the earth." Probably some remained at Babel, on the Euphrates—the forefathers of the Israelites when they dwelt in Chaldea. It is not probable that every man spoke a different language, but that there was a great division of language, corresponding with the great division of families, so that the posterity of Shem took one course, that of Japhet another, and that of Ham the third—dividing themselves into three separate nations, each speaking substantially the same tongue, afterward divided into different dialects from their peculiar circumstances.

The Confusion of tongues.

Much learning and ingenuity have been expended in tracing the different races and languages of the earth to the grand confusion of Babel. But the subject is too complicated, and in the present state of science, too unsatisfactory to make it expedient to pursue ethnological and philological inquiries in a work so limited as this. We refer students to Max Muller, and other authorities.

Dispersion of nations.

But that there was a great tripartite division of the human family can not be doubted. The descendants of Japhet occupied a great zone running from the high lands of Armenia to the southeast, into the table-lands of Iran, and to Northern India, and to the west into Thrace, the Grecian peninsula, and Western Europe. And all the nations which subsequently sprung from the children of Japhet, spoke languages the roots of which bear a striking affinity. This can be proved. The descendants of Japhet, supposed to be the oldest son of Noah, possessed the fairest lands of the world—most favorable to development and progress—most favorable to ultimate supremacy. They

The settlements of the children of Japhet.

composed the great Caucasian race, which spread over Northern and Western Asia, and over Europe—superior to other races in personal beauty and strength, and also intellectual force. From the times of the Greek and Romans this race has held the supremacy of the world, as was predicted to Noah. "God shall enlarge Japhet, and he shall dwell in the tents of Shem, and Canaan shall be his servant." The conquest of the descendants of Ham by the Greeks and Romans, and their slavery, attest the truth of Scripture.

The settlements of the descendants of Shem.

The descendants of Shem occupied another belt or zone. It extended from the southeastern part of Asia Minor to the Persian Gulf and the peninsula of Arabia. The people lived in tents, were not ambitious of conquest, were religious and contemplative. The great theogonies of the East came from this people. They studied the stars. They meditated on God and theological questions. They were a chosen race with whom sacred history dwells. They had, compared with other races, a small territory between the possessions of Japhet on the north, and that of Ham on the south. Their destiny was not to spread over the world, but to exhibit the dealings of God's providence. From this race came the Jews and the Messiah. The most enterprising of the descendants of Shem were the Phœnicians, who pursued commerce on a narrow strip of the eastern shore of the Mediterranean, and who colonized Carthage and North Africa, but were not powerful enough to contend successfully with the Romans in political power.

The descendants of Ham.

The most powerful of the posterity of Noah were the descendants of Ham, for more than two thousand years, since they erected great monarchies, and were warlike, aggressive, and unscrupulous. They lived in Egypt, Ethiopia, Palestine, and the countries around the Red Sea. They commenced their empire in Babel, on the great plain of Babylonia, and extended it northward into the land of Asshur (Assyria). They built the great cities of Antioch, Rehoboth, Calah and Resen. Their empire was the oldest in the world—that established by a Cushite dynasty on the plains of Babylon, and in the highlands of Persia. They cast off the patriarchal law, and indulged in a restless passion for dominion. And they were the most civilized of the ancient nations in arts and material life. They built cities and monuments of power. These temples, their palaces, their pyramids were the wonders of the ancient world. Their grand and somber architecture lasted for centuries. They were the wickedest of the nations of the earth, and effeminacy, pride and sensuality followed naturally from their material civilization unhallowed by high religious ideas. They were hateful conquerors and tyrants, and yet slaves. They were permitted to prosper until their vices wrought out their own destruction, and they became finally subservient to the posterity of Japhet. But among some of the descendants of Ham civilization never advanced. The negro race of Africa ever has been degraded and enslaved. It has done nothing to advance human society. None of these races, even the most successful, have left durable monuments of intellect or virtue: they have left gloomy monuments of tyrannical and physical power. The Babylonians and Egyptians laid the foundation of some of the sciences and arts, but nothing remains at the present day which civilization values.

How impressive and august the ancient prophecy to Noah! How strikingly have all the predictions been fulfilled! These give to history an imperishable interest and grandeur.

CHAPTER III.

THE HEBREW RACE FROM ABRAHAM TO THE SALE OF JOSEPH.

We postpone the narrative of the settlements and empires which grew up on the banks of the Euphrates and the Nile, the oldest monarchies, until we have contemplated the early history of the Jews—descended from one of the children of Shem. This is not in chronological order, but in accordance with the inimitable history of Moses. The Jews did not become a nation until four hundred and thirty years after the call of Abram—and Abram was of the tenth generation from Noah. When he was born, great cities existed in Babylon, Canaan, and Egypt, and the descendants of Ham were the great potentates of earth. The children of Shem were quietly living in tents, occupied with agriculture and the raising of cattle. Those of Japhet were exploring all countries with zealous enterprise, and founding distant settlements—adventurers in quest of genial climates and fruitful fields.

Abram.

Abram was born in Ur, a city of the Chaldeans, in the year 1996 before Christ—supposed by some to be the Edessa of the Greeks, and by others to be a great maritime city on the right bank of the Euphrates near its confluence with the Tigris.

From this city his father Terah removed with his children and kindred to Haran, and dwelt there. It was in Mesopotamia—a rich district, fruitful in pasturage. Here Abram remained until he was 75, and had become rich.

While sojourning in this fruitful plain the Lord said unto him, "get thee out of thy country, and from thy kindred, and from thy father's house, unto a land which I will show thee." "And I will make thee a great nation, and will bless thee, and make thy name great, and thou shalt be a blessing. And I will bless them that bless thee, and curse him that curseth thee. And in thee shall all the families of the earth be blessed." So Abram departed with Lot, his nephew, and Sarai, his wife, with all his cattle and substance, to the land of Canaan, then occupied by that Hamite race which had probably proved unfriendly to his family in Chaldea. We do not know by what route he passed the Syrian desert, but he halted at Shechem, situated in a fruitful valley, one of the passes of the hills from Damascus to Canaan. He then built an altar to the Lord, probably among an idolatrous people. From want of pasturage, or some cause not explained, he removed from thence into a mountain on the east of Bethel, between that city and Hai, or Ai, when he again erected an altar, and called upon the living God. But here he did not long remain, being driven by a famine to the fertile land of Egypt, then ruled by the Pharaohs, whose unscrupulous character he feared, and which tempted him to practice an unworthy deception, yet in accordance with profound worldly sagacity. It was the dictate of expediency rather than faith. He pretended that Sarai was his sister, and was well treated on her account by the princes of Egypt, and not killed, as he feared he would be if she was known to be his wife. The king, afflicted by great plagues in consequence of his attentions to this beautiful woman, sent Abram away, after a stern rebuke for the story he had told, with all his possessions.

The wanderings and settlements of Abraham.

The patriarch returned to Canaan, enriched by the princes of Egypt, and resumed his old encampment near Bethel. But there was not enough pasturage for his flocks, united with those of Lot. So, with magnanimous generosity, disinclined to strife or greed, he gave his nephew the choice of lands, but insisted on a division. "Is not the whole land before thee," said he: "Separate thyself, I pray thee: if thou wilt take the left hand, I will go to the right, and if thou depart to the right

The separation of Abraham and Lot.

hand, then I will go to the left." The children of Ham and of Japhet would have quarreled, and one would have got the ascendency over the other. Not so with the just and generous Shemite—the reproachless model of all oriental virtues, if we may forget the eclipse of his fair name in Egypt.

Lot chose, as was natural, the lower valley of the Jordan, a fertile and well-watered plain, but near the wicked cities of the Canaanites, which lay in the track of the commerce between Arabia, Syria, Egypt, and the East. The worst vices of antiquity prevailed among them, and Lot subsequently realized, by a painful experience, the folly of seeking, for immediate good, such an accursed neighborhood.

The settlements of Lot.

Abram was contented with less advantages among the hills, and after a renewed blessing from the Lord, removed his tents to the plain of Mamre, near Hebron, one of the oldest cities of the world.

The first battle that we read of in history was fought between the Chaldean monarch and the kings of the five cities of Canaan, near to the plain which Lot had selected. The kings were vanquished, and, in the spoliation which ensued, Lot himself and his cattle were carried away by Chederlaomer.

The first recorded battle in history.

The news reached Abram in time for him to pursue the Chaldean king with his trained servants, three hundred and eighteen in number. In a midnight attack the Chaldeans were routed, since a panic was created, and Lot was rescued with all his goods, from which we infer that Abram was a powerful chieftain, and was also assisted directly by God, as Joshua subsequently was in his unequal contest with the Canaanites.

The victory of Abraham.

The king of Sodom, in gratitude, went out to meet him on his return from the successful encounter, and also the king of Salem, Melchizedek, with bread and wine. This latter was probably of the posterity of Shem, since he was also a priest of the most high God. He blessed Abram, and gave him tithes, which Abram accepted.

Melchizedek.

But Abram would accept nothing from the king of Sodom—not even to a shoe-latchet—from patriarchal pride, or disinclination to have any intercourse with idolators. But he did not prevent his young warriors from eating his bread in their hunger. It was not the Sodomites he wished to rescue, but Lot, his kinsman and friend.

The pride of Abraham.

Abram, now a powerful chieftain and a rich man, well advanced in years, had no children, in spite of the promise of God that he should be the father of nations. His apparent heir was his chief servant, or steward, Elizur, of Damascus. He then reminds the Lord of the promise, and the Lord renewed the covenant, and Abram rested in faith.

His prospects.

Not so his wife Sarai. Skeptical that from herself should come the promised seed, she besought Abram to make a concubine or wife of her Egyptian maid, Hagar. Abram listens to her, and grants her request. Sarai is then despised by the woman, and lays her complaint before her husband. Abram delivers the concubine into the hands of the jealous and offended wife, who dealt hardly with her, so that she fled to the wilderness. Thirsty and miserable, she was found by an angel, near to a fountain of water, who encouraged her by the promise that her child should be the father of a numerous nation, but counseled her to return to Sarai, and submit herself to her rule. In due time the child was born, and was called Ishmael—destined to be a wild man, with whom the world should be at enmity. Abram was now eighty-six years of age.

Hagar.

Fourteen years later the Lord again renewed his covenant that he should be the father of many nations, who should possess forever the land of Canaan. His name was changed to Abraham (father of a multitude), and Sarai's was changed to Sarah. The Lord promised that from Sarah should come the predicted blessing. The patriarch is still incredulous, and laughs within himself; but God renews the promise, and henceforth Abraham be-

The renewed Covenant with Abraham.

lieves, and, as a test of his faith, he institutes, by divine direction, the rite of circumcision to Ishmael and all the servants and slaves of his family—even those "bought with money of the stranger."

The birth of Isaac.

In due time, according to prediction, Sarah gave birth to Isaac, who was circumcised on the eighth day, when Abraham was 100 years old. Ishmael, now a boy of fifteen, made a mockery of the event, whereupon Sarah demanded that the son of the bondwoman, her slave, should be expelled from the house, with his mother. Abraham was grieved also, and, by divine counsel, they were both sent away, with some bread and a bottle of water. The water was soon expended in the wilderness of Beersheba, and Hagar sat down in despair and wept. God heard her lamentations, and she opened her eyes and saw that she was seated near a well. The child was preserved, and dwelt in the wilderness of Paran, pursuing the occupation of an archer, or huntsman, and his mother found for him a wife out of the land of Egypt. He is the ancestor of the twelve tribes of Bedouin Arabs, among whom the Hamite blood predominated.

The destruction of Sodom.

Meanwhile, as Abraham dwelt on the plains of Mamre, the destruction of Sodom and Gomorrah took place, because not ten righteous persons could be found therein. But Lot was rescued by angels, and afterward dwelt in a cave, for fear, his wife being turned into a pillar of salt for daring to look back on the burning cities. He lived with his two daughters, who became the guilty mothers of the Moabites and the Ammonites, who settled on the hills to the east of Jordan and the Dead Sea.

The duplicity of Abraham.

Before the birth of Isaac, Abraham removed to the South, and dwelt in Gerah, a city of the Philistines, and probably for the same reason that he had before sought the land of Egypt. But here the same difficulty occurred as in Egypt. The king, Abimelech, sent and took Sarah, supposing she was merely Abraham's sister; and Abraham equivocated and deceived in this instance to save his own life. But the king, warned by God in a dream, restored unto Abraham his wife, and gave him sheep, oxen, men servants and women servants, and one thousand pieces of silver, for he knew he was a prophet. In return Abraham prayed for him, and removed from him and his house all impediments for the growth of his family. The king, seeing how Abraham was prospered, made a covenant with him, so that the patriarch lived long among the Philistines, worshiping "the everlasting God."

Then followed the great trial of his faith, when requested to sacrifice Isaac. And when he was obedient to the call, and did not withhold his son, his only son, from the sacrificial knife, having faith that his seed should still possess the land of Canaan, he was again blessed, and in the most emphatic language. After this he dwelt in Beersheba.

The Trial of Abraham.

At the age of 120 Sarah died at Hebron, and Abraham purchased of Ephron the Hittite, the cave of Machpelah, with a field near Mamre, for four hundred shekels of silver, in which he buried his wife.

Death of Sarah.

Shortly after, he sought a wife for Isaac. But he would not accept any of the daughters of the Canaanites, among whom he dwelt, but sent his eldest and most trusted servant to Mesopotamia, with ten loaded camels, to secure one of his own people. Rebekah, the grand-daughter of Nahor, the brother of Abraham, was the favored damsel whom the Lord provided. Her father and brother accepted the proposal of Abraham's servant, and loaded with presents, jewels of silver and jewels of gold, and raiment, the Mesopotamian lady departed from her country and her father's house, with the benediction of the whole family. "Be thou the mother of thousands of millions, and let thy seed possess the gate of those which hate them." Thus was "Isaac comforted after his mother's death."

The marriage of Isaac.

Abraham married again, and had five sons by Keturah; but, in his life-time, he gave all he had unto Isaac, except some gifts to his other children, whom he sent away, that they might not dispute the inheritance with Isaac. He died at a good old age, 175 years, and was buried by his sons, Isaac and Ishmael, in the cave of Machpelah, which had been purchased of the sons of Heth. Isaac thus became the head of the house, with princely possessions, living near a well.

Second marriage of Abraham.

But a famine arose, as in the days of his father, and he went to Gerar, and not to Egypt. He, however, was afraid to call Rebekah his wife, for the same reason that Abraham called Sarah his sister. But the king happening from his window to see Isaac "sporting with Rebekah," knew he had been deceived, yet abstained from taking her, and even loaded Isaac with new favors, so that he became very great and rich—so much so that the Philistines envied him, and maliciously filled up the wells which Abraham had dug. Here again he was befriended by Abimelech, who saw that the Lord was with him, and a solemn covenant of peace was made between them, and new wells were dug.

He deceives the Philistines.

Isaac, it seems, led a quiet and peaceful life—averse to all strife with the Canaanites, and gradually grew very rich. He gave no evidence of remarkable strength of mind, and was easily deceived. His greatest affliction was the marriage of his eldest and favorite son Esau with a Hittite woman, and it was probably this mistake and folly which confirmed the superior fortunes of Jacob.

The affliction of Isaac.

Esau was a hunter. On returning one day from hunting he was faint from hunger, and cast a greedy eye on some pottage that Jacob had prepared. But Jacob would not give his hungry brother the food until he had promised, by a solemn oath, to surrender his birthright to him. The clever man of enterprise, impulsive and passionate, thought more, for the moment, of the pangs of hunger than of his future prospects, and the quiet, plain, and cunning man of tents availed himself of his brother's rashness.

Jacob and Esau.

But the birthright was not secure to Jacob without his father's blessing. So he, with his mother's contrivance, for he was *her* favorite, deceived his father, and appeared to be Esau. Isaac, old and dim and credulous, supposing that Jacob, clothed in Esau's vestments as a hunter, and his hands covered with skins, was his eldest son, blessed him. The old man still had doubts, but Jacob falsely declared that he was Esau, and obtained what he wanted. When Esau returned from the hunt he saw what Jacob had done, and his grief was bitter and profound. He cried out in his agony, "Bless me even me, also, O my father." And Isaac said: "Thy brother came with subtilty, and hath taken away thy blessing." And Esau said, "Is he not rightly named Jacob—that is, a supplanter—for he hath supplanted me these two times: he took away my birthright, and behold now he hath taken away my blessing." "And he lifted up his voice and wept." Isaac, then moved, declared that his dwelling should be the fatness of the earth, even though he should serve his brother,—that he should live by the sword, and finally break the yoke from off his neck. This was all Esau could wring from his father. He hated Jacob with ill-concealed resentment, as was to be expected, and threatened to kill him on his father's death. Rebekah advised Jacob to flee to his uncle, giving as an excuse to Isaac, that he sought a wife in Mesopotamia. This pleased Isaac, who regarded a marriage with a Canaanite as the greatest calamity. So he again gave him his blessing, and advised him to select one of the daughters of Laban for his wife. And Jacob departed from his father's house, and escaped the wrath of Esau. But Esau, seeing that his Hittite wife was offensive to his father, married also one of the daughters of Ishmael, his cousin.

Jacob obtains the birthright.

The despair of Esau.

Jacob meanwhile pursued his journey. Arriving at a certain place after sunset, he lay down to sleep, with stones for his pillow, and he dreamed that a ladder set up on the earth reached the heavens, on which the angels of God ascended and descended, and above it was the Lord himself, the God of his father, who renewed all the promises that had been made to Abraham of the future prosperity of his house. He then continued his journey till he arrived in Haran, by the side of a well. Thither Rachel, the daughter of Laban, came to draw water for the sheep she tended. Jacob rolled away the stone from the mouth of the well, and watered her flock, and kissed her, and wept, for he had found in his cousin his bride. He then told her who he was, and she ran and told her father that his nephew had come, Isaac's son, and Laban was filled with joy, and kissed Jacob and brought him to his house, where he dwelt a month as a guest.

Jacob's wanderings.

An agreement was then made that Jacob should serve Laban seven years, and receive in return for his services his youngest daughter Rachel, whom he loved. But Laban deceived him, and gave him Leah instead, and Jacob was compelled to serve another seven years before he obtained her. Thus he had two wives, the one tender-eyed, the other beautiful. But he loved Rachel and hated Leah.

He served Laban.

Jacob continued to serve Laban until he was the father of eleven sons and a daughter, and then desired to return to his own country. But Laban, unwilling to lose so profitable a son-in-law, raised obstacles. Jacob, in the mean time, became rich, although his flocks and herds were obtained by a sharp bargain, which he turned to his own account. The envy of Laban's sons was the result. Laban also was alienated, whereupon Jacob fled, with his wives and children and cattle. Laban pursued, overtook him, and after an angry altercation, in which Jacob recounted his wrongs during twenty years of servitude, and Laban claimed every thing as his—daughters, children and cattle, they made a covenant on a heap of stones not to pass either across it for the other's harm, and Laban returned to his home and Jacob went on his way.

The quarrel with Laban.

But Esau, apprised of the return of his brother, came out

of Edom against him with four hundred men. Jacob was afraid, and sought to approach Esau with presents. The brothers met, but whether from fraternal impulse or by the aid of God, they met affectionately, and fell into each other's arms and wept. Jacob offered his presents, which Esau at first magnanimously refused to take, but finally accepted: peace was restored, and Jacob continued his journey till he arrived in Thalcom—a city of Shechem, in the land of Canaan, where he pitched his tent and erected an altar.

Meeting of Esau and Jacob.

Here he was soon brought into collision with the people of Shechem, whose prince had inflicted a great wrong. Levi and Simeon avenged it, and the city was spoiled.

Jacob, perhaps in fear of the other Amorites, retreated to Bethel, purged his household of all idolatry, and built an altar, and God again appeared to him, and blessed him and changed his name to Israel.

Jacob in Bethel.

Soon after, Rachel died, on the birth of her son, Benjamin, and Jacob came to see his father in Mamre, now 180 years of age, and about to die. Esau and Jacob buried him in the cave of Machpelah.

Death of Rachel.

Esau dwelt in Edom, the progenitor of a long line of dukes or princes. The seat of his sovereignty was Mount Seir.

Jacob continued to live in Hebron—a patriarchal prince, rich in cattle, and feared by his neighbors. His favorite son was Joseph, and his father's partiality excited the envy of the other sons. They conspired to kill him, but changed their purpose through the influence of Reuben, and cast him into a pit in the wilderness. While he lay there, a troop of Ishmaelites appeared, and to them, at the advice of Judah, they sold him as a slave, but pretended to their father that he was slain by wild beasts, and produced, in attestation, his lacerated coat of colors. The Ishmaelites carried Joseph to Egypt, and sold him to Potaphar, captain of Pharaoh's guard. Before we follow his fortunes, we will turn our attention to the land whence he was carried.

The sale of Joseph.

CHAPTER IV.

EGYPT AND THE PHARAOHS.

The original inhabitants of Egypt.

THE first country to which Moses refers, in connection with the Hebrew history, is Egypt. This favored land was the seat of one of the oldest monarchies of the world. Although it would seem that Assyria was first peopled, historians claim for Egypt a more remote antiquity. Whether this claim can be substantiated or not, it is certain that Egypt was one of the primeval seats of the race of Ham. Mizraim, the Scripture name for the country, indicates that it was settled by a son of Ham. But if this is true even, the tide of emigration from Armenia probably passed to the southeast through Syria and Palestine, and hence the descendants of Ham had probably occupied the land of Canaan before they crossed the desert between the Red Sea and the Mediterranean. I doubt if Egypt had older cities than Damascus, Hebron, Zoar, and Tyre.

But Egypt certainly was a more powerful monarchy than any existing on the earth in the time of Abraham.

Their peculiarities.

Its language, traditions, and monuments alike point to a high antiquity. It was probably inhabited by a mixed race, Shemitic as well as Hamite; though the latter had the supremacy. The distinction of castes indicates a mixed population, so that the ancients doubted whether Egypt belonged to Asia or Africa. The people were not black, but of a reddish color, with thick lips, straight black hair, and elongated eye, and sunk in the degraded superstitions of the African race.

The geographical position indicates not only a high antiquity, but a state favorable to great national wealth and power. The river Nile, issuing from a great lake under the equator, runs 3,000 miles nearly due north to the Mediterranean. Its annual inundations covered the valley with a rich soil brought down from the mountains of Abyssinia, making it the most fertile in the world. The country, thus so favored by a great river, with its rich alluvial deposits, is about 500 miles in length, with an area of 115,000 square miles, of which 9,600 are subject to the fertilizing inundation. But, in ancient times, a great part of the country was irrigated, and abounded in orchards, gardens, and vineyards. Every kind of vegetable was cultivated, and grain was raised in the greatest abundance, so that the people lived in luxury and plenty while other nations were subject to occasional famines.

The fertility of Egypt.

Among the fruits, were dates, grapes, figs, pomegranates, apricots, peaches, oranges, citrons, lemons, limes, bananas, melons, mulberries, olives. Among vegetables, if we infer from what exist at present, were beans, peas, lentils, luprins, spinach, leeks, onions, garlic, celery, chiccory, radishes, carrots, turnips, lettuce, cabbage, fennel, gourds, cucumbers, tomatoes, egg-plant. What a variety for the sustenance of man, to say nothing of the various kinds of grain,—barley, oats, maize, rice, and especially wheat, which grows to the greatest perfection.

The productions of Egypt.

In old times the horses were famous, as well as cattle, and sheep, and poultry. Quails were abundant, while the marshes afforded every kind of web-footed fowl. Fish, too, abounded in the Nile, and in the lakes. Bees were kept, and honey was produced, though inferior to that of Greece.

The climate also of this fruitful land was salubrious without being enervating. The soil was capable of supporting a large population, which amounted, in the time of Herodotus, to seven millions. On the banks of the Nile were great cities, whose ruins still astonish travelers. The land, except that owned by the priests, belonged

The castes of Egypt.

to the king, who was supreme and unlimited in power. The people were divided into castes, the highest being priests, and the lowest husbandmen. The kings were hereditary, but belonged to the priesthood, and their duties and labors were arduous. The priests were the real governing body, and were treated with the most respectful homage. They were councilors of the king, judges of the land, and guardians of all great interests. The soldiers were also numerous, and formed a distinct caste.

When Abram visited Egypt, impelled by the famine in Canaan, it was already a powerful monarchy. This was about 1921 years before Christ, according to the received chronology, when the kings of the 15th dynasty reigned.

Egyptian dynasties.

These dynasties of ancient kings are difficult to be settled, and rest upon traditions rather than well defined historical grounds,—or rather on the authority of Manetho, an Egyptian priest, who lived nearly 300 years before Christ. His list of dynasties has been confirmed, to a great extent, by the hieroglyphic inscriptions which are still to be found on ancient monuments, but they give us only a barren catalogue of names without any vital historical truths. Therefore these old dynasties, before Abraham, are only interesting to antiquarians, and not satisfactory to them, since so little is known or can be known. These, if correct, would give a much greater antiquity to Egypt than can be reconciled with Mosaic history. But all authorities agree in ascribing to Moses the commencement of the first dynasty, 2712 years before Christ, according to Hales, but 3893 according to Lepsius, and 2700 according to Lane. Neither Menes nor his successors of the first dynasty left any monuments. It is probable, however, that Memphis was built by them, and possibly hieroglyphics were invented during their reigns.

But here a chronological difficulty arises. The Scriptures ascribe ten generations from Shem to Abram. Either the generations were made longer than in our times, or the seventeen dynasties, usually supposed to have reigned when

Abram came to Egypt, could not have existed; for, according to the received chronology, he was born 1996, B. C., and the Deluge took place 2349, before Christ; leaving but 353 years from the Deluge to the birth of Abraham. How could seventeen dynasties have reigned in Egypt in that time, even supposing that Egypt was settled immediately after the Flood, unless either more than ten generations existed from Noah to Abram, or that these generations extended over seven or eight hundred years? Until science shall reconcile the various chronologies with the one usually received, there is but little satisfaction in the study of Egyptian history prior to Abram. Nor is it easy to settle when the Pyramids were constructed. If they existed in the time of Abram a most rapid advance had been made in the arts, unless a much longer period elapsed from Noah to Abraham than Scripture seems to represent.

Nothing of interest occurs in Egyptian history until the fourth dynasty of kings, when the pyramids of Ghizeh, were supposed to have been built—a period more remote than Scripture ascribes to the Flood itself, according to our received chronology. These were the tombs of the Memphian kings, who believed in the immortality of the soul, and its final reunion with the body after various forms of transmigration. Hence the solicitude to preserve the body in some enduring monument, and by elaborate embalmment. What more durable monument than these great masses of granite, built to defy the ravages of time, and the spoliations of conquerors! The largest of these pyramids, towering above other pyramids, and the lesser sepulchres of the rich, was built upon a square of 756 feet, and the height of it was 489 feet 9 inches, covering an area of 571,536 feet, or more than thirteen acres. The whole mass contained 90,000,000 cubic feet of masonry, weighing 6,316,000 tons. Nearly in the centre of this pile of stone, reached by a narrow passage, were the chambers where the royal sarcophagi were deposited. At whatever period these vast monuments were actu-

The Pyramids.

ally built, they at least go back into remote antiquity, and probably before the time of Abram.

The first great name of the early Egyptian kings was Sesertesen, or Osirtasin I., the founder of the twelfth dynasty of kings, B.C. 2080. He was a great conqueror, and tradition confounds him with the Sesostris of the Greeks, which gathered up stories about him as the Middle Ages did of Charlemagne and his paladins. The real Sesostris was Ramenes the Great, of the nineteenth dynasty. By the kings of this dynasty (the twelfth) Ethiopia was conquered, the Labyrinth was built, and Lake Moevis dug, to control the inundations. Under them Thebes became a great city. The dynasty lasted 100 years, but became subject to the Shepherd kings. These early Egyptian monarchs were fond of peace, and their subjects enjoyed repose and prosperity.

Thebes.

The Shepherd kings, who ruled 400 years, were supposed by Manetho, to be Arabs, but leaves us to infer that they were Phœnicians—as is probable—a roving body of conquerors, who easily subdued the peaceful Egyptians. They have left no monumental history. They were alien to the conquered race in language and habits, and probably settled in Lower Egypt where the land was most fertile, and where conquests would be most easily retained.

The Shepherd kings.

It was under their rule that Abram probably visited Egypt when driven by a famine from Canaan. And they were not expelled till the time of Joseph, by the first of the eighteenth dynasty. The descendants of the old kings, we suppose, lived in Thebes, and were tributary princes for 400 years, but gained sufficient strength, finally, to expel the Shemite invaders, even as the Gothic nations of Spain, in the Middle Ages, expelled their conquerors, the Moors.

But it was under the Shepherd kings that the relations between Egypt and the Hebrew patriarchs took place. We infer this fact from the friendly intercourse and absence of national prejudices. The Phœnicians belonged to the same Shemitic stock

Friendly relations of the Hebrews with the Shepherd kings.

from which Abraham came. They built no temples. They did not advance a material civilization. They loaded Abram and Joseph with presents, and accepted the latter as a minister and governor. We read of no great repulsion of races, and see a great similarity in pursuits.

Meanwhile, the older dynasties under whom Thebes was built, probably B. C. 2200, gathered strength in misfortune and subjection. They reigned, during five dynasties, in a subordinate relation, tributary and oppressed. The first king of the eighteenth dynasty seems to have been a remarkable man—the deliverer of his nation. His name was Aah-mes, or Amosis, and he expelled the shepherds from the greater part of Egygt, B. C. 1525. In his reign we see on the monuments chariots and horses. He built temples both in Thebes and Memphis, and established a navy. This was probably the king who knew not Joseph. His successors continued the work of conquest, and extended their dominion from Ethiopia to Mesopotamia, and obtained that part of Western Asia formerly held by the Chaldeans. They built the temple of Karnak, the "Vocal Memnon," and the avenue of Sphinxes in Thebes.

Expulsion of the Shepherd kings.

The grandest period of Egyptian history begins with the nineteenth dynasty, founded by Sethee I., or Sethos, B. C. 1340. He built the famous "Hall of Columns," in the temple of Karnak, and the finest of the tombs of the Theban kings. On the walls of this great temple are depicted his conquests, especially over the Hittites. But the glories of the monarchy, now decidedly military, culminated in Ramesis II.—the Sesostris of the Greeks. He extended his dominion as far as Scythia and Thrace, while his naval expeditions penetrated to the Erythræan Sea. The captives which he brought from his wars were employed in digging canals, which intersected the country, for purposes of irrigation, and especially that great canal which united the Mediterranean with the Red Sea. He added to the temple of Karnak, built the Memnonium on the western side of the Nile, opposite

Greatness of Ramesis II.

His architectural works.

to Thebes, and enlarged the temple of Ptah, at Memphis, which he adorned by a beautiful colossal statue, the fist of which is (now in the British Museum) thirty inches wide across the knuckles. But the Rameseum, or Memnonium, was his greatest architectural work, approached by an avenue of sphinxes and obelisks, in the centre of which was the great statue of Ramesis himself, sixty feet high, carved from a single stone of the red granite of Syene.

The twentieth dynasty was founded by Sethee II., B. C. 1220 (or 1232 B. C., according to Wilkinson), when Gideon ruled the Israelites and Theseus reigned at Athens and Priam at Troy. The third king of this dynasty—Ramesis III.—built palaces and tombs scarcely inferior to any of the Theban kings, but under his successors the Theban power declined. Under the twenty-first dynasty, which began B. C. 1085, Lower Egypt had a new capital, Zoan, and gradually extended its power over Upper Egypt. It had a strong Shemetic element in its population, and strengthened itself by alliances with the Assyrians.

Decline of Thebes.

The twenty-second dynasty was probably Assyrian, and began about 1009 B. C. It was hostile to the Jews, and took and sacked Jerusalem.

From this period the history of Egypt is obscure. Ruled by Assyrians, and then by Ethiopians, the grandeur of the old Theban monarchy had passed away. On the rise of the Babylonian kingdom, over the ruins of the old Assyrian Empire, Egypt was greatly prostrated as a military power. Babylon became the great monarchy of the East, and gained possession of all the territories of the Theban kings, from the Euphrates to the Nile.

Obscurity of Egyptian history.

Leaving, then, the obscure and uninteresting history of Egypt, which presents nothing of especial interest until its conquest by Alexander, B. C. 332, with no great kings even, with the exception of Necho, of the twenty-sixth dynasty, B. C. 611, we will present briefly the religion, manners, customs, and attainments of the ancient Egyptians.

Their religion was idolatrous. They worshiped various divinities: Num, the soul of the universe; Amen, the generative principle; Khom, by whom the productiveness of nature was emblematized; Ptah, or the creator of the universe; Ra, the sun; Thoth, the patron of letters; Athor, the goddess of beauty; Mu, physical light; Mat, moral light; Munt, the god of war; Osiris, the personification of good; Isis, who presided over funeral rites; Set, the personification of evil; Anup, who judged the souls of the departed.

Religion of the Egyptians.

These were principal deities, and were worshiped through sacred animals, as emblems of divinity. Among them were the bulls, Apis, at Memphis, and Muenis, at Heliopolis, both sacred to Osiris. The crocodile was sacred to Lebak, whose offices are unknown; the asp to Num; the cat to Pasht, whose offices were also unknown; the beetle to Ptah. The worship of these and of other animals was conducted with great ceremony, and sacrifices were made to them of other animals, fruits and vegetables.

The Deities.

Man was held accountable for his actions, and to be judged according to them. Be was to be brought before Osiris, and receive from him future rewards or punishments.

The penal laws of the Egyptians were severe. Murder was punished with death. Adultery was punished by the man being beaten with a thousand rods. The woman had her nose cut off. Theft was punished with less severity—with a beating by a stick. Usury was not permitted beyond double of the debt, and the debtor was not imprisoned.

Laws of the Egyptians.

The government was a monarchy, only limited by the priesthood, into whose order he was received, and was administered by men appointed by the king. On the whole, it was mild and paternal, and exercised for the good of the people.

Government

Polygamy was not common, though concubines were allowed. In the upper classes women were treated with great respect, and were regarded as the equals

Habits of the people.

of men. They ruled their households. The rich were hospitable, and delighted to give feasts, at which were dancers and musicians. They possessed chariots and horses, and were indolent and pleasure-seeking. The poor people toiled, with scanty clothing and poor fare.

Literary culture.

Hieroglyphic writing prevailed from a remote antiquity. The papyrus was also used for hieratic writing, and numerous papyri have been discovered, which show some advance in literature. Astronomy was cultivated by the priests, and was carried to the highest point it could attain without modern instruments. Geometry also reached considerable perfection. Mechanics must have been carried to a great extent, when we remember that vast blocks of stone were transported 500 miles and elevated to enormous heights. Chemistry was made subservient to many arts, such as the working of metals and the tempering of steel. But architecture was the great art in which the Egyptians excelled, as we infer from the ruins of temples and palaces; and these wonderful fabrics were ornamented with paintings which have preserved their color to this day. Architecture was massive, grand, and imposing. Magical arts were in high estimation, and chiefly exercised by the priests. The industrial arts reached great excellence, especially in the weaving of linen, pottery, and household furniture. The Egyptians were great musicians, using harps, flutes, cymbals, and drums. They were also great gardeners. In their dress they were simple, frugal in diet, though given to occasional excess; fond of war, but not cruel like the Assyrians; hospitable among themselves, shy of strangers, patriotic in feeling, and contemplative in character.

CHAPTER V.

THE JEWS UNTIL THE CONQUEST OF CANAAN.

WHEN Joseph was sold by the Midianites to Potiphar, Egypt was probably ruled by the Shepherd kings, who were called Pharaoh, like all the other kings, by the Jewish writers. Pitiphar (Pet-Pha, dedicated to the sun) was probably the second person in the kingdom. Joseph, the Hebrew slave, found favor in his sight, and was gradually promoted to the oversight of his great household. Cast into prison, from the intrigues of Potiphar's wife, whose disgraceful overtures he had virtuously and honorably rejected, he found favor with the keeper of the prison, who intrusted him with the sole care of the prisoners, although himself a prisoner,—a striking proof of his transparent virtue. In process of time two other high officers of the king, having offended him, were cast into the same prison. They had strange dreams. Joseph interpreted them, indicating the speedy return of the one to favor, and of the other to as sudden an execution. These things came to pass. After two years the king himself had a singular dream, and none of the professional magicians or priests of Egypt could interpret it. It then occurred to the chief butler that Joseph, whom he had forgotten and neglected, could interpret the royal dream which troubled him. He told the king of his own dream in prison, and the explanation of it by the Hebrew slave. Whereupon Joseph was sent for, shaven and washed, and clothed with clean raiment to appear in the royal palace, and he interpreted the king's dream, which not only led to his promotion to be governor over Egypt, with the State chariots

Potiphar and Joseph.

Elevation of Joseph.

for his use, and all the emblems of sovereignty about his person—a viceroy whose power was limited only by that of the king—but he was also instrumental in rescuing Egypt from the evils of that terrible famine which for seven years afflicted Western Asia. He was then thirty years of age, 1715 B. C., and his elevation had been earned by the noblest qualities—fidelity to his trusts, patience, and high principle—all of which had doubtless been recounted to the king.

His rule as Viceroy.

The course which Joseph pursued toward the Egyptians was apparently hard. The hoarded grain of seven years' unexampled plenty was at first sold to the famishing people, and when they had no longer money to buy it, it was only obtained by the surrender of their cattle, and then by the alienation of their land, so that the king became possessed of all the property of the realm, personal as well as real, except that of the priests. But he surrendered the land back again to the people subsequently, on condition of the payment of one-fifth of the produce annually (which remained to the time of Moses)—a large tax, but not so great as was exacted of the peasantry of France by their feudal and royal lords. This proceeding undoubtedly strengthened the power of the Shepherd kings, and prevented insurrections.

The famine in Egypt.

The severity of the famine compels the brothers of Joseph to seek corn in Egypt. Their arrival of course, is known to the governor, who has unlimited rule. They appear before him, and bowed themselves before him, as was predicted by Joseph's dreams. But clothed in the vesture of princes, with a gold chain around his neck, and surrounded by the pomp of power, they did not know him, while he knows them. He speaks to them, through an interpreter, harshly and proudly, accuses them of being spies, obtains all the information he wanted, and learns that his father and Benjamin are alive. He even imprisons them for three days. He releases them on the condition that they verify their statement; as a proof of which, he demands the appearance of Benjamin himself.

They return to Canaan with their sacks filled with corn, and the money which they had brought to purchase it, secretly restored, leaving Simeon as surety for the appearance of Benjamin. To this Jacob will not assent. But starvation drives them again to Egypt, the next year, and Jacob, reluctantly is compelled to allow Benjamin to go with them. The unexpected feast which Joseph made for them, sitting himself at another table—the greater portions given to Benjamin, the deception played upon them by the secretion of Joseph's silver cup in Benjamin's sack, as if he were a thief, the distress of all the sons of Jacob, the eloquent pleadings of Judah, the restrained tears of Joseph, the discovery of himself to them, the generosity of Pharaoh, the return of Jacob's children laden not only with corn but presents, the final migration of the whole family, to the land of Goshen, in the royal chariots, and the consummation of Joseph's triumphs, and happiness of Jacob—all these facts and incidents are told by Moses in the most fascinating and affecting narrative ever penned by man. It is absolutely transcendent, showing not only the highest dramatic skill, but revealing the Providence of God—that overruling power which causes good to come from evil, which is the most impressive lesson of all history, in every age. That single episode is worth more to civilization than all the glories of ancient Egypt; nor is there any thing in the history of the ancient monarchies so valuable to all generations as the record by Moses of the early relations between God and his chosen people. And that is the reason why I propose to give them, in this work, their proper place, even if it be not after the fashion with historians. The supposed familiarity with Jewish history ought not to preclude the narration of these great events, and the substitution for them of the less important and obscure annals of the Pagans.

Benjamin and his brothers.

Moses as an historian.

Joseph remained the favored viceroy of Egypt until he died, having the supreme satisfaction of seeing the prosperity of his father's house, and their rapid increase in the land of

Goshen, on the eastern frontier of the Delta of the Nile,—a land favorable for herds and flocks. The capital of this district was On—afterward Heliopolis, the sacred City of the Sun, a place with which Joseph was especially connected by his marriage with the daughter of the high priest of On. Separated from the Egyptians by their position as shepherds, the children of Jacob retained their patriarchal constitution. In 215 years, they became exceedingly numerous, but were doomed, on the change of dynasty which placed Ramesis on the throne, to oppressive labors. Joseph died at the age of 110—eighty years after he had become governor of Egypt. In his latter years the change in the Egyptian dynasty took place. The oppression of his people lasted eighty years; and this was consummated by the cruel edict which doomed to death the infants of Israel; made, probably, in fear and jealousy from the rapid increase of the Israelites. The great crimes of our world, it would seem, are instigated by these passions, rather than hatred and malignity, like the massacre of St. Bartholomew and the atrocities of the French Revolution.

Prosperity of the Hebrews.

Their subsequent miseries.

But a deliverer was raised up by God in the person of Moses, the greatest man in human annals, when we consider his marvelous intellectual gifts, his great work of legislation, his heroic qualities, his moral excellence, and his executive talents. His genius is more powerfully stamped upon civilization than that of any other one man—not merely on the Jews, but even Christian nations. He was born B. C. 1571, sixty-four years after the death of Joseph. Hidden in his birth, to escape the sanguinary decree of Pharaoh he was adopted by the daughter of the king, and taught by the priests in all the learning of the Egyptians. He was also a great warrior, and gained great victories over the Ethiopians. But seeing the afflictions of his brethren, he preferred to share their lot than enjoy all the advantages of his elevated rank in the palace of the king—an act of self-renunciation unparalleled in history. Seeing an Egyptian

Moses.

smite a Hebrew, he slew him in a burst of indignation, and was compelled to fly. He fled to Jethro, an Arab chieftain, among the Midianites. He was now forty years of age, in the prime of his life, and in the full maturity of his powers. The next forty years were devoted to a life of contemplation, the best preparation for his future duties. In the most secret places of the wilderness of Sinai, at Horeb, he communed with God, who appeared in the burning bush, and revealed the magnificent mission which he was destined to fulfill. He was called to deliver his brethren from bondage; but forty years of quiet contemplation, while tending the flocks of Jethro, whose daughter he married, had made him timid and modest. God renewed the covenant made to Abraham and Jacob, and Moses returned to Egypt to fulfill his mission. He joined himself with Aaron, his brother, and the two went and gathered together all the elders of the children of Israel, and after securing their confidence by signs and wonders, revealed their mission.

They then went to Pharaoh, a new king, and entreated of him permission to allow the people of Israel to go into the wilderness and hold a feast in obedience to the command of God. But Pharaoh said, who is the Lord that I should obey his voice. I know not the Lord—*your God.* The result was, the anger of the king and the increased burdens of the Israelites, which tended to make them indifferent to the voice of Moses, from the excess of their anguish.

The slavery of the Israelites.

Then followed the ten plagues which afflicted the Egyptians, and the obstinacy of the monarch, resolved to suffer any evil rather than permit the Israelites to go free. But the last plague was greater than the king could bear—the destruction of all the first-born in his land—and he hastily summoned Moses and Aaron in the night, under the impulse of a mighty fear, and bade them to depart with all their hosts and all their possessions. The Egyptians seconded the command, anxious to be relieved from further evils, and the Israelites, after spoiling the Egyptians, de-

The ten plagues.

parted in the night—"a night to be much observed" for all generations, marching by the line of the ancient canal from Rameses, not far from Heliopolis, toward the southern frontier of Palestine. But Moses, instructed not to conduct his people at once to a conflict with the warlike inhabitants of Canaan, for which they were unprepared, having just issued from slavery, brought them round by a sudden turn to the south and east, upon an arm or gulf of the Red Sea. To the eyes of the Egyptians, who repented that they had suffered them to depart, and who now pursued them with a great army, they were caught in a trap. Their miraculous deliverance, one of the great events of their history, and the ruin of the Egyptian hosts, and their three months' march and countermarch in the wilderness need not be enlarged upon.

The deliverance of the Israelites.

The exodus took place 430 years from the call of Abraham, after a sojourn in Egypt of 215 years, the greater part of which had been passed in abject slavery and misery. There were 600,000 men, besides women and children and strangers.

The exodus.

It was during their various wanderings in the wilderness of Sinai—forty years of discipline—that Moses gave to them the rules they were to observe during all their generations, until a new dispensation should come. These form that great system of original jurisprudence that has entered, more or less, into the codes of all nations, and by which the genius of the lawgiver is especially manifested; although it is not to be forgotten he framed his laws by divine direction.

Hebrew jurisprudence.

Let us examine briefly the nature and character of these laws. They have been ably expounded by Bishop Warburton, Prof. Wines and others.

The great fundamental principle of the Jewish code was to establish the doctrine of the unity of God. Idolatry had crept into the religious system of all the other nations of the world, and a degrading polytheism was everywhere prevalent. The Israelites had not

The principles of the Jewish code.

probably escaped the contagion of bad example, and the suggestions of evil powers. The most necessary truth to impress upon the nation was the God of Abraham, and Isaac, and Jacob. Jehovah was made the supreme head of the Jewish state, whom the Hebrews were required, first and last, to recognize, and whose laws they were required to obey. And this right to give laws to the Hebrews was deduced, not only because he was the supreme creator and preserver, but because he had also signally and especially laid the foundation of the state by signs and miracles. He had spoken to the patriarchs, he had brought them into the land of Egypt, he had delivered them when oppressed. Hence, they were to have no other gods than this God of Abraham —this supreme, personal, benevolent God. The violation of this fundamental law was to be attended with the severest penalties. Hence Moses institutes the worship of the Supreme Deity. It was indeed ritualistic, and blended with sacrifices and ceremonies; but the idea—the spiritual idea of God as the supreme object of all obedience and faith, was impressed first of all upon the minds of the Israelites, and engraven on the tables of stone—"Thou shalt have no other gods before me."

Having established the idea and the worship of God, Moses then instituted the various rites of the service, and laid down the principles of civil government, as the dictation of this Supreme Deity, under whose supreme guidance they were to be ruled.

But before the details of the laws were given to guide the Israelites in their civil polity, or to regulate the worship of Jehovah, Moses, it would seem, first spake the word of God, amid the thunders and lightnings of Sinai, to the assembled people, and delivered the ten fundamental commandments which were to bind them and all succeeding generations. Whether these were those which were afterward written on the two tables of stone, or not, we do not know. We know only that these great obligations were declared soon after the Israelites had encamped around Sinai, and to the whole people orally.

The Ten Commandments.

4

And, with these, God directed Moses more particularly to declare also the laws relating to man-servants, and to manslaughter, to injury to women, to stealing, to damage, to the treatment of strangers, to usury, to slander, to the observance of the Sabbath, to the reverence due to magistrates, and sundry other things, which seem to be included in the ten commandments.

Moses on Mount Sinai.

After this, if we rightly interpret the book of Exodus, Moses went up into the mountain of Sinai, and there abode forty days and forty nights, receiving the commandments of God. Then followed the directions respecting the ark, and the tabernacle, and the mercy-seat, and the cherubim. And then were ordained the priesthood of Aaron and his vestments, and the garments for Aaron's sons, and the ceremonies which pertained to the consecration of priests, and the altar of incense, and the brazen laver.

The tables of stone.

After renewed injunctions to observe the Sabbath, Moses received of the Lord the two tables of stone, "written with the finger of God." But as he descended the mountain with these tables, after forty days, and came near the camp, he perceived the golden calf which Aaron had made of the Egyptian ear-rings and jewelry,—made to please the murmuring people, so soon did they forget the true God who brought them out of Egypt. And Moses in anger, cast down the tables and brake them, and destroyed the calf, and caused the slaughter of three thousand of the people by the hands of the children of Levi.

The idolatry of the Jews.

But God forgave the iniquity and renewed the tables, and made a new covenant with Moses, enjoining upon him the utter destruction of the Canaanites, and the complete extirpation of idolatry. He again gathered together the people of Israel, and renewed the injunction to observe the Sabbath, and then prepared for the building of the tabernacle, as the Lord directed, and also for the making of the sacred vessels and holy garments, and the various ritualistic form of worship. He then established the sacrificial rites, consecrated Aaron and his sons as priests, laid down the law for them in their sacred functions, and made other divers laws for the nation, in their social and political relations.

The substance of these civil laws was the political equality of the people; the distribution of the public domains among the free citizens which were to remain inalienable and perpetual in the families to which they were given, thus making absolute poverty or overgrown riches impossible; the establishment of a year of jubilee, once every fifty years, when there should be a release of all servitude, and all debts, and all the social inequalities which half a century produced; a magistracy chosen by the people, and its responsibility to the people; a speedy and impartial administration of justice; the absence of a standing army and the prohibition of cavalry, thus indicating a peaceful policy, and the preservation of political equality; the establishment of agriculture as the basis of national prosperity; universal industry, inviolability of private property, and the sacredness of family relations. These were fundamental principles. Moses also renewed the Noahmic ideas of the sacredness of human life. He further instituted rules for the education of the people, that "sons may be as plants grown up in their youth, and daughters as corner stones polished after the similitude of a palace." Such were the elemental ideas of the Hebrew commonwealth, which have entered, more or less, into all Christian civilizations. I can not enter upon a minute detail of these primary laws. Each of the tribes formed a separate state, and had a local administration of justice, but all alike recognized the theocracy as the supreme and organic law. To the tribe of Levi were assigned the duties of the priesthood, and the general oversight of education and the laws. The members of this favored tribe were thus priests, lawyers, teachers, and popular orators—a literary aristocracy devoted to the cultivation of the sciences. The chief magistrate of the united tribes was not prescribed, but Moses remained the highest magistrate until his death, when the command was given to

The Mosaic legislation.

Joshua. Both Moses and Joshua convened the states general, presided over their deliberations, commanded the army, and decided all appeals in civil questions. The office of chief magistrate was elective, and was held for life, no salary was attached to it, no revenues were appropriated to it, no tribute was raised for it. The chief ruler had no outward badges of authority; he did not wear a diadem; he was not surrounded with a court. His power was great as commander of the armies and president of the assemblies, but he did not make laws or impose taxes. He was assisted by a body of seventy elders—a council or senate, whose decisions, however, were submitted to the congregation, or general body of citizens, for confirmation. These senators were elected; the office was not hereditary; neither was a salary attached to it.

The great congregation—or assembly of the people, in which lay the supreme power, so far as any human power could be supreme in a theocracy,—was probably a delegated body chosen by the people in their tribes. They were representatives of the people, acting for the general good, without receiving instructions from their constituents. It was impossible for the elders, or for Moses, to address two million of people. They spoke to a select assembly. It was this assembly which made or ratified the laws, and which the executioner carried out into execution.

The Jewish theocracy.

The oracle of Jehovah formed an essential part of the constitution, since it was God who ruled the nation. The oracle, in the form of a pillar of cloud, directed the wanderings of the people in the wilderness. This appeared amid the thunders of Sinai. This oracle decided all final questions and difficult points of justice. It could not be interrogated by private persons, only by the High Priest himself, clad in his pontifical vestments, and with the sacred insignia of his office, by "urim and thummim." Within the most sacred recesses of the tabernacle, in the Holy of Holies, the Deity made known his will to the most sacred personage of the nation, in order that no rash resolution of the people, or senate, or judge might be executed. And this response,

The Oracle.

given in an audible voice, was final and supreme, and not like the Grecian oracles, venal and mendacious. This oracle of the Hebrew God "was a wise provision to preserve a continual sense of the principal design of their constitution—to keep the Hebrews from idolatry, and to the worship of the only true God as their immediate protector; and that their security and prosperity rested upon adhering to his counsels and commands."

The designation and institution of high priest belonged not to the council of priests—although he was of the tribe of Levi, but to the Senate, and received the confirmation of the people through their deputies. "But the priests belonged to the tribe of Levi, which was set apart to God—the king of the commonwealth." "They were thus, not merely a sacerdotal body, appointed to the service of the altar, but also a temporal magistracy having important civil and political functions, especially to teach the people the laws." The high priest, as head of the hierarchy, and supreme interpreter of the laws, had his seat in the capital of the nation, while the priests of his tribe were scattered among the other tribes, and were hereditary. The Hebrew priests simply interpreted the laws; the priests of Egypt made them. Their power was chiefly judicial. They had no means of usurpation, neither from property, nor military command. They were simply the expositors of laws which they did not make, which they could not change, and which they themselves were bound to obey. The income of a Levite was about five times as great as an ordinary man, and this, of course, was derived from the tithes. But a greater part of the soil paid no tithes. The taxes to the leading class, as the Levites were, can not be called ruinous when compared with what the Egyptian priesthood received, especially when we remember that all the expenses connected with sacrifice and worship were taken from the tithes. The treasures which flowed into the sacerdotal treasury belonged to the Lord, and of these the priests were trustees rather than possessors.

The Priesthood.

Such, in general terms, briefly presented, was the Hebrew constitution framed by Moses, by the direction of God. It was eminently republican in spirit, and the power of the people through their representatives, was great and controlling. The rights of property were most sacredly guarded, and crime was severely and rigidly punished. Every citizen was eligible to the highest offices. That the people were the source of all power is proven by their voluntary change of government, against the advice of Samuel, against the oracle, and against the council of elders. We look in vain to the ancient constitutions of Greece and Rome for the wisdom we see in the Mosaic code. Under no ancient government were men so free or the laws so just. It is not easy to say how much the Puritans derived from the Hebrew constitution in erecting their new empire, but in many aspects there is a striking resemblance between the republican organization of New England and the Jewish commonwealth.

The Hebrew Constitution.

The Mosaic code was framed in the first year after the exodus, while the Israelites were encamped near Sinai. When the Tabernacle was erected, the camp was broken up, and the wandering in the desert recommenced. This was continued for forty years—not as a punishment, but as a discipline, to enable the Jews to become indoctrinated into the principles of their constitution, and to gain strength and organization, so as more successfully to contend with the people they were commanded to expel from Canaan. In this wilderness they had few enemies, and some friends, and these were wandering Arab tribes.

We can not point out all the details of the wanderings under the leadership of Moses, guided by the pillar of fire and the cloud. After forty years, they reached the broad valley which runs from the eastern gulf of the Red Sea, along the foot of Mount Seir, to the valley of the Dead Sea. Diverted from a direct entrance into Canaan by hostile Edomites, they marched to the hilly country to the east of Jordan, inhabited by the Amor-

The wanderings of the Israelites.

ites. In a conflict with this nation, they gained possession of their whole territory, from Mount Hermon to the river Arnon, which runs into the Dead Sea. The hills south of this river were inhabited by pastoral Moabites—descendants of Lot, and beyond them to the Great Desert were the Ammonites, also descendants of Lot. That nation formed an alliance with the Midianites, hoping to expel the invaders then encamped on the plains of Moab. Here Moses delivered his farewell instructions, appointed his successor, and passed away on Mount Pisgah, from which he could see the promised land, but which he was not permitted to conquer. That task was reserved for Joshua, but the complete conquest of the Canaanites did not take place till the reign of David.

CHAPTER VI.

THE CONQUEST OF CANAAN TO THE ESTABLISHMENT OF THE KINGDOM OF DAVID.

THE only survivors of the generation that had escaped from Egypt were Caleb and Joshua. All the rest had offended God by murmurings, rebellion, idolatries, and sundry offenses, by which they were not deemed worthy to enter the promised land. Even Moses and Aaron had sinned against the Lord.

So after forty years' wanderings, and the children of Israel were encamped on the plains of Moab, Moses finally addressed them, forbidding all intercourse with other nations, enjoining obedience to God, requiring the utter extirpation of idolatry, and rehearsing in general, the laws which he had previously given them, and which form the substance of the Jewish code, all of which he also committed to writing, and then ascended to the top of Pisgah, over against Jericho, from which he surveyed all the land of Judah and Napthali, and Manasseh and Gilead unto Dan—the greater part of the land promised unto Abraham.

Non-intercourse of the Jews with other nations.

He then died, at the age of 120, B. C. 1451 and no man knew the place of his burial.

Death of Moses.

The Lord then encouraged Joshua his successor, and the conquest of the country began—by the passage over the Jordan and the fall of Jericho. The manna, with which the Israelites for forty years had been miraculously fed, now was no longer to be had, and supplies of food were obtained from the enemy's country. None of the inhabitants of Jericho were spared except Rahab the harlot, and her father's household, in reward for

Joshua.

her secretion of the spy which Joshua had sent into the city. At the city of Ai, the three thousand men sent to take it were repulsed, in punishment for the sin of Achan, who had taken at the spoil of Jericho, a Babylonian garment and three hundred sheckels of silver and a wedge of gold. After he had expiated this crime, the city of Ai was taken, and all its inhabitants were put to death. The spoil of the city was reserved for the nation.

The fall of these two cities alarmed the Hamite nations of Palestine west of the Jordan, and five kings of the Amorites entered into a confederation to resist the invaders. The Gibeonites made a separate peace with the Israelites. Their lives were consequently spared, but they were made slaves forever. Thus was fulfilled the prophecy that Canaan should serve Shem.

His victories.

Meantime the confederate kings—more incensed with the Gibeonites than with the Israelites, since they were traitors to the general cause, marched against Gibeon, one of the strongest cities of the land. It invoked the aid of Joshua, who came up from Gilgal, and a great battle was fought, and resulted in the total discomfiture of the five Canaanite kings. The cities of Makkedah, Libnah, Gizu, Eglon, Hebron, successively fell into the hands of Joshua, as the result of their victory.

Combination of the Canaanites against Joshua.

The following year a confederation of the Northern kings, a vast host with horses and chariots, was arrayed against the Israelites; but the forces of the Canaanites were defeated at the "Waters of Merom," a small lake, formerly the Upper Jordan. This victory was followed by the fall of Hazor, and the conquest of the whole land from Mount Halak to the Valley of Lebanon. Thirty-one kings were smitten "in the mountains, in the plains, in the wilderness, in the south country: the Hittites, the Amorites, the Canaanites, the Perizites, the Hivites, and the Jebusites." There only remained the Philistines, whose power was formidable. The conquered country was divided among the different tribes, half of which were settled on the west of Jordan. The tabernacle was now removed to Shiloh, in the central hill country between Jordan and the Mediterranean, which had been assigned to the tribe of Ephraim. Jacob had prophetically declared the ultimate settlements of the twelve tribes in the various sections of the conquered country. The pre-eminence was given to Judah, whose territory was the most considerable, including Jerusalem, the future capital, then in the hands of the Jebusites. The hilly country first fell into the hands of the invaders, while the low lands were held tenaciously by the old inhabitants where their cavalry and war chariots were of most avail.

Conquest of Canaan.

The Israelites then entered, by conquest, into a fruitful land, well irrigated, whose material civilization was already established, with orchards and vineyards, and a cultivated face of nature, with strong cities and fortifications.

Death of Joshua.

Joshua, the great captain of the nation, died about the year 1426 B. C., and Shechem, the old abode of Abraham and Jacob, remained the chief city until the fall of Jerusalem. Here the bones of Joseph were deposited, with those of his ancestors.

The Judges.

The nation was ruled by Judges from the death of Joshua for about 330 years—a period of turbulence and of conquest. The theocracy was in full force, administered by the high priests and the council of elders. The people, however, were not perfectly cured of the sin of idolatry, and paid religious veneration to the gods of Phœnicia and Moab. The tribes enjoyed a virtual independence, and central authority was weak. In consequence, there were frequent dissensions and jealousies and encroachments.

Their wars.

The most powerful external enemies of this period were the kings of Mesopotamia, of Moab, and of Hazor, the Midianites, the Amalekites, the Ammonites, and the Philistines. The great heroes of the Israelites in their contests with these people were Othnie, Ehud, Barak, Gideon, Jepthna, and Samson. After the victories of Gideon over the Midianites, and of Jepthna over the

Ammonites, the northern and eastern tribes enjoyed comparative repose, and when tranquillity was restored Eli seems to have exercised the office of high priest with extraordinary dignity, but his sons were a disgrace and scandal, whose profligacy led the way to the temporary subjection of the Israelites for forty years to the Philistines, who obtained possession of the sacred ark.

A deliverer of the country was raised up in the person of Samuel, the prophet, who obtained an ascendancy over the nation by his purity and moral wisdom. He founded the "School of the Prophets" in Ramah, and to him the people came for advice. He seems to have exercised the office of judge. Under his guidance the Israelites recovered their sacred ark, which the Philistines, grievously tormented by God, sent back in an impulse of superstitious fear. Moreover, these people were so completely overthrown by the Irsaelites that they troubled them no longer for many years.

Samuel.

Samuel, when old, made his sons judges, but their rule was venal and corrupt. In disgust, the people of Israel then desired a king. Samuel warned them of the consequences of such a step, and foretold the oppression to which they would be necessarily subject; but they were bent on having a king, like other nations—a man who should lead them on to conquest and dominion. Samuel then, by divine command, granted their request, and selected Saul, of the tribe of Benjamin, as a fit captain to lead the people against the Philistines—the most powerful foe which had afflicted Israel.

The Israelites demand a King.

After he had anointed the future king he assembled the whole nation together, through their deputies, at Mizpeh, who confirmed the divine appointment. Saul, who appeared reluctant to accept the high dignity, was fair and tall, and noble in appearance, patriotic, warlike, generous, affectionate—the type of an ancient hero, but vacillating, jealous, moody, and passionate. He was a man to make conquests, but not to elevate the dignity of the

Anointment of Saul.

nation. Samuel retired into private life, and Saul reigned over the whole people.

His first care was to select a chosen band of experienced warriors, and there was need, for the Philistines gathered together a great army, with 30,000 chariots and 6,000 horsemen, and encamped at Michmash. The Israelites, in view of this overwhelming force, hid themselves from fear, in caves and amid the rocks of the mountain fastnesses. In their trouble it was found necessary to offer burnt sacrifices; but Saul, impulsive and assuming, would not wait to have the rites performed according to the divine direction, but offered the sacrifices himself. By this act he disobeyed the fundamental laws which Moses had given, violated, as it were, the constitution; and, as a penalty for this foolish and rash act, Samuel pronounced his future deposition; but God confounded, nevertheless, the armies of the Philistines, and they were routed and scattered. Saul then turned against the Amalekites, and took their king, whom he spared in an impulse of generosity, even though he utterly destroyed his people. Samuel reproved him for this leniency against the divine command. Saul attempted to justify himself by the sacrifice of all the enemies' goods and oxen, to which Samuel said, "Hath the Lord as great delight in burnt sacrifices and offerings as in obeying the voice of the Lord? Behold! to obey is better than sacrifice, and to hearken than the fat of rams; for rebellion is as the sin of witchcraft, and stubbornness as iniquity and idolatry." Most memorable words! thus setting virtue and obedience over all rites and ceremonies—a final answer to all ritualism and phariseeism.

His wars with the Philistines.

The remainder of the life of Saul was embittered by the consciousness that the kingdom would depart from his house; and by his jealousy of David, and his unmanly persecution of him; in whom he saw his successor. He was slain, with three of his sons, at the battle of Gilboa, when the Philistines gained a great victory—B. C. 1056.

The unhappiness of Saul.

David, meanwhile had been secretly anointed by Samuel as king over Israel. Nothing could exceed his grief when he heard of the death of Saul, and of Jonathan, whom he loved, and who returned his love with a love passing that of women, and who had protected him against the wrath and enmity of his father.

David.

David, of the tribe of Judah, after his encounter with Goliah, was the favorite of the people, and was rewarded by a marriage with the daughter of Saul—Michal, who admired his gallantry and heroism. Saul too had dissembled his jealousy, and heaped honors on the man he was determined to destroy. By the aid of his wife, and of Jonathan, and especially protected by God, the young warrior escaped all the snares laid for his destruction, and even spared the life of Saul when he was in his power in the cave of Engedi. He continued loyal to his king, patiently waiting for his future exaltation.

The enmity of Saul.

On the death of Saul, he was anointed king over Judah, at Hebron; but the other tribes still adhered to the house of Saul. A civil war ensued, during which Abner, the captain-general of the late king, was treacherously murdered, and also Ishboseth, the feeble successor of Saul. The war lasted seven and a half years, when all the tribes gave their allegiance to David, who then fixed his seat at Jerusalem, which he had wrested from the Jebusites, and his illustrious reign began, when he was thirty years of age, B. C. 1048, after several years of adversity and trial.

The elevation of David.

CHAPTER VII.

THE JEWISH MONARCHY.

We can not enter upon a detail of the conquests of David, the greatest warrior that his nation has produced. In successive campaigns, extending over thirty years, he reduced the various Canaanite nations that remained unconquered—the Amalekites, the Moabites, the Philistines, the Edomites, and the Syrians of Tobah. Hiram, king of Tyre, was his ally. His kingdom extended from the borders of Egypt to the Euphrates, and from the valley of Cœlo-Syria to the eastern gulf of the Red Sea. But his reign, if glorious and successful, was marked by troubles. He was continually at war; his kingdom was afflicted with a plague as the punishment for his vanity in numbering the people; his son Amnon disgraced him; Absalom, his favorite son, revolted and was slain; he himself was expelled for a time from his capital.

The reign of David.

But David is memorable for his character, and his poetry, his romantic vicissitudes of life, and as the founder of a dynasty rather than for his conquests over the neighboring nations. His magnificent virtues blended with faults, his piety in spite of his sins, his allegiance to God, and his faith in his promises invest his character with singular interest. In his Psalms he lives through all the generations of men. He reigned thirty-three years at Jerusalem, and seven at Hebron, and transmitted his throne to Solomon—his youngest child, a youth ten years of age, precocious in wisdom and culture.

Character of David.

The reign of Solomon is most distinguished for the magnificent Temple he erected in Jerusalem, after the designs furnished by his father, aided by the

The reign of Solomon.

friendship of the Phœnicians. This edifice, "beautiful for situation—the joy of the whole earth," was the wonder of those times, and though small compared with subsequent Grecian temples, was probably more profusely ornamented with gold, silver, and precious woods, than any building of ancient times. We have no means of knowing its architectural appearance, in the absence of all plans and all ruins, and much ingenuity has been expended in conjectures, which are far from satisfactory. It most probably resembled an Egyptian temple, modified by Phœnician artists. It had an outer court for worshipers and their sacrifices, and an inner court for the ark and the throne of Jehovah, into which the high priest alone entered, and only once a year. It was erected upon a solid platform of stone, having a resemblance to the temples of Paestum. The portico, as rebuilt, in the time of Herod, was 180 feet high, and the temple itself was entered by nine gates thickly coated with silver and gold. The inner sanctuary was covered on all sides by plates of gold, and was dazzling to the eye. It was connected with various courts and porticoes which gave to it an imposing appearance. Its consecration by Solomon, amid the cloud of glories in which Jehovah took possession of it, and the immense body of musicians and singers, was probably the grandest religious service ever performed. That 30,000 men were employed by Solomon, in hewing timber on Mount Lebanon, and 70,000 more in hewing stones, would indicate a very extensive and costly edifice. The stones which composed the foundation were of extraordinary size, and rivaled the greatest works of the Egyptians. The whole temple was overlaid with gold—a proof of its extraordinary splendor, and it took seven years to build it.

His architectural works.

The palace of Solomon must also have been of great magnificence, on which the resources of his kingdom were employed for thirteen years. He moreover built a palace for his wife, the daughter of Pharaoh, composed of costly stones, the foundation-stones of which were fifteen feet

The palace.

in length, surrounded with beautiful columns. But these palaces did not include all his works, for the courts of the temple were ornamented with brazen pillars, with elaborate capitals, brazen seas standing upon bronze oxen, brazen bases ornamented with figures of various animals, brazen lavers, one of which contained forty baths, altars of gold, tables, candelabras, basins, censers and other sacred vessels of pure gold,—all of which together were of enormous expense and great beauty.

The wisdom of Solomon.

During the execution of these splendid works, which occupied thirteen years or more, Solomon gave extraordinary indications of wisdom, as well as signs of great temporal prosperity. His kingdom was the most powerful of Western Asia, and he enjoyed peace with other nations. His fame spread through the East, and the Queen of Sheba, among others, came to visit him, and witness his wealth and prosperity. She was amazed and astonished at the splendor of his life, the magnificence of his court, and the brilliancy of his conversation, and she burst out in the most unbounded panegyrics. "The half was not told me." She departed leaving a present of one hundred and twenty talents of gold, besides spices and precious stones; and he gave, in return, all she asked. We may judge of the wealth of Solomon from the fact that in one year six hundred and sixty-six talents of gold flowed into his treasury, besides the spices, and the precious stones, and ivory, and rare curiosities which were brought to him from Arabia and India. The voyages of his ships occupied three years, and it is supposed that they doubled the Cape of Good Hope. All his banqueting cups and dishes were of pure gold, and "he exceeded all the kings of the earth for riches and wisdom," who made their contributions with royal munificence. In his army were 1,400 chariots and 12,000 horses, which it would seem were purchased in Egypt.

His apostasy.

Intoxicated by this splendor, and enervated by luxury, Solomon forgot his higher duties, and yielded to the fascination of oriental courts. In his harem were 700 wives, princesses, and 300 concubines, who turned his heart to idolatry. In punishment for his apostacy, God declared that his kingdom should be divided, and that his son should reign only over the single tribe of Judah, which was spared him for the sake of his father David. In his latter days he was disturbed in his delusions by various adversaries who rose up against him—by Hadad, a prince of Edom, and Rezon, king of Damascus, and Jeroboam, one of his principal officers, who afterward became king of the ten revolted tribes. Solomon continued, however, to reign over the united tribes for forty years, when he was gathered to his fathers.

His latter days.

The apostacy of Solomon is the most mournful fall recorded in history, thereby showing that no intellectual power can rescue a man from the indulgence of his passions and the sins of pride and vainglory. How immeasurably superior to him in self-control was Marcus Aurelius, who had the whole world at his feet! It was women who estranged him from allegiance to God—the princesses of idolatrous nations. Although no mention is made of his repentance, the heart of the world will not accept his final impenitence; and we infer from the book of Ecclesiastes, written when all his delusions were dispelled—that sad and bitter and cynical composition,—that he was at least finally persuaded that the fear of the Lord constitutes the beginning and the end of all wisdom in this probationary state. And we can not but feel that he who urged this wisdom upon the young with so much reason and eloquence at last was made to feel its power upon his own soul.

The rebellion of Jeroboam.

The government of Solomon, nevertheless had proved arbitrary, and his public works oppressive. The monarch whom he most resembled, in his taste for magnificence, in the splendor of his reign, and in the vexations and humiliations of his latter days, was Louis XIV. of France, who sowed the seeds of future revolutions. So Solomon prepared the way for rebellion, by his grievous exactions. Under his son Rehoboam, a vain and frivolous, and obstinate young man, who ascended the throne B. C. 975, the revolt took place. He would not listen to his father's councillors, and increased rather than mitigated the burdens of the people. And this revolt was successful: ten tribes joined the standard of Jeroboam, with 800,000 fighting men. Judah remained faithful to Rehoboam, and the tribe of Benjamin subsequently joined it, and from its geographical situation, it remained nearly as powerful as the other tribes, having 500,000 fighting men. But the area of territory was only quarter as large.

The Jewish nation is now divided. The descendants of David reign at Jerusalem; the usurper and rebel Jeroboam reigns over the ten tribes, at Shechem.

Division of the nation.

For the sake of clearness of representation we will first present the fortunes of the legitimate kings who reigned over the tribe of Judah.

Rehoboam reigned forty-one years at Jerusalem, but did evil in the sight of the Lord. In the fifth year of his reign his capital was rifled by the king of Egypt, who took away the treasures which Solomon had accumulated. He was also at war with Jeroboam all his days. He was succeeded by his son Abijam, whose reign was evil and unfortunate, during which the country was afflicted with wars which lasted for ninety years between Judah and Israel. But his reign was short, lasting only three years, and he was succeeded by Asa, his son, an upright and warlike prince, who removed the idols which his father had set up. He also formed a league with Ben-Hadad, king of Syria, and, with a large bribe, induced him to break with Baasha, king of Israel. His reign lasted forty years, and he was succeeded by his son Jehoshaphat, B. C. 954. Under this prince the long wars between Judah and Israel terminated, probably on account of the marriage of Jehoram, son of Jehoshaphat, with the daughter of Ahab, king of Israel—an unfortunate alliance on moral, if not political grounds. Jehoshaphat reigned thirty-five years, prosperously and virtuously, and his ships visited Ophir for gold as in the time of

The reign of Rehoboam.

His successors.

Solomon, being in alliance with the Phœnicians. His son Jehoram succeeded him, and reigned eight years, but was disgraced by the idolatries which Ahab encouraged. It was about this time that Elijah and Elisha were prophets of the Lord, whose field of duties lay chiefly among the idolatrous people of the ten tribes. During the reign of Jehoram, Edom revolted from Judah, and succeeded in maintaining its independence, according to the predictions made to Esau, that his posterity, after serving Israel, should finally break their yoke.

His son Ahaziah succeeded him at Jerusalem B. C. 885, but formed an alliance with Jehoram, king of Israel, and after a brief and wicked reign of one year, he was slain by Jehu, the great instrument of divine vengeance on the idolators. Of his numerous sons, the infant Joash alone was spared by Athaliah, the daughter of Ahab and Jezebel, who usurped authority in the name of the infant king, until she was overthrown by the high priest Jehoiada. The usurpations of this queen have furnished a subject for one of the finest tragedies of Racine. Jehoiada restored the temple worship, and instituted many other reforms, having supreme power, like Dunstan over the Saxon kings, when they were ruled by priests. His death left Judah under the dominion of the patriarchal rulers (the princes of Judah), who opposed all reforms, and even slew the son of Jehoida, Zechariah the prophet, between the altar and the temple. It would seem that Joash ruled wisely and benignantly during the life of Jehoiada, by whom he was influenced—a venerable old man of 130 years of age when he died. After his death Joash gave occasion for reproach, by permitting or commanding the assassination of Zechariah, who had reproved the people for their sins, and his country was invaded by the Syrians under Hazaal, and they sent the spoil of Jerusalem to Damascus. Joash reigned in all forty years, and was assassinated by his servants.

The princes of Judah at Jerusalem.

His son Amaziah succeeded him B. C. 839, and reigned twenty-nine years. He was on the whole a good and able prince, and gained great victories over the Edomites whom he attempted to reconquer. He punished also the murderers of his father, and spared their sons, according to the merciful provision of the laws of Moses. But he worshiped the gods of the Edomites, and was filled with vainglory from his successes over them. It was then he rashly challenged the king of Israel, who replied haughtily: "The thistle that was in Lebanon sent to the cedar that was in Lebanon, saying, give thy daughter to my son to wife, and there passed by a wild beast that was in Lebanon, and trode down the thistle." "So thou hast smitten the Edomites, and thine heart lifteth thee up to boast. Abide now at home; why shouldst thou meddle to thine hurt, that thou shouldst fall, even thou and Judah with thee." But Amaziah would not heed, and the two kings encountered each other in battle, and Judah suffered a disastrous defeat, and Joash, the king of Israel, came to Jerusalem and took all the gold and silver and all the sacred vessels of the temple and the treasures of the royal palace, and returned to Samaria. After this humiliation Amaziah reigned, probably wisely, more than fifteen years, until falling into evil courses, he was slain in a conspiracy, B. C. 810, and his son Uzziah or Azariah, a boy of sixteen, was made king by the people of Judah.

The reign of Amaziah.

This monarch enjoyed a long and prosperous reign of fifty-two years. He reorganized the army and refortified his capital. He conquered the Philistines, and also the Arabs, on his borders: received tribute from the Ammonites, and spread his name unto Egypt. During his reign the kingdom of Judah and Benjamin had great prosperity and power. The army numbered 307,500 men well equipped and armed, with military engines to shoot arrows and stones from the towers and walls. He also built castles in the desert, and digged wells for his troops stationed there. He developed the resources of his country, and devoted himself especially to the arts of agriculture and the cultivation of the vine, and the raising of cattle. But he could not stand prosperity, and in his presumption, attempted even to force

Uzziah.

himself in the sacred part of the temple to offer sacrifices, which was permitted to the priests alone; for which violation of the sacred laws of the realm, he was smitten with leprosy—the most loathsome of all the deseases which afflict the East. As a leper, he remained isolated the rest of his life, not even being permitted by the laws to enter the precincts of the temple to worship, or administer his kingdom. It was during his reign that the Assyrians laid Samaria under contribution.

His prosperity.

He was succeeded by Jotham, his son, B. C. 758, who carried on his father's reforms and wars, and was therefore prospered. It is worthy of notice that the kings of Judah, who were good, and abstained from idolatry, enjoyed great temporal prosperity. Jotham reigned sixteen years, receiving tribute from the Ammonites, and was succeeded by Ahaz, who walked in the ways of the kings of Israel, and restored idolatrous and superstitious rites. Besieged in Jerusalem by the forces of Rezin, king of Syria, and Pekah, king of Israel, and afflicted by the Edomites and Philistines, he invoked the aid of Tiglath-pileser, king of Assyria, offering him the treasure of the temple and his royal palace. The Assyrian monarch responded, and took Damascus, and slew its king. Ahaz, in his distress, yet sinned still more against the Lord by sacrificing to the gods of Damascus whither he went to meet the Assyrian king. He died in the year B. C. 726, after a reign of sixteen years, and Hezekiah, his son, reigned in his stead.

Jotham.

This prince was one of the best and greatest of the kings of Judah. He carried his zeal against idolatry so far as to break in pieces the brazen serpent of Moses, which had become an object of superstitious homage. He proclaimed a solemn passover, which was held in Jerusalem with extraordinary ceremony, and at which 2,000 bullocks and 17,000 sheep were slaughtered. No such day of national jubilee had been seen since the reign of Solomon. He cut down the groves in which idolatrous priests performed their mysterious rites, and overthrew their altars

Hezekiah.

throughout the land. The temple was purified, and the courses of the priests were restored. Under his encouragement the people brought in joyfully their tithes to the priests and levites, and offerings for the temple.

In all his reforms he was ably supported by Isaiah, the most remarkable of all the prophets who flourished during the latter days of the Hebrew monarchy. Under his direction he made war successfully against the Philistines, and sought to recover the independence of Judah. In the fourteenth year of his reign, Sennacherib invaded Palestine. Hezekiah purchased his favor by a present of three hundred talents of silver and thirty talents of gold, which stripped his palace and the temple of all their treasure. But whether he neglected to pay further tribute or not, he offended the king of Assyria, who marched upon Jerusalem, but was arrested in his purpose by the miraculous destruction of his army, which caused him to retreat with shame into his own country. After this his reign was peaceful and splendid, and he accumulated treasures greater than had been seen in Jerusalem since the time of Solomon. He also built cities, and diverted the course of the river Gihar to the western side of his capital, and made pools and conduits. It was in these years of prosperity that he received the embassadors of the king of Babylon, and showed unto them his riches, which led to his rebuke by Isaiah, and the prophecy of the future captivity of his people.

His wars.

He was succeeded by his son, Manasseh, B. C. 698, who reigned fifty-five years; but he did not follow out the policy of his father, or imitate his virtues. He restored idolatry, and "worshiped all the hosts of heaven," and built altars to them, as Ahab had done in Samaria. He was also cruel and tyrannical, and shed much innocent blood; wherefore, for these and other infamous sins, the Lord, through the mouth of the prophets, declared that "he would wipe Jerusalem as a man wipeth a dish," and would deliver the people into the hands of their enemies.

Manasseh.

His son, Amon, followed in the steps of his father, but after a brief reign of two years, was killed by his servants, B. C. 639, and was buried in the sepulchre of his family, in the garden of Uzza.

Amon.

Then followed the noble reign of Josiah—the last independent king of Judah—whose piety and zeal in destroying idolatry, and great reforms, have made him the most memorable of all the successors of David. He repaired the temple, and utterly destroyed every vestige of idolatry, assisted by the high priest Hilkiah, who seems to have been his prime minister. He kept the great feast of the passover with more grandeur than had ever been known, either in the days of the judges, or of the kings, his ancestors; nor did any king ever equal him in his fidelity to the laws of Moses. But notwithstanding all his piety and zeal, God was not to be turned from chastising Judah for the sins of Manasseh, and the repeated idolatries of his people; and all that Josiah could secure was a promise from the Lord that the calamities of his country should not happen in his day.

Josiah.

His noble reign.

In the thirty-first year of his reign, Necho, the king of Egypt, made war against the king of Babylon, who had now established his empire on the banks of the Euphrates, over the ruins of the old Assyrian monarchy. Josiah rashly embarked in the contest, either with a view of giving his aid to the king of Babylon, or to prevent the march of Necho, which lay through the great plain of Esdrælon. Josiah, heedless of all warnings, ventured in person against the Egyptian army, though in disguise, and was slain by an arrow. His dead body was brought to Jerusalem, and was buried in one of the sepulchres of his fathers; and all Judah and Israel mourned for the loss of one of the greatest, and certainly the best of their kings.

His death.

The prophet Jeremiah pronounced his eulogy, and led the lamentations of the people for this great calamity, B. C. 608.

The people proclaimed one of his sons, Shallum, to be king, under the name of Jehoahaz, but the Egyptian conqueror deposed him and set up his brother Jehoiakim as a tributary vassal. He reigned ingloriously for eleven years—an idolator and a tyrant.

His successor.

In his days Nebuchadnezzar, king of Babylon, came up against him, having driven the Egyptians out of Palestine. Jehoiakim made his submission to the conqueror of Egypt, who now reigned over the whole Assyrian empire, but did not escape captivity in Babylon, with many other of the first men of the nation, including Daniel, and the spoil of Jerusalem. He was restored to the throne, on promise of paying a large tribute. He served the king of Babylon three years and then rebelled, hoping to secure the assistance of Egypt. But he leaned on a broken reed. A Chaldean army laid siege to Jerusalem, and Jehoiakim was killed in a sally, B. C. 597. His son Jehoiachin had reigned only three months when Nebuchadnezzar, a great general, came to carry on the siege in person. The city fell, the king was carried into captivity, with 10,000 of his subjects, among whom were Ezekiel and Mordecai, and only the poorer class remained behind. Over these people Nebuchadnezzar set up Zedekiah, the youngest son of Josiah, as tributary king. Yet even in this state of degradation and humiliation the Jews, wrought upon by false prophets, expected deliverance, against the solemn warnings of Jeremiah, who remained at Jerusalem. Zedekiah, encouraged by the partial successes of the Egyptians, rebelled, upon which the king of Babylon resolved upon the complete conquest and utter ruin of the country. Jerusalem fell into his hands, by assault, and was leveled with the ground, and the temple was destroyed. Zedekiah, in attempting to escape, was taken, had his eyes put out, and was carried captive to Babylon, together with the whole nation, and the country was reduced to utter desolation. It was not, however, repeopled by heathen settlers, as was Samaria. The

Nebuchadnezzar wars against Judah.

The fall of Jerusalem.

Captivity of the Jews.

small remnant that remained, under the guidance of Jeremiah, recovered some civil rights, and supported themselves by the cultivation of the land, and in their bitter misery learned those lessons which prepared them for a renewed prosperity after the seventy years captivity. Never afterward was idolatry practiced by the Jews. But no nation was ever more signally humiliated and prostrated. Can we hence wonder at the mournful strains of Jeremiah, or the bitter tears which the captive Jews, now slaves, shed by the rivers of Babylon when they remembered the old prosperity of Zion.

Jeremiah.

The Jewish monarchy ended by the capture of Zedekiah. The kingdom of the ten tribes had already fallen to the same foes, and even more disastrously, because the kings of Israel were uniformly wicked, without a single exception, and were hopelessly sunk into idolatry; whereas the kings of Judah were good as well as evil, and some of them were illustrious for virtues and talents. The descendants of David reigned in Jerusalem in an unbroken dynasty for more than 500 years, while the monarchs of Samaria were a succession of usurpers. The degenerate kings were frequently succeeded by the captains of their guards, who in turn gave way for other usurpers, all of whom were bad. The dynasty of David was uninterrupted to the captivity of the nation. And the kingdom of Judah was also more powerful and prosperous than that of the ten tribes, in spite of their superior numbers.

The character of the kings of Judah.

But it is time to consider these ten tribes which revolted under Jeroboam. Their history is uninteresting, and, were it not for the beautiful episodes which relate to the prophets who were sent to reclaim the people from idolatry, would be without significance other than that which is drawn from the lives of wicked and idolatrous kings.

The ten tribes.

Jeroboam commenced his reign B. C. 975, by setting up for worship two golden calves in Bethel and Dan, and thus inaugurated idolatry: for which his dynasty was short. His son Nadah was murdered in a military revolution, B. C. 953, and the usurper of his throne, Baasha, destroyed his whole house. He, too, was a wicked prince, and his son Elah was slain by Zimri, captain of his guard, who now reigned over Israel, after exterminating the whole family of Elah, but was in his turn assassinated after a reign of seven years, B. C. 929. Omri, the captain of the guard, was now raised by the voice of the people to the throne; but he had a rival in Tibni, whom he succeeded in conquering. Omri reigned twelve years, and bought the hill of Samaria, on which he built the capital of his kingdom. But he exceeded all his predecessors in iniquity, and was succeeded by his son Ahab, who reigned twenty-two years. He was the most infamous of all the kings of Israel, both for cruelty and idolatry, and his queen, Jezebel, was also unique in crime—the Messalina and Fredigonde of her age. It was through her influence that the worship of Baal became the established religion, thus showing that the general influence of woman on man is evil whenever she is not Christian. And this is perhaps the reason that the ancients represented women as worse than men.

Jeroboam.

His wicked reign.

It was during the reign of this wicked king that God raised up the greatest of the ancient prophets—Elijah, and sent him to Ahab with the stern intelligence that there should be no rain until the prophet himself should invoke it. After three years of grievous famine, during which he sought to destroy the man who prophesied so much evil, but who was miraculously fed in his flight by the ravens, Ahab allowed Elijah to do his will.

Elijah.

Ahab.

Thereupon he caused the king to assemble together the whole people of Israel, through their representatives, upon Mount Carmel, together with the four hundred and fifty priests of Baal, and the four hundred false prophets of the grove, whom Jezebel supported. He then invoked the people, who, it seems, vacillated in their opinions in respect to Jehovah and Baal, to choose finally,

The destruction of the priests of Baal.

of these two deities, the God whom they *would* worship. Having discomfited the priests of Baal in the trial of sacrifices, and mocked them with the fiercest irony, thereby showing to the people how they had been imposed upon, Elijah incited them to the slaughter of these false prophets and foreign priests, and then set up an altar to the true God. But all the people had not fallen into idolatry; there still had remained seven thousand who had not bowed unto Baal.

Rain descended almost immediately, and Ahab departed and told Jezebel what had transpired. Hereupon, she was transported with rage and fury, and sought the life of the prophet. He again escaped, and by divine command went to the wilderness of Damascus and anointed Hazael to be king over Syria, and Jehu to be king over Israel, and Elisha to be his successor as prophet.

Wrath of Jezebel.

Soon after this, Benhadad, the king of Syria, came from Damascus with a vast army and thirty-two allied kings, to besiege Samaria. Defeated in a battle with Ahab, the king of Syria fled, but returned the following year with a still larger army for the conquest of Samaria. But he was again defeated, with the loss of one hundred thousand men in a single day, and sought to make peace with the king of Israel. Ahab made a treaty with him, instead of taking his life, for which the prophet of the Lord predicted evil upon him and his people. But the anger of God was still further increased by the slaughter of Naboth, through the wiles of Jezebel, and the unjust possession of the vineyard which Ahab had coveted. Elijah, after this outrage on all the fundamental laws of the Jews, met the king for the last time, and pronounced a dreadful penalty—that his own royal blood should be licked up by dogs in the very place where Naboth was slain, and that his posterity should be cut off from reigning over Israel; also, that his wicked queen should be eaten by dogs.

War with Damascus.

Curse upon Ahab.

In three years after, while attempting to recover Ramoth, in Gilead, from Benhadad, he lost his life, and was brought in his chariot to Samaria to be buried. And the dogs came and licked the blood from the chariot where it was washed.

Ahaziah.

He was succeeded by Ahaziah, his son, B. C. 913, who renewed the worship of Baal, and died after a short and inglorious reign, B. C. 896, without leaving any son, and Jehoram, his brother, succeeded him. In reference to this king the Scripture accounts are obscure, and he is sometimes confounded with Jehoram, the son of Jehoshaphat, king of Judah, who married a daughter of Ahab. This accounts for the alliance between Jehoshaphat and Ahab, and also between the two Jehorams, since they were brothers-in-law, which brought to an end the long wars of seventy years, which had wasted both Israel and Judah.

Jehoram did evil in the sight of the Lord, but was not disgraced by idolatry. In his reign the Moabites, who paid a tribute of one hundred thousand sheep and one hundred thousand lambs, revolted. Jehoram, assisted by the kings of Judah, and of Edom, marched against them, and routed them, and destroyed their cities, and filled up their wells, and felled all their good trees, and covered their good land with stones.

Meanwhile, it happened that there was a grievous famine in Samaria, so that an ass's head sold for eighty pieces of silver. Benhadad, in this time of national distress, came with a mighty host and besieged the city; but in the night, in his camp was heard a mighty sound of chariots and horses, and a panic ensued, and the Syrians fled, leaving every thing behind them. The spoil of their camp furnished the starving Samaritans with food.

Famine in Samaria.

After this, Jehoram was engaged in war with the Syrians, now ruled by Hazael, one of the generals of Benhadad, who had murdered his master. In this war, Jehoram, or Joram, was wounded, and went to be healed of his wounds at Jezreel, where he was visited by his kinsman, Ahaziah, who had succeeded to the throne of Judah. While he lay sick in this place, Jehu, one of his generals, conspired against him, and drew a bow against him, and the arrow pierced him so that he died, and his

Wars with the Syrians.

body was cast into Naboth's vineyard. Thus was the sin against Naboth again avenged. Jehu prosecuted the work of vengeance assigned to him, and slew Ahaziah, the king of Judah, also, and then caused Jezebel, the queen mother, to be thrown from a window, and the dogs devoured her body. He then slew the seventy sons of Ahab, and all his great men, and his kinsfolk, and his priests, so that none remained of the house of Ahab, as Elijah had predicted. His zeal did not stop here, but he collected together, by artifice, all the priests of Baal, and smote them, and brake their images.

Jehu.

But Jehu, now king of Israel, though he had destroyed the priests of Baal, fell into the idolatry of Jehoram, and was therefore inflicted with another invasion of the Syrians, who devastated his country, and decimated his people. He died, after a reign of twenty-eight years, B. C. 856, and was succeeded by his son, Jehoahaz.

His successors.

This king also did evil in the sight of the Lord, so that he was made subject to Hazael, king of Syria, all his days, who ground down and oppressed Israel, as the prophet had predicted. He reigned seventeen years, in sorrow and humiliation, and was succeeded by his son Johash, who followed the wicked course of his predecessors. His reign lasted sixteen years, during which Elisha died. There is nothing in the Scriptures more impressive than the stern messages which this prophet, as well as Elijah, sent to the kings of Israel, and the bold rebukes with which he reproached them. Nor is any thing more beautiful than those episodes which pertain to the cure of Naaman, the Syrian, and the restoration to life of the son of the Shunamite woman, in reward for her hospitality, and the interview with Hazael before he became king. All his predictions came to pass. He seems to have lived an isolated and ascetic life, though he had great influence with the people and the king, like other prophets of the Lord.

Their short reigns.

Jeroboam II. succeeded Johash, B. C. 825, and reigned successfully, and received all the territory which the Syrians had gained, but he did not depart from the idolatry of the golden calves. His son and successor, Zachariah, followed his evil courses, and was slain by Shallum, after a brief reign of six months, and the dynasty of Jehu came to an end, B. C. 772.

Shallum was murdered one month afterward by Menahem, who reigned ingloriously ten years. It was during his reign that Pul, king of Assyria, invaded his territories, but was induced to retire for a sum of one thousand talents of silver, which he exacted from his subjects. He was succeeded by Pekaiah, a bad prince, who was assassinated at the end of two years by Pekah, one of his captains, who seized his throne. During his reign, which lasted twenty years, Tiglath-Pilaser, king of Assyria, made war against him, by invitation of Ahaz, and took his principal cities, and carried their inhabitants captive to Nineveh. He was assassinated by Hosea, who reigned in his stead. He also was a bad prince, and became subject to Shalmanezer, king of Assyria, who came up against him. In the ninth year of his reign, having proved treacherous to Shalmanezer, the king of Assyria besieged Samaria, and carried him captive to his own capital. Thus ended the kingdom of the ten tribes, who were now carried into captivity beyond the Euphrates, and who settled in the eastern provinces of Assyria, and probably relapsed hopelessly into idolatry, without ever revisiting their native land. In all probability most of them were absorbed among the nations which composed the Assyrian empire, B. C. 721.

Fall of Samaria.

Nineteen sovereigns thus reigned over the children of Israel in Samaria—a period of two hundred and fifty-four years, not one of whom was obedient to the laws of God, and most of whom perished by assassination, or in battle. There is no record in history of more inglorious kings. There was not a great man nor a good man among them all. They were, with one or two exceptions, disgraced by the idolatry of Jeroboam, in whose steps they followed. Nor was their kingdom ever raised to any considerable height of political power. The history of the re-

The kings of Israel.

volted and idolatrous tribes is gloomy and disgraceful, only relieved by the stern lives of Elijah and Elisha, the only men of note who remained true to the God of their fathers, and who sought to turn the people from their sins. "Whereupon the Lord was very angry with Israel, and removed them out of his sight."

CHAPTER VIII.

THE OLD CHALDEAN AND ASSYRIAN MONARCHIES.

The plains of Babylon.

On a great plain, four hundred miles in length and one hundred miles in width, forming the valley of the Euphrates, bounded on the north by Mesopotamia, on the east by the Tigris, on the south by the Persian Gulf, and on the west by the Syrian Desert, was established, at a very early period, the Babylonian monarchy. This plain, or valley, contains about twenty-three thousand square miles, equal to the Grecian territories. It was destitute of all striking natural features—furnishing an unbroken horizon. The only interruptions to the view on this level plain were sand-hills and the embankments of the river. The river, like the Nile, is subject to inundations, though less regular than the Nile, and this, of course, deposits a rich alluvial soil. The climate in summer is intensely hot, and in winter mild and genial. Wheat here is indigenous, and the vine and other fruits abound in rich luxuriance. The land was as rich as the valley of the Nile, and was favorable to flocks and herds. The river was stocked with fish, and every means of an easy subsistence was afforded.

Into this goodly land a migration from Armenia—the primeval seat of man—came at a period when history begins. Nimrod and his hunters then gained an ascendency over the old settlers, and supplanted them—Cushites, of the family of Ham, and not the descendants of Shem.

The Tower of Babel.

The beginning of the kingdom of Nimrod was Babel, a tower, or temple, modeled after the one which was left unfinished, or was destroyed. This was erected, probably, B. C. 2334. It was square, and arose with successive stories, each one smaller than the one below, presenting an analogy to the pyramidical form. The highest stage supported the sacred ark. The temple was built of burnt brick. Thus the race of Ham led the way in the arts in Chaldea as in Egypt, and soon fell into idolatry. We know nothing, with certainty, of this ancient monarchy, which lasted, it is supposed, two hundred and fifty-eight years, from B. C. 2234 to 1976. It was not established until after the dispersion of the races. The dynasty of which Nimrod was the founder came to an end during the early years of Abraham.

The foundation of the Assyrian monarchy.

The first king of the new dynasty is supposed to be Chedorlaomer, though Josephus represents him as a general of the Chaldean king who extended the Chaldean conquests to Palestine. His encounters with the kings of Sodom, Gomorrah, and others in the vale of Siddim, tributary princes, and his slaughter by Abraham's servants, are recounted in the fourteenth chapter of Genesis, and put an end to Chaldean conquests beyond the Syrian desert. From his alliance, however, with the Tidal, king of nations; Amrapher, king of Shinar; and Arioch, king of Ellasar, we infer that other races, besides the Hamite, composed the population of Chaldea, of which the subjects of Chedorlaomer were pre-eminent.

His empire was subverted by Arabs from the desert, B. C. 1518; and an Arabian dynasty is supposed to have reigned for two hundred and forty-five years.

Extension of the kingdom.

This came to an end in consequence of a grand irruption of Assyrians—of Semitic origin. "Asshur (Gen. 10, 11), the son of Shem, built Nineveh," which was on the Tigris. The name Assyria came to be extended to the whole of Upper Mesopotamia, from the Euphrates to the Tagros mountains. This country consisted of undulating pastures, diversified by woodlands, and watered by streams running into the Tigris. Its valleys were rich, its hills were beautiful, and its climate was cooler than the Chaldean plain.

It would seem from the traditions preserved by the Greeks, that Nineveh was ruled by a viceroy of the Babylonian king. This corresponds with the book of Genesis, which makes the dynasty Chaldean, while the people were Semitic, since the kingdom of Asshur was derived from that of Nimrod. "Ninus, the viceroy," says Smith, "having revolted from the king of Babylon, overruns Armenia, Asia Minor, and the shores of the Euxine, as far as Tanais, subdues the Medes and Persians, and makes war upon the Bactrians. Semiramis, the wife of one of the chief nobles, coming to the camp before Bactria, takes the city by a bold stroke. Her courage wins the love of Ninus, and she becomes his wife. On his death she succeeds to the throne, and undertakes the conquest of India, but is defeated." These two sovereigns built Nineveh on a grand scale, as well as added to the edifices of Babylon.

Nineveh.

This king was the founder of the northwest palace of Nineveh, three hundred and sixty feet long and three hundred wide, standing on a raised platform overlooking the Tigris, with a grand façade to the north fronting the town, and another to the west commanding the river. It was built of hewn stone, and its central hall was one hundred and twenty feet long and ninety wide. The ceilings were of cedar brought from Lebanon. The walls were paneled with slabs of marble ornamented with bas-reliefs. The floors were paved with stone. (See Rawlinson's Herodotus.)

All this is tradition, but recent discoveries in cuneiform literature shed light upon it. From these, compared with the fragments of Berosus, a priest of Babylon in the third century before Christ, and the scattered notices of Scripture history, we infer that the dynasty which Belus founded reigned more than five hundred years, from 1272 to 747 before Christ. Of these kings, Sardanapalus, the most famous, added Babylonia to the Assyrian empire, and built vast architectural works. He employed three hundred and sixty thousand men in the construction of this palace, some of whom were employed in making brick, and others in

The palaces.

cutting timber on Mount Hermon. It covered an area of eight acres. The palaces of Nineveh were of great splendor, and the scenes portrayed on the walls, as discovered by Mr. Layard, lately disinterred from the mounds of earth, represent the king as of colossal stature, fighting battles, and clothed with symbolic attributes. He appears as a great warrior, leading captives, and storming cities, and also in the chase, piercing the lion, and pursuing the wild ass. This monarch should not be confounded with the Sardanapalus of the Greeks, the last of the preceding dynasty. His son, Shalmanezer, was also a great prince, and added to the dominion of the Assyrian empire. Distant nations paid tribute to him, the Phœnicians, the Syrians, the Jews, and the Medians beyond the Tagros mountains. He defeated Benhadad and routed Hazael. His reign ended, it is supposed, B. C. 850. Two other kings succeeded him, who extended their conquests to the west, the last of whom is identified by Smith with Pul, the reigning monarch when Jonah visited Nineveh, B. C. 770.

Assyrian kings.

The next dynasty commences with Tiglath-Pileser II., who carried on wars against Babylon and Syria and Israel. This was in the time of Ahaz, B. C. 729.

His son, Shalmanezer, made Hosea, king of Israel, his vassal, and reduced the country of the ten tribes to a province of his empire, and carried the people away into captivity. Hezekiah was also, for a time, his vassal. He was succeeded by Sargon, B. C. 721, according to Smith, but 715 B. C., according to others. He reigned, as Geseneus thinks, but two or three years; but fifteen according to Rawlinson, and built that splendid palace, the ruins of which, at Khorsabad, have supplied the Louvre with its choicest remains of Assyrian antiquity. He was one of the greatest of the Assyrian conquerors. He invaded Babylon and drove away its kings; he defeated the Philistines, took Ashdod and Tyre, received tribute from the Greeks at Cyprus, invaded even Egypt, whose king paid him tribute, and conquered Media.

Conquests of Shalmanezer.

His son, Sennacherib, who came to the throne, B. C. 702, is an interesting historical personage, and under him the Assyrian empire reached its culminating point. He added to the palace of Nineveh, and built one which exceeded all that had existed before him. No monarch surpassed this one in the magnificence of his buildings. He erected no less than thirty temples, shining with silver and gold. One of the halls of his palace was two hundred and twenty feet long, and one hundred and one wide. He made use of Syrian, Greek, and Phœnician artists. It is from the ruins of this palace at *Koyunjik* that Mr. Layard made those valuable discoveries which have enriched the British Museum. He subdued Babylonia, Upper Mesopotamia, Syria, Phœnicia, Philistia, Idumæa, and a part of Egypt, which, with Media, a part of Armenia, and the old Assyrian territory, formed his vast empire—by far greater than the Egyptian monarchy at any period. He chastised also the Jews for encouraging a revolt among the Philistines, and carried away captive two hundred thousand people, and only abstained from laying siege to Jerusalem by a present from Hezekiah of three hundred talents of silver and thirty of gold. The destruction of his host, as recorded by Scripture, is thought by some to have occurred in a subsequent invasion of Judea, when it was in alliance with Egypt. That "he returned to Nineveh and dwelt there" is asserted by Scripture, but only to be assassinated by his sons, B. C. 680.

Sennacherib.

Culmination of the power of Nineveh.

His son Esar-Haddon succeeded him, a warlike monarch, who fought the Egyptians, and colonized Samaria with Babylonian settlers. He also built the palace of Nimrod, and cultivated art.

Assyrian civilization.

The civilization of the Assyrians shows a laborious and patient people. Its chief glory was in architecture. Sculpture was imitated from nature, but had neither the grace nor the ideality of the Greeks. War was the grand business of kings, and hunting their pleasure. The people were ground down by the double tyranny of kings and priests. There is little of interest in the Assyrian annals, and what little we know of their life and manners is chiefly drawn by inductions from the monuments excavated by Botta and Layard. The learned treatise of Rawlinson sheds a light on the annals of the monarchy, which, before the discoveries of Layard, were exceedingly obscure, and this treatise has been most judiciously abridged by Smith, whom I have followed. It would be interesting to consider the mythology of the Assyrians, but it is too complicated for a work like this.

Decline of the monarchy.

Under his successors, the empire rapidly declined. Though it nominally included the whole of Western Asia, from the Mediterranean to the desert of Iran, and from the Caspian Sea and the mountains of Armenia to the Persian Gulf, it was wanting in unity. It embraced various kingdoms, and cities, and tribes, which simply paid tribute, limited by the power of the king to enforce it. The Assyrian armies, which committed so great devastations, did not occupy the country they chastised, as the Romans and Greeks did. Their conquests were like those of Tamerlane. As the monarchs became effeminated, new powers sprung up, especially Media, which ultimately completed the ruin of Assyria, under Cyaxares. The last of the monarchs was probably the Sardanapalus of the Greeks.

Destruction of Nineveh.

The decline of this great monarchy was so rapid and complete, that even Nineveh, the capital city, was blotted out of existence. No traces of it remained in the time of Herodotus, and it is only from recent excavations that its site is known. Still, it must have been a great city. The eastern wall of it, as it now appears from the excavations, is fifteen thousand nine hundred feet (about three miles); but the city probably included vast suburbs, with fortified towers, so as to have been equal to four hundred and eighty stadias in circumference, or sixty miles—the three days' journey of Jonah. It is supposed, with the suburbs, to have contained five hundred thousand people. The palaces of the great were large and magnificent; but the dwellings of the people were mean, built of brick dried in the sun. The palaces consisted of a large number of chambers around a central hall, open to the sky, since no pillars are found necessary to support a roof. No traces of windows are found in the walls, which were lined with slabs of coarse marble, with cuneiform inscriptions. The façade of the palaces we know little about, except that the entrances to them were lined by groups of colossal bulls. These are sculptured with considerable spirit, but *art*, in the sense that the Greeks understood it, did not exist. In the ordinary appliances of life the Assyrians were probably on a par with the Egyptians; but they were debased by savage passions and degrading superstitions. They have left nothing for subsequent ages to use. Nothing which has contributed to civilization remains of their existence. They have furnished no *models* of literature, art, or government.

Its remains.

While Nineveh was rising to greatness, Babylon was under an eclipse, and thus lasted six hundred and fifty years. It was in the year 1273 that this eclipse began. But a great change took place in the era of Narbonassar, B. C. 747, when Babylon threatened to secure its independence, and which subsequently compelled Esar-Haddon, the Assyrian monarch, to assume, in his own person, the government of Babylon, B. C. 680.

Growth of Babylon.

In 625 B. C. the old Chaldeans recovered their political importance, probably by an alliance with the Medes, and Nabopolassar obtained undisputed possession of Babylon, and founded a short but brilliant dynasty. He obtained a share of the captives of Nineveh, and increased the population of his capital. His son, Nebuchadnezzar, was sent as general against the Egyptians, and defeated their king, Neko, reconquered all the lands bordering on Egypt, and received the submission of Jehoiakim, of Jerusalem. The death of Nabopolassar recalled his son to Babylon, and his great reign began B. C. 604.

The Chaldean monarchy.

It was he who enlarged the capital to so great an extent that he may almost be said to have built it. It was in the form of a square, on both banks of the Euphrates, forty-eight miles in circuit, according to Herodotus, with an area of two hundred square miles—large enough to support a considerable population by agriculture alone. The walls of this city, if we accept the testimony of Herodotus, were three hundred and fifty feet high, and eighty-seven feet thick, and were strengthened by two hundred and fifty towers, and pierced with one hundred gates of brass. The river was lined by quays, and the two parts of the city were united by a stone bridge, at each end of which was a fortified palace. The greatest work of the royal architect was the new palace, with the adjoining hanging garden—a series of terraces to resemble hills, to please his Median queen. This palace, with the garden, was eight miles in circumference, and splendidly decorated with statues of men and animals. Here the mighty monarch, after his great military expeditions, solaced himself, and dreamed of omnipotence, until a sudden stroke of madness—that form which causes a man to mistake himself for a brute animal—sent him from his luxurious halls into the gardens he had planted. His madness lasted seven years, and he died, after a reign of forty-three years, B. C. 561, and Evil-Merodach, his son, reigned in his stead.

Nebuchadnezzar.

Magnificence of Babylon.

He was put to death two years after, for lawlessness and intemperance, and was succeeded by his brother-in-law and murderer, Neriglissar. So rapid was the decline of the monarchy, that after a few brief reigns Babylon was entered by the army of Cyrus, and the last king, Bil-shar-utzur, or Bilshassar, associated with his father Nabonadius, was slain, B. C. 538. Thus ended the Chaldean monarchy, seventeen hundred and ninety-six years after the building of Babel by Nimrod, according to the chronology it is most convenient to assume.

Fall of the monarchy.

CHAPTER IX.

THE EMPIRE OF THE MEDES AND PERSIANS.

The third of the great Oriental monarchies brought in contact with the Jews was that of the Medes and Persians, which arose on the dissolution of the Assyrian and Babylonian empires. The nations we have hitherto alluded to were either Hamite or Shemite. But our attention is now directed to a different race, the descendants of Japhet. Madai, the third son of Japhet, was the progenitor of the Medes, whose territory extended from the Caspian Sea on the north, to the mountains of Persia on the south, and from the highlands of Armenia and the chain of Tagros on the west, to the great desert of Iran on the east. It comprised a great variety of climate, and was intersected by mountains whose valleys were fruitful in corn and fruits. "The finest part of the country is an elevated region inclosed by the offshoots of the Armenian mountains, and surrounding the basin of the great lake Urumizu, four thousand two hundred feet above the sea, and the valleys of the ancient Mardus and the Araxes, the northern boundary of the land. In this mountain region stands Tabris, the delightful summer seat of the modern Persian shahs. The slopes of the Tagros furnish excellent pasture; and here were reared the famous horses which the ancients called Nisæan. The eastern districts are flat and pestilential, where they sink down to the shores of the Caspian Sea; rugged and sterile where they adjoin the desert of Iran." The people who inhabited this country were hardy and bold, and were remarkable for their horsemanship. They were the greatest warriors

The country of the Medes and Persians.

The martial character of the people.

of the ancient world, until the time of the Greeks. They were called Aryians by Herodotus. They had spread over the highlands of Western Asia in the primeval ages, and formed various tribes. The first notice of this Aryan (or Arian) race, appears in the inscriptions on the black obelisk of Nimrod, B. C. 880, from which it would appear that this was about the period of the immigration into Media, and they were then exposed to the aggressions of the Assyrians. "The first king who menaced their independence was the monarch whose victories are recorded on the black obelisk in the British Museum." He made a raid into, rather than a conquest of, the Median country. Sargon, the third monarch of the Lower Empire, effected something like a conquest, and peopled the cities which he founded with Jewish captives from Samaria, B. C. 710. Media thus became the most eastern province of his empire, but the conquest of it was doubtless incomplete. The Median princes paid tribute to the kings of Nineveh, or withheld it, according to their circumstances.

Early kings of Media.

According to Ctesias, the Median monarchy commenced B. C. 875; but Herodotus, with greater probable accuracy, places the beginning of it B. C. 708. The revolt of Media from Assyria was followed by the election of Deioces, who reigned fifty-three years. The history of this king is drawn through Grecian sources, and can not much be depended upon. According to the legends, the seven tribes of the Medes, scattered over separate villages, suffered all the evils of anarchy, till the reputation of Deioces made him the arbiter of their disputes. He then retired into private life; anarchy returned, a king was called for, and Deioces was elected. He organized a despotic power, which had its central seat in Ecbatana, which he made his capital, built upon a hill, on the summit of which was the royal palace, where the king reigned in seclusion, transacting all business through spies, informers, petitions, and decrees. Such is the account which Rawlinson gives, and which Smith follows.

Deioces.

The great Median kingdom really began with Cyaxares, about the year B. C. 633, when the Assyrian empire was waning. He emerges from the obscurity like Attila and Gengis Khan, and other eastern conquerors, at the head of irresistible hordes, sweeps all away before him, and builds up an enormous power. This period was distinguished by a great movement among the Turanian races (Cimmerians), living north of the Danube, which, according to Herodotus, made a great irruption into Asia Minor, where some of the tribes effected a permanent settlement; while the Scythians, from Central Asia, overran Media, crossed the Zagros mountains, entered Mesopotamia, passed through Syria to Egypt, and held the dominion of Western Asia, till expelled by Cyaxares. He only established his new kingdom after a severe conflict between the Scythian and Aryan races, which had hitherto shared the possession of the tablelands of Media.

Cyaxares.

From age to age the Turanian races have pressed forward to occupy the South, and it was one of these great movements which Cyaxares opposed, and opposed successfully—the first recorded in history. These nomads of Tartary, or Scythian tribes, which overran Western Asia in the seventh century before Christ, under the new names of Huns, Avari, Bulgarians, Magyars, Turks, Mongols, devastated Europe and Asia for fifteen successive centuries. They have been the scourge of the race, and they commenced their incursions before Grecian history begins.

The irruption of the Turanian races.

Learning from these Scythian invaders many arts, not before practiced in war, such as archery and cavalry movements, Cyaxares was prepared to extend his empire to the west over Armenia and Asia Minor, as far as the river Halys. He made war in Lydia with the father of Crœsus. But before these conquests were made, he probably captured Nineveh and destroyed it, B. C. 625. He was here assisted by the whole force of the Babylonians, under Nabopolassar, an old general of the Assyrians, but who had rebelled. In reward he obtained for his son, Nebu-

Conquests of Cyaxares.

chadnezzar, the hand of the daughter of Cyaxares. The last of the Assyrian monarchs, whom the Greeks have called Sardanapalus, burned himself in his palace rather than fall into the hands of the Median conqueror.

The fall of Nineveh led to the independence of Babylon, and its wonderful growth, and also to the conquests of the Medes as far as Lydia to the west. The war with Lydia lasted six years, and was carried on with various success, until peace was restored by the mediation of a Babylonian prince. The reason that peace was made was an eclipse of the sun, which happened in the midst of a great battle, which struck both armies with superstitious fears. On the conclusion of peace, the son of the Median king, Astyages, married the daughter of the Lydian monarch, Alyattes, and an alliance was formed between Media and Lydia.

War with Lydia.

At this time Lydia comprised nearly all of Asia Minor, west of the Halys. The early history of this country is involved in obscurity. The dynasty on the throne, when invaded by the Medes, was founded by Gyges, B. C. 724, who began those aggressions on the Grecian colonies which were consummated by Crœsus. Under the reign of Ardys, his successor, Asia Minor was devastated by the Cimmerians, a people who came from the regions north of the Black Sea, between the Danube and the Sea of Azov, being driven away by an inundation of Scythians, like that which afterward desolated Media. These Cimmerians, having burned the great temple of Diana, at Ephesus, and destroyed the capital city of Sardis, were expelled from Lydia by Alyattes, the monarch against whom Cyaxares had made war.

The Lydian monarchy.

Cyaxares reigned forty years, and was succeeded by Astyages, B. C. 593, whose history is a total blank, till near the close of his long reign of thirty-five years, when the Persians under Cyrus arose to power. He seems to have resigned himself to the ordinary condition of Oriental kings—to effeminacy and luxury—brought

Astyages.

about by the prosperity which he inherited. He was contemporary with Crœsus, the famous king of Lydia, whose life has been invested with so much romantic interest by Herodotus—the first of the Asiatic kings who commenced hostile aggression on the Greeks. After making himself master of all the Greek States of Asia Minor, he combated a power which was destined to overturn the older monarchies of the East—that of the Persians—a race closely connected with the Medes in race, language, and religion.

The Persians first appear in history as a hardy, warlike people, simple in manners and scornful of luxury. They were uncultivated in art and science, but possessed great wit, and a poetical imagination. They lived in the mountainous region on the southwest of Iran, where the great plain descends to the Persian Gulf. The sea-coast is hot and arid, as well as the eastern region where the mountains pass into the table-land of Iran. Between these tracts, resembling the Arabian desert, lie the high lands at the extremity of the Zagros chain. These rugged regions, rich in fruitful valleys, are favorable to the cultivation of corn, of the grape, and fruits, and afford excellent pasturage for flocks. In the northern part is the beautiful plain of Shiraz, which forms the favorite residence of the modern shahs. In the valley of Bend-amir was the old capital of Persepolis, whose ruins attest the magnificent palaces of Darius and Xerxes. Persia proper was a small country, three hundred miles from north to south, and two hundred and eighty from east to west, inhabited by an Aryan race, who brought with them, from the country beyond the Indus, a distinctive religion, language, and political institutions. Their language was closely connected with the Aryan dialects of India, and the tongues of modern Europe. Hence the Persians were noble types of the great Indo-European family, whose civilization has spread throughout the world. Their religion was the least corrupted of the ancient races, and was marked by a keen desire to arrive at truth, and entered, in the time of the Gnostics, into the

The early history of the Persians.

speculations of the Christian fathers, of whom Origen was the type. Their teachers were the Magi, a wise and learned caste, some of whom came to Jerusalem in the time of Herod, guided by the star in the East, to institute inquiries as to the birth of Christ. They attempted to solve the mysteries of creation, but their elemental principle of religion was worship of all the elements, especially of fire. But the Persians also believed in the two principles of good and evil, which were called the principle of dualism, and which they brought from India. It is thought by Rawlinson that the Persians differed in their religion from the primeval people of India, whose Vedas, or sacred books, were based on monotheism, in its spiritual and personal form, and that, for the heresy of "dualism," they were compelled to migrate to the West. The Medes, with whom they subsequently became associated, were inclined to the old elemental worship of nature, which they learned from the Turanian or Scythic population.

Zoroaster.

The great man among the Persians was Zoroaster—or Zerdusht, born, probably, B. C. 589. He is immortal, not from his personal history, the details of which we are ignorant, but from his ideas, which became the basis of the faith of the Persians. He stamped his mind on the nation, as Mohammed subsequently did upon Arabia. His central principle was "dualism"—the two powers of good and evil—the former of which was destined ultimately to conquer. But with this dualistic creed of the old Persian, he also blended a reformed Magian worship of the elements, which had gained a footing among the Chaldean priests, and which originally came from the Scythic invaders. Magism could not have come from the Semitic races, whose original religion was theism, like that of Melchisedek and Abraham; nor from the Japhetic races, or Indo-European, whose worship was polytheism—that of personal gods under distinct names, like Jupiter, Juno, and Minerva. The first to yield to this Magism were the Medes, who adopted the religion of older settlers,—the Scythic tribes,

His religion.

their subjects,—and which faith superseded the old Aryan religion.

Character of the Persians

The Persians, the flower of the Aryan races, were peculiarly military in all their habits and aspirations. Their nobles, mounted on a famous breed of horses, composed the finest cavalry in the world. Nor was their infantry inferior, armed with lances, shields, and bows. Their military spirit was kept alive by their mountain life and simple habits and strict discipline.

Astyages, we have seen, was the last of the Median kings. He married his daughter, according to Herodotus, to Cambyses, a Persian noble, preferring him to a higher alliance among the Median princes, in order that a dream might not be fulfilled that her offspring should conquer Asia. On the return of the dream he sought to destroy the child she was about to bear, but it was preserved by a herdsman; and when the child was ten years of age he was chosen by his playfellows on the mountains to be their king. As such he caused the son of a noble Median to be scourged for disobedience, who carried his complaint to Astyages. The Median monarch finds out his pedigree from the herdsman, and his officer, Harpagus, to whom he had intrusted the commission for his destruction. He invites, in suppressed anger, this noble to a feast, at which he serves up the flesh of his own son. Harpagus, in revenge, conspires with some discontented nobles, and invites Cyrus, this boy-king, now the bravest of the youths of his age and country, to a revolt. Cyrus leads his troops against Astyages, and gains a victory, and also the person of the sovereign, and his great reign began, B. C. 558.

Rise of Cyrus.

The dethronement of Astyages caused a war between Lydia and Persia. Crœsus hastens to attack the usurper and defend his father-in-law. He forms a league with Babylonia and Egypt. Thus the three most powerful monarchs of the world are arrayed against Cyrus, who is prepared to meet the confederation. Crœsus is defeated, and retreats to his capital, Sardis; and the next

His wars.

spring, while summoning his allies, is attacked unexpectedly by Cyrus, and is again defeated. He now retires to Sardis, which is strongly fortified, and the city is besieged by the Persians, and falls after a brief siege. Crœsus himself is spared, and in his adversity gives wise counsel to his conqueror.

Cyrus leaves a Lydian in command of the captured city, and departs for home. A revolt ensues, which leads to a collision between Persia and the Greek colonies, and the subjection of the Grecian cities by Harpagus, the general of Cyrus. Then followed the conquest of Asia Minor, which required several years, and was conducted by the generals of Cyrus. He was required in Media, to consolidate his power. He then extended his conquests to the East, and subdued the whole plateau of Iran, to the mountains which divided it from the Indus. Thus fifteen years of splendid military successes passed before he laid siege to Babylon, B. C. 538.

His great empire.

On the fall of that great city Cyrus took up his residence in it, as the imperial capital of his vast dominion. Here he issued his decree for the return of the Jews to their ancient territory, and for the rebuilding of their temple, after seventy years' captivity. This decree was dictated by the sound military policy of maintaining the frontier territory of Palestine against his enemies in Asia Minor, which he knew the Jews would do their best to preserve, and this policy he carried out with noble generosity, and returned to the Jews the captured vessels of silver and gold which Nebuchadnezzar had carried away; and for more than two centuries Persia had no warmer friends and allies than the obedient and loyal subjects of Judea.

He makes Babylon his capital.

Cyrus fell in battle while fighting a tribe of Scythians at the east of the Caspian Sea, B. C. 529. He was the greatest general that the Oriental world ever produced, and well may rank with Alexander himself. His reign of twenty-nine years was one constant succession of wars, in which he was uniformly successful, and in which

Greatness of the reign of Cyrus.

success was only equaled by his magnanimity. His empire extended from the Indus to the Hellespont and the Syrian coast, far greater than that of either Assyria or Babylonia.

Degeneracy of the Persian conquerors.

The result of the Persian conquest on the conquerors themselves was to produce habits of excessive luxury, a wide and vast departure from their original mode of life, which enfeebled the empire, and prepared the way for a rapid decline.

Cambyses.

Cambyses, however, the son and successor of Cyrus, carried out his policy and conquests. He was, unlike his father, a tyrant and a sensualist, but possessed considerable military genius. He conquered Phœnicia, and thus became master of the sea as well as of the land. He then quarreled with Amasis, the king of Egypt, and subdued his kingdom.

His follies.

Like an eastern despot, he had, while in Egypt, in an hour of madness and caprice, killed his brother, Smerdis. It happened there was a Magian who bore a striking resemblance to the murdered prince. With the help of his brother, whom the king had left governor of his household, this Magian usurped the throne of Persia, while Cambyses was absent, the death of the true Smerdis having been carefully concealed.

Usurpation of the Magians.

The news of the usurpation reached Cambyses while returning from an expedition to Syria. An accidental wound from the point of his sword proved mortal, B. C. 522. But Cambyses, about to die, called his nobles around him, and revealed the murder of his brother, and exhorted them to prevent the kingdom falling into the hands of the Medes. He left no children.

Darius.

The usurper proved a tyrant. A conspiracy of Persians followed, headed by the descendants of Cyrus; and Darius, the chief of these—the son of Hystaspes, became king of Persia, after Smerdis had reigned seven months. But this reign, brief as it was, had restored the old Magian priests to power, who had, by their magical arts, great popularity with the people, not only Medes, but Persians.

Darius restored the temples and the worship which the Magian priests had overthrown, and established the religion of Zoroaster. The early years of his reign were disturbed by rebellions in Babylonia and Media, but these were suppressed, and Darius prosecuted the conquests which Cyrus had begun. He invaded both India and Scythia, while his general, Megabazus, subdued Thrace and the Greek cities of the Hellespont.

His conquests.

The king of Macedonia acknowledged the supremacy of the great monarch of Asia, and gave the customary present of earth and water. Darius returned at length to Susa to enjoy the fruit of his victories, and the pleasures which his great empire afforded. For twenty years his glories were unparalleled in the East, and his life was tranquil.

His greatness.

But in the year B. C. 500, a great revolt of the Ionian cities took place. It was suppressed, at first, but the Atticans, at Marathon, defeated the Persian warriors, B. C. 490, and the great victory changed the whole course of Asiatic conquest. Darius made vast preparations for a new invasion of Greece, but died before they were completed, after a reign of thirty-six years, B. C. 485, leaving a name greater than that of any Oriental sovereign, except Cyrus.

The revolt of the Ionian cities.

Unfortunately for him and his dynasty, he challenged the spirit of western liberty, then at its height among the cities of Greece. His successor, Xerxes, inherited his power, but not his genius, and rashly provoked Europe by new invasions, while he lived ingloriously in his seraglio. He was murdered in his palace, the fate of the great tyrants of eastern monarchies, for in no other way than by the assassin's dagger could a change of administration take place—a poor remedy, perhaps, but not worse than the disease itself. This tyrant was the Ahasuerus of the Scriptures.

Xerxes.

Fate of the Persian empire.

We need not follow the fortunes of the imbecile princes who succeeded Xerxes, for the Persian monarchy was now degenerate and weakened, and easily fell under the dominion of Alexander, who finally overthrew the power of Persia, B. C. 330.

Its characteristics.

And this was well. The Persian monarchy was an absolute despotism, like that of Turkey, and the monarch not only controlled the actions of his subjects, but was the owner even of their soil. He delegated his power to satraps, who ruled during his pleasure, but whose rule was disgraced by every form of extortion—sometimes punished, however, when it became outrageous and notorious. The satraps, like pashas, were virtually independent princes, and exercised all the rights of sovereigns so long as they secured the confidence of the supreme monarch, and regularly remitted to him the tribute which was imposed. The satrapies were generally given to members of the royal family, or to great nobles connected with it by marriage. The monarch governed by no council, and the laws centered in the principle that the will of the king was supreme. The only check which he feared was assassination, and he generally spent his life in the retirement of his seraglio, at Susa, Babylon, or Ecbatana.

The Persian empire was the last of the great monarchies of the Oriental world, and these flourished for a period of two thousand years. When nations became wicked or extended over a large territory, the patriarchal rule of the primitive ages no longer proved an efficient government. Men must be ruled, however, in some way, and the irresponsible despotism of the East, over all the different races, Semitic, Hamite, and Japhetic, was the government which Providence provided, in a state of general rudeness, or pastoral simplicity, or oligarchal usurpations. The last great monarchy was the best; it was that which was exercised by the descendants of Japhet, according to the prediction that he should dwell in the tents of Shem, and Canaan should be his servant.

Before we follow the progress of the descendants of Japhet in Greece, among whom a new civilization arose, designed to improve the condition of society by the free agency displayed in art, science, literature, and government — the rise, in short, of free institutions — we will glance at the nations in Asia Minor which were brought in contact with the powers we have so briefly considered.

CHAPTER X.

ASIA MINOR AND PHŒNICIA.

CONCERNING the original inhabitants of Asia Minor our information is very scanty. The works of Strabo shed an indefinite light, and the author of the Iliad seems to have been but imperfectly acquainted with either the geography or the people of that extensive country. According to Herodotus, the river Halys was the most important geographical limit; nor does he mention the great chain of Taurus, which begins from the southern coast of Lycia, and strikes northeastward as far as Armenia — the most important boundary line in the time of the Romans. Northward of Mount Taurus, on the upper portion of the river Halys, was situated the spacious plain of Asia Minor. The northeast and south of this plain was mountainous, and was bounded by the Euxine, the Ægean, and the Pamphylian seas. The northwestern part included the mountainous region of Ida, Temnus, and Olympus. The peninsula was fruitful in grains, wine, fruit, cattle, and oil.

Original inhabitants of Asia Minor.

Along the western shores of this great peninsula were Pelasgians, Mysians, Bythinians, Phrygians, Lydians, and other nations, before the Greeks established their colonies. Further eastward were Lycians, Pisidians, Phrygians, Cappadocians, Paphlagonians, and others. The Phrygians, Mysians, and Teucrians were on the northwest. These various nations were not formed into large kingdoms or confederacies, nor even into large cities, but were inconsiderable tribes, that presented no formidable resistance to external enemies. The most powerful people were the Lydians, whose capital was Sardis, who were ruled by

Its various nations.

Gyges, 700 B. C. This monarchy extinguished the independence of the Greek cities on the coast, without impeding their development in wealth and civilization. All the nations west of the river Halys were kindred in language and habits. East of the Halys dwelt Semitic races, Assyrians, Syrians, Cappadocians, and Cilicians. Along the coast of the Euxine dwelt Bythinians, Marandynians, and Paphlagonians — branches of the Thracian race. Along the southern coast of the Propontis were the Doliones and Pelasgians. In the region of Mount Ida were the Teucrians and Mysians. All these races had a certain affinity with the Thracians, and all modified the institutions of the Greeks who settled on the coast for purposes of traffic or colonization. The music of the Greeks was borrowed from the Phrygians and Lydians. The flute is known to have been invented, or used by the Phrygians, and from them to have passed to Greek composers.

The Phrygians.

The ancient Phrygians were celebrated chiefly for their flocks and agricultural produce, while the Lydians, dwelling in cities, possessed much gold and silver. But there are few great historical facts connected with either nation. There is an interesting legend connected with the Phrygian town of Gordium. The primitive king, Gordius, was originally a poor husbandman, upon the yoke of whose team, as he tilled the field, an eagle perched. He consulted the augurs to explain the curious portent, and was told that the kingdom was destined for his family. His son was Midas, offspring of a maiden of prophetic family. Soon after, dissensions breaking out among the Phrygians, they were directed by an oracle to choose a king, whom they should first see approaching in a wagon. Gordius and his son Midas were the first they saw approaching the town, and the crown was conferred upon them. The wagon was consecrated, and became celebrated for a knot which no one could untie. Whosoever should untie that knot was promised the kingdom of Asia. It remained untied until Alexander the Great cut it with his sword.

The Lydians became celebrated for their music, of which the chief instruments were the flute and the harp. Their capital, Sardis, was situated on a precipitous rock, and was deemed impregnable. Among their kings was Crœsus, whose great wealth was derived from the gold found in the sands of the river Pactolus, which flowed toward the Hermus from Mount Tmolus, and also from the industry of his subjects. They were the first on record to coin gold and silver. The antiquity of the Lydian monarchy is very great, and was traced to Heracles. The Heracleid dynasty lasted five hundred and five years, and ended with Myrsus, or Kandaules. His wife was of exceeding beauty, and the vanity of her husband led him to expose her person to Gyges, commander of his guard. The affronted wife, in revenge, caused her husband to be assassinated, and married Gyges. A strong party opposed his ascent to the throne, and a civil war ensued, which was terminated by a consultation of the oracle, which decided in favor of Gyges, the first historical king of Lydia, about the year 715 B. C.

The Lydians.

Gyges.

With this king commenced the aggressions from Sardis on the Asiatic Greeks, which ended in their subjection. How far the Lydian kingdom of Sardis extended during the reign of Gyges is not known, but probably over the whole Troad, to Abydus, on the Hellespont. Gyges reigned thirty-eight years, and was succeeded by his son Ardys, during whose reign was an extensive invasion of the Cimmerians, and a collision between the inhabitants of Lydia and those of Upper Asia, under the Median kings, who first acquired importance about the year 656 B. C., under a king called, by the Greeks, Phraortes, son of Deioces, who built the city of Ecbatana.

His prosperous reign.

Phraortes greatly extended the empire of the Medes, and conquered the Persians, but was defeated and slain by the Assyrians of Nineveh. His son, Cyaxares (636—595 B. C.), continued the Median conquests to the river Halys, which was the boundary between the

Alliance of Lydia with Persia.

Lydian and Median kingdoms. A war between these two powers was terminated by the marriage of the daughter of the Lydian king with the son of the Median monarch, Cyaxares, who shortly after laid siege to Nineveh, but was obliged to desist by a sudden inroad of Scythians.

This inroad of the Scythians in Media took place about the same time that the Cimmerians invaded Lydia, a nomad race which probably inhabited the Tauric Chersonessus (Crimea), and had once before desolated Asia Minor before the time of Homer. The Cimmerians may have been urged forward into Asia Minor by an invasion of the Scythians themselves, a nomadic people who neither planted nor reaped, but lived on food derived from animals—prototypes of the Huns, and also progenitors—a formidable race of barbarians, in the northern section of Central Asia, east of the Caspian Sea. The Cimmerians fled before this more warlike race, abandoned their country on the northern coast of the Euxine, and invaded Asia Minor. They occupied Sardis, and threatened Ephesus, and finally were overwhelmed in the mountainous regions of Cilicia. Some, however, effected a settlement in the territory where the Greek city of Sinope was afterward built.

Scythian inroads.

Their characteristics.

Ardys was succeeded by his son Tadyattes, who reigned twelve years; and his son and successor, Alyattes, expelled the Cimmerians from Asia Minor. But the Scythians, who invaded Media, defeated the king, Cyaxares, and became masters of the country, and spread as far as Palestine, and enjoyed their dominion twenty-eight years, until they were finally driven away by Cyaxares. These nomadic tribes from Tartary were the precursors of Huns, Avars, Bulgarians, Magyars, Turks, Mongols, and Tartars, who, at different periods, invaded the civilized portions of Asia and Europe, and established a dominion more or less durable.

Scythian conquests.

Cyaxares, after the expulsion of the Scythians, took Nineveh, and reduced the Assyrian empire, while Alyattes, the king of Lydia, after the Cimmerians were subdued, made war on the Greek city of Miletus, and reduced the Milesians to great distress, and also took Smyrna. He reigned fifty-seven years with great prosperity, and transmitted his kingdom to Crœsus, his son by an Ionian wife. His tomb was one of the architectural wonders of that day, and only surpassed by the edifices of Egypt and Babylon.

Crœsus.

Crœsus made war on the Asiatic Greeks, and as the twelve Ionian cities did not co-operate with any effect, they were subdued. He extended his conquests over Asia Minor, until he had conquered the Phrygians, Mysians, and other nations, and created a great empire, of which Sardis was the capital. The treasures he amassed exceeded any thing before known to the Greeks, though inferior to the treasures accumulated at Susa and other Persian capitals when Alexander conquered the East.

His prosperity.

But the Lydian monarchy under Crœsus was soon absorbed in the Persian empire, together with the cities of the Ionian Greeks, as has been narrated.

But there was another power intimately connected with the kingdom of Judea,—the Phœnician, which furnished Solomon artists and timber for his famous temple. We close this chapter with a brief notice of the greatest merchants of the ancient world, the Phœnicians.

The Phœnicians.

They belonged, as well as the Assyrians, to the Semitic or Syro-Arabian family, comprising, besides, the Syrians, Jews, Arabians, and in part the Abyssinians. They were at a very early period a trading and mercantile nation, and the variegated robes and golden ornaments fabricated at Sidon were prized by the Homeric heroes. They habitually traversed the Ægean Sea, and formed settlements on its islands.

Their Semitic origin.

The Phœnician towns occupied a narrow slip of the coast of Syria and Palestine, about one hundred and twenty miles in length, and generally about twenty in breadth—between Mount Libanus and the sea. Aradus was the northernmost, and Tyre the southernmost city. Between these were situated Sidon, Berytus, Tripolis, and Byblus. Within this confined territory was concentrated a greater degree of commercial wealth and enterprise, also of manufacturing skill, than could be found in the other parts of the world at the time. Each town was an independent community, having its own surrounding territory, and political constitution and hereditary prince. Tyre was a sort of presiding city, having a controlling political power over the other cities. Mount Libanus, or Lebanon, touched the sea along the Phœnician coast, and furnished abundant supplies for ship-building.

The country.

The great Phœnician deity was Melkarth, whom the Greeks called Hercules, to whom a splendid temple was erected at Tyre, coeval, perhaps, with the foundation of the city two thousand three hundred years before the time of Herodotus. In the year 700 B. C., the Phœnicians seemed to have reached their culminating power, and they had colonies in Africa, Sicily, Sardinia, and Spain. Carthage, Utica, and Gades were all flourishing cities before the first Olympiad. The commerce of the Phœnicians extended through the Red Sea and the coast of Arabia in the time of Solomon. They furnished the Egyptians, Assyrians, and Persians with the varied productions of other countries at a very remote period.

Phœnician cities.

The most ancient colonies were Utica and Carthage, built in what is now called the gulf of Tunis; and Cades, now Cadiz, was prosperous one thousand years before the Christian era. The enterprising mariners of Tyre coasted beyond the pillars of Hercules without ever losing sight of land. The extreme productiveness of the southern region of Spain in the precious metals tempted the merchants to that distant country. But Carthage was by far the most important centre for Tyrian trade, and became the mistress of a large number of dependent cities.

Phœnician colonies.

When Psammetichus relaxed the jealous exclusion of ships from the mouth of the Nile, the incitements to traffic were greatly increased, and the Phœnicians, as well as Ionian merchants, visited Egypt. But the Phœnicians were jealous of rivals in profitable commerce, and concealed their tracks, and magnified the dangers of the sea. About the year 600 B. C., they had circumnavigated Africa, starting from the Red Sea, and going round the Cape of Good Hope to Gades, and from thence returning by the Nile.

It would seem that Nechos, king of Egypt, anxious to procure a water communication between the Red Sea and the Mediterranean, began digging a canal from one to the other. In the prosecution of this project he dispatched Phœnicians on an experimental voyage round Libya, which was accomplished in three years. The mariners landed in the autumn, and remained long enough to plant corn and raise a crop for their supplies. They reached Egypt through the Straits of Gibraltar, and recounted a tale, which, says Herodotus, "others may believe it if they choose, but I can not believe, that in sailing round Libya, they had the sun on their right and—to the north." In going round Africa they had no occasion to lose sight of land, and their vessels were amply stored. The voyage, however, was regarded as desperate and unprofitable, and was not repeated.

Voyage of the Phœnicians.

Besides the trade which the Phœnicians carried on along the coasts, they had an extensive commerce in the interior of Asia. But we do not read of any great characters who arrested the attention of their own age or succeeding ages. Phœnician history is barren in political changes and great historical characters, as is that of Carthage till the Roman wars.

Between the years 700 and 530 B. C., there was a great decline of Phœnician power, which was succeeded by the rise of the Greek maritime cities. Nebuchadnezzar reduced the Phœnician cities to the same dependence that the Ionian cities were reduced by Crœsus and Cyrus. The opening of the Nile to the Grecian commerce contributed to the decline of Phœnicia. But to this country the Greeks owed the alphabet and the first standard of weights and measures.

Decline of Phœnician power.

Carthage, founded 819 B. C., by Dido, had a flourishing commerce in the sixth century before Christ, and also commenced, at this time, their encroachments in Sicily, which led to wars for two hundred and fifty years with the Greek settlements. It contained, it is said, at one time, seven hundred thousand people. But a further notice of their great city is reserved until allusion is made to the Punic wars which the Romans waged with this powerful State.

Carthage.

CHAPTER XI.

JEWISH HISTORY FROM THE BABYLONIAN CAPTIVITY TO THE BIRTH OF CHRIST.—THE HIGHP RIESTS AND THE ASMONEAN AND IDUMEAN KINGS.

Absorption of the ten tribes.

WE have seen how the ten tribes were carried captive to Assyria, on the fall of Samaria, by Shalmanezer, B. C., 721. From that time history loses sight of the ten tribes, as a distinct people. They were probably absorbed with the nations among whom they settled, although imagination has loved to follow them into inaccessible regions where they await their final restoration. But there are no reliable facts which justify this conclusion. They may have been the ancestors of the Christian converts afterward found among the Nestorians. They may have retained in the East, to a certain extent, some of their old institutions. But nothing is known with certainty. All is vain conjecture respecting their ultimate fortunes.

The Jews at Babylon.

The Jews of the tribes of Judah and Benjamin never entirely departed from their ancient faith, and their monarchs reigned in regular succession till the captivity of the family of David. They were not carried to Babylon for one hundred and twenty-three years after the dispersion of the ten tribes, B. C. 598.

During the captivity, the Jews still remained a separate people, governed by their own law and religion. It is supposed that they were rather colonists than captives, and were allowed to dwell together in considerable bodies—that they were not sold as slaves, and by degrees became possessed of considerable wealth. What region, from time immemorial, has not witnessed their thrift and their love of money? Well may a Jew say, as well as a Greek, " *Quæ regio in terris nostri non plena laboris.*" Taking the advice of Jeremiah they built houses, planted gardens, and submitted to their fate, even if they bewailed it "by the rivers of Babylon," in such sad contrast to their old mountain homes. They had the free enjoyment of their religion, and were subjected to no general and grievous religious persecutions. And some of their noble youth, like Daniel, were treated with great distinction during the captivity. Daniel had been transported to Babylon before Jerusalem fell, as a hostage, among others, of the fidelity of their king. These young men, from the highest Jewish families, were educated in all the knowledge of the Babylonians, as Joseph had been in Egyptian wisdom. They were the equals of the Chaldean priests in knowledge of astronomy, divination, and the interpretation of dreams. And though these young hostages were maintained at the public expense, and perhaps in the royal palaces, they remembered their distressed countrymen, and lived on the simplest fare. It was as an interpreter of dreams that Daniel maintained his influence in the Babylonian court. Twice was he summoned by Nebuchadnezzar, and once by Belshazzar to interpret the handwriting on the wall. And under the Persian monarch, when Babylon fell, Daniel became a vizier, or satrap, with great dignity and power.

Daniel.

When the seventy years' captivity, which Jeremiah had predicted, came to an end, the empire of the Medes and Persians was in the hands of Cyrus, under whose sway he enjoyed the same favor and rank that he did under Darius, or any of the Babylonian princes. The miraculous deliverance of this great man from the lion's den, into which he had been thrown from the intrigues of his enemies and the unalterable law of the Medes, resulted in a renewed exaltation. Josephus ascribes to Daniel one of the noblest and most interesting characters in Jewish history, a great skill in architecture, and it is to him that the splendid mausoleum at Ecbatana is attributed. But Daniel, with all his honors, was not corrupted, and it was probably

His beautiful character.

through his influence, as a grand vizier, that the exiled Jews obtained from Cyrus the decree which restored them to their beloved land.

Return of the Jews.

The number of the returned Jews, under Zerubbabel, a descendant of the kings of Judah, were forty-two thousand three hundred and sixty men—a great and joyful caravan—but small in number compared with the Israelites who departed from Egypt with Moses. On their arrival in their native land, they were joined by great numbers of the common people who had remained. They bore with them the sacred vessels of the temple, which Cyrus generously restored. They arrived in the spring of the year B. C. 536, and immediately made preparations for the restoration of the temple; not under those circumstances which enabled Solomon to concentrate the wealth of Western Asia, but under great discouragements and the pressure of poverty. The temple was built on the old foundation, but was not completed till the sixth year of Darius Hystapes, B. C. 515, and then without the ancient splendor.

Dedication of the Temple.

It was dedicated with great joy and magnificence, but the sacrifice of one hundred bullocks, two hundred rams, four hundred lambs, and twelve goats, formed a sad contrast to the hecatombs which Solomon had offered.

Nothing else of importance marked the history of the dependent, impoverished, and humiliated Jews, who had returned to the country of their ancestors during the reign of Darius Hystaspes.

Mordecai and Ahasuerus.

It was under his successor, Xerxes, he who commanded the Hellespont to be scourged — that mad, luxurious, effeminated monarch, who is called in Scripture Ahasuerus,—that Mordecai figured in the court of Persia, and Esther was exalted to the throne itself. It was in the seventh year of his reign that this inglorious king returned, discomfited, from the invasion of Greece. Abandoning himself to the pleasures of his harem, he marries the Jewess maiden, who is the instrument, under Providence, of averting the greatest calamity with which the Jews were ever threatened. Haman, a descendant of the Amalekitish kings, is the favorite minister and grand vizier of the Persian monarch. Offended with Mordecai, his rival in imperial favor, the cousin of the queen, he intrigues for the wholesale slaughter of the Jews wherever they were to be found, promising the king ten thousand talents of silver from the confiscation of Jewish property, and which the king needed, impoverished by his unsuccessful expedition into Greece. He thus obtains a decree from Ahasuerus for the general massacre of the Jewish nation, in all the provinces of the empire, of which Judea was one. The Jews are in the utmost consternation, and look to Mordecai. His hope is based on Esther, the queen, who might soften, by her fascinations, the heart of the king. She assumes the responsibility of saving her nation at the peril of her own life — a deed of not extraordinary self-devotion, but requiring extraordinary tact. What anxiety must have pressed the soul of that Jewish woman in the task she undertook! What a responsibility on her unaided shoulders? But she dissembles her grief, her fear, her anxiety, and appears before the king radiant in beauty and loveliness. The golden sceptre is extended to her by her weak and cruel husband, though arrayed in the pomp and power of an Oriental monarch, before whom all bent the knee, and to whom, even in his folly, he appears as demigod. She does not venture to tell the king her wishes. The stake is too great. She merely invites him to a grand banquet, with his minister Haman. Both king and minister are ensnared by the cautious queen, and the result is the disgrace of Haman, the elevation of Mordecai, and the deliverance of the Jews from the fatal sentence — not a perfect deliverance, for the decree could not be changed, but the Jews were warned and allowed to defend themselves, and they slew seventy-five thousand of their enemies. The act of vengeance was followed by the execution of

The story of Esther.

the ten sons of Haman, and Mordecai became the real governor of Persia. We see in this story the caprice which governed the actions, in general, of Oriental kings, and their own slavery to their favorite wives. The charms of a woman effect, for evil or good, what conscience, and reason, and policy, and wisdom united can not do. Esther is justly a favorite with the Christian and Jewish world; but Vashti, the proud queen who, with true woman's dignity, refuses to grace with her presence the saturnalia of an intoxicated monarch, is also entitled to our esteem, although she paid the penalty of disobedience; and the foolish edict which the king promulgated, that all women should implicitly obey their husbands, seems to indicate that unconditional obedience was not the custom of the Persian women.

Return to Palestine of Jews under Ezra.

The reign of Artaxerxes, the successor of Xerxes, was favorable to the Jews, for Judea was a province of the Persian empire. In the seventh year of his reign, B. C. 458, a new migration of Jews from Babylonia took place, headed by Ezra, a man of high rank at the Persian court. He was empowered to make a collection among the Jews of Babylonia for the adornment of the temple, and he came to Jerusalem laden with treasures. He was, however, affected by the sight of a custom which had grown up, of intermarriage of the Jews with adjacent tribes. He succeeded in causing the foreign wives to be repudiated, and the old laws to be enforced which separated the Jews from all other nations. And it is probably this stern law, which prevents the Jews from marriage with foreigners, that has preserved their nationality, in all their wanderings and misfortunes, more than any other one cause.

Nehemiah.

A renewed commission granted to Nehemiah, B. C. 445, resulted in a fresh immigration of Jews to Palestine, in spite of all the opposition which the Samaritan and other nations made. Nehemiah was cup-bearer to the Persian king, and devoted to the Persian interests. At that time Persia had suffered a fatal blow at the battle of Cindus, and among the humiliating articles of peace with the Athenian admiral was the stipulation that the Persians should not advance within three days' journey of the sea. Jerusalem being at this distance, was an important post to hold, and the Persian court saw the wisdom of intrusting its defense to faithful allies. In spite of all obstacles, Nehemiah succeeded, in fifty-two days, in restoring the old walls and fortifications; the whole population, of every rank and order having devoted themselves to the work. Moreover, contributions for the temple continued to flow into the treasury of a once opulent, but now impoverished and decimated people. After providing for the security of the capital and the adornment of the temple, the leaders of the nation turned their attention to the compilation of the sacred books and the restoration of religion. Many important literary works had been lost during their captivity, including the work of Solomon on national history, and the ancient book of Jasher. But the books on the law, the historical books, the prophetic writings, the Psalms, Proverbs, Ecclesiastes, and the Songs of Solomon, were collected and copied. The law, revised and corrected, was publicly read by Ezra; the Feast of Tabernacles was celebrated with considerable splendor; and a renewed covenant was made by the people to keep the law, to observe the Sabbath, to avoid idolatry, and abstain from intermarriage with strangers. The Jewish constitution was restored, and Nehemiah, a Persian satrap in reality, lived in a state of considerable magnificence, entertaining the chief leaders of the nation, and reforming all disorders. Jerusalem gradually regained political importance, while the country of the ten tribes, though filled with people, continued to be the seat of idolaters.

Rebuilding of Jerusalem.

Revival of ancient laws.

On the death of Nehemiah, B. C. 415, the history of the Jews becomes obscure, and we catch only scattered glimpses of the state of the country, till the accession of Antiochus Epiphanes, B. C. 175, when the Syrian monarch had erected a new kingdom on the ruins of the Persian empire. For more than two centuries, when the Greeks and Romans flourished, Jewish history is a blank, with here and there some scattered notices and traditions which Josephus has recorded. The Jews, living in vassalage to the successors of Alexander during this interval, had become animated by a martial spirit, and the Maccabaic wars elevated them into sufficient importance to become allies of Rome—the new conquering power, destined to subdue the world. During this period the Jewish character assumed the hard, stubborn, exclusive cast which it has ever since maintained—an intense hostility to polytheism and all Gentile influences. The Jewish Scriptures took their present shape, and the Apocryphal books came to light. The sects of the Jews arose, like Pharisees and Sadducees, and religious and political parties exhibited an unwonted fierceness and intolerance. While the Greeks and Romans were absorbed in wars, the Jews perfected their peculiar economy, and grew again into political importance. The country, by means of irrigation and cultivation, became populous and fertile, and poetry and the arts regained their sway. The people took but little interest in the political convulsions of neighboring nations, and devoted themselves quietly to the development of their own resources. The captivity had cured them of war, of idolatry, and warlike expeditions.

Obscurity of Jewish history after Nehemiah.

During this two hundred years of obscurity, but real growth, unnoticed and unknown by other nations, a new capital had arisen in Egypt; Alexandria became a great mart of commerce, and the seat of revived Grecian learning. The sway of the Ptolemaic kings, Grecian in origin, was favorable to letters, and to arts. The Jews settled in their magnificent city, translated their Scriptures into Greek, and cultivated the Greek philosophy.

Obscurity and growth of the Jews.

Meanwhile the internal government of the Jews fell into the hands of the high priests—the Persian governors exercising only a general superintendence. At length the country, once again favored, was subjected to the invasion of Alexander. After the fall of Tyre, the conqueror advanced to

Gaza, and totally destroyed it. He then approached Jerusalem, in fealty to Persia. The high priest made no resistance, but went forth in his pontifical robes, followed by the people in white garments, to meet the mighty warrior. Alexander, probably encouraged by the prophesies of Daniel, as explained by the high priest, did no harm to the city or nation, but offered gifts, and, as tradition asserts, even worshiped the God of the Jews. On the conquest of Persia, Judea came into the possession of Laomedon, one of the generals of Alexander, B. C. 321. On his defeat by Ptolemy, another general, to whom Egypt had fallen as his share, one hundred thousand Jews were carried captive to Alexandria, where they settled and learned the Greek language. The country continued to be convulsed by the wars between the generals of Alexander, and fell into the hands, alternately, of the Syrian and Egyptian kings—successors of the generals of the great conqueror.

The ascendency of the high priests.

On the establishment of the Syro-Grecian kingdom by Seleucus, Antioch, the capital, became a great city, and the rival of Alexandria. Syria, no longer a satrapy of Persia, became a powerful monarchy, and Judea became a prey to the armies of this ambitious State in its warfare with Egypt, and was alternately the vassal of each—Syria and Egypt. Under the government of the first three Ptolemies—those enlightened and magnificent princes, Soter, Philadelphus, and Evergetes, the Jews were protected, both at home and in Alexandria, and their country enjoyed peace and prosperity, until the ambition of Antiochus the Great again plunged the nation in difficulties. He had seized Judea, which was then a province of the Egyptian kings, but was defeated by Ptolemy Philopator. This monarch made sumptuous presents to the temple, and, even ventured to enter the sanctuary, but was prevented by the high priest. Although filled with fear in view of the tumult which this act provoked, he henceforth hated and persecuted the Jews. Under his successor, Judea was again invaded by Antiochus, and again was Jerusalem wrested

Persecution of the Jews by Antiochus.

from his grasp by Scopas, the Egyptian general. Defeated, however, near the source of the Jordan, the country fell into the hands of Antiochus, who was regarded as a deliverer. And it continued to be subject to the kings of Syria, until, with Jerusalem, it suffered calamities scarcely inferior to those inflicted by the Babylonians.

It is difficult to trace, with any satisfaction, the internal government of the Jews during the two hundred years when the chief power was in the hands of the high priests—this period marked by the wars between Syria and Egypt, or rather between the successors of the generals of Alexander. The government of the high priests at Jerusalem was not exempt from those disgraceful outrages which occasionally have marked all the governments of the world—whether in the hands of kings, or in an oligarchy of nobles and priests. Nehemiah had expelled from Jerusalem, Manasseh, the son of Jehoiada, who succeeded Eliashib in the high priesthood, on account of his unlawful marriage with a stranger. Manasseh, invited to Samaria by the father of the woman he had married, became high priest of the temple on Mount Gerizim, and thus perpetuated the schism between the two nations. Before the conquests of Alexander, while the country was under the dominion of Persia, a high priest by the name of John murdered his brother Jesus within the precincts of the sanctuary, which crime was punished by the Persian governor, by a heavy fine imposed upon the whole nation. Jaddua was the high priest in the time of Alexander, and by his dignity and tact won over the conqueror of Asia. Onias succeeded Jaddua, and ruled for twenty-one years, and he was succeeded by Simon the Just, a pontiff on whose administration Jewish tradition dwells with delight. Simon was succeeded by his uncles, Eleazar and Manasseh, and they by Onias II., son of Simon, through whose misconduct, or indolence, in omitting the customary tribute to the Egyptian king, came near involving the country in fresh calamities—averted, however, by his nephew Joseph, who pacified the

The reign of the high priests.

Their turbulent reigns.

Egyptian court, and obtained the former generalship of the revenues of Judea, Samaria, and Phœnicia, which he enjoyed to the time of Antiochus the Great. Onias II. was succeeded by his son Simon, under whose pontificate the Egyptian monarch was prevented from entering the temple, and he by Onias III., under whose rule a feud took place with the sons of Joseph, disgraced by murders, which called for the interposition of the Syrian king, who then possessed Judea. Joshua, or Jason, by bribery, obtained the pontificate, but he allowed the temple worship to fall into disuse, and was even alienated from the Jewish faith by his intimacy with the Syrian court. He was outbidden in his high office by Onias, his brother, who was disgraced by savage passions, and who robbed the temple of its golden vessels. The people, indignant, rose in a tumult, and slew his brother, Lysimachus. Meanwhile, Jason, the dispossessed high priest, recovered his authority, and shut up Onias, or Menelaus, as he called himself, in a castle. This was interpreted by Antiochus as an insurrection, and he visited on Jerusalem a terrible penalty—slaughtering forty thousand of the people, and seizing as many more for slaves. He then abolished the temple services, seized all the sacred vessels, collected spoil to the amount of eighteen hundred talents, defiled the altar by the sacrifice of a sow, and suppressed every sign of Jewish independence. He meditated the complete extirpation of the Jewish religion, dismantled the capitol, harassed the country people, and inflicted unprecedented barbarities. The temple itself was dedicated to Jupiter Olympius, and the reluctant and miserable Jews were forced to join in all the rites of pagan worship, including the bacchanalia, which mocked the virtue of the older Romans.

Popular tumults.

Misery of the Jews.

From this degradation and slavery the Jews were rescued by a line of heroes whom God raised up—the Asmoneans, or Maccabees. The head of this heroic family was Mattathias, a man of priestly origin, living in the town of Modin, commanding a view of the sea—an old man of wealth and influence who refused to depart from the faith

The Maccabees.

of his fathers, while most of the nation had relapsed into the paganism of the Greeks. He slew with his own hand an apostate Jew, who offered sacrifice to a pagan deity, and then killed the royal commissioner, Apelles, whom Antiochus had sent to enforce his edicts. The heroic old man, who resembled William Tell, in his mission and character, summoned his countrymen, who adhered to the old faith, and intrenched himself in the mountains, and headed a vigorous revolt against the Syrian power, even fighting on the Sabbath day. The ranks of the insurrectionists were gradually filled with those who were still zealous for the law, or inspired with patriotic desires for independence. Mattathias was prospered, making successful raids from his mountain fastnesses, destroying heathen altars, and punishing apostate Jews. Two sects joined his standard with peculiar ardor—the Zadikim, who observed the written law of Moses, from whom the Sadducees of later times sprang, and the more zealous and austere Chasidim, who added to the law the traditions of the elders, from whom the Pharisees came.

Mattathias.

His successes.

Old men are ill suited to conduct military expeditions when great fatigue and privation are required, and the aged Mattathias sank under the weight which he had so nobly supported, and bequeathed his power to Judas, the most valiant of his sons.

This remarkable man, scarcely inferior to Joshua and David in military genius and heroic qualities, added prudence and discretion to personal bravery. When his followers had gained experience and courage by various gallant adventures, he led them openly against his enemies. The governor of Samaria, Apollonius, was the first whom he encountered, and whom he routed and slew. Seron, the deputy governor of Cœlesyria, sought to redeem the disgrace of the Syrian arms; but he also was defeated at the pass of Bethoron. At the urgent solicitation of Philip, governor of Jerusalem, Antiochus then sent a strong force of forty thousand foot and seven thousand horse to

His son Judas.

subdue the insurgents, under the command of Ptolemy Macron. Judas, to resist these forces, had six thousand men; but he relied on the God of Israel, as his fathers had done in the early ages of Jewish history, and in a sudden attack he totally routed a large detachment of the main army, under Gorgias, and spoiled their camp. He then defeated another force beyond the Jordan, and the general fled in the disguise of a slave, to Antioch. Thus closed a triumphant campaign.

His heroic deeds.

The next year, Lysias, the lieutenant-general of Antiochus, invaded Judea with a large force of sixty-five thousand men. Judas met it with ten thousand, and gained a brilliant victory, which proved decisive, and which led to the re-establishment of the Jewish power at Jerusalem. Judas fortified the city and the temple, and assumed the offensive, and recovered, one after another, the cities which had fallen under the dominion of Syria. In the mean time, Antiochus, the bitterest enemy which the Jews ever had, died miserably in Persia—the most powerful of all the Syrian kings.

Syria invades Palestine.

On the accession of Antiochus Eupater, Lysias again attempted the subjugation of Judea. This time he advanced with one hundred thousand foot, twenty thousand horse, and thirty-two elephants. But this large force wasted away in an unsuccessful attack on Jerusalem, harassed by the soldiers of the Maccabees. A treaty of peace was concluded, by which full liberty of worship was granted to the Jews, with permission to be ruled by their own laws.

Another unsuccessful invasion.

Demetrius, the lawful heir of Antiochus the Great, had been detained at Rome as a hostage, in consequence of which Antiochus Eupater had usurped his throne. Escaping from Rome, he overpowered his enemies and recovered his kingdom. But he was even more hostile to the Jews than his predecessor, and succeeded in imposing a high priest on the nation friendly to his interests. His cruelties and crimes once more aroused

Continued hostilities between Syria and Palestine.

the Jews to resistance, and Judas gained another decisive victory, and Nicanor, the Syrian general, was slain.

The Jews form an alliance with the Romans.

Judas then adopted a policy which was pregnant with important consequences. He formed a league with the Romans, then bent on the conquest of the East. The Roman senate readily entered into a coalition with the weaker State, in accordance with its uniform custom of protecting those whom they ultimately absorbed in their vast empire: but scarcely was the treaty ratified when the gallant Judas died, leaving the defense of his country to his brothers, B. C. 161.

Jonathan Maccabeus master of Judea.

Jonathan, on whom the leadership fell, found the forces under his control disheartened by the tyranny of the high priest, Alcimus, whom the nation had accepted. Leagued with Bacchides, the Syrian general, the high priest had every thing his own way, until Jonathan, emerging from his retreat, delivered his countrymen once again, and another peace was made. Several years then passed in tranquillity, Jonathan being master of Judea. A revolution in Syria added to his power, and his brother Simon was made captain-general of all the country from Tyre to Egypt. Jonathan, unfortunately, was taken in siege, and the leadership of the nation devolved upon Simon, the last of this heroic family. He ruled with great wisdom, consolidated his power, strengthened his alliance with Rome, repaired Jerusalem, and restored the peace of the country. He was, on a present of one thousand pounds of gold to the Romans, decreed to be prince of Judea, and taken under the protection of his powerful ally. But the peace with Syria, from the new complications to which that kingdom was subjected from rival aspirants to the throne, was broken in the old age of Simon, and he was treacherously murdered, with his oldest son, Judas, at a banquet in Jerusalem. The youngest son, John Hyrcanus, inherited the vigor of his family, and was declared high priest, and sought to revenge the murder of his father and brother. Still, a Syrian army

His rule.

John Hyrcanus as high priest.

overran the country, and John Hyrcanus, shut up in Jerusalem, was reduced to great extremities. A peace was finally made between him and the Syrian monarch, Antiochus, by which Judea submitted to vassalage to the king of Syria. An unfortunate expedition of Antiochus into Parthia enabled Hyrcanus once again to throw off the Syrian yoke, and Judea regained its independence, which it maintained until compelled to acknowledge the Roman power. Hyrcanus was prospered in his reign, and destroyed the rival temple on Mount Gerizim, while the temple of Jerusalem resumed its ancient dignity and splendor.

At this period the Jews, who had settled in Alexandria, devoted themselves to literature and philosophy in that liberal and elegant city, and were allowed liberty of worship. But they became entangled in the mazes of Grecian speculation, and lost much of their ancient spirit. By compliance with the opinions and customs of the Greeks, they reached great honors and distinction, and even high posts in the army.

The Jews in Alexandria.

Hyrcanus, supreme in Judea, now reduced Samaria and Idumea, and was only troubled by the conflicting parties of Pharisees and Sadducees, whose quarrels agitated the State. He joined the party of the Sadducees, who asserted free will, and denied the more orthodox doctrines of the Pharisees, a kind of epicureans, opposed to severities and the authority of traditions. It is one proof of the advance of the Hebrew mind over the simplicity of former ages, that the State could be agitated by theological and philosophical questions, like the States of Greece in their highest development.

The rule of John Hyrcanus.

Hyrcanus reigned twenty-nine years, and was succeeded by his son, Aristobulus, B. C. 106. His brief and inglorious reign was disgraced by his starving to death his mother in a dungeon, and imprisoning his three brothers, and assassinating a fourth, Antigonus, who was a victorious general. This prince died in an agony of remorse and horror on the spot where his brother was assassinated.

Succeeded by his son.

Alexander Jannaus succeeded to the throne of the Asmonean princes, who possessed the whole region of Palestine, except the part of Ptolemais, and the city of Gaza. In an attempt to recover the former he was signally defeated, and came near losing his throne. He was more successful in his attack on Gaza, which finally surrendered, after Alexander had incurred immense losses.

While this priest-king was celebrating the Feast of Tabernacles, a meeting, incited by the Pharisaic party, broke out, which resulted in the slaughter of ten thousand people. While invading the country to the east of the Jordan, the rebellion was renewed, and the nation, for six years, suffered all the evils of civil war. Routed in a battle with the Syrian monarch, whose aid the insurgents had invoked, he was obliged to flee to the mountains; but recovering his authority, at the head of sixty thousand men,—which shows the power of Judea at this period,—he marched upon Jerusalem, and inflicted a terrible vengeance, eight hundred men being publicly crucified, and eight thousand more forced to abandon the city. Under his iron sway, the country recovered its political importance, for his kingdom comprised the greater part of Palestine. He died, after a turbulent reign of twenty-seven years, B. C. 77, invoking his queen to throw herself into the arms of the Pharisaic party, which advice she followed, as it was the most powerful and popular.

Turbulent reign of Alexander.

The high priesthood devolved on his eldest son, Hyrcanus II., while the reins of government were held by his queen, Alexandra. She reigned vigorously and prosperously for nine years, punishing the murderers of the eight hundred Pharisees who had been executed.

Queen Alexandra.

Hyrcanus was not equal to his task amid the bitterness of party strife. His brother Aristobulus, belonging to the party of the Sadducees, and who had taken Damascus, was popular with the people, and compelled his elder brother to abdicate in his favor, and an end came to Pharisaic rule.

But now another family appears upon the stage, which

ultimately wrested the crown from the Asmodean princes. Antipater, a noble Idumean, was the chief minister of the feeble Hyrcanus. He incited, from motives of ambition, the deposed prince to reassert his rights, and influenced by his counsels, he fled to Aretas, the king of Arabia, whose capital, Petra, had become a great commercial emporium. Aretas, Antipater, and Hyrcanus, marched with an army of fifty thousand men against Aristobulus, who was defeated, and fled to Jerusalem.

The Idumean family.

At this time Pompey was pursuing his career of conquests in the East, and both parties invoked his interference, and both offered enormous bribes. This powerful Roman was then at Damascus, receiving the homage and tribute of Oriental kings. The Egyptian monarch sent as a present a crown worth four thousand pieces of gold. Aristobulus, in command of the riches of the temple, sent a golden vine worth five hundred talents. Pompey, intent on the conquest of Arabia, made no decision; but, having succeeded in his object, assumed a tone of haughtiness irreconcilable with the independence of Judea. Aristobulus, patriotic yet vacillating,—"too high-minded to yield, too weak to resist,"—fled to Jerusalem and prepared for resistance.

All parties invoke the aid of Pompey.

Pompey approached the capital, weakened by those everlasting divisions to which the latter Jews were subjected by the zeal of their religious disputes. The city fell, after a brave defense of three months, and might not have fallen had the Jews been willing to abate from the rigid observance of the Sabbath, during which the Romans prepared for assault. Pompey demolished the fortifications of the city, and exacted tribute, but spared the treasures of the temple which he profaned by his heathen presence. He nominated Hyrcanus to the priesthood, but withheld the royal diadem, and limited the dominions of Hyrcanus to Judea. He took Aristobulus to Rome to grace his triumph.

Jerusalem falls into the hands of Pompey.

But he contrived to escape, and, with his son Alexander, again renewed the civil strife; but taken prisoner, he was again sent as a captive to the "eternal city." Gabinius, the Roman general—for Hyrcanus had invoked the aid of the Romans—now deprived the high priest of the royal authority, and reorganized the whole government of Judea; establishing five independent Sanhedrims in the principal cities, after the form of the great Sanhedrim, which had existed since the captivity. This form lasted until Julius Cæsar reinvested Hyrcanus with the supreme dignity.

Reorangization of the government.

Jerusalem was now exposed to the rapacity of the Roman generals who really governed the country. Crassus plundered all that Pompey spared. He took from the temple ten thousand talents—about ten million dollars when gold and silver had vastly greater value than in our times. These vast sums had been accumulated from the contributions of Jews scattered over the world—some of whom were immensely wealthy.

Jerusalem governed by Roman generals.

Aristobulus and his son Alexander were assassinated during the great civil war between the partisans of Cæsar and Pompey. After the fall of the latter, Cæsar confirmed Hyrcanus in the high priesthood, and allowed him to rebuild the walls of Jerusalem. But Antipater, presuming on the incapacity of Hyrcanus, renewed his ambitious intrigues, and contrived to make his son, Phasael, governor of Jerusalem, and Herod, a second son, governor of Galilee.

Herod governor of Galilee.

Herod developed great talents, and waited for his time. After the battle of Philippi Herod made acceptable offerings to the conquering party, and received the crown of Judea, which had been recently ravaged by the Parthians, through the intrigues of Antigonas, the surviving son of Aristobulus. By his marriage with Mariamne, of the royal line of the Asmoneans, he cemented the power he had won by the sword and the favor of Rome. He was the last of the independent sovereigns of Palestine. He reigned tyrannically, and was guilty of great crimes, having caused the death of the aged Hyrcanus, and the imprison-

Receives the crown of Judea.

ment and execution of his wife on a foul suspicion. He paid the same court to Augustus that he did to Antony, and was confirmed in the possession of his kingdom. The last of the line of the Asmonæans had perished on the scaffold, beautiful, innocent, and proud, the object of a boundless passion to a tyrant who sacrificed her to a still greater one—suspicion. Alternating between his love and resentment, Herod sank into a violent fit of remorse, for he had more or less concern in the murder of the father, the grandfather, the brother, and the uncle of his beautiful and imperious wife. At all times, even amid the glories of his palace, he was haunted with the image of the wife he had destroyed, and loved with passionate ardor. He burst forth in tears, he tried every diversion, banquets and revels, solitude and labor—still the murdered Mariamne is ever present to his excited imagination. He settles down in a fixed and indelible gloom, and his stern nature sought cruelty and bloodshed. His public administration was, on the whole, favorable to the peace and happiness of the country, although he introduced the games and the theatres in which the Romans sought their greatest pleasures. For these innovations he was exposed to incessant dangers; but he surmounted them all by his vigilance and energy. He rebuilt Samaria, and erected palaces. But his greatest work was the building of Cæsarea—a city of palaces and theatres. His policy of reducing Judea to a mere province of Rome was not pleasing to his subjects, and he was suspected of a design of heathenizing the nation. Neither his munificence nor severities could suppress the murmurs of an indignant people. The undisguised hostility of the nation prompted him to an act of policy by which he hoped to conciliate it forever. The pride and glory of the Jews was their temple. This Herod determined to rebuild with extraordinary splendor, so as to approach its magnificence in the time of Solomon. He removed the old structure, dilapidated by the sieges, and violence, and wear of five hundred years; and the new edifice gradually arose, glittering with gold, and imposing with marble pinnacles.

And reigns tyrannically.

His miserable life.

But in spite of all his magnificent public works, whether to gratify the pride of his people, or his own vanity—in spite of his efforts to develop the resources of the country over which he ruled by the favor of Rome—in spite of his talents and energies—one of the most able of the monarchs who had sat on the throne of Judea, he was obnoxious to his subjects for his cruelties, and his sympathy with paganism, and he was visited in his latter days by a terrible disorder which racked his body with pain, and inflamed his soul with suspicions, while his court was distracted with cabals from his own family, which poisoned his life, and led him to perpetrate unnatural cruelties. He had already executed two favorite sons, by Mariamne whom he loved, all from court intrigues and jealousy, and he then executed his son and heir, by Doris, his first wife, whom he had divorced to marry Mariamne, and under circumstances so cruel that Augustus remarked that he had rather be one of his swine than one of his sons. Among other atrocities, he had ordered the massacre of the Innocents to prevent any one to be born "as king of the Jews." His last act was to give the fatal mandate for the execution of his son Antipater, whom he hoped to make his heir, and then almost immediately expired in agonies, detested by the nation, and leaving a name as infamous as that of Ahab, B. C. 4.

The hatred in which he was held.

His death.

Herod had married ten wives, and left a numerous family. By his will, he designated the sons of Malthace, his sixth wife, and a Samaritan, as his successors. These were Archelaus, Antipas, and Olympias. The first inherited Idumea, Samaria, and Judea; to the second were assigned Galilee and Peræa. Archelaus at once assumed the government at Jerusalem; and after he had given his father a magnificent funeral, and the people a funeral banquet, he entered the temple, seated himself on a golden throne, and made, as is usual with monarchs, a conciliatory speech, promising reform and alleviations from taxes and oppression. But even this did not prevent one of those disgraceful seditions which have ever marked the people of

His kingdom is divided among his sons.

Jerusalem, in which three thousand were slain, caused by religious animosities. After quelling the tumult by the military, he set out for Rome, to secure his confirmation to the throne. He encountered opposition from various intrigues by his own family, and the caprice of the emperor. His younger brother, Antipas, also went to Rome to support his claim to the throne by virtue of a former will. While the cause of the royal litigants was being settled in the supreme tribunal of the civilized world, new disturbances broke out in Judea, caused by the rapacities of Sabinus, the Roman procurator of Syria. The whole country was in a state of anarchy, and adventurers flocked from all quarters to assert their claims in a nation that ardently looked forward to national independence, or the rise of some conqueror who should restore the predicted glory of the land now rent with civil feuds, and stained with fratricidal blood. Varus, the prefect of Syria, attempted to restore order, and crucified some two thousand ringleaders of the tumults. Five hundred Jews went to Rome to petition for the restoration of their ancient constitution, and the abolition of kingly rule.

The claims of the rival princes.

At length the imperial edict confirmed the will of Herod, and Archelaus was appointed to the sovereignty of Jerusalem, Idumea, and Samaria, under the title of ethnarch; Herod Antipas obtained Galilee and Peræa; Philip, the son of Herod and Cleopatra of Jerusalem, was made tetrarch of Ituræa. Archelaus governed his dominions with such injustice and cruelty, that he was deposed by the emperor, and Judea became a Roman province. The sceptre departed finally from the family of David, of the Asmonæans, and of Herod, and the kingdom sank into a district dependent on the prefecture of Syria, though administered by a Roman governor.

The Romans confirm the will of Herod.

CHAPTER XII.

THE ROMAN GOVERNORS.

THE history of the Jews after the death of Herod is marked by the greatest event in human annals. In four years after he expired in agonies of pain and remorse, Jesus Christ was born in Bethlehem, whose teachings have changed the whole condition of the world, and will continue to change all institutions and governments until the seed of the woman shall have completely triumphed over all the wiles of the serpent. We can not, however, enter upon the life or mission of the Saviour, or the feeble beginnings of the early and persecuted Church which he founded, and which is destined to go on from conquering to conquer. We return to the more direct history of the Jewish nation until their capital fell into the hands of Titus, and their political existence was annihilated.

Birth of Christ.

They were now to be ruled by Roman governors—or by mere vassal kings whom the Romans tolerated and protected. The first of these rulers was P. Sulpicius Quirinus—a man of consular rank, who, as proconsul of Syria, was responsible for the government of Judea, which was intrusted to Coponius. He was succeeded by M. Ambivius, and he again by Annius Rufus. A rapid succession of governors took place till Tiberius appointed Valerius Gratus, who was kept in power eleven years, on the principle that a rapid succession of rulers increased the oppression of the people, since every new governor sought to be enriched. Tiberius was a tyrant, but a wise emperor, and the affairs of the Roman world were never better administered than during his reign. These provincial governors, like the

The rule of Roman governors.

Herodian kings, appointed and removed the high priests, and left the internal management of the city of Jerusalem to them. They generally resided themselves at Cæsarea, to avoid the disputes of the Jewish sects, and the tumults of the people.

Pontius Pilate succeeded Gratus A. D. 27,—under whose memorable rule Jesus Christ was crucified and slain—a man cruel, stern, and reckless of human life, but regardful of the peace and tranquillity of the province. He sought to transfer the innocent criminal to the tribunal of Herod, to whose jurisdiction he belonged as a Galilean, but yielded to the importunities of the people, and left him at the mercy of the Jewish priesthood.

Pontius Pilate.

The vigilant jealousy of popular commotion, and the reckless disregard of human life, led to the recall of Pilate; but during the forty years which had elapsed since the death of Herod, his sons had quietly reigned over their respective provinces. Antipas at Sepphoris, the capital of Galilee, and Philip beyond the Jordan. The latter prince was humane and just, and died without issue, and his territorry was annexed to Syria.

Herod Antipas was a different man. He seduced and married his niece Herodias, wife of Herod Philip, daughter of Aristobolus, and granddaughter of Mariamne, whom Herod the Great had sacrificed in jealousy—the last scion of the Asmonæan princes. It was for her that John the Baptist was put to death. But this marriage proved unfortunate, since it involved him in difficulties with Aretas, king of Arabia, father of his first and repudiated wife. He ended his days in exile at Lyons, having provoked the jealousy or enmity of Caligula, the Roman emperor, through the intrigues of Herod Agrippa, the brother of Herodias, and consequently, a grandson of Herod the Great and Mariamne. The Herodian family, of Idumean origin, never was free from disgraceful quarrels and jealousies and rivalries.

Herod Antipas.

The dominions of Herod Antipas were transferred to Herod Agrippa, who had already obtained from Caligula the tetrarchate of Ituræa, on the death of Philip, with the title of king. The fortunes of this prince, in whose veins flowed the blood of the Asmonæans and the Herodians, surpassed in romance and vicissitude any recorded of Eastern princes; alternately a fugitive and a favorite, a vagabond and a courtier, a pauper and a spendthrift—according to the varied hatred and favor of the imperial family at Rome. He had the good luck to be a friend of Caligula before the death of Tiberius. When he ascended the throne of the Roman world, he took his friend from prison and disgrace, and gave him a royal title and part of the dominions of his ancestors.

Herod Agrippa.

Agrippa did all he could to avert the mad designs of Caligula of securing religious worship as a deity from the Jews, and he was moderate in his government and policy. On the death of the Roman tyrant, he received from his successor Claudius the investiture of all the dominions which belonged to Herod the Great. He reigned in great splendor, respecting the national religion, observing the Mosaic law with great exactness, and aiming at the favor of the people. He inherited the taste of his great progenitor for palace building, and theatrical representations. He greatly improved Jerusalem, and strengthened its fortifications, and yet he was only a vassal king. He reigned by the favor of Rome, on whom he was dependent, and whom he feared, like other kings and princes of the earth, for the emperor was alone supreme.

His brilliant reign.

Agrippa sullied his fair fame by being a persecutor of the Christians, and died in the forty-fourth year of his age, having reigned seven years over part of his dominions, and three over the whole of Palestine. He died in extreme agony from internal pains, being "eaten of worms." He left one son, Agrippa, and three daughters, Drusilla, Berenice, and Mariamne, the two first of whom married princes.

Persecutes the Christians.

On his death Judea relapsed into a Roman province, his son, Agrippa, being only seventeen years of age, and too young to manage such a turbulent, unreasonable, and stiff-necked people as the Jews, rent

Judea a Roman province.

by perpetual feuds and party animosities, and which seem to have characterized them ever since the captivity, when they renounced idolatry forever.

What were these parties? For their opinions and struggles and quarrels form no inconsiderable part of the internal history of the Jews, both under the Asmonæan and Idumean dynasties.

Jewish parties.

The most powerful and numerous were the Pharisees, and most popular with the nation. The origin of this famous sect is involved in obscurity, but probably arose not long after the captivity. They were the orthodox party. They clung to the Law of Moses in its most minute observances, and to all the traditions of their religion. They were earnest, fierce, intolerant, and proud. They believed in angels, and in immortality. They were bold and heroic in war, and intractable and domineering in peace. They were great zealots, devoted to proselytism. They were austere in life, and despised all who were not. They were learned and decorous, and pragmatical. Their dogmatism knew no respite or palliation. They were predestinarians, and believed in the servitude of the will. They were seen in public with ostentatious piety. They made long prayers, fasted with rigor, scrupulously observed the Sabbath, and paid tithes to the cheapest herbs. They assumed superiority in social circles, and always took the uppermost seats in the synagogue. They displayed on their foreheads and the hem of their garments, slips of parchment inscribed with sentences from the law. They were regarded as models of virtue and excellence, but were hypocrites in the observance of the weightier matters of justice and equity. They were, of course, the most bitter adversaries of the faith which Christ revealed, and were ever in the ranks of persecution. They resembled the most austere of the Dominican monks in the Middle Ages. They were the favorite teachers and guides of the people, whom they incited in their various seditions. They were theologians who stood at the summit of legal Judaism. "They fenced round their

The Pharisees.

Their doctrines and character.

law hedges whereby its precepts were guarded against any possible infringement." And they contrived, by an artful and technical interpretation, to find statutes which favored their ends. They wrought out asceticism into a system, and observed the most painful ceremonials—the ancestors of rigid monks; and they united a specious casuistry, not unlike the Jesuits, to excuse the violation of the *spirit* of the law. They were a hierarchal caste, whose ambition was to govern, and to govern by legal technicalities. They were utterly deficient in the virtues of humility and toleration, and as such, peculiarly offensive to the Great Teacher when he propounded the higher code of love and forgiveness. Outwardly, however, they were the most respectable as well as honorable men of the nation—dignified, decorous, and studious of appearances.

The next great party was that of the Sadducees, who aimed to restore the original Mosaic religion in its purity, and expunge every thing which had been added by tradition. But they were deficient in a profound sense of religion, denied the doctrine of immortality, and hence all punishment in a future life. They made up for their denial of the future by a rigid punishment of all crimes. They inculcated a belief of Divine Providence by whom all crime was supposed to be avenged in this world. The party was not so popular as that of their rivals, but embraced men of high rank. In common with the Pharisees, they maintained the strictness of the Jewish code, and professed great uprightness of morals. They had, however, no true, deep religious life, and were cold and heartless in their dispositions. They were mostly men of ease and wealth, and satisfied with earthly enjoyments, and inclined to the epicureanism which marked many of the Greek philosophers. Nor did they escape the hypocrisy which disgraced the Pharisees, and their bitter opposition to the truths of Christianity.

The Sadducees.

In addition to these two great parties which controlled the people, were the Essenes. But they lived apart from men, in the deserts round the Dead Sea, and

The Essenes.

dreaded cities as nurseries of vice. They allowed no women to come within their settlements. They were recruited by strangers and proselytes, who thought all pleasure to be a sin. They established a community of goods, and prosecuted the desire of riches. They were clothed in white garments which they never changed, and regulated their lives by the severest forms. They abstained from animal food, and lived on roots and bread. They worked and ate in silence, and observed the Sabbath with great precision. They were great students, and were rigid in morals, and believed in immortality. They abhorred oaths, and slavery, and idolatry. They embraced the philosophy of the Orientals, and supposed that matter was evil, and that mind was divine. They were mystics who reveled in the pleasures of abstract contemplation. Their theosophy was sublime, but Brahminical. Practically they were industrious, ascetic, and devout—the precursors of those monks who fled from the abodes of man, and filled the solitudes of Upper Egypt and Arabia and Palestine, the loftiest and most misguided of the Christian sects in the second and third centuries. But the Essenes had no direct influence over the people of Judea like the Pharisees and Sadducees, except in encouraging obedience and charity.

State of the country.

All these sects were in a flourishing state on the death of Agrippa. Judea was henceforth to be ruled directly by Roman governors. Cuspius Fadus, Tiberius Alexander, Ventidius Cumanus, Felix Portius, Festus Albinus, and Gessius Florus successively administered the affairs of a discontented province. Their brief administrations were marked by famines and tumults. King Agrippa, meanwhile, with mere nominal power, resided in Jerusalem, in the palace of the Asmonæan princes, which stood on Mount Zion, toward the temple. Robbers infested the country, and murders and robbery were of constant occurrence. High priests were set up, and dethroned. The people were oppressed by taxation and irritated by pillage. Prodigies, wild and awful, filled the land with dread of approaching calamities. Fanatics alarmed the people. The Christians predicted the ruin of the State. Never was a population of three millions of people more discontented and oppressed. Outrage, and injustice, and tumults, and insurrections, marked the doomed people. The governors were insulted, and massacred the people in retaliation. Florus, at one time, destroyed three thousand six hundred people, A. D. 66. Open war was apparent to the more discerning. Agrippa in vain counseled moderation and reconciliation, showing the people how vain resistance would be to the overwhelming power of Rome, which had subdued the world; and that the refusal of tribute, and the demolition of Roman fortifications, were overt acts of war. But he talked to people doomed. Every day new causes of discord arose. Some of the higher orders were disposed to be prudent, but the people generally were filled with bigotry and fanaticism. Some of the boldest of the war party one day seized the fortress of Masada, near the Dead Sea, built by Jonathan the Maccabean, and fortified by Herod. The Roman garrison was put to the sword, and the banner of revolt was unfolded. In the city of Jerusalem, the blinded people refused to receive, as was customary, the gifts and sacrifices of foreign potentates offered in the temple to the God of the Jews. This was an insult and a declaration of war, which the chief priests and Pharisees attempted in vain to prevent.

Miserable condition of the Jews.

Popular commotions.

The insurgents, urged by zealots and assassins, even set fire to the palace of the high priest and of Agrippa and Berenice, and also to the public archives, where the bonds of creditors were deposited, which destroyed the power of the rich. They then carried the important citadel of Antonia, and stormed the palace. A fanatic, by the name of Manahem, son of Judas of Galilee, openly proclaimed the doctrine that it was impious to own any king but God, and treason to pay tribute to Cæsar. He became the leader of the war party because he was the most unscrupulous and zealous, as is always the case in times of excitement and passion. He entered the city, in the pomp of a conqueror, and became the captain of the forces, which took the palace and killed the defenders. The high priest, Ananias, striving to secure order, was stoned. Then followed dissensions between the insurgents themselves, during which Manahem was killed. Eleazar, another chieftain, pressed the siege of the towers, defended by Roman soldiers, which were taken, and the defenders massacred. Meanwhile, twenty thousand Jews were slain by the Greeks in Cæsarea, which drove the nation to madness, and led to a general insurrection in Syria, and a bloody strife between the Greco-Syrians and Jews. There were commotions in all quarters—wars and rumors of wars, so that men fled to the mountains. Wherever the Jews had settled were commotions and massacres, especially at Alexandria, when fifty thousand bodies were heaped up for burial.

Wars and rumors of wars.

Nero was now on the imperial throne, and stringent measures were adopted to suppress the revolt of the Jews, now goaded to desperation by the remembrance of their oppressions, and the conviction that every man's hand was against them. Certius, the prefect of Syria, advanced with ten thousand Roman troops and thirteen hundred allies, and desperate war seemed now inevitable. Agrippa, knowing how fatal it would be to the Jewish nation, attempted to avert it. He argued to infatuated men. Certius undertook to storm Jerusalem, the head-quarters of the insurrection, but failed, and was obliged to retreat, with loss of a great part of his army—a defeat such as the Romans had not received since Varus was overpowered in the forests of Germany.

Incipient rebellion.

Judea was now in open rebellion against the whole power of Rome—a mad and desperate revolt, which could not end but in the political ruin of the nation. Great preparations were made for the approaching contest, in which the Jews were to fight single-handed and unassisted by allies. The fortified posts were in the hands of the insurgents, but they had no organized and disciplined forces, and were divided among themselves. Agrippa, the representa-

Open rebellion of Judea.

tive of the Herodian kings, openly espoused the cause of Rome. The only hope of the Jews was in their stern fanaticism, their stubborn patience, and their daring valor. They were to be justified for their insurrection by all those principles which animate oppressed people striving to be free, and they had glorious precedents in the victories of the Maccabees; but it was their misfortune to contend against the armies of the masters of the world. They were not strong enough for revolt.

Sensation at Rome.

The news of the insurrection, and the defeat of a Roman prefect, made a profound sensation at Rome. Although Nero affected to treat the affair with levity, he selected, however, the ablest general of the empire, Vespasian, and sent him to Syria. The storm broke out in Galilee, whose mountain fastnesses were intrusted by the Jews to Joseph, the son of Matthias—lineally descended from an illustrious priestly family, with the blood of the Asmonæan running in his veins—a man of culture and learning—a Pharisee who had at first opposed the insurrection, but drawn into it after the defeat of Certius. He is better known to us as the historian Josephus. His measures of defence were prudent and vigorous, and he endeavored to unite the various parties in the contest which he knew was desperate. He raised an army of one hundred thousand men, and introduced the Roman discipline, but was impeded in his measures by party dissensions and by treachery. In the city of Jerusalem, Ananias, the high priest, took the lead, but had to contend with fanatics and secret enemies.

Roman preparations for war.

The first memorable event of the war was the unsuccessful expedition against Ascalon, sixty-five miles from Jerusalem, in which Roman discipline prevailed against numbers. This was soon followed by the advance of Vespasian to Ptolemais, while Titus, his lieutenant and son, sailed from Alexandria to join him. Vespasian had an army of sixty thousand veterans. Josephus could not openly contend against this force, but strengthened his fortified

Expedition against Ascalon.

cities. Vespasian advanced cautiously in battle array, and halted on the frontiers of Galilee. The Jews, under Josephus, fled in despair. Gabaia was the first city which fell, and its inhabitants were put to the sword—a stern vengeance which the Romans often exercised, to awe their insurgent enemies. Josephus retired to Tiberius, hopeless and discouraged, and exhorted the people of Jerusalem either to re-enforce him with a powerful army, or make submission to the Romans. They did neither. He then threw himself into Jotaphata, where the strongest of the Galilean warriors had intrenched themselves. Vespasian advanced against the city with his whole army, and drew a line of circumvallation around it, and then commenced the attack. The city stood on the top of a lofty hill, and was difficult of access, and well supplied with provisions. As the works of the Romans arose around the city, its walls were raised thirty-five feet by the defenders, while they issued out in sallies and fought with the courage of despair. The city could not be taken by assault, and the siege was converted into a blockade. The besieged, supplied with provisions, issued out from behind their fortifications, and destroyed the works of the Romans. The fearful battering-rams of the besiegers were destroyed by the arts and inventions of the besieged. The catapults and scorpions swept the walls, and the huge stones began to tell upon the turrets and the towers. The whole city was surrounded by triple lines of heavy armed soldiers, ready for assault. The Jews resorted to all kinds of expedients, even to the pouring of boiling oil on the heads of their assailants. The Roman general was exasperated at the obstinate resistance, and proceeded by more cautious measures. He raised the embankments, and fortified them with towers, in which he placed slingers and archers, whose missiles told with terrible effect on those who defended the walls. Forty-seven days did the gallant defenders resist all the resources of Vespasian. But they were at length exhausted, and their ranks were thinned. Once again a furious assault was made by the whole army, and Titus scaled the walls. The city fell

Fall of Jotaphata.

with the loss of forty thousand men on both sides, and Josephus surrendered to the will of God, but was himself spared by the victors by adroit flatteries, in which he predicted the elevation of Vespasian to the throne of Nero.

It would be interesting to detail the progress of the war, but our limits forbid. The reader is referred to Josephus.

Fall of Joppa.

City after city gradually fell into the hands of Vespasian, who now established himself in Cæsarea. Joppa shared the fate of Jotaphata; the city was razed, but the citadel was fortified by the Romans.

The intelligence of these disasters filled Jerusalem with consternation and mourning, for scarcely a family had not to deplore the loss of some of its members. Tiberius and Tarichea, on the banks of the beautiful lake of Galilee, were the next which fell, followed by atrocious massacres, after the fashion of war in those days. Galilee stood appalled,

Fall of Gamala.

and all its cities but three surrendered. Of these Gamala, the capital, was the strongest, and more inaccessible than Jotaphata. It was built upon a precipice, and was crowded with fugitives, and well provisioned. But it was finally taken, as well as Gischala and Itabyriun, and all Galilee was in the hands of the Romans.

Jerusalem, meanwhile, was the scene of factions and dissen-

Factions at Jerusalem.

sions. It might have re-enforced the strongholds of Galilee, but gave itself up to party animosities, which weakened its strength. Had the Jews been united, they might have offered a more successful resistance. But their fate was sealed. I can not describe the various intrigues and factions which paralyzed the national arm, and forewarned the inhabitants of their doom.

Meanwhile, Nero was assassinated, and Vespasian was elevated to the imperial throne. He sent his son Titus to complete the subjugation which had hitherto resisted his conquering legions.

Jerusalem, in those days of danger and anxiety, was still rent by factions, and neglected her last chance of organizing her forces to resist the common enemy. Never was a city more insensible of its doom. Three distinct parties were at war with each other, shedding each others' blood, reckless of all consequences, callous, fierce, desperate. At length the army of Titus advanced to the siege of the sacred city, still strong and well provisioned. Four legions, with mercenary troops and allies, burning to avenge the past, encamped beneath the walls, destroying the orchards and olive-grounds and gardens which everywhere gladdened the beautiful environs. The city was fortified with three walls where not surrounded by impassable ravines, not one within the other, but inclosing distinct quarters; and these were of great strength, the stones of which were in some parts thirty-five feet long, and so thick that even the heaviest battering-rams could make no impression. One hundred and sixty-four towers surmounted these heavy walls, one of which was one hundred and forty feet high, and forty-three feet square; another, of white marble, seventy-six feet in height, was built of stones thirty-five feet long, and seventeen and a half wide, and eight and a half high, joined together with the most perfect masonry. Within these walls and towers was the royal palace, surrounded by walls and towers of equal strength. The fortress of Antonia, seventy feet high, stood on a rock of ninety feet elevation, with precipitous sides. High above all these towers and hills, and fortresses, stood the temple, on an esplanade covering a square of a furlong on each side. The walls which surrounded this fortress-temple were built of vast stones, and were of great height; and within these walls, on each side, was a spacious double portico fifty-two and a half feet broad, with a ceiling of cedar exquisitely carved, supported by marble columns forty-three and three-quarters feet high, hewn out of single stones. There were one hundred and sixty-two of these beautiful columns. Within this quadrangle was an inner wall, seventy feet in height, inclosing the inner court, around which, in the interior, was another still more splendid portico, entered by brazen gates adorned with gold. These doors, or gates,

Infatuation of the city.

Its fortifications.

The temple.

were fifty-two and a half feet high and twenty-six and a quarter wide. Each gateway had two lofty pillars, twenty-one feet in circumference. The gate called Beautiful was eighty-seven and a half feet high, made of Corinthian brass, and plated with gold. The quadrangle, entered by nine of these gates, inclosed still another, within which was the temple itself, with its glittering façade. This third and inner quadrangle was entered by a gateway tower one hundred and thirty-two and a half feet high and forty-three and a half wide. "At a distance the temple looked like a mountain of snow fretted with golden pinnacles." With what eomtions Titus must have surveyed this glorious edifice, as the sun rising above Mount Moriah gilded its gates and pinnacles—soon to be so utterly demolished that not one stone should be left upon another.

The siege.

Around the devoted city Titus erected towers which overlooked the walls, from which he discharged his destructive missiles, while the battering-rams played against the walls, where they were weakest. The first wall was soon abandoned, and five days after the second was penetrated, after a furious combat, and Titus took possession of the lower city, where most of the people lived.

The precipitous heights of Zion, the tower of Antonia and the temple still remained, and although the cause was hopeless, the Jews would hear of no terms of surrender. Titus used every means. So did Josephus, who harangued the people at a safe distance. The most obstinate fury was added to presumptuous, vain confidence, perhaps allied with utter distrust of the promises of enemies whom they had offended past forgiveness.

Famine in the city.

At length famine pressed. No grain was to be bought. The wealthy secreted their food. All kind feelings were lost in the general misery. Wives snatched the last morsel from their family and weary husbands, and children from their parents. The houses were full of dying and the dead, a heavy silence oppressed every one, yet no complaints were made. They suffered in sullen gloom and despair. From the 14th of April to the 19th of July, A. D. 70, from one hundred thousand to five hundred thousand, according to different estimates, were buried or thrown from the walls. A measure of wheat sold for a talent, and the dunghills were raked for subsistence.

When all was ready, the assault on the places which remained commenced. On the 5th of July the fortress of Antonia was taken, and the siege of the temple was pressed. Titus made one more attempt to persuade its defenders to surrender, wishing to save the sacred edifice, but they were deaf and obstinate. They continued to fight, inch by inch, exhausted by famine, and reduced to despair. They gnawed their leathern belts, and ate their very children. On the 8th of August the wall inclosing the portico, or cloisters, was scaled. On the 10th the temple itself, a powerful fortress, fell, with all its treasures, into the hands of the victors. The soldiers gazed with admiration on the plates of gold, and the curious workmanship of the sacred vessels. All that could be destroyed by fire was burned, and all who guarded the precincts were killed.

The assault of Jerusalem

The fall.

Still the palace and the upper city held out. Titus promised to spare the lives of the defenders if they would instantly surrender. But they still demanded terms. Titus, in a fury, swore that the whole surviving population should be exterminated. It was not till the 7th of September that this last bulwark was captured, so obstinately did the starving Jews defend themselves. A miscellaneous slaughter commenced, till the Romans were weary of their work of vengeance. During the whole siege one million one hundred thousand were killed, and ninety-seven thousand made prisoners, since a large part of the population of Judea had taken refuge within the walls. During the whole war one million three hundred and fifty-six thousand were killed.

The siege and sack of the city.

Thus fell Jerusalem, after a siege of five months, the most desperate defense of a capital in the history of war. It fell never to rise again as a Jewish metropolis. Never had a city greater misfortunes. Never was heroism accompanied with greater fanaticism. Never was a prophecy more signally fulfilled.

Consequences of the fall of Jerusalem.

The fall of Jerusalem was succeeded by bloody combats before the whole country was finally subdued. With the final conquest the Jews were dispersed among the nations, and their nationality was at an end. Their political existence was annihilated. The capital was destroyed, the temple demolished, and the royal house extinguished, and the high priesthood buried amid the ruins of the sacred places.

With the occupation of Palestine by strangers, and the final dispersion of the Jews over all nations, who, without a country, and without friends, maintained their institutions, their religion, their name, their peculiarities, and their associations, we leave the subject—so full of mournful interest, and of impressive lessons. The student of history should see in their prosperity and misfortunes the overruling Providence vindicating his promises, and the awful majesty of eternal laws.

BOOK II.

THE GRECIAN STATES.

CHAPTER XIII.

THE GEOGRAPHY OF ANCIENT GREECE AND ITS EARLY INHABITANTS.

We have seen that the Oriental world, so favored by nature, so rich in fields, in flocks, and fruits, failed to realize the higher destiny of man. In spite of all the advantages of nature, he was degraded by debasing superstitions, and by the degeneracy which wealth and ease produced. He was enslaved by vices and by despots. The Assyrian and Babylonian kingdom, that "head of gold," as seen in Nebuchadnezzar's dream, became inferior to the "breast and arms of silver," as represented by the Persian Empire, and this, in turn, became subject to the Grecian States, "the belly and the thighs of brass." It is the nobler Hellenic race, with its original genius, its enterprise, its stern and rugged nature, strengthened by toil, and enterprise, and war, that we are now to contemplate. It is Greece—the land of song, of art, of philosophy—the land of heroes and freemen, to which we now turn our eyes—the most interesting, and the most famous of the countries of antiquity.

Degeneracy of the oriental states.

Let us first survey that country in all its stern ruggedness and picturesque beauty. It was small compared with Assyria or Persia. Its original name was Hellas, designated by a little district of Thessaly, which lay on the southeast verge of Europe, and extended in length from the thirty-sixth to the fortieth degree of latitude. It

Boundaries of Greece.

contained, with its islands, only twenty-one thousand two hundred and ninety square miles—less than Portugal or Ireland, but its coasts exceeded the whole Pyrenean peninsula. Hellas is itself a peninsula, bounded on the north by the Cambunian and Ceraunian mountains, which separated it from Macedonia; on the east by the Æægean Sea, (Archipelago), which separated it from Asia Minor; on the south by the Cretan Sea, and on the west by the Ionian Sea.

The mountains of Greece.

The northern part of this country of the Hellenes is traversed by a range of mountains, commencing at Acra Ceraunia, on the Adriatic, and tending southeast above Dodona, in Epirus, till they join the Cambunian mountains, near Mount Olympus, which run along the coast of the Ægean till they terminate in the southeastern part of Thessaly, under the names of Ossa, Pelion, and Tissæus. The great range of Pindus enters Greece at the sources of the Peneus, where it crosses the Cambunian mountains, and extends at first south, and then east to the sea, nearly inclosing Thessaly, and dividing it from the rest of Greece. After throwing out the various spurs of Othrys, Œta, and Corax, it loses itself in those famous haunts of the Muses—the heights of Parnassus and Helicon, in Phocis and Bœotia. In the southern part of Greece are the mountains which intersect the Peloponnesus in almost every part, the principal of which are Scollis, Aroanii, and Taygetus. We can not enumerate the names of all these mountains; it is enough to say that no part of Europe, except Switzerland, is so covered with mountains as Greece, some of which attain the altitude of perpetual snow. Only a small part of the country is level.

Between Ossa and Olympus is the famous vale of Tempe.

The rivers.

The rivers, again, are numerous, but more famous for associations than for navigable importance. The Peneus which empties itself into the Ægean, a little below Tempe; the Achelous, which flows into the Ionian Sea; the Alpheus, flowing into the Ionian Sea; and the Eurotas, which enters the Laconican Gulf, are among the most considerable. The lakes are numerous, but not large. The coasts are lined by bays and promontories, favorable to navigation in its infancy, and for fishing. The adjacent seas are full of islands, memorable in Grecian history, some of which are of considerable size.

Natural advantages for political independence.

Thus intersected in all parts with mountains, and deeply indented by the sea, Greece was both mountainous and maritime. The mountains, the rivers, the valleys, the sea, the islands contributed to make the people enterprising and poetical, and as each State was divided from every other State by mountains, or valleys, or gulfs, political liberty was engendered. The difficulties of cultivating a barren soil on the highlands inured the inhabitants to industry and economy, as in Scotland and New England, while the configuration of the country strengthened the powers of defense, and shut the people up from those invasions which have so often subjugated a plain and level country. These natural divisions also kept the States from political union, and fostered a principle of repulsion, and led to an indefinite multiplication of self-governing towns, and to great individuality of character.

Natural productions.

Situated in the same parallels of latitude as Asia Minor, and the south of Italy and Spain, Greece produced wheat, barley, flax, wine, oil, in the earliest times. The cultivation of the vine and the olive was peculiarly careful. Barley cakes were more eaten than wheaten. All vegetables and fish were abundant and cheap. But little fresh meat was eaten. Corn also was imported in considerable quantities by the maritime States in exchange for figs, olives, and oil. The climate, clear and beautiful to modern Europeans, was less genial than that of Asia Minor, but more bracing and variable. It also varied in various sections.

These various sections, or provinces, or states, into which Greece was divided, claim a short notice.

Epirus.

The largest and most northerly State was Epirus, containing four thousand two hundred and sixty square miles, bounded on the north by Macedonia, on the east by Thessaly, on the south by Acarnania, and on the west by the Ionian Sea. Though mountainous, it was fertile, and produced excellent cattle and horses. Of the interesting places of Epirus, memorable in history, ranks first Dodona, celebrated for its oracle, the most ancient in Greece, and only inferior to that of Delphi. It was founded by the Pelasgi before the Trojan war, and was dedicated to Jupiter. The temple was surrounded by a grove of oak, but the oracles were latterly delivered by the murmuring of fountains. On the west of Epirus is the island of Corcyra (Corfu), famous for the shipwreck of Ulysses, and for the gardens of Alcinous, and for having given rise to the Peloponnesian war. Epirus is also distinguished as the country over which Pyrrhus ruled. The Acheron, supposed to communicate with the infernal regions, was one of its rivers.

Thessaly.

West of Epirus was Thessaly, and next to it in size, containing four thousand two hundred and sixty square miles. It was a plain inclosed by mountains; next to Bœotia, the most fertile of all the States of Greece, abounding in oil, wine, and corn, and yet one of the weakest and most insignificant, politically. The people were rich, but perfidious. The river Peneus flowed through the entire extent of the country, and near its mouth was the vale of Tempe, the most beautiful valley in Greece, guarded by four strong fortresses.

The famous places.

At some distance from the mouth of the Peneus was Larissa, the city of Achilles, and the general capital of the Pelasgi. At the southern extremity of the lake Cælas, the largest in Thessaly, was Pheræ, one of the most ancient cities in Greece, and near it was the fountain of Hyperia. In the southern part of Thessaly was Pharsalia, the battle-ground between Cæsar and Pompey, and near it was Pyrrha, formerly called Hellas, where was the tomb of Hellen, son of Deucalion, whose descendants, Æolus, Dorus and Ion, are said to have given name to the three nations, Æolians, Dorians, and Ionians. Still further south, between the inaccessible cliffs of Mount Œta and the marshes which skirt the Maliacus Bay, were the defiles of Thermopylæ, where Leonidas and three hundred heroes died defending the pass, against the army of Xerxes, and which in one place was only twenty-five feet wide, so that, in so narrow a defile, the Spartans were able to withstand for three days the whole power of Persia. In this famous pass the Amphictyonic council met annually to deliberate on the common affairs of all the States.

South of Epirus, on the Ionian Sea, and west of Ætolia, was Acarnania, occupied by a barbarous people before the Pelasgi settled in it. It had no historic fame, except as furnishing on its waters a place for the decisive battle which Augustus gained over Antony, at Actium, and for the islands on the coast, one of which, Ithaca, a rugged and mountainous island, was the residence of Ulysses. Acarnania.

Ætolia, to the east of Acarnania, and south of Thessaly, and separated from Achaia by the Corinthian Gulf, contained nine hundred and thirty square miles. Its principal city was Thermon, considered impregnable, at which were held splendid games and festivals. The Ætolians were little known in the palmy days of Athens and Sparta, except as a hardy race, but covetous and faithless. Ætolia.

Doris was a small tract to the east of Ætolia, inhabited by one of the most ancient of the Greek tribes—the Dorians, called so from Dorus, son of Deucalion, and originally inhabited that part of Thessaly in which were the mountains of Olympus and Ossa. From this section they were driven by the Cadmeans. Doris was the abode of the Heraclidæ when exiled from the Peloponnesus, and which was given to Hyllas, the son of Hercules, in gratitude by Ægiminius, the king, who was reinstated by the hero in his dispossessed dominion. Doris.

Locri Ozolæ was another small State, south of Doris, from which it is separated by the range of the Parnassus, situated on the Corinthian Gulf, the most important city of which was Salona, surrounded on all sides by hills. Naupactus was also a considerable place, known Locri Ozolæ in the Middle Ages as Lepanto, where was fought one of the decisive naval battles of the world, in which the Turks were defeated by the Venetians. It contained three hundred and fifty square miles.

Phocis.

Phocis was directly to the east, bounded on the north by Doris and the Locri Epicnemidii, and south by the Corinthian Gulf. This State embraced six hundred and ten square miles. The Phocians are known in history from the sacred or Phocian war, which broke out in 357 B. C., in consequence of refusing to pay a fine imposed by the Amphictyonic council. The Thebans and Locrians carried on this war successfully, joined by Philip of Macedon, who thus paved the way for the sovereignty of Greece. One among the most noted places was Crissa, famed for the Pythian games, and Delphi, renowned for its oracle sacred to Apollo. The priestess, Pythia, sat on a sacred tripod over the mouth of a cave, and pronounced her oracles in verse or prose. Those who consulted her made rich presents, from which Delphi became vastly enriched. Above Delphi towers Parnassus, the highest mountain in central Greece, near whose summit was the supposed residence of Deucalion.

Bœotia.

Bœotia was the richest State in Greece, so far as fertility of soil can make a State rich. It was bounded on the north by the territory of the Locri, on the west by Phocis, on the south by Attica, and on the east by the Eubœan Sea. It contained about one thousand square miles. Its inhabitants were famed for their stolidity, and yet it furnished Hesiod, Pindar, Corinna, and Plutarch to the immortal catalogue of names. Its men, if stupid, were brave, and its women were handsome. It was originally inhabited by barbarous tribes, all connected with the Leleges. In its southwestern part was the famous Helicon, famed as the seat of Apollo and the Muses, and on the southern border was Mount Cithæron, to the north of which was Platea, where the Persians were defeated by the confederate Greeks under Pausanias. Bœotia contained the largest lake in Greece—Copaias, famed for eels. On the borders of this lake was

Coronea, where the Thebans were defeated by the Spartans. To the north of Coronea was Chæronea, where was fought the great battle with Philip, which subverted the liberties of Greece. To the north of the river Æsopus, a sluggish stream, was Thebes, the capital of Bœotia, founded by Cadmus, whose great generals, Epaminondas and Pelopidas, made it, for a time, one of the great powers of Greece.

The most famous province of Greece was Attica, bounded on the north by the mountains Cithæron and Parnes, on the west by the bay of Saronicus, on the east by the Myrtoum Sea. It contained but seven hundred square miles. It derived its name from Atthis, a daughter of Cranaus; but its earliest name was Cecropia, from its king, Cecrops. It was divided, in the time of Cecrops, into four tribes. On its western extremity, on the shores of the Saronic Gulf, stood Eleusis, the scene of the Eleusinian mysteries, the most famous of all the religious ceremonials of Greece, sacred to Ceres, and celebrated every four years, and lasting for nine days. Opposite to Eleusis was Salamis, the birthplace of Ajax, Teucer, and Solon. There the Persian fleet of Xerxes was defeated by the Athenians. The capital, Athens, founded by Cecrops, 1556 B. C., received its name from the goddess Neith, an Egyptian deity, known by the Greeks as Athena, or Minerva. Its population, in the time of Pericles, was one hundred and twenty thousand. The southernmost point of Attica was Sunium, sacred to Minerva; Marathon, the scene of the most brilliant victory which the Athenians ever fought, was in the eastern part of Attica. To the southeast of Athens was Mount Hymettus, celebrated for its flowers and honey. Between Hymettus and Marathon was Mount Pentelicus, famed for its marbles.

Attica.

Megaris, another small State, was at the west of Attica, between the Corinthian and the Saronican gulfs. Its chief city, Megara, was a considerable place, defended by two citadels on the hills above it. It was celebrated as the seat of the Megaric school of philosophy, founded by Euclid.

Megaris.

The largest of the Grecian States was the famous peninsula known as the Peloponnesus, entirely surrounded by water, except the isthmus of Corinth, four geographical miles wide. On the west was the Ionian Sea; on the east the Saronic Gulf and the Myrtoum Sea; on the north the Corinthian Gulf. It contained six thousand seven hundred and forty-five square miles. It was divided into several States. It was said to be left by Hercules on his death to the Heraclidæ, which they, with the assistance of the Dorians, ultimately succeeded in regaining, about eighty years after the Trojan war.

The Peloponnesus and its states.

Of the six States into which the Peloponnesus was divided, Achaia was the northernmost, and was celebrated for the Achæan league, composed of its principal cities, as well as Corinth, Sicyon, Phlius, Arcadia, Argolis, Laconia, Megaris, and other cities and States.

Elis.

Southwest of Achaia was Elis, on the Ionian Sea, in which stood Olympia, where the Olympic games were celebrated every four years, instituted by Hercules.

Arcadia.

Arcadia occupied the centre of the Peloponnesus, surrounded on all sides by lofty mountains—a rich and pastoral country, producing fine horses and asses. It was the favorite residence of Pan, the god of shepherds, and its people were famed for their love of liberty and music.

Argolis.

Argolis was the eastern portion of the Peloponnesus, watered by the Saronic Gulf, whose original inhabitants were Pelasgi. It boasted of the cities of Argos and Mycenæ, the former of which was the oldest city of Greece. Agamemnon reigned at Mycenæ, the most powerful of the kings of Greece during the Trojan war.

Laconia.

Laconia, at the southeastern extremity of the peninsula, was the largest and most important of the States of the Peloponnesus. It was rugged and mountainous, but its people were brave and noble. Its largest city, Sparta, for several generations controlled the fortune of Greece, the most warlike of the Grecian cities.

Messenia was the southwestern part of the peninsula—mountainous, but well watered, and abounding in pasture. It was early coveted by the Lacedæmonians, inhabitants of Laconia, and was subjugated in a series of famous wars, called the Messenian.

Messenia.

Such were the principal States of Greece. But in connection with these were the islands in the seas which surrounded it, and these are nearly as famous as the States on the main land.

The most important of these was Crete, at the southern extremity of the Ægean Sea. It was the fabled birthplace of Jupiter. To the south of Thrace were Thasos, remarkable for fertility, and for mines of gold and silver; Samothrace, celebrated for the mysteries of Cybele; Imbros, sacred to Ceres and Mercury. Lemnos, in latitude forty, equidistant from Mount Athos and the Hellespont, rendered infamous by the massacre of all the male inhabitants of the island by the women. The island of Eubœa stretched along the coast of Attica, Locris, and Bœotia, and was exceedingly fertile, and from this island the Athenians drew large supplies of corn—the largest island in the Archipelago, next to Crete. Its principal city was Chalcis, one of the strongest in Greece.

Crete.

To the southeast of Eubœa are the Cyclades—a group of islands of which Delos, Andros, Tenos, Myconos, Naxos, Paros, Olearos, Siphnos, Melos, and Syros, were the most important. All these islands are famous for temples and the birthplace of celebrated men.

The Cyclades.

The islands called the Sporades lie to the south and east of the Cyclades, among which are Amorgo, Ios, Sicinos, Thera, and Anaphe—some of which are barren, and others favorable to the vine.

The Sporades.

Besides these islands, which belong to the continent of Europe, are those which belong to Asia—Tenedos, small but fertile; Lesbos, celebrated for wine, the fourth in size of all the islands of the Ægean; Chios, also famed for wine; Samos, famous for the worship of Juno, and

Lesbos, and other islands.

the birthplace of Pythagoras; Patmcs, used as a place of banishment; Cos, the birthplace of Apelles and Hippocrates, exceedingly fertile; and south of all, Rhodes, the largest island of the Ægean, after Crete and Eubœa. It was famous for the brazen and colossal statue of the sun, seventy cubits high. Its people were great navigators, and their maritime laws were ultimately adopted by all the Greeks and Romans. It was also famous for its schools of art.

Such were the States and islands of Greece, mountainous, in many parts sterile, but filled with a hardy, bold, and adventurous race, whose exploits and arts were the glory of the ancient world.

The various tribes and nations all belonged to that branch of the Indo-European race to which ethnographers have given the name of Pelasgian. They were a people of savage manners, but sufficiently civilized to till the earth, and build walled cities. Their religion was polytheistic—a personification of the elemental powers and the heavenly bodies. The Pelasgians occupied insulated points, but were generally diffused throughout Greece; and they were probably a wandering people before they settled in Greece. The Greek traditions about their migration rests on no certain ground. Besides this race, concerning which we have no authentic history, were the Leleges and Carians. But all of them were barbarous, and have left no written records. Argos and Sicyon are said to be Pelasgian cities, founded as far back as one thousand eight hundred and fifty-six years before Christ. It is also thought that Oriental elements entered into the early population of Greece. Cecrops imported into Attica Egyptian arts. Cadmus, the Phœnician, colonized Bœotia, and introduced weights and measures. Danaus, driven out of Egypt, gave his name to the warlike Danai, and instructed the Pelasgian women of Argos in the mystic rites of Demetus. Pelope is supposed to have passed from Asia into Greece, with great treasures, and his descendants occupied the throne of Argos.

Origin of the Grecian nations.

The Pelasgians.

At a period before written history commences, the early

inhabitants of Greece, whatever may have been their origin, which is involved in obscurity, were driven from their settlements by a warlike race, akin, however, to the Pelasgians. These conquerors were the Hellenes, who were believed to have issued from the district of Thessaly, north of Mount Othrys. They gave their name ultimately to the whole country. Divided into small settlements, they yet were bound together by language and customs, and cherished the idea of national unity. There were four chief divisions of this nation, the Dorians, Æolians, Achæans, and Ionians, traditionally supposed to be descended from the three sons of Hellen, the son of Deucalion, Dorus, Æolus, and Xuthus, the last the father of Achæus, and Ion. So the Greek poets represented the origin of the Hellenes—a people fond of adventure, and endowed by nature with vast capacities, subsequently developed by education.

The Hellenes.

The Æolians.

The Achæans.

Of these four divisions of the Hellenic race, the Æolians spread over northern Greece, and also occupied the western coast of the Peloponnesus and the Ionian islands. It continued, to the latest times, to occupy the greater part of Greece. The Achæans were the most celebrated in epic poetry, their name being used by Homer to denote all the Hellenic tribes which fought at Troy. They were the dominant people of the Peloponnesus, occupying the south and east, and the Arcadians the centre. The Dorians and Ionians were of later celebrity; the former occupying a small patch of territory on the slopes of Mount Œta, north of Delphi; the latter living on a narrow slip of the country along the northern coast of the Peloponnesus, and extending eastward into Attica.

The Dorians and Ionians.

The principal settlements of the Æolians lay around the Pagasæan Gulf, and were blended with the Minyaus, a race of Pelasgian adventurers known in the Argonautic expedition, under Æolian leaders. In the north of Bœotia arose the city of Orchomenus, whose treasures were compared by Homer to those of the Egyptian

Settlements of the Æolians.

Thebes. Another seat of the Æolians was Ephyra, afterward known as Corinth, where the "wily Sisyphus" ruled. He was the father of Phocus, who gave his name to Phocis. The descendants of Æolus led also a colony to Elis, and another to Pylus. In general, the Æolians sought maritime settlements in northern Greece, and the western side of the Peloponnesus.

Of the Achæans.

The Achæans were the dominant race, in very early times, of the south of Thessaly, and the eastern side of the Peloponnesus, whose chief seats were Phthia, where Achilles reigned, and Argolis. Thirlwall seems to think they were a Pelasgian, rather than an Hellenic people. The ancient traditions represent the sons of Achæus as migrating to Argos, where they married the daughters of Danaus the king, but did not mount the throne.

Of the Dorians.

The early fortunes of the Dorians are involved in great obscurity, nor is there much that is satisfactory in the early history of any of the Hellenic tribes. Our information is chiefly traditional, derived from the poets. Dorus, the son of Deucalion, occupied the country over against Peloponnesus, on the opposite side of the Corinthian Gulf, comprising Ætolia, Phocis, and the Ozolian Locrians. Nor can the conquests of the Dorians on the Peloponnesus be reconciled upon any other ground than that they occupied a considerable tract of country.

Of the Ionians.

The early history of the Ionians is still more obscure. Ion, the son of Xuthus, is supposed to have led his followers from Thessaly to Attica, and to have conquered the Pelasgians, or effected peaceable settlements with them. Then follows a series of legends which have more poetical than historical interest, but which will be briefly noticed in the next chapter.

CHAPTER XIV.

THE LEGENDS OF ANCIENT GREECE.

THE Greeks possessed no authentic written history of that period which included the first appearance of the Hellenes in Thessaly to the first Olympiad, B. C. 776. This is called the heroic age, and is known to us only by legends and traditions, called myths. They pertain both to gods and men, and are connected with what we call mythology, which possesses no historical importance, although it is full of interest for its poetic life. And as mythology is interwoven with the literature and the art of the ancients, furnishing inexhaustible subjects for poets, painters, and sculptors, it can not be omitted wholly in the history of that classic people, whose songs and arts have been the admiration of the world.

The heroic ages of Greece.

We have space, however, only for those legends which are of universal interest, and will first allude to those which pertain to gods, such as appear most prominent in the poems of Hesiod and Homer.

The legends.

Zeus, or Jupiter, is the most important personage in the mythology of Greece. Although, chronologically, he comes after Kronos and Uranos, he was called the "father of gods and men," whose power it was impossible to resist, and which power was universal. He was supposed to be the superintending providence, whose seat was on Mount Olympus, enthroned in majesty and might, to whom the lesser deities were obedient. With his two brothers, Poseidon, or Neptune, and Hades, or Pluto, he reigned over the heavens, the earth, the sea, and hell. Mythology represents him as born in Crete; and when he had gained suffi-

Zeus.

cient mental and bodily force, he summoned the gods to Mount Olympus, and resolved to wrest the supreme power from his father, Kronos, and the Titans. Ten years were spent in the mighty combat, in which all nature was convulsed, before victory was obtained, and the Titans hurled into Tartarus. With Zeus now began a different order of beings. He is represented as having many wives and a numerous offspring. From his own head came Athene, fully armed, the goddess of wisdom, the patron deity of Athens. By Themis he begat the Horæ; by Eurynome, the three Graces; by Mnemosyne, the Muses; by Leto (Latona), Apollo, and Artemis (Diana); by Demeter (Ceres), Persephone; by Here (Juno), Hebe, Ares (Mars), and Eileithyia; by Maia, Hermes (Mercury).

The other deities.

Under the presidency of Zeus were the twelve great gods and goddesses of Olympus—Poseidon (Neptune), who presided over the sea; Apollo, who was the patron of art; Ares, the god of war; Hephaestos (Vulcan), who forged the thunderbolts; Hermes, who was the messenger of omnipotence and the protector of merchants; Here, the queen of heaven, and general protector of the female sex; Athene (Minerva), the goddess of wisdom and letters; Artemis (Diana), the protectress of hunters and shepherds; Aphrodite (Venus), the goddess of beauty and love; Hertia (Vesta), the goddess of the hearth and altar, whose fire never went out. Demeter (Ceres), mother earth, the goddess of agriculture.

Scarcely inferior to these Olympian deities were Hades (Pluto), who presided over the infernal regions; Helios, the sun; Hecate, the goddess of expiation; Dionysus (Bacchus), the god of the vine; Leto (Latona), the goddess of the concealed powers; Eos (Aurora), goddess of the morn; Nemesis, god of vengeance; Æolus, the god of winds; Harmonia; the Graces, the Muses, the Nymphs, the Nereids, marine nymphs—these were all invested with great power and dignity.

Besides these were deities who performed special services to the greater gods, like the Horæ; and monsters, offspring of gods, like the gorgons, chimera, the dragon of the Hesperides, the Lernæan hydra, the Nemean lion, Scylla and Charybdis, the centaurs, the sphinx, and others.

Who represent the powers of Nature.

It will be seen that these gods and goddesses represent the powers of nature, and the great attributes of wisdom, purity, courage, fidelity, truth, which belong to man's higher nature, and which are associated with the divine. It was these powers and attributes which were worshiped—superhuman and adorable. Homer and Hesiod are the great authorities of the theogonies of the pagan world, and we can not tell how much of this was of their invention, and how much was implanted in the common mind of the Greeks, at an age earlier than 700 B. C. The Orphic theogony belongs to a later date, but acquired even greater popular veneration than the Hesiodic.

The worship of these deities.

The worship of these divinities was attended by rites more or less elevated, but sometimes by impurities and follies, like those of Bacchus and Venus. Sometimes this worship was veiled in mysteries, like those of Eleusis. To all these deities temples were erected, and offerings made, sometimes of fruits and flowers, and then of animals. Of all these deities there were legends—sometimes absurd, and these were interwoven with literature and religious solemnities. The details of these fill many a large dictionary, and are to be read in dictionaries, or in poems. Those which pertain to Ceres, to Apollo, to Juno, to Venus, to Minerva, to Mercury, are full of poetic beauty and fascination. They arose in an age of fertile imagination and ardent feeling, and became the faith of the people.

Legends which pertain to heroes.

Besides the legends pertaining to gods and goddesses, are those which relate the heroic actions of men. Grote describes the different races of men as they appear in the Hesiodic theogony—the offspring of gods. First, the golden race: first created, good and happy, like the gods themselves, and honored after death by being made the unseen guardians of men—"terrestrial demons." Second, the silver race, inferior in body and mind, was next created, and being disobedient, are buried in the earth. Third, the brazen race, hard, pugnacious, terrible, strong, which was continually at war, and ultimately destroyed itself, and descended into Hades, unhonored and without privilege. Fourth, the race of heroes, or demigods, such as fought at Thebes and Troy, virtuous but warlike, which also perished in battle, but were removed to a happier state. And finally, the iron race, doomed to perpetual guilt, care, toil, suffering—unjust, dishonest, ungrateful, thoughtless—such is the present race of men, with a small admixture of good, which will also end in due time. Such are the races which Hesiod describes in his poem of the "Works and Days,"—penetrated with a profound sense of the wickedness and degeneracy of human life, yet of the ultimate rewards of virtue and truth. His demons are not gods, nor men, but intermediate agents, essentially good—angels, whose province was to guard and to benefit the world. But the notions of demons gradually changed, until they were regarded as both good and bad, as viewed by Plato, and finally they were regarded as the causes of evil, as in the time of the Christian writers. Hesiod, who lived, it is supposed, four hundred years before Herodotus, is a great ethical poet, and embodied the views of his age respecting the great mysteries of nature and life.

The legends which Hesiod, Homer, and other poets made so attractive by their genius, have a perpetual interest, since they are invested with all the fascinations of song and romance. We will not enter upon those which relate to gods, but confine ourselves to those which relate to men—the early heroes of the classic land and age; nor can we allude to all—only a few—those which are most memorable and impressive.

The Danaides.

Among the most ancient was the legend relating to the Danaides, which invest the early history of Argos with peculiar interest. Inachus, who reigned 1986 B. C., according to ancient chronology, is also the name of the river flowing beneath the walls of the ancient city, situated in the eastern part of the Peloponnesus. In the reign of

Krotopos, one of his descendants, Danaus came with his fifty daughters from Egypt to Argos in a vessel of fifty oars, in order to escape the solicitations of the fifty sons of Ægyptos, his brother, who wished to make them their wives. Ægyptos and the sons followed in pursuit, and Danaus was compelled to assent to their desires, but furnished each of his daughters with a dagger, on the wedding night, who thus slew their husbands, except one, whose husband, Lynceus, ultimately became king of Argos. From Danaus was derived the name of Danai, applied to the people of the Argeian territory, and to the Homeric Greeks generally. We hence infer that Argos—one of the oldest cities of Greece, was settled in part by Egyptians, probably in the era of the shepherd kings, who introduced not only the arts, but the religious rites of that ancient country. Among the regal descendants of Lynceus was Danae, whose son Perseus performed marvelous deeds, by the special favor of Athene, among which he brought from Libya the terrific head of the Gorgon Medusa, which had the marvelous property of turning every one to stone who looked at her. Stung with remorse for the accidental murder of his grandfather, the king, he retired from Argos, and founded the city of Mycenæ, the ruins of whose massive walls are still to be seen—Cyclopean works, which seem to show that the old Pelasgians derived their architectural ideas from the Egyptian Danauns. The Perseids of Mycenæ thus boasted of an illustrious descent, which continued down to the last sovereign of Sparta.

Hercules.

The grand-daughter of Perseus was Alcmena, whom mythology represents as the mother of Hercules by Jupiter. The labors of Hercules are among the most interesting legends of pagan antiquity, since they are types of the endless toils of a noble soul, doomed to labor for others, and obey the commands of worthless persecutors. But the hero is finally rewarded by admission to the family of the gods, and his descendants are ultimately restored to the inheritance from which they were deprived by the wrath and jealousy of Juno. A younger branch of the Perseid family reigned in Lacædemon—Eurystheus, to whom Hercules was subject; but he, with all his sons, lost their lives in battle, so that the Perseid family was represented only by the sons of Hercules—the Heracleids, or Heraclidæ. They endeavored to regain their possessions, and invaded the Peloponnesus, from which they had been expelled. Hyllos, the oldest son, proposed to the army of Ionians, Achæans, and Arcadians, which met them in defense, that the combat should be decided between himself and any champion of the invading army, and that, if he were victorious, the Heracleids should be restored to their sovereignty, but if defeated, should forego their claim for three generations. Hyllos was vanquished, and the Heracleids retired and resided with the Dorians. When the stipulated period had ended, they, assisted by the Dorians, gained possession of the Peloponnesus. Hence the great Dorian settlement of Argos, Sparta, and Messenia, effected by the return of the Heracleids.

Deucalion.

Another important legend is that which relates to Deucalion and the deluge, as it is supposed to shed light on the different races that colonized Greece. The wickedness of the world induced Zeus to punish it by a deluge; a terrible rain laid the whole of Greece under water, except a few mountain tops. Deucalion was saved in an ark, or chest, which he had been forewarned to construct. After floating nine days, he landed on the summit of Mount Parnassus. Issuing from his ark, he found no inhabitants, they having been destroyed by the deluge. Instructed, however, by Zeus, he and his wife, Pyrrha, threw stones over their heads, and those which he threw became men, and those thrown by his wife became women. Thus does mythology account for the new settlement of the country—a tradition doubtless derived from the remote ages through the children of Japhet, from whom the Greeks descended, and who, after many wanderings and migrations, settled in Greece.

Hellen and Pyrrha.

Deucalion and Pyrrha had two sons, Hellen and Amphictyon. The eldest, Hellen, by a nymph was the father of Dorus, Æolus, and Xuthus, and he gave his name to the nation—Hellenas. In dividing the country among his sons, Æolus received Thessaly; Xuthus, Peloponnesus; and Dorus, the country lying opposite, on the northern side of the Corinthian Gulf, as has been already mentioned in the preceding chapter. Substitute Deucalion for Noah, Greece for Armenia, and Dorus, Æolus, and Xuthus for Shem, Ham, and Japhet, and we see a reproduction of the Mosaic account of the second settlement of mankind.

As it is natural for men to trace their origin to illustrious progenitors, so the Greeks, in their various settlements, cherished the legends which represented themselves as sprung from gods and heroes—those great benefactors, whose exploits occupy the heroic ages. As Hercules was the Argive hero of the Peloponnesus, so Æolus was the father of heroes sacred in the history of the Æolians, who inhabited the largest part of Greece. Æolus reigned in Thessaly, the original seat of the Hellenes.

Among his sons was Salmoneus, whose daughter, Tyro, became enamored of the river Eneipus, and frequenting its banks, the god Poseidon fell in love with her. The fruits of this alliance were the twin brothers, Pelias and Neleus, who quarreled respecting the possession of Iolchos, situated at the foot of Mount Pelion, celebrated afterward as the residence of Jason. Pelias prevailed, and Neleus returned into Peloponnesus and founded the kingdom of Pylos. His beautiful daughter, Pero, was sought in marriage by princes from all the neighboring countries, but he refused to entertain the pretensions of any of them, declaring that she should only wed the man who brought him the famous oxen of Iphiklos, in Thessaiy. Melampus, the nephew of Neleus, obtained the oxen for his brother Bias, who thus obtained the hand of Pero. Of the twelve sons of Neleus, Nestor was the most celebrated. It was he who assembled the various chieftains for the siege of Troy, and was pre-eminent over all for wisdom.

Pelias and Neleus.

Another descendant of Æolus was the subject of a beautiful legend. Admetus, who married a daughter of Pelias, and whose horses were tended by Apollo, for a time incarnated as a slave in punishment for the murder of the Cyclopes. Apollo, in gratitude, obtained from the Fates the privilege that the life of Admetus should be prolonged if any one could be found to die voluntarily for him. His wife, Alkestes, made the sacrifice, but was released from the grasp of death (Thanatos) by Hercules, the ancient friend of Admetus.

Admetus.

But a still more beautiful legend is associated with Jason, a great grandson of Æolus. Pelias, still reigning at Iolchos, was informed by the oracle to beware of the man who should appear before him with only one sandal. He was celebrating a festival in honor of Poseidon when Jason appeared, having lost one of his sandals in crossing a river. As a means of averting the danger, he imposed upon Jason the task, deemed desperate, of bringing back to Iolchos the "Golden Fleece." The result was the memorable Argonautic expedition of the ship Argo, to the distant land of Colchis, on the eastern coast of the Black Sea. Jason invited the noblest youth of Greece to join him in this voyage of danger and glory. Fifty illustrious persons joined him, including Hercules and Theseus, Castor and Pollux, Mopsus, and Orpheus. They proceeded along the coast of Thrace, up the Hellespont, past the southern coast of the Propontis, through the Bosphorus, onward past Bithynia and Pontus, and arrived at the river Phasis, south of the Caucasian mountains, where dwelt Æetes, whom they sought. But he refused to surrender the golden fleece except on conditions which were almost impossible. Medea, however, his daughter, fell in love with Jason, and by her means, assisted by Hecate, he succeeded in yoking the ferocious bulls and plowing the field, and sowing it with dragons' teeth. Still Æetes refused the reward, and meditated the murder of the Argonauts; but Medea lulled to sleep the dragon which guarded the fleece, and fled with her lover and his companions on board the Argo. The adventurers returned to Iolchos in safety, after innumerable perils, and by courses irreconcil-

Jason and the Argonauts.

able with all geographical truths. But Jason could avenge himself on Pelias only through the stratagem of his wife, and by her magical arts she induced the daughters of Pelias to cut up their father, and to cast his limbs into a caldron, believing that by this method he would be restored to the vigor of youth, and Jason was thus revenged, and obtained possession of the kingdom, which he surrendered to a son of Pelias, and retired with his wife to Corinth. Here he lived ten years in prosperity, but repudiated Medea in order to marry Glauce, the daughter of the king of Corinth; Medea avenged the insult by the poisoned robe she sent to Glauce as a marriage present, while Jason perished, while asleep, from a fragment of his ship Argo, which fell upon him. Such is the legend of the Argonauts, which is typical of the naval adventures of the maritime Greeks, and their restless enterprises.

Sisyphus.

The legend of Sisyphus is connected with the early history of Corinth. Sisyphus was the son of Æolus, and founded this wealthy city. He was distinguished for cunning and deceit. He detected Antolycus, the son of Hermes, by marking his sheep under the foot, so that the arch-thief was obliged to acknowledge the superior craft of the Æolid, and restore the plunder. He discovered the amour of Zeus with the nymph Ægina, and told her mother where she was carried, which so incensed the "father of gods and men," that he doomed Sisyphus, in Hades, to the perpetual punishment of rolling up a hill a heavy stone, which, as soon as it reached the summit, rolled back again in spite of all his efforts. This legend illustrates the never ending toils and disappointments of men.

Bellerophon.

Sisyphus was the grandfather of Bellerophon, whose beauty made him the object of a violent passion on the part of Antea, the wife of a king of Argos. He rejected her advances, and became as violently hated. She made false accusations, and persuaded her husband to kill him. Not wishing to commit the murder directly, he sent him to his son-in-law, the king of Sykia, in Asia Minor, with a folded tablet full of destructive symbols, which required him to perform perilous undertakings, which he successfully performed. He was then recognized as the son of a god, and married the daughter of the king. This legend reminds us of Joseph in Egypt.

Æolus.

We are compelled to omit other interesting legends of the Æolids, the sons and daughters of Æolus, among which are those which record the feats of Atalanta, and turn to those which relate to the Pelopids, who gave to the Peloponnesus its early poetic interest. Of this remarkable race were Tantalus, Pelops, Atreus, Thyestes, Agamemnon, Menelaus, Helen, and Hermione, all of whom figured in the ancient legendary genealogies.

Tantalus.

Tantalus resided, at a remote antiquity, near Mount Sipylus, in Lydia, and was a man of immense wealth, and pre-eminently favored both by gods and men. Intoxicated by prosperity, he stole nectar and ambrosia from the table of the gods, and revealed their secrets, for which he was punished in the under world by perpetual hunger and thirst, yet placed with fruit and water near him, which eluded his grasp when he attempted to touch them. He had two children, Pelops and Niobe. The latter was blessed with seven sons and seven daughters, which so inflamed her with pride that she claimed equality with the goddesses Latona and Diana, who favored her by their friendship. This presumption so incensed the goddesses, that they killed all her children, and Niobe wept herself to death, and was turned into a stone, a striking image of excessive grief.

Pelops.

Pelops was a Lydian king, but was expelled from Asia by Ilus, king of Troy, for his impieties. He came to Greece, and beat Hippodamenia, whose father was king of Pisa, near Olympia, in Elis, in a chariot race, when death was the penalty of failure. He succeeded by the favor of Poseidon, and married the princess, and became king of Pisa. He gave his name to the whole peninsula, which he was enabled to do from the great wealth he brought from Lydia, thus connecting the early settlements of the Peloponnesus with Asia Minor. He had numerous children, who became the sovereigns of different cities and states in Argos, Elis, Laconia, and Arcadia. One of them, Atreus, was king of Mycenæ, who inherited the sceptre of Zeus, and whose wealth was proverbial. The sceptre was made by Hephæstus (Vulcan) and given to Zeus; he gave it to Hermes; Hermes presented it to Pelops; and Pelops gave it to Atreus, the ruler of men. Atreus and his brother, Thyestes, bequeathed it to Agamemnon, who ruled at Mycenæ, while his brother, Menelaus, reigned at Sparta. It was the wife of Menelaus, Helen, who was carried away by Paris, which occasioned the Trojan war. Agamemnon was killed on his return from Troy, through the treachery of his wife Clytemnestra, who was seduced by Ægisthus, the son of Thyestes. His only son, Orestes, afterward avenged the murder, and recovered Mycenæ. Hermione, the only daughter of Menelaus and Helen, was given in marriage to the son of Achilles, Neoptolemas, who reigned in Thessaly. Mycenæ maintained its independence to the Persian invasion, and is rendered immortal by the Iliad and Odyssey. On the subsequent ascendency of Sparta, the bones of Orestes were brought from Tegea, where they had reposed for generations, in a coffin seven cubits long.

The other States of the Peloponnesus, have also their genealogical legends, which trace their ancestors to gods and goddesses, which I omit, and turn to those which belong to Attica.

The Deucalian deluge.

The great Deucalian deluge, according to legend, happened during the reign of Ogyges, 1796 years B. C., and 1020 before the first Olympiad. After a long interval, Cecrops, half man and half serpent, became king of the country. By some he is represented as a Pelasgian, by others, as an Egyptian. He introduced the first elements of civilized life—marriage, the twelve political divisions of Attica, and a new form of worship, abolishing the bloody sacrifices to Zeus. He gave to the country the name of Cecropia. During his reign there ensued a dispute between Athenæ and Poseidon, respecting the possession of the Acropolis.

Poseidon struck the rocks with his trident, and produced a well of salt water; Athenæ planted an olive tree. The twelve Olympian gods decided the dispute, and awarded to Athenæ the coveted possession, and she ever afterward remained the protecting deity of Athens.

Theseus.

Among his descendants was Theseus, the great legendary hero of Attica, who was one of the Argonauts, and also one of those who hunted the Calidomian boar. He freed Attica from robbers and wild beasts, conquered the celebrated Minotaur of Crete, and escaped from the labyrinth by the aid of Ariadne, whom he carried off and abandoned. In the Iliad he is represented as fighting against the centaurs, and in the Hesiodic poems he is an amorous knight-errant, misguided by the beautiful Ægle. Among his other feats, inferior only to those of Hercules, he vanquished the Amazons—a nation of courageous and hardy women, who came from the country about Caucasus, and whose principal seats were near the modern Trezibond. They invaded Thrace, Asia Minor, Greece, Syria, Egypt, and the islands of the Ægean. The foundation of several towns in Asia Minor is ascribed to them. In the time of Theseus, this semi-mythical and semi-historical race of female warriors invaded Attica, and even penetrated to Athens, but were conquered by the hero king. Allusion is made to their defeat throughout the literature of Athens. Although Theseus was a purely legendary personage, the Athenians were accustomed to regard him as a great political reformer and legislator, who consolidated the Athenian commonwealth, distributing the people into three classes.

Theban legends.

The legends pertaining to Thebes occupy a prominent place in Grecian mythology. Cadmus, the son of Agenor, king of Phœnicia, leaves his country in search of his sister Europa, with whom Zeus, in the form of a bull, had fallen in love, and carried on his back to Crete. He first goes to Thrace, and thence to Delphi, to learn tidings of Europa, but the god directs him not to prosecute his search; he is to follow the guidance of a cow, and to found a city where the animal should lie down. The cow stops at the site of Thebes. He marries Harmonia, the daughter of Ares and Aphrodite, after having killed the dragons which guarded the fountain Allia, and sowed their teeth. From these armed men sprang up, who killed each other, except five. From these arose the five great families of Thebes, called Sparti. One of the Sparti marries a daughter of Cadmus, whose issue was Pentheus, who became king. It was in his reign that Dionysus appears as a god in Bœotia, the giver of the vine, and obtains divine honors in Thebes. Among the descendants of Cadmus was Laius. He is forewarned by an oracle that any son he should beget would destroy him, and hence he caused the infant Œdipus to be exposed on Mount Cithæron. Here the herdsmen of Polybus, king of Corinth, find him, and convey him to their lord who brings him up as his own child. Distressed by the taunts of companions as to his unknown parentage, he goes to Delphi, to inquire the name of his real father. He is told not to return to his own country, for it was his destiny to kill his father and become the husband of his mother. Knowing no country but Corinth, he pursues his way to Bœotia, and meets Laius in a chariot drawn by mules. A quarrel ensues from the insolence of attendants, and Œdipus kills Laius. The brother of Laius, Creon, succeeds to the throne of Thebes. The country around is vexed with a terrible monster, with the face of a woman, the wings of a bird, and the tail of a lion, called the Sphinx, who has learned from the Muses a riddle, which she proposed to the Thebans, and on every failure to resolve it one of them was devoured. But no person can solve the riddle. The king offers his crown and his sister Jocasta, wife of Laius, in marriage to any one who would explain the riddle. Œdipus solves it, and is made king of Thebes, and marries Jocasta. A fatal curse rests upon him. Jocasta, informed by the gods of her relationship, hangs herself in agony. Œdipus endures great miseries, as well as his children, whom he curses, and who quarrel about their inheritance, which quarrel leads to

Cadmus.

Œdipus.

the siege of Thebes by Adrastus, king of Argos, who seeks to restore Polynices—one of the sons of Œdipus, to the throne of which he was dispossessed. The Argeian chieftains readily enter into the enterprise, assisted by numerous auxiliaries from Arcadia and Messenia. The Cadmeans, assisted by the Phocians, march out to resist the invaders, who are repulsed, in consequence of the magnanimity of a generous youth, who offers himself a victim to Ares. Eteocles then proposed to his brother, Polynices, the rival claimants, to decide the quarrel by single combat. It resulted in the death of both, and then in the renewal of the general contest, and the destruction of the Argeian chiefs, and Adrastus's return to Argos in shame and woe.

Creon.

But Creon, the father of the self-sacrificing Menœceus, succeeds on the death of the rival brothers, to the administration of Thebes. A second siege takes place, conducted by Adrastus, and the sons of those who had been slain. Thebes now falls, and Thersander, the son of Polynices, is made king. The legends of Thebes have furnished the great tragedians Sophocles and Euripides, with their finest subjects. In the fable of the Sphinx we trace a connection between Thebes and ancient Egypt.

But all the legends of ancient Greece yield in interest to that of Troy, which Homer chose as the subject of his immortal epic.

Dardanus.

Dardanus, a son of Zeus, is the primitive ancestor of the Trojan kings, whose seat of power was Mount Ida. His son, Erichthonius, became the richest of mankind, and had in his pastures three thousand mares. His son, Tros, was the father of Ilus, Assaracus, and Ganymede. The latter was stolen by Zeus to be his cup-bearer.

Ilus.

Ilus was the father of Laomedon, under whom Apollo and Poseidon, in mortal form, went through a temporary servitude—the former tending his flocks, the latter building the walls of Ilium. Laomedon was killed by Hercules, in punishment for his perfidy in giving him mortal horses for his destruction of a sea monster, instead of the immortal horses, as he had promised, the gift of Zeus to Tros.

Among the sons of Laomedon was Priam, who was placed upon the throne. He was the father of illustrious sons, among whom were Hector and Paris. The latter was exposed on Mount Ida, to avoid the fulfillment of an evil prophecy, but grew up beautiful and active among the flocks and herds. Is was to him that the three goddesses, Here, Athenæ, and Aphrodite (Juno, Minerva, and Venus), presented their respective claims to beauty, which he awarded to Aphrodite, and by whom he was promised, in recompense, Helen, wife of the Spartan king, Menelaus, and daughter of Zeus. Aphrodite caused ships to be built for him, and he safely arrived in Sparta, and was hospitably entertained by the unsuspecting monarch. In the absence of Menelaus in Crete, Paris carries away to Troy both Helen, and a large sum of money belonging to the king. Menelaus hastens home, informed of the perfidy, and consults his brother, Agamemnon, and the venerable Nestor. They interest the Argeian chieftains, who resolve to recover Helen. Ten years are spent in preparations, consisting of one thousand one hundred and eighty-six ships, and one hundred thousand men, comprised of heroes from all parts of Greece, among whom are Ajax, Diomedes, Achilles, and Odysseus. The heroes set sail from Aulis, and after various mistakes, reach Asia.

Priam.

Helen.

Meanwhile the Trojans assemble, with a large body of allies, to resist the invaders, who demand the redress of a great wrong. The Trojans are routed in battle, and return within their walls. After various fortunes, the city is taken, at the end of ten years, by stratagem, and the Grecian chieftains who were not killed seek to return to their own country, with Helen among the spoils. They meet with many misfortunes, from the anger of the gods, for not having spared the altars of Troy. Their chieftains quarrel among themselves, and even Agamemnon and Menelaus lose their fraternal friendship. After long wanderings, and

The Trojan war.

bitter disappointments, and protracted hopes, the heroes return to their homes—such as war had spared—to recount their adventures and sufferings, and reconstruct their shattered States, and mend their broken fortunes—a type of war in all the ages, calamitous even to conquerors. The wanderings of Ulysses have a peculiar fascination, since they form the subject of the Odyssey, one of the noblest poems of antiquity. Nor are the adventures of Æneas scarcely less interesting, as presented by Virgil, who traces the first settlement of Latium to the Trojan exiles. We should like to dwell on the siege of Troy, and its great results, but the subject is too extensive and complicated. The student of the great event, whether historical or mystical, must read the detailed accounts in the immortal epics of Homer. We have only space for the grand outlines, which can be scarcely more than allusions.

The legend of the Heraclidæ.

Scarcely inferior to the legend of Troy, is that which recounts the return of the descendants of Hercules to the ancient inheritance on the Peloponnesus, which, it is supposed, took place three or four hundred years before authentic history begins, or eighty years after the Trojan war.

We have briefly described the geographical position of the most important part of ancient Greece—the Peloponnesus—almost an island, separated from the continent only by a narrow gulf, resembling in shape a palm-tree, indented on all sides by bays, and intersected with mountains, and inhabited by a simple and warlike race.

We have seen that the descendants of Perseus, who was a descendant of Danaus, reigned at Mycenæ in Argolis—among whom was Amphitryon, who fled to Thebes, on the murder of his uncle, with Alemena his wife. Then Hercules, to whom the throne of Mycenæ legitimately belonged, was born, but deprived of his inheritance by Eurystheus—a younger branch of the Perseids—in consequence of the anger and jealousy of Juno, and to whom, by the fates, Hercules was made subject. We have seen how the sons of Hercules, under Hyllos, attempted to regain their kingdom, but were defeated, and retreated among the Dorians.

After three generations, the Heraclidæ set out to regain their inheritance, assisted by the Dorians. They at length, after five expeditions, gained possession of the country, and divided it among the various chieftains, who established their dominion in Argos, Mycenæ, and Sparta, which, at the time of the Trojan war, was ruled by Agamemnon and Menelaus, descendants of Pelops. In the next generation, Corinth was conquered by the Dorians, under an Heraclide prince.

Their settlement in Sparta.

The Achæans, thus expelled by the Dorians from the south and east of the Peloponnesus, fell back upon the northwest coast, and drove away the Ionians, and formed a confederacy of twelve cities, which in later times became of considerable importance. The dispossessed Ionians joined their brethren of the same race in Attica, but the rugged peninsula was unequal to support the increased population, and a great migration took place to the Cyclades and the coasts of Lydia. The colonists there built twelve cities, about one hundred and forty years after the Trojan war. Another body of Achæans, driven out of the Peloponnesus by the Dorians, first settled in Bœotia, and afterward, with Æolians, sailed to the isle of Lesbos, where they founded six cities, and then to the opposite mainland. At the foot of Mount Ida they founded the twelve Æolian cities, of which Smyrna was the principal.

The wanderings of the dispossessed Achæans.

Crete was founded by a body of Dorians and conquered Achæans. Rhodes received a similar colony. So did the island of Cos. The cities of Lindus, Ialysus, Camirus, Cos, with Cnidus and Halicarnassus, on the mainland, formed the Dorian Hexapolis of Caria, inferior, however, to the Ionian and Æolian colonies.

Crete.

At the beginning of the mythical age the dominant Hellenic races were the Achæans and Æolians; at the close, the Ionians and Dorians were predominant. The Ionians extended their maritime pos-

The Dorians and Ionians become the leading tribes.

sessions from Attica to the Asiatic colonies across the Ægean, and gradually took the lead of the Asiatic Æolians, and formed a great maritime empire under the supremacy of Athens. The Hellenic world ultimately was divided and convulsed by the great contest for supremacy between the Dorians and Ionians, until the common danger from the Persian invasion united them together for a time.

Thus far we have only legend to guide us in the early history of Greece. The historical period begins with the first Olympiad, B. C. 776. Before this all is uncertain, yet as probable as the events of English history in the mythical period between the departure of the Romans and the establishment of the Anglo-Saxon kingdom. The history is not all myth; neither is it clearly authenticated.

First Olympiad the era of the historic period.

The various Hellenic tribes, though separated by political ambition, were yet kindred in language and institutions. They formed great leagues, or associations, of neighboring cities, for the performance of religious rites. The Amphictyonic Council, which became subsequently so famous, was made up of Thessalians, Bœotians, Dorians, Ionians, Achæans, Locrians, and Phocians—all Hellenic in race. Their great centre was the temple of Apollo at Delphi. The different tribes or nations also came together regularly to take part in the four great religious festivals or games—the Olympic, Pythian, Isthmian, and Nemæan—the two former of which were celebrated every four years.

Grecian leagues.

In the Homeric age the dominant State was Achæa, whose capital was Mycenæ. The next in power was Lacedæmon. After the Dorian conquest, Argos was the first, Sparta the second, and Messenia the third State in importance. Argos, at the head of a large confederacy of cities on the northeast of the Peloponnesus, was governed by Phidon—an irresponsible ruler, a descendant of Hercules, to whom is inscribed the coinage of silver and copper money, and the introduction of weights and measures. He flourished B. C. 747.

Early dominant states.

All these various legends, though unsupported by history, have a great ethical importance, as well as poetic interest. The passions, habits, and adventures of a primitive and warlike race are presented by the poets with transcendent effect, and we read lessons of human nature as in the dramas of Shakespeare. Hence, one of the most learned and dignified of the English historians deems it worthy of his pen to devote to these myths a volume of his noble work. Nor is it misplaced labor. These legends furnished subjects to the tragic and epic poets of antiquity, as well as to painters and sculptors, in all the ages of art. They are identified with the development of Grecian genius, and are as imperishable as history itself. They were to the Greeks realities, and represent all that is vital in their associations and worship. They stimulated the poëtic faculty, and taught lessons of moral wisdom which all nations respect and venerate. They contributed to enrich both literature and art. They make Æschylus, Euripides, Pindar, Homer, and Hesiod great monumental pillars of the progress of the human race. Therefore, we will not willingly let those legends die in our memories or hearts.

Interest to be attached to the legends of Greece.

They are particularly important as shedding light on the manners, customs, and institutions of the ancient Greeks, although they give no reliable historical facts. They are memorials of the first state of Grecian society, essentially different from the Oriental world. We see in them the germs of political constitutions—the rise of liberty—the pre-eminence of families which forms the foundation for oligarchy, or the ascendency of nobles. We see also the first beginnings of democratic influence—the voice of the people asserting a claim to be heard in the market-place. We see again the existence of slavery—captives taken in war doomed to attendance in princely palaces, and ultimately to menial labor on the land. In those primitive times a State was often nothing but a city, with the lands surrounding it, and therefore it was possible for all the inhabitants to assemble in the agora with the king and nobles. We find, in

Their historical importance.

the early condition of Greece, kings, nobles, citizens, and slaves.

The early government of the Hellenes.

The king was seldom distinguished by any impassable barrier between himself and subjects. He was rather the chief among his nobles, and his supremacy was based on descent from illustrious ancestors. It passed generally to the eldest son. In war he was a leader; in peace, a protector. He offered up prayers and sacrifices for his people to the gods in whom they all alike believed. He possessed an ample domain, and the produce of his lands was devoted to a generous but rude hospitality. He had a large share of the plunder taken from an enemy, and the most alluring of the female captives. It was, however, difficult for him to retain ascendency without great personal gifts and virtues, and especially bravery on the field of battle, and wisdom in council. To the noblest of these kings the legends ascribe great bodily strength and activity.

The king.

The councils.

The kings were assisted by a great council of chieftains or nobles, whose functions were deliberation and consultation; and after having talked over their intentions with the chiefs, they announced them to the people, who assembled in the market-place, and who were generally submissive to the royal authority, although they were regarded as the source of power. Then the king, and sometimes his nobles, administered justice and heard complaints. Public speaking was favorable to eloquence, and stimulated intellectual development, and gave dignity to the people to whom the speeches were addressed.

Religious and social life.

In those primitive times there was a strong religious feeling, great reverence for the gods, whose anger was deprecated, and whose favor was sought. The ties of families were strong. Paternal authority was recognized and revered. Marriage was a sacred institution. The wife occupied a position of great dignity and influence. Women were not secluded in a harem, as were the Asiatics, but employed in useful labors. Children were obedient, and brothers, sisters, and cousins were united together by strong attachments. Hospitality was a cherished virtue, and the stranger was ever cordially welcome, nor questioned even until refreshed by the bath and the banquet. Feasts were free from extravagance and luxury, and those who shared in them enlivened the company by a recital of the adventures of gods and men. But passions were unrestrained, and homicide was common. The murderer was not punished by the State, but was left to the vengeance of kindred and friends, appeased sometimes by costly gifts, as among the ancient Jews.

Early forms of civilization.

There was a rude civilization among the ancient Greeks, reminding us of the Teutonic tribes, but it was higher than theirs. We observe the division of the people into various trades and occupations—carpenters, smiths, leather-dressers, leeches, prophets, bards, and fishermen, although the main business was agriculture. Cattle were the great staple of wealth, and the largest part of the land was devoted to pasture. The land was tilled chiefly by slaves, and women of the servile class were doomed to severe labor and privations. They brought the water, and they turned the mills. Spinning and weaving were, however, the occupations of all, and garments for men and women were alike made at home. There was only a limited commerce, which was then monopolized by the Phœnicians, who exaggerated the dangers of the sea. There were walled cities, palaces, and temples. Armor was curiously wrought, and arms were well made. Rich garments were worn by princes, and their palaces glittered with the precious metals. Copper was hardened so as to be employed in weapons of war. The warriors had chariots and horses, and were armed with sword, dagger, and spear, and were protected by helmets, breastplates, and greaves. Fortified cities were built on rocky elevations, although the people generally lived in unfortified villages. The means of defense were superior to those of offense, which enabled men to preserve their acquisitions, for the ancient chieftains resembled the feudal barons of the Middle Ages in the passion for robbery and adventure. We do not read of coined money nor the art of writing, nor sculpture, nor ornamental architecture among the Homeric Greeks; but they were fond of music and poetry. Before history commences, they had their epics, which, sung by the bards and minstrels, furnished Homer and Hesiod with materials for their noble productions. It is supposed by Grote that the Homeric poems were composed eight hundred and fifty years before Christ, and preserved two hundred years without the aid of writing—of all poems the most popular and natural, and addressed to unlettered minds.

Such were the heroic ages with their myths, their heroes, their simple manners, their credulity, their religious faith, their rude civilization. We have now to trace their progress through the historical epoch.

CHAPTER XV.

THE GRECIAN STATES AND COLONIES TO THE PERSIAN WARS.

We come now to consider those States which grew into importance about the middle of the eighth century before Christ, at the close of the legendary period.

The most important of these was Sparta, which was the leading State. We have seen how it was conquered by Dorians, under Heraclic princes. Its first great historic name was Lycurgus, whom some historians, however, regard as a mythical personage.

Lycurgus.

Sparta was in a state of anarchy in consequence of the Dorian conquest, a contest between the kings, aiming at absolute power, and the people, desirous of democratic liberty. At this juncture the king, Polydectes, died, leaving Lycurgus, his brother, guardian of the realm, and of the infant heir to the throne. The future lawgiver then set out on his travels, visiting the other States of Greece, Asia Minor, Egypt, and other countries, and returned to Sparta about the period of the first Olympiad, B. C. 776, with a rich store of wisdom and knowledge. The State was full of disorders, but he instituted great reforms, aided by the authority of the Delphic oracle, and a strong party of influential men. His great object was to convert the citizens of Sparta into warriors united by the strongest bonds, and trained to the severest discipline, governed by an oligarchy under the form of the ancient monarchy. In other words, his object was to secure the ascendency of the small body of Dorian invaders that had conquered Laconia.

His legislation.

The descendants of these invaders, the Spartans, alone possessed the citizenship, and were equal in political rights.

They were the proprietors of the soil, which was tilled by Helots. The Spartans disdained any occupation but war and government. They lived within their city, which was a fortified camp, and ate in common at public tables, and on the simplest fare. Every virtue and energy were concentrated on self-discipline and sacrifice, in order to fan the fires of heroism and self-devotion. They were a sort of stoics—hard, severe, proud, despotic, and overbearing. They cared nothing for literature, or art, or philosophy. Even eloquence was disdained, and the only poetry or music they cultivated were religious hymns and heroic war songs. Commerce was forbidden by the constitution, and all the luxuries to which it leads. Only iron was allowed for money, and the precious metals were prohibited. Every exercise, every motive, every law, contributed to make the Spartans soldiers, and nothing but soldiers. Their discipline was the severest known to the ancients. Their habits of life were austere and rigid. They were trained to suffer any hardship without complaint.

Spartan citizens.

Besides these Spartan citizens were the *Periœci*—remnants of the old Achæan population, but mixed with an inferior class of Dorians. They had no political power, but possessed personal freedom. They were landed proprietors, and engaged in commerce and manufactures.

The old Achæan population.

Below this class were the Helots—pure Greeks, but reduced to dependence by conquest. They were bound to the soil, like serfs, but dwelt with their families on the farms they tilled. They were not bought and sold as slaves. They were the body servants of the Spartan citizens, and were regarded as the property of the State. They were treated with great haughtiness and injustice by their masters, which bred at last an intense hatred.

The Helots.

All political power was in the hands of the citizen warriors, only about nine thousand in number in the time of Lycurgus. From them emanated all delegated authority, except that of kings. This assembly, or *ecclesia*, of Spartans over thirty years of age, met at stated intervals to decide

The Ecclesia.

on all important matters submitted to them, but they had no right of amendment—only a simple approval or rejection.

The body to which the people, it would seem, delegated considerable power, was the Senate, composed of thirty members, not under sixty years of age, and elected for life. They were a deliberative body, and judges in all capital charges against Spartans. They were not chosen for noble birth or property qualifications, but for merit and wisdom.

The Senate.

At the head of the State, at least nominally, were two kings, who were numbered with the thirty senators. They had scarcely more power than the Roman consuls; they commanded the armies, and offered the public sacrifices, and were revered as the descendants of Hercules.

The kings.

The persons of most importance were the ephors, chosen annually by the people, who exercised the chief executive power, and without responsibility. They could even arrest kings, and bring them to trial before the Senate. Two of the five ephors accompanied the king in war, and were a check on his authority.

The Ephors.

It would thus seem that the government of Sparta was a republic of an aristocratic type. There were no others nobler than citizens, but these citizens composed but a small part of the population. They were Spartans—a handful of conquerors, in the midst of hostile people—a body of lords among slaves and subjects. They sympathized with law and order, and detested the democratical turbulence of Athens. They were trained, by their military education, to subordination, obedience, and self-sacrifice. They, as citizens or as soldiers, existed only for the *State*, and to the State every thing was subordinate. In our times, the State is made for the people; in Sparta, the people for the State. This generated an intense patriotism and self-denial. It also permitted a greater interference of the State in personal matters than would now be tolerated in any despotism in Europe. It made the citizens submissive to a division of property, which if not

Aristocratic form of government.

The citizen lost in the State.

a perfect community of goods, was fatal to all private fortunes. But the property which the citizens thus shared was virtually created by the Helots, who alone tilled the ground. The wealth of nations is in the earth, and it is its cultivation which is the ordinary source of property. The State, not individual masters, owned the Helots; and they toiled for the citizens. In the modern sense of liberty, there was very little in Sparta, except that which was possessed by the aristocratic citizens—the conquerors of the country—men, whose very occupation was war and government, and whose very amusement were those which fostered warlike habits. The Roman citizens did not disdain husbandry, nor the Puritan settlers of New England, but the Spartan citizens despised both this and all trade and manufacture. Never was a haughtier class of men than these Spartan soldiers. They exceeded in pride the feudal chieftain.

Such an exclusive body of citizens, however, jealous of their political privileges, constantly declined in numbers, so that, in the time of Aristotle, there were only one thousand Spartan citizens; and this decline continued in spite of all the laws by which the citizens were compelled to marry, and those customs, so abhorrent to our Christian notions, which permitted the invasion of marital rights for the sake of healthy children.

Number of citizens.

As it was to war that the best energies of the Spartans were directed, so their armies were the admiration of the ancient world for discipline and effectiveness. They were the first who reduced war to a science. The general type of their military organization was the phalanx, a body of troops in close array, armed with a long spear and short sword. The strength of an army was in the heavy armed infantry; and this body was composed almost entirely of citizens, with a small mixture of Periœci. From the age of twenty to sixty, every Spartan was liable to military service; and all the citizens formed an army, whether congregated at Sparta, or absent on foreign service.

Spartan armies.

Such, in general, were the social, civil, and military institutions of Sparta, and not peculiar to her alone, but to all the Dorians, even in Crete; from which we infer that it was not Lycurgus who shaped them, but that they existed independent of his authority. He may have re-established the old regulations, and gave his aid to preserve the State from corruption and decay. And when we remember that the constitution which he re-established resisted both the usurpations of tyrants and the advances of democracy, by which other States were revolutionized, we can not sufficiently admire the wisdom which so early animated the Dorian legislators.

The Spartans obtain the ascendency on the Peninsula.

The Spartans became masters of the country after a long struggle, and it was henceforth called Laconia. The more obstinate Achæans became Helots. After the conquest, the first memorable event in Spartan history was the reduction of Messenia, for which it took two great wars.

Messenia.

Messenia has already been mentioned as the southwestern part of the Peloponnesus, and resembling Laconia in its general aspects. The river Parnisus flows through its entire length, as Eurotas does in Laconia, forming fertile valleys and plains, and producing various kinds of cereals and fruits, even as it now produces oil, silk, figs, wheat, maize, cotton, wine, and honey. The area of Messenia is one thousand one hundred and ninety-two square miles, not so large as one of our counties. The early inhabitants had been conquered by the Dorians, and it was against the descendants of these conquerors that the Spartans made war. The murder of a Spartan king, Teleclus, at a temple on the confines of Laconia and Messenia, where sacrifices were offered in common, gave occasion for the first war, which lasted nineteen years, B. C. 743. Other States were involved in the quarrel—Corinth on the side of Sparta, and Sicyon and Arcadia on the part of the Messenians. The Spartans having the superiority in the field, the Messenians retreated to their stronghold of Ithome, where they defended themselves fifteen years. But at

The war with Sparta.

last they were compelled to abandon it, and the fortress was razed to the ground. The conquered were reduced to the condition of Helots—compelled to cultivate the land and pay half of its produce to their new masters. The Spartan citizens became the absolute owners of the whole soil of Messenia.

Aristomenes.

After thirty-nine years of servitude, a hero arose among the conquered Messenians, Aristomenes, like Judas Maccabeus, or William Wallace, who incited his countrymen to revolt. The whole of the Peloponnesus became involved in the new war, and only Corinth became the ally of Sparta; the remaining States of Argos, Sicyon, Arcadia, and Pisa, sided with the Messenians. The Athenian poet, Tyrtæus, stimulated the Spartans by his war-songs. In the first great battle, the Spartans were worsted; in the second, they gained a signal victory, so that the Messenians were obliged to leave the open country and retire to the fortress on Mount Ira. Here they maintained themselves eleven years, the Spartans being unused to sieges, and trained only to conflict in the open field. The fortress was finally taken by treachery, and the hero who sought to revive the martial glories of his State fled to Rhodes. Messenia became now, B. C. 668, a part of Laconia, and it was three hundred years before it appeared again in history.

Conquest of Messenia.

Aggrandizement of Sparta.

The Spartans, after the conquest of Messenia, turned their eyes upon Arcadia—that land of shepherds, free and simple and brave like themselves. The city of Tegea long withstood the arms of the Spartans, but finally yielded to superior strength, and became a subject ally, B. C. 560. Sparta was further increased by a part of Argos, and a great battle, B. C. 547, between the Argives and Spartans, resulted in the complete ascendency of Sparta in the southern part of the Peloponnesus, about the time that Cyrus overthrew the Lydian empire. The Ionian Greeks of Asia Minor invoked their aid against the Persian power, and Sparta proudly rallied in their defens

Meanwhile, a great political revolution was going on in the other States of Greece, in no condition to resist the pre-eminence of Sparta. The patriarchal monarchies of the heroic ages had gradually been subverted by the rising importance of the nobility, enriched by conquered lands. Every conquest, every step to national advancement, brought the nobles nearer to the crown, and the government passed into the hands of those nobles who had formerly composed the council of the king. With the growing power of nobles was a corresponding growth of the political power of the people or citizens, in consequence of increased wealth and intelligence. The political changes were rapid. As the nobles had usurped the power of the kings, so the citizens usurped the power of the nobles. The everlasting war of classes, where the people are intelligent and free, was signally illustrated in the Grecian States, and democracy succeeded to the oligarchy which had prostrated kings. Then, when the people had gained the ascendency, ambitious and factious demagogues in turn, got the control, and these adventurers, now called Tyrants, assumed arbitrary powers. Their power was only maintained by cruelty, injustice, and unscrupulous means, which caused them finally to be so detested that they were removed by assassination. These natural changes, from a monarchy, primitive and just and limited, to an oligarchy of nobles, and the gradual subversion of their power by wealthy and enlightened citizens, and then the rise of demagogues, who became tyrants, have been illustrated in all ages of the world. But the rapidity of these changes in the Grecian States, with the progress of wealth and corruption, make their history impressive on all generations. It is these rapid and natural revolutions which give to the political history of Greece its permanent interest and value. The age of the Tyrants is generally fixed from B. C. 650 to B. C. 500—about one hundred and fifty years.

Political changes.

The age of Tyrants.

No State passed through these changes of government more signally than Corinthia, which, with Megaris, formed the isthmus which connected the Peloponnesus with Greece Proper.

Corinthia. It was a small territory, covered with the ridges and the spurs of the Geranean and and Oneian mountains, and useless for purposes of agriculture. Its principal city was Corinth; was favorably situated for commerce, and rapidly grew in population and wealth. It also commanded the great roads which led from Greece Proper through the defiles of the mountains into the Peloponnesus. It rapidly monopolized the commerce of the Ægean Sea, and the East through the Saronic Gulf; and through the Corinthian Gulf it commanded the trade of the Ionian and Sicilian seas.

Changes in Corinth. Corinth, by some, is supposed have been a Phœnician colony. Before authentic history begins, it was inhabited by a mixed population of Æolians and Ionians, the former of whom were dominant. Over them reigned Sisyphus, according to tradition, the grandfather of Bellerophon who laid the foundation of mercantile prosperity. The first historical king was Aletes, B. C. 1074, the leader of Dorian invaders, who subdued the Æolians, and incorporated them with their own citizens. The descendants of Aletes reigned twelve generations, when the nobles converted the government into an oligarchy, under Bacchis, who greatly increased the commercial importance of the city. In 754, B. C., Corinth began to colonize, and fitted out a war fleet for the protection of commerce. The oligarchy was supplanted by Cypselus, B. C. 655, a man of the people, whose mother was of noble birth, but rejected by her family, of the ruling house of the Bacchiadæ, on account of lameness. His son Periander reigned forty years with cruel despotism, but made Corinth the leading commercial city of Greece, and he subjected to her sway the colonies planted on the islands of the Ionian Sea, one of which was Corcyra (Corfu), which gained a great mercantile fame. It was under his reign that the poet Arion, or Lesbos, flourished, to whom he gave his patronage. In three years after the death of Periander, 585 B. C., the oligarchal power was restored, and Corinth allied herself with Sparta in her schemes of aggrandizement.

The same change of government was seen in Megara, a neighboring State, situated on the isthmus, between Corinth and Attica, and which attained great commercial distinction. As a result of commercial opulence, the people succeeded in overthrowing the government, an oligarchy of Dorian conquerors, and elevating a demagogue, Theagenes, to the supreme power, B. C. 630. He ruled tyrannically, in the name of the people, for thirty years, but was expelled by the oligarchy, which regained power. During his reign all kinds of popular excesses were perpetrated, especially the confiscation of the property of the rich.

Changes in Megara.

Other States are also illustrations of this change of government from kings to oligarchies, and oligarchies to demagogues and tyrants, as on the isle of Lesbos, where Pittacus reigned dictator, but with wisdom and virtue—one of the seven wise men of Greece—and in Samos, where Polycrates rivaled the fame of Periander, and adorned his capital with beautiful buildings, and patronized literature and art. One of his friends was Anacreon, the poet. He was murdered by the Persians, B. C. 522.

Changes in other States.

But the State which most signally illustrates the revolutions in government was Athens.

> "Where on the Ægean shore a city stands,—
> Built nobly; pure the air, and light the soil:
> Athens, the eye of Greece, mother of arts
> And eloquence, native to famous wits."

Every thing interesting or impressive in the history of classical antiquity clusters round this famous city, so that without Athens there could be no Greece. Attica, the little State of which it was the capital, formed a triangular peninsula, of about seven hundred square miles. The country is hilly and rocky, and unfavorable to agriculture; but such was the salubrity of the climate, and the industry of the people, all kinds of plants and animals flourished. The history of the country, like that of the other States, is mythical, to the period of the first Olympiad. Ogyges has the reputation of being the first king of a people who

Early history of Athens.

claimed to be indigenous, about one hundred and fifty years before the arrival of Cecrops, who came, it is supposed, from Egypt, and founded Athens, and taught the simple but savage natives a new religion, and the elements of civilized life, 1556 B. C. It received its name from the goddess Neith, introduced by him from Egypt, under the name of Athena, or Minerva. It was also called Cecropia, from its founder. Until the time of Theseus it was a small town, confined to the Acropolis and Mars Hill. This hero is the great name of ancient Athenian legend, as Hercules is to Greece generally. He cleared the roads of robbers, and formed an aristocratical constitution, with a king, who was only the first of his nobles. But he himself, after having given political unity, was driven away by a conspiracy of nobles, leaving the throne to Menesthius, a descendant of the ancient kings. This monarch reigned twenty-four years, and lost his life at the siege of Troy. The whole period of the monarchy lies within the mythical age. Tradition makes Codrus the last king, who was slain during an invasion of the Dorians, B. C. 1045. Resolving to have no future king, the Athenians substituted the office of archon, or ruler, and made his son, Medus, the superior magistrate. This office remained hereditary in the family of Codrus for thirteen generations. In B. C. 752, the duration of the office was fixed for ten years. It remained in the family of Codrus thirty-eight years longer, when it was left open for all the nobles. In 683 B. C., nine archons were annually elected from the nobles, the first having superior dignity

Theseus.

Codrus.

The first of these archons, of whom any thing of importance is recorded, was Draco, who governed Athens in the year 624 B. C., who promulgated written laws, exceedingly severe, inflicting capital punishment for slight offenses. The people grew weary of him and his laws, and he was banished to Ægina, where he died, from a conspiracy headed by Cylon, one of the nobles, who seized the Acropolis, B. C. 612. His insurrection, however, failed, and he was treacherously put to death by one of the archons,

Draco.

which led to the expulsion of the whole body, and a change in the constitution.

This was effected by Solon, the Athenian sage and lawgiver—himself of the race of Codrus, whom the Athenians chose as archon, with full power to make new laws. Intrusted with absolute power, he abstained from abusing it—a patriot in the most exalted sense, as well as a poet and philosopher. Urged by his friends to make himself tyrant, he replied that tyranny might be a fair country, only there was no way out of it.

Solon.

When he commenced his reforms, the nobles, or Eupatridæ, were in possession of most of the fertile land of Attica, while the poorer citizens possessed only the sterile highlands. This created an unhappy jealousy between the rich and poor. Besides, there was another class that had grown rich by commerce, animated by the spirit of freedom. But their influence tended to widen the gulf between the rich and poor. The poor got into debt, and fell in the power of creditors, and sunk to the condition of serfs, and many were even sold in slavery, for the laws were severe against debtors, as in ancient Rome. Solon, like Moses in his institution of the Year of Jubilee, set free all the estates and persons that had fallen in the power of creditors, and ransomed such as were sold in slavery.

His institutions.

Having removed the chief source of enmity between the rich and poor, he repealed the bloody laws of Draco, and commenced to remodel the political constitution. The fundamental principles which he adopted was a distribution of power to all citizens according to their wealth. But the nobles were not deprived of their ascendency, only the way was opened to all citizens to reach political distinction, especially those who were enriched by commerce. He made an assessment of the landed property of all the citizens, taking as the medium a standard of value which was equivalent to a drachma of annual produce. The first class, who had no aristocratic titles, were called Pentacosio medimni, from possessing five hundred medimni or upward.

Loss of aristocratic power.

They alone were eligible to the archonship and other high offices, and bore the largest share of the public burdens. The second class was called Knights, because they were bound to serve as cavalry. They filled the inferior offices, farmed the revenue, and had the commerce of the country in their hands.

Different classes.

The third class was called Zeugitæ (yokesmen), from their ability to keep a yoke of oxen. They were small farmers, and served in the heavy-armed infantry, and were subject to a property-tax. All those whose incomes fell short of two hundred medimni formed the fourth class, and served in the light-armed troops, and were exempt from property-tax, but disqualified for public office, and yet they had a vote in popular elections, and in the judgment passed upon archons at the expiration of office. "The direct responsibility of all the magistrates to the popular assembly, was the most democratic of all the institutions of Solon; and though the government was still in the hands of the oligarchy, Solon clearly foresaw, if he did not purposely prepare for, the preponderance of the popular element." "To guard against hasty measures, he also instituted the Senate of four hundred, chosen year by year, from the four Ionic tribes, whose office was to prepare all business for the popular assembly, and regulate its meetings. The Areopagus retained its ancient functions, to which Solon added a general oversight over all the public institutions, and over the private life of the citizens. He also enacted many other laws for the administration of justice, the regulation of social life, the encouragement of commerce, and the general prosperity of the State." His whole legislation is marked by wisdom and patriotism, and adaptation to the circumstances of the people who intrusted to him so much power and dignity. The laws were, however, better than the people, and his legislative wisdom and justice place him among the great benefactors of mankind, for who can tell the ultimate influence of his legislation on Rome and on other nations. The most beautiful feature was the responsibility of the chief magis-

Other political changes.

trates to the people who elected them, and from the fact that they could subsequently be punished for bad conduct was the greatest security against tyranny and peculation.

After having given this constitution to his countrymen, the lawgiver took his departure from Athens, for ten years, binding the people by a solemn oath to make no alteration in his laws. He visited Egypt, Cyprus, and Asia Minor, and returned to Athens to find his work nearly subverted by one of his own kinsmen. Pisistratus, of noble origin, but a demagogue, contrived, by his arts and prodigality, to secure a guard, which he increased, and succeeded in seizing the Acropolis, B. C. 560, and in usurping the supreme authority—so soon are good laws perverted, so easily are constitutions overthrown, when demagogues and usurpers are sustained by the people. A combination of the rich and poor drove him into exile; but their divisions and hatreds favored his return. Again he was exiled by popular dissension, and a third time he regained his power, but only by a battle. He sustained his usurpation by means of Thracian mercenaries, and sent the children of all he suspected as hostages to Naxos. He veiled his despotic power under the forms of the constitution, and even submitted himself to the judgment of the Areopagus on the charge of murder. He kept up his popularity by generosity and affability, by mingling freely with the citizens, by opening to them his gardens, by adorning the city with beautiful edifices, and by a liberal patronage of arts and letters. He founded a public library, and collected the Homeric poems in a single volume. He ruled beneficently, as tyrants often have,—like Cæsar, like Richelieu, like Napoleon,—identifying his own glory with the welfare of the State. He died after a successful reign of thirty-three years B. C. 527, and his two sons, Hippias and Hipparchus, succeeded him in the government, ruling, like their father, at first wisely but despotically, cultivating art and letters and friendship of great men. But sensual passions led to outrages which resulted in the assassination of Hipparchus. Hippias, having

Departure of Solon from Athens.

Pisistratus.

His reign.

punished the conspirators, changed the spirit of the government, imposed arbitrary taxes, surrounded himself with an armed guard, and ruled tyrannically and cruelly. After four years of despotic government, Athens was liberated, chiefly by aid of the Lacedæmonians, now at the highest of their power. Hippias retired to the court of Persia, and planned and guided the attack of Darius on Greece—a traitor of the most infamous kind, since he combined tyranny at home with the coldest treachery to his country. His accursed family were doomed to perpetual banishment, and never succeeded in securing a pardon. Their power had lasted fifty years, and had been fatal to the liberties of Athens.

Hippias.

The Lacedæmonians did not retire until their king Cleomenes formed a close friendship with Isagoras, the leader of the aristocratic party—and no people were prouder of their birth than the old Athenian nobles. Opposed to him was Cleisthenes, of the noble family of the Alcmæonids, who had been banished in the time of Megacles, for the murder of Cylon, who had been treacherously enticed from the sanctuary at the altar of Athena. Cleisthenes gained the ear of the people, and prevailed over Isagoras, and effected another change in the constitution, by which it became still more democratic. He remodeled the basis of citizenship, heretofore confined to the four Ionic tribes; and divided the whole country into demes, or parishes, each of which managed its local affairs. All freemen were enrolled in the demes, and became members of the tribes, now ten in number, instead of the old four Ionian tribes. He increased the members of the senate from four to five hundred, fifty members being elected from each tribe. To this body was committed the chief functions of executive government. It sat in permanence, and was divided into ten sections, one for each tribe, and each section or committee, called *prytany*, had the presidency of the senate and ecclesia during its term. Each prytany of fifty members was subdivided into committees of ten, each of which held the

Cleisthenes.

The increase of the Senate.

presidency for seven days, and out of these a chairman was chosen by lot every day, to preside in the senate and assembly, and to keep the keys of the Acropolis and treasury, and public seal. Nothing shows jealousy of power more than the brief term of office which the president exercised.

The ecclesia. The ecclesia, or assembly of the people, was the arena for the debate of all public measures. The archons were chosen according to the regulations of Solon, but were stripped of their power, which was transferred to the senate and ecclesia. The generals were elected by the people annually, one from each tribe. They were called strategi, and had also the direction of foreign affairs. It was as first strategus that Pericles governed—"prime minister of the people."

Ostracism. In order to guard against the ascendency of tyrants—the great evil of the ancient States, Cleisthenes devised the institution of *ostracism*, by which a suspected or obnoxious citizen could be removed from the city for ten years, though practically abridged to five. It simply involved an exclusion from political power, without casting a stigma on the character. It was virtually a retirement, during which his property and rights remained intact, and attended with no disgrace. The citizens, after the senate had decreed the vote was needful, were required to write a name in an oyster shell, and he who had less than six thousand votes was obliged to withdraw within ten days from the city. The wisdom of this measure is proved in the fact that no tyrannical usurpation occurred at Athens after that of Pisistratus. This revolution which Cleisthenes effected was purely democratic, to which the aristocrats did not submit without a struggle. The aristocrats called to their aid the Spartans, but without other effect than creating that long rivalry which existed between democracy and oligarchy in Greece, in which Sparta and Athens were the representatives.

About this time began the dominion of Athens over the islands of the Ægean, and the system of colonizing conquered

States. This was the period which immediately preceded the Persian wars, when Athens reached the climax of political glory.

Bœotia. Next in importance to the States which have been briefly mentioned was Bœotia, which contained fourteen cities, united in a confederacy, of which Thebes took the lead. They were governed by magistrates, called bœtarchs, elected annually. In these cities aristocratic institutions prevailed. The people were chiefly of Æolian descent, with a strong mixture of the Dorian element, and were dull and heavy, owing, probably, to the easy facilities of support, in consequence of the richness of the soil.

Phocis. At the west of Bœotia, Phocis, with its small territory, gained great consideration from the possession of the Delphic oracle; but its people thus far, of Achæan origin, played no important part in the politics of Greece.

Thessaly. North of the isthmus lay the extensive plains of Thessaly, inclosed by lofty mountains. Nature favored this State more than any other in Greece for political pre-eminence, but inhabitants of Æolian origin were any thing but famous. At first they were governed by kings, but subsequently an aristocratic government prevailed. They were represented in the Amphictyonic Council.

Macedonia. The history of Macedonia is obscure till the time of the Persian wars; but its kings claimed an Heraclid origin. The Doric dialect predominated in a rude form.

Epirus. Epirus, west of Thessaly and Macedonia, was inhabited by various tribes, under their own princes, until the kings of Molossus, claiming descent from Achilles, founded the dynasty which was so powerful under Pyrrus.

There is but little interest connected with the States of Greece, before the Persian wars, except Sparta, Athens, and Corinth; and hence a very brief notice is all that is needed.

But the Grecian colonies are of more importance. They

were numerous in the islands of the Ægean Sea, in Epirus, and in Asia Minor, and even extended into Italy, Sicily, and Gaul. They were said to be planted as early as the Trojan war by the heroes who lived to return—by Agamemnon on the coast of Asia; by the sons of Theseus in Thrace; by Ialmenus on the Euxine; by Diomed and others in Italy. But colonization, to any extent, did not take place until the Æolians invaded Bœotia, and the Dorians, the Peloponnesus. The Achæans, driven from their homes by the Dorians, sought new seats in the East, under chieftains who claimed descent from Agamemnon and other heroes who went to the siege of Troy. They settled, first, on the Isle of Lesbos, where they founded six cities. Others made settlements on the mainland, from the Hermes to Mount Ida. But the greatest migration was made by the Ionians, who, dislodged by Achæans, went first to Attica, and thence to the Cyclades and the coasts of Asia, afterward called Ionia. Twelve independent States were gradually formed of divers elements, and assumed the Ionian name. Among those twelve cities, or States, were Samos, Chios, Miletus, Ephesus, Colophon, and Phocæa. The purest Ionian blood was found at Miletus, the seat of Neleus. These cities were probably inhabited by other races before the Ionians came. To these another was subsequently added—Smyrna, which still retains its ancient name. The southwest corner of the Asiatic peninsula, about the same time, was colonized by a body of Dorians, accompanied by conquered Achæans, the chief seat of which was Halicarnassus. Crete, Rhodes, Cos, and Cnidus, were colonized also by the same people; but Rhodes is the parent of the Greek colonies on the south coast of Asia Minor. A century afterward, Cyprus was founded, and then Sicily was colonized, and then the south of Italy. They were successively colonized by different Grecian tribes, Achæan or Æolian, Dorian, and Ionian. But all the colonists had to contend with races previously established, Iberians, Phœnicians, Sicanians, and Sicels. Among the Greek cities in

Grecian colonies.

The Ionian cities in Asia Minor.

Sicily, Syracuse, founded by Dorians, was the most important, and became, in turn, the founder of other cities. Sybaris and Croton, in the south of Italy, were of Achæan origin. The Greeks even penetrated to the northern part of Africa, and founded Cyrene; while, on the Euxine, along the north coast of Asia Minor, Cyzicus and Sinope arose. These migrations were generally undertaken with the approbation and encouragement of the mother States. There was no colonial jealousy, and no dependence. The colonists, straitened for room at home, carried the benedictions of their fathers, and were emancipated from their control. Sometimes the colony became more powerful than the parent State, but both colonies and parent States were bound together by strong ties of religion, language, customs, and interests. The colonists uniformly became conquerors where they settled, but ever retained their connection with the mother country. And they grew more rapidly than the States from which they came, and their institutions were more democratic. The Asiatic colonies especially, made great advances in civilization by their contact with the East. Music, poetry, and art were cultivated with great enthusiasm. The Ionians took the lead, and their principal city, Miletus, is said to have planted no less than eighty colonies. The greatness of Ephesus was of a later date, owing, in part, to the splendid temple of Artemis, to which Asiatics as well as Greeks made contributions. One of the most remarkable of the Greek colonies was Cyrene, on the coast of Africa, which was of peculiar beauty, and was famous for eight hundred years.

Political importance of the colonies.

So the Greeks, although they occupied a small territory, yet, by their numerous colonies in all those parts watered by the Mediterranean, formed, if not politically, at least socially, a powerful empire, and exercised a vast influence on the civilized world. From Cyprus to Marseilles—from the Crimea to Cyrene, numerous States spoke the same language, and practiced the same rites, which were observed in Athens and Sparta. Hence the great extent of country in Asia and Europe to which the Greek language was familiar, and still more the arts which made Athens the centre of a new civilization. Some of the most noted philosophers and artists of antiquity were born in these colonies. The power of Hellas was not a centralized empire, like Persia, or even Rome, but a domain in the heart and mind of the world. It was Hellas which worked out, in its various States and colonies, great problems of government, as well as social life. Hellas was the parent of arts, of poetry, of philosophy, and of all æsthetic culture—the pattern of new forms of life, and new modes of cultivation. It is this Grecian civilization which appeared in full development as early as five hundred years before the Christian era, which we now propose, in a short chapter, to present—the era which immediately preceded the Persian wars.

CHAPTER XVI.

GRECIAN CIVILIZATION BEFORE THE PERSIAN WARS.

Early civilization.

WE understand by civilization the progress which nations have made in art, literature, material strength, social culture, and political institutions, by which habits are softened, the mind enlarged, the soul elevated, and a wise government, by laws established, protecting the weak, punishing the wicked, and developing wealth and national resources.

Such a civilization did exist to a remarkable degree among the Greeks, which was not only the admiration of their own times, but a wonder to all succeeding ages, since it was established by the unaided powers of man, and affected the relations of all the nations of Europe and Asia which fell under its influence.

It is this which we propose briefly to present in this chapter, not the highest developments of Grecian culture and genius, but such as existed in the period immediately preceding the Persian wars.

Legislation.

One important feature in the civilization of Greece was the progress made in legislation by Lycurgus and Solon. But as this has been alluded to, we pass on to consider first those institutions which were more national and universal.

The peculiar situations of the various States, independent of each other, warlike, encroaching, and ambitious, led naturally to numerous wars, which would have been civil wars had all these petty States been united under a common government. But incessant wars, growing out of endless causes of irritation, would have soon ruined these States, and they could have had no proper development. Something was needed to restrain passion and heal dissensions without a resort to arms, ever attended by dire calamities. And something was needed to unite these various States, in which the same language was spoken, and the same religion and customs prevailed. This union was partially effected by the Amphictyonic Council. It was a congress, composed of deputies from the different States, and deliberating according to rules established from time immemorial. Its meetings were held in two different places, and were convened twice a year, once in the spring, at Delphi, the other in the autumn, near the pass of Thermopylæ. Delphi was probably the original place of meeting, and was, therefore, in one important sense, the capital of Greece. Originally, this council or congress was composed of deputies from twelve States, or tribes—Thessalians, Bœotians, Dorians, Ionians, Perrhæbians, Magnetes, Locrians, Oetæans, Phthiots, Achæans, Melians, and Phocians. These tribes assembled together before authentic history commences, before the return of the Heracleids. There were other States which were not represented in this league—Arcadia, Elis, Æolia, and Acarnania; but the league was sufficiently powerful to make its decisions respected by the greater part of Greece. Each tribe, whether powerful or weak, had two votes in the assembly. Beside those members who had the exclusive power of voting, there were others, and more numerous, who had the privilege of deliberation. The object of the council was more for religious purposes than political, although, on rare occasions and national crises, subjects of a political nature were discussed. The council laid down the rules of war, by which each State that was represented was guaranteed against complete subjection, and the supplies of war were protected. There was no confederacy against foreign powers. The functions of the league were confined to matters purely domestic; the object of the league was the protection of temples against sacrilege. But the council had no common army to execute its decrees, which were often disregarded. In particular, the protection of the Del-

The Amphictyonic Council.

phic oracle, it acted with dignity and effect, whose responses were universally respected.

The Delphic oracle. As the Delphic oracle was the object which engrossed the most important duties of the council, and the responses of this oracle in early times was a sacred law, the deliberations of the league had considerable influence, and were often directed to political purposes. But the immediate management of the oracle was in the hands of the citizens of Delphi. In process of time the responses of the oracle, by the mouth of a woman, which were thus controlled by the Delphians, lost much of their prestige, in consequence of the presents or bribery by which favorable responses were gained.

The Olympic games. More powerful than this council, as an institution, were the Olympic games, solemnized every four years, in which all the States of Greece took part. These games lasted four days, and were of engrossing interest. They were supposed to be founded by Hercules, and were of very ancient date. During these celebrations there was a universal truce, and also during the time it was necessary for the people to assemble and retire to their homes. Elis, in whose territory Olympia was situated, had the whole regulation of the festival, the immediate object of which were various trials of strength and skill. They included chariot races, foot races, horse races, wrestling, boxing, and leaping. They were open to all, even to the poorest Greeks; no accidents of birth or condition affected these honorable contests. The palm of honor was given to the men who had real merit. A simple garland of leaves was the prize, but this was sufficient to call out all the energies and ambition of the whole nation. There were, however, incidental advantages to successful combatants. At Athens, the citizen who gained a prize was rewarded by five hundred drachmas, and was entitled to a seat at the table of the magistrates, and had a conspicuous part on the field of battle. The victors had statues erected to them, and called forth the praises of the poets, and thus these primitive sports incidentally gave an impulse to art and poetry. In later times, poets and historians recited their compositions, and were rewarded with the garland of leaves. The victors of these games thus acquired a social pre-eminence, and were held in especial honor, like those heroes in the Middle Ages who obtained the honor of tournaments and tilts, and, in modern times, those who receive decoration at the hands of kings.

The celebrity of the Olympic games, which drew spectators from Asia as well as all the States of Greece, led to similar institutions or festivals in other places. The Pythian games, in honor of Apollo, were celebrated near Delphi every third Olympic year; and various musical contests, exercises in poetry, exhibitions of works of art were added to gymnastic exercises and chariot and horse races. The sacrifices, processions, and other solemnities, resemble those at Olympia in honor of Zeus. They lasted as long as the Olympic games, down to A. D. 394. Wherever the worship of Apollo was introduced, there were imitations of these Pythian games in all the States of Greece.

The Pythian games.

The Nemæan and Ithmian games were celebrated each twice in every Olympiad, the former on the plain of Nemæa, in Argolis; the latter in the Corinthian Isthmus, under the presidency of Corinth. These also claimed a high antiquity, and at these were celebrated the same feats of strength as at Olympia. But the Olympic festival was the representation of all the rest, and transcended all the rest in national importance. It was viewed with so much interest, that the Greeks measured time itself by them. It was Olympiads, and not years, by which the date of all events was determined. The Romans reckoned their years from the foundation of their city; modern Christian nations, by the birth of Christ; Mohammedans, by the flight of the prophet to Medina; and the Greeks, from the first recorded Olympiad, B. C. 776.

The Nemæan and Ithmian games.

It was in these festivals, at which no foreigner, however, eminent, was allowed to contend for prizes, that the Greeks buried their quarrels, and incited each

Effect of these festivals.

other to heroism. The places in which they were celebrated became marts of commerce like the mediæval fairs of Germany; and the vast assemblage of spectators favored that communication of news, and inventions, and improvements which has been produced by our modern exhibitions. These games answered all the purposes of our races, our industrial exhibitions, and our anniversaries, religious, political, educational, and literary, and thus had a most decided influence on the development of Grecian thought and enterprise. The exhibition of sculpture and painting alone made them attractive and intellectual, while the athletic exercises amused ordinary minds. They were not demoralizing, like the sports of the amphitheatre, or a modern bull-fight, or even fashionable races. They were more like tournaments in the martial ages of Europe, but superior to them vastly, since no woman was allowed to be present at the Olympic games under pain of death.

Changes in government.

It has already been shown that the form of government in the States of Ancient Greece, in the Homeric ages, was monarchical. In two or three hundred years after the Trojan war, the authority of kings had greatly diminished. The great immigration and convulsions destroyed the line of the ancient royal houses. The abolition of royalty was in substance rather than name. First, it was divided among several persons, then it was made elective, first for life, afterward for a definite period. The nobles or chieftains gained increasing power with the decline of royalty, and the government became, in many States, aristocratic. But the nobles abused their power by making an oligarchy, which is a perverted aristocracy. This aroused hatred and opposition on the part of the people, especially in the maritime cities, where the increase of wealth by commerce and the arts raised up a body of powerful citizens. Then followed popular revolutions under leaders or demagogues. These leaders in turn became tyrants, and their exactions gave rise to more hatred than that produced by the government of powerful families. They gained power by stratagem, and perverted it by violence. But to amuse the people whom they oppressed, or to please them, they built temples, theatres, and other public buildings, in which a liberal patronage was extended to the arts. Thus Athens and Corinth, before the Persian wars, were beautiful cities, from the lavish expenditure of the public treasury by the tyrants or despots who had gained ascendency. In the mean time, those who were most eminent for wealth, or power, or virtue, were persecuted, for fear they would effect a revolution. But the parties which the tyrants had trampled upon were rather exasperated than ruined, and they seized every opportunity to rally the people under their standard, and effect an overthrow of the tyrants. Sparta, whose constitution remained aristocratic, generally was ready to assist any State in throwing off the yoke of the usurpers. In some States, like Athens, every change favored the rise of the people, who gradually obtained the ascendency. They instituted the principle of legal equality, by which every freeman was supposed to exercise the attributes of sovereignty. But democracy invariably led to the ascendency of factions, and became itself a tyranny. It became jealous of all who were distinguished for birth, or wealth, or talents. It encouraged flatterers and sycophants. It was insatiable in its demands on the property of the rich, and listened to charges which exposed them to exile and their estates to confiscation. It increased the public burdens by unwise expenditures to please the men of the lower classes who possessed political franchise.

Erection of temples.

Legal equality and political rights.

But different forms of government existed in different States. In Sparta there was an oligarchy of nobles which made royalty a shadow, and which kept the people in slavery and degradation. In Athens the democratic principle prevailed. In Argos kings reigned down to the Persian wars. In Corinth the government went through mutations as at Athens. In all the States and cities experiments in the various forms of government were perpetually made and perpetually failed. They existed for a time, and

Different forms of government.

were in turn supplanted. The most permanent government was that of Sparta; the most unstable was that of Athens. The former promoted a lofty patriotism and public morality and the national virtues; the latter inequalities of wealth, the rise of obscure individuals, and the progress of arts.

Commercial enterprise.

The fall of the ancient monarchies and aristocracies was closely connected with commercial enterprise and the increase of a wealthy class of citizens. In the beginning of the seventh century before Christ, a great improvement in the art of ship-building was made, especially at Corinth. Colonial settlements kept pace with maritime enterprise; and both of these fostered commerce and wealth. The Euxine lost its terrors to navigators, and the Ægean Sea was filled with ships and colonists. The Adriatic Sea was penetrated, and all the seas connected with the Mediterranean. From the mouth of the Po was brought amber, which was highly valued by the ancients. A great number of people were drawn to Egypt, by the liberal offers of its kings, who went there for the pursuit of knowledge and of wealth, and from which they brought back the papyrus as a cheap material for writing. The productions of Greece were exchanged for the rich fabrics which only Asia furnished, and the cities to which these were brought, like Athens and Corinth, rapidly grew rich, like Venice and Genoa in the Middle Ages.

Increase of wealth.

Wealth of course introduced art. The origin of art may have been in religious ideas—in temples and the statues of the gods—in tombs and monuments of great men. But wealth immeasurably increased the facilities both for architecture and sculpture. Artists in old times, as in these, sought a pecuniary reward—patrons who could afford to buy their productions, and stimulate their genius. Art was cultivated more rapidly in the Asiatic colonies than in the mother country, both on account of their wealth, and the objects of interest around them. The Ionian cities, especially, were distinguished for luxury and refinement. Corinth took the lead in the early patronage

Introduction of art.

of art, as the most wealthy and luxurious of the Grecian cities.

The first great impulse was given to architecture. The Pelasgi had erected Cyclopean structures fifteen hundred years before Christ. The Dorians built temples on the severest principles of beauty, and the Doric column arose, massive and elegant. Long before the Persian wars the temples were numerous and grand, yet simple and harmonious. The temple of Here, at Samos, was begun in the eighth century, B. C., and built in the Doric style, and, soon after, beautiful structures ornamented Athens.

Architecture.

Sculpture rapidly followed architecture, and passed from the stiffness of ancient times to that beauty which afterward distinguished Phidias and Polynotus. Schools of art, in the sixth century, flourished in all the Grecian cities. We can not enter upon the details, from the use of wood to brass and marble. The temples were filled with groups from celebrated masters, and their deep recesses were peopled with colossal forms. Gold, silver, and ivory were used as well as marble and brass. The statues of heroes adorned every public place. Art, before the Persian wars, did not indeed reach the refinement which it subsequently boasted, but a great progress was made in it, in all its forms. Engraving was also known, and imperfect pictures were painted. But this art, and indeed any of the arts, did not culminate until after the Persian wars.

Sculpture.

Literature made equal if not greater progress in the early ages of Grecian history. Hesiod lived B. C. 735; and lyric poetry flourished in the sixth and seventh centuries before Christ, especially the elegiac form, or songs for the dead. Epic poetry was of still earlier date, as seen in the Homeric poems. The Æolian and Ionic Greeks of Asia were early noted for celebrated poets. Alcæus and Sappho lived on the Isle of Lesbos, and were surrounded with admirers. Anacreon of Teos was courted by the rulers of Athens.

Literature.

Even philosophy was cultivated at this early age. Thales

of Miletus flourished in the middle of the seventh century, and Anaximander, born B. C. 610—one of the great original mathematicians of the world, speculated like Thales, on the origin of things. Pythagoras, born in Samos, B. C. 580—a still greater name, grave and majestic, taught the harmony of the spheres long before the Ionian revolt.

Philosophy.

But neither art, nor literature, nor philosophy reached their full development till a later era. It is enough for our purpose to say that, before the Persian wars, civilization was by no means contemptible, in all those departments which subsequently made Greece the teacher and the glory of the world.

CHAPTER XVII.

THE PERSIAN WAR.

We come now to the most important and interesting of Grecian history—the great contest with Persia—the age of heroes and of battle-fields, when military glory was the master passion of a noble race. What inspiration have all ages gained from that noble contest in behalf of liberty!

We have seen how Asiatic cities were colonized by Greeks, among whom the Ionians were pre-eminent. The cities were governed by tyrants, who were sustained in their usurpation by the power of Persia, then the great power of the world. Darius, then king, had absurdly invaded Scythia, with an immense army of six hundred thousand men, to punish the people for their inroad upon Western Asia, subject to his sway, about a century before. He was followed by his allies, the tyrants of the Ionian cities, to whom he intrusted the guardianship of the bridge of boats by which he had crossed the Danube, B. C. 510. As he did not return within the time specified—sixty days—the Greeks were left at liberty to return. A body of Scythians then appeared, who urged the Greeks to destroy the bridge, as Darius was in full retreat, and thus secure the destruction of the Persian army and the recovery of their own liberty. Miltiades, who ruled the Chersonese—the future hero of Marathon, seconded the wise proposal of the Scythians, but Histiæus, tyrant of Miletus, feared that such an act would recoil upon themselves, and favor another inroad of Scythians—a fierce nation of barbarians. The result was that the bridge was not destroyed, but the further end of it was severed from the shore. Night arrived, and the

Condition of the Ionian cities.

Invasion of Scythia by Darius.

Persian hosts appeared upon the banks of the river, but finding no trace of it, Darius ordered an Egyptian who had a trumpet-voice to summon to his aid Histiæus, the Milesian. He came forward with a fleet and restored the bridge, and Darius and his army were saved, and the opportunity was lost to the Ionians for emancipating themselves from the Persians. The bridge was preserved, not from honorable fidelity to fulfill a trust, but selfish regard in the despot of Miletus to maintain his power. For this service he was rewarded with a principality on the Strymon. Exciting, however, the suspicion of Darius, by his intrigues, he was carried captive to the Persian court, but with every mark of honor. Darius left his brother Artaphernes as governor of all the cities in Western Asia Minor.

A few years after this unsuccessful invasion of Scythia by Darius, a political conflict broke out in Naxos, an island of the Cyclades, B. C. 502, which had not submitted to the Persian yoke, and the oligarchy, which ruled the island, were expelled. They applied for aid to Aristagoras, the tyrant of Miletus, the largest of the Ionian cities, who persuaded the Persian satrap to send an expedition against the island. The expedition failed, which ruined the credit of Aristagoras, son-in-law to Histiæus, who was himself incensed at his detention in Susa, and who sent a trusty slave with a message urging the Ionians to revolt. Aristagoras, as a means of success, conciliated popular favor throughout Asiatic Greece, by putting down the various tyrants—the instruments of Persian ascendency. The flames of revolt were kindled, the despots were expelled, the revolted towns were put in a state of defense, and Aristagoras visited Sparta to invoke its aid, inflaming the mind of the king with the untold wealth of Asia, which would become his spoil. Sparta was then at war with her neighbors, and unwilling to become involved in so uncertain a contest. Rejected at Sparta, Aristagoras proceeded to Athens, then the second power in Greece, and was favorably received, for the Athenians had a powerful sympathy with the revolted

Revolt of the Ionian cities from Persia.

Ionians; they agreed to send a fleet of twenty ships. When Aristagoras returned, the Persians had commenced the siege of Miletus. The twenty ships soon crossed the Ægean, and were joined by five Eretrian ships coming to the succor of Miletus. An unsuccessful attempt of Aristagoras on Sardis disgusted the Athenians, who abandoned the alliance. But the accidental burning of the city, including the temple of the goddess Cybele, encouraged the revolters, and incensed the Persians. Other Greek cities on the coast took part in the revolt, including the island of Cyprus. The revolt now assumed a serious character. The Persians rallied their allies, among whom were the Phœnicians. An armament of Persians and Phœnicians sailed against Cyprus, and a victory on the land gave the Persians the control of the island. A large army of Persians and their allies collected at Sardis, and, under different divisions reconquered all their principal Ionian cities, except Miletus; but the Ionian fleet kept its ascendency at sea. Aristagoras as the Persians advanced, lost courage and fled to Myrkinus, where he shortly afterward perished.

Defeat of the Ionian cities.

Meanwhile Histiæus presented himself at the gates of Miletus, having procured the consent of Darius to proceed thither to quell the revolt. He was, however, suspected by the satrap, Artaphernes, and fled to Chios, whose people he gained over, and who carried him back to Miletus. On his arrival, he found the citizens averse to his reception, and was obliged to return to Chios, and then to Lesbos, where he abandoned himself to piracy.

Histiæus.

A vast Persian host, however, had been concentrated near Miletus, and with the assistance of the Phœnicians, invested the city by sea and land. The entire force of the confederated cities abandoned the Milesians to their fate, and took to their ships, three hundred and fifty-three in number, with a view of fighting the Phœnicians, who had six hundred ships. But there was a want of union among the Ionian commanders, and the sailors abandoned themselves to disorder and carelessness; upon which

Want of union among the Ionian cities.

Dionysius, of Phocæa, which furnished but three ships, rebuked the Ionians for their neglect of discipline. His rebuke was not thrown away, and the Ionians having their comfortable tents on shore, submitted themselves to the nautical labors imposed by Dionysius. At last, after seven days of work, the Ionian sailors broke out in open mutiny, and refused longer to be under the discipline of a man whose State furnished the smallest number of ships. They left their ships, and resumed their pleasures on the shore, unwilling to endure the discipline so necessary in so great a crisis. Their camp became a scene of disunion and mistrust. The Samians, in particular, were discontented, and on the day of battle, which was to decide the fortunes of Ionia, they deserted with sixty ships, and other Ionians followed their example. The ships of Chios, one hundred in number, fought with great fidelity and resolution, and Dionysius captured, with his three ships, three of the Phœnicians'. But these exceptional examples of bravery did not compensate the treachery and cowardice of the rest, and the consequence was a complete defeat of the Ionians at Lade. Dionysius, seeing the ruin of the Ionian camp, did not return to his own city, and set sail for the Phœnician coast, doing all he could as a pirate.

Their signal defeat.

This victory of Lade enabled the Persians to attack Miletus by sea as well as land; the siege was prosecuted with vigor, and the city shortly fell. The adult male population was slain, while the women and children were sent as slaves to Susa. The Milesian territory was devastated and stripped of its inhabitants. The other States hastened to make their submission, and the revolt was crushed, B. C. 496, five years after its commencement. The Persian forces reconquered all the Asiatic Greeks, insular and continental, and the Athenian Miltiades escaped with difficulty from his command in the Chersonese, to his native city. All the threats which were made by the Persians were realized. The most beautiful virgins were distributed among the Persian nobles; the

Attack of Miletus.

Complete conquest of the Ionian Greeks.

cities were destroyed; and Samos alone remained, as a reward for desertion at the battle of Lade.

The reconquest of Ionia being completed, the satrap Artaphernes proceeded to organize the future government, the inhabitants now being composed of a great number of Persians. Meanwhile, Darius made preparations for the complete conquest of Greece. The wisdom of the advice of Miltiades, to destroy the bridge over the Danube, when Darius and his army would have been annihilated by the Scythians, was now apparent. Mardonius was sent with a large army into Ionia, who deposed the despots in the various cities, whom Artaphernes had reinstated, and left the people to govern themselves, subject to the Persian dominion and tribute. He did not remain long in Ionia, but passed with his fleet to the Hellespont, and joined his land forces. He transported his army to Europe, and began his march through Thrace. Thence he marched into Macedonia, and subdued a part of its inhabitants. He then sent his fleet around Mount Athos, with a view of joining it with his army at the Gulf of Therma. But a storm overtook his fleet near Athos, and destroyed three hundred ships, and drowned twenty thousand men. This disaster compelled a retreat, and he recrossed the Hellespont with the shame of failure. He was employed no more by the Persian king.

Artaphernes organizes the government.

Darius prepares for the invasion of Greece.

Darius, incited by the traitor Hippias, made new preparation for the invasion of Greece. He sent his heralds in every direction, demanding the customary token of submission—earth and water. Many of the continental cities sent in their submission, including the Thebans, Thessalians, and the island of Ægina, which was on bad terms with Athens. The heralds of Darius were put to death at Athens and Sparta, which can only be explained from the fiercest resentment and rage. These two powers made common cause, and armed all the other States over which they had influence, to resist the Persian domination. Hellas, headed by Sparta, now resolved to put forth all its energies, and

His immense preparations.

embarked, in desperate hostility. A war which Sparta had been waging for several years against Argos crippled that ancient State, and she was no longer the leading power. The only rival which Sparta feared was weakened, and full scope was given for the prosecution of the Persian war. Ægina, which had submitted to Darius, was visited by Cleomenes, king of Sparta, and hostages were sent to Athens for the neutrality of that island. Athens and Sparta suspended their political jealousies, and acted in concert to resist the common danger.

His vast army.

By the spring of 490 B. C., the preparations of Darius were completed, and a vast army collected on a plain upon the Cilician shore. A fleet of six hundred ships convoyed it to the rendezvous at Samos. The exiled tyrant Hippias was present to guide the forces to the attack of Attica. The Mede Datis, and Artaphernes, son of the satrap of Sardis, nephew to Darius, were the Persian generals. They had orders from Darius to bring the inhabitants of Athens as slaves to his presence.

The Persian fleet.

The Persian fleet, fearing a similar disaster as happened near Mount Athos, struck directly across the Ægean, from Samos to Eubœa, attacking on the way the intermediate islands. Naxos thus was invaded and easily subdued. From Naxos, Datis sent his fleet round the other Cyclades Islands, demanding reinforcements and hostages from all he visited, and reached the southern extremity of Eubœa in safety. Etruria was first subdued, unable to resist. After halting a few days at this city, he crossed to Attica, and landed in the bay of Marathon, on the eastern coast. The despot Hippias, son of Pisistratus, twenty years after his expulsion from Athens, pointed out the way.

Political change at Athens.

But a great change had taken place at Athens since his expulsion. The city was now under democratic rule, in its best estate. The ten tribes had become identified with the government and institutions of the city. The senate of the areopagus, renovated by the annual archons, was in sympathy with the people. Great men had arisen under the amazing stimulus of liberty, among whom Miltiades, Themistocles, and Aristides were the most distinguished. Miltiades, after an absence of six years in the Chersonesus of Thrace, returned to the city full of patriotic ardor. He was brought to trial before the popular assembly on the charge of having misgoverned the Chersonese; but he was honorably acquitted, and was chosen one of the ten generals of the republic annually elected. He was not, however, a politician of the democratic stamp, like Themistocles and Aristides, being a descendant of an illustrious race, which traced their lineage to the gods; but he was patriotic, brave, and decided. His advice to burn the bridge over the Danube illustrates his character—bold and far-seeing. Moreover, he was peculiarly hostile to Darius, whom he had so grievously offended.

Miltiades, and other generals.

Themistocles was a man of great native genius and sagacity. He comprehended all the embarrassments and dangers of the political crisis in which his city was placed, and saw at a glance the true course to be pursued. H was also bold and daring. He was not favored by the accidents of birth, and owed very little to education. He had an unbounded passion for glory and for display. He had great tact in the management of party, and was intent on the aggrandizement of his country. His morality was reckless, but his intelligence was great—a sort of Mirabeau: with his passion, his eloquence, and his talents. His unfortunate end—a traitor and an exile—shows how little intellectual pre-eminence will avail, in the long run, without virtue, although such talents as he exhibited will be found useful in a crisis.

Themistocles.

Aristides was inferior to both Alcibiades and Themistocles in genius, in resource, in boldness, and in energy; but superior in virtue, in public fidelity, and moral elevation. He pursued a consistent course, was no demagogue, unflinching in the discharge of trusts, just, upright, unspotted. Such a man, of course, in a corrupt society, would be exposed to many enmities and jealousies.

Aristides.

But he was, on the whole, appreciated, and died, in a period of war and revolution, a poor man, with unbounded means of becoming rich—one of the few examples which our world affords of a man who believed in virtue, in God, and a judgment to come, and who preferred the future and spiritual to the present and material—a fool in the eyes of the sordid and bad—a wise man according to the eternal standards.

Aristides, Miltiades, and perhaps Themistocles, were elected among the ten generals, by the ten tribes, in the year that Datis led his expedition to Marathon. Each of the ten generals had the supreme command of the army for a day. Great alarm was felt at Athens as tidings reached the city of the advancing and conquering Persians. Couriers were sent in hot haste to the other cities, especially Sparta, and one was found to make the journey to Sparta on foot—one hundred and fifty miles—in forty-eight hours. The Spartans agreed to march, without delay, after the last quarter of the moon, which custom and superstition dictated. This delay was fraught with danger, but was insisted upon by the Spartans.

Athens allies herself with Sparta.

Meanwhile the dangers multiplied and thickened. The Persians were at Marathon. It was urged by Miltiades that not a moment should be lost in bringing the Persians into action. Five of the generals counseled delay. The polemarch, Calimachus, who then had the casting vote, decided for immediate action. Themistocles and Aristides had seconded the advice of Miltiades, to whom the other generals surrendered their days of command—a rare example of patriotic disinterestedness. The Athenians marched at once to Marathon to meet their foes, and were joined by the Platæans, one thousand warriors, from a little city—the whole armed population, which had a great moral effect.

Prominence of the dangers.

The Athenians had only ten thousand hoplites, including the one thousand from Platæa. The Persian army is variously estimated at from one hundred and ten thousand to six hundred thousand. The Greeks

Marshaling of the Grecian forces at Marathon.

were encamped upon the higher ground overlooking the plain which their enemies occupied. The fleet was ranged along the beach. The Greeks advanced to the combat in rapid movement, urged on by the war-cry, which ever animated their charges. The wings of the Persian army were put to flight by the audacity of the charge, but the centre, where the best troops were posted, resisted the attack until Miltiades returned from the pursuit of the retreating soldiers on the wings. The defeat of the Persians was the result. They fled to their ships, and became involved in the marshes. Six thousand four hundred men fell on the Persian side, and only one hundred and ninety-two on the Athenian. The Persians, though defeated, still retained their ships, and sailed toward Cape Sunium, with a view of another descent upon Attica. Miltiades, the victor in the most glorious battle ever till then fought in Greece, penetrated the designs of the Persians, and rapidly retreated to Athens on the very day of battle. Datis arrived at the port of Phalerum to discover that his plans were baffled, and that the Athenians were still ready to oppose him. The energy and promptness of Miltiades had saved the city. Datis, discouraged, set sail, without landing, to the Cyclades.

The battle of Marathon.

The battle of Marathon, B. C. 490, must be regarded as one of the great decisive battles of the world, and the first which raised the political importance of the Greeks in the eyes of foreign powers. It was fought by Athens twenty years after the expulsion of the tyrants, and as a democratic State. On the Athenians rest the glory forever. It was not important for the number of men who fell on either side, but for giving the first great check to the Persian domination, and preventing their conquest of Europe. And its moral effect was greater than its political. It freed the Greeks from that fear of the Persians which was so fatal and universal, for the tide of Persian conquest had been hitherto uninterrupted. It animated the Greeks with fresh courage, for the bravery of the Athenians

Results of the battle.

had been unexampled, as had been the generalship of Miltiades. Athens was delivered by the almost supernatural bravery of its warriors, and was then prepared to make those sacrifices which were necessary in the more desperate struggles which were to come. And it inspired the people with patriotic ardor, and upheld the new civil constitution. It gave force and dignity to the democracy, and prepared it for future and exalted triumphs. It also gave force to the religious sentiments of the people, for such a victory was regarded as owing to the special favor of the gods.

The Spartans did not arrive until after the battle had been fought, and Datis had returned with his Etrurian prisoners to Asia.

The victory of Marathon raised the military fame of Miltiades to the most exalted height, and there were no bounds to the enthusiasm of the Athenians. But the victory turned his head, and he lost both prudence and patriotism. He persuaded his countrymen, in the full tide of his popularity, to intrust him with seventy ships, with an adequate force, with powers to direct an expedition according to his pleasure. The armament was cheerfully granted. But he disgracefully failed in an attack on the island of Paros, to gratify a private vindictive animosity. He lost all his *éclat*, and was impeached. He appealed, wounded and disabled from a fall he had received, to his previous services. He was found guilty, but escaped the penalty of death, but not of a fine of fifty talents. He did not live to pay it, or redeem his fame, but died of the injury he had received. Thus this great man fell from a pinnacle of glory to the deepest disgrace and ruin—a fate deserved, for he was not true to himself or country. The Athenians were not to blame, but judged him rightly. It was not fickleness, but a change in their opinions, founded on sufficient grounds, from the deep disappointment in finding that their hero was unworthy of their regards. No man who had rendered a favor has a claim to pursue a course of selfishness and unlawful ambi-

Fame of Miltiades.

His subsequent reverses.

His death.

tion. No services can offset crimes. The Athenians, in their unbounded admiration, had given unbounded trust, and that trust was abused. And as the greatest despots who had mounted to power had earned their success by early services, so had they abused their power by imposing fetters, and the Athenians, just escaped from the tyranny of these despots, felt a natural jealousy and a deep repugnance, in spite of their previous admiration. The Athenians, in their treatment of Miltiades, were neither ungrateful nor fickle, but acted from a high sense of public morality, and in a stern regard to justice, without which the new constitution would soon have been subverted. On the death of Miltiades Themistocles and Aristides became the two leading men of Athens, and their rivalries composed the domestic history of the city, until the renewed and vast preparations of the Persians caused all dissensions to be suspended for the public good.

Jealousies between Aristides and Themistocles.

But the jealousies and rivalries of these great men were not altogether personal. They were both patriotic, but each had different views respecting the course which Athens should adopt in the greatness of the dangers which impended. The policy of Aristides was to strengthen the army—that of Themistocles, the navy. Both foresaw the national dangers, but Themistocles felt that the hopes of Greece rested on ships rather than armies to resist the Persians. And his policy was adopted. As the world can not have two suns, so Athens could not be prospered by the presence of two such great men, each advocating different views. One or the other must succumb to the general good, and Aristides was banished by the power of ostracism.

Not altogether on personal grounds.

The wrath of Darius—a man of great force of character, but haughty and self-sufficient, was tremendous when he learned the defeat of Datis, and his retreat into Asia. He resolved to bring the whole force of the Persian empire together to subdue the Athenians, from whom he had suffered so great a disgrace. Three years were

Renewed preparations of Darius.

spent in active preparations for a new expedition which should be overwhelming. All the allies of Persia were called upon for men and supplies. Nor was he deterred by a revolt of Egypt, which broke out about this time, and he was on the point of carrying two gigantic enterprises—one for the reconquest of Egypt, and the other for the conquest of Greece—when he died, after a reign of thirty-six years, B. C. 485.

His death.

He was succeeded by his son Xerxes, who was animated by the animosities, but not the genius of his father. Though beautiful and tall, he was faint-hearted, vain, blinded by a sense of power, and enslaved by women. Yet he continued the preparations which Darius projected. Egypt was first subdued by his generals, and he then turned his undivided attention to Greece. He convoked the dignitaries of his empire—the princes and governors of provinces, and announced his resolution to bridge over the Hellespont and march to the conquest of Europe. Artabanus, his uncle, dissuaded him from the enterprise, setting forth especially the probability that the Greeks, if victorious at sea, would destroy the bridge, and thus prevent his safe return. Mardonius advised differently, urging ambition and revenge, motives not lost on the Persian monarch. For four years the preparations went forward from all parts of the empire, including even the islands in the Ægean. In the autumn of 481 B. C., the largest army this world has ever seen assembled at Sardis. Besides this, a powerful fleet of one thousand two hundred and seven ships of war, besides transports, was collected at the Hellespont. Large magazines of provisions were formed along the coast of Asia Minor. A double bridge of boats, extending from Abydos to Sestos—a mile in length across the Hellespont, was constructed by Phœnicians and Egyptians; but this was destroyed by a storm. Xerxes, in a transport of fury, caused the heads of the engineers to be cut off, and the sea itself scourged with three hundred lashes. This insane wrath being expended, the monarch caused the work to be at once reconstructed,

Xerxes.

His enormous preparations.

this time by the aid of Greek engineers. Two bridges were built side by side upon more than six hundred large ships, moored with strong anchors, with their heads toward the Ægean. Over each bridge were stretched six vast cables, which held the ships together, and over these were laid planks of wood, upon which a causeway was formed of wood and earth, with a high palisade on each side. To facilitate his march, Xerxes also constructed a canal across the isthmus which connects Mount Athos with the main land, on which were employed Phœnician engineers. The men employed in digging the canal worked under the whip. Bridges were also thrown across the river Strymon.

His bridges over the Hellespont.

These works were completed while Xerxes wintered at Sardis. From that city he dispatched heralds to all the cities of Greece, except Sparta and Athens, to demand the usual tokens of submission—earth and water. He also sent orders to the maritime cities of Thrace and Macedonia to prepare dinner for himself and hosts, as they passed through. Greece was struck with consternation as the news reached the various cities of the vast forces which were on the march to subdue them. The army proceeded from Sardis, in the spring, in two grand columns, between which was the king and guards and select troops—all native Persians, ten thousand foot and ten thousand horse. From Sardis the hosts of Xerxes proceeded to Abydos, through Ilium, where his two bridges across the Hellespont awaited him. From a marble throne the proud and vainglorious monarch saw his vast army defile over the bridges, perfumed with frankincense and strewed with myrtle boughs. One bridge was devoted to the troops, the other to the beasts and baggage. The first to cross were the ten thousand household troops, called Immortals, wearing garlands on their heads; then followed Xerxes himself in his gilded chariot, and then the rest of the army. It occupied seven days for the vast hosts to cross the bridge. Xerxes then directed his march to Doriscus, in Thrace, near the mouth of the Hebrus, where he joined his fleet. There he

His advance.

He crosses the Hellespont.

took a general review, and never, probably, was so great an army marshaled before or since, and composed of so many various nations. There were assembled nations from the Indus, from the Persian Gulf, the Red Sea, the Levant, the Ægean and the Euxine—Egyptian, Ethiopian, and Lybian. Forty-six nations were represented —all that were tributary to Persia. From the estimates made by Herodotus, there were one million seven hundred thousand foot, eighty thousand horse, besides a large number of chariots. With the men who manned the fleet and those he pressed into his service on the march, the aggregate of his forces was two million six hundred and forty thousand. Scarcely an inferior number attended the soldiers as slaves, sutlers, and other persons, swelling the amount of the males to five million two hundred and eighty-three thousand two hundred and twenty—the whole available force of the Eastern world—Asia against Europe: as in mediæval times it was Europe against Asia. It is, however, impossible for us to believe in so large a force, since it could not have been supplied with provisions. But with every deduction, it was still the largest army the world ever saw.

His review of his army.

After the grand enumeration of forces, Xerxes passed in his chariot to survey separately each body of contingents, to which he put questions. He then embarked in a gilded galley, and sailed past the prows of the twelve hundred ships moored four hundred feet from the shore. That such a vast force could be resisted was not even supposed to be conceivable by the blinded monarch. But Demaratus, the exiled king of Sparta, told him he would be resisted unto death, a statement which was received with derision.

The magnitude of his forces.

After the review, the grand army pursued its course westward in three divisions and roads along Thrace, levying enormous contributions on all the Grecian towns, which submitted as the Persian monarch marched along, for how could they resist? The mere provisioning this great host for a single day impoverished the country.

Progress of the Persians.

But there was no help, for to mortal eyes the success of Xerxes was certain. At Acanthus, Xerxes separated from his fleet, which was directed to sail round Mount Athos, while he pursued his march through Pæonia and Crestonia, and rejoin him at Therma, on the Thermaic Gulf, in Macedonia, within sight of Mount Olympus.

Meanwhile, the Athenians, fully alive to their danger, strained every nerve to make preparations to resist the enemy. Fortunately, there was in the treasury a large sum derived from the Lamian mines, and this they applied, on the urgent representations of Themistocles, to building ships and refitting their navy. A Panhellenic congress, under the presidency of Athens and Sparta, assembled at the Isthmus of Corinth—the first great league since the Trojan war. The representatives of the various States buried their dissensions, the most prominent of which were between Athens and Ægina. In reconciling these feuds, Themistocles took a pre-eminent part. Indeed, there was need, for the political existence of Hellas was threatened, and despair was seen in most every city. Even the Delphic oracle gave out replies discouraging and terrible, intimating, however, that the safety of Athens lay in the wooden wall, which, with extraordinary tact, was interpreted by Themistocles to mean that the true defense lay in the navy. Salamis was the place designated by the oracle for the retreat, which was now imperative, and thither the Athenians fled, with their wives and children, guarded by their fleet. It was decided by the congress that Sparta should command the land forces, and Athens the united navy of the Greeks; but many States, in deadly fear of the Persians, persisted in neutrality, among which were Argos, Cretes, Corcyra. The chief glory of the defense lay with Sparta and Athens. The united army was sent into Thessaly to defend the defile of Tempe, but discovering that they were unable to do this, since another pass over Mount Olympus was open in the summer, they retreated to the isthmus of Corinth, and left all Greece north of

Preparations of the Athenians.

Sparta commands the land forces and Athens the naval.

Mount Citheron and the Megarid territory without defense. Had the Greeks been able to maintain the passes of Olympus and Ossa, all the northern States would probably have joined in the confederation against Persia; but, as they were left defenseless, we can not wonder that they submitted, including even the Achæans, Bœotians, and Dorians.

The pass of Thermopylæ.

The Pass of Thermopylæ was now fixed upon as the most convenient place of resistance, next to the vale of Tempe. Here the main land was separated from the island of Eubœa by a narrow strait two miles wide. On the northern part of the island, near the town of Histiæa, the coast was called Artemisium, and here the fleet was mustered, to co-operate with the land forces, and oppose, in a narrow strait, the progress of the Persian fleet. The defile of Thermopylæ itself, at the south of Thessaly, was between Mount Œta and an impassable morass on the Maliac Gulf. Nature had thus provided a double position of defense—a narrow defile on the land, and a narrow strait on the water, through which the army and the fleet must need pass if they would co-operate.

Interruption of military preparations by the Olympic games.

While the congress resolved to avail themselves of the double position, by sea and land, the Olympic games, and the great Dorian, of the Carneia, were at hand. These could not be dispensed with, even in the most extraordinary crisis to which the nation could be exposed. While, therefore, the Greeks assembled to keep the national festivals, probably from religious and superstitious motives, auguring no good if they were disregarded, Leonidas, king of Sparta, with three hundred Spartans, two thousand one hundred and twenty Arcadians, four hundred Corinthians, two hundred men from Philius, and eighty from Mycenæ—in all three thousand one hundred hoplites, besides Helots and light troops, was sent to defend the pass against the Persian hosts. On the march through Bœotia one thousand men from Thebes and Thespiæ joined them, though on the point of submission to Xerxes. The Athenians sent their whole force on board their ships, joined by the Platæans.

It was in the summer of 480 B. C. when Xerxes reached Therma, about which time the Greeks arrived at their allotted posts. Leonidas took his position in the middle of the Pass —a mile in length, with two narrow openings. He then repaired the old wall built across the Pass by the Phocians, and awaited the coming of the enemy, for it was supposed his force was sufficient to hold it till the games were over. It was also thought that this narrow pass was the only means of access possible to the invading army; but it was soon discovered that there was also a narrow mountain path from the Phocian territory to Thermopylæ. The Phocians agreed to guard this path, and leave the defense of the main pass to the Peloponnesian troops. But Leonidas painfully felt that his men were insufficient in number, and found it necessary to send envoys to the different States for immediate re-enforcements.

Leonidas defends the pass of Thermopylæ.

The Greek fleet, assembled at Artemisium, was composed of two hundred and seventy-one triremes and nine penteconters, commanded by Themistocles, but furnished by the different States. A disaster happened to the Greeks very early; three triremes were captured by the Persians, which caused great discouragement, and in a panic the Greeks abandoned their strong naval position, and sailed up the Eubœan Strait to Chalcis. This was a great misfortune, since the rear of the army of Leonidas was no longer protected by the fleet. But a destructive storm dispersed the fleet of the Persians at this imminent crisis, so that it was impossible to lend aid to their army now arrived at Thermopylæ.. Four hundred ships of war, together with a vast number of transports, were thus destroyed. The storm lasted three days. After this disaster to the Persians, the Greek fleet returned to Artemisium. Xerxes encamped within sight of Thermopylæ four days, without making an attack, on account of the dangers to which his fleet were exposed. On the fifth day he became wroth at the impudence and boldness of the petty force which quietly remained to dispute his passage, for the Spartans

The Greek fleet.

Disaster to the Persian fleet.

amused themselves with athletic sports and combing their hair. Nor was it altogether presumption on the part of the Greeks, for there were four or five thousand heavily-armed men, the bravest in the land, to defend a passage scarcely wider than a carriage-road—with a wall and other defenses in front.

Attack on the Greeks by the Persians.

The first attack on the Greeks was made by the Medes—the bravest of the Persian army, but their arrows and short spears were of little avail against the phalanx which opposed, armed with long spears, and protected by shields. For two days the attack continued, and was constantly repulsed, for only a small detachment of Greeks fought at a time. Even the "Immortals"—the chosen band of Xerxes—were repulsed with a great loss, to the agony and shame of Xerxes.

Leonidas defends the pass, but is slain.

On the third day, a Malian revealed to the Persian king the fact that a narrow path, leading over the mountains, was defended only by Phocians, and that this path led to the rear of the Spartans. A strong detachment of Persians was sent in the night to secure this path, and the Phocian guardians fled. The Persians descended the path, and attacked the Greeks in their rear. Leonidas soon became apprised of his danger, but in time to send away his army. It was now clear that Thermopylæ could no longer be defended, but the heroic and self-sacrificing general resolved to remain, and sell his life as dearly as possible, and retard, if he could not resist, the march of the enemy. Three hundred Spartans, with seven hundred Thespians and four hundred Thebans joined him, while the rest retired to fight another day. It required all the efforts of the Persian generals, assisted by the whip, to force the men to attack this devoted band. The Greeks fought with the most desperate bravery, till their spears were broken, and no weapons remained but their swords and daggers. At last, exhausted, they died, surrounded by vast forces, after having made the most heroic defense in the history of the war. Only one man, Aristodemus,

Heroic death of the three hundred Spartans.

returned to his home of all the three hundred Spartans, but only to receive scorn and infamy. The Theban band alone yielded to the Persians, but only at the last hour.

Nothing could exceed the blended anger and admiration of Xerxes as he beheld this memorable resistance. He now saw, for the first time, the difficulty of subduing such a people as the Greeks, resolved to resist unto death. His mind was perplexed, and he did not know what course to adopt. Had he accepted the advice of Demaratus, to make war on the southern coast of Laconia, and thus distract the Spartans and prevent their co-operation with Athens, he would have probably succeeded.

The dismay and indignation of Xerxes.

But he followed other councils. Meanwhile, the Persian fleet rallied after the storm, and was still formidable, in spite of losses. The Greeks were disposed to retire and leave the strait open to the enemy. The Eubœans, seeing the evil which would happen to them if their island was unprotected, sent to Themistocles a present of thirty talents, if he would keep his position. This money he spent in bribing the different commanders who wished to retire, and it was resolved to remain. The Persians, confident of an easy victory, sent round the island of Eubœa a detachment of two hundred ships, to cut off all hopes of escape to the ships which they expected to capture. A deserter revealed the intelligence to Themistocles, and it was resolved to fight the Persians, thus weakened, at once, but at the close of the day, so that the battle would not be decisive. The battle of Artemisium was a sort of skirmish, to accustom the Greeks to the Phœnician mode of fighting. It was, however, successful, and thirty ships of the Persians were taken or disabled.

Naval battle of Artemisium.

But the Greeks derived a greater succor than ships and men. Another storm overtook the Persians, damaged their fleet, and destroyed the squadron sent round the island of Eubœa. Another sea-fight was the result, since the Greeks were not only aided by the storm, but new re-enforcements; but this second fight was indecisive.

Themistocles sails for Salamis.

Themistocles now felt he could not hold the strait against superior numbers, and the disaster of Thermopylæ being also now known, he resolved to retreat farther into Greece, and sailed for Salamis.

Despair of the Greeks.

At this period the Greeks generally were filled with consternation and disappointment. Neither the Pass of Thermopylæ, nor the strait which connected the Malicas Gulf with the Ægean, had been successfully defended. The army of Xerxes was advancing through Phocis and Bœotia to the Isthmus of Corinth, while the navy sailed unobstructed through the Eubœan Sea. On the part of the Greeks there had been no preparations commensurate with the greatness of the crisis, while, had they rallied to Thermopylæ, instead of wasting time at the festivals, they would have saved the pass, and the army of Xerxes, strained for provisions, would have been compelled to retreat. The Lacedæmonians, aroused by the death of their king, at last made vigorous efforts to fortify the Isthmus of Corinth, too late, however, to defend Bœotia and Attica. The situation of Athens was now hopeless, and it was seen what a fatal mistake had been made not to defend, with the whole force of Greece, the Pass of Thermopylæ. There was no help from the Spartans, for they had all flocked to the Isthmus of Corinth, as the last chance of protecting the Peloponnesus. In despair, the Athenians resolved to abandon Athens, with their families, and take shelter at Salamis. Themistocles alone was undismayed, and sought to encourage his countrymen that the "wooden wall" would still be their salvation. The Athenians, if dismayed, did not lose their energies. The recall of the exiles was decreed by Themistocles' suggestion. With incredible efforts the whole population of Attica was removed to Salamis, and the hopes of all were centered in the ships. Xerxes took possession of the deserted city, but found but five hundred captives. He ravaged the country, and a detachment of Persians even penetrated to Delphi, to rob the shrine, but were defeated. Athens was, however, sacked.

Themistocles revives courage by his "wooden wall."

The combined fleet of the Greeks now numbered three hundred and sixty-six ships, more than half of which were Athenian. Many wished to retreat to the Isthmus of Corinth, and co-operate with the Spartans. Dissensions came near wrecking the last hopes of Greece, and Themistocles only prevailed by threatening to withdraw the Athenian ships unless a battle were at once fought. He resorted to stratagem to compel the fleet to remain together, with no outlet of escape if conquered. Aristides came in the night from Ægina, and informed the Greeks that their whole fleet was surrounded by the Persians—just what Themistocles desired. There was nothing then left but to fight with desperation, for on the issue of the battle depended the fortunes of Greece. Both fleets were stationed in the strait between the bay of Eleusis and the Saronic Gulf, on the west of the island of Salamis.

The hostile fleets at Salamis.

Xerxes, seated upon a throne upon one of the declivities of Mount Ægaleos, surveyed the armaments and the coming battle. Both parties fought with bravery; but the space was too narrow for the Persians to engage their whole fleet, and they had not the discipline of the Greeks, schooled by severe experience. The Persian fleet became unmanageable, and the victory was gained by the Greeks. Two hundred ships fell into the hands of the victors. But a sufficient number remained to the Persians to renew the battle with better hopes. Xerxes, however, was intimidated, and in a transport of rage, disappointment, and fear, gave the order to retreat. He distrusted the fidelity of the allies, and feared for his own personal safety; he feared that the victors would sail to the Hellespont, and destroy the bridges. Themistocles, on the retreat of the Persians, employed his fleet in levying fines and contributions upon the islands which had supported the Persians, while Xerxes made his way back to the Hellespont, and crossed to Asia, leaving Mardonius in Thessaly, with a large army, to pursue the conquest on land.

Self-confidence of Xerxes.

Battle of Salamis and retreat of Xerxes.

Thus Greece was saved by the battle of Salamis, and the

distinguished services of Themistocles, which can not be too highly estimated. The terrific cloud was dispersed, and the Greeks abandoned themselves to joy. Unparalleled honors were bestowed upon the victor, especially in Sparta, and his influence, like that of Alcibiades, after the battle of Marathon, was unbounded. No man ever merited greater reward.

The important results.

Though the Persians now abandoned all hopes of any further maritime attack, yet still great success was anticipated from the immense army which Mardonius commanded. The Greeks in the northern parts still adhered to him, and Thessaly was prostrate at his feet. He sent Alexander, of Macedon, to Athens to offer honorable terms of peace, which were nobly rejected, and he was sent back with this message: "Tell Mardonius that as long as the sun shall continue in his present path we will never contract alliance with a foe who has shown no reverence to our gods and heroes, and who has burned their statues and houses." The league was renewed with Sparta for mutual defense and offense, in spite of seductive offers from Mardonius; but the Spartans displayed both indifference and selfishness to any interests outside the Peloponnesus. They fortified the Isthmus of Corinth, but left Attica undefended. Mardonius accordingly marched to Athens, and again the city was the spoil of the Persians. The Athenians again retreated to Salamis, with bitter feelings against Sparta for her selfishness and ingratitude. Again Mardonius sought to conciliate the Athenians, and again his overtures were rejected with wrath and defiance. The Athenians, distressed, sent envoys to Sparta to remonstrate against her slackness and selfishness, not without effect, for, at last, a large Spartan force was collected under Pausanias. Meanwhile Mardonius ravaged Attica and Bœotia, and then fortified his camp near Platæa, ten furlongs square. Platæa was a plain favorable to the action of the cavalry, not far from Thebes; but his army was discouraged after so many disasters—in modern military language, demoralized—while Ar-

Mardonius left in command of the Persians.

He ravishes Attica and Bœotia.

tabazus, the second in command, was filled with jealousy. Nor could much be hoped from the Grecian allies, who secretly were hostile to the invaders. The Thebans and Bœotians appeared to be zealous, but were governed by fear merely of a superior power, and hence were unreliable. It can not be supposed that the Thebans, who sided with the Persians, by compulsion, preferred their cause to that of their countrymen, great as may have been national jealousy and rivalries.

The Greeks assemble against the Persians at Platæa.

The total number of Lacedæmonians, Corinthians, Athenians, and other Greeks, assembled to meet the Persian army, B. C. 479, was thirty-eight thousand seven hundred men, heavily armed, and seventy-one thousand three hundred light armed, without defensive armor; but most of these were simply in attendance on the hoplites. The Persians, about three hundred thousand in number, occupied the line of the river Asopus, on a plain; the Greeks stationed themselves on the mountain declivity near Erythæ. The Persian cavalry charged, to dislodge the Greeks, unwilling to contend on the plain; but the ground was unfavorable for cavalry operations, and after a brief success, was driven back, while the general, Masistias, who commanded it, was slain. His death, and the repulse of the cavalry, so much encouraged Pausanias, the Spartan general, that he quitted his ground on the mountain declivity, and took position on the plain beneath. The Lacedæmonians composed the right wing; the Athenians, the left; and various other allies, the centre. Mardonius then slightly changed his position, crossing the Asopus, nearer his own camp, and took post on the left wing, opposite the right wing of the Greeks, commanded by Pausanias. Both armies then offered sacrifices to the gods, but Mardonius was able to give constant annoyance to the Greeks by his cavalry, and the Thebans gave great assistance. Ten days were thus spent by the two armies, without coming into general action, until Mardonius, on becoming impatient, against the advice of Artabazus, second in command, resolved to commence the attack. The Greeks were forewarned of his in-

Preparations for battle.

tention, by Alexander of Macedon, who came secretly to the Greek camp at night—a proof that he, as well as others, were impatient of the Persian yoke. The Lacedæmonians, posted in the right wing, against the Persians, changed places with the Athenians, who were more accustomed to Persian warfare; but this manœuvre being detected, Mardonius made a corresponding change in his own army—upon which Pausanias led back again his troops to the right wing, and a second movement of Mardonius placed the armies in the original position.

A vigorous attack of the Persian cavalry now followed, which so annoyed the Greeks, that Pausanias in the night resolved to change once again his position, and retreated to the hilly ground, north of Platæa, about twenty furlongs distant, not without confusion and mistrust on the part of the Athenians. Mardonius, astonished at this movement, pursued, and a general engagement followed. Both armies fought with desperate courage, but discipline was on the side of the Greeks, and Mardonius was slain, fighting gallantly with his guard. Artabazus, with the forty thousand Persians under his immediate command, had not taken part, and now gave orders to retreat, and retired from Greece. The main body, however, of the defeated Persians retired to their fortified camp. This was attacked by the Lacedæmonians, and carried with immense slaughter, so that only three thousand men survived out of the army of Mardonius, save the forty thousand which Artabazus—a more able captain—had led away. The defeat of the Persians was complete, and the spoils which fell to the victors was immense—gold and silver, arms, carpets, clothing, horses, camels, and even the rich tent of Xerxes himself, left with Mardonius. The booty was distributed among the different contingents of the army. The real victors were the Lacedæmonians, Athenians, and Tegeans; the Corinthians did not reach the field till the battle was ended, and thus missed their share of the spoil.

Battle of Platæa.

There was one ally of the Persians which Pausanias resolved to punish—the city of Thebes when a merited chastisement was inflicted, and the customary solemnities were observed, and honors decreed for the greatest and most decisive victory which the Greeks had ever gained. A confederacy was held at Platæa, in which a permanent league was made between the leading Grecian States, not to separate until the common foe was driven back to Asia.

Chastisement of Thebes.

While these great events were transpiring in Bœotia, the fleet of the Greeks, after the battle of Salamis, undertook to rescue Samos from the Persians, and secure the independence of the Ionian cities in Asia. The Persian fleet, now disheartened, abandoned Samos and retired to Mycale, in Ionia. The Greek fleet followed, but the Persians abandoned or dismissed their fleet, and joined their forces with those of Tigranes, who, with an army of sixty thousand men, guarded Ionia. The Greeks disembarked, and prepared to attack the enemy just as the news reached them of the battle of Platæa. This attack was successful, partly in consequence of the revolt of the Ionians in the Persian camp, although the Persians fought with great bravery. The battle of Mycale was as complete as that of Platæa and Marathon, and the remnants of the Persian army retired to Sardis. The Ionian cities were thus, for the time, delivered of the Persians, as well as Greece itself, chiefly by means of the Athenians and Corinthians. The Spartans, with inconceivable narrowness, were reluctant to receive the continental Ionians as allies, and proposed to transport them across the Ægean into Western Greece, which proposal was most honorably rejected by the Athenians. In every thing, except the defense of Greece Proper, and especially the Peloponnesus, the Spartans showed themselves inferior to the Athenians in magnanimity and enlarged views. After the capture of Sestos, B. C. 478, which relieved the Thracian Chersonese from the Persians, the fleet of Athens returned home. The capture of this city concludes the narration of Herodotus, which ended virtually the Persian war, although hostilities were continued in Asia. The battle

Battle of Mycale.

of Marathon had given the first effective resistance to Persian conquests, and created confidence among the Greeks. The battle of Salamis had destroyed the power of Persia on the sea, and prevented any co-operation of land and naval forces. The battle of Platæa freed Greece altogether of the invaders. The battle of Mycale rescued the Ionian cities.

Rivalry between Athens and Sparta.

Athens had, on the whole, most distinguished herself in this great and glorious contest, and now stood forth as the guardian of Hellenic interests on the sea and the leader of the Ionian race. Sparta continued to take the lead of the military States, to which Athens had generously submitted. But a serious rivalry now was seen between these leading States, chiefly through the jealousy of Sparta, which ultimately proved fatal to that supremacy which the Greeks might have maintained over all the powers of the world. Sparta wished that Athens might remain unfortified, in common with all the cities of Northern Greece, while the isthmus should be the centre of all the works of defense. But Athens, under the sagacious and crafty management of Themistocles, amused the Spartans by delays, while the whole population were employed upon restoring its fortifications.

Disgrace and death of Pausanias.

Although the war against the Persians was virtually concluded by the capture of Sestos, an expedition was fitted out by Sparta, under Pausanias, the hero of Platæa, to prosecute hostilities on the shores of Asia. After liberating most of the cities of Cyprus, and wresting Byzantium from the Persians, which thus left the Euxine free to Athenian ships, from which the Greeks derived their chief supplies of foreign corn, Pausanias, giddy with his victories, unaccountably began a treasonable correspondence with Xerxes, whose daughter he wished to marry, promising to bring all Greece again under his sway. He was recalled to Sparta, before this correspondence was known, having given offense by adopting the Persian dress, and surrounding himself with Persian and Median guards. When his treason was at last detected, he attempted to raise a rebellion among the Helots, but failed, and died miserably by hunger in the temple in which he had taken sanctuary.

A fall scarcely less melancholy came to the illustrious Themistocles. In spite of his great services, his popularity began to decline. He was hated by the Spartans for the part he took in the fortification of the city, who brought all their influence against him. He gave umbrage to the citizens by his personal vanity, continually boasting of his services. He erected a private chapel in honor of Artemis. He prostituted his great influence for arbitrary and corrupt purposes. He accepted bribes without scruple, to the detriment of the State, and in violation of justice and right. And as the Persians could offer the highest bribes, he was suspected of secretly favoring their interests. The old rivalries between him and Aristides were renewed; and as Aristides was no longer opposed to the policy which Athens adopted, of giving its supreme attention to naval defenses, and, moreover, constantly had gained the respect of the city by his integrity and patriotism, especially by his admirable management at Delos, where he cemented the confederacy of the maritime States, his influence was perhaps greater than that of Themistocles, stained with the imputation of *Medism*. Cimon, the son of Miltiades, also became a strong opponent. Though acquitted of accepting bribes from Persia, Themistocles was banished by a vote of ostracism, as Aristides had been before—a kind of exile which was not dishonorable, but resorted to from regard to public interests, and to which men who became unpopular were often subjected, whatever may have been their services or merits. He retired to Argos, and while there the treason of Pausanias was discovered. Themistocles was involved in it, since the designs of Pausanias were known by him. Joint envoys from Sparta and Athens were sent to arrest him, which, when known, he fled to Corcyra, and thence to Admetus, king of the Molossians. The Epirotic prince shielded him in spite of his former hostility, and furnished him with guides to Pydna, across the mountains, from

Fall of Themistocles.

Cimon.

which he succeeded in reaching Ephesus, and then repaired to the Persian court. At Athens he was proclaimed a traitor, and his property, amounting to one hundred talents, accumulated by the war, was confiscated. In Persia, he represented himself as a deserter, and subsequently acquired influence with Artaxerxes, and devoted his talents to laying out schemes for the subjugation of Greece. He received the large sum of fifty talents yearly, and died at sixty-five years of age, with a blighted reputation, such as no previous services could redeem from infamy.

Death of Themistocles.

Aristides died four years after the ostracism of Themistocles, universally respected, and he died so poor as not to have enough for his funeral expenses. Nor did any of his descendants ever become rich.

Death of Aristides.

Xerxes himself, the Ahasuerus of the Scriptures, who commanded the largest expedition ever recorded in human annals, reached Sardis, eight months after he had left it, disgusted with active enterprise, and buried himself amid the intrigues of his court and seraglio, in Susa, as recorded in the book of Esther. He was not deficient in generous impulses, but deficient in all those qualities which make men victorious in war. He died fifteen years after, the victim of a conspiracy, in his palace, B. C. 465—six years after Themistocles had sought his protection.

Death of Xerxes.

CHAPTER XVIII.

THE AGE OF PERICLES.

WITH the defeat of the Persian armies, Athens and Sparta became, respectively, the leaders of two great parties in Greece. Athens advocated maritime interests and democratic institutions; Sparta was the champion of the continental and oligarchal powers. The one was Ionian, and organized the league of Delos, under the management of Aristides; the other was Dorian, and chief of the Peloponnesian confederacy. The rivalries between these leading States involved a strife between those ideas and interests of which each was the recognized representative. Those States which previously had been severed from each other by geographical position and diversity of interests, now rallied under the guidance either of Athens or Sparta. The intrigues of Themistocles and Pausanias had prevented that Panhellenic union, so necessary for the full development of political power, and which was for a time promoted by the Persian war. Athens, in particular, gradually came to regard herself as a pre-eminent power, to which the other States were to be tributary. Her empire, based on maritime supremacy, became a tyranny to which it was hard for the old allies to submit.

Rivalry between the Grecian States.

But the rivalry between Sparta and Athens was still more marked. Sparta had thus far taken the lead among the Grecian States, and Athens had submitted to it in the Persian invasion. But the consciousness of new powers, which naval warfare developed, the *éclat* of the battles of Marathon and Salamis, and the confederacy of Delos, changed the relative position of the two States. Moreover, to Athens the highest glory of resisting

Pre-eminently between Athens and Sparta.

the Persians was due, while her patriotic and enlarged spirit favorably contrasted with the narrow and selfish policy of Sparta.

Opposition by Sparta to the fortifications of Athens.

And this policy was seen in nothing more signally than in the oppositions he made to the new fortifications of Athens, so that Themistocles was obliged to go to Sparta, and cover up by deceit and falsehood the fact that the Athenians were really repairing their walls, which they had an undoubted right to do, but which Ægina beheld with fear and Sparta with jealousy. And this unreasonable meanness and injustice on the part of Sparta, again reacted on the Athenians, and created great bitterness and acrimony.

The city nevertheless fortified.

But in spite of the opposition of Sparta, the new fortifications arose, to which all citizens, rich and poor, lent their aid, and on a scale which was not unworthy of the grandeur of a future capital. The circuit of the walls was fifty stadia or seven miles, and they were of sufficient strength and height to protect the city against external enemies. And when they were completed Themistocles—a man of great foresight and genius, persuaded the citizens to fortify also their harbor, as a means of securing the ascendency of the city in future maritime conflicts. He foresaw that the political ascendency of Athens was based on those "wooden walls" which the Delphic oracle had declared to be her hope in the Persian invasion. The victory at Salamis had confirmed the wisdom of the prediction, and given to Athens an imperishable glory. Themistocles persuaded his countrymen that the open roadstead of Phalerum was insecure, and induced them to inclose the more spacious harbors of Peireus and Munychia, by a wall as long as that which encircled Athens itself,—so thick and high that all assault should be hopeless, while within its fortifications the combined fleets of Greece could safely be anchored, and to which the citizens of Athens could also retire in extreme danger. Peireus accordingly was inclosed at vast expense and labor by a wall fourteen feet in thickness, which

The Peireus.

served not merely for a harbor, but a dock-yard and arsenal. Thither resorted metics or resident foreigners, and much of the trade of Athens was in their hands, since they were less frequently employed in foreign service. They became a thrifty population of traders and handy craftsmen identified with the prosperity of Athens. These various works, absorbed much of the Athenian force and capital, yet enough remained to build annually twenty new triremes—equivalent to our modern ships of the line. Athens now became the acknowledged head and leader of the allied States, instead of Sparta, whose authority as a presiding State was now openly renunciated by the Athenians. The Panhellenic union under Sparta was now broken forever, and two rival States disputed the supremacy,—the maritime States adhering to Athens, and the land States, which furnished the larger part of the army at Platæa, adhering to Sparta. It was then that the confederacy of Delos was formed, under the presidency of Athens, which Aristides directed. His assessment was so just and equitable that no jealousies were excited, and the four hundred and sixty talents which were collected from the maritime States were kept at Delos for the common benefit of the league, managed by a board of Athenian officers. It was a common fear which led to this great contribution, for the Phœnician fleet might at any time reappear, and, co-operating with a Persian land force, destroy the liberties of Greece. Although Athens reaped the chief benefit of this league, it was essentially national. It was afterward indeed turned to aggrandize Athens, but, when it was originally made, was a means of common defense against a power as yet unconquered though repulsed.

Increase of the navy.

Confederacy of Delos.

During all the time that the fortifications of Athens and the Peireus were being made, Themistocles was the ruling spirit at Athens, while Aristides commanded the fleet and organized the confederacy of Delos. It was thus several years before he became false to his countrymen, and the change was only gradually wrought in his

Confederacy of Delos.

character, owing chiefly to his extravagant habits and the arrogance which so often attends success.

Change in the Athenian constitution.

During this period, a change was also made in the civil constitution of Athens. All citizens were rendered admissible to office. The State became still more democratic. The archons were withdrawn from military duties, and confined to civil functions. The stategi or generals gained greater power with the extending political relations, and upon them was placed the duty of superintending foreign affairs. Athens became more democratical and more military at the same time.

The political growth of Athens.

From this time, 479 B. C., we date the commencement of the Athenian empire. It gradually was cemented by circumstances rather than a long-sighted and calculating ambition. At the head of the confederacy of Delos, opportunities were constantly presented of centralizing power, while its rapid increase of population and wealth favored the schemes which political leaders advanced for its aggrandizement. The first ten years of the Athenian hegomony or headship were years of active warfare against the Persians. The capture of Eion, on the Strymon, with its Persian garrison, by Cimonon, led to the settlement of Amphipolis by the Athenians; and the fall of the cities which the Persians had occupied in Thrace and in the various islands of the Ægean increased the power of Athens.

The Confederate States.

The confederate States at last grew weary of personal military service, and prevailed upon the Athenians to provide ships and men in their place, for which they imposed upon themselves a suitable money-payment. They thus gradually sunk to the condition of tributary allies, unwarlike and averse to privation, while the Athenians, stimulated by new and expanding ambition, became more and more enterprising and powerful.

Unpopularity of Athens.

But with the growth of Athens was also the increase of jealousies. Athens became unpopular, not only because she made the different maritime States her tributaries, but because she embarked in war against them to secure a still greater aggrandizement. Naxos revolted, but was conquered, B.C. 467. The confederate State was stripped of its navy, and its fortifications were razed to the ground. Next year the island of Thasos likewise seceded from the alliance, and was subdued with difficulty, and came near involving Athens in a war with Sparta. The Thasians invoked the aid of Sparta, which was promised though not fulfilled, which imbittered the relations between the two leading Grecian States.

During this period, from the formation of the league at Delos, and the fall of Thasos, about thirteen years, Athens was occupied in maintaining expeditions against Persia, being left free from embarrassments in Attica. The towns of Platæa and Thespiæ were restored and repeopled under Athenian influence.

Expeditions against Persia.

The jealousy of Sparta, in view of the growing power of Athens, at last gave vent in giving aid to Thebes, against the old policy of the State, to enable that city to maintain supremacy over the lesser Bœotian towns. The Spartans even aided in enlarging her circuit and improving her fortifications, which aid made Thebes a vehement partisan of Sparta. Soon after, a terrible earthquake happened in Sparta, 464 B. C., which calamity was seized upon by the Helots as a fitting occasion for revolt. Defeated, but not subdued, the insurgents retreated to Ithome, the ancient citadel of their Messenian ancestors, and there intrenched themselves. The Spartans spent two years in an unsuccessful siege, and were forced to appeal to their allies for assistance. But even the increased force made no impression on the fortified hill, so ignorant were the Greeks, at this period, of the art of attacking walls. And when the Athenians, under Cimon, still numbered among the allies of Sparta, were not more successful, their impatience degenerated to mistrust and suspicion, and summarily dismissed the Athenian contingent. This ungracious and jealous treatment exasperated the Athenians, whose feelings were worked upon by Pericles who had opposed the policy of

Sparta.

Rebellion of the Helots.

sending troops at all to Laconia. Cimon here was antagonistic to Pericles, and wished to cement the more complete union of Greece against Persia, and maintain the union with Sparta. Cimon, moreover, disliked the democratic policy of Pericles. But the Athenians rallied under Pericles, and Cimon lost his influence, which had been paramount since the disgrace of Themistocles. A formal resolution was passed at Athens to renounce the alliance with Sparta against the Persians, and to seek alliance with Argos, which had been neutral during the Persian invasion, but which had regained something of its ancient prestige and power by the conquest of Mycenæ and other small towns. The Thessalians became members of this new alliance which was intended to be antagonistic to Sparta. Megara, shortly after, renounced the protection of the Peloponnesian capital, and was enrolled among the allies of Athens,— a great acquisition to Athenian power, since this city secured the passes of Mount Gerania, so that Attica was protected from invasion by the Isthmus of Corinth. But the alliance of Megara and Athens gave deep umbrage to Corinth as well as Sparta, and a war with Corinth was the result, in which Ægina was involved as the ally of Sparta and Corinth.

Cimon opposed to Pericles.

Alliance of different states with Athens.

The Athenians were at first defeated on the land; but this defeat was more than overbalanced by a naval victory over the Dorian seamen, off the island of Ægina, by which the naval force of *Ægina*, hitherto great, was forever prostrated. The Athenians captured seventy ships and commenced the siege of the city itself. Sparta would have come to the rescue, but was preoccupied in suppressing the insurrection of the Helots. Corinth sent three hundred hoplites to Ægina and attacked Megara. But the Athenians prevailed both at Ægina and Megara, which was a great blow to Corinth.

Defeat of Athens on the land and victory on the sea.

Fearing, however, a renewed attack from Corinth and the Peloponnesian States, now full of rivalry and enmity, the Athenians, under the leadership of

Pericles begins his career.

Pericles, resolved to connect their city with the harbor of Peireus by a long wall—a stupendous undertaking at that time. It excited the greatest alarm among the enemies of Athens, and was a subject of contention among different parties in the city. The party which Cimon, now ostracised, had headed, wished to cement the various Grecian States in a grand alliance against the Persians, and dreaded to see this long wall arise as a standing menace against the united power of the Peloponnesus. Moreover, the aristocrats of Athens disliked a closer amalgamation with the maritime people of the Peireus, as well as the burdens and taxes which this undertaking involved. These fortifications doubtless increased the power of Athens, but weakened the unity of Hellenic patriotism; and increased those jealousies which ultimately proved the political ruin of Greece.

Cimon banished.

Under the influence of these rivalries and jealousies the Lacedæmonians, although the Helots were not subdued, undertook a hostile expedition out of the Peloponnesus, with eleven thousand five hundred men, ostensibly to protect Doris against the Phœcians, but really to prevent the further aggrandizement of Athens, and this was supposed to be most easily effected by strengthening Thebes and securing the obedience of the Bœotian cities. But there was yet another design, to prevent the building of the long walls, to which the aristocratical party of Athens was opposed, but which Pericles, with long-sighted views, defended.

Hostilities between Sparta and Athens.

This extraordinary man, with whom the glory and greatness of Athens are so intimately associated, now had the ascendency over all his rivals. He is considered the ablest of all the statesmen which Greece produced. He was of illustrious descent, and spent the early part of his life in retirement and study, and when he emerged from obscurity his rise was rapid, until he gained the control of his countrymen, which he retained until his death. He took the side of the democracy, and, in one sense, was a demagogue, as well as a statesman, since he appealed to

Ascendency of Pericles.

popular passions and interests. He was very eloquent, and was the idol of the party which was dominant in the State. His rank and fortune enabled him to avail himself of every mode of culture and self-improvement known in his day. He loved music, philosophy, poetry, and art. The great Anaxagoras gave a noble direction to his studies, so that he became imbued with the sublimest ideas of Grecian wisdom. And his eloquence is said to have been of the most lofty kind. His manners partook of the same exalted and dignified bearing as his philosophy. He never lost his temper, and maintained the severest self-control. His voice was sweet, and his figure was graceful and commanding. He early distinguished himself as a soldier, and so gained upon his countrymen that, when Themistocles and Aristides were dead, and Cimon engaged in military expeditions, he supplanted all who had gone before him in popular favor. All his sympathies were with the democratic party, while his manners and habits and tastes and associations were those of the aristocracy. His political career lasted forty years from the year 469 B. C. He was unremitting in his public duties, and was never seen in the streets unless on his way to the assembly or senate. He was not fond of convivial pleasures, and was, though affable, reserved and dignified. He won the favor of the people by a series of measures which provided the poor with amusement and means of subsistence. He caused those who served in the courts to be paid for their attendance and services. He weakened the power of the court of the Areopagus, which was opposed to popular measures. Assured of his own popularity, he even contrived to secure the pardon of Cimon, his great rival, when publicly impeached.

His character and accomplishments.

Pericles was thus the leading citizen of his country, when he advocated the junction of the Peireus with Athens by the long walls which have been alluded to, and when the Spartan army in Bœotia threatened to sustain the oligarchal party in the city. The Athenians, in view of this danger, took decisive measures. They took

The union of the Peireus with Athens.

the field at once against their old allies, the Lacedæmonians. The unfortunate battle of Tanagra was decided in favor of the Spartans, chiefly through the desertion of the Thessalian horse.

Cimon, though ostracised, appeared in the field of battle, and requested permission to fight in the ranks. Though the request was refused, he used all his influence with his friends to fight with bravery and fidelity to his country's cause, which noble conduct allayed the existing jealousies, and through the influence of Pericles, his banishment of ten years was revoked. He returned to Athens, reconciled with the party which had defeated him, and so great was the admiration of his magnanimity that all parties generously united in the common cause. Another battle with the enemy was fought in Bœotia, this time attended with success, the result of which was the complete ascendency of the Athenians over all Bœotia. They became masters of Thebes and all the neighboring towns, and reversed all the acts of the Spartans, and established democratic governments, and forced the aristocratical leaders into exile. Phocis and Locris were added to the list of dependent allies, and the victory cemented their power from the Corinthian Gulf to the strait of Thermopylæ.

Magnanimity of Cimon.

Then followed the completion of the long walls, B. C. 455, and the conquest of Ægina. Athens was now mistress of the sea, and her admiral displayed his strength by sailing round the Peloponnesus, and taking possession of many cities in the Gulf of Corinth. But the Athenians were unsuccessful in an expedition into Thessaly, and sustained many losses in Egypt in the great warfare with Persia.

Completion of the long walls.

After the success of the Lacedæmonians at Tanagra they made no expeditions out of the Peloponnesus for several years, and allowed Bœotia and Phocis to be absorbed in the Athenian empire. They even extended the truce with Athens for five years longer, and this was promoted by Cimon, who wished to resume offensive operations against

16

the Persians. Cimon was allowed to equip a fleet of two hundred triremes and set sail to Cyprus, where he died. The expedition failed under his successor, and this closed all further aggressive war with the Persians.

Death of Cimon.

The death of Cimon, whose interest it was to fight the Persians, and thus by the spoils and honors of war keep up his influence at home, left Pericles without rivals, and with opportunities to develop his policy of internal improvements, and the development of national resources, to enable Athens to maintain her ascendency over the States of Greece. So he gladly concluded peace with the Persians, by the terms of which they were excluded from the coasts of Asia Minor and the islands of the Ægean; while Athens stipulated to make no further aggression on Cyprus, Phœnicia, Cilicia, and Egypt.

Pericles without rivals.

Athens, at peace with all her enemies, with a large empire of tributary allies, a great fleet, and large accumulations of treasure, sought now to make herself supreme in Greece. The fund of the confederacy of Delos was transferred to the Acropolis. New allies sought her alliance. It is said the tributary cities amounted to one thousand. She was not only mistress of the sea, but she was the equal of Sparta on the land. Beside this political power, a vast treasure was accumulated in the Acropolis. Such rapid aggrandizement was bitterly felt by Corinth, Sicyon, and Sparta, and the feeling of enmity expanded until it exploded in the Peloponnesian war.

Aggrandizement of Athens.

It was while Athens was at this height of power and renown that further changes were made in the constitution by Pericles. Great authority was still in the hands of the court of the Areopagus, which was composed exclusively of ex-archons, sitting for life, and hence of very aristocratic sentiments. It was indeed a judicial body, but its functions were mixed; it decided all disputes, inquired into crimes, and inflicted punishments. And it was enabled to enforce its own mandates, which were without appeal, and led to great injustice and oppression.

Change in the constitution by Pericles.

The magistrates, serving without pay, were generally wealthy, and though their offices were eligible to all the citizens, still, practically, only the rich became magistrates, as is the case with the British House of Commons. Hence, magistrates possessing large powers, and the senate sitting for life, all belonging to the wealthy class, were animated by aristocratic sympathies. But a rapidly increasing democracy succeeded in securing the selection of archons by lot, in place of election. This threw more popular elements into the court of Areopagus. The innovations which Pericles effected, of causing the jury courts, or Dikasteries, to be regularly paid, again threw into public life the poorer citizens. But the great change which he effected was in transferring to the numerous dikasts, selected from the citizens, a new judicial power, heretofore exercised by the magistrates, and the senate of the Areopagus.

Increase of democratic power.

The dikasts.

The magistrate, instead of deciding causes and inflicting punishment beyond the imposition of a small fine, was constrained to impanel a jury to try the cause. In fact, the ten dikasts became the leading judicial tribunals, and as these were composed, each, of five hundred citizens, judgments were virtually made by the people, instead of the old court. The pay of each man serving as a juror was determined and punctually paid. The importance of this revolution will be seen when these dikasts thus became the exclusive assemblies, of course popular, in which all cases, civil and criminal, were tried. The magistrates were thus deprived of the judicial functions which they once enjoyed, and were confined to purely administrative matters. The commanding functions of the archon were destroyed, and he only retained power to hear complaints, and fix the day of trial, and preside over the dikastic assembly. The senate of the Areopagus, which had exercised an inquisitorial power over the lives and habits of the citizens, and supervised the meetings of the assembly—a power uncertain but immense, and sustained by ancient customs,—now became a mere nominal tribunal. And this change was called for, since the members of the court were open to bribery and corruption, and had abused their powers, little short of paternal despotism. And when the great public improvements, the growth of a new population, the rising importance of the Penæus, the introduction of nautical people, and the active duties of Athens as the head of the Delian confederacy—all, together, gave force to the democratic elements of society, the old and conservative court became stricter, and more oppressive, instead of more popular and conciliatory.

Ascendency of the democratic power.

But beside this great change in the constitution, Pericles effected others also. Under his influence, a general power of supervision, over the magistrates and the assembly, was intrusted to seven men called Nomophylakes, or Law Guardians, changed every year, who sat with the president in the senate and assembly, and interposed when any step was taken contrary to existing laws. Other changes were also effected with a view to the enforcement of laws, upon which we can not enter. It is enough to say that it was by means of Pericles that the magistrates were stripped of judicial power, and the Areopagus of all its jurisdiction, except in cases of homicide, and numerous and paid and popular dikasts were substituted to decide judicial cases, and repeal and enact laws; this, says Grote, was the consummation of the Athenian democracy. And thus it remained until the time of Demosthenes.

Other political changes effected by Pericles.

But the influence of Pericles is still more memorable from the impulse he gave to the improvements of Athens and his patronage of art and letters. He conceived the idea of investing his city with intellectual glory, which is more permanent than any conquests of territory. And since he could not make Athens the centre of political power, owing to the jealousies of other States, he resolved to make her the great attraction to all scholars, artists, and strangers. And his countrymen were prepared to second his glorious objects, and were in a condition to do so, enriched by commerce, rendered independent by successes over the Persians, and jealous Grecian rivals, and stimulated by

Improvements of Athens.

the poets and philosophers who flourished in that glorious age. The age of Pericles is justly regarded as the epoch of the highest creation genius ever exhibited, and gave to Athens an intellectual supremacy which no military genius could have secured.

The Persian war despoiled and depopulated Athens. The city was rebuilt on a more extensive plan, and the streets were made more regular. The long walls to the Peiræus were completed—a double wall, as it were, with a space between them large enough to secure the communication between the city and the port, in case an enemy should gain a footing in the wide space between the Peiræan and Thaleric walls. The port itself was ornamented with beautiful public buildings, of which the Agora was the most considerable. The theatre, called the Odeon, was erected in Athens for musical and poetical contests. The Acropolis, with its temples, was rebuilt, and the splendid Propylæa, of Doric architecture, formed a magnificent approach to them. The temple of Athenæ—the famous Parthenon—was built of white marble, and adorned with sculptures in the pediments and frieze by the greatest artists of antiquity, while Phidias constructed the statue of the goddess of ivory and gold. No Doric temple ever equaled the severe proportions and chaste beauty of the Parthenon, and its ruins still are one of the wonders of the world. The Odeon and Parthenon were finished during the first seven years of the administration of Pericles, and many other temples were constructed in various parts of Attica. The genius of Phidias is seen in the numerous sculptures which ornamented the city, and the general impulse he gave to art. Other great artists labored in generous competition,—sculptors, painters, and architects,—to make Athens the most beautiful city in the world.

The public buildings.

"It was under the administration of Pericles that Greek literature reached its culminating height in the Attic drama, a form of poetry which Aristotle justly considers as the most perfect; and it shone with undiminished

Impulse given to literature.

splendor to the close of the century. It was this branch of literature which peculiarly marked the age of Pericles—the period between the Persian and Peloponnesian wars. The first regular comedies were produced by Epicharmus, who was born in Cos, B. C. 540, and exhibited at Syracuse. Comedy arose before tragedy, and was at first at the celebration of Dionysus by rustic revelers in the season of the vintage, in the form of songs and dances. But these were not so appropriate in cities, and the songs of the revelers were gradually molded into the regular choral dithyramb, while the performers still preserved the wild dress and gestures of the satyrs—half goat and half man—who accompanied Dionysus." The prevalence of tales of crime and fate and suffering naturally impressed spectators with tragic sentiments, and tragedy was thus born and separated from comedy. Both forms received their earliest development in the Dorian States, and were particularly cultivated by the Megarians. "Thespis, a native of Icaria, first gave to tragedy its dramatic character, in the time of Pisistratus, B. C. 535. He introduced the dialogue, relieved by choral performances, and the recitation of mythological and heroic adventures. He traveled about Attica in a wagon, which served him for a stage; but the art soon found its way to Athens, where dramatic contests for prizes were established in connection with the festivals of Dionysus. These became State institutions. Chœrilus, B.C. 523, and Phrynichus followed Thespis, and these ventured from the regions of mythology to contemporaneous history."

The drama.

It was at this time that Æschylus, the father of tragedy, exhibited his dramas at Athens, B. C. 500. He added a second actor, and made the choral odes subordinate to the action. The actors now made use of masks, and wore lofty head-dresses and magnificent robes. Scenes were painted according to the rules of perspective, and an elaborate mechanism was introduced upon the stage. New figures were invented for the dancers of the chorus. Sophocles still further improved tragedy by

Æschylus.

Sophocles.

adding the third actor, and snatched from Æschylus the tragic prize. He was not equal to Æschylus in the boldness and originality of his characters, or the loftiness of his sentiments, or the colossal grandeur of his figures; but in the harmony of his composition, and the grace and vigor displayed in all the parts—the severe unity, the classic elegance of his style, and the charm of his expressions he is his superior. These two men carried tragedy to a degree of perfection never afterward attained in Greece. It was not merely a spectacle to the people, but was applied to moral and religious purposes. The heroes of Æschylus are raised above the sphere of real life, and often they are the sport of destiny, or victims of a struggle between superior beings. The characters of Sophocles are rarely removed beyond the sphere of mortal sympathy, and they are made to rebuke injustice and give impressive warnings.

Comedy.

Comedy also made a great stride during the administration of Pericles; but it was not till his great ascendency was at its height that Aristophanes was born, B. C. 444. The comedians of the time were allowed great license, which they carried even into politics, and which was directed against Pericles himself.

Power of the stage.

The Athenian stage at this epoch was the chief means by which national life and liberty were sustained. It answered the functions of the press and the pulpit in our day, and quickened the perceptions of the people. The great audiences which assembled at the theatres were kindled into patriotic glow, and were moved by the noble thoughts, and withering sarcasm, and inexhaustible wit of the poets. "The gods and goddesses who swept majestically over the tragic stage were the objects of religious and national faith, real beings, whose actions and sufferings claimed their deepest sympathy, and whose heroic fortitude served for an example, or their terrific fate for a warning. So, too, in the old comedy, the persons, habits, manners, principles held up to ridicule were all familiar to the audience in their daily lives; and the poet might exhibit in a humorous light objects which to attack seriously would have been a treason or a sacrilege, and might recommend measures which he could only have proposed in the popular assembly with a halter round his neck." This susceptibility of the people to grand impressions, and the toleration of rulers, alike show a great degree of popular intelligence and a great practical liberty in social life.

The histo-rians and philosophers.

The age of Pericles was also adorned by great historians and philosophers. Herodotus and Thucydides have never been surpassed as historians, while the Sophists who succeeded the more earnest philosophers of a previous age, gave to Athenian youth a severe intellectual training. Rhetoric, mathematics and natural history supplanted speculation, led to the practice of eloquence as an art, and gave to society polish and culture. The Sophists can not indeed be compared with those great men who preceded or succeeded them in philosophical wisdom, but their influence in educating the Grecian mind, and creating polished men of society, can not be disproved. Politics became a profession in the democratic State, which demanded the highest culture, and an extensive acquaintance with the principles of moral and political science. This was the age of lectures, when students voluntarily assembled to learn from the great masters of thought that knowledge which would enable them to rise in a State where the common mind was well instructed.

Athens de-clines in mo-ral power.

But it must also be admitted that while the age of Pericles furnished an extraordinary stimulus to the people, in art, in literature, in political science, and in popular institutions, the great teachers of the day inculcated a selfish morality, and sought an æsthetic enjoyment irrespective of high moral improvement, and the inevitable result was the rapid degeneracy of Athens, and the decline even in political influence, and strength, as was seen in the superior power of Sparta in the great contest to which the two leading States of Greece were hurried by their jealousies and animosities. The prosperity was delusive and outside; for no intellectual triumph, no glories of art, no fascinations of literature, can balance the moral forces which are generated in self-denial and lofty public virtue.

It was while the power and glory of Pericles were at their height that he formed that memorable attachment to Aspasia, a Milesian woman, which furnished a fruitful subject for the attacks of the comic poets. She was the most brilliant and intellectual woman of the age, and her house was the resort of the literary men and philosophers and artists of Athens until the death of Pericles. He formed as close a union with her as the law allowed, and her influence in creating a sympathy with intellectual excellence can not be questioned. But she was charged with pandering to the vices of Pericles, and corrupting society by her example and influence.

Aspasia.

The latter years of Pericles were marked by the outbreak of that great war with Sparta, which crippled the power of Athens and tarnished her glories. He also was afflicted by the death of his children by the plague which devastated Athens in the early part of the Peloponnesian war, to which attention is now directed. The probity of Pericles is attested by the fact that during his long administration he added nothing to his patrimonial estate. His policy was ambitious, and if it could have been carried out, it would have been wise. He sought first to develop the resources of his country—the true aim of all enlightened statesmen—and then to make Athens the centre of Grecian civilization and political power, to which all other States would be secondary and subservient. But the rivalries of the Grecian States and inextinguishable jealousies would not allow this. He made Athens, indeed, the centre of cultivated life; he could not make it the centre of national unity. In attempting this he failed, and a disastrous war was the consequence.

Latter days of Pericles.

Policy of Pericles.

Pericles lived long enough to see the commencement of the contest which ultimately resulted in the political ruin of Athens, and which we now present.

CHAPTER XIX.

THE PELOPONNESIAN WAR.

Causes of the war.

THE great and disastrous war between the two leading States of Greece broke out about two years and a half before the death of Pericles, but the causes of the war can be traced to a period shortly after the Persians were driven out of the Ionian cities. It arose primarily from the rapid growth and power of Athens, when, as the leader of the maritime States, it excited the envy of Sparta and other republics. A thirty years' truce was made between Athens and Sparta, B. C. 445, after the revolution in Bœotia, when the ascendency of Pericles was undisputed, which forced his rival, Thucydides, a kinsman of Cimon, to go into temporary exile. The continuance of the truce is identical with the palmy days of Athens, and the glory of Pericles, during which the vast improvements to the city were made, and art and literature flourished to a degree unprecedented in the history of the ancient world.

After the conquest of Samos the jealousy of Sparta reached a point which made it obvious that the truce could not much longer be maintained, though both powers shrunk from open hostilities, foreseeing the calamities which would result. The storm burst out in an unexpected quarter. The city of Epidamnus had been founded by colonists from Corcyra, on the eastern side of the Adriatic. It was, however, the prey of domestic factions, and in a domestic revolution a part of the inhabitants became exiles. These appealed to the neighboring barbarians, who invested the city by sea and land. The city, in distress, invoked the aid of Corcyra, the parent State, which aid being disregarded, the city transferred its allegiance to Corinth. The Corinthians, indulging a hatred of

Corcyra, took the distressed city under their protection. This led to a war between Corcyra and Corinth, in which the Corinthians were defeated. But Corinth, burning to revenge the disaster, fitted out a still larger force against Corcyra. The Corcyræans, in alarm, then sent envoys to Athens to come to their assistance. The Corinthians also sent embassadors to frustrate their proposal. Two assemblies were held in Athens in reference to the subject. The delegates of Corcyra argued that peace could not long be maintained with Sparta, and that in the coming contest the Corcyræans would prove useful allies. The envoys of Corinth, on the other hand, maintained that Athens could not lend aid to Corcyra without violating the treaty with Corinth. The Athenians decided to assist Corcyra, and ten ships were sent, under the command of Lacedæmonicus, the son of Cimon. This was considered a breach of faith by the Corinthians, and a war resulted between Corinth and Athens. The Corinthians then invited the Lacedæmonians to join them and make common cause against an aggressive and powerful enemy, that aimed at the supremacy of Greece. In spite of the influence of Athenian envoys in Sparta, who attempted to justify the course their countrymen had taken, the feeling against Athens was bitter and universally hostile. Instant hostilities were demanded in defense of the allies of Sparta, and war was decided upon.

War between Corcyra and Corinth.

Both parties appealed to Athens.

Athens decides in favor of Corcyra.

Thus commenced the Peloponnesian war, which led to such disastrous consequences, and which was thus brought about by the Corinthians, B. C. 433, sixteen years before the conclusion of the truce.

To Athens the coming war was any thing but agreeable. It had no hopes of gain, and the certainty of prodigious loss. But the Spartans were not then prepared for the contest, and hostilities did not immediately commence. They contented themselves, at first, with sending envoys to Athens to multiply demands and enlarge the grounds of quarrel. The offensive was plainly with Sparta. The first requisition which Sparta made was the expulsion of the Alcmæonidæ from Athens, to which family Pericles belonged —a mere political manœuvre to get rid of so commanding a statesman. The enemies of Pericles, especially the comic actors at Athens, seized this occasion to make public attacks upon him, and it was then that the persecution of Aspasia took place, as well as that against Anaxagoras, the philosopher, the teacher, and friend of Pericles. He was also accused of peculation in complicity with Phidias. But he was acquitted of the various charges made by his enemies. Nor could his services be well dispensed with in the great crisis of public affairs, even had he been guilty, as was exceedingly doubtful.

Intrigues of Sparta.

The reluctance on the part of the Athenians to go to war was very great, but Pericles strenuously urged his countrymen to resent the outrageous demands of Sparta, which were nothing less than the virtual extinction of the Athenian empire. He showed that the Spartans, though all-powerful on the Peloponnesus, had no means of carrying on an aggressive war at a distance, neither leaders nor money, nor habits of concert with allies; while Athens was mistress of the sea, and was impregnable in defense; that great calamities would indeed happen in Attica, but even if overrun by Spartan armies, there were other territories and islands from which a support could be derived. "Mourn not for the loss of land," said the orator, "but reserve your mourning for the men that acquire land." His eloquence and patriotism prevailed with a majority of the assembly, and answer was made to Sparta that the Athenians were prepared to discuss all grounds of complaint pursuant to the truce, by arbitration, but that they would yield nothing to authoritative command. This closed the negotiations, which Pericles foresaw would be vain and useless, since the Spartans were obstinately bent on war. The first blow was struck by the Thebans—allies of Sparta. They surprised Platæa in the night. The gates were opened by the oligarchal party; a party of Thebans

Pericles urges the Athenians to support a war.

Imperious demands of Sparta.

were admitted into the agora; but the people rallied, and the party was overwhelmed. Meanwhile another detachment of Thebans arrived in the morning, and, discovering what had happened, they laid waste the Platæan territory without the walls. The Platæans retaliated by slaughtering their prisoners. Messengers left the city, on the entrance of the Thebans, to carry the news to Athens, and the Athenians issued orders to seize all the Bœotians who could be found in Attica, and sent re-enforcements to Platæa. This aggression of the Thebans silenced the opponents of Pericles, who now saw that the war had actually begun, and that active preparations should be made. Athens immediately sent messengers to her allies, tributary as well as free, and contributions flowed in from all parts of the Athenian empire. Athens had soon three hundred triremes fit for service, twelve hundred horsemen, sixteen hundred bowmen, and twenty-nine thousand hoplites. The Acropolis was filled with the treasure which had long been accumulating, not less than six thousand talents—about $7,000,000 of our money—an immense sum at that time, when gold and silver were worth twenty or thirty times as much as at present. Moreover, the various temples were rich in votive offerings, in deposits, plate, and sacred vessels, while the great statue of the goddess, lately set up in the Parthenon by Phidias, composed of gold and ivory, was itself valued at four hundred talents. The contributions of allies swelled the resources of Athens to one thousand talents, or over $11,000,000.

Preparations for war.

Wealth of Athens.

Sparta, on the other hand, had but few ships, no funds, and no powers of combination, and it would seem that success would be on the side of Athens, with her unrivaled maritime skill, and the unanimity of the citizens. Pericles did not promise successful engagements on the land, but a successful resistance, and the maintenance of the empire. His policy was purely defensive. But if Sparta was weak in money and ships, she was rich in allies. The entire strength of the Peloponnesus was brought out, assisted by Megarians, Bœotians, Phocians, Locrians, and other States. Corinth, Megara, Sicyon, Elis, and other maritime cities furnished ships, while Bœotians, Phocians, and Locrians furnished cavalry. Not even to resist the Persian hosts was so large a land force collected, as was now assembled to destroy the supremacy of Athens. And this great force was animated with savage hopes, while the Athenians were not without desponding anticipations, for there was little hope of resisting the Spartans and their allies on the field. The Spartans, moreover, resolved, by means of their allies, to send a fleet able to cope with that of Athens, and even were so transported with enmity and jealousy as to lay schemes for invoking the aid of Persia.

Immense array of forces against Athens.

The invasion of Attica was the primary object of Sparta and her allies; and at the appointed time the Lacedæmonian forces were mustered on the Isthmus of Corinth, under the command of Archidamus. Envoys were sent to Athens to summon a surrender, but Pericles would not receive them, nor allow them to enter the city, upon which the Lacedæmonian army commenced its march to Attica. It required all the eloquence and tact of Pericles to induce the proprietors of Attica to submit to the devastation of their cultivated territory, and fly with their families and movable property to Athens or the neighboring islands, without making an effort to resist the invaders. But this was the policy of Pericles. He knew he could not contend with superior forces on the land. It was hard for the people to submit to the cruel necessity of seeing their farms devastated without opposition. But they made the sacrifice, and intrenched themselves behind the fortifications of Athens. Then was seen the wisdom of the long walls which connected Athens with the Piræus.

Invasion of Attica.

Defensive policy of Pericles.

Meanwhile the Spartan forces—sixty thousand hoplites, advanced through Attica, burning and plundering every thing on their way, and reached Acharnæ, within seven miles of Athens. The Athenians, pent up behind their walls, and seeing the destruction of their property, were eager to go forth and fight, but were dissuaded by Pericles. Then came to him the trying hour. He was denounced as the cause of the existing sufferings, and was reviled as a coward. But nothing disturbed his equanimity, and he refused even to convene the assembly. As one of the ten generals he had this power; but it was a remarkable thing that the people should have respected the democratic constitution so far as to submit, when their assembly would have been justified by the exigency of the crisis. But while the Athenians remained inactive behind their walls, the cavalry was sent out on skirmishing expeditions, and a large fleet was sent to the Peloponnesus with orders to devastate the country in retaliation. The Spartans, after having spent thirty or forty days in Attica, retired for want of provisions. Ægina was also invaded, and the inhabitants were expelled and sent to the Peloponnesus. Megara was soon after invaded by an army under Pericles himself, and its territory was devastated—a retribution well deserved, for both Megara and Ægina had been zealous in kindling the war.

Retreat of the Lacedæmonians.

Expecting a prolonged struggle, the Athenians now made arrangements for putting Attica in permanent defense, both by sea and land, and set apart one thousand talents, out of the treasure of the Acropolis, which was not to be used except in certain dangers previously prescribed, and a law was passed making it a capital offense for any citizen to propose its use for any other purpose.

Athens sets aside 1,000 talents for future contingencies

The first year of the war closed without decisive successes on either side. The Athenians made a more powerful resistance than was anticipated. It was supposed they could not hold out against the superior forces of their enemies more than a year. They had the misfortune to see their territory wasted, and their treasures spent in a war which they would gladly have avoided. But, on the other hand, they inflicted nearly equal damages upon the Peloponnesus, and still remained masters of the sea, Pericles pronounced a funeral oration on those who had fallen and stimulated his countrymen to continued resistance, and

Results of the first year of the war.

excited their patriotic sentiments. Thus far the anticipations of the statesman and orator had been more than realized.

The Spartans again invade Attica.

The second year of the war opened with another invasion of Attica by the Spartans and their allies. They inflicted even more injury than in the preceding year, but they found the territory deserted, all the population having retired within the defenses of Athens.

The plague at Athens.

But a new and unforeseen calamity now fell upon the Athenians, and against which they could not guard. A great pestilence broke out in the city, which had already overrun Western Asia. Its progress was rapid and destructive, and the overcrowded city was but too favorable for its ravages. Thucydides has left a graphic and mournful account of this pestilence, analogous to the plague of modern times. The victims generally perished on the seventh or ninth day, and no treatment was efficacious. The sufferings and miseries of the people were intense, and the calamity by many was regarded as resulting from the anger of the gods. The pestilence demoralized the population, who lost courage and fortitude. The sick were left to take care of themselves. The utmost lawlessness prevailed. The bonds of law and morality were relaxed, and the thoughtless people abandoned themselves to every species of folly and excess, seeking, in their despair, to seize some brief moments of joy before the hand of destiny should fall upon them. For three years did this calamity desolate Athens, and the loss of life was deplorable, both in the army and among private citizens. Pericles lost both his children and his sister; four thousand four hundred hoplites died, and a greater part of the horsemen.

Naval expedition against Sparta.

And yet, amid the devastation which the pestilence inflicted, Pericles led another expedition against the coasts of the Peloponnesus. But the soldiers carried infection with them, and a greater part of them died of the disease at the siege or blockade of Potidæa. The Athenians were nearly distracted by the double ravages of pestilence and war, and became incensed against Pericles, and sent messengers to Sparta to negotiate peace. But the Spartans turned a deaf ear, which added to the bitterness against their heroic leader, whose fortitude and firmness were never more effectively manifested. He was accused, and condemned to pay a fine, and excluded from re-election. Though he was restored to power and confidence, his affliction bore heavily upon his exalted nature, and he died, B. C. 430, in the early period of the war. He had, indeed, many enemies, and was hunted down by the comic writers, whose trade it was to deride all political characters, yet his wisdom, patriotism, eloquence, and great services are indisputable, and he died, leaving on the whole, the greatest name which had ever ennobled the Athenians.

Death of Pericles.

The war, of course, languished during the prevalence of the epidemic, and much injury was done to Athenian commerce by Peloponnesian privateers, who put to death all their prisoners. It was then that Sparta sent envoys to Persia to solicit money and troops against Athens, which shows that no warfare is so bitter as civil strife, and that no expedients are too disgraceful not to be made use of, in order to gratify malignant passions. But the envoys were seized in Thrace by the allies of Athens, and delivered up to the Athenians, and by them were put to death.

Sparta invokes the aid of the Persians.

In January, B. C. 429, Potidæa surrendered to the Athenian generals, upon favorable terms, after enduring all the miseries of famine. The fall of this city cost Athens two thousand talents. The Lacedæmonians, after two years, had accomplished nothing. They had not even relieved Potidæa.

Results of the second year of the war.

On the third year, the Lacedæmonians, instead of ravaging Attica, marched to the attack of Platæa. The inhabitants resolved to withstand the whole force of the enemies. Archidemus, the Lacedæmonian general, commenced the siege, defended only by four hundred native citi-

Siege of Platæa.

zens and eighty Athenians. So unskilled were the Greeks in the attack of fortified cities, that the besiegers made no progress, and were obliged to resort to blockade. A wall of circumvallation was built around the city, which was now left to the operations of famine.

At the same time the siege was pressed, an Athenian armament was sent to Thrace, which was defeated; but in the western part of Greece the Athenian arms were more successful. The Spartans and their allies suffered a repulse at Stratus, and their fleet was defeated by Phormio, the Athenian admiral. Nothing could exceed the rage of the Lacedæmonians at these two disasters. They collected a still larger fleet, and were again defeated with severe loss near Naupactus, by inferior forces. But the defeated Lacedæmonians, under the persuasion of the Megarians, undertook the bold enterprise of surprising the Piræus, during the absence of the Athenian fleet; but the courage of the assailants failed at the critical hour, and the port of Athens was saved. The Athenians then had the precaution to extend a chain across the mouth of the harbor, to guard against such surprises in the future.

Naval defeat of the Spartans.

Athens, during the summer, had secured the alliance of the Odrysians, a barbarous but powerful nation in Thrace. Their king, Sitalces, with an army of fifteen thousand men, attacked Perdiccas, the king of Macedonia, and overran his country, and only retired from the severity of the season and the want of Athenian co-operation. Such were the chief enterprises and events of the third campaign, and Athens was still powerful and unhumbled.

Results of the third campaign.

The fourth year of the war was marked by a renewed invasion of Attica, without any other results than such as had happened before. But it was a more serious calamity to the Athenians to learn that Mitylene and the most of Lesbos had revolted—one of the most powerful of the Athenian allies. Nothing was left to Athens but to subjugate the city. A large force was sent for this purpose, but the inhabitants of Mitylene appealed to the Spartans for

Renewed invasion of Attica.

aid, and prepared for a vigorous resistance. But the treasures of Athens were now nearly consumed, and the Athenians were obliged to resort to contributions to force the siege, which they did with vigor. The Lacedæmonians promised succor, and the Mitylenæans held out till their provisions were exhausted, when they surrendered to the Athenians. The Lacedæmonians advanced to relieve their allies, but were too late. The Athenian admiral pursued them, and they returned to the Peloponnesus without having done any thing. Paches, the Athenian general, sent home one thousand Mitylenæan prisoners, while it was decreed to slaughter the whole remaining population—about six thousand—able to carry arms, and make slaves of the women and children. This severe measure was prompted by Cleon. But the Athenians repented, and a second decree of the assembly, through the influence of Diodotus, prevented the barbarous revenge; but the Athenians put to death the prisoners which Paches had sent, razed the fortifications of Mitylene, took possession of all her ships of war, and confiscated all the land of the island except that which belonged to one town that had been faithful. So severe was ancient warfare, even among the most civilized of the Greeks.

Revolt and subjugation of Mitylene.

The surrender of Platæa to the Lacedæmonians took place not long after; but not until one-half of the garrison had sallied from the city, scaled the wall of circumvallation, and escaped safely to Athens. The Platæans were sentenced to death by the Spartan judges, and barbarously slain. The captured women were sold as slaves, and the town and territory were handed over to the Thebans.

Surrender of Platæa.

Scenes not less bloody took place in the western part of Greece, in the island of Corcyra, before which a naval battle was fought between the Lacedæmonians and the Athenians. The island had been governed by oligarchies, under the protection of Sparta, but the retirement of the Lacedæmonian fleet enabled the Athenian general to wreak his vengeance on the party which had held supremacy, which was exterminated in the most cruel manner,

Cruelties of the Athenians at Corcyra.

which produced a profound sensation, and furnished Thucydides a theme for the most profound reflections on the acerbity and ferocity of the political parties, which, it seems, then divided Greece, and were among the exciting causes of the war itself—the struggle between the advocates of democratic and aristocratic institutions.

Nicias.

A new character now appears upon the stage at Athens—Nicias—one of the ten generals who, in rank and wealth, was the equal of Pericles. He belonged to the oligarchal party, and succeeded Cimon and Thucydides in the control of it. But he was moderate in his conduct, and so won the esteem of his countrymen, that he retained power until his death, although opposed to the party which had the ascendency. He was incorruptible as to pecuniary gains, and adopted the conservative views of Pericles, avoiding new acquisitions at a distance, or creating new enemies. He surrounded himself, not as Pericles did, with philosophers, but religious men, avoided all scandals, and employed his large fortune in securing popularity. Pericles disdained to win the people by such means, cultivated art, and patronized the wits who surrounded Aspasia. Nicias was zealous in the worship of the gods, was careful to make no enemies, and conciliated the poor by presents. Yet he increased his private fortune, so far as he could, by honorable means, and united thrift and sagacity with honesty and piety. He was not a man of commanding genius, but his character was above reproach, and was never assailed by the comic writers. He was the great opponent of Alcibiades, the oracle of the democracy—one of those memorable demagogues who made use of the people to forward his ambitious projects. He was also the opponent of Cleon, whose office it was to supervise official men for the public conduct—a man of great eloquence, but fault-finding and denunciatory.

He continues the policy of Pericles.

Opposed by Alcibiades and Cleon.

The fifth year of the war.

The fifth year of the war was not signalized by the usual invasion of Attica, which gave the Athenians leisure to send an expedition under Nicias against the island of Melos, inhabited by ancient colonists from Sparta. Demosthenes, another general, was sent around the Peloponnesus to attack Acarnania, and he ravaged the whole territory of Leucas. He also attacked Ætolia, but was completely beaten, and obliged to retire with loss; but this defeat was counterbalanced by a great victory, the next year, over the enemy at Olpæ, when the Lacedæmonian general was slain. He returned in triumph to Athens with considerable spoil. The attention of the Athenians was now directed to Delos, the island sacred to Apollo, and a complete purification of the island was made, and the old Delian festivals renewed with peculiar splendor.

The war had now lasted six years, without any grand or decisive results on either side. The expeditions of both parties were of the nature of raids—destructive, cruel, irritating, but without bringing any grand triumphs. Though the seventh year was marked by the usual enterprise on the part of the Lacedæmonians—the invasion of Attica—Corcyra promised to be the principal scene of military operations. Both an Athenian and Spartan fleet was sent thither. But an unforeseen incident gave a new character to the war. In the course of the voyage to Corcyra, Demosthenes, the Athenian general, stopped at Pylus, with the intention of erecting a fort on the uninhabited promontory, since it protected the spacious basin now known as the bay of Navarino, and was itself easily defended. Eurymedon, the admiral, insisted on going directly to Corcyra, but the fleet was driven by a storm into the very harbor which Demosthenes proposed to defend. The place was accordingly fortified by Demosthenes, where he himself remained with a garrison, while the fleet proceeded to Corcyra. Intelligence of this insult to Sparta—the attempt to plant a hostile fort on its territory—induced the Lacedæmonians to send their fleet to Pylus, instead of Corcyra. Forty-three triremes, under Thrasymelidas, and a powerful land force, advanced to attack Demosthenes, intrenched with his small army on the

The sixth year of the war.

Undecisive nature of the conflict.

rocky promontory. When the news of this new diversion reached the Athenian fleet at Corcyra, it returned to Pylus, to succor Demosthenes. Here a naval battle took place, in which the Lacedæmonians were defeated. This defeat jeopardized the situation of the Spartan army which had occupied the island of Shacteria, cut off from supplies from the main land, as well as the existence of the fleet. So great was this exigency, that the ephors came from Sparta to consult on operations. They took a desponding view, and sent a herald to the Athenian generals to propose an armistice, in order to allow time for envoys to go to Athens and treat for peace. But Athens demanded now her own terms, elated by the success. Cleon, the organ of the popular mind, excited and sanguine, gave utterance to the feelings of the people, and insisted on the restoration of all the territory they had lost during the war. The Lacedæmonian envoys, unable to resist a vehement speaker like Cleon, which required qualities they did not possess, and which could only be acquired from skill in managing popular assemblies, to which they were unused, returned to Pylus. And it was the object of Cleon to prevent a hearing of the envoys by a select committee (what they desired) for fear that Nicias and other conservative politicians would accede to their proposals. Thus the best opportunity that could be presented for making an honorable peace and reuniting Greece was lost by the arts of a demagogue, who inflamed and shared the popular passions. Had Pericles been alive, the treaty would probably have been made, but Nicias had not sufficient influence to secure it.

Great defeat of the Lacedæmonians at Pylus.

Sparta seeks peace.

Peace prevented by Cleon.

War therefore recommenced, with fresh irritation. The Athenian fleet blockaded the island where the Spartan hoplites were posted, and found in the attempt, which they thought so easy, unexpected obstacles. Provisions clandestinely continually reached the besieged. Week after week passed without the expected surrender. Demosthenes, baffled for want of provisions and water for

Renewed hostilities.

his own fleet, sent urgently to Athens for re-enforcements, which caused infinite mortification. The people now began to regret that they had listened to Cleon, and not to the voice of wisdom. Cleon himself was sent with the re-enforcements demanded, against his will, although he was not one of the ten generals. The island of Sphacteria now contained the bravest of the Lacedæmonian troops—from the first families of Sparta—a prey which Cleon and Demosthenes were eager to grasp. They attacked the island with a force double of that of the defenders, altogether ten thousand men, eight hundred of whom were hoplites. The besieged could not resist this overwhelming force, and retreated to their last redoubt, but were surrounded and taken prisoners. This surrender caused astonishment throughout Greece, since it was supposed the Spartan hoplites would die, as they did at Thermopylæ, rather than allow themselves to be taken alive, and this calamity diminished greatly the lustre of the Spartan arms. A modern army, surrounded with an overwhelming force, against which all resistance was madness, would have done the same as the Spartans. But it was a sad blow to them. Cleon, within twenty days of his departure, arrived at Athens with his three hundred Lacedæmonian prisoners, amid universal shouts of joy, for it was the most triumphant success which the Athenians had yet obtained. The war was prosecuted with renewed vigor, and the Lacedæmonians again made advances for peace, but without effect. The flushed victors would hear of no terms but what were disgraceful to the Spartans. The chances were now most favorable to Athens. Nicias invaded the Corinthian territory with eighty triremes, two thousand hoplites, and two hundred horsemen, to say nothing of the large number which supported these, and committed the same ravages that the Spartans and their allies had inflicted upon Attica.

Surrender of Sphacteria.

Triumph of the Athenians.

Who refuse all overtures of peace.

Among other events, the Athenians this year captured the Persian embassador, Artaphernes, on his way to Sparta. He was brought to Athens, and his dispatches were translated and made public. He was sent back to Ephesus, with Athenian envoys, to the great king, to counteract the influence of the Spartans, but Artaerxes had died when they reached Susa.

Situation of Athens in eighth year of the war.

The capture of Sphacteria, and the surrender of the whole Lacedæmonian fleet, not only placed Athens, on the opening of the eighth year of the war, in a situation more commanding than she had previously enjoyed, but stimulated her to renewed operations on a grander scale, not merely against Sparta, but to recover the ascendency in Bœotia, which was held before the thirty years' truce. The Lacedæmonians, in concert with the revolted Chalcidic allies of Athens in Thrace, and Perdiccas, king of Macedonia, also made great preparations for more decisive measures. The war had dragged out seven years, and nothing was accomplished which seriously weakened either of the contending parties.

The first movement was made by the Athenians on the Laconian coast. The island of Cythera was captured by an expedition led by Nicias, of sixty triremes and two thousand hoplites, beside other forces, and the coast was ravaged. Then Thyrea, an Æginetan settlement, between Laconia and Argolis, fell into the hands of the Athenians, and all the Æginetans were either killed in the assault, or put to death as prisoners. These successive disasters alarmed the Lacedæmonians, and they now began to fear repeated assaults on their own territory, with a discontented population of Helots. This fear prompted an act of cruelty and treachery which had no parallel in the history of the war. Two thousand of the bravest Helots were entrapped, as if especial honors were to be bestowed upon them, and barbarously slain. None but the five ephors knew the bloody details. There was even no public examination of this savage inhumanity, which shows that Sparta was governed, as Venice was in the Middle Ages, by a small but exceedingly powerful oligarchy.

Despair of the Lacedæmonians and slaughter of the Helots.

After this cruelty was consummated, envoys came from Perdiccas and the Chalcidians of Thrace, invoking aid against Athens. It was joyfully granted, and Brasidas, at the request of Perdiccas and the Chalcidians, was sent with a large force of Peloponnesian hoplites.

Meanwhile the Athenians formed plans to attack Megara, whose inhabitants had stimulated the war, and had been the greatest sufferers by it. A force was sent under Hippocrates and Demosthenes to surprise the place, and also Nisæa. The long walls of Megara, similar to those of Athens, were taken by surprise, and the Athenians found themselves at the gates of the city, which came near falling into their hands by treachery. Baffled for the moment, the Athenians attacked Clisaca, which lay behind it, and succeeded.

Attack of Megara.

But Brasidas, the Lacedæmonian general, learning that the long walls had fallen into the hands of the Athenians, got together a large force of six thousand hoplites and six hundred cavalry, and relieved Megara, and the Athenians were obliged to retire. Ultimately the Megarians regained possession of the long walls, and instituted an oligarchal government.

Relieved by Brasidas.

The Athenians, disappointed in getting possession of Megara, which failed by one of those accidents ever recurring in war, organized a large force for the attack of Bœotia, on three sides, under Hippocrates and Demosthenes. The attack was first made at Siphac, by Demosthenes, on the Corinthian Gulf, but failed. In spite of this failure by sea, Hippocrates marched with a land force to Delium, with seven thousand hoplites, and twenty-five thousand other troops, and occupied the place, which was a temple consecrated to Apollo, and strongly fortified it. When the work of fortification was completed, the army prepared to return to Athens.

Occupation of Delium by the Athenians.

Forces from all parts of Bœotia rallied, and met the Athenians. Among the forces of the Bœotians was the famous Theban band of three hundred select warriors, accustomed to fight in pairs, each man attached to his companion by peculiar ties of friendship. At Delium was fought the great battle of the war, in which the Athenians were routed, and the general, Hippocrates, with a thousand hoplites, were slain. The victors refused the Athenians the sacred right of burying their dead, unless they retired altogether from Delium—the post they had fortified on Bœotian territory. To this the Athenians refused to submit, the consequence of which was the siege and capture of Delium.

Battle of Delium.

Among the hoplites who fought in this unfortunate battle, which was a great discouragement to the Athenian cause, was the philosopher Socrates. The famous Alcibiades also served in the cavalry, and helped to protect Socrates in his retreat, after having bravely fought.

Diasters of the Athenians in Thrace.

The disasters of the Athenians in Thrace were yet more considerable. Brasidas, with a large force, including seventeen hundred hoplites, rapidly marched through Thrace and Thessaly, and arrived in Macedonia safely, and attacked Acanthus, an ally of Athens. It fell into his hands, as well as Stageirus, and he was thus enabled to lay plans for the acquisition of Amphipolis, which was founded by Athenian colonists. He soon became master of the surrounding territory. He then offered favorable terms of capitulation to the citizens of the town, which were accepted, and the city surrendered—the most important of all the foreign possessions of Athens. The bridge over the Strymon was also opened, by which all the eastern allies of Athens were approachable by land. This great reverse sent dismay into the hearts of the Athenians, greater than had before been felt. The bloody victory at Delium, and the conquests of Brasidas, more than balanced the capture of Sphacteria. Sparta, under the victorious banner of Brasidas, a general of great probity, good faith, and moderation, now proclaimed herself liberator of Greece. Athens, discouraged and baffled, lost all the prestige she had gained.

Successes of Brasidas.

But Amphipolis was lost by the negligence of the Athenian commanders. Eucles and Thucydides, the historian, to whom the defense of the place was intrusted, had means ample to prevent the capture had they employed ordinary precaution. The Athenians, indignant, banished Thucydides for twenty years, and probably Eucles also—a just sentence, since they did not keep the bridge over the Strymon properly guarded, nor retained the Athenian squadron at Eion. The banishment of Thucydides gave him leisure to write the history on which his great fame rests—the most able and philosophical of all the historical works of antiquity.

Loss of Amphipolis.

Brasidas, after the fall of Amphipolis, extended his military operations with success. He took Torone, Lecythus, and other places, and then went into winter quarters. The campaign had been disastrous to the Athenians, and a truce of one year was agreed upon by the belligerent parties—Athens of the one party, and Sparta, Corinth, Sicyon, Epidaurus, and Megara, of the other.

Truce of one year.

The conditions of this truce stipulated that Delphi might be visited by all Greeks, without distinction; that all violations of the property of the Delphian god should be promptly punished; that the Athenian garrisons at Pylus, Cythera, Nisæa, and Methana, should remain unmolested; that the Lacedæmonians should be free to use the sea for trading purposes; and that neither side should receive deserters from the other—important to both parties, since Athens feared the revolt of subject allies, and Sparta the desertion of Helots.

Its conditions.

But two days had elapsed after the treaty was made before Scione in Thrace revolted to Brasidas—a great cause of exasperation to the Athenians, although the revolt took place before the treaty was known. Mendes, a neighboring town, also revolted. Brasidas sent the inhabitants a garrison to protect themselves, and departed with his forces for an expedition into the interior of Macedonia, but was soon compelled to retreat before the Illyrians.

An Athenian force, under Nicias and Nicostratus, however, proceeded to Thrace to recover the revolted cities. Everywhere else the truce was observed. It was intended to give terms for more complete negotiations. This was the policy of Nicias. But Cleon and his party, the democracy, was opposed to peace, and wished to prosecute the war vigorously in Thrace. Brasidas, on his part, was equally in favor of continued hostilities. And this was the great question of the day in Greece.

Both Cleon and Brasidas opposed to the truce.

The war party triumphed, and Cleon, by no means an able general, was sent with an expedition to recover Amphipolis, B. C. 422. He succeeded in taking Torone, but Amphipolis, built on a hill in the peninsula formed by the river Strymon, as it passes from the Strymonic Gulf to Lake Kerkernilis, was a strongly fortified place in which Brasidas intrenched. He was obliged to remain inactive at Eion, at the mouth of the river, three miles distant from Amphipolis, which excited great discontent in his army, but which was the wiser course, until his auxiliaries arrived. But the murmur of the hoplites compelled him to some sort of action, and while he was reconnoitering, he was attacked by Brasidas. Cleon was killed, and his army totally defeated. Brasidas, the ablest general of the day, however, was also mortally wounded, and carried from the field. This unsuccessful battle compelled the Athenians to return home, deeply disgusted with their generals. But they embarked in the enterprise reluctantly, and with no faith in their leader, and this was one cause of their defeat. The death of Brasidas, however, converted the defeat into a substantial victory, since there remained no Spartan with sufficient ability to secure the confidence of the allies. Brasidas, when he died, was the first man in Greece, and universally admired for his valor, intelligence, probity, and magnanimity.

Death of Cleon and of Brasidas.

The battle of Amphipolis was decisive; it led to a peace between the contending parties. It is called the peace of Nicias, made in March, B. C. 421. By the provisions of this treaty of peace, which was made

Consequences of the battle of Amphipolis.

for fifty years, Amphipolis was restored to the Athenians, all persons had full liberty to visit the public temples of Greece, the Athenians restored the captive Spartans, and the various towns taken during the war were restored on both sides. This peace was concluded after a ten years' war, when the resources of both parties were exhausted. It was a war of ambition and jealousy, without sufficient reasons, and its consequences were disastrous to the general welfare of Greece. In some respects it must be considered, not merely as a war between Sparta and Athens to gain supremacy, but a war between the partisans of aristocratic and democratic institutions throughout the various States.

The peace of Nicias.

The peace made by Nicias between Athens and Sparta for fifty years was not of long continuance. It was a truce rather than a treaty, since neither party was overthrown—but merely crippled—like Rome and Carthage after the first Punic war. The same causes which provoked the contest still remained—an unextinguishable jealousy between States nearly equal in power, and the desire of ascendency at any cost. But we do not perceive in either party that persistent and self-sacrificing spirit which marked the Romans in their conquest of Italy. The Romans abandoned every thing which interfered with their aggressive policy: the Grecian States were diverted from political aggrandizement by other objects of pursuit—pleasure, art, wealth.

Causes of the war still continued.

There was needed only a commanding demagogue, popular, brilliant, and unprincipled, to embroil Greece once more in war, and such a man was Alcibiades, who appeared upon the stage at the death of Cleon. And hostilities were easily kindled, since the allies on both sides were averse to the treaty which had been made, and the conditions of the peace were not fulfilled. Athens returned the captive Spartans she had held since the battle of Sphacteria, but Amphipolis was not restored, from the continued enmity of the Thracian cities. Both parties were full of intrigues,

Alcibiades.

and new combinations were constantly being formed. Argos became the centre of a new Peloponnesian alliance. A change of ephors at Sparta favored hostile measures, and an alliance was made between the Bœotians and Lacedæmonians. The Athenians, on their side, captured Scione, and put to death the prisoners.

Character of Alcibiades.

It was in this unsettled state of things, when all the late contending States were insincere and vacillating, that Alcibiades stood forth as a party leader. He was thirty-one years of age, belonged to an ancient and powerful family, possessed vast wealth, had great personal beauty and attractive manners, but above all, was unboundedly ambitious, and grossly immoral — the most insolent, unprincipled, licentious, and selfish man that had thus far scandalized and adorned Athenian society. The only redeeming feature in his character was his friendship for Socrates, who, it seems, fascinated him by his talk, and sought to improve his morals. He had those brilliant qualities, and luxurious habits, and ostentatious prodigality, which so often dazzle superficial people, especially young men of fashion and wealth, but more even than they, the idolatrous rabble. So great was his popularity and social prestige, that no injured person ever dared to bring him to trial, and he even rescued his own wife from the hands of the law when she sought to procure a divorce—a proof that even in democratic Athens all bowed down to the insolence of wealth and high social position.

His intellectual training under Socrates.

Alcibiades, though luxurious and profligate, saw that a severe intellectual training was necessary to him if he would take rank as a politician, for a politician who can not make a speech stands a poor chance of popular favor. So he sought the instructions of Socrates, Prodicus, Protagoras, and others—not for love of learning, but as means of success, although it may be supposed that the intellectual excitement, which the discourse, cross-examination, and ironical sallies of Socrates produced, was not without its force on so bright a mind.

Alcibiades commenced his public life with a sullied reputation, and with numerous enemies created by his unbearable insolence, but with a flexibility of character which enabled him to adapt himself to whatever habits circumstances required. He inspired no confidence, and his extravagant mode of life was sure to end in ruin, unless he reimbursed himself out of the public funds; and yet he fascinated the people who mistrusted and hated him. The great comic poet, Aristophanes, said of him to the Athenians: "You ought not to keep a lion's whelp in your city at all, but if you choose to keep him, you must submit to his behavior."

His abandoned habits.

Alcibiades, in commencing his political life, departed from his family traditions; for he was a relative of Pericles, and became a partisan of the oligarchal party. But he soon changed his politics, on receiving a repulse from the Spartans, who despised him, and he became a violent democrat. His first memorable effort was to bring Argos, then in league with Sparta, into alliance with Athens, in which he was successful. He then cheated the Lacedæmonian envoys who were sent to protest against the alliance and make other terms, and put them in a false position, and made them appear deceitful, and thus arrayed against them the wrath of the Athenians. As Alcibiades had prevailed upon these envoys, by false promises and advice, to act a part different from what they were sent to perform, Nicias was sent to Sparta to clear up embarrassments, but failed in his object, upon which Athens concluded an alliance with Argos, Elis, and Mantinea, which only tended to complicate existing difficulties.

His intrigues.

Shortly after this alliance was concluded, the Olympic games were celebrated with unusual interest, from which the Athenians had been excluded during the war. Here Alcibiades appeared with seven chariots, each with four horses, when the richest Greeks had hitherto possessed but one, and gained two prizes. He celebrated his success by a magnificent banquet more stately and expensive than those given by kings. But while the Athenians thus

His extravagance at the Olympic games.

appeared at the ninetieth Olympiad, the Lacedæmonians were excluded by the Eleians, who controlled the festival, from an alleged violation of the Olympic truce, but really from the intrigues of Alcibiades.

Renewal of hostilities.

The subsequent attack of Argos and Athens on Epidaurus proved that the peace between Athens and Sparta existed only in name. It was distinctly violated by the attack of Argos by the Lacedæmonians, Bœotians, and Corinthians, and the battle of Mantinea opened again the war. This was decided in favor of the Lacedæmonians, with a great loss to the Athenians and their allies, including both their generals, Laches and Nicostratus.

Effect of the battle of Mantinea.

The moral effect of the battle of Mantinea, B. C. 418, was overwhelming throughout Greece, and re-established the military prestige of Sparta. It was lost by the withdrawal of three thousand Eleians before the battle, illustrating the remark of Pericles that numerous and equal allies could never be kept in harmonious co-operation. One effect of the battle was a renewed alliance between Sparta and Argos, and the re-establishment of an oligarchal government in the latter city. Mantinea submitted to Sparta, and the Achaian towns were obliged to submit to a remodeling of their political institutions, according to the views of Sparta. The people of Argos, however, took the first occasion which was presented for regaining their power, assisted by an Athenian force under Alcibiades, and Argos once again became an ally of Athens.

Siege of Melos.

The next important operation of the war was the siege and conquest of Melos, a Dorian island, by the Athenians, B. C. 416. The inhabitants were killed, and the women and children were sold as slaves, and an Athenian colony was settled on the island. But this massacre, exceeding even the customary cruelty of war in those times, raised a general indignation among the allies of Sparta.

The invasion of Sicily.

But an expedition of far greater importance was now undertaken by the Athenians—the most gigantic effort which they ever made, but which terminated disastrously, and led to the ruin and subjugation of their proud and warlike city, as a political power. This was the invasion of Sicily and siege of Syracuse.

Before we present this unfortunate expedition, some brief notice is necessary of the Grecian colonies in Sicily.

The Grecian colonies in Sicily.

In the eighth century before Christ Sicily was inhabited by two distinct races of barbarians—the Sikels and Sikans—besides Phœnician colonies, for purposes of trade. The Sikans were an Iberian tribe, and were immigrants of an earlier date than the Sikels, by whom they were invaded. The earliest Grecian colony was (B. C. 735) at Naxos, on the eastern coast of the island, between the Straits of Messina and Mount Ætna, founded by Theocles, a Chalcidian mariner, who was cast by storms upon the coast, and built a fort on a hill called Taurus, to defend himself against the Sikels, who were in possession of the larger half of the island. Other colonists followed, chiefly from the Peloponnesus. In the year following that Naxos was founded, a body of settlers from Corinth landed on the islet Ortygia, expelled the Sikel inhabitants, and laid the foundation of Syracuse. Successive settlements were made forty-five years after at Gela, in the southwestern part of the island. Other settlements continued to be made, not only from Greece, but from the colonies themselves; so that the old inhabitants were gradually Hellenized and merged with Greek colonists, while the Greeks, in their turn, adopted many of the habits and customs of the Sikels and Sikans. The various races lived on terms of amity, for the native population was not numerous enough to become formidable to the Grecian colonists.

Syracuse.

Agrigentum and Gela.

Five hundred years before Christ the most powerful Grecian cities in Sicily were Agrigentum and Gela, on the south side of the island. The former, within a few years of its foundation, B. C. 570, fell under the dominion of one of its rich citizens, Phalasaris, who proved a cruel despot, but after a reign of sixteen years he was killed in an insurrection, and an oligarchal government was established, such as then existed in most of the Grecian cities. Syracuse was governed in this way by the descendants of the original settlers. Gela was, on the other hand, ruled by a despot called Gelo, the most powerful man on the island. He got possession of Syracuse, B. C. 485, and transferred the seat of his power to this city, by bringing thither the leading people and making slaves of the rest. Under Gelo Syracuse became the first city on the island, to which other towns were tributary. When the Greeks confederated against Xerxes, they sent to solicit his aid as the imperial leader of Sicily, and he could command, according to Herodotus, twenty thousand hoplites, two hundred triremes, two thousand cavalry, two thousand archers, and two thousand light-armed horse. So great was then the power of this despot, who now sought to expel the Carthaginians and unite all the Hellenic colonies in Sicily under his sway. But the aid was not given, probably on account of a Carthaginian invasion simultaneous with the expedition of the Persian king. The Carthaginians, according to the historian, arrived at Panormus B. C. 480, with a fleet of three thousand ships and a land force of three hundred thousand men, besides chariots and horses, under Hamilcar—a mercenary army, composed of various African nations. Gelo marched against him with fifty thousand foot and five thousand horse, and gained a complete victory, so that one hundred and fifty thousand, on the side of the Carthaginians, were slain, together with their general. The number of the combatants is doubtless exaggerated, but we may believe that the force was very great. Gelo was now supreme in Sicily, and the victory of Himera, which he had gained, enabled him to distribute a large body of prisoners, as slaves, in all the Grecian colonies. It appears that he was much respected, but he died shortly after his victory, leaving an infant son to the guardianship of two of his brothers, Polyzelus and Hiero, who became the supreme governors of the island. A victory gained by Hiero over the tyrant of Agrigentum gave him the same

The reign of Gelo.

His power in Sicily.

His successor Hiero.

supremacy which Gelo had enjoyed. On his death, B. C. 467, the succession was disputed between his brother, Thrasybulus, and his nephew, the son of Gelo; but Thrasybulus contrived to make away with his nephew, and reigned alone, cruelly and despotically, until a revolution took place which resulted in his expulsion and the fall of the Gelonian dynasty. Popular governments were now established in all the Sicilian cities, but these were distracted by disputes and confusions. Syracuse became isolated from the other cities, and a government whose powers were limited by the city. The expulsion of the Gelonian dynasty left the Grecian cities to reorganize free and constitutional governments; but Syracuse maintained a proud pre-eminence, and her power was increased from time to time by conquests in the interior over the old population. Agrigentum was next in power, and scarcely inferior in wealth. The temple of Zeus, in this city, was one of the most magnificent in the world. The population was large, and many were the rich men who kept chariots and competed at the Olympic games. In these Sicilian cities the intellectual improvement kept pace with the material, and the little town of Elea supported the two greatest speculative philosophers of Greece—Parmenides and Zeno. Empedocles, of Agrigentum, was scarcely less famous.

Grandeur of Syracuse.

Such was the state of the Sicilian cities on the outbreak of the Peloponnesian war. Being generally of Dorian origin, they sympathized with Sparta, and great expectations were formed by the Lacedæmonians of assistance from their Sicilian allies. The cities of Sicily could not behold the contest between Athens and Sparta without being drawn into the quarrel, and the result was that the Dorian cities made war on the Ionian cities, which, of course, sympathized with Athens. As these cities were weaker than the Dorian, they solicited aid from Athens, and an expedition was sent to Sicily under Laches, B. C. 426. Another one, under Polydorus, followed, but without decisive results. The next year still another and larger expedi-

The Dorian cities of Sicily make war on the Ionian.

tion, under Eurymedon and Sophocles, arrived in Sicily, while Athens was jubilant by the possession of the Spartan prisoners, and the possession of Pylus and Cythera. The Sicilian cities now fearing that their domestic strife would endanger their independence and make them subject to Athens, the most ambitious and powerful State in Greece, made a common league with each other. Eurymedon acceded to the peace and returned to Athens, much to the displeasure of the war party, which embraced most of the people, and he and his colleague were banished.

Intervention of Athens.

But wars between the Sicilian cities again led to the intervention of Athens. Egesta especially sent envoys for help in her struggle against Selinus, which was assisted by Syracuse. Alcibiades warmly seconded these envoys, and inflamed the people with his ambitious projects. He, more than any other man, was the cause of the great Sicilian expedition which proved the ruin of his country. He was opposed by Nicias, who foretold all the miserable consequences of so distant an expedition, when so little could be gained and so much would be jeopardized, and when, on the first reverse, the enemies of Athens would rally against her. He particularly cautioned his countrymen not only against the expedition, but against intrusting the command of it to an unprincipled and selfish man who squandered his own patrimony in chariot races and other extravagances, and would be wasteful of the public property—a man without the experience which became a leader in so great an enterprise. Alcibiades, in reply, justified his extravagance at the Olympic games, where he contested with seven chariots, as a means to impress Sparta with the wealth and power of Athens, after a ten years' war. He inflamed the ambition of the assembly, held out specious hopes of a glorious conquest which would add to Athenian power, and make her not merely pre-eminent, but dominant in Greece. The assembly, eager for war and glory, sided with the youthful and magnificent demagogue, and disre-

Opposed by Nicias, but favored by Alcibiades.

garded the counsels of the old patriot, whose wisdom and experience were second to none in the city.

Consequently the expedition was fitted out for the attack of Syracuse—the largest and most powerful which Athens ever sent against an enemy; for all classes, maddened by military glory, or tempted by love of gain, eagerly embarked in the enterprise. Nicias, finding he could not prevent the expedition, demanded more than he thought the people would be willing to grant. He proposed a gigantic force. But in proposing this force, he hoped he might thus discourage the Athenians altogether by the very greatness of the armament which he deemed necessary. But so popular was the enterprise, that the large force he suggested was voted. Alcibiades had flattered the people that their city was mistress of the sea, and entitled to dominion over all the islands, and could easily prevail over any naval enemy.

Athenian expedition against Syracuse.

Three years had now elapsed since the peace of Nicias, and Athens had ample means. The treasury was full, and triremes had accumulated in the harbor. The confidence of the Athenians was as unbounded as was that of Xerxes when he crossed the Hellespont, and hence there had been great zeal and forwardness in preparation.

Self-confidence of the Athenians.

When the expedition was at last ready, an event occurred which filled the city with gloom and anxious forebodings. The half statues of the god Hermes were distributed in great numbers in Athens in the most conspicuous situations, beside the doors of private houses and temples, and in the agora, so that the people were accustomed to regard the god as domiciled among them for their protection. In one night, at the end of May, B. C. 415, these statues were nearly all mutilated. The heads, necks, and busts were all destroyed, leaving the lower part of them—mere quadrangular pillars, without arms, or legs, or body—alone standing. The sacrilege sent universal dismay into the city, and was regarded as a most depressing omen,

Unfavorable auguries.

and was done, doubtless, with a view of ruining Alcibiades and frustrating the expedition. But all efforts were vain to discover the guilty parties.

Alcibiades accused of divulging the Eleusinian mysteries.

And this was not the only means adopted to break down the power of a man whom the more discerning perceived was the evil genius of Athens. Alcibiades was publicly accused of having profaned and divulged the Eleusinian mysteries. The charge was denied by Alcibiades, who demanded an immediate trial. It was eluded by his enemies, who preferred to have the charge hanging over his head, in case of the failure of the enterprise which he had projected.

Sailing of the Athenian fleet.

So the fleet sailed from Piræus amid mingled sentiments of anxiety and popular enthusiasm. It consisted of one hundred triremes, with a large body of hoplites. It made straight for Corcyra, where the contingents of the allies were assembled, which nearly doubled its force. The Syracusans were well informed as to its destination, and made great exertions to meet this great armament, under Nicias, Alcibiades, and Lamachus. The latter commander recommended an immediate attack of Syracuse, as unprepared and dismayed.

Alcibiades wished first to open negotiations with the Sikels, of the interior, to detach them from the aid of Syracuse. His plan was followed, but before he could carry it into operation he was summoned home to take his trial.

Escape of Alcibiades to Sparta.

Fearing the result of the accusations against him, for, in his absence, the popular feeling had changed respecting him—fear and reason had triumphed over the power of his personal fascination—Alcibiades made his escape to the Peloponnesus.

Nicias commands the expedition.

The master spirit of the expedition was now removed, and its operations were languid and undecided, for Nicias had no heart in it. The delays which occurred gave the Syracusans time to prepare, and more confidence in their means of defense. So that when the forces of the Athenians were landed in the great harbor, they found a powerful army ready to resist them. In spite of a victory which Nicias gained near Olympeion, the Syracusans were not dejected, and the Athenian fleet was obliged to seek winter quarters at Catana, and also send for additional re-enforcements. Nicias unwisely delayed, but his inexcusable apathy afforded the enemy leisure to enlarge their fortifications. The Syracusans constructed an entirely new wall around the inner and outer city, and which also extended across the whole space from the outer sea to the great harbor, so that it would be difficult for the Athenians, in the coming siege, to draw lines of circumvallation around the city. Syracuse also sent envoys to Corinth and Sparta for aid, while Alcibiades, filled now with intense hatred of Athens, encouraged the Lacedæmonians to send a force to the Sicilian capital. He admitted that it was the design of Athens first to conquer the Sicilian Greeks, and then the Italian Greeks; then to make an attempt on Carthage, and then, if that was successful, to bring together all the forces of the subjected States and attack the Peloponnesus itself, and create a great empire, of which Athens was to be the capital. Such an avowal was doubtless the aim of the ambitious Alcibiades when he first stimulated the enterprise, which, if successful, would have made him the most powerful man in Greece; but he was thwarted by his enemies at home, and so he turned all his energies against his native State. His address made a powerful effect on the Lacedæmonians, who, impelled by hatred and jealousy, now resolved to make use of the services of the traitor, and send an auxiliary force to Syracuse.

Rebellion and treason of Alcibiades.

That city then consisted of two parts—an inner and an outer city. The outer city was defended on two sides by the sea, and a sea wall. On the land side a long wall extended from the sea to the fortified high land of Achradina, so that the city could only be taken by a wall of circumvallation, so as to cut off supplies by land; at the same time it was blockaded by sea. But the delay of Nicias had enabled the Syracusans to construct a new wall,

Situation of Syracuse.

covering both the outer and inner city, and extending from the great port to the high land near the bay of Magnesi, so that any attack, except from a single point, was difficult, unless the wall of circumvallation was made much larger than was originally intended. Amid incredible difficulties the Athenians constructed their works, and in an assault from the cliff of Epipolæ, where they were intrenched, their general, Lamachus, was slain. But the Athenians had gained an advantage, and the siege was being successfully prosecuted. It was then that the Lacedæmonians arrived under Gylippus, who was unable to render succor. But Nicias, despising him, allowed him to land at Himera, from whence he marched across Sicily to Syracuse. A Corinthian fleet, under Gorgylus, arrived only just in time to prevent the city from capitulating, and Gylippus entered Syracuse unopposed. The inaction of Nicias, who could have prevented this, is unaccountable. But the arrival of Gylippus turned the scale, and he immediately prosecuted vigorous and aggressive measures. He surprised an Athenian fort, and began to construct a third counter-wall on the north side of the Athenian circle. The Athenians, now shut up within their lines, were obliged to accept battle, and were defeated, and even forced to seek shelter within their fortified lines. Under this discouragement, Nicias sent to Athens for another armament, and the Athenians responded to his call. But Sparta also resolved to send re-enforcements, and invade Attica besides. Sicilian forces also marched in aid of Syracuse. The result of all these gathering forces, in which the whole strength of Greece was employed, was the total defeat of the Athenian fleet in the Great Harbor, in spite of the powerful fleet which had sailed from Athens under Demosthenes. The Syracusans pursued their advantage by blocking up the harbor, and inclosing the whole Athenian fleet. The Athenians resolved then to force their way out, which led to another general engagement, in which the Athenians were totally defeated. Nicias once again attempted to force his way out,

Inaction of Nicias.

Athenian fleet inclosed by the Syracusans.

with the remainder of his defeated fleet, but the armament was too much discouraged to obey, and the Athenians sought to retreat by land. But all the roads were blockaded. The miserable army, nevertheless, began its hopeless march completely demoralized, and compelled to abandon the sick and wounded. The retreating army was harassed on every side, no progress could be made, and the discouraged army sought in the night to retreat by a different route. The rear division, under Demosthenes, was overtaken and forced to surrender, and were carried captives to Syracuse—some six thousand in number. The next day, the first division, under Nicias, also was overtaken and made prisoners. No less than forty thousand who had started from the Athenian camp, six days before, were either killed or made prisoners, with the two generals who commanded them. The prisoners at first were subjected to the most cruel and inhuman treatment, and then sold as slaves. Both Nicias and Demosthenes were put to death, B. C. 413.

Retreat of Athenians.

Such was the disastrous close of the Sicilian expedition. Our limits prevent an extended notice. We can only give the barren outline. But never in Grecian history had so large a force been arrayed against a foreign power, and never was ruin more complete. The enterprise was started at the instance of Alcibiades. It was he who brought this disaster on his country. But it would have been better to have left the expedition to his management. Nicias was a lofty and religious man, but was no general. He grossly mismanaged from first to last. The confidence of the Athenians was misplaced; and he, after having spent his life in inculcating a conservative policy, which was the wiser, yet became the unwilling instrument of untold and unparalleled calamities. His fault was over-confidence. He was personally brave, religious, incorruptible, munificent, affable—in all respects honorable and respectable, but he had no military genius.

Mismanagement of Nicias.

The Lacedæmonians, at the suggestion of Alcibiades, had permanently occupied Decelea—a fortified post within fifteen miles of Athens, and instead of spending a few weeks in ravaging Attica, now intrenched themselves, and issued out in excursions until they had destroyed all that was valuable in the neighborhood of Athens. The great calamities which the Athenians had suffered prevented them from expelling the invaders, and the city itself was now in the condition of a post besieged. All the accumulations in her treasury were exhausted, and she was compelled to dismiss even her Thracian mercenaries. They were sent back to their own country under Dotrephes; but after inflicting great atrocities in Bœotia, were driven back by the Thebans.

Exhaustion of Athens.

The Athenian navy was now so crippled that it could no longer maintain the supremacy of the sea. The Corinthians were formidable rivals and enemies. A naval battle at Naupactus, at the mouth of the Corinthian Gulf, between the Athenians and Corinthians, though indecisive, yet really was to the advantage of the latter.

The Athenian navy hopelessly crippled.

The full effects of the terrible catastrophe at Syracuse were not at first made known to the Athenians, but gradually a settled despair overspread the public mind. The supremacy of Athens in Greece was at an end, and the city itself was endangered. The inhabitants now put forth all the energies that a forlorn hope allowed. The distant garrisons were recalled; all expenses were curtailed; timber was collected for new ships, and Cape Sunium was fortified. But the enemies of Athens were also stimulated to renewed exertions, and subject-allies were induced to revolt. Persia sent envoys to Sparta. The Eubœans and Chians applied to the same power for aid in shaking off the yoke of Athens now broken and defenseless. Although a Peloponnesian fleet was defeated by the Athenians on its way to assist Chios in revolt, yet new dangers multiplied. The infamous Alcibiades crossed with a squadron to Chios, and the Athenians were obliged to make use of their reserved fund of one thousand talents, which Peri-

Effects of the disastrous expedition against Syracuse.

cles had set aside for the last extremity, in order to equip a fleet, under the command of Strombichides. Alcibiades passed over to Miletus, and induced this city also to revolt. A shameful treaty was made between Sparta and Persia to carry on war against Athens; and the first step in the execution of the treaty was to hand Miletus over to a Persian general. Ionia now became the seat of war, and a victory was gained near Miletus by the Athenians, but this was balanced by the capture of Iasus by the Lacedæmonians. The Athenians rallied at Samos, which remained faithful, and still controlled one hundred and twenty-eight triremes at this island. Alternate successes and defeats happened to the contending parties, with no decided result.

The Athenians compelled to make use of their reserved fund.

The want of success on the coast of Asia led the Lacedæmonians to suspect Alcibiades of treachery. Moreover, his intrigue with the wife of Agis made the king of Sparta his relentless enemy. Agis accordingly procured a decision of the ephors to send out instructions for his death. He was warned in time, and made his escape to the satrap Tissaphernes, who commanded the forces of Persia. He persuaded the Persian not to give a decisive superiority to either of the contending parties, who followed his advice, and kept the Peloponnesian fleet inactive, and bribed the Spartan general. Having now gratified his revenge against Athens and lost the support of Sparta, Alcibiades now looked to his native country as the best field for his unprincipled ambition. "He opened negotiations with the Athenian commanders at Samos, and offered the alliance of Persia as the price of his restoration, but proposed as a further condition the overthrow of the democratic government at Athens."

Escape of Alcibiades from Sparta.

Then followed the political revolution which Alcibiades had planned, in conjunction with oligarchal conspirators. The rally of the city, threatened with complete ruin, had been energetic and astonishing, and she was now, a year after the disaster at Syracuse, able to carry

Popular revolution in Athens.

on a purely defensive system, though with crippled resources. But for this revolution Athens might have secured her independence.

The proposal of Alcibiades to change the constitution was listened to by the rich men, on whom the chief burden of the war had fallen. With the treasures of Persia to help them, they hoped to carry on the war against Sparta without cost to themselves. It was hence resolved at Samos, among the Athenians congregated there, to send a deputation to Athens, under Pisander, to carry out their designs. But they had no other security than the word of Alcibiades, that restless and unpatriotic schemer, that they would secure the assistance of Persia. And it is astonishing that such a man—so faithless—could be believed.

Restless schemes of Alcibiades.

One of the generals of the fleet at Samos, Phrynichus, strongly opposed this movement, and gave good reasons; but the tide of opinion among the oligarchal conspirators ran so violently against him, that Pisander was at once dispatched to Athens. He laid before the public assembly the terms which Alcibiades proposed. The people, eager at any cost to gain the Persian king as an ally, in their extremity listened to the proposal, though unwilling, and voted to relinquish their political power. Pisander made them believe it was a choice between utter ruin and the relinquishment of political privileges, since the Lacedæmonians had an overwhelming force against them. It was while Chios seemed likely to be recovered by the Athenians, and while the Peloponnesian fleet was paralyzed at Rhodes by Persian intrigues, that Pisander returned to Ionia to open negotiations with Alcibiades and Tissaphernes. But Alcibiades had promised too much, the satrap having no idea of lending aid to Athens, and yet he extricated himself by such exaggerated demands, which he knew the Athenians would never concede to Persia, that negotiations were broken off, and a reconciliation was made between Persia and Sparta. The oligarchal conspirators had, however, gone so far that a retreat was impossible.

Vain promises of Alcibiades.

Aid invoked from Persia.

The democracy of Athens was now subverted. Instead of the Senate of Five Hundred and the assembled people, an oligarchy of Four Hundred sat in the Senate house, and all except five thousand were disfranchised—and these were not convened. The oligarchy was in full power when Pisander returned to Athens. All democratic magistrates had been removed, and no civil functionaries were paid. The Four Hundred had complete control. Thus perished, through the intrigues of Alcibiades, the democracy of Athens. He had organized the unfortunate expedition to Sicily; he had served the bitterest enemies of his country; and now, he had succeeded in overturning the constitution which had lasted one hundred years, during which Athens had won all her glories. Why should the Athenians receive back to their confidence so bad a man? But whom God wishes to destroy, he first makes mad, and Alcibiades, it would seem, was the instrument by which Athens was humiliated and ruined as a political power. The revolution was effected in an hour of despair, and by delusive promises. The character and conduct of the insidious and unscrupulous intriguer were forgotten in his promises. The Athenians were simply cheated.

An oligarchy at Athens.

Alcibiades cheats the Athenians.

The Four Hundred, installed in power, solemnized their installation by prayer and sacrifice, put to death some political enemies, imprisoned and banished others, and ruled with great rigor and strictness. They then sought to make peace with Sparta, which was declined. The army at Samos heard of these changes with exceeding wrath, especially the cruelties which were inflicted on all citizens who spoke against the new tyranny. A democratic demonstration took place at Samos, by which the Samians and the army were united in the strongest ties, for the Samians had successfully resisted a like revolution on their island. The army at Samos refused to obey any orders from the oligarchy, and constituted a democracy by themselves. Yet the man who had been instrumental in creating this oligarchy, with characteristic

Athens seeks peace with Sparta.

Unprincipled conduct of Alcibiades.

versatility and impudence, joined the democracy at Samos. He came to Samos by invitation of the armament, and pledged himself to secure Persian aid, and he was believed and again trusted. He then launched into a new career, and professed to take up again the interests of the democracy at Athens. The envoys of the Four Hundred which were sent to Samos were indignantly sent back, and the general indignation against the oligarchy was intensified. Envoys from Argos also appeared at Samos, offering aid to the Athenian democracy. There was now a strong and organized resistance to the Four Hundred, and their own divisions placed them further in a precarious situation. Theramenes demanded that the Five Thousand, which body had been thus far nominal, should be made a reality. The Four Hundred again solicited aid from Sparta, and constructed a fort for the admission of a Spartan garrison, while a Lacedæmonian fleet hovered near the Piræus.

The long-suppressed energies of the people at length burst forth. A body of soldiers seized the fortress the oligarchy were constructing for a Spartan garrison, and demolished it.

Subversion of the oligarchy.

The Four Hundred made important concessions, and agreed to renew the public assembly. While these events occurred a naval battle took place near Eretria between the Lacedæmonians and the Athenians, in which the latter were defeated. The victory, if they had pushed their success, would have completed the ruin of Athens, since her home fleet was destroyed, and that at Samos was detained by Alcibiades. When it was seen the hostile fleet did not enter the harbor, the Athenians recovered their dismay and prosecuted their domestic revolution by deposing the Four Hundred and placing the whole government in the hands of the Five Thousand, and this body was soon enlarged to that of universal citizenship. The old constitution was restored, except that part of it which allowed pay to the judges. Most of the oligarchal leaders fled, and a few of them were tried and executed—those who had sought Spartan aid. Thus this selfish movement terminated, after

Restoration of the old constitution.

the oligarchy had enjoyed a brief reign of only a few months.

While Athens was distracted by changes of government, the war was conducted on the coasts of Asia between the belligerents with alternate success and defeat. Abydos, connected with Miletus by colonial ties, revolted from Athens, and Lampsacus, a neighboring town, followed its example two days afterward. Byzantium also went over to the Lacedæmonians, which enabled them to command the strait. Alcibiades pursued still his double game with Persia and Athens. An Athenian fleet was sent to the Hellespont to contend with the Lacedæmonian squadron, and gained an incomplete victory at Cynossema, whose only effect was to encourage the Athenians. The Persians gave substantial aid to the Lacedæmonians, withheld for a time by the intrigues of Alcibiades, who erturned to Samos, but was shortly after seized by Tissaphernes and sent to Sardis, from which he contrived to escape. He partially redeemed his infamy by a victory over the Peloponnesian fleet at Cyzicus, and captured it entirely, which disaster induced the Spartans to make overtures of peace, which were rejected through the influence of Cleophon, the demagogue.

Alternate successes and failures of the belligerents.

The Athenian fleet now reigned alone in the Propontis, the Bosphorus, and the Hellespont, and levied toll on all the ships passing through the straits, while Chrysopolis, opposite to Byzantium, was occupied by Alcibiades. Athens now once more became hopeful and energetic. Thrasyllus was sent with a large force to Ionia, and joined his forces with the fleet which Alcibiades commanded at Sestos, but the conjoined forces were unable to retake Abydos, which was relieved by Pharnabazus, the Persian satrap.

Revival of the hopes of the Athenians.

The absence of the fleet from Athens encouraged the Lacedæmonians, who retook Pylus, B. C. 409, while the Athenians captured Chalcedon, and the following year Byzantium itself. Such was the state of the

Cyrus sent to Phrygia.

contending parties when Cyrus the younger was sent by his father Darius as satrap of Lydia, Phrygia, and Cappadocia, and whose command in Asia Minor was attended by important consequences. Tissaphernes and Pharnabazus were still left in command of the coast.

Union of Cyrus with Lysander.

Cyrus, a man of great ambition and self-control, came to Asia Minor with a fixed purpose of putting down the Athenian power, which for sixty years had humbled the pride of the Persian kings. He formed a hearty and cordial alliance with Lysander, the Spartan admiral, and the most eminent man, after Brasidas, whom the Lacedæmonians had produced during the war. He was a man of severe Spartan discipline and virtue, but ambitious and cruel. He visited Cyrus at Sardis, was welcomed with every mark of favor, and induced Cyrus to grant additional pay to every Spartan seaman.

Return of Alcibiades to Athens.

His exploits.

Meanwhile Alcibiades re-entered his native city in triumph, after eight years' exile, and was welcomed by all parties as the only man who had sufficient capacity to restore the fallen fortunes of Athens. His confiscated property was restored, and he was made captain-general with ample powers, while all his treasons were apparently forgotten, which had proved so fatal to his country—the sending of Gylippus to Syracuse, the revolt of Chios and Miletus, and the conspiracy of the Four Hundred. The effect of this treatment, so much better than what he deserved, intoxicated this wayward and unprincipled, but exceedingly able man. His first exploit was to sail to Andros, now under a Lacedæmonian garrison, whose fields he devastated, but was unable to take the town. He then went to Samos, and there learned that all his intrigues with Persia had failed, and that Persia was allied still more strongly with the Lacedæmonians under Lysander.

His reverses.

This great general, now at Ephesus, pursued a cautious policy, and refused to give battle to the Athenian forces under Alcibiades, who then retired to Phocæa, leaving his fleet under the command of Antiochus, his favorite pilot. Antiochus, in the absence of his general, engaged the Lacedæmonian fleet, but was defeated and slain at Notium. The conduct of Alcibiades produced great dissaffection at Athens. He had sailed with a fleet not inferior to that which he commanded at Syracuse, and had made great promises of future achievements, yet in three months he had not gained a single success. He was therefore dismissed from his command, which was given to ten generals, of whom Conon was the most eminent, while he retired to the Chersonese. Lysander, at the same time, was superseded in the command of the Lacedæmonians by Callicratidas, in accordance with Spartan custom, his term being expired.

Lysander recalled to Sparta.

Callicratidas was not welcomed by Cyrus, and he was also left without funds by Lysander, who returned to the Persians the sums he had received. This conduct so much enraged the Spartan admiral that he sailed with his whole fleet—the largest which had been assembled during the war, one hundred and forty triremes, of which only ten were Lacedæmonian—the rest being furnished by allies—to Lesbos, and liberated the Athenian captives and garrison at Methymna, and seemed animated by that old Panhellenic patriotism which had united the Greeks half a century before against the Persian invaders, declaring that not a single Greek should be reduced to slavery if he could help it. But while he was thus actuated by these noble sentiments, he also prosecuted the war of his country, which had been intrusted to him to conduct. He blocked up the Athenian fleet at Mitylene, which had no provisions to sustain a siege. The Athenians now made prodigious efforts to relieve Conon, and one hundred and ten triremes were sent from the Piræus, and sailed to Samos. Callicratidas, apprised of the approach of the large fleet, went out to meet it. At Arginusæ was fought a great battle, in which the Spartan admiral was killed, and his forces completely defeated. Sixty-nine Lacedæmonian ships were destroyed; the Athenians lost twenty-

Vigorous measures of the Lacedæmonians.

The battle of Arginusæ.

five, a severe loss to Greece, since, if Callicratidas had gained the victory, he would, according to Grote, have closed the Peloponnesian war, and united the Greeks once more against Persia.

The battle of Arginusæ now gave the Athenians the control of the Asiatic seas, and so discouraged were the Lacedæmonians, that they were induced to make proposals of peace. This is doubted, indeed, by Grote, since no positive results accrued to Athens.

The Chians and other allies of Sparta, in conjunction with Cyrus, now sent envoys to the ephors, to request the restoration of Lysander to the command of the fleet. They acceded to the request substantially, and Lysander reached Ephesus, B. C. 405, to renovate the Lacedæmonian power and turn the fortunes of war.

Lysander returns to power.

The victorious Athenian fleet was now at Ægospotami, in the Hellespont, opposite Lampsacus, having been inactive for nearly a year. There the fleet was exposed to imminent danger, which was even seen by Alcibiades, in his forts opposite, on the Chersonese. He expostulated with the Athenian admirals, but to no purpose, and urged them to retire to Sestos. As he feared, the Athenian fleet was surprised, at anchor, on this open shore, while the crews were on shore in quest of a meal. One hundred and seventy triremes were thus ingloriously captured, without the loss of a man—the greatest calamity which had happened to Athens since the beginning of the war, and decisive as to its result. The captive generals were slaughtered, together with four thousand Athenian prisoners. Conon, however, made his escape. So disgraceful and unnecessary was this great calamity, that it is supposed the fleet was betrayed by its own commanders; and this supposition is strengthened by its inactivity since the battle of Arginusæ. This crowning disaster happened in September, B. C. 405, and caused a dismay at Athens such as had never before been felt—not even when the Persians were marching through Attica. Nothing was now

Capture of the Athenian fleet.

Despair of Athens.

left to the miserable city but to make what preparation it could for the siege, which everybody foresaw would soon take place. The walls were put in the best defense it was possible, and two of the three ports were blocked up. Not only was Athens deprived of her maritime power, but her very existence was now jeopardized.

Lysander was in no haste to march upon Athens, since he knew that no corn ships could reach the city from the Euxine, and that a famine would soon set in. The Athenian empire was annihilated, and nothing remained but Athens herself. The Athenians now saw that nothing but union between the citizens could give them any hope of success, and they made a solemn pledge in the Acropolis to bury their dissensions and cultivate harmonious feelings.

Annihilation of the Athenian empire.

In November, Lysander, with two hundred triremes, blockaded the Piræus. The whole force of Sparta, under King Pausanias, went out to meet him, and encamped at the gates of Athens. The citizens bore the calamity with fortitude, and, when they began to die of hunger, sent propositions for capitulation. But no proposition was received which did not include the demolition of the long walls which Pericles had built. As famine pressed, and the condition of the people had become intolerable, Athens was obliged to surrender on the hard conditions that the Piræus should be destroyed, the long walls demolished, all foreign possessions evacuated, all ships surrendered, and, most humiliating of all, that Athens should become the ally of Sparta, and follow her lead upon the sea and upon the land.

Surrender of Athens to the Spartans.

Thus fell imperial Athens, after a glorous reign of one hundred years. Lysander entered the city as a conqueror. The ships were surrendered, all but twelve, which the Athenians were allowed to retain; the unfinished ships in the dockyards were burned, the fortifications demolished, and the Piræus dismantled. The constitution of the city was annulled, and a board of thirty was nominated,

Fate of Athens.

under the dictation of Lysander, for the government of the city. The conqueror then sailed to Samos, which was easily reduced, and oligarchy was restored on that island, as at Athens.

Close of the war.

The fall of Athens virtually closed the Peloponnesian war, after a bitter struggle between the two leading States of Greece for thirty years. Lysander became the leading man in Greece, and wielded a power greater than any individual Greek before or after him. Sparta, personified in him, became supreme, and ruled over all the islands, and over the Asiatic and Thracian cities. The tyrants whom he placed over Athens exercised their power with extreme rigor--sending to execution all who were obnoxious, seizing as spoil the property of the citizens, and disarming the remaining hoplites in the city. They even forbade intellectual teaching, and shut the mouth of Socrates. Such was Athens, humbled, deprived of her fleet, and rendered powerless, with a Spartan garrison occupying the Acropolis, and discord reigning even among the Thirty Tyrants themselves.

Cause of the fall of Athens.

In considering the downfall of Athens, we perceive that the unfortunate Sicilian expedition which Alcibiades had stimulated proved the main cause. Her maritime supremacy might have been maintained but for this aggression, which Pericles never would have sanctioned, and which Nicias so earnestly disapproved. After that disaster, the conditions of the State were totally changed, and it was a bitter and desperate struggle to retain the fragments of empire. And the catastrophe proved, ultimately, the political ruin of Greece herself, since there was left no one State sufficiently powerful to resist foreign attacks. The glory of Athens was her navy, and this being destroyed, Greece was open to invasion, and to the corruption brought about by Persian gold. It was Athens which had resisted Persia, and protected the maritime States and islands. When Athens was crippled, the decline of the other States was rapid, for they had all exhausted themselves in the war. And the war itself has few redeeming features. It was a wicked contest carried on by rivalry and jealousy. And it produced, as war generally does, a class of unprincipled men who aggrandize themselves at the expense of their country. Nothing but war would have developed such men as Alcibiades and Lysander, and it is difficult to say which of the two brought the greatest dishonor on their respective States. Both were ambitious, and both hoped to gain an ascendency incompatible with free institutions. To my mind, Alcibiades is the worst man in Grecian history, and not only personally disgraced by the worst vices, but his influence was disastrous on his country. Athens owed her political degradation more to him than any other man. He was insolent, lawless, extravagant, and unscrupulous, from his first appearance in public life. He incited the Sicilian expedition, and caused it to end disastrously by sending Gylippus to Syracuse. He originated the revolt of Chios and Miletus, the fortification of Decelea, and the conspiracy of the Four Hundred. And though he partially redeemed his treason by his three years' services, after his exile, yet his vanity, and intrigues, and prodigality prevented him from accomplishing what he promised. It is true he was a man of great resources, and was never defeated either by sea or land; "and he was the first man in every party he espoused—Athenian, Spartan, or Persian, oligarchal or democratical, but he never inspired confidence with any party, and all parties successively threw him off." The end of such a man proclaims the avenging Nemesis in this world. He died by the hands of Persian assassins, at the instance of both Lysander and Cyrus, who felt that there could be nothing settled so long as this restless schemer lived. And he died, unlamented and unhonored, in spite of his high birth, wealth, talents, and personal accomplishments.

Miserable spirit of the war.

Alcibiades the evil genius of Athens.

His inglorious death.

Lysander was more fortunate; he gained a great ascendency in Sparta, but his ambition proved ruinous to his country, by involving it in those desperate wars which are yet to be presented.

Glory of Lysander.

CHAPTER XX.

MARCH OF CYRUS AND RETREAT OF THE TEN THOUSAND GREEKS.

Effect of the Peloponnesian war.

The Peloponnesian war being closed, a large body of Grecian soldiers were disbanded, but rendered venal and restless by the excitements and changes of the past thirty years, and ready to embark in any warlike enterprise that promised money and spoil. They were unfitted, as is usually the case, for sober and industrial pursuits. They panted for fresh adventures.

The real ends of Cyrus disguised.

This restless passion which war ever kindles, found vent and direction in the enterprise which Cyrus led from Western Asia to dethrone his brother Artaxerxes from the throne of Persia. Some fourteen thousand Greeks from different States joined his standard—not with a view of a march to Babylon and an attack on the great king, but to conquer and root out the Pisidian mountaineers, who did much mischief from their fastnesses in the southeast of Asia Minor. This was the ostensible object of Cyrus, and he found no difficulty in enlisting Grecian mercenaries, under promise of large rewards. All these Greeks were deceived but one man, to whom alone Cyrus revealed his real purpose. This was Clearchus, a Lacedæmonian general of considerable ability and experience, who had been banished for abuse of authority at Byzantium, which he commanded. He repaired to Sardis and offered his services to Cyrus, who had been sent thither by his father Darius to command the Persian forces. Cyrus accepted the overtures of Clearchus, who secured his confidence so completely that he gave him the large sum of ten thousand darics, which he employed in hiring Grecian mercenaries.

Other Greeks of note also joined the army of Cyrus with a view of being employed against the Pisidians. Among them were Aristippus and Menon, of a distinguished family in Thessaly; Proxenus, a Bœotian; Agis, an Arcadian; Socrates, an Achæan, who were employed to collect mercenaries, and who received large sums of money. A considerable body of Lacedæmonians were also taken under pay.

Mercenary Greeks enlist under Cyrus.

The march of these men to Babylon, and their successful retreat, form one of the most interesting episodes in Grecian history, and it is this march and retreat which I purpose briefly to present.

Cyrus was an extraordinary man. The younger son of the Persian king, he aimed to secure the sovereignty of Persia, which fell to his elder brother, Artaxerxes, on the death of Darius. During his residence at Sardis, as satrap or governor, he perceived and felt the great superiority of the Greeks to his own countrymen, not only intellectually, but as soldiers. He was brave, generous, frank, and ambitious. Had it been his fortune to have achieved the object of his ambition, the whole history of Persia would have been changed, and Alexander would have lived in vain. Perceiving and appreciating the great qualities of the Greeks, and learning how to influence them, he sought, by their aid, to conquer his way to the throne.

Character of Cyrus.

High estimation in which he held the Greeks.

But he dissembled his designs so that they were not suspected, even in Persia. As has been remarked, he communicated them only to the Spartan general, Clearchus. Neither Greek nor Persian divined his object as he collected a great army at Sardis. At first he employed his forces in the siege of Miletus and other enterprises, which provoked no suspicion of his real designs.

He dissembles his designs.

When all was ready, he commenced his march from Sardis, in March, B. C. 401, with about eight thousand Grecian hoplites and one hundred thousand native troops, while a joint Lacedæmonian and Persian fleet coasted around the south of Asia Minor to co-operate with the land forces.

He commences his march.

These Greeks who thus joined his standard under promise of large pay, and were unwittingly about to plunge into unknown perils, were not outcasts and paupers, but were men of position, reputation, and, in some cases, of wealth. About half of them were Arcadians. Young men of good family, ennuied of home, restless and adventurous, formed the greater part, although many of mature age had been induced by liberal offers to leave their wives and children. They simply calculated on a year's campaign in Pisidia, from which they would return to their homes enriched. So they were assured by the Greek commanders at Sardis, and so these commanders believed, for Cyrus stood high in popular estimation for liberality and good faith.

Character of the Greeks who joined his standard.

Among other illustrious Greeks that were thus to be led so far from home was Xenophon, the Athenian historian, who was induced by his friend Proxenus, of Bœotia, to join the expedition. He was of high family, and a pupil of Socrates, but embarked against the wishes and advice of his teacher.

Xenophon.

When the siege of Miletus was abandoned, and Cyrus began his march, his object was divined by the satrap Tissaphernes, who hastened to Persia to put the king on his guard.

At Celenæ, or Kelænæ, a Phrygian city, Cyrus halted and reviewed his army. Grecian re-enforcements here joined him, which swelled the number of Greeks to thirteen thousand men, of whom eleven thousand were hoplites. As this city was on the way to Pisidia, no mistrust existed as to the object of the expedition, not even when the army passed into Lycaonia, since its inhabitants were of the same predatory character as the Pisidians. But when it had crossed Mount Taurus, which bounded Cilicia, and reached

Cyrus reviews his army.

Tarsus, the Greeks perceived that they had been cheated, and refused to advance farther. Clearchus attempted to suppress the mutiny by severe measures, but failed. He then resorted to stratagem, and pretended to yield to the wishes of the Greeks, and likewise refused to march, but sent a secret dispatch to Cyrus that all would be well in the end, and requested him to send fresh invitations, that he might answer by fresh refusals. He then, with the characteristic cunning and eloquence of a Greek, made known to his countrymen the extreme peril of making Cyrus their enemy in a hostile country, where retreat was beset with so many dangers, and induced them to proceed. So the army continued its march to Issus, at the extremity of the Issican Gulf, and near the mountains which separate Cilicia from Syria. Here Cyrus was further re-enforced, making the grand total of Greeks in his army fourteen thousand.

The Greeks perceive that they have been deceived.

He expected to find the passes over the mountains, a day's journey from Issus, defended, but the Persian general Abrocomas fled at his approach, and Cyrus easily crossed into Syria by the pass of Beilan, over Mount Amanus. He then proceeded south to Myriandus, a Phœnician maritime town, where he parted from his fleet. Eight days' march brought his army to Thapsacus, on the Euphrates, where he remained five days to refresh his troops. Here again the Greeks showed a reluctance to proceed, but, on the promise of five minæ a head, nearly one hundred dollars more than a year's pay, they consented to advance. It was here Cyrus crossed the river unobstructed, and continued his march on the left bank for nine days, until he came to the river Araxes, which separates Syria from Arabia. Thus far his army was well supplied with provisions from the numerous villages through which they passed; but now he entered a desert country, entirely without cultivation, where the astonished Greeks beheld for the first time wild asses, antelopes, and ostriches. For eighteen days the army marched without other provisions than what

Cyrus crosses into Syria.

He crosses the Euphrates.

they brought with them, parched with thirst and exhausted by heat. At Pylæ they reached the cultivated territory of Babylonia, and the alluvial plains commenced. Three days' further march brought them to Cunaxa, about seventy miles from Babylon, where the army of Artaxerxes was marshaled to meet them. It was an immense force of more than a million of men, besides six thousand horse-guards and two hundred chariots. But so confident was Cyrus of the vast superiority of the Greeks and their warfare, that he did not hesitate to engage the overwhelming forces of his brother with only ten thousand Greeks and one hundred thousand Asiatics. The battle of Cunaxa was fatal to Cyrus; he was slain and his camp was pillaged. The expedition had failed.

Battle of Cunaxa.

Dismay now seized the Greeks, as well it might—a handful of men in the midst of innumerable enemies, and in the very centre of the Persian empire. But such men are not driven to despair. They refused to surrender, and made up their minds to retreat—to find their way back again to Greece, since all aggressive measures was madness.

Dismay of the Greeks.

They retreat.

This retreat, amid so many difficulties, and against such powerful and numerous enemies, is one of the most gallant actions in the history of war, and has made those ten thousand men immortal.

Ariæus, who commanded the Asiatic forces on the left wing of the army at the battle of Cunaxa, joined the Greeks with what force remained, in retreat, and promised to guide them to the Asiatic coast, not by the route which Cyrus had taken, for this was now impracticable, but by a longer one, up the course of the Tigris, through Armenia, to the Euxine Sea. The Greeks had marched ninety days from Sardis, about fourteen hundred and sixty-four English miles, and rested ninety-six days in various places. Six months had been spent on the expedition, and it would take more than that time to return, considering the new difficulties which it was necessary to surmount. The condition of the Greeks, to all appearance, was hopeless. How were they to ford rivers and cross mountains, with a hostile cavalry in their rear, without supplies, without a knowledge of roads, without trustworthy guides, through hostile territories?

Their forlorn condition.

The Persians still continued their negotiations, regarding the advance or retreat of the Greeks alike impossible, and curious to learn what motives had brought them so far from home. They replied that they had been deceived, that they had no hostility to the Persian king, that they had been ashamed to desert Cyrus in the midst of danger, and that they now desired only to return home peaceably, but were prepared to repel hostilities.

Deceitful negotiations of the Persians.

It was not pleasant to the Persian monarch to have thirteen thousand Grecian veterans, whose prestige was immense, and whose power was really formidable, in the heart of the kingdom. It was not easy to conquer such brave men, reduced to desperation, without immense losses and probable humiliation. So the Persians dissembled. It was their object to get the Greeks out of Babylonia, where they could easily intrench and support themselves, and then attack them at a disadvantage. So Tissaphernes agreed to conduct them home by a different route. They acceded to his proposal, and he led them to the banks of the Tigris, and advanced on its left bank, north to the Great Zab River, about two hundred miles from Babylon. The Persians marched in advance, and the Greeks about three miles in the rear. At the Great Zab they halted three days, and then Tissaphernes enticed the Greek generals to his tent, ostensibly to feast them and renew negotiations. There they were seized, sent prisoners to the Persian court, and treacherously murdered.

The Persian king aims at their overthrow.

Utter despair now seized the Greeks. They were deprived of their generals, in the heart of Media, with unscrupulous enemies in the rear, and the mountains of Armenia in their front, whose passes were defended

The despair of the Greeks.

by hostile barbarians, and this in the depth of winter, deprived of guides, and exposed to every kind of hardship, difficulty, and danger. They were apparently in the hands of their enemies, without any probability of escape. They were then summoned to surrender to the Persians, but they resolved to fight their way home, great as were their dangers and insurmountable the difficulties—a most heroic resolution. And their retreat, under these circumstances, to the Euxine, is the most extraordinary march in the whole history of war.

Xenophon rallies the Greeks.

But a great man appeared, in this crisis, to lead them, whose prudence, sagacity, moderation, and courage can never be sufficiently praised, and his successful retreat places him in the ranks of the great generals of the world. Xenophon, the Athenian historian, now appears upon the stage with all those noble qualities which inspired the heroes at the siege of Troy—a man as religious as he was brave and magnanimous, and eloquent even for a Greek. He summoned together the captains, and persuaded them to advance, giving the assurance of the protection of Zeus. He then convened the army, and inspired them by his spirit, with surpassing eloquence, and acquired the ascendency of a Moses by his genius, piety, and wisdom. His military rank was not great, but in such an emergency talents and virtues have more force than rank.

Their retreat to the Tigris.

So, under his leadership, the Greeks crossed the Zab, and resumed their march to the north, harassed by Persian cavalry, and subjected to great privations. The army no longer marched, as was usual, in one undivided hollow square, but in small companies, for they were obliged to cross mountains and ford rivers. So long as they marched on the banks of the Tigris, they found well-stocked villages, from which they obtained supplies; but as they entered the country of the Carducians, they were obliged to leave the Tigris to their left, and cross the high mountains which divided it from Armenia. They were also compelled to burn their baggage, for the roads were nearly impassable, not only on account of the narrow defiles, but from the vast quantities of snow which fell. Their situation was full of peril, and fatigue, and privation. Still they persevered, animated by the example and eloquence of their intrepid leader. At every new pass they were obliged to fight a battle, but the enemies they encountered could not withstand their arms in close combat, and usually fled, contented to harass them by rolling stones down the mountains on their heads, and discharging their long arrows.

Their perils and hardships.

The march through Armenia was still more difficult, for the inhabitants were more warlike and hardy, and the passage more difficult. They also were sorely troubled for lack of guides. The sufferings of the Greeks were intense from cold and privation. The beasts of burden perished in the snow, while the soldiers were frost-bitten and famished. It was their good fortune to find villages, after several days' march, where they halted and rested, but assailed all the while by hostile bands. Yet onward they pressed, wearied and hungry, through the country of the Taochi, of the Chalybes, of the Scytheni, of the Marones, of the Colchians, and reached Trapezus (Trebizond) in safety. The sight of the sea filled the Greeks with indescribable joy after so many perils, for the sea was their own element, and they could now pursue their way in ships rather than by perilous marches.

The march through Armenia.

They reach the Euxine.

But the delays were long and dreary. There were no ships to transport the warriors to Byzantium. They were exposed to new troubles from the indifference or hostility of the cities on the Euxine, for so large a force created alarm. And when the most pressing dangers were passed, the license of the men broke out, so that it was difficult to preserve order and prevent them from robbing their friends. They were obliged to resort to marauding expeditions among the Asiatic people, and it was difficult to support themselves. Not being able to get ships, they marched along the coast to Cotyora, exposed to incessant hostilities. It was now the desire of Xenophon to found a new city on

New troubles and dangers.

the Euxine with the army; but the army was eager to return home, and did not accede to the proposal. Clamors arose against the general who had led them so gloriously from the heart of Media, and his speeches in his defense are among the most eloquent on Grecian record. He remonstrated against the disorders of the army, and had sufficient influence to secure reform, and completely triumphed over faction as he had over danger.

At last ships were provided, and the army passed by sea to Sinope—a Grecian colony—where the men were hospitably received, and fed, and lodged. From thence the army passed by sea to Heracleia, where the soldiers sought to extort money against the opposition of Xenophon and Cherisophus, the latter of whom had nobly seconded the plans of Xenophon, although a Spartan of superior military rank. The army, at this opposition, divided into three factions, but on suffering new disasters, reunited. It made a halt at Calpe, where new disorders broke out. Then Cleander, Spartan governor of Byzantium, arrived with two triremes, who promised to conduct the army, and took command of it, but subsequently threw up his command from the unpropitious sacrifices. Nothing proved the religious character of the Greeks so forcibly as their scrupulous attention to the rites imposed by their pagan faith. They undertook no enterprise of importance without sacrifices to the gods, and if the auguries were unfavorable, they relinquished their most cherished objects.

They pass by sea to Sinope.

Their courage and faith.

From Calpe the army marched to Chalcedon, turning into money the slaves and plunder which it had collected. There it remained seven days. But nothing could be done without the consent of the Spartan admiral at Byzantium, Anaxibius, since the Lacedæmonians were the masters of Greece both by sea and land. This man was bribed by the Persian satrap Pharnabazus, who commanded the northwestern region of Asia Minor, to transport the army to the European side of the Bosphorus. It accordingly

They reach Byzantium.

crossed to Byzantium, but was not allowed to halt in the city, or even to enter the gates.

The wrath of the soldiers was boundless when they were thus excluded from Byzantium. They rushed into the town and took possession, which conduct gave grave apprehension to Xenophon, who mustered and harangued the army, and thus prevented anticipated violence. They at length consented to leave the city, and accepted the services of the Theban Coeratidas, who promised to conduct them to the Delta of Thrace, for purposes of plunder, but he was soon dismissed. After various misfortunes the soldiers at length were taken under the pay of Seuthes, a Thracian prince, who sought the recovery of his principality, but who cheated them out of their pay. A change of policy among the Lacedæmonians led to the conveyance of the Cyrenian army into Asia in order to make war on the satraps. Xenophon accordingly conducted his troops, now reduced to six thousand men, over Mount Ida to Pergamus. He succeeded in capturing the Persian general Asidates, and securing a valuable booty, B. C. 399. The soldiers whom he had led were now incorporated with the Lacedæmonian army in Asia, and Xenophon himself enlisted in the Spartan service. His subsequent fortunes we have not room to present. An exile from Athens, he settled in Scillus, near Olympia, with abundant wealth, but ultimately returned to his native city after the battle of Leuctra.

But are excluded from the city.

They enlist in the service of Sparta.

The impression produced on the Grecian mind by the successful retreat of the Ten Thousand was profound and lasting. Its most obvious effect was to produce contempt for Persian armies and Persian generals, and to show that Persia was only strong by employing Hellenic strength against the Hellenic cause. The real weakness of Persia was thus revealed to the Greeks, and sentiments were fostered which two generations afterward led to the expeditions of Alexander and the subjection of Asia to Grecian rule.

Moral effect of the expedition.

CHAPTER XXI.

THE LACEDÆMONIAN EMPIRE.

I HAVE already shown that Sparta, after a battle with the Argives, B. C., 547, obtained the ascendency in the southern part of the Peloponnesus, and became the leading military State of Greece. This prestige and power were not lost. The severe simplicity of Spartan life, the rigor of political and social institutions, the aristocratic form of government, and above all the military spirit and ambition, gave permanence to all conquests, so that in the Persian wars Sparta took the lead of the land forces. The great rival power of Sparta was Athens, but this was founded on maritime skill and enterprise. It was to the navy of Athens, next after the hoplites of Sparta, that the successful resistance to the empire of Persia may be attributed.

Sparta never lost her power.

After the Persian wars the rivalship between Athens and Sparta is the most prominent feature in Grecian history. The confederacy of Delos gave to Athens supremacy over the sea, and the great commercial prosperity of Athens under Pericles, and the empire gained over the Ionian colonies and the islands of the Ægæan, made Athens, perhaps, the leading State. It was the richest, the most cultivated, and the most influential of the Grecian States, and threatened to absorb gradually all the other States of Greece in her empire.

Continued glory of Athens also.

This ascendency and rapid growth in wealth and power were beheld with jealous eyes, not only by Sparta, but other States which she controlled, or with which she was in alliance. The consequence was, the Peloponnesian war, which lasted half a generation, and which, after various vicissitudes and fortunes, terminated auspiciously for Sparta, but disastrously to Greece as a united nation. The Persian wars bound all the States together by a powerful Hellenic sentiment of patriotism. The Peloponnesian war dissevered this Panhellenic tie. The disaster at Syracuse was fatal to Athenian supremacy, and even independence. But for this Athens might have remained the great power of Greece. The democratic organization of the government gave great vigor and enterprise to all the ambitious projects of Athens. If Alcibiades had lent his vast talents to the building up of his native State, even then the fortunes of Athens might have been different. But he was a traitor, and threw all his energies on the side of Sparta, until it was too late for Athens to recover the prestige she had won. He partially redeemed his honor, but had he been animated by the spirit of Pericles or Nicias, to say nothing of the self-devotion of Miltiades, he might have raised the power of Athens to a height which nothing could have resisted.

Consequences of the Peloponnesian war.

Lysander completed the war which Brasidas had so nobly carried on, and took possession of Athens, abolished the democratic constitution, demolished the walls, and set up, as his creatures, a set of tyrants, and also a Spartan governor in Athens. Under Lysander, the Lacedæmonian rule was paramount in Greece. At one time, he had more power than any man in Greece ever enjoyed. He undertook to change the government of the allied cities, and there was scarcely a city in Greece where the Spartans had not the ascendency. In most of the Ionian cities, and in all the cities which had taken the side of Athens, there was a Spartan governor, so that when Xenophon returned with his Ten Thousand to Asia Minor, he found he could do nothing without the consent of the Spartan governors. Moreover, the rule of Sparta was hostile to all democratic governments. She sought to establish oligarchal institutions everywhere. Perhaps this difference between Athens

Paramount authority of Sparta after the victories of Lysander.

and Sparta respecting government was one great cause of the Peloponnesian war.

Sparta incurs the jealousy of Greece.

But the same envy which had once existed among the Grecian States of the prosperity of Athens, was now turned upon Sparta. Her rule was arrogant and hard, and she in turn had to experience the humiliation of revolt from her domination. "The allies of Sparta," says Grote, "especially Corinth and Thebes, not only relented in their hatred of Athens, now she had lost her power, but even sympathized with her suffering exiles, and became disgusted with the self-willed encroachments of Sparta; while the Spartan king, Pausanias, together with some of the ephors, were also jealous of the arbitrary and oppressive conduct of Lysander. He refused to prevent the revival of the democracy. It was in this manner that Athens, rescued from that sanguinary and rapacious *régime* of the Thirty Tyrants, was enabled to reappear as a humble and dependent member of the Spartan alliance—with nothing but the recollection of her former power, yet with her democracy again in vigorous action for internal government.

Her oppressive superiority.

The victory of Ægospotami, which annihilated the Athenian navy, ushered in the supremacy of Sparta, both on the land and sea, and all Greece made submission to the ascendant power. Lysander established in most of the cities an oligarchy of ten citizens, as well as a Spartan harmost, or governor. Everywhere the Lysandrian dekarchy superseded the previous governments, and ruled oppressively, like the Thirty at Athens, with Critias at their head. And no justice could be obtained at Sparta against the bad conduct of the harmosts who now domineered in every city. Sparta had embroiled Greece in war to put down the ascendency of Athens, but exercised a more tyrannical usurpation than Athens ever meditated. The language of Brasidas, who promised every thing, was in striking contrast to the conduct of Lysander, who put his foot on the neck of Greece.

The rule of the Thirty at Athens came to an end by the noble efforts of Thrasybulus and the Athenian democracy, and the old constitution was restored because the Spartan king was disgusted with the usurpations and arrogance of Lysander, and forbore to interfere. Had Sparta been wise, with this vast accession of power gained by the victories of Lysander, she would have ruled moderately, and reorganized the Grecian world on sound principles, and restored a Panhellenic stability and harmony. She might not have restored, as Brasidas had promised, a universal autonomy, or the complete independence of all the cities, but would have bound together all the States under her presidency, by a just and moderate rule. But Sparta had not this wisdom. She was narrow, hard, and extortionate. She loved her own, as selfish people generally do, but nothing outside her territory with any true magnanimity. And she thus provoked her allies into rebellion, so that her chance was lost, and her dominion short-lived. Athens would have been more enlightened, but she never had the power, as Sparta had, of organizing a general Panhellenic combination. The nearest approach which Athens ever made was the confederacy of Delos, which did not work well, from the jealousy of the cities. But Sparta soon made herself more unpopular than Athens ever was, and her dream of empire was short.

Effect of the tyrannical policy of Sparta.

The first great movement of Sparta, after the establishment of oligarchy in all the cities which yielded to her, was a renewal of the war with Persia. The Asiatic Greek cities had been surrendered to Persia according to treaty, as the price for the assistance which Persia rendered to Sparta in the war with Athens. But the Persian rule, under the satraps, especially of Tissaphernes, who had been rewarded by Artaxerxes with more power than before, became oppressive and intolerable. Nothing but aggravated slavery impended over them. They therefore sent to Sparta for aid to throw off the Persian yoke. The ephors, with nothing more to gain from Persia, and inspired with contempt for the Persian armies—contempt created by the expedition of the Ten Thousand—readily

Renewal of the war with Persia.

listened to the overtures, and sent a considerable force into Asia, under Thimbron. He had poor success, and was recalled, and Dercyllidas was sent in his stead. He made a truce with Tissaphernes, in order to attack Pharnabazus, against whom he had an old grudge, and with whom Tissaphernes himself happened for the time to be on ill terms. Dercyllidas overran the satrapy of Pharnabazus, took immense spoil, and took up winter-quarters in Bythinia. Making a truce with Pharnabazus, he crossed over into Europe and fortified the Chersonesus against the Thracians. He then renewed the war both against Pharnabazus and Tissaphernes upon the Mæander, the result of which was an agreement, on the part of the satraps, to exempt the Grecian cities from tribute and political interference, while the Spartan general promised to withdraw from Asia his army, and the Spartan governors from the Grecian cities.

Agesilaus, king of Sparta.

At this point, B. C. 397, Dercyllidas was recalled to Sparta, and King **Agesilaus**, who had recently arrived with large re-enforcements, superseded him in command of the Lacedæmonian army. Agesilaus was the son of king Archidamus, and half-brother to King Agis. He was about forty when he became king, through the influence of Lysander, in preference to his nephew, and having been brought up without prospects of the throne, had passed through the unmitigated rigor of the Spartan drill and training. He was distinguished for all the Spartan virtues—obedience to authority, extraordinary courage and energy, simplicity and frugality.

Agesilaus was assisted by large contingents from the allied Greek cities for his war in Asia; but Athens, Corinth, and Thebes stood aloof. Lysander accompanied him as one of the generals, but gave so great offense by his overweening arrogance, that he was sent to command at the Hellespont. The truce between the Spartans and Persians being broken, Agesilaus prosecuted the war vigorously against both Tissaphernes and Pharnabazus. He gained a considerable victory over the Persians near Sardis, invaded Phrygia, and laid waste the satrapy of Pharnabazus. He even surprised the camp of the satrap, and gained immense booty. But in the midst of his victories he was recalled by Sparta, which had need of his services at home. A rebellion of the allies had broken out, which seriously threatened the stability of the Spartan empire.

Recall of Agesilaus from the war.

"The prostration of the power of Athens had removed that common bond of hatred and alarm which attached the allied cities to the headship of Sparta; while her subsequent conduct had given positive offense, and had excited against herself the same fear of unmeasured imperial ambition which had before run so powerfully against Athens. She had appropriated to herself nearly the whole of the Athenian maritime empire, with a tribute of one thousand talents. But while Sparta had gained so much by the war, not one of her allies had received the smallest remuneration. Even the four hundred and seventy talents which Lysander brought home out of the advances made by Cyrus, together with the booty acquired at Decelea, was all detained by the Lacedæmonians. Hence there arose among the allies not only a fear of the grasping dominion, but a hatred of the monopolizing rapacity of Sparta. This was manifested by the Thebans and Corinthians when they refused to join Pausanias in his march against Thrasybulus and the Athenian exiles in Piræus. But the Lacedæmonians were strong enough to despise this alienation of the allies, and even to take revenge on such as incurred their displeasure. Among these were the Elians, whose territory they invaded, but which they retreated from, on the appearance of an earthquake."

Discontent of the Grecian States.

Alienation of the allies of Sparta.

The following year the Spartans, under King Agis, again invaded the territory of Elis, enriched by the offerings made to the temple of Olympeia. Immense booty in slaves, cattle, and provisions was the result of this invasion, provoked by the refusal of the Elians to furnish aid in the war against Athens. The Elians were obliged to submit to hard terms of peace, and all the enemies of Sparta were rooted out of the Peloponnesus.

Such was the triumphant position of Sparta at the close of the Peloponnesian war. And a great change had also taken place in her internal affairs. The people had become enrich-

Enrichment of Sparta.

ed by successful war, and gold and silver were admitted against the old institution of Lycurgus, which recognized only iron money. The public men were enriched by bribes. The strictness of the old rule of Spartan discipline was gradually relaxed.

It was then, shortly after the accession of Agesilaus to the throne, on the death of Agis, that a dangerous conspiracy

Conspiracy against the States.

broke out in Sparta itself, headed by Cinadon, a man of strength and courage, who saw that men of his class were excluded from the honors and distinctions of the State by the oligarchy—the ephors and the senate. But the rebellion, though put down by the energy of Agesilaus, still produced a dangerous discontent which weakened the power of the State.

The Lacedæmonian naval power, at this crisis, was seriously threatened by the union of the Persian and Athenian

Lacedæmonian fleet threatened.

fleet under Conon. That remarkable man had escaped from the disaster of Ægospotami with eight triremes, and sought the shelter of Cyprus, governed by his friend Evagoras, where he remained until the war between Sparta and the Persians gave a new direction to his enterprising genius. He joined Pharnabazus, enraged with the Spartans on account of the invasion of his satrapy by Lysander and Agesilaus, and by him was intrusted with the command of the Persian fleet. He succeeded in detaching Rhodes from the Spartan alliance, and gained, some time

Naval victory over the Lacedæmonians.

after, a decisive victory over Pisander—the Spartan admiral, off Cnidus, which weakened the power of Sparta on the sea, B. C. 394. More than half of the Spartan ships were captured and destroyed.

This great success emboldened Thebes and other States to throw off the Spartan yoke. Lysander was detached from his command at the Hellespont to act against Bœotia while Pausanias conducted an army from the Peloponnesus. The Thebans, threatened by the whole power of Sparta, applied to Athens, and Athens responded, no longer under the control of the Thirty Tyrants. Lysander was killed before Haliartus, an irreparable blow to Sparta, since he was her ablest general. Pausanias was compelled to evacuate Bœotia, and the enemies of Sparta took courage. An alliance between Athens, Corinth, Thebes, and Argos was now made to carry on war against Sparta.

Revolt of Thebes.

Thebes at this time steps from the rank of a secondary power, and gradually rises to the rank of an ascendant city. Her leading citizen was Ismenias, one of the great organizers of the anti-Spartan movement—the precursor of Pelopidas and Epaminondas. He conducted successful operations in the northern part of Bœotia, and captured Heracleia.

Renewed power of the city.

Such successes induced the Lacedæmonians to recall Agesilaus from Asia, and to concentrate all their forces against this new alliance, of which Thebes and Corinth were then the most powerful cities. The allied forces were also considerable—some twenty-four thousand hoplites, besides light troops and cavalry, and these were mustered at Corinth, where they took up a defensive position. The Lacedæmonians advanced to attack them, and gained an indecisive victory, B. C. 394, which secured their ascendency within the Peloponnesus, but no further. Agesilaus advanced from Asia through Thrace to co-operate, but learned, on the confines of Bœotia, the news of the great battle of Cnidus. At Coronæa another battle was fought between the Spartan and anti-Spartan forces, which was also indecisive, but in which the Thebans displayed great heroism. This battle compelled Agesilaus, with the Spartan forces, which he commanded, to retire from Bœotia.

Battle of Coronæa.

This battle was a moral defeat to Sparta. Nearly all her maritime allies deserted her—all but Abydos, which was held by the celebrated Dercyllidas. Pharnabazus and Conon now sailed with their fleet to Corinth, but the Persian satrap soon left, and Conon remained sole admiral, assisted with Persian money. With this aid he rebuilt the long walls of Athens, with the hearty co-operation of those allies which had once been opposed to Athens.

Decline of Sparta.

Conon had large plans for the restoration of the Athenian power. He organized a large mercenary force at Corinth, which had now become the seat of war. But as many evils resulted from the presence of so many soldiers in the city, a conspiracy headed by the oligarchal party took place, with a view of restoring the Lacedæmonian power. Pasimelus, the head of the conspirators, admitted the enemy within the long walls of the city, which, as in Athens, secured a communication between the city and the port. And between these walls a battle took place, in which the Lacedæmonians were victorious with a severe loss. They pulled down a portion of the walls between Corinth and the port of Lechæum, sallied forth, and captured two Corinthian dependencies, but the city of Corinth remained in the hands of their gallant defenders, under the Athenian Iphicrates. The long walls were soon restored, by aid of the Athenians, but were again retaken by Agesilaus and the Spartans, together with Lechæum. This success alarmed Thebes, which unsuccessfully sued for peace. The war continued, with the loss, to the Corinthians, of Piræum, an important island port, which induced the Thebans again to open negotiations for peace, which were contemptuously rejected.

Corinth becomes the seat of war.

In the midst of these successes, tidings came to Agesilaus of a disaster which was attended with important consequences, and which spoiled his triumph. This was the destruction of a detachment of six hundred Lacedæmonian hoplites by the light troops of Iphicrates—an unprecedented victory—for the hoplites, in their heavy defensive armor, held in contempt the peltarts with their darts and arrows, even as the knights of mediæval Europe despised an encounter with the peasantry. This event revived the courage of the anti-Spartan allies, and intensely humiliated

Great disaster to Sparta.

the Lacedæmonians. It was not only the loss of the aristocratic hoplites, but the disgrace of being beaten by peltarts. Iphicrates recovered the places which Agesilaus had taken, and Corinth remained undisturbed.

Sparta, in view of these great disasters, now sought to detach Persia from Athens. She sent Antalcidas to Ionia, offering to surrender the Asiatic Greeks, and promising a universal autonomy throughout the Grecian world. These overtures were disliked by the allies, who sent Conon to counteract them. But Antalcidas gained the favor of the Persian satrap Tiribasus, who had succeeded Tissaphernes, and he privately espoused the cause of Sparta, and seized Conon and caused his death. Tiribasus, however, was not sustained by the Persian court, which remained hostile to Sparta. Struthas, a Persian general, was sent into Ionia, to act more vigorously against the Lacedæmonians. He gained a victory, B. C. 390, over the Spartan forces, commanded by Thimbron, who was slain.

Sparta invokes the aid of Persia.

The Lacedæmonians succeeded, after the death of Conon, in concentrating a considerable fleet near Rhodes. Against this, Thrasybulus was sent from Athens with a still larger one, and was gaining advantages, when he was slain near Aspendus, in Pamphylia, in a mutiny, and Athens lost the restorer of her renovated democracy, and an able general and honest citizen, without the vindictive animosities which characterized the great men of his day.

Death of Thrasybulus.

Rhodes still held out against the Lacedæmonians, who were now commanded by Anaxibius, in the place of Dercyllidas. He was surprised by Iphicrates, and was slain, and the Athenians, under this gallant leader, again became masters of the Hellespont. But this success was balanced by the defection of Ægina, which island was constrained by the Lacedæmonians into war with Athens. I need not detail the various enterprises on both sides, until Antalcidas returned from Susa with the treaty confirmed between the Spartans and the court of Persia, which closed the war between the various contending parties,

Investment of Rhodes.

B. C. 387. This treaty was of great importance, but it indicates the loss of all Hellenic dignity when Sparta, too, descends so far as to comply with the demands of a Persian satrap.

Evil consequences of the rivalries of the Grecian States.

Athens and Sparta, both, at different times, invoked the aid of Persia against each other—the most mournful fact in the whole history of Greece, showing how much more powerful were the rivalries of States than the sentiment of patriotism, which should have united them against their common enemy. The sacrifice of Ionia was the price which was paid by Sparta, in order to retain her supremacy over the rest of Greece, and Persia ruled over all the Greeks on the Asiatic coast. Sparta became mistress of Corinth and of the Corinthian Isthmus. She organized anti-Theban oligarchies in the Bœotian cities, with a Spartan harmost. She decomposed the Grecian world into small fragments. She crushed Olythus, and formed a confederacy between the Persian king and the Dionysius of Syracuse. In short, she ruled with despotic sway over all the different States.

We have now to show how Sparta lost the ascendency she had gained, and became involved in a war with Thebes, and how Thebes became, under Pelopidas and Epaminondas, for a time the dominant State of Greece.

CHAPTER XXII.

THE REPUBLIC OF THEBES.

AFTER Sparta and Athens, no State of Greece arrived at pre-eminence, until the Macedonian empire arose, except Thebes, the capital of Bœotia; and the empire of this city was short, though memorable, from the extraordinary military genius of Epaminondas.

Thebes.

In the year B. C. 379, Sparta was the ascendant power of Greece, and was feared, even as Athens was in the time of Pericles. She had formed an alliance with the Persian king and with Dionysius of Syracuse. All Greece, within and without the Peloponnesus, except Argos and Attica and some Thessalian cities, was enrolled in a confederacy under the lead of Sparta, and Spartan governors and garrisons occupied the principal cities.

Thebes especially was completely under Spartan influence and control, and was apparently powerless. Her citadel, the Cadmea, was filled with Spartan soldiers, and the independence of Greece was at an end. Confederated with Macedonians, Persians, and Syracusans, nobody dared to call in question the headship of Sparta, or to provoke her displeasure.

Under the dominion of Sparta.

This destruction of Grecian liberties, with the aid of the old enemies of Greece, kindled great indignation. The orator Lysias, at Athens, gave vent to the general feeling, in which he veils his displeasure under the form of surprise, that Sparta, as the chief of Greece, should permit the Persians, under Artaxerxes, and the Syracusans, under Dionysius, to enslave Greece. The orator Isocrates spoke still more plainly, and denounced the

Invectives of the orators against Sparta.

Lacedæmonians as "traitors to the general security and freedom of Greece, and seconding foreign kings to aggrandize themselves at the cost of autonomous Grecian cities—all in the interest of their own selfish ambition." Even Xenophon, with all his partiality for Sparta, was still more emphatic, and accused the Lacedæmonians with the violation of their oaths.

In Thebes the discontent was most apparent, for their leading citizens were exiled, and the oligarchal party, headed by Leontiades and the Spartan garrison, was oppressive and tyrannical. The Theban exiles found at Athens sympathy and shelter. Among these was Pelopidas, who resolved to free his country from the Spartan yoke. Holding intimate correspondence with his friends in Thebes, he looked forward patiently for the means of effecting deliverance, which could only be effected by the destruction of Leontiades and his colleagues, who ruled the city. Philidas, secretary of the polemarchs, entered into the conspiracy, and, being sent in an embassy to Athens, concocted the way for Pelopidas and his friends to return to Thebes and effect a revolution. Charon, an eminent patriot, agreed to shelter the conspirators in his house until they struck the blow. Epaminondas, then living at Thebes, dissuaded the enterprise as too hazardous, although all his sympathies were with the conspirators.

Discontent in Thebes.

When all was ready, Philidas gave a banquet at his house to the polemarchs, agreeing to introduce into the company some women of the first families of Thebes, distinguished for their beauty. In concert with the Theban exiles at Athens, Pelopidas, with six companions, crossed Cithæron and arrived at Thebes, in December, B. C. 379, disguised as hunters, with no other arms than concealed daggers. By a fortunate accident they entered the gates and sought shelter in the house of Charon until the night of the banquet. They were introduced into the banqueting chamber when the polemarchs were full of wine, disguised in female attire, and, with the aid of their Theban conspira-

Rebellion under Philidas.

tors, dispatched three of the polemarchs with their daggers. Leontiades was not present, but the conspirators were conducted secretly to his house, and effected their purpose. Leontiades was slain, in the presence of his wife. The conspirators then proceeded to the prison, slew the jailor, and liberated the prisoners, and then proclaimed, by heralds, in the streets, at midnight, that the despots were slain and Thebes was free. But the Spartans still held possession of the citadel, and, apprised of the *coup d'état*, sent home for re-enforcements. But before they could arrive Pelopidas and the enfranchised citizens stormed the Cadmea, dispersed the garrison, put to death the oligarchal Thebans, and took full possession of the city.

Its success.

This unlooked-for revolution was felt throughout Greece like an electric shock, and had a powerful moral effect. But the Spartans, although it was the depth of winter, sent forth an expedition, under King Cleombrotus—Agesilaus being disabled—to reconquer Thebes. He conducted his army along the Isthmus of Corinth, through Megara, but did nothing, and returned, leaving his lieutenant, Sphodrias, to prosecute hostilities. Sphodrias, learning that the Piræus was undefended, undertook to seize it, but failed, which outrage so incensed the Athenians, that they dismissed the Lacedæmonian envoys, and declared war against Sparta. Athens now exerted herself to form a second maritime confederacy, like that of Delos, and Thebes enrolled herself a member. As the Athenian envoys, sent to the islands of the Ægean, promised the most liberal principles, a new confederacy was formed. The confederates assembled at Athens and threatened war on an extensive scale. A resolution was passed to equip twenty thousand hoplites, five hundred horsemen, and two hundred triremes. A new property-tax was imposed at Athens to carry on the war.

The Theban revolution produces a great sensation.

Thebes forms an alliance with Athens.

At Thebes there was great enthusiasm, and Pelopidas, with Charon and Melon, were named the first bœotarchs. The Theban government became demo-

Theban government.

cratic in form and spirit, and the military force was put upon a severe training. A new brigade of three hundred hoplites, called the Sacred Band, was organized for the special defense of the citadel, composed of young men from the best families, distinguished for strength and courage. The Thebans had always been good soldiers, but the popular enthusiasm raised up the best army for its size in Greece.

Epaminondas.

Epaminondas now stands forth as a leader of rare excellence, destined to achieve the greatest military reputation of any Greek, before or since his time, with the exception of Alexander the Great—a kind of Gustavus Adolphus, introducing new tactics into Grecian warfare. He was in the prime of life, belonging to a poor but honorable family, younger than Pelopidas, who was rich. He had acquired great reputation for his gymnastic exercises, and was the most cultivated man in Thebes, a good musician, and a still greater orator. He learned to play on both the lyre and flute from the teachings of the best masters, sought the conversation of the learned, but was especially eloquent in speech, and effective, even against the best Athenian opponents. He was modest, unambitious, patriotic, intellectual, contented with poverty, generous, and disinterested. When the Cadmea was taken, he was undistinguished, and his rare merits were only known to Pelopidas and his friends. He was among the first to join the revolutionists, and was placed by Pelopidas among the organizers of the military force.

His accomplishments.

The Spartans now made renewed exertions, and King Agesilaus, the greatest military man of whom Sparta can boast, marched with a large army, in the spring of B. C. 378, to attack Thebes. He established his head-quarters in Thespiæ, from which he issued to devastate the Theban territory.

Sparta attacks Thebes.

The Thebans and Athenians, unequal in force, still kept the field against him, acting on the defensive, declining battle, and occupying strong positions. After a month of desultory warfare, Agesilaus retired, leaving Phœbidas in command at Thespiæ, who was slain in an incautious pursuit of the enemy.

In the ensuing summer Agesilaus undertook a second expedition into Bœotia, but gained no decided advantage, while the Thebans acquired experience, courage, and strength. Agesilaus having strained his lame leg, was incapacitated for active operation, and returned to Sparta, leaving Cleombrotus to command the Spartan forces. He was unable to enter Bœotia, since the passes over Mount Cithæron were held by the Thebans, and he made an inglorious retreat, without even reaching Bœotia.

Second unsuccessful expedition of Agesilaus.

The Spartans now resolved to fit out a large naval force to operate against Athens, by whose assistance the Thebans had maintained their ground for two years. The Athenians, on their part, also fitted out a fleet, assisted by their allies, under the command of Chabrias, which defeated the Lacedæmonian fleet near Naxos, B. C. 376. This was the first great victory which Athens had gained since the Peloponnesian war, and filled her citizens with joy and confidence, and led to a material enlargement of their maritime confederacy. Phocion, who had charge of a squadron detached from the fleet of Chabrias, also sailed victorious round the Ægean, took twenty triremes, three thousand prisoners, with one hundred and ten talents in money, and annexed seventeen cities to the confederacy. Timotheus, the son of Conon, was sent with the fleet of Chabrias, to circumnavigate the Peloponnesus, and alarm the coast of Laconia. The important island of Corcyra entered into the confederation, and another Spartan fleet, under Nicolochus, was defeated, so that the Athenians became once again the masters of the sea. But having regained their ascendency, Athens became jealous of the growing power of Thebes, now mistress of Bœotia, and this jealousy, inexcusable after such reverses, was increased when Pelopidas gained a great victory over the Lacedæmonians near Tegyra, which led to the expulsion of their enemies from all parts of Bœotia, except Orchomenus, on the borders of Phocis.

Naval victory of the Athenians.

Victory of Pelopidas.

That territory was now attacked by the victorious Thebans, upon which Athens made peace with the Lacedæmonians.

The jealousy of the Grecian republics.

It would thus seem that the ancient Grecian States were perpetually jealous of any ascendant power, and their policy was not dissimilar from that which was inaugurated in modern Europe since the treaty of Westphalia—called the balance of power. Greece, thus far, was not ambitious to extend her rule over foreign nations, but sought an autonomous independence of the several States of which she was composed. Had Greece united under the leadership of Sparta or Athens, her foreign conquests might have been considerable, and her power, centralized and formidable, might have been a match even for the Romans. But in the anxiety of each State to secure its independence, there were perpetual and unworthy jealousies of each rising State, when it had reached a certain point of prosperity and glory. Hence the various States united under Sparta, in the Peloponnesian war, to subvert the ascendency of Athens. And when Sparta became the dominant power of Greece, Athens unites with Thebes to break her domination. And now Athens becomes jealous of Thebes, and makes peace with Sparta, in the same way that England in the eighteenth century united with Holland and other States, to prevent the aggrandizement of France, as different powers of Europe had previously united to prevent the ascendency of Austria.

Humiliation of Sparta.

The Spartan power was now obviously humbled, and one of the greatest evidences of this was the decline of Sparta to give aid to the cities of Thessaly, in danger of being conquered by Jason, the despot of Pheræ, whose formidable strength was now alarming Northern Greece.

The peace which Sparta had concluded with Athens was of very short duration. The Lacedæmonians resolved to attack Corcyra, which had joined the Athenian confederation. An armament collected from the allies, under Mnasippus, in the spring of B. C. 373, proceeded against Corcyra. The inhabitants, driven within the walls of the city, were in danger of famine, and invoked Athenian aid. Before it arrived, however, the Corcyræans made a successful sally upon the Spartan troops, over-confident of victory, in which Mnasippus was slain, and the city became supplied with provisions. After the victory, Iphicrates, in command of the Athenian fleet, which had been delayed, arrived and captured the ships which Dionysius of Syracuse had sent to the aid of the Lacedæmonians. These reverses induced the Spartans to send Antalcidas again to Persia to sue for fresh intervention, but the satraps, having nothing more to gain from Sparta, refused aid. But Athens was not averse to peace, since she no longer was jealous of Sparta, and was jealous of Thebes. In the mean time Thebes seized Platæa, a town of Bœotia, unfriendly to her ascendency, and expelled the inhabitants who sought shelter in Athens, and increased the feeling of disaffection toward the rising power. This event led to renewed negotiations for peace between Athens and Sparta, which was effected at a congress held in the latter city. The Athenian orator Callistratus, one of the envoys, proposed that Sparta and Athens should divide the headship of Greece between them, the former having the supremacy on land, the latter on the sea. Peace was concluded on the basis of the autonomy of each city.

Hostilities between Athens and Sparta.

Peace between Athens and Sparta.

Epaminondas was the Theban deputy to this congress. He insisted on taking the oath in behalf of the Bœotian confederation, even as Sparta had done for herself and allies. But Agesilaus required he should take the oath for Thebes alone, as Athens had done for herself alone. He refused, and made himself memorable for his eloquent speeches, in which he protested against the pretensions of Sparta. "Why," he maintained, "should not Thebes respond for Bœotia, as well as Sparta for Laconia, since Thebes had the same ascendency in Bœotia that Sparta had in Laconia?" Agesilaus, at last, indignantly started

Epaminondas at the congress of Sparta.

21

from his seat, and said to Epaminondas: "Speak plainly. Will you, or will you not, leave to each of the Bœotian cities its separate autonomy?" To which the other replied: "Will you leave each of the Laconian towns autonomous?" Without saying a word, Agesilaus struck the name of the Thebans out of the roll, and they were excluded from the treaty.

The war now is to be prosecuted between Sparta and Thebes, since peace was sworn between all the other States.

Renewal of hostilities between Sparta and Thebes.

The deputies of Thebes returned home discouraged, knowing that their city must now encounter, single-handed, the whole power of the dominant State of Greece. "The Athenians—friendly with both, yet allies with neither—suffered the dispute to be fought out without interfering." The point of it was, whether Thebes was in the same relation to the Bœotian towns that Sparta was to the Laconian cities. Agesilaus contended that the relations between Thebes and other Bœotian cities was the same as what subsisted between Sparta and her allies. This was opposed by Epaminondas.

After the congress of B. C. 371, both Sparta and Athens fulfilled the conditions to which their deputies had sworn. The latter gave orders to Iphicrates to return home with his fleet, which had threatened the Lacedæmonian coast; the

Great preparations of Sparta.

former recalled her harmosts and garrisons from all the cities which she occupied, while she made preparations, with all her energies, to subdue Thebes. It was anticipated that so powerful a State as Sparta would soon accomplish her object, and few out of Bœotia doubted her success.

King Cleombrotus was accordingly ordered to march out of Phocis, where he was with a powerful force, into Bœotia. Epaminondas, with a body of Thebans, occupied a narrow pass near Coronea, between a spur of Mount Helicon and the Lake Copais. But instead of forcing this pass, the Spar-

Defeat of a Theban force.

tan king turned southward by a mountain road, over Helicon, deemed scarcely practicable, and defeated a Theban division which guarded it, and marched to

Creusis, on the Gulf of Alcyonis, and captured twelve Theban triremes in the harbor. He then left a garrison to occupy the post, and proceeded over a mountainous road in the territory of Thespiæ, on the eastern declivity of Helicon, to Leuctra, where he encamped. He was now near Thebes, having a communication with Sparta through the port of Creusis. The Thebans were dismayed, and it required all the tact and eloquence of Epaminondas and Pelopidas to rally them. They marched out at length from Thebes, under their seven bœotrarchs, and posted themselves opposite the Spartan camp. Epaminondas was one of these generals, and urged immediate battle, although the Theban forces were inferior.

Military tactics of Epaminondas.

It was through him that a change took place in the ordinary Grecian tactics. It was customary to fight simultaneously along the whole line, in which the opposing armies were drawn up. Departing from this custom, he disposed his troops obliquely, or in échelon, placing on his left chosen Theban hoplites to the depth of fifty, so as to bear with impetuous force on the Spartan right, while his centre and right were kept back for awhile from action. Such a combination, so unexpected, was completely successful. The Spartans could not resist the concentrated and impetuous assault made on their right, led by the Sacred Band, with fifty shields propelling behind. Cleombrotus, the Spartan king, was killed, with the most distinguished of his staff, and the Spartans were driven back to their camp. The allies, who fought without spirit or heart, could not be rallied.

Great victory obtained by Thebes.

The victory was decisive, and made an immense impression throughout Greece; for it was only twenty days since Epaminondas had departed from Sparta, excluded from the general peace. The Spartans bore the defeat with their characteristic fortitude, but their prestige was destroyed. A new general had arisen in Bœotia, who carried every thing before him. The Athenians heard of the victory with ill-concealed jealousy of the rising power.

Jason, the tyrant of Pheræ, now joined the Theban camp

and the Spartan army was obliged to evacuate Bœotia.

The Spartans evacuate Bœotia.

The great victory of Leuctra gave immense extension to the Theban power, and broke the Spartan rule north of the Peloponnesus. All the cities of Bœotia acknowledged the Theban supremacy, while the harmosts which Sparta had placed in the Grecian cities were forced to return home. Sparta was now discouraged and helpless, and even many Peloponnesian cities put themselves under the presidency of Athens. None were more affected by the Spartan overthrow than the Arcadians, whose principal cities had been governed by an oligarchy in the interest of Sparta, such as Tegea and Orchomenus, while Mantinea was broken up into villages. The Arcadians, free from Spartan governors, and ceasing to look henceforth for victory and plunder in the service of Sparta, became hostile, and sought their political independence. A Pan-Arcadian union was formed.

Agesilaus marches into Arcadia.

Sparta undertook to recover her supremacy over Arcadia, and Agesilaus was sent to Mantinea with a considerable force, for the city had rebuilt its walls, and resumed its former consolidation, which was a great offense in the eyes of Sparta. The Arcadians, invaded by Spartans, first invoked the aid of Athens, which being refused, they turned to Thebes, and Epaminondas came to their relief with a great army of auxiliaries—Argeians, Elians, Phocians, Locrians, as well as Thebans, for his fame now drew adventurers from every quarter to his standard. These forces urged him to invade Laconia itself, and his great army, in four divisions, penetrated the country through different passes. He crossed the Eurotas and advanced to Sparta, which was in the greatest consternation, not merely from the near presence of Epaminondas with a powerful army of seventy thousand men, but from the discontent of the Helots. But Agesilaus put the city in the best possible defense, while every means were used to secure auxiliaries from other cities. Epaminondas dared not to attempt to take the city by storm, and after ravaging Laco-

Epaminondas invades Sparta.

nia, returned into Arcadia. This insult to Sparta was of great moral force, and was an intense humiliation, greater even than that felt after the battle of Leuctra.

This expedition, though powerless against Sparta herself, prepared Epaminondas to execute the real object which led to the assistance of the Arcadians. This was the re-establishment of Messenia, which had been conquered by Sparta two hundred years before. The new city of Messenia was built on the site of Mount Ithome, where the Messenians had defended themselves in their long war against the Laconians, and the best masons and architects were invited from all Greece to lay out the streets, and erect the public edifices, while Epaminondas superintended the fortifications. All the territory westward and south of Ithome—the southwestern corner of the Peloponnesus, richest on the peninsula, was now subtracted from Sparta, while the country to the east was protected by the new city in Arcadia, Megalopolis, which the Arcadians built. This wide area, the best half of the Spartan territory, was thus severed from Sparta, and was settled by Helots, who became free men, with inextinguishable hatred of their old masters. But these Helots were probably the descendants of the old Messenians whom Sparta had conquered. This renovation of Messenia, and the building of the two cities, Messenia and Megalopolis, was the work of Epaminondas, and were the most important events of the day. The latter city was designed as the centre of a new confederacy, comprising all Arcadia.

Restores the independence of Messenia.

The Spartan kingdom dismembered.

Sparta being thus crippled, dismembered, and humbled, Epaminondas evacuated the Peloponnesus, filled, however, with undiminished hostility. Sparta condescends to solicit aid from Athens, so completely was its power broken by the Theban State, and Athens consents to assist her, in the growing fear and jealousy of Thebes, thereby showing that the animosities of the Grecian States grew out of political jealousy rather than from revenge or injury. To rescue Sparta was a wise policy, if it were

Sparta forms an alliance with Athens.

necessary to maintain a counterpoise against the ascendency of Thebes. An army was raised, and Iphicrates was appointed general. He first marched to Corinth, and from thence into Arcadia, but made war with no important results.

Such were the great political changes which occurred within two years under the influence of such a hero as Epaminondas. Laconia had been invaded and devastated, the Spartans were confined within their walls, Messenia had been liberated from Spartan rule, two important cities had been built, to serve as great fortresses to depress Sparta, Helots were converted into freemen, and Greece generally had been emancipated from the Spartan yoke. Such were the consequences of the battle of Leuctra.

Greece emancipated from the Spartan yoke.

And this battle, which thus destroyed the prestige of Sparta, also led to renewed hopes on the part of the Athenians to regain the power they had lost. Athens already had regained the ascendency on the sea, and looked for increased maritime aggrandizement. On the land she could only remain a second class power, and serve as a bulwark against Theban ascendency.

Athens sought also to recover Amphipolis—a maritime city, colonized by Athenians, at the head of the Strymonican Gulf, in Macedonia, which was taken from her in the Peloponnesian war, by Brasidas. Amyntas, the king of Macedonia, seeking aid against Jason of Pheræ, whose Thessalian dominion and personal talents and ambition combined to make him a powerful potentate, consented to the right of Athens to this city. But Amyntas died not long after the assassination of Jason, and both Thessaly and Macedonia were ruled by new kings, and new complications took place. Many Thessalian cities, hostile to Alexander, the son of Jason, invoked the aid of Thebes, and Pelopidas was sent into Thessaly with an army, who took Larissa and various other cities under his protection. A large part of Thessaly thus came under the protection of Thebes. On the other hand, Alexander,

Athens seeks to recover Amphipolis.

A part of Thessaly under the protection of Thebes.

who succeeded Amyntas in Macedonia, found it difficult to maintain his own dominion without holding Thessalian towns in garrison. He was also harassed by interior commotions, headed by Pausanias, and was slain. Ptolemy, of Alorus, now became regent, and administered the kingdom in the name of the minor children of Amyntas—Perdiccas and Philip. The mother of these children, Eurydice, presented herself, with her children, to Iphicrates, and invoked protection. He declared in her favor, and expelled Pausanias, and secured the sceptre of Amyntas, who had been friendly to the Athenians, to his children, under Ptolemy as regent. The younger of these children lived to overthrow the liberties of Greece.

But Iphicrates did not recover Amphipolis, which was a free city, and had become attached to the Spartans after Brasidas had taken it. Iphicrates was afterward sent to assist Sparta in the desperate contest with Thebes. The Spartan allied army occupied Corinth, and guarded the passes which prevented the Thebans from penetrating into the Peloponnesus. Epaminondas broke through the defenses of the Spartans, and opened a communication with his Peloponnesian allies, and with these increased forces was more than a match for the Spartans and Athenians. He ravaged the country, induced Sicyon to abandon Sparta, and visited Arcadia to superintend the building of Megalopolis. Meanwhile Pelopidas, B. C. 368, conducted an expedition into Thessaly, to protect Larissa against Alexander of Pheræ, and to counterwork the projects of that despot, who was in league with Athens. He was successful, and then proceeded to Macedonia, and made peace with Ptolemy, who was not strong enough to resist him, taking, among other hostages to Thebes, Philip, the son of Amyntas. The Thebans and Macedonians now united to protect the freedom of Amphipolis against Athens, Pelopidas returned to Thebes, having extended her ascendency over both Thessaly and Macedonia.

The Theban supremacy in Thessaly and Macedonia.

Thebes, now ambitious for the headship of Greece, sent

Pelopidas on a mission to the Persian king at Susa, who obtained a favorable rescript. The States which were summoned to Thebes to hear the rescript read refused to accept it; and even the Arcadian deputies protested against the headship of Thebes. So powerful were the sentiments of all the Grecian States, from first to last, against the complete ascendency of any one power, either Athens, or Sparta, or Thebes. The rescript was also rejected at Corinth. Pelopidas was now sent to Thessaly to secure the recognition of the headship of Thebes; but in the execution of his mission he was seized and detained by Alexander of Pheræ.

Thebes now aspires to the leadership of Greece.

The Thebans then sent an army into Thessaly to rescue Pelopidas. Unfortunately, Epaminondas did not command it. Having given offense to his countrymen, he was not elected that year as bœotrarch, and served in the ranks as a private hoplite. Alexander, assisted by the Athenians, triumphed in his act of treachery, and treated his illustrious captive with harshness and cruelty, and the Theban army, unsuccessful, returned home.

Thebes rescues Pelopidas.

The Thebans then sent another army, under Epaminondas, into Thessaly for the rescue of Pelopidas, and such was the terror of his name, that Alexander surrendered his prisoner, and sought to make peace. But the rescue of Pelopidas disabled Thebes from prosecuting the war in the Peloponnesus. As soon, however, as this was effected, Epaminondas was sent as an envoy into Arcadia to dissuade her from a proposed alliance with Athens, and there had to contend with the Athenian orator Callistratus. The relations of the different Grecian States now became so complicated, that it is useless, in a book like this, to attempt to unravel them. Negotiations between Athens and Persia, the efforts of Corinth and other cities to secure peace, the ambition of Athens to maintain ascendency on the sea, the creation of a Theban navy—these and other events must be passed by.

Complicated political relations of the Grecian States.

But we can not omit to notice the death of Pelopidas.

He had been sent with an army into Thessaly against Alexander of Pheræ, who was at the height of his power, holding in dependence a considerable part of Thessaly, and having Athens for an ally. In a battle which took place between Pelopidas and Alexander, near Pharsalus, the Thessalians were routed. Pelopidas, seeing his enemy apparently within his reach, and remembering only his injuries, sallied forth, unsupported, like Cyrus, on the field of Cunaxa, at the sight of his brother, to attack him when surrounded by his guards, and fell while fighting bravely. Nothing could exceed the grief of the victorious Thebans in view of this disaster, which was the result of inexcusable rashness. He was endeared by uninterrupted services from the day he slew the Spartan governors and recovered the independence of his city. He had taken a prominent part in all the struggles which had raised Thebes to unexpected glory, and was second in abilities to Epaminondas alone, whom he ever cherished with more than fraternal friendship, without envy and without reproach. All that Thebes could do was to revenge his death. Alexander was stripped of all his Thessalian dependencies, and confined to his own city, with its territory, near the Gulf of Pegasæ.

Death of Pelopidas.

Grief of the Thebans.

It was while Pelopidas was engaged in his Thessalian campaign, that a conspiracy against the power of Thebes took place in the second city of Bœotia—Orchomenus, on Lake Copais. This city was always disaffected, and in the absence of Pelopidas in Thessaly, and Epaminondas with a fleet on the Hellespont, some three hundred of the richest citizens undertook to overthrow the existing government. The plot was discovered before it was ripe for execution, the conspirators were executed, the town itself was destroyed, the male adults were killed, and the women and children were sold into slavery. This barbarous act was but the result of long pent up Theban hatred, but it kindled a great excitement against Thebes throughout Greece. The city, indeed, sympathized with the Spartan cause, and would have been

Orchomenus revolts from Thebes.

Unfortunate fate of the city.

destroyed before but for the intercession of Epaminondas, whose policy was ever lenient and magnanimous. It was a matter of profound grief to this general, now re-elected as one of the bœotarchs, that Thebes had stained her name by this cruel vengeance, since he knew it would intensify the increasing animosity against the power which had arrived so suddenly to greatness.

Renewed hostilities.

Hostilities, as he feared, soon broke out with increased bitterness between Sparta and Thebes. And these were precipitated by difficulties in Arcadia, then at war with Elis, and the appropriation of the treasures of Olympia by the Arcadians. Sparta, Elis, and Achaia formed an alliance, and Arcadia invoked the aid of Thebes. The result was that Epaminondas marched with a large army into the Peloponnesus, and mustered his forces at Tegea, which was under the protection of Thebes. His army comprised, besides Thebans and Bœotians, Eubœans, Thessalians, Locrians, and other allies from Northern Greece. The Spartans, allied with Elians, Achæans, and Athenians, united at Mantinea, under the command of Agesilaus, now an old man of eighty, but still vigorous and strong. Tegea lay in the direct road from Sparta to Mantinea, and while Agesilaus was moving by a more circuitous route to the westward, Epaminondas resolved to attempt a surprise on Sparta. This movement was unexpected, and nothing saved Sparta except the accidental information which Agesilaus received of the movement from a runner, in time to turn back to Sparta and put it in a condition of defense before Epaminondas arrived, for Tegea was only about thirty miles from Sparta. The Theban general was in no condition to assault the city, and his enterprise failed, from no fault of his. Seeing that Sparta was defended, he marched back immediately to Tegea, and dispatched his cavalry to surprise Mantinea, about fifteen miles distant. The surprise was baffled by the unexpected arrival of Athenian cavalry. An encounter took place between these two bodies of cavalry, in which

Epaminondas attempts to surprise Sparta.

the Athenians gained an advantage. Epaminondas saw then no chance left for striking a blow but by a pitched battle, with all his forces. He therefore marched from Tegea toward the enemy, who did not expect to be attacked, and was unprepared. He adopted the same tactics that gave him success at Leuctra, and posted himself, with his Theban phalanx on the left, against the opposing right, and bore down with irresistible force, both of infantry and cavalry, while he kept back the centre and right, composed of his trustworthy troops, until the battle should be decided. His column, not far from fifty shields in depth, pressed upon the opposing column of only eight shields in depth, like the prow of a trireme impelled against the midships of an antagonist in a sea-fight. This mode of attack was completely successful. Epaminondas broke through the Lacedæmonian line, which turned and fled, but he himself, pressing on to the attack, at the head of his column, was mortally wounded. He was pierced with a spear—the handle broke, leaving the head sticking in his breast. He at once fell, and his own troops gathered around his bleeding body, giving full expression to their grief and lamentations.

His great victory over the Lacedæmonians at Mantinea.

His death.

Thebes gained, by the battle of Mantinea, the preservation of her Arcadian allies and of her anti-Spartan frontier; while Sparta lost, beyond hope, her ancient prestige and power. But the victory was dearly purchased by the death of Epaminondas, who has received, and probably deserves, more unmingled admiration than any hero whom Greece ever produced. He was a great military genius, and introduced new tactics into the art of war. He was a true patriot, thinking more of the glory of his country than his own exaltation. He was a man of great political insight, and merits the praise of being a great statesman. He was, above all, unsullied by vices, generous, devoted, merciful in war, magnanimous in victory, and laborious in peace. He was also learned, eloquent, and wise, ruling by moral wisdom as well as by genius. His death

His great military genius.

His character.

was an irreparable loss—one of those great men whom his country could not spare, and whose services no other man could render. Of modern heroes he most resembles Gustavus Adolphus. And as the Thirty Years in Germany loses all its interest after the battle of Leutzen, when the Swedish hero laid down his life in defense of his Protestant brethren, so the Theban contest with Sparta has no great significance after the battle of Mantinea. The only great blunder which Epaminondas made was to encourage his countrymen to compete with Athens for the sovereignty of the seas. That sovereignty was the natural empire of Athens, even as the empire of the land was the glory of Sparta. If these two powers had been contented with their own peculiar sphere, and joined in a true alliance with each other, the empire of Greece might have resisted the encroachments of Philip and Alexander, and defied the growing ascendency of Rome.

Death of Agesilaus.

Shortly after the death of Epaminondas, B. C. 362, the greatest man of Spartan annals disappeared from the stage of history. Agesilaus died in Egypt, having gone there to assist the king in his revolt from Persia. He also possessed all the great qualities of a prince, a soldier, a statesman and a man. He, too, was ambitious, but only to perpetuate the power of Sparta. It was his misfortune to contend with a greater man, but he did all that was in the power of a king of Sparta to retrieve her fortunes, and died deeply lamented and honored.

Death of Artaxerxes.

Artaxerxes died B. C. 358, after having subdued the revolt of his satraps and of Egypt, having reigned forty-five years, and Ochus succeeded to his throne, taking his father's name.

Philip of Macedon.

Athens recovered, during the wars between Sparta and Thebes, much of her former maritime power, and succeeded in retaking the Chersonese. But another great character now arises to our view—Philip of Macedon, who succeeded in overturning the liberties of Greece. But before we present his career, that of Dionysius of Syracuse, demands a brief notice, and the great power of Sicily, as a Grecian State, during his life.

CHAPTER XXIII.

DIONYSIUS AND SICILY.

We have already seen how the Athenian fleet was destroyed at the siege of Syracuse, where Nicias and Demosthenes were so lamentably defeated, which defeat resulted in the humiliation of Athens and the loss of her power as the leading State of Greece.

The destruction of this great Athenian armament in September, B. C. 413, created an intoxication of triumph in the Sicilian cities. Nearly all of them had joined Syracuse, except Naxos and Catana, which sided with Athens. Agrigentum was neutral.

Syracuse after the failure of Nicias.

The Syracusans were too much exhausted by the contest to push their victory to the loss of the independence of these cities, but they assisted their allies, the Lacedæmonians, with twenty triremes against Athens, under Hermocrates, while Rhodes furnished a still further re-enforcement, under Dorieus. But the Peloponnesian war was not finished as soon as the Syracusans anticipated. Even the combined Peloponnesian and Syracusan fleets sustained two defeats in the Hellespont. The battle of Cyzicus was even still more calamitous, since the Spartan admiral Mindarus was slain, and the whole of his fleet was captured and destroyed. The Syracusans suffered much by this latter defeat, and all their triremes were burned to prevent them falling into the hands of their enemies, and the seamen were left destitute on the Propontis, in the satrapy of Pharnabazus. These adverse events led to the disgrace of Hermocrates, who stimulated the movement and promised what he could not perform. But his conduct had been good, and his treatment was unjust and harsh. War recognizes only success, whatever may be the virtues and talents of the commanders; and this is one of the worst phases of war, when accident and circumstances contribute more to military rewards than genius itself.

The banishment of Hermocrates was followed by the triumph of the democratical party, and Diocles, an influential citizen, was named, with a commission of ten, to revise the constitution and the laws. The laws of Diocles did not remain in force long, and were exceeding severe in their penalties. But they were afterward revived, and copied by other Sicilian cities, and remained in force to the Grecian conquest of the island.

Internal condition of the city.

The Syracusans then prosecuted war with vigor against Naxos, which sided with Athens, until it was brought to a sudden close by an invasion of the Carthaginians, the ancient foes of Greece. As far back as the year 480 B. C.—that year which witnessed the invasion of Greece by Xerxes—the Carthaginians had invaded Sicily, with a mercenary army under Hamilcar, for the purpose of reinstating the tyrant of Himera, expelled by Theron of Agrigentum. The Carthaginian army was routed, and Hamilcar was slain by Gelon, the tyrant of Syracuse. This defeat was so signal, that it was seventy years before the Carthaginians again invaded Sicily, shortly after the destruction of Athenian power at Syracuse. No sooner was the protecting naval power of Athens withdrawn from Greece, than the Persians and the Carthaginians pressed upon the Hellenic world.

The wars of the Syracusans with Carthage.

It is singular that so little is known of the early history of Carthage, which became the great rival of Rome. It was founded by the Phœnicians, and became a considerable commercial city before Athens had reached the naval supremacy of Greece. Her possessions were extensive on the coast of Africa, both east and west, comprehending Sardinia and the Balearic isles. At the maximum of her power, before the first Punic war, the popu-

Carthage.

lation was nearly a million of people. It was built on a fortified peninsula of about twenty miles in circumference, with the isthmus. Upon this isthmus was the citadel Byrsa, surrounded with a triple wall, and crowned at its summit by a magnificent temple of Æsculapius. It possessed three hundred tributary cities in Libya, which was but a small part of the great empire which belonged to it in the fourth century before Christ. All the towns on the coast, even those founded by the Phœnicians, like Hippo and Utica, were tributary, with the exception of Utica. Although the Carthaginians were averse to land service, yet no less than forty thousand hoplites, with one thousand cavalry and two thousand war chariots, marched out from the gates to resist an enemy. But the Carthaginian armies were mostly composed of mercenaries—Gauls, Iberians, and Libyans, and forming a discordant host in language and custom.

Its maritime power.

The political constitution of Carthage was oligarchal. Two kings were elected annually, and presided over the Senate, of three hundred persons, made up from the principal families. The great families divided between them, as in Rome, the offices and influence of the State, and maintained an insolent distinction from the people. It was an aristocracy, based on wealth, and created by commerce, as in Venice, in the Middle Ages. There was a demos, or people, at Carthage, who were consulted on particular occasions; but, whether numerous or not, they were kept in dependence to the rich families by banquets and lucrative employments. The government was stable and well conducted, both for internal tranquillity and commercial aggrandizement.

Its political constitution.

The first eminent historical personage was Mago, B. C. 500, who greatly extended the dominions of Carthage. Of his two sons, Hamilcar was defeated and slain by Gelon of Syracuse. The other son, Hasdrubal, perished in Sardinia. His sons remained the most powerful citizens of the State, carrying on war against the Moors and

Its eminent men.

other African tribes. Hannibal, grandson of Hamilcar, distinguished himself in an invasion of Sicily, B. C. 410, and with a large army, of one hundred thousand men, stormed and took Selinus, and killed one hundred and sixty thousand of the inhabitants, and carried away captive five thousand more. He then laid siege to Himera, which he also took, and slaughtered three thousand of the inhabitants, in expiation of the memory of his grandfather. These were Grecian cities, and the alarm throughout Greece was profound for this new enemy. These events took place about the time that Hermocrates was banished for an unsuccessful maritime war. Hermocrates afterward attempted to enter Syracuse, but was defeated and slain.

At this period Dionysius appears upon the stage—for the next generation the most formidable name in the Grecian world. He had none of the advantages of family or wealth—but was well educated, and espoused the cause of Hermocrates, and rose to distinction during the intestine commotions which resulted from the death of Hermocrates and the banishment of Diocles, the lawgiver.

Dionysius at Syracuse.

In 406 B. C., Sicily was again invaded by a large force from Carthage, estimated by some writers as high as three hundred thousand men, who were chiefly mercenaries. Hannibal was the leader of these forces. All the Greek cities now prepared for vigorous war. The Syracusans sent to Sparta and the Italian Greek cities for aid. Agrigentum was most in danger, and most alarmed of the Greek Sicilian cities. It was second only to Syracuse in numbers and wealth, having a population of eight hundred thousand people, though this is probably an exaggeration. It was rich in temples and villas and palaces; its citizens were wealthy, luxurious, and hospitable.

Carthaginians invade Sicily.

The army of Hannibal advanced against this city, which was strongly fortified, and re-enforced by a strong body of troops from Syracuse, under Daphneus. He defeated the Iberian mercenaries, but did not preserve his victory, so that the Carthaginians were enabled to take and plunder Agrigentum. There was, of course, bitter complaint against the Syracusan generals, who might have prevented this calamity. In the discontent which succeeded, Dionysius was elevated to the command. He procured a vote to restore the Hermocratean exiles, and procured, also, a body of paid guards, and established himself as despot of Syracuse; and he arrived at this power by demagogic arts, allying himself with the ultra democratic party.

Rise of Dionysius.

Soon after his elevation, the Carthaginians advanced, under Imolco, to attack Gela, which was relieved by Dionysius with a force of fifty thousand men. Intrenching himself between Gela and the sea, opposite the Carthaginians, he resolved to attack the invaders, but was defeated and obliged to retreat, so that Gela fell into the hands of the Carthaginians, who perpetrated their usual cruelties. This defeat occasioned a mutiny at Syracuse, and his house was plundered of the silver and gold and valuables which he had already collected. But he rapidly returned to Syracuse, and punished the mutineers, and became master of the city, driving away the rich citizens who had vainly obstructed his elevation. He abolished every remnant of freedom, and ruled despotically with the aid of his mercenaries, and the common people who rallied to his standard.

Defeated by the Carthaginians.

It was fortunate for him that the Carthaginians, although victors at Gela, made proposals of peace, which were accepted. Dionysius accepted a peace, the terms of which were favorable to Carthage, in order to secure his own power. He betrayed the interests of Sicily to an enemy from selfish and unworthy motives. The whole south of Sicily was consigned to the Carthaginians, and Syracuse to Dionysius.

Carthaginians make peace.

Dionysius now concentrated all his efforts to centralize and maintain his power. He greatly strengthened the fortifications of Syracuse. He constructed a new wall, with lofty towers and elaborate defenses, outside the mole which connected the islet Ortygia with Sicily. He also erected a citadel. He then had an impregnable

Dionysius centralizes his power.

stronghold, powerful for attack and defense. The fortress he erected in the islet of Ortygia he filled with his devoted adherents, consisting mostly of foreigners, to whom he assigned a permanent support and residence. He distributed anew the Syracusan territory, reserving the best lands for his friends, who thus became citizens. By this wholesale confiscation he was enabled to support ten thousand mercenary troops, devoted to him and his tyranny. The contributions he extorted were enormous, so that in five years twenty per cent of the whole property of Syracuse was paid into his hands.

Marches against the Sikels.

Having thus strengthened his power in Syracuse, he marched against the Sikels, in the interior of the island. But his absence was taken advantage of by the discontented citizens, who attempted to regain their freedom. He returned at once to Syracuse, and intrenched himself in his fortress, where he was besieged by the insurgents. The tyrant was now driven to desperation, and nothing saved him but the impregnable fortifications which he had erected. But his situation was so desperate that his adherents melted away, and he began to abandon all hope of retaining his position. As a last resource, he purchased the aid of a body of Campanian cavalry, in the Carthaginian service, which was stationed at Gela, while he amused the Syracusans, to gain time, by a pretended submission. They agreed to allow him to depart with five triremes, and relaxed the siege, supposing him already subdued. Meanwhile the Carthaginian mercenaries arrived and defeated the Syracusans, already dispersed and divided. Dionysius, finding himself rescued and re-established in his dominions, strengthened the fortifications of Ortygia, and employed his forces, now that Syracuse was subdued, in conquering the Grecian cities of Naxos, Catana, and Leontini. Strengthened at home and in the interior, Dionysius then prepared to attack the Carthaginians, but previously took measures to insure the defensibility of Syracuse. Six thousand persons were employed on a wall three and a half

His critical condition.

miles in length, from the fort of Trogilus to Euryalus, the summit of the slope of Epipolæ, a high cliff, which commanded the roads to the city. Six thousand teams of oxen were employed in drawing the stones from the quarries. This wall was not like Ortygia, a guard-house against the people of Syracuse, but a defense against external enemies. As it was a great public work of defense, the citizens worked with cheerfulness and vigor, and so enthusiastically did they labor, that the work was completed in twenty days. The city being now impregnable, he commenced preparations for offensive war, and changed his course toward the citizens, pursuing a mild and conciliatory policy. He made peace with Messene and Rhegium, and married a lady from Locri. He collected all the best engineers, mechanics, and artisans from Sicily and Italy, constructed immense machines, provided arms from every nation around the Mediterranean, so that he collected or fabricated one hundred and forty thousand shields and fourteen thousand breastplates, destined for his body-guard and officers, together with a vast number of helmets, spears, and daggers. All these were accumulated in his impregnable fortress of Ortygia. His naval preparations were equally stupendous. The docks of Syracuse were filled with workmen, and two hundred triremes were added to the one hundred and ten which already were housed in the docks. The trireme was the largest ship of war which for three hundred years had sailed in the Grecian or Mediterranean waters. But Dionysius constructed triremes with five banks of oars, and had a navy vastly superior to what Athens ever possessed. He now hired soldiers from every quarter, enlisting Syracusans and the inhabitants of the cities depending upon her. He sent envoys to Italy and the Peloponnesus for recruits, offering the most liberal pay.

Strengthens the fortifications of Syracuse.

His vast military preparations.

When all his preparations were completed, he married, on the same day, two wives—the Locrian (Doris), and the Syracusan (Aristomache), and both of these

His marriage.

women lived with him at the same table in equal dignity. He had three children by Doris, the eldest of whom was Dionysius the Younger, and four by Aristomache. When his nuptials had been celebrated with extraordinary magnificence, and banquets, and fêtes, in which the whole population shared, he convoked a public assembly, and exhorted the citizens to war against Carthage, as the common enemy of Greece, B. C. 397. He then granted permission to plunder the Carthaginian ships in the harbor, and shortly after marched out from Syracuse with an army against the Carthaginians in Sicily, consisting of eighty thousand men, while a fleet of two hundred triremes and five hundred transports accompanied its march along the coast—the largest military force hitherto assembled under Grecian command.

Marches against the Carthaginians.

The first place he attacked was Motya, north of Cape Lilybæum, in the western extremity of the island, all the Grecian cities under Carthaginian leadership having revolted. This city was both populous and wealthy, built on an islet, which was separated from Sicily by a narrow strait two-thirds of a mile in width, bridged over by a narrow mole. The Motyans, seeing the approach of so formidable an army, broke up their mole, and insulated themselves from Sicily. The Carthaginians sent a large fleet to assist Motya, under Imilco, but being inferior to that of Dionysius, it could not venture on a pitched battle. Motya made a desperate defense, but a road across the strait being built by the besiegers, the new engines of war carried over it were irresistible, the town was at length carried and plundered, and the inhabitants slaughtered or sold as slaves.

His success.

The siege occupied the summer, and Dionysius, triumphant, returned to Syracuse. But Imilco being elevated to the chief magistracy of Carthage, brought over to Sicily an overwhelming force, collected from all Africa and Iberia, amounting to one hundred thousand men, afterward re-enforced by thirty thousand more, at the lowest estimate, with four hundred ships and six hundred

He returns to Syracuse.

transports. This army disembarked at Panormus, on the northwestern side of the island (Palermo) retook Motya, regained Eryx, then marched east and captured Messene, at the extreme eastern part of the island near Italy, which prevented Dionysius from getting aid from Italy. The Sikels also rebelled, and Dionysius, greatly disquieted by the loss of all his conquests, and by approaching dangers, strengthened the fortifications of Syracuse, to which he had retired, and made preparations to resist the enemy. He had still a force of thirty thousand foot and three thousand horse, and one hundred and eighty ships of war. He sent also to Sparta for aid. He then advanced to Catana. A naval battle took place off this city, gained by the Carthaginians, from superior numbers. One hundred of the Syracusan ships were destroyed, with twenty thousand men, B. C. 395.

His naval defeat at Catana.

After this defeat, Dionysius retreated to Syracuse with his land forces, amid great discontent, and invoked the aid of Sparta and Corinth. Imilco advanced also to Syracuse, while his victorious fleet occupied the great harbor—a much more imposing armament than that the Athenians had at the close of the Persian war. The total number of vessels was two thousand. Imilco established his head-quarters at the temple of Zeus Olympius, one mile and a half from the city, and allowed his troops thirty days for plunder over the Syracusan territory; then he established fortified posts, and encircled his camp with a wall, and set down in earnest to reduce the city to famine. But as he was not master of Epipolæ, as Nicias was, Syracuse was able to communicate with the country around, both west and north, and also found means to secure supplies by sea.

Imilco lays siege to Syracuse.

Meanwhile the Syracusans defeated a portion of the Carthaginian fleet, and a terrific pestilence overtook the army before the city. The military strength of the Carthaginians was prostrated by the terrible malady, which swept away one hundred and fifty thousand persons

Disasters of the Carthaginians.

in the camp. When thus weakened and demoralized, the Carthaginians were attacked by the Syracusans, and were completely routed. The fleet was also defeated and set on fire, and the conflagration reached the camp, which was thus attacked by pestilence, fire, and sword. The disaster was fatal to the Carthaginians, and retreat was necessary. Imilco dispatched a secret envoy to Dionysius, offering three hundred talents if the fleet was allowed to sail away unmolested to Africa. This could not be permitted, but Imilco and the native Carthaginians were allowed to retire. The remaining part of the army, deprived of their head, was destroyed, with the exception of the Sikels, who knew the roads, and made good their escape.

They retire from Syracuse.

This immense disaster, greater than that the Athenians had suffered under Nicias, produced universal mourning and distress at Carthage, while the miserable Imilco vainly endeavoring to disarm the wrath of his countrymen, shut himself up in his house, and starved himself to death. This misfortune led also to a revolt of the African allies, which was subdued with difficulty, while the power of Carthage in Sicily was reduced to the lowest ebb. Dionysius was now left to push his conquests in other directions, and Syracuse was rescued from impending ruin.

Death of Imilco.

Dionysius had now reigned eleven years, with absolute power. The pestilence, and the treachery of Imilco, had freed him of the Carthaginians. But a difficulty arose as to the payment of his mercenaries, which he compromised by giving them the rich territory of Leontini, so that ten thousand quitted Syracuse, and took up their residence in the town. The cost of maintaining a large standing army was exceeding burdensome, and we only wonder how the tyrant found means to pay it, and prosecute at the same time such great improvements.

Financial embarrassments of Dionysius.

He now directed his attention to the Sikels, in the interior of the island, and took several of their towns, but from one of them he met with desperate

Makes himself master of Messene.

resistance, and came near losing his life from a wound by a spear which penetrated his cuirass. This repulse caused the Carthaginians to rally in the west of the island, under Magon, with an army of eighty thousand. But he was repulsed by Dionysius, and concluded a truce with him, which gave the latter leisure to make himself master of Messene and Taurominium—the two most important maritime posts on the Italian side of Sicily, and thus prepare for the invasion of the Greek cities in the south of Italy, B. C. 391.

Dionysius departed from Syracuse, B. C. 389, with a powerful force, to subdue the Italiot Greeks, and laid siege to Caulonia. He defeated their army, and slew their general. The victor treated the defeated Greeks with lenity, and then laid siege to Rhegium, to which he granted peace on severe terms. Caulonia and Hipponium, two cities whose territory occupied the breadth of the Calabrian peninsula, fell into his hands. Rhegium surrendered after a desperate defense, and Phyton, who commanded the town, was treated with brutal inhumanity. The town was dismantled, and all the territory of Southern Calabria was united to Locri. It was at this time that the peace of Antalcidas took place, which put an end to the Spartan wars in Asia Minor. The ascendant powers of Greece were now Sparta and Syracuse, each fortified by alliance with the other.

Invades Italy.

Croton, the largest city in Magna Grecia, was now conquered by Dionysius, who plundered the temple of Here, near Cape Lacinium, and among its treasure was a splendid robe, decorated in the most costly manner, which the conqueror sold to the Carthaginians, which long remained one of the ornaments of their city. The value and beauty of the robe may be estimated at the price paid for it—one hundred and twenty talents, more than one hundred thousand dollars.

Conquers Croton.

He now undertook a maritime expedition along the coast of Latium and Etruria, and pillaged the rich temple at Agylla, stripping it of gold and ornaments to the value of one thousand talents. So great was the celebrity he acquired, that the Gauls of Northern Italy, who had recently sacked Rome, proffered their alliance and aid. Master of Sicily and Southern Italy, he inspired, by his unscrupulous plundering of temples, the greatest terror and dislike throughout Central Greece. He then entered as competitor at the festivals of Greece for the prize of tragic poetry. But so contemptible were his poems, they were disgracefully hissed and ridiculed. Especially those poems which were recited at Olympeia—where he sent legations decked in the richest garments, furnished with gold and silver, and provided with splendid tents—were received with a storm of hisses, which plunged him in an agony of shame and grief, and drove him nearly mad, and made him conscious of the deep hatred which everywhere existed toward him. All his rich displays, which surpassed every thing that had ever before been seen in that holy plain, were worse than a failure—because they came from him. Not all his grandeur in Syracuse could save him from the disgrace and insults which he had received in Olympeia.

Becomes master of Southern Italy.

Hissed at the Grecian games.

It was at this time, B. C. 387, that Plato visited Sicily on a voyage of inquiry and curiosity, chiefly to see Mount Ætna, and was introduced to Dion, then a young man in Syracuse, and brother-in-law to Dionysius. Dion was so impressed with the conversation of Plato, that he invited the tyrant to talk with him also. Plato discoursed on virtue and justice, showing that happiness belonged only to the virtuous, and that despots could not lay claim even to the merit of true courage—most unpalatable doctrine to the tyrant, who became bitterly hostile to the philosopher. He even caused Plato to be exposed in the market as a slave, and sold for twenty minæ, which his friends paid and released him. On his voyage home, through the influence of the tyrant, he was again sold at Egina, and again repurchased, and set at liberty. So bitter are tyrants of the virtues which contrast with their misdeeds; and

Dion.

so vindictive especially was the despot who reigned at Syracuse.

Dionysius was now occupied by the new defenses and fortifications of his capital, so that the whole slope of Epipolæ was bordered and protected by massive walls and towers, and five divisions of the city had each its separate fortifications, so that it was the largest fortified city in all Greece—larger than Athens herself.

Power and wealth of Dionysius.

The plunder the tyrant had accumulated enabled him to make new preparations for a war with Carthage. But he was defeated in a great battle at Cronium, with terrible loss, by the youthful son of Magon, which compelled him to make peace, and cede to Carthage all the territory of Sicily west of the river Halycus, and pay a tribute of one thousand talents.

Defeated in a war with Carthage.

Very little is recorded of Dionysius after this peace, B. C. 382, for thirteen years, during which the Spartans had made themselves master of Thebes, and placed a garrison in Cadmea. In the year 368 he made war again with Carthage, but was defeated near Lilybæum, and forced to return to Syracuse. In the year 367 it would seem that he was at last successful with his poems, for he gained the prize of tragedy at the Lenæan festival at Athens, which so intoxicated him with joy, that he invited his friends to a splendid banquet, and died from the effects of excess and wine, after a reign of thirty-eight years. He was a man of restless energy and unscrupulous ambition. His personal bravery was great, and he was vigilant and long sighted—a man of great abilities, sullied by cruelty and jealousy. In his spare time he composed tragedies to compete for prizes. No other Greek had ever arrived at so great power from a humble position, or achieved so striking exploits abroad, or preserved his grandeur so unimpared at his death. But he was greatly favored by fortune, especially when the pestilence destroyed the hosts of Imilco. He maintained his power by intimidation of his subjects, careful organization, and liberal pay to his

Again defeated

Gains a prize for poetry dies from a fit of debauchery.

His character.

mercenaries. He cared nothing for money excepting as a means to secure dominion. His exactions were exorbitant, and his rapacity boundless. He trusted no one, and his suspicion was extended even to his wives. He allowed no one to shave him, and searched his most intimate friends for concealed weapons before they were allowed in his presence. He made Syracuse a great fortress, to the injury of Sicily and Italy, and fancied that he left his dominions fastened by chains of adamant. He could point to Ortygia with its impregnable fortifications, to a large army of mercenaries—to four hundred ships of war, and to vast magazines of arms and military stores.

Dion.

He left no successor competent to rivet the chains he had forged. His son Dionysius succeeded to his throne at the age of twenty-five. His brother-in-law Dion was the next prominent member of his family, and possessed a fortune of one hundred talents—a man of great capacity, ambitious, luxurious, but fond of literature and philosophy. He was, however, so much influenced by Plato, whose Socratic talk and democratic principles enchained and fascinated him, that his character became essentially modified, and he learned to hate the despotism under which he grew up, and formed large schemes for political reform. He aspired to cleanse Syracuse of slavery, and clothe her in the dignity of freedom, by establishing an improved constitutional polity, with laws which secured individual rights. He exchanged his luxurious habits for the simple fare of a philosopher. Never before had Plato met with a pupil who so profoundly and earnestly profited from his instructions. The harsh treatment which Plato received from the tyrant was a salutary warning to Dion. He saw that patience was imperatively necessary, and he so conducted as to maintain the favor of Dionysius.

Dionysius II.

Dionysius II. was twenty-five years old when his father died, and though he possessed generous impulses, was both weak and vain, given to caprice, and insatiate of praise. He had been kept from business from the excessive jealousy of his father, and his life had been passed in idleness and luxury at the palace of Ortygia. His father's taste for poetry had introduced guests to his table whose conversation opened his mind to generous sentiments, but the indecision of his character prevented his profiting from any serious studies. Dion supported this feeble novice on the throne of his father, and tried to gain influence over him, and frankly suggested the measures to be adopted, and Dionysius listened at first to his wise counsels. Dion wished to make Syracuse a free city, with good laws, to expel the Carthaginians from Sicily, and replant the semi-barbarian Hellenic cities. He also endeavored to reform the life of Dionysius as well as Syracuse, and actually wrought a signal change in his royal pupil, so that he desired to see and converse with the great sage who had so completely changed the life of Dion, and inspired him with patriotic enthusiasm. Accordingly, Plato was sent for, who reluctantly consented to visit Syracuse. He had no great faith in the despot who sought his wisdom, and he did not wish, at sixty-one, to leave his favorite grove, with admiring disciples from every part of Greece, where he reigned as monarch of the mind. He went to Syracuse, not with the hope so much of converting a weak tyrant, as from unwillingness to desert his friend, and be taunted with the impotence of his philosophy. He was received with great distinction at court, and a royal carriage conveyed him to his lodgings. The banquets of the Acropolis became distinguished for simplicity, and the royal pupil commenced at once in taking lessons in geometry. The old courtiers were alarmed, and disgusted. "A single Athenian sophist," they said, "with no force but his tongue and reputation, has achieved the conquest of Syracuse." Dionysius seemed to have abdicated in favor of Plato, and the noble objects for which Dion labored seemed to be on the way of fulfillment. But Plato acted injudiciously, and spoiled his influence by unreasonable vigor. It was absurd to expect that the despot would go

His feeble character.

Plato visits Syracuse.

His injudicious teachings.

to school like a boy, and insist upon a mental regeneration before he gave him lessons of practical wisdom in politics. All the necessary reforms were postponed on the ground that the royal pupil was not yet ripe for them, and every influence was exerted to show him his own unworthiness—that his whole past life had been vicious—delicate ground for any teacher to assume, since he irritated rather than reformed. He was even averse to any political changes until Dionysius had gone through his schooling. Plato also maintained a proud, philosophical dignity, showing no respect to persons, and refusing to the defects of his pupil any more indulgence than he granted to those who listened to his teachings at home.

Such a mistake was attended soon with difficulties. The old courtiers recovered their influence. Dion was calumniated and slandered, as seeking to usurp the sovereign powers, and that Plato was brought to Syracuse as an agent in the conspiracy. Plato tried to counterwork this mischief, but in vain. Dionysius lost all inclination to reform, and Dion was hated, for he was superior to his nephew in dignity and ability, and was haughty and austere in his manners. He was accordingly banished from Syracuse, and Plato was retained *in the Acropolis*, but was otherwise well treated, and entreated to remain. The tyrant, however, refused to recall Dion, but consented to the departure of Plato. Another visit to Syracuse, which he made with the hope of securing the recall of Dion, was a splendid captivity, and although he was treated with extraordinary deference, he was not at rest until he obtained permission to depart. He had failed in his mission of benevolence and friendship. All the vast possessions of Dion were confiscated, and Plato had the mortification to hear of this injury in the very palace to which he went as a reformer.

Banishment of Dion.

Second visit of Plato.

Incensed at the seizure of his property, and hopeless of permission to return, and of all those reforms which he had projected, Dion now meditated the over-

Dion in exile.

throw of the power of Dionysius, and his own restoration at the point of the sword. During his exile he had chiefly resided in Athens, enjoying the teaching of his friend Plato, and dispensing his vast wealth in generous charities. Nor did Plato fully approve of his plans for the overthrow of Dionysius, anticipating little good from such violence, although he fully admitted his wrongs. But other friends, less judicious and more interested, warmly seconded his projects. With aid from various sources, he at last could muster eight hundred veterans, with which he ventured to attack the most powerful despot in Greece, and in his own stronghold. And so enthusiastic was Dion, all disparity of forces was a matter of indifference. Moreover, he accounted it glory and honor to perish in so just and noble a cause as the liberation of Sicily from a weak and cruel despot, every way inferior to his father in character, though as strong in resources.

Meditates the overthrow of Dionysius.

But the friends of Dion did not dream of throwing away their lives. They calculated on a rising of the Syracusans to throw off an insupportable yoke, and they had utter contempt for the tyrant himself, knowing his drunken habits, and effeminate character, and personal incompetency. So, after ten years' exile, Dion, with his followers, landed in Sicily, at Heracleia, also in the absence of Dionysius, who had quitted Syracuse for Italy, with eighty triremes, so that the city was easy of access.

He lands in Sicily.

This unaccountable mistake of the tyrant in leaving his capital at such a crisis, was regarded with great joy by the small army of Dion, which marched out at once from Heracleia, and was joined in the Agrigentian territory with two hundred horsemen. As he approached Syracuse, other bands joined him, so that he had five thousand men as he approached the capital. Timocrates, the husband of Dion's late wife, for his wife was taken away from him, was left in command at Syracuse with a large force of mercenaries. But as Dion advanced to the city, there was a general rising of the citizens, and Timocrates was obliged to return, leaving the fortresses garrisoned. Dion entered the city by the principal street, which was decorated as on a day of jubilee, and proclaimed liberty to all. He was also chosen general, with his brother Megacles, and approached Ortygia, and challenged the garrison to come out and fight. He then succeeded in capturing Epipolæ and Eurylæ, those fortified quarters, and erected a cross wall from sea to sea to block up Ortygia.

Enters Syracuse in triumph.

At the end of seven days, when all these results had been accomplished, Dionysius returned to Syracuse, but Ortygia was the only place which remained to him, and that, too, shut up on the land side by a blockading wall. The rest of the city was in possession of his enemies, though those enemies were subjects. His abdication was imperatively demanded by Dion, who refused all conciliation and promises of reform. Rallying, then, his soldiers, he made a sally to surprise the blockading wall, and was nearly successful, but Dion, at length, repulsed his forces, and recovered the wall. Ortygia was again blockaded, but as Dionysius was still master of the sea, he ravaged the coasts for provisions, and maintained his position, until the arrival of Heraclides, with a Peloponnesian fleet, gave the Syracusans a tolerable naval force. Philistus commanded the fleet of Dionysius, but in a battle with Heraclides, he lost his life.

Demands the abdication of Dionysius.

Dionysius now lost all hope of recovering his power by force, and resorted to intrigues, stimulating the rivalry of Heraclides, and exposing the defects of Dion, whose arrogance and severity were far from making him popular. Calumnies now began to assail Dion, and he was mistrusted by the Syracusans, who feared only an exchange of tyrants. There was also an unhappy dissension between Dion and Heraclides, which resulted in the deposition of Dion, and he was forced to retreat from Syracuse, and seek shelter with the people of Leontini, who stood by him. Dionysius again had left Ortygia for Italy, leaving his son in command, and succeeded in

Dionysius resorts to intrigues.

Unpopularity of Dion.

sending re-enforcements from Locri, under Nypsius, so that the garrison of Ortygia was increased to ten thousand men, with ample stores. Nypsius sallied from the fortress, mastered the blockading wall, and entered Neapolis and Achradina, fortified quarters of the city. The Syracusans, in distress, then sent to Leontini to invoke the aid of Dion, who returned as victor, drove Nypsius into his fortress, and saved Syracuse. He also magnanimously pardoned Heraclides, and prosecuted the blockade of Ortygia, and was again named general. Still Heraclides, who was allowed to command the fleet, continued his intrigues, and frustrated the operations against Dionysius. At last, Ortygia surrendered to Dion, who entered the fortress, where he found his wife and sister, from whom he had been separated twelve years. At first, Arete, his wife, who had consented to marry Timocrates, was afraid to approach him, but he received her with the tenderest emotion and affection. His son, however, soon after died, having fallen into the drunken habits of Dionysius.

But Ortygia surrenders to him.

Dion master of Syracuse.

Dion was now master of Syracuse, and on the pinnacle of power. His enterprise had succeeded against all probabilities. But prosperity, which the Greeks were never able to bear, poisoned all his good qualities and exaggerated his bad ones. He did not fall into the luxury of his predecessors. He still wore the habit of a philosopher, and lived with simplicity, but he made public mistakes. His manners, always haughty, became repulsive. He despised popularity. He conferred no real liberty. He retained his dictatorial power. He preserved the fortifications of Ortygia. He did not meditate a permanent despotism, but meant to make himself king, with a modified constitution, like that of Sparta. He had no popular sympathies, and sought to make Syracuse, like Corinth, completely oligarchal. He took no step to realize any measure of popular freedom, and, above all, refused to demolish the fortress, behind whose fortifications the tyrants of Syracuse had intrenched themselves in danger. He also caused Hera-

His mistakes.

clides to be privately assassinated, so that the Syracusans began to hate him as cordially as they had hated Dionysius. This unpopularity made him irritable, and suspicious and disquieted. A conspiracy, headed by Callippus, put an end to his reign. He was slain by the daggers of assassins. Thus perished one of the noblest of the Greeks, but without sufficient virtue to bear success. His great defect was inexperience in government, and it may be doubted whether Plato himself could have preserved liberty in so corrupt a city as Syracuse. The character of Dion also changed greatly by his banishment, since vindictive sentiments were paramount in his soul. He had a splendid opportunity of becoming a benefactor to his country, but this was thrown away, and instead of giving liberty he only ruled by force, and moved from bad to worse, until he made a martyr of the man whom once he magnanimously forgave. Had he lived longer, he probably would have proved a remorseless tyrant like Tiberius. So rare is it for men to be temperate in the use of power, and so much easier is it to give expression to grand sentiments than practice the self-restraint which has immortalized the few Washingtons of the world.

His death.

His character.

The Athenian Callippus, who overturned Dion, remained master of Syracuse for more than a year, but its condition was miserable and deplorable, convulsed by passions and hostile interests. In the midst of the anarchy which prevailed, Dionysius contrived to recover Ortygia, and establish himself as despot. The Syracusans endured more evil than before, for the returned tyrant had animosities to gratify. There was also fresh danger from Carthage, so that the Syracusans appealed to their mother city, Corinth, for aid. Timoleon was chosen as the general of the forces to be sent—an illustrious citizen of Corinth, then fifty years of age, devoted to the cause of liberty, with hatred of tyrants and wrongs, who had even slain his brother when he trampled on the liberties of Corinth—and a brother whom he loved.

Dionysius recovers Ortygia.

Syracuse invokes the aid of Corinth.

Timoleon sent as general.

But he was forced to choose between him and his country, and he chose his country, securing the gratitude of Corinth, but the curses of his mother and the agonies of self-reproach, so that he left for years the haunts of men, and buried himself in the severest solitude. Twenty years elapsed from the fratricide to his command of a force to relieve the Syracusans from their tyrant Dionysius.

Timoleon commenced his preparations of ships and soldiers with alacrity, but his means were scanty, not equal even to those of Dion when he embarked on his expedition. He was prevented with his small force from reaching Sicily by a Carthaginian fleet of superior force, but he effected his purpose by stratagem, and landed at Taurominiun under great discouragements. He defeated Hicetas, who had invoked the aid of Carthage, at Adranum, and marched unimpeded to the walls of Syracuse. Dionysius, blocked up at Ortygia, despaired of his position, and resolved to surrender the fortress, stipulating for a safe conveyance and shelter at Corinth. This tyrant, broken by his drunken habits, did not care to fight, as his father did, for a sceptre so difficult to be maintained, and only sought his ease and self-indulgence. So he passed into the camp of Timoleon with what money he could raise, and the fortress was surrendered. A re-enforcement from Corinth enabled Timoleon to maintain his ground.

His wonderful successes.

The appearance of the fallen tyrant in Corinth produced a great sensation. Some from curiosity, others from sympathy, and still more from derision, went to see a man who had enjoyed so long despotic power, now suing only for a humble domicile. But his conduct, considering his drunken habits, was marked by more dignity than was to be expected from so weak a man. He is said to have even opened a school to teach boys to read, and to have instructed the public singers in reciting poetry. His career, at least, was an impressive commentary on the mutability of fortune, to which the Greeks were fully alive.

Dionysius an exile in Corinth.

Timoleon, in possession of Ortygia, with its numerous

stores, found himself able to organize a considerable force to oppose the Carthaginians who sought to get possession of the fortress. Hicetas, now assisted by a Carthaginian force under Magon, attacked Ortygia, but was defeated by the Corinthian Neon, who acquired Achradina, and joined it by a wall to Ortygia. But Magon now distrusted Hicetas, and suddenly withdrew his army. Timoleon thus became master of Syracuse, and Hicetas was obliged to retire to Leontini. Timoleon ascribed his good fortune to the gods, but purchased a greater hold on men's minds than fortune gave him by his moderation in the hour of success—a striking contrast to Dion and the elder Dionysius. He invited the Syracusans to demolish the stronghold of tyranny, where the despots had so long intrenched themselves. He erected courts of justice on its site. He recalled the exiles, and invited new colonists to the impoverished city, so that sixty thousand immigrants arrived. He relieved the poverty and distress of the people by selling the public lands, and employed his forces to expel remaining despots from the island.

Timoleon demolishes the stronghold of tyranny.

His noble administration.

But Hicetas again invited the Carthaginians to Sicily. They came, with a vast army of seventy thousand men and twelve hundred ships, under Hasdrubal and Hamilcar, B. C. 340. Timoleon could only assemble twelve thousand to meet this overwhelming force, but with these he marched against the Carthaginians, and gained a great victory, by the aid of a terrible storm which pelted the Carthaginians in the face. No victory was ever more complete than this at Crimisus. Ten thousand of the invaders were slain, and fifteen thousand made prisoners, together with an enormous spoil.

His great victory over the Carthaginians.

Timoleon had now to deal with two Grecian enemies—Hicetas and Mamercus—tyrants of Leontini and Catana. Over these he gained a complete victory, and put them to death. He then, after having delivered Syracuse, and defeated his enemies, laid down his power, and became a private citizen. But his influence re-

He lays down his power.

mained, as it ought to have been, as great as ever, for he was a patriot of most exalted virtue, a counselor whom all could trust—a friend who sacrificed his own interests. And he exerted his influence for the restoration of Syracuse, for the introduction of colonists, and the enforcement of wise laws. The city was born anew, and the gratitude and admiration of the citizens were unbounded. In his latter years he became blind, but his presence could not then even be spared when any serious difficulty arose—ruling by the moral power of wisdom and sanctity—one of the best and loftiest characters of all antiquity. And nothing was more remarkable than his patience under contradiction, and his eagerness to insure freedom of speech, even against himself.

Thus, by the virtues and wisdom of this remarkable man, were freedom and comfort diffused throughout Sicily for twenty-four years, until the despotism of Agathocles. Timoleon died B. C. 337—a father and benefactor—and the Syracusans solemnized his funeral with lavish honors, which was attended by a countless procession, and passed a vote to honor him for all future time with festive matches, in music and chariot-races, and such gymnastics as were practiced at the Grecian games. A magnificent monument was erected to his memory. "The mournful letters written by Plato after the death of Dion contrasts strikingly with the enviable end of Timoleon, and with the grateful inscription of the Syracusans on his tomb."

His death and character.

CHAPTER XXIV.

PHILIP OF MACEDON.

No one would have supposed, B. C. 400, that the destruction of Grecian liberties would come from Macedonia—a semi-barbarous kingdom which, during the ascendency of Sparta, had so little political importance. And if any new power threatened to rise over the ruins of the Spartan State, and become paramount in Greece, it was Thebes. The successes of Pelopidas and Epaminondas had effectually weakened the power of Sparta. She no longer enjoyed the headship of Greece. She no longer was the leader of dependent allies, submitting to her dictation in all external politics, serving under the officers she appointed, administering their internal affairs by oligarchies devoted to her purposes, and even submitting to be ruled by governors whom she put over them. She had lost her foreign auxiliary force and dignity, and even half of her territory in Laconia. The Peloponnesians, who once rallied around her were disunited, and Megalopolis and Messene were hostile. Corinth, Sicyon, Epidaurus, and other cities, formerly allies, stood aloof, and the grand forces of Hellas now resided outside of the Peloponnesus. Athens and Thebes were the new seats of power. Athens had regained her maritime supremacy, and Thebes was formidable on the land, having absorbed one-third of the Bœotian territory, and destroyed three or four autonomous cities, and secured powerful allies in Thessaly.

Unexpected rise of Macedonia.

When the battle of Mantinea was fought, at which Epaminondas lost his life, Perdiccas, son of Amyntas, was the king of Macedonia. He was slain, in the flower of his life, in a battle with the Illyrians, B. C. 359. On the advice of Plato, who had been his teacher, he was induced to bestow upon his brother Philip a portion of territory in Macedonia, who for three years preceding had been living in Thebes as a hostage, carried there by Pelopidas at fifteen years of age, when he had reduced Macedonia to partial submission.

Philip of Macedon.

At Thebes the young prince was treated with courtesy, and resided with one of the principal citizens, and received a good education. He was also favored with the society of Pelopidas and Epaminondas, and witnessed with great interest the training of the Theban forces by these two remarkable men—one the greatest organizer, and the other the greatest tactician of the age. When transferred from Thebes to a subordinate government of a district in his brother's kingdom, he organized a military force on the principles he had learned in Thebes. The unexpected death of Perdiccas, leaving an infant son, opened to him the prospect of succeeding to the throne. He first assumed the government as guardian of his young nephew Amyntas, but the difficulties with which he was surrounded, having many competitors from other princes of the family of Amyntas, his father, that he assumed the crown, putting to death one of his half-brothers, while the other two fled into exile.

Philip at Thebes.

His first proceeding as king was to buy the Thracians, his enemies, by presents and promises, so that only the Athenians and the Illyrians remained formidable. But he made peace with Athens by yielding up Amphipolis, for the possession of which the Athenians had made war in Macedonia.

Surrender of Amphipolis.

The Athenians, however, neglected to take possession of Amphipolis, being engaged in a struggle to regain the island of Eubœa, then under the dominion of Thebes. It also happened that a revolt of a large number of the islands of the Ægean, which belonged to the confederacy of which Athens was chief, took place—Lesbos, Chios, Samos, Cos, and Rhodes, including Byzantium. This

Revolt from Athens of Lesbos, Chios, Samos, &c.

revolt is called the social war, caused by the selfishness of Athens in acting more for her own interest than that of her allies, and neglecting to pay the mercenaries in her service. The revolt was also stimulated by the intrigues of the Carian prince, Mausolus. But it was a serious blow to the foreign ascendency of Athens, and in a battle to recover these islands, the Athenians, under Chabrias, were defeated at Chios. They were also unsuccessful on the Hellespont from quarrels among their generals—Timotheus, Iphicrates, and Chares. The popular voice at Athens laid the blame of defeat on the two former unjustly, in consequence of which Timotheus was fined one hundred talents, the largest fine ever imposed at Athens, and shortly after died in exile—a distinguished man, who had signally maintained the honor and glory of his country. Iphicrates also was never employed again. The loss of these two generals could scarcely be repaired. Soon after, peace was made with the revolted cities, by which their independence and autonomy were guaranteed. This was an inglorious result of the war to Athens, and fatally impaired her power and dignity, so that she was unable to make a stand against the aggressions of Philip.

Death of Timotheus.

One of the first things he did after defeating the Illyrians was to lay siege to Amphipolis, although he had ceded the city to Athens. For this treachery there was no other reason than ambition and the weakened power of Athens. Amphipolis had long remained free, and was not disposed to give up its liberties, and sent to Athens for aid. Philip, an arch politician, contrived by his intrigues to prevent Athens from giving assistance. The neglect of Athens was a great mistake, for Amphipolis commanded the passage over the Strymon, and shut up Macedonia from the east, and was, moreover, easily defensible by sea. Deprived of aid from Athens, the city fell into the hands of Philip, and was an acquisition of great importance. It was the most convenient maritime station in Thrace, and threw open to him all the country east of the Strymon, and

Philip lays siege to Amphipolis.

Fall of the city.

especially the gold region near Mount Pangæus. This place henceforward became one of the bulwarks of Macedonia, until the Roman conquest.

Having obtained this place, he commenced, without a declaration of war against Athens, a series of hostile measures, while he professed to be her friend. He deprived her of her hold upon the Thermaic Gulf, conquered Pydna and Potidæa, and conciliated Olynthus. His power was thus so far increased that he founded a new city, called Philippi, in the regions where his gold mines yielded one thousand talents yearly. He then married Olympias, daughter of a prince of the Molossi, who gave birth, in the year B. C. 356, to a son destined to conquer the world.

Duplicity of Philip.

The capture of Amphipolis by Philip was, of course, followed by war with Athens, which lasted twelve years. And this war commenced at a time Athens was in great embarrassments, owing to the social war. But he was aided by another event of still greater importance—the sacred war, which for a time convulsed the Hellenic world, and which grew out of the accusation of Thebes, before the Amphictyonic Council, that Sparta had seized her citadel in time of profound peace. The sentence of the council, that Sparta should pay a fine of five hundred talents, was a departure of Grecian custom, and Sparta refused to pay it, which refusal led to her exclusion from the council, the Delphic temple, and the Pythian games, and this exclusion again arrayed the different States of Greece against each other, as to the guardianship of the Oracle itself.

War with Athens.

The sacred war.

Philip of Macedon seized this opportunity, when so many States were engaged in war, to prosecute his schemes. He attacked Methone, the last remaining possession of Athens on the Macedonian coast, and captured the city, and then advanced into Thessaly against the despots of Pheræ, who invoked the aid of Onomarchus, now very powerful.

It was at this time, B. C. 353, that Demosthenes, the orator, appeared before the Athenian people. He was about twenty-seven years of age, and the wealth of his father secured him great advantages in education. His father died while he was young, and his property was confided to the care of guardians, named in his father's will. But they administered the property with such negligence, that only a small sum came to Demosthenes when he attained his civil majority, at the age of sixteen. After repeated complaints, he brought a judicial action against one of the guardians, and obtained verdict against him to the extent of ten talents. But the guardian delayed the payment, and Demosthenes lost nearly all his patrimony. He had, however, received a good education, and in spite of a feeble constitution, he mastered all the learning of the age. His family influence enabled him to get an early introduction to public affairs, and he proceeded to train himself as a speaker, and a writer of speeches for others. He put himself under the teaching of a famous rhetorician, Isæus, and profited by the discourses of Plato and Isocrates then in the height of their fame. He also was a great student of Thucydides, and copied his whole history, with his own hand, eight times. He still had to contend against a poor voice, and an ungraceful gesticulation; but by unwearied labor he overcame his natural difficulties so as to satisfy the most critical Athenian audience. But this conquest in self-education was only made by repeated trials and humiliations, and it is said he even spoke with pebbles in his mouth, and prepared himself to overcome the noise of the Assembly by declaiming in stormy weather on the sea-shore. He sometimes passed two or three months in a subterranean chamber, practicing by day and by night, both in composition and declamation, such pains did those old Greeks take to perfect themselves in art; for public speaking is an art, as well as literary composition. He learned Sophocles by heart, and took lessons from actors even to get the true accent. It was several years before he was rewarded with success, and then his delivery was full of vehemence and energy, but elaborate and artificial. But it was not mere labor which made De-

Demosthenes.

His accomplishments.

mosthenes the greatest orator of antiquity, and perhaps, of all ages and nations, but also natural genius. His self-training merely developed the great qualities of which he was conscious, as was Disraeli when he made his early failures in Parliament. Without natural gifts of eloquence, he might have worked till doomsday without producing the extraordinary effect which is ascribed to him, for his speeches show great insight, genius, and natural force, as well as learning, culture, and practice; so that they could be read like the speeches of Burke and Webster, with great effect. He had great political sagacity, moral wisdom, elevation of sentiment, and patriotic ardor, as well as art. He would have been great, if he had stammered all his life. He composed speeches for other great orators before he had confidence in his own eloquence.

His great eloquence.

In contrast with Demosthenes, who was rich, was Phocion, who remained poor, and would receive neither money nor gifts. He went barefoot, like Socrates, and had only one female slave in his household, was personally incorruptible, and also brave in battle, so that he was elected to the office of strategus, or general, forty-five times, without ever having solicited place or been present at the election. He had great contempt of fine speeches, yet was most effective as an orator for his brevity, good sense, and patriotism, and despised the "warlike eloquence, unwarlike despotism, paid speech-writing, and delicate habits of Demosthenes."

Phocion.

This Athenian, with Spartan character and habits, was opposed to the war with Philip, and was therefore the leading opponent of Demosthenes, whose foresight and cacacity led him to penetrate the schemes of the Macedonian king. But the Athenians were generally induced to a peace policy in degenerate times, and did not sympathize with the lofty principles which Demosthenes declared, and hence the influence of Phocion, though of commanding patriotism and morality, was mischievous, while that of Demosthenes was good. The citizens of Athens, enrich-

Different policy of these two leaders.

ed by commerce and enervated by leisure, were at this time averse to the burdens of military service, and formed a striking contrast to their ancestors one hundred years earlier, in the time of Pericles. In the time of Demosthenes, they sought home pleasures, the refinements of art, and the enjoyments of cultivated life, not warlike enterprises. And this decline in military spirit was equally noticeable in the cities of the Peloponnesus. And hence the cities of Greece resorted to mercenaries, like Carthage, and intrusted to them the defense of their liberties. The warlike spirit of ancient Sparta and Athens now was pre-eminent in Macedonia, where the people were poor, hardy, adventurous and bold.

It was against these warlike Macedonians, rude and hardy, that the refined Athenians were now to contend, led by a prince of uncommon military talents and insatiable ambition, and who joined craft to bravery and genius. Demosthenes in vain invoked the ancient spirit which had inspired the heroes of Marathon.

In the year 353 B. C., Philip attacked Lycophron, of Pheræ, in Thessaly. Onomarchus, then victorious over the Thebans, advanced against Philip, and defeated him in two battles, so that the Macedonian army withdrew from Thessaly. But Philip repaired his losses, marched again into Thessaly, defeated the Phocians, and slew Onomarchus. His conquest of Pheræ was now easy, and he rapidly made himself master of all Thessaly, and expelled Lycophron. He then marched to Thermopylæ, to the great alarm of Athens, which sent a force to resist him, which force succeeded in defending the pass, and keeping Philip, for a time, from entering Southern Greece. The Phocians also rallied, again availed themselves of the treasure of Delphi, and melted down the golden ornaments and vessels which Crœsus, the Lydian king, had given one hundred years before, among which were three hundred and sixty golden goblets, from the proceeds of which a new army of mercenaries was raised.

Conquests of Philip in Thessaly.

Threatens Central Greece.

The power of Philip was now exceedingly formidable, and

his successes inspired great alarm throughout Greece, as would appear from the first Philippic of Demosthenes, delivered in B. C. 352. But the Grecian States had no general able to cope with him on the land, while he created a navy to annoy the Athenians at sea.

No generals fit to cope with him.

For a time, however, the efforts of Philip were diverted from Southern and Central Greece, in order to conquer the Olynthians. They were his neighbors, and had been his allies; but the expulsion of the Athenians from the coast of Thrace and Macedonia now alarmed the Olynthians, together with the increasing power of Philip, so that they concluded a treaty of peace with Athens. Hostilities broke out in the year 350 B. C., and Demosthenes put forward all his eloquence to excite his countrymen to vigorous war. Athens, partially aroused, sent a body of mercenaries to the assistance of Olynthus, one of the most flourishing of the cities of Chalcidia, southeast of Macedonia. But before effective aid could be rendered, the island of Eubœa, through the intrigues of Philip, revolted from Athens. It was in an expedition to recover that island that Demosthenes served as a hoplite in the army, under Phocion as general. It was not till the summer of B. C. 348 that this territory was recovered by Athens. In the year following, Athens made great exertions in behalf of Olynthus, and amid great financial embarrassments. Three expeditions were sent into Chalcidia, under the command of Chares, numbering altogether four thousand Athenians and ten thousand mercenaries. But they were powerless against the conquering arms of Philip, who completely overrun and devastated the peninsula, taking thirty-two cities, and selling the people for slaves. At last Olynthus fell, B. C. 347, and the spoils of this old Hellenic city were divided among the soldiers of the conqueror, who celebrated his victories by a splendid festival.

Philip conquers the Olynthians.

Revolt of Eubœa.

Ravages of Philip.

No such calamity had befallen Greece for a century as the conquest of Chalcidia, and it filled Athens with unspeakable alarms. Æschines, the rival of Demosthenes as an orator, now joined with him in denouncing Philip as the common enemy of Greece. Aristodemus was sent to him with propo sitions of peace, and Philip professed to entertain them favorably, with his characteristic duplicity.

Meanwhile the sacred war had impoverished the Phocians, and there were dissensions among themselves. Their temple of Delphi had already been stripped of the enormous sum or ten thousand talents, eleven million five hundred thousand dollars, probably equal in our times to two hundred and thirty million dollars; so that it must have been richer, when the relative value of gold and silver is considered, than any church in Christendom. The treasures of the temple, enriched for three hundred years by offerings from all parts of the world, still enabled the Phocians to maintain war with Thebes. At last the Thebans invoked the aid of Philip, and a Macedonian army, under Parmenio, advanced as far as Thessaly. But the Phocians, in alarm, entreated both Sparta and Athens for assistance. The crisis was great, for if Philip should once secure the Pass of Thermopylæ, all Southern Greece was in imminent danger. The whole defense of Greece now turned upon this Pass, of as much importance to Philip as to Athens and Sparta, for it was the only road into Greece. Envoys were again sent from Athens to Philip, to learn on what conditions peace could be secured, among whom were Demosthenes and Æschines. But he would grant no better terms than that each party should retain what they already possessed, and the Athenians consented. Philip reaped all the advantages of a peace, which gave him the possession of the cities and territory he had taken. The Phocians were left out in the negotiations, a fatal step, since it required the united forces of Greece from preventing the further encroachments of the Macedonian king. He had now leisure for the completion of the conquest of Thrace. When this was completed, he marched toward Thermopylæ, which was held by the Phocians, carefully veiling his real intentions, and even pretending that his advance to the south

The temple of Delphi robbed.

Encroachments of Philip.

His duplicities and intrigues.

was for the purpose of reconstituting the Bœotian cities and putting down Thebes. His real object was to surprise the Pass, for he was a man who had very little respect to treaties, promises, or oaths. All this while he contrived to deceive Athens and the Phocians, with the connivance of Æschines, whom he had bribed or cheated. But he did not deceive Demosthenes, who entreated his countrymen to make a stand against him, even at the eleventh hour, for he was then within three days' march of the Pass. But the eloquence and warnings of Demosthenes were in vain. The people went with Æschines, who persuaded them that Philip was friendly to Athens and only hostile to Thebes. It was the design of Philip to detach Athens from the Phocians, and thus make his conquest easier; and he succeeded by his falsehoods and intrigues. Under these circumstances, the Phocians surrendered to Philip the pass, which they ought to have defended at all hazard, and the king retired to Phocis, but still professed the greatest friendship for Athens, with whom he made peace.

Philip obtains possession of the pass of Thermopylæ.

Master now of Phocis, with a triumphant army, he openly joined the Thebans and restored the Temple of Delphi to its inhabitants, and convoked the Amphictyonic Council, which dispossessed the Phocians of their place in the assembly, and conferred it upon Philip. The unhappy Phocians were now reduced to a state of utter ruin. Their towns were dismantled, and their villages were not allowed to contain over fifty houses each. They were stripped, and slain, and their fields laid waste. Philip was now master of the keys of Greece, and the recognized leader of the Amphictyonic Council. Athens had secured an inglorious peace with her enemy, through the corruption of her own envoys, B. C. 346, and was soon to reap the penalty of her credulity and indolence. She allowed herself to be deceived, and Philip, in co-operation with Thebes, the enemy of Athens, presently threw off the mask and disgracefully renewed the war with Athens. He had gained his object by bribery and falsehood. It is mournful that the Athenians

And is master of the keys of Greece.

should not have listened to the warnings of the most sagacious patriot who adorned those degenerate times, but the influence of Æschines was then paramount, and he was sold to Philip. He cried peace, when there was no peace. The great error of Athens was in not rendering timely assistance to the Phocians, who possessed the Pass of Thermopylæ, although they had brought upon themselves the indignation of Greece by the seizure of the Delphic treasures.

Lamentations of Demosthenes.

The victories and encroachments of Philip, within the line of common Grecian defense, were profoundly lamented by Demosthenes, and he now felt that it was expedient to keep on terms of peace with so powerful and unscrupulous and cunning a man. Isocrates wished Philip to reconcile the four great cities of Greece, Sparta, Athens, Thebes, and Argos, put himself at the head of their united forces, and Greece generally, invade Persia, and liberate the Asiatic Greeks. But this was putting the Hellenic world under one man, and renouncing the independence of States and the autonomy of cities—the great principles of Grecian policy from the earliest historic times, and therefore a complete subversion of Grecian liberties, and the establishment of a centralized power under Philip, whose patrimonial kingdom was among the least civilized in Greece.

Philip's continued encroachments.

The peace between Philip and Athens lasted, without any formal renunciation, for six years, during which the Macedonian king pursued his aggressive policy and his intrigues in all the States of Greece. His policy was precisely that of Rome when it meditated the conquest of the world, only his schemes were confined chiefly to Greece. Every year his power increased, while the States of Greece remained inactive and uncombined—a proof of the degeneracy of the times—certainly in regard to self-sacrifices to secure their independence. Demosthenes plainly saw the approaching absorption of Greece in the Macedonian dominion, unless the States should unite for common defense; and he took every occasion

His insatiate ambition.

to denounce Philip, not only in Athens, but to the envoys of the different States. The counsels of the orator were a bitter annoyance to the despot, who sent to Athens letters of remonstrance.

At last an occasion was presented for hostilities by the refusal of the Athenians to allow Philip to take possession of the island of Halicarnassus, claiming the island as their own. Reprisals took place, and Philip demanded the possession of the Hellespont and Bosphorus, and the Greek cities on their coast, of the greatest value to Athens, since she relied upon the possession of the straits for the unobstructed importation of corn. The Athenians now began to realize the encroaching ambition of Philip, and to listen to Demosthenes, who, about this time, B. C. 341, delivered his third Philippic. From this time to the battle of Chæronea, the influence of Demosthenes was greater than that of any other man in Athens, which too late listened to his warning voice. Through his influence, Eubœa was detached from Philip, and also Byzantium, and they were brought into alliance with Athens. Philip was so much chagrined that he laid siege to Perinthus, and marched through the Chersonese, which was part of the Athenian territory, upon which Athens declared war. Philip, on his side, issued a manifesto declaring his wrongs, as is usual with conquerors, and announced his intention of revenge. The Athenians fitted out a fleet and sent it under Chares to the Hellespont. Philip prosecuted, on his part, the siege of Perinthus, on the Propontis, with an army of thirty thousand men, with a great number of military engines. One of his movable towers was one hundred and twenty feet high, so that he was able to drive away the defenders of the walls by missiles. He succeeded in driving the citizens of this strong town into the city, and it would have shared the fate of Olynthus, had it not been relieved by the Byzantine and Grecian mercenaries. Philip was baffled, after a siege of three months, and turned his

Athens at last aroused by Demosthenes.

Siege of Perinthus.

forces against Byzantium, but this town was also relieved by the Athenians, and the inhabitants from the islands of the Ægean. These operations lasted six months, and were the greatest adverses which Philip had as yet met with. A vote of thanks was decreed by the Athenians to Demosthenes, who had stimulated these enterprises. Philip was obliged to withdraw from Byzantium, and retreated to attack the Scythians. An important reform in the administration of the marine was effected by Demosthenes, although opposed by the rich citizens and by Æschines.

Philip withdraws from Byzantium.

While these events transpired, a new sacred war was declared by the Amphictyonic Council against the Locrians of Amphissa, kindled by Æschines, which more than compensated Philip for his repulse at Byzantium, bringing advantage to him and ruin to Grecian liberty. But the Athenians stood aloof from this suicidal war, when all the energies of Greece were demanded to put down the encroachments of Philip. As was usual in these intestine troubles, the weaker party invoked the aid of a foreign power, and the Amphictyonic Assembly, intent on punishing Amphissa, sought assistance from Philip. He, of course, accepted the invitation, and marched south through Thermopylæ, proclaiming his intention to avenge the Delphian god. In his march he took Nicæa from the Thebans, and entered Phocis, and converted Elatea into a permanent garrison. Hitherto he had only proclaimed himself as a general acting under the Amphictyonic vote to avenge the Delphian god,—now he constructed a military post in the heart of Greece.

Another sacred war.

Ruinous to Grecian liberties.

Thebes, ever since the battle of Leuctra, had been opposed to Athens, and even now unfriendly relations existed between the two cities, and Philip hoped that Thebes would act in concert with him against Athens. But this last outrage of Philip exceedingly alarmed Athens, and Demosthenes stood up in the Assembly to propose an embassy to Thebes with offers of alliance. His advice was adopted, and he was dispatched with other envoys to

Alliance of Thebes and Athens.

Thebes. The Athenian orator, in spite of the influence of the Macedonian envoys, carried his point with the Theban Assembly, and an alliance was formed between Thebes and Athens. The Athenian army marched at once to Thebes, and vigorous measures were made at Athens for the defensive war which so seriously threatened the loss of Grecian liberty. The alliance was a great disappointment to Philip, who remained at Phocis, and sent envoys to Sparta, inviting the Peloponnesians to join him against Amphissa. But the Thebans and Athenians maintained their ground against him, and even gained some advantages. Among other things, they reconstituted the Phocian towns. The Athenians and their allies had a force of fifteen thousand infantry and two thousand cavalry, and Demosthenes was the war minister by whom these forces were collected. These efforts on the part of Thebes and Athens led to renewed preparations on the part of Philip. He defeated a large body of mercenaries, and took Amphissa. Unfortunately, the Athenians had no general able to cope with him, and it was the work of Demosthenes merely to keep up the courage of his countrymen and incite them to effort.

Renewed military preparations of Philip.

At last, in the month of August, Philip, with thirty thousand foot and two thousand horse, met the allied Greeks at Chæronea, the last Bœotian town on the frontiers of Phocis. The command of the armies of the allies was shared between the Thebans and Athenians, but their movements were determined by a council of civilians and generals, of which Demosthenes was the leading spirit. Philip, in this battle, which decided the fortunes of Greece, commanded the right wing, opposed to the Athenians, and his son Alexander, the left wing, opposed to the Thebans. The Macedonian phalanx, organized by Philip, was sixteen deep, with veteran soldiers in the front. The Theban "Sacred Band" was overpowered and broken by its tremendous force, much increased by the long pikes which projected in front of the foremost

Battle of Chæronea.

Its decisive character.

soldiers. But the battle was not gained by the phalanx alone. The organization of the Macedonian army was perfect, with many other sorts of troops, body-guards, light hoplites, light cavalry, bowmen, and slingers. One thousand Athenians were slain, and two thousand more were made captives. The Theban loss was still greater.

Macedonian phalanx.

Unspeakable was the grief and consternation of Athens, when the intelligence reached her of this decisive victory. A resolution was at once taken for a vigorous defense of the city. All citizens sent in their contributions, and every hand was employed on the fortifications. The temples were stripped of arms, and envoys were sent to various places for aid.

Desperate measures of Athens.

Thebes was unable to rally, and fell into the hands of the victors, and a Macedonian garrison was placed in the Cadmea, or citadel. From Athens, envoys were sent to Philip for peace, which was granted on the condition that he should be recognized as the chief of the Hellenic world. It was a great humiliation to Athens to concede this, after having defeated the Persian hosts, and keeping out so long all foreign domination. But times had changed, and the military spirit had fled.

Fall of Thebes.

Athens was not prostrated by the battle of Chæronea. She still retained her navy, and her civic rights. Thebes was utterly prostrated, and never rallied again.

Philip, having now subjugated Thebes, and constrained Athens into submission, next proceeded to carry his arms into the Peloponnesus. He found but little resistance, except in Laconia. The Corinthians, Argeians, Messenians, Elians, and Arcadians submitted to his power. Even Sparta could make but feeble resistance. He laid waste Laconia, and then convened a congress of Grecian cities at Corinth, and announced his purpose to undertake an expedition against the king of Persia, avenge the invasion of Greece by Xerxes, and liberate the Asiatic Greeks. A large force of two hundred thousand foot and fifteen thousand horse was promised him, and all the States

Philip invades the Peloponnesus.

of Greece concurred, except Sparta, which held aloof from the congress. Athens was required to furnish a well equipped fleet. All the States, and all the islands, and all the cities of Greece, were now subservient to Philip, and no one State could exercise control over its former territories.

Collects a large force against the Persians.

It was in the year B. C. 337, that this great scheme for the invasion of Persia was concerted, which created no general enthusiasm, since Persia was no longer a power to be feared. The only power to be feared now was Macedonia. While preparations were going on for this foolish and unnecessary expedition, the prime mover of it was assassinated, and his career, so disastrous to Grecian liberty, came to an end. It seems that he had repudiated his wife, Olympias, disgusted with the savage impulses of her character, and married, for his last wife, for he had several, Cleopatra, which provoked bitter dissensions among the partisans of the two queens, and also led to a separation between himself and his son Alexander, although a reconciliation afterward took place. It was while celebrating the marriage of his daughter by Olympias, with Alexander, king of Epirus, and also the birth of a son by Cleopatra, that Pausanias, one of the royal body-guard, who nourished an implacable hatred of Philip, chose his opportunity, and stabbed him with a short sword he had concealed under his garment.

Death of Philip.

Alexander, the son of Philip by Olympias, was at once declared king, whose prosecution of the schemes of his father are to be recounted in the next chapter. Philip perished at the age of forty-seven, after a most successful reign of twenty-three years. On his accession he found his kingdom a narrow territory around Pella, excluded from the sea-coast. At his death the Macedonian kingdom was the most powerful in Greece, and all the States and cities, except Sparta, recognized its ascendency. He had gained this great power, more from the weakness and dissensions of the Grecian States, than from his own strength, great as were his talents. He became the arbiter of Greece

Alexander.

by unscrupulous perjury and perpetual intrigues. But he was a great organizer, and created a most efficient army. Without many accomplishments, he affected to be a patron of both letters and religion. His private life was stained by drunkenness, gambling, perfidy, and wantonness. His wives and mistresses were as numerous as those of an Oriental despot. He was a successful man, but it must be borne in mind that he had no opponents like Epaminondas, or Agesilaus, or Iphicrates. Demosthenes was his great opponent, but only in counsels and speech. The generals of Athens, and Sparta, and Thebes had passed away, and with the decline of military spirit, it is not remarkable that Philip should have ascended to a height from which he saw the Grecian world suppliant at his feet.

Character of Philip.

CHAPTER XXV.

ALEXANDER THE GREAT.

WE come now to consider briefly the career of Alexander, the son of Philip—the most successful, fortunate, and brilliant hero of antiquity. I do not admire either his character or his work. He does not compare with Cæsar or Napoleon in comprehensiveness of genius, or magnanimity, or variety of attainments, or posthumous influences. He was a meteor—a star of surprising magnitude, which blazed over the whole Oriental world with unprecedented brilliancy. His military genius was doubtless great—even transcendent, and his fame is greater than his genius. His prestige is wonderful. He conquered the world more by his name than by his power. Only two men, among military heroes, dispute his pre-eminence in the history of nations. After more than two thousand years, his glory shines with undiminished brightness. His conquests extended over a period of only twelve years, yet they were greater and more dazzling than any man ever made before in a long reign. Had he lived to be fifty, he might have subdued the whole world, and created a universal empire equal to that of the Cæsars—which was the result of five hundred years' uninterrupted conquests by the greatest generals of a military nation. Though we neither love nor reverence Alexander, we can not withhold our admiration for his almost superhuman energy, courage, and force of will. He looms up as one of the prodigies of earth—yet sent by Providence as an avenger—an instrument of punishment on those effeminated nations, or rather dynasties, which had triumphed over human misery. I look

Alexander the Great.

Sent by Providence to do a great work.

upon his career, as the Christians of the fifth century looked upon that of Alaric or Attila, whom they called the scourge of God.

Which was prepared by his father.

His conquests and dominions were, however, prepared by one perhaps greater than himself in creative genius, and as unscrupulous and cruel as he. Philip found his kingdom a little brook; he left it a river—broad, deep, and grand. Under Alexander, this river became an irresistible torrent, sweeping every thing away which impeded its course. Philip created an army, and a military system, and generals, all so striking, that Greece succumbed before him, and yielded up her liberties. Alexander had only to follow out his policy, which was to subdue the Persians. The Persian empire extended over all the East—Asia Minor, Syria, Egypt, Parthia, Babylonia, Mesopotamia, Armenia, Bactria, and other countries—the one hundred and twenty provinces of Nebuchadnezzar and Cyrus, from the Mediterranean to India, from the Euxine and Caspian Seas to Arabia and the Persian Gulf—a monstrous empire, whose possession was calculated to inflame the monarchs who reigned at Susa and Babylon with more than mortal pride and self-sufficiency. It had been gradually won by successive conquerors, from Nimrod to Darius. It was the gradual absorption of all the kingdoms of the East in the successive Assyrian, Babylonian, and Persian empires—for these three empires were really one under different dynasties, and were ruled by the same precedents and principles. The various kingdoms which composed this empire, once independent, yielded to the conquerors who reigned at Babylon, or Nineveh, or Persepolis, and formed satrapies paying tribute to the great king. The satraps of Cyrus were like the satraps of Nebuchadnezzar, members or friends of the imperial house, who ruled the various provinces in the name of the king of Babylon, or Persia, without much interference with the manners, or language, or customs, or laws, or religion of the conquered, contented to receive tribute merely, and troops in case of war. And so great was the accumulation

Extent of the Persian empire.

of treasure in the various royal cities where the king resided part of the year, that Darius left behind him on his flight, in Ecbatana alone, one hundred and eighty thousand talents, or two hundred million dollars. It was by this treasure that the kings of Persia lived in such royal magnificence, and with it they were able to subsidize armies to maintain their power throughout their vast dominions, and even gain allies like the Greeks, when they had need of their services. Their treasures were inexhaustible—and were accumulated with the purpose of maintaining empire, and hence were not spent, but remained as a sacred deposit.

The accumulation of riches in the royal cities.

It was to overthrow this empire that Philip aspired, after he had conquered Greece, in part to revenge the injuries inflicted by the Persian invasions, but more from personal ambition. And had he lived, he would have succeeded, and his name would have been handed down as the great conqueror, rather than that of his more fortunate son. Philip knew what a rope of sand the Persian military power was. Xenophon had enlightened the Greeks as to the inefficiency of the Persian armies, if they needed any additional instruction after the defeat of Xerxes and his generals. The vast armies of the Persians made a grand show, and looked formidable when reviewed by the king in his gilded chariot, surrounded by his nobles, the princes of his family, and the women of his harem. And these armies were sufficient to keep the empire together. The mighty prestige attending victories for one thousand years, and all the pomp of millions in battle array, was adequate to keep the province together, for the system of warfare and the character of the forces were similar in all the provinces. It was external enemies, with a different system of warfare, that the Persian kings had to dread—not the revolt of enervated States, and unwarlike cities. The Orientals were never warlike in the sense that Greece and Rome were. The armies of Greece and Rome were small, but efficient. It was seldom that any Grecian

Philip had aspired to overturn the empire.

Knowing its internal weakness.

or Roman army exceeded fifty thousand men, but they were veterans, and they had military science and skill and discipline. The hosts of Xerxes or Darius were undisciplined, and they were mercenaries, unlike the original troops of Cyrus.

But this work is reserved for Alexander.

Now it was the mission of Alexander to overturn the dynasties which reigned so ingloriously on the banks of the Euphrates—to overrun the Persian empire from north to south and east to west—to cut it up, and form new kingdoms of the dismembered provinces, and distribute the hoarded treasures of Susa, Persepolis, and Ecbatana—to introduce Greek satraps instead of Persian—to favor the spread of the Greek language and institutions—to found new cities where Greeks might reign, from which they might diffuse their spirit and culture. Alexander spent only one year of his reign in Greece, all the rest of his life was spent in the various provinces of Persia. He was the conqueror of the Oriental world. He had no hard battles to fight, like Cæsar or Napoleon. All he had to do was to appear with his troops, and the enemy fled. Cities were surrendered as he approached. The two great battles which decided the fate of Persia—Issus and Arbela—were gained at the first shock of his cavalry. Darius fled from the field, in both instances, at the very beginning of the battle, and made no real resistance. The greater the number of Persian soldiers, the more disorderly was the rout. The Macedonian soldiers fought retreating armies in headlong flight. The slaughter of the Persians was mere butchery. It was something like collecting a vast number of birds in a small space, and shooting them when collected in a corner, and dignifying the slaughter with a grand name—not like chasing the deer over rocks and hills.

Who was the conqueror of the Oriental world?

What constituted his military genius.

The military genius of Alexander was seen in the siege of the few towns which *did* resist, like Tyre and Gaza; in his rapid marches; in the combination of his forces; in the system, foresight, and sagacity he displayed, conquering at the right time, marching upon the right place, husbanding his energies, wasting no time in expeditions which did not bear on the main issue, and concentrating his men on points which were vital and important. Philip, if he had lived, might have conquered the Persian empire; but he would not have conquered so rapidly as Alexander, who knew no rest, and advanced from conquering to conquer, in some cases without ulterior objects, as in the Indian campaigns—simply from the love and excitement of conquest. He only needed time. He met no enemies who could oppose him—more, I apprehend, from the want of discipline among his enemies, than from any irresistible strength of his soldiers, for he embodied the conquered soldiers in his own army, and they fought like his own troops, when once disciplined. Nor did he dream of reconstruction, or building up a great central power. He would, if he had lived, have overrun Arabia, and then Italy, and Gaul. But he did not live to measure his strength with the Romans. His mission was ended when he had subdued the Persian world. And he left no successor. His empire was divided among his generals, and new kingdoms arose on the ruins of the Persian empire.

It was his passion to conquer, not reconstruct.

"Alexander was born B. C. 356, and like his father, Philip, was not Greek, but a Macedonian and Epirot, only partially imbued with Grecian sentiment and intelligence." He inherited the ambition of Philip, and the violent and headstrong temperament of his furious mother, Olympias. His education was good, and he was instructed by his Greek tutors in the learning common to Grecian princes. His taste inclined him to poetry and literature, rather than to science and philosophy. At thirteen he was intrusted to the care of the great Aristotle, and remained under his teaching three years. At sixteen he was left regent of the Macedonian kingdom, whose capital was Pella, while his father was absent in the siege of Byzantium. At eighteen he commanded one of the wings of the army at the battle of Chæronea. His prospects were uncertain up to the very day when Philip was assassinated, on account of family dissen-

His early history.

sions, and the wrath of his father, whom he had displeased. But he was proclaimed king on the death of Philip, B. C., 336 and celebrated his funeral with great magnificence, and slew many of his murderers. The death of Philip had excited aspirations of freedom in the Grecian States, but there was no combination to throw off the Macedonian yoke. Alexander well understood the discontent of Greece, and his first object was to bring it to abject submission. With the army of his father he marched from State to State, compelling submission, and punishing with unscrupulous cruelty all who resisted. After displaying his forces in various portions of the Peloponnesus, he repaired to Corinth and convened the deputies from the Grecian cities, and was chosen to the headship of Greece, as his father, Philip, had been. He was appointed the keeper of the peace of Greece. Each Hellenic city was declared free, and in each the existing institutions were recognized, but no new despot was to be established, and each city was forbidden to send armed vessels to the harbor of any other, or build vessels, or engage seamen there. Such was the melancholy degradation of the Grecian world. Its freedom was extinguished, and there was no hope of escaping the despotism of Macedonia, but by invoking aid from the Persian king. Had he been wise, he would have subsidized the Greeks with a part of his vast treasures, and raised a force in Greece able to cope with Alexander. But he was doomed, and the Macedonian king was left free to complete the conquest of all the States. He first marched across Mount Hæmus, and subdued the Illyrians, Pæonians, and Thracians. He even crossed the Danube, and defeated the Gætæ.

His conquest of the Grecian States.

Just as he had completed the conquest of the barbarians north of Macedonia, he heard that the Thebans had declared their independence, being encouraged by his long absence in Thrace, and by reports of his death. But he suddenly appeared with his victorious army, and as the Thebans had no generals equal to Pelopidas and Epaminondas, they were easily subdued. Thebes

He annihilates the Theban power.

was taken by assault, and the population was massacred—even women and children, whether in their houses or in temples. Thirty thousand captives were reserved for sale. The city was razed to the ground, and the Cadmea alone was preserved for a Macedonian garrison. The Theban territory was partitioned among the reconstructed cities of Orchomenus and Platæa. This severity was unparaleled in the history of Greece, but the remorseless conqueror wished to strike with terror all other cities, and prevent rebellion. He produced the effect he desired. All the cities of Greece hastened to make peace with so terrible an enemy. He threatened a like doom on Athens because she refused to surrender the anti-Macedonian leaders, including Demosthenes, but was finally appeased through the influence of Phocion, since he did not wish to drive Athens to desperate courses, which might have impeded his contemplated conquest of Persia, for the city was still strong in naval defenses, and might unite with the Persian king. So Athens was spared, but the empire of Thebes was utterly destroyed. He then repaired to Corinth to make arrangements for his Persian campaign, and while in that city he visited the cynical philosopher, Diogenes, who lived in a tub. It is said that when the philosopher was asked by Alexander if he wished any thing, he replied: "Nothing, except that you would stand a little out of my sunshine"—a reply which extorted from the conqueror the remark: "If I were not Alexander, I would be Diogenes."

Moral effect of his merciless severity.

He is master of Greece.

It took Alexander a year and a few months to crush out what little remained of Grecian freedom, subdue the Thracians, and collect forces for his expedition into Persia. In the spring of 334 B. C., his army was mustered between Pella and Amphipolis, while his fleet was at hand to render assistance. In April he crossed the strait from Sestos to Abydos, and never returned to his own capital—Pella—or to Europe. The remainder of his life, eleven years and two months, was spent in Asia, in continued and increas-

Prepares to invade Persia.

ing conquests; and these were on such a gigantic scale that Greece dwindled into insignificance.

He marshals his forces in Asia.

When marshalled on the Asiatic shore, the army of Alexander presented a total of thirty thousand infantry, and four thousand five hundred cavalry—a small force, apparently, to overthrow the most venerable and extensive empire in the world. But these troops were veterans, trained by Philip, and commanded by able generals. Of these troops twelve thousand were Macedonians, armed with the sarissa, a long pike, which made the phalanx, sixteen deep, so formidable. The sarissa was twenty-one feet in length, and so held by both hands as to project fifteen feet before the body of the pikeman. The soldier of the phalanx was also provided with a short sword, a circular shield, a breastplate, leggings, and broad-brimmed hat. But, besides the phalanx of heavy armed men, there were hoplites lightly armed, hypaspists for the assault of walled places, and troops with javelins and with bows. The cavalry was admirable, distributed into squadrons, among whom were the body-guards—all promoted out of royal pages and the picked men of the army, sons of the chief people in Macedonia, and these were heavily armed.

His phalanx and the armor of his troops.

His generals.

The generals who served under Alexander were all Macedonians, and had been trained by Philip. Among these were Hephæstion, the intimate personal friend of Alexander, Ptolemy, Perdiccas, Antipater, Clitus, Parmenio, Philotas, Nicanor, Seleucus, Amyntas, Phillipes, Lysimachus, Antigonas, most of whom reached great power. Parmenio and Antipater were the highest in rank, the latter of whom was left as viceroy of Macedonia. Eumenes was the private secretary of Alexander, the most long-headed man in his army.

Alexander is unobstructed in crossing the Hellespont.

Alexander had landed, unopposed, against the advice of Memnon and Mentor—two Rhodians, in the service of Darius, the king—descendants of one of the brothers of Artaxerxes Mnemon—the children of King Ochus, after his assassination, having all been murdered by the eunuch Bagoas. As the Persians were superior by sea to the Macedonians, it was an imprudence to allow Alexander to cross the Hellespont without opposition; but Memnon was overruled by the Persian satraps, who supposed that they were more than a match for Alexander on the land, and hoped to defeat him. Arsites, the Phrygian satrap, commanded the Persian forces, assisted by other satraps, and Persians of high rank, among whom were Spithridates, satrap of Lydia and Ionia. The cavalry of the Persians greatly outnumbered that of the Macedonians, but the infantry was inferior. Memnon advised the satraps to avoid fighting on the land, and to employ the fleet for aggressive movements in Macedonia and Greece, but Arsites rejected his advice. The Persians took post on the river Granicus, near the town of Parium, on one of the declivities of Mount Ida. Alexander at once resolved to force the passage of the river, taking the command of the right wing, and giving the left to Parmenio. The battle was fought by the cavalry, in which Alexander showed great personal courage. At one time he was in imminent danger of his life, from the cimeter of Spithridates, but Clitus saved him by severing the uplifted arm of the satrap from his body with his sword. The victory was complete, and great numbers of the satraps were slain. There remained no force in Asia Minor to resist the conqueror, and the Asiatics submitted in terror and alarm. Alexander then sent Parmenio to subdue Dascyleum, the stronghold of the satrap of Phrygia, while he advanced to Sardis, the capital of Lydia, and the main station of the Persians in Asia Minor. The citadel was considered impregnable, yet such was the terror of the Persians, that both city and citadel surrendered without a blow. Phrygia and Lydia then fell into his hands, with immense treasure, of which he stood in need. He then marched to Ephesus, and entered the city without resistance, and thus was placed in communication with his fleet, under the command of Nicanor. He found no opposition

Error of the Persians.

Battle of the Granicus.

Alexander dispenses with his fleet.

until he reached Miletus, which was encouraged to resist him from the approach of the Persian fleet, four hundred sail, chiefly of Phœnician and Cyprian ships, which, a few weeks earlier, might have prevented his crossing into Asia. But the Persian fleet did not arrive until the city was invested, and the Macedonian fleet, of one hundred and sixty sail, had occupied the harbor. Alexander declined to fight on the sea, but pressed the siege on the land, so that the Persian fleet, unable to render assistance, withdrew to Halicarnassus.

Fall of Miletus. The city fell, and Alexander took the resolution of disbanding his own fleet altogether, and concentrating all his operations on the land—doubtless a wise, but desperate measure. He supposed, and rightly, that after he had taken the cities on the coast, the Persian fleet would be useless, and the country would be insured to his army.

Alexander found some difficulty at the siege of Halicarnassus, from the bravery of the garrison, commanded by Memnon, and the strength of the defenses, aided by the Persian fleet.

The siege of Halicarnassus. But his soldiers, "protected from missiles by movable pent-houses, called tortoises, gradually filled up the deep and wide ditch round the town, so as to open a level road for his engines (rolling towers of wood) to come up close to the walls." Then the battering-rams overthrew the towers of the city wall, and made a breach in them, so that the city was taken by assault. Memnon, forced to abandon his defenses, withdrew the garrison by sea, and Alexander entered the city. The ensuing winter months

Conquest of Asia Minor. were employed in the conquest of Lydia, Pamphylia, and Pisidia, which was effected easily, since the terror of his arms led to submission wherever he appeared. At Gordium, in Phrygia, he performed the exploit familiarly known as the cutting of the Gordian knot, which was a cord so twisted and entangled, that no one could untie it. The oracle had pronounced that to the person who should untie it, the empire of Persia was destined. Alexander, after many futile attempts to disentangle the knot, in a fit of impatience, cut it with his sword, and this was accepted as the solution of the problem.

Meanwhile Memnon, to whom Darius had intrusted the guardianship of the whole coast of Asia Minor, with a large Phœnician fleet and a considerable body of Grecian mercenaries, acquired the important island of Chios, and a large part of Lesbos. But in the midst of his successes, he died of sickness, and no one was left able to take his place. Had his advice been taken, Alexander could not have landed in Asia. His death was an irreparable loss to the Persian cause, and with his death vanished all hope of employing the Persian force with wisdom and effect. Darius now changed his policy, and resolved to carry on offensive measures on the land. He therefore summoned a vast army, from all parts of his empire, of five hundred thousand infantry, and one hundred thousand cavalry. An eminent Athenian, Charidemus, advised the Persian king to employ his great treasure in subsidizing the Greeks, and not to dream, with his undisciplined Asiatics, to oppose the Macedonians in battle. But the advice was so unpalatable to the proud and self-reliant king, in the midst of his vast forces, that he looked upon Charidemus as a traitor, and sent him to execution.

The Persians resolve on offensive operations.

It would not have been difficult for Darius to defend his kingdom, had he properly guarded the mountain passes through which Alexander must needs march to invade Persia. Here again Darius was infatuated, and he, in his self-confidence, left the passes over Mount Taurus and Mount Amanus undefended. Alexander, with re-enforcements from Macedonia, now marched from Gordium through Paphlagonia and Cappadocia, whose inhabitants made instant submission, and advanced to the Cilician Gates—an impregnable pass in the Taurus range, which opened the way to Cilicia. It had been traversed seventy years before by Cyrus the Younger, with the ten thousand Greeks, and was the main road from Asia Minor into Cilicia and Syria. The narrowest part

Neglect to guard the mountain passes.

Which Alexander passes through unobstructed.

of this defile allowed only four soldiers abreast, and here Darius should have taken his stand, even as the Greeks took possession of Thermopylæ in the invasion of Xerxes. But the pass was utterly undefended, and Alexander marched through unobstructed without the loss of a man. He then found himself at Tarsus, where he made a long halt, from a dangerous illness which he got by bathing in the river Cydnus. When he recovered, he sent Parmenio to secure the pass over Mount Amanus, six days' march from Tarsus, called the Cilician Gates. These were defended, but the guard fled at the approach of the Macedonians, and this important defile was secured. Alexander then marched through Issus to Myriandrus, to the south of the Cilician Gates, which he had passed. The Persians now advanced from Sochi, and appeared in his rear at Issus—a vast host, in the midst of which was Darius with his mother, his wife, his harem, and children, who accompanied him to witness his anticipated triumph, for it seemed to him an easy matter to overwhelm and crush the invaders, who numbered only about forty thousand men. So impatient was Darius to attack Alexander that he imprudently advanced into Cilicia by the northern pass, now called Beylan, with all his army, so that in the narrow defiles of that country his cavalry was nearly useless. He encamped near Issus, on the river Pinarus. Alexander, learning that Darius was in his rear, retraced his steps, passed north through the Gates of Cilicia, through which he had marched two days before, and advanced to the river Pinarus, on the north bank of which Darius was encamped. And here Darius resolved to fight. He threw across the river thirty thousand cavalry and twenty thousand infantry, to insure the undisturbed formation of his main force. His main line was composed of ninety thousand hoplites, of which thirty thousand were Greek in the centre. On the mountain to his left, he posted twenty thousand, to act against the right wing of the Macedonian army. He then recalled the thirty thousand cavalry and twenty thousand infantry, which he had sent

Infatuation and errors of the Persians.

The Persians advance to Issus.

across the river, and awaited the onset of Alexander. Darius was in his chariot, in the centre, behind the Grecian hoplites. But the ground was so uneven, that only a part of his army could fight. A large proportion of it were mere spectators.

Alexander advanced to the attack. The left wing was commanded by Parmenio, and the right by himself, on which were placed the Macedonian cavalry. The divisions of the phalanx were in the centre, and the Peloponnesian cavalry and Thracian light infantry on the left. The whole front extended only one and a half mile. Crossing the river rapidly, Alexander, at the head of his cavalry, light infantry, and some divisions of the phalanx, fell suddenly upon the Asiatic hoplites which were stationed on the Persian left. So impetuous and unexpected was the charge, that the troops instantly fled, vigorously pressed by the Macedonian right. Darius, from his chariot, saw the flight of his left wing, and, seized with sudden panic, caused his chariot to be turned, and fled also among the foremost fugitives. In his terror he cast away his bow, shield, and regal mantle. He did not give a single order, nor did he remain a moment after the defeat of his left, as he ought, for he was behind thirty thousand Grecian hoplites, in the centre, but abandoned himself to inglorious flight, and this was the signal for a general flight also of all his troops, who turned and trampled each other down in their efforts to get beyond the reach of the enemy.

The great and decisive battle of Issus.

Thus the battle was lost by the giving way of the Asiatic hoplites on the left, and the flight of Darius in a few minutes after. The Persian right showed some bravery, till Alexander, having completed the rout of the left, turned to attack the Grecian mercenaries in the flank and rear, when all fled in terror. The slaughter of the fugitives was prodigious. The camp of Darius was taken, with his mother, wife, sister, and children. One hundred thousand Persians were slain, not in *fight*, but in *flight*, and among them were several eminent

The mistakes of the Persians, and the cowardice of Darius.

satraps and grandees. The Persian hosts were completely dispersed, and Darius did not stop till he had crossed the Euphrates. The booty acquired was immense, in gold, silver, and captives.

Such was the decisive battle of Issus, where the cowardice and incompetency of Darius were more marked than the generalship of Alexander himself. No victory was ever followed by more important consequences. It dispersed the Persian hosts, and opened Persia to a victorious enemy, and gave an irresistible prestige to the conqueror. The fall of the empire was rendered probable, and insured successive triumphs to Alexander.

Important consequences of the battle.

But before he proceeded to the complete conquest of the Persian empire, Alexander, like a prudent and far-reaching general, impetuous as he was, concluded to subdue first all the provinces which lay on the coast, and thus make the Persian fleet useless, and ultimately capture it, and leave his rear without an enemy. Accordingly he sent Parmenio to capture Damascus, where were collected immense treasures. It was surrendered without resistance, though it was capable of sustaining a siege. There were captured vast treasures, with prodigious numbers of Persians of high rank, and many illustrious Greek exiles. Master of Damascus, Alexander, in the winter of B. C. 331, advanced upon Phœnicia, the cities of which mostly sent letters of submission. While at Maranthus, Darius wrote to Alexander, asking for the restitution of his wife, mother, sister, and daughter, and tendering friendship, to which Alexander replied in a haughty letter, demanding to be addressed, not as an equal, but as lord of Asia.

The flight and inaction of Darius.

The last hope of Darius was in the Phœnicians, who furnished him ships; and one city remained firm in its allegiance—Tyre—the strongest and most important place in Phœnicia. But even this city would have yielded on fair and honorable conditions. This did not accord with Alexander's views, who made exorbitant demands, which could not be accepted by the Tyrians without hazarding their all. Accordingly they prepared for a siege, trusting to the impregnable defenses of the city. It was situated on an islet, half a mile from the main land, surrounded by lofty walls and towers of immense strength and thickness. But nothing discouraged Alexander, who loved to surmount difficulties. He constructed a mole from the main land to the islet, two hundred feet wide, of stone and timber, which was destroyed by a storm and by the efforts of the Tyrians. Nothing daunted, he built another, still wider and stronger, and repaired to Sidon, where he collected a great fleet, with which he invested the city by sea, as well as land. The doom of the city was now sealed, and the Tyrians could offer no more serious obstructions. The engines were then rolled along the mole to the walls, and a breach was at last made, and the city was taken by assault. The citizens then barricaded the streets, and fought desperately until they were slain. The surviving soldiers were hanged, and the women and children sold as slaves. Still the city resisted for seven months, and its capture was really the greatest effort of genius that Alexander had shown, and furnished an example to Richelieu in the siege of La Rochelle.

The siege of Tyre.

Its fall.

On the fall of this ancient and wealthy capital, whose pride and wealth are spoken of in the Scriptures, Alexander received a second letter from Darius, offering ten thousand talents, his daughter in marriage, with the cession of all the provinces of his empire west of the Euphrates, for the surrender of his family. To which the haughty and insolent conqueror replied: "I want neither your money nor your cession. All your money and territory are mine already, and you are tendering me a part instead of the whole. If I choose to marry your daughter I *shall* marry her, whether you give her to me or not. Come hither to me, if you wish for friendship."

Offer of Darius.

Rejected by Alexander.

Darius now saw that he must risk another desperate battle, and summoned all his hosts. Yet Alexander did not immediately march against him, but undertook first the conquest of Egypt. Syria, Phœnicia, and Palestine were now his, as well as Asia Minor. He had also defeated the Persian fleet, and was master of all the islands of the Ægean. He stopped on his way to Egypt to take Gaza, which held out against him, built on a lofty artificial mound two hundred and fifty feet high, and encircled with a lofty wall. The Macedonian engineers pronounced the place impregnable, but the greater the difficulty the greater the eagerness of Alexander to surmount it. He accordingly built a mound all around the city, as high as that on which Gaza was built, and then rolled his engines to the wall, effected a breach, and stormed the city, slew all the garrison, and sold all the women and children for slaves. As for Batis, the defender of the city, he was dragged by a chariot around the town, as Achilles, whom Alexander imitated, had done to the dead body of Hector. The siege of these two cities, Tyre and Gaza, occupied nine months, and was the hardest fighting that Alexander ever encountered.

Who conquers Egypt.

He entered and occupied Egypt without resistance, and resolved to found a new city, near the mouth of the Nile, not as a future capital of the commercial world, but as a depot for his ships. While he was preparing for this great work, he visited the temple of Jupiter Ammon in the desert, and was addressed by the priests as the Son of God, not as a mortal, which flattery was agreeable to him, so that ever afterward he claimed divinity, in the arrogance of his character, and the splendor of his successes, and even slew the man who saved his life at the Granicus, because he denied his divine claims—the most signal instance of self-exaggeration and pride recorded in history, transcending both Nebuchadnezzar and Napoleon.

Founding of Alexandria.

After arranging his affairs in Egypt, and obtaining re-enforcements of Greeks and Thracians, he set out for the Euphrates, which he crossed at Thapsacus, unobstructed—another error of the Persians. But Darius was paralyzed by the greatness of his mis-

Alexander marches to the Euphrates.

fortunes, and by the capture of his family, and could not act with energy or wisdom. He collected his vast hosts on a plain near Arbela, east of the Tigris, and waited for the approach of the enemy. He had one million of infantry, forty thousand cavalry, and two hundred scythed chariots, besides a number of elephants. He placed himself in the centre, with his choice troops, including the horse and foot-guards, and mercenary Greeks. In the rear stood deep masses of Babylonians, and on the left and right, Bactrians, Cadusians, Medes, Albanians, and troops from the remote provinces. In the front of Darius, were the scythed chariots with advanced bodies of cavalry.

Marshalling of the armies at Arbela.

Alexander, as he approached, ranged his forces with great care and skill, forty thousand foot and seven thousand horse. His main line was composed, on the right, of choice cavalry; then, toward the left, of hypaspists; then the phalanx, in six divisions, which formed the centre; then Greek cavalry on the extreme left. Behind the main line was a body of reserves, intended to guard against attack on the flanks and rear. In front of the main line were advanced squadrons of cavalry and light troops. The Thracian infantry guarded the baggage and camp. He himself commanded the right, and Parmenio the left.

Utter discomfiture of Darius.

His inglorious flight.

Darius, at the commencement of the attack, ordered his chariots to charge, and the main line to follow, calculating on disorder. But the horses of the chariots were terrified and wounded by the Grecian archers and darters in front, and most turned round, or were stopped. Those that pressed on were let through the Macedonian lines without mischief. As at Issus, Alexander did not attack the centre, where Darius was surrounded with the choicest troops of the army, but advanced impetuously upon the left wing, turned it, and advanced by a flank movement toward the centre, where Darius was posted. The Persian king, seeing the failure of the chariots, and the advancing troops of Alexander, lost his self-possession, turned his chariot, and fled, as at Issus. Such folly and cowardice led, of course, to instant defeat and rout; and nothing was left for the victor, but to pursue and destroy the disorderly fugitives, so that the slaughter was immense. But while the left and centre of the Persians were put to flight, the right fought vigorously, and might have changed the fortune of the day, had not Alexander seasonably returned from the pursuit, and attacked the left in the rear and flank. Then all was lost, and headlong flight marked the Persian hosts. The battle was lost by the cowardice of Darius, who insisted, with strange presumption, on commanding in person. Half the troops, under an able general, would have overwhelmed the Macedonian army, even with Alexander at the head. But the Persians had no leader of courage and skill, and were a mere rabble. According to some accounts, three hundred thousand Persians were slain, and not more than one hundred Macedonians. There was no attempt on the part of Darius to rally or collect a new army. His cause and throne were irretrievably lost, and he was obliged to fly to his farthest provinces, pursued by the conqueror. The battle of Arbela was the death-blow to the Persian empire. We can not help feeling sentiments of indignation in view of such wretched management on the part of the Persians, thus throwing away an empire. But, on the other hand, we are also compelled to admit the extraordinary generalship of Alexander, who brought into action every part of his army, while at least three-quarters of the Persians were mere spectators, so that his available force was really great. His sagacious combinations, his perception of the weak points of his adversary, and the instant advantage which he seized—his insight, rapidity of movement, and splendid organization, made him irresistible against any Persian array of numbers, without skill. Indeed, the Persian army was too large, since it could not be commanded by one man with any effect, and all became confusion and ruin on the first misfortune. The great generals of antiquity, Greek and Roman, rarely commanded over fifty thousand men on the field of battle; and fifty thousand, under Alex-

The battle of Arbela a death-blow to Persia.

Military genius of the conqueror.

ander's circumstances, were more effective, perhaps, than two hundred thousand. In modern times, when battles are not decided by personal bravery, but by the number and disposition of cannon, and the excellence of fire-arms, an army of one hundred thousand can generally overwhelm an army of fifty thousand, with the same destructive weapons. But in ancient times, the impetuous charge of twenty thousand men on a single point, followed by success, would produce a panic, and then a rout, when even flight is obstructed by numbers. Thus Alexander succeeded both at Issus and Arbela. He concentrated forces upon a weak point, which, when carried, produced a panic, and especially sent dismay into the mind of Darius, who had no nerve or self-control. Had he remained firm, and only fought on the defensive, the Macedonians might not have prevailed. But he fled; and confusion seized, of course, his hosts.

Both Babylon and Susa, the two great capitals of the empire, immediately surrendered after the decisive battle of Arbela, and Alexander became the great king and Darius a fugitive. The treasure found at Susa was even greater than that which Babylon furnished—about fifty thousand talents, or fifty million dollars, one-fifth of which, three years before, would have been sufficient to subsidize Greece, and present a barrier to the conquests of both Philip and Alexander.

Surrender of Babylon and Susa.

The victor spent a month in Babylon, sacrificing to the Babylonian deities, feasting his troops, and organizing his new empire. He then marched into Persia proper, subdued the inhabitants, and entered Persepolis. Though it was the strongest place in the empire, it made no resistance. Here were hoarded the chief treasures of the Persian kings, no less than one hundred and twenty thousand talents, or about one hundred and twenty million dollars of our money—an immense sum in gold and silver in that age, a tenth of which, judiciously spent, would have secured the throne to Darius against any exterior enemy. He was now a fugitive in Media, and thither Alex-

The enormous treasures of the Persian kings.

ander went at once in pursuit, giving himself no rest. He established himself at Ecbatana, the capital, without resistance, and made preparations for the invasion of the eastern part of the Persian empire, beyond the Parthian desert, even to the Oxus and the Indus, inhabited by warlike barbarians, from which were chiefly recruited the Persian armies.

It would be tedious to describe the successive conquests of Sogdiana, Margiana, Bactriana, and even some territory beyond the Indus. Alexander never met from these nations the resistance which Cæsar found in Gaul, nor were his battles in these eastern countries remarkable. He only had to appear, and he was master. At last his troops were wearied of these continual marchings and easy victories, when their real enemies were heat, hunger, thirst, fatigue, and toil. They refused to follow their general and king any further to the east, and he was obliged to return. Yet some seven years were consumed in marches and conquests in these remote countries, for he penetrated to Scythia at the north, and the mouth of the Indus to the south.

Successive conquests of Alexander.

It was in the expeditions among these barbarians that some of the most disgraceful events of his life took place. He seldom rested, but when he had leisure he indulged in great excesses at the festive board. His revelries with his officers were prolonged often during the night, and when intoxicated, he did things which gave him afterward the deepest remorse and shame. Thus he killed, with his own hand, Clitus, at a feast, because Clitus ventured to utter some truths which were in opposition to his notions of omnipotence. But the agony of remorse was so great, that he remained in bed three whole days and nights immediately after, refusing all food and drink. He also killed Philotas, one of his most trusted generals, and commander of his body-guard, on suspicion of treachery, and then, without other cause than fear of the anger of his father, Parmenio, he caused that old general to be assassinated at Ecbatana, in command of the post—the most important in his dominions—

He kills his friend Clitus.

Agony and remorse of Alexander.

where his treasures were deposited. He savagely mutilated Bessus, the satrap, who stood out against him in Bactria. Callisthenes, one of the greatest philosophers of the age, was tortured and assassinated for alleged complexity in a conspiracy, but he really incurred the hatred of the monarch for denying his claim to divinity.

In the spring of B. C. 326, Alexander crossed the Indus, but met with no resistance until he reached the river Hydaspes (Jhylum) on the other side of which, Porus, an Indian prince, disputed his passage, with a formidable force and many trained elephants—animals which the Macedonians had never before encountered. By a series of masterly combinations Alexander succeeded in crossing the river, and the combat commenced. But the Indians could not long withstand the long pikes and close combats of the Greeks, and were defeated with great loss. Porus himself, a prince of gigantic stature, mounted on an elephant, was taken, after having fought with great courage. Carried into the presence of the conqueror, Alexander asked him what he wished to be done for him, for his gallantry and physical strength excited admiration. Porus replied that he wished to be treated as a king, which answer still more excited the admiration of the Greeks. He was accordingly treated with the utmost courtesy and generosity, and retained as an ally. Alexander was capable of great magnanimity, when he was not opposed. He was kind to the family of Darius, both before and after his assassination by the satrap Bessus. And his munificence to his soldiers was great, and he never lost their affections. But he was cruel and sanguinary in his treatment of captives who had made him trouble, putting thousands to the sword in cold blood.

He penetrates to the Indus.

Porus.

As before mentioned, the soldiers were wearied with victories and hardships, without enjoyments, and longed to return to Europe. Hence Sangala, in India, was the easternmost point to which he penetrated. On returning to the river Hydaspes, he constructed a fleet of two thousand boats, in which a part of his

The soldiers of Alexander refuse to advance further to the East.

army descended the river with himself, while another part marched along its banks. He sailed slowly down the river to its junction with the Indus, and then to the Indian ocean. This voyage occupied nine months, but most of the time was employed in subduing the various people who opposed his march. On reaching the ocean, he was astonished and interested by the ebbing and flowing of the tide—a new phenomenon to him. The fleet was conducted from the mouth of the Indus, round by the Persian Gulf to the mouth of the Tigris—a great nautical achievement in those days; but he himself, with the army, marched westward through deserts, undergoing great fatigues and sufferings, and with a great loss of men, horses, and baggage. At Carmania he halted, and the army for seven days was abandoned to drunken festivities.

He returns to Persepolis.

On returning to Persepolis, in Persia, he visited and repaired the tomb of Cyrus, the greatest conqueror the world had seen before himself. In February, B. C. 324, he marched to Susa, where he spent several months in festivities and in organizing his great government, since he no longer had armies to oppose. He now surrounded himself with the pomp of the Persian kings, wore their dress, and affected their habits, much to the disgust of his Macedonian generals. He had married a beautiful captive—Roxana, in Bactria, and he now took two additional wives, Statira, daughter of Darius, and Parysatis, daughter of King Ochus. He also caused his principal officers to marry the daughters of the old Persian grandees, and seemed to forget the country from which he came, and which he was destined never again to see. Here also he gave a donation to his soldiers of twenty thousand talents—about five hundred dollars to each man. But even this did not satisfy them, and when new re-enforcements arrived, the old soldiers mutinied. He disbanded the whole of them in anger, and gave them leave to return to their homes, but they were filled with shame and regret, and a reconciliation took place.

His abandonment to pleasure.

It was while he made a visit to Ecbatana, in the summer of B. C. 324, that his favorite, Hephæstion, died. His sorrow and grief were unbounded. He cast himself upon the ground, cut his hair close, and refused food and drink for two days. This was the most violent grief he ever manifested, and it was sincere. He refused to be comforted, yet sought for a distraction from his grief in festivals and ostentation of life.

Death of Hephæstion and grief of Alexander.

In the spring of B. C. 323, he marched to Babylon, where were assembled envoys from all the nations of the known world to congratulate him for his prodigious and unprecedented successes, and invoke his friendship, which fact indicates his wide-spread fame. At Babylon he laid plans and made preparations for the circumnavigation and conquest of Arabia, and to found a great maritime city in the interior of the Persian Gulf. But before setting out, he resolved to celebrate the funeral obsequies of Hephæstion with unprecedented splendor. The funeral pile was two hundred feet high, loaded with costly decorations, in which all the invention of artists was exhausted. It cost twelve thousand talents, or twelve million dollars of our money. The funeral ceremonies were succeeded by a general banquet, in which he shared, passing a whole night in drinking with his friend Medius. This last feast was fatal. His heated blood furnished fuel for the raging fever which seized him, and which carried him off in a few days, at the age of thirty-two, and after a reign of twelve years and eight months, June, B. C 323.

His entrance into Babylon.

Splendor of the funeral of Hephæstion.

Death of Alexander.

He indicated no successor. Nor could one man have governed so vast an empire with so little machinery of government. His achievements threw into the shade those of all previous conquerors, and he was, most emphatically, the Great King—the type of all worldly power. "He had mastered, in defiance of fatigue, hardship, and combat, not merely all the eastern half of the Persian empire, but unknown Indian regions beyond. Besides Mace-

His boundless ambition.

don, Greece, and Thrace, he possessed all the treasures and forces which rendered the Persian king so formidable," and he was exalted to all this power and grandeur by conquest at an age when a citizen of Athens was intrusted with important commands, and ten years less than the age for a Roman consul. But he was unsatisfied, and is said to have wept that there were no more worlds to conquer. He would, had he lived, doubtless have encountered the Romans, and all their foes, and added Italy and Spain and Carthage to his empire. But there is a limit to human successes, and when his work of chastisement of the nations was done, he died. But he left a fame never since surpassed, and "he overawes the imagination more than any personage of antiquity." He had transcendent merits as a general, but he was much indebted to fortunate circumstances. He thought of new conquests, rather than of consolidating what he had made, so that his empire must naturally be divided and subdivided at his death. Though divided and subdivided, the effect of those conquests remained to future generations, and had no small effect on civilization, and yet, instead of Hellenizing Asia, he rather Asiatized Hellas. That process, so far as it was carried out, is due to his generals—the Diadochi—Antigonas, Ptolemy, Seleucus, Lysimachus, &c., who divided between them the empire. But Hellenism in reality never to a great extent passed into Asia. The old Oriental habits and sentiments and intellectual qualities remained, and have survived all succeeding conquests. Oriental habits and opinions rather invaded the western world with the progress of wealth and luxury. Asia, by the insidious influences of effeminated habits, undermined Greece, and even Rome, rather than received from Europe new impulses or sentiments, or institutions. A new and barbarous country may prevail, by the aid of hardy warriors, adventurous and needy, over the civilized nations which have been famous for a thousand years, but the conquered country almost invariably has transmitted its habits and institutions among the conquerors, so much more majes-

His death a fortunate event.

Effects of his conquests.

tic are ideas than any display of victorious brute forces. Dynasties are succeeded by dynasties, but civilization survives, when any material exists on which it can work.

Athens was never a greater power in the world than at the time her political ruin was consummated. Hence the political changes of nations, which form the bulk of all histories, are insignificant in comparison with those ideas and institutions which gradually transform the habits and opinions of ordinary life. Yet it is these silent and gradual changes which escape the notice of historians, and are the most difficult to be understood and explained, for lack of sufficient and definite knowledge. Moreover, it is the feats of extraordinary individuals in stirring enterprise and heroism which have thus far proved the great attraction of past ages to ordinary minds. No history, truly philosophical, would be extensively read by any people, in any age, and least of all by the young, in the process of education.

The remaining history of Greece has little interest until the Roman conquests, which will be presented in the next book.

BOOK III.

THE ROMAN EMPIRE.

CHAPTER XXVI.

ROME IN ITS INFANCY, UNDER KINGS.

In presenting the growth of that great power which gradually absorbed all other States and monarchies so as to form the largest empire ever known on earth, I shall omit a notice of all other States, in Italy and Europe, until they were brought into direct collision with Rome herself.

Obscurity of the early history of Rome.

The early history of Rome is involved in obscurity, and although many great writers have expended vast learning and ingenuity in tracing the origin of the city and its inhabitants, still but little has been established on an incontrovertible basis. We look to poetry and legends for the foundation of the "Eternal City."

Æneas.

These legends are of peculiar interest. Æneas, in his flight from Troy, after many adventures, reaches Italy, marries the daughter of Latinus, king of the people, who then lived in Latium, and builds a city, which he names Lavinium, and unites his Trojan followers with the aboriginal inhabitants.

Latium.

Latium was a small country, bounded on the north by the Tiber, on the east by the Liris and Vinius, and on the south and west by the Tuscan Sea. It was immediately surrounded by the Etruscans, Sabines, Equi, and

Marsi. When Latium was originally settled we do not know, but the people doubtless belonged to the Indo-European race, kindred to the early settlers of Europe. Latium was a plain, inclosed by mountains and traversed by the Tiber, of about seven hundred square miles. Between the Alban Lake and the Alban Mount, was Alba—the original seat of the Latin race, and the mother city of Rome. Here, according to tradition, reigned Ascanius, the son of Æneas, and his descendants for three hundred years were the Latin tribes. After eleven generations of kings, Amulius usurps the throne, which belonged to Numitor, the elder brother, and dooms his only daughter, Silvia, to perpetual virginity as a Vestal. Silvia, visited by a god, gives birth to twins, Romulus and Remus. The twins, exposed by the order of Amulius, are suckled by a she-wolf, and brought up by one of the king's herdsmen. They feed their flocks on the Palatine, but a quarrel ensuing between them and the herdsmen of Numitor on the Aventine, their royal origin is discovered, and the restoration of Numitor is effected. But the twins resolve to found a city, and Rome arises on the Palatine, an asylum for outlaws and slaves, who are provided with wives by the "rape of the Sabine women."

Foundation of Rome.

Thus, according to the legends, was the foundation of Rome, on a hill about fourteen miles from the mouth of the Tiber, and on a site less healthy than the old Latin towns, B. C. 751, or 753. According to the speculations of Mommsen, it would seem that Rome was at a very early period the resort of a lawless band of men, who fortified themselves on the Palatine, and perhaps other hills, and robbed the small merchants, who sailed up and down the Tiber, as well as the neighboring rural population, even as the feudal barons intrenched themselves on hills overlooking plains and rivers. But all theories relating to the foundation of Rome are based either on legend or speculation. Until we arrive at certain facts, I prefer those based on legend, such as have been accepted for more than two thousand years.

The early inhabitants.

It is but little consequence whether Romulus and Remus are real characters, or poetic names. This is probable, that the situation of Rome was favorable in ancient times for rapine, even if it were not a healthy locality. The first beginnings of Rome were violence and robbery, and the murder of Remus by Romulus is a type of its early history, and whole subsequent career.

Rome founded in violence.

Romulus and his associate outlaws, now intrenched on the Palatine, organize a city and government, and extend the limits. The rape of the Sabines leads to war, and Titus Tatius, king of the Sabines, obtains possession of the Capitoline Hill—the smallest but most famous of the seven hills on which Rome was subsequently built. In the valley between, on which the forum was afterward built, the combatants are separated by the Sabine wives of the outlaws, and the tribes or nations are united under the name of Ramnes and Tities, the Sabines retaining the capitol and the Quirinal, and the Romans the Palatine. Some Etruscans, in possession of the Cælian Hill, are incorporated as a third tribe, called Luceres. But it is probable that the Sabine element prevailed. Each tribe contains ten curiæ of a hundred citizens, which, with the three hundred horsemen, form a body of three thousand three hundred citizens, who alone enjoyed political rights.

The Sabine element of Rome.

The government, though monarchical, was limited. The king was bound to lay all questions of moment before the assembly of the thirty duriæ, called the *Comitia Curiata.* But the king had a council called the *Senate*, composed of one hundred members, who were called *Patres*, or Fathers, and doubtless were the heads of clans called *Gentes.* The Gentes were divided into *Familiæ*, or families. These *Patres* were the heads of the patrician houses—that class who alone had political rights, and who were Roman citizens.

The constitution.

Romulus is said to have reigned justly and ably for thirty-seven years, and no one could be found worthy to succeed him. At length the Roman tribe, the

Numa Pompilius.

Ramnes, elected Numa Pompilius, from the Sabines, a man of wisdom and piety, and said to have acquired his learning from Pythagoras. This king instituted the religious and civil legislation of Rome, and built the temple of Janus in the midst of the Forum, whose doors were shut in peace and opened in war, but were never closed from his death to the reign of Augustus, but a brief period after the first Punic war.

He established the College of Pontiffs, who directed all the ceremonies of religion and regulated festivals and the system of weights and measures; also the College of Augurs, who interpreted by various omens the will of the gods; and also the College of Heralds, who guarded the public faith. He fixed the boundaries of fields, divided the territory of Rome into districts, called *paji*, and regulated the calendar.

Establishment of religion.

According to the legends, Tullus Hostilius was the third king of Rome, elected by the curiæ. He assigned the Cælian Mount for the poor, and the strangers who flocked to Rome, and was a warlike sovereign. The great event of his reign was the destruction of Alba. The growing power of Rome provoked the jealousy of this ancient seat of Latin power, and war ensued. The armies of the two States were drawn up in battle array, when it was determined that the quarrel should be settled by three champions, chosen from each side. Hence the beautiful story of the Curiatii and the Horatii, three brothers on each side. Two of the Horatii were slain, and the three Curiatii were wounded. The third of the Horatii affected to fly, and was pursued by the Curiatii, but as they were wounded, the third Roman subdued them in detail, and so the Albans became subjects of the Romans. The conqueror met his sister at one of the gates, who, being betrothed to one of the Curiatii, reproached him for the death of her lover, which so incensed him that he slew her. Thus early does patriotism surmount natural affections among the Romans. But Horatius was nevertheless tried for his life by

Tullus Hostilius.

The Horatii and the Curiatii.

two judges and condemned. He appealed to the people, who reversed the judgment—the first instance on record of an appeal in a capital case to the people, which subsequently was the right of Roman citizens.

Hostilities again breaking out between Alba and Rome, the former city was demolished and the inhabitants removed to the Cælian Mount and enrolled among the citizens. By the destruction of Alba, Rome obtained the presidency over the thirty cities of the Latin confederacy. Tullus, it would seem, was an unscrupulous king, but able, and to him is ascribed the erection of the Curia Hostilia, where the Senate had its meetings.

Destruction of Alba.

The Sabine Ancus Martius was the fourth king, B. C. 640, who pursued the warlike policy of his predecessor, conquering many Latin towns, and incorporating their inhabitants with the Romans, whom he settled on Mount Aventine. They were freemen, but not citizens. They were called plebeians, with modified civil, but not political rights, and were the origin of that great middle class which afterward became so formidable. The plebeians, though of the same race as the Romans, were a conquered people, and yet were not reduced to slavery like most conquered people among the ancients. They had their Gentes and Familiæ, but they could not intermarry with the patricians. Though they were not citizens, they were bound to fight for the State, for which, as a compensation, they retained their lands, that is, their old possessions.

The origin of plebeians.

On the death, B. C. 616, of Ancus Martius, Lucius Tarquinius, of an Etruscan family, became king, best known as Tarquinius Priscus. He had been guardian of the two sons of Ancus, but offered himself as candidate for the throne, from which it would appear that the monarchs were elected by the people.

Tarquinius Priscus.

He carried on successful war against the Latins and Sabines, and introduced from Etruria, by permission of the Senate, a golden crown, an ivory chain, a sceptre topped with an eagle, and a crimson robe studded with gold—

emblems of royalty. But he is best known for various public works of great magnificence at the time, as well as of public utility. Among these was the Cloaca Maxima, to drain the marshy land between the Palatine and the Tiber—a work so great, that Niebuhr ranks it with the pyramids. It has lasted, without the displacement of a stone, for more than two thousand years. It shows that the use of the arch was known at that period. The masonry of the stones is perfect, joined together without cement. Tarquin also instituted public games, and reigned with more splendor than we usually associate with an infant State.

His public work.

This king, who excited the jealousy of the patricians, was assassinated B. C. 578, and Servius Tullius reigned in his stead. He was the greatest of the Roman kings, and arose to his position by eminent merit, being originally obscure. He married the daughter of Tarquin, and shared all his political plans.

Servius Tullius.

He is most celebrated for remodeling the constitution. He left the old institutions untouched, but added new ones. He made a new territorial division of the State, and created a popular assembly. He divided the whole population into thirty tribes, at the head of each of which was a tribune. Each tribe managed its own local affairs, and held public meetings. These tribes included both patricians and plebeians. This was the commencement of the power of the plebs, which was seen with great jealousy by the patricians.

His reforms.

The basis or principle of the new organization of Servius was the possession of property. All free citizens, whether patricians or plebeians, were called to defend the State, and were enrolled in the army. The equites, or cavalry, took the precedence in the army, and was com posed of the wealthy citizens. There were eighteen centu ries of these knights, six patrician and twelve plebeian, all having more than one hundred thousand ases. They were armed with sword, spear, helmet, shield, greaves, and cuirass. The infantry was composed of the classes, variously armed,

Based on property.

of which, including equites, there were one hundred and ninety-four centuries, one hundred of whom were of the first rank, heavily armed—all men possessing one hundred thousand ases. Each class was divided into seniores—men between forty-five and sixty, and juniores—from seventeen to forty-five. The former were liable to be called out only in emergencies. This division of the citizens was a purely military one, and each century had one vote. But as the first class numbered one hundred centuries, each man of which was worth land valued at one hundred thousand ases, it could cast a larger vote than all the other classes, which numbered only ninety-four together. Thus the rich controlled all public affairs.

New division of the people.

To this military body of men, in which the rich preponderated, Servius committed all the highest functions of the State, for the Comitia Centuriata possessed elective, judicial, and legislative functions. Servius also rendered many other benefits to the plebeians. He divided among them the lands gained from the Etruscans. He inclosed the city with a wall, which remained for centuries, embracing the seven hills on which Rome was built. But it is as the hero of the plebeian order that he is famous, and paid the penalty for being such. He was assassinated, probably by the instigation of the patricians, by his son-in-law, Lucius Tarquinius, who mounted his throne as Tarquinius Superbus, the last king of Rome, B. C. 534. The daughter of the murdered king, Tullia, who rode in her chariot over his bleeding body, is enrolled among the infamous women of antiquity.

Comitia Centuriata.

Tarquinius Superbus, a usurper and murderer, abrogated the popular laws of Servius Tullius, and set aside even the assembly of the Curiæ, and degraded and decimated the Senate, and appropriated the confiscated estates of those whom he destroyed. He reigned as a despot, making treaties without consulting the Senate, and living for his pleasure alone. But he ornamented the city with magnificent edifices, and completed the Circus Maxi-

The despotism of Tarquin.

mus as well as the Capitoline Temple, which stood five hundred years. He was also successful in war, and exalted the glory of the Roman name.

An end came to his tyranny by one of these events on which poetry and history have alike exhausted all their fascinations. It was while Tarquin was conducting a war against Ardea, and the army was idly encamped before the town, that the sons of Tarquin, with their kinsmen, were supping in the tent of Sextus, that conversation turned upon the comparative virtue of their wives. By a simultaneous impulse, they took horse to see the manner in which these ladies were at the time employed. The wives of Tarquin's sons at Rome were found in luxurious banquets with other women. Lucretia, the wife of Collatinus, was discovered carding wool in the midst of her maidens. The boast of Collatinus that his wife was the most virtuous was confirmed. But her charms or virtues made a deep impression on the heart or passions of Sextus, and he returned to her dwelling in Collatia to propose infamous overtures. They were proudly rejected, but the disappointed lover, by threats and force, accomplished his purpose. Lucrétia, stung with shame, made known the crime of Sextus to her husband and father, who hastened to her house, accompanied with Brutus. They found the ravished beauty in agonies of shame and revenge, and after she had revealed the scandalous facts, she plunged a dagger in her own bosom and died, invoking revenge. Her relatives and friends carried her corpse to the marketplace, revealed the atrocity of the crime of Sextus, and demanded vengeance. The people rallied in the Forum at Rome, and the assembled Curiæ deprived Tarquin of his throne, and decreed the banishment of his accursed family. On the news of the insurrection, the tyrant started for the city with a band of chosen followers, but Brutus reached the army after the king had left, recounted the wrongs, and marched to Rome, whose gates were already shut against Tarquin. He fled to Etruria,

The legend of Lucretia.

Death of Lucretia.

Banishment of the Tarquins.

with two of his sons, but Sextus was murdered by the people of Gabii.

Thus were the kings driven out of Rome, never to return. In the revolution which followed, the patricians recovered their power, and a new form of government was instituted, republican in name, but oligarchal and aristocratic in reality, two hundred and forty-five years after the foundation of the city, B. C. 510. Historical criticism throws doubt on the chronology which assigns two hundred and forty-five years to seven elective kings, and some critics think that a longer period elapsed from the reign of Romulus to that of Tarquin than legend narrates, and that there must have been a great number of kings whose names are unknown. As the city advanced in wealth and numbers, the popular influence increased. The admission of commons favored the establishment of despotism, and its excesses led to its overthrow. It would have been better for the commons had Brutus established a monarchy with more limited powers, for the plebeians were now subjected to the tyranny of a proud and grasping oligarchy, and lost a powerful protector in the king, and the whole internal history of Rome, for nearly two centuries, were the conflicts between the plebeians and their aristocratic masters for the privileges they were said to possess under the reign of Tullius. Under the patricians the growth of the city was slow, and it was not till the voices of the tribunes were heard that Rome advanced in civilization and liberty. Under the kings, the progress in arts and culture had been rapid.

The restoration of power to the patricians.

Mommsen, in his learned and profound history of Rome, enumerates the various forms of civilization that existed on the expulsion of the Tarquins, a summary of which I present. Law and justice were already enforced on some of the elemental principles which marked the Roman jurisprudence. The punishment of offenses against order was severe, and compensation for crime, where injuries to person and property were slight, was somewhat similar to the penalties of the Mosaic code. The idea of property was asso-

Jurisprudence.

ciated with estate in slaves and cattle, and all property passed freely from hand to hand; but it was not in the power of the father arbitrarily to deprive his children of their hereditary rights. Contracts between the State and a citizen were valid without formalities, but those between private persons were difficult to be enforced. A purchase only founded an action in the event of its being a transaction for ready money, and this was attested by witnesses. Protection was afforded to minors and for the estate of persons not capable of bearing arms. After a man's death, his property descended to his nearest heirs. The emancipation of slaves was difficult, and that of a son was attended with even greater difficulties. Burgesses and clients were equally free in their private rights, but foreigners were beyond the pale of the law. The laws indicated a great progress in agriculture and commerce, but the foundation of law was the State. The greatest liberality in the permission of commerce, and the most rigorous procedure in execution, went hand in hand. Women were placed on a legal capacity with men, though restricted in the administration of their property. Personal credit was extravagant and easy, but the creditor could treat the debtor like a thief. A freeman could not, indeed, be tortured, but he could be imprisoned for debt with merciless severity. From the first, the laws of property were stringent and inexorable.

Religion.

In religion, the ancient Romans, like the Greeks, personified the powers of nature, and also abstractions, like sowing, field labor, war, boundary, youth, health, harmony, fidelity. The profoundest worship was that of the tutelary deities, who presided over the household. Next to the deities of the house and forest, held in the greatest veneration, was Hercules, the god of the inclosed homestead, and, therefore, of property and gain. The souls of departed mortals were supposed to haunt the spot where the bodies reposed, but dwelt in the depths below. The hero worship of the Greeks was uncommon, and even Numa was never worshiped as a god. The central object

Objects of worship.

of worship was Mars, the god of war, and this was conducted by imposing ceremonies and rites. The worship of Vesta was held with peculiar sacredness, and the vestal virgins were the last to yield to Christianity. The worshipers of the gods often consulted priests and augurs, who had great colleges, but little power in the State. The Latin worship was grounded on man's enjoyment of earthly pleasures, and not on his fear of the wild forces of nature, and it gradually sunk into a dreary round of ceremonies. The Italian god was simply an instrument for the attainment of worldly ends, and not an object of profound awe or love, and hence the Latin worship was unfavorable to poetry, as well as philosophical speculation.

Agriculture.

Agriculture is ever a distinguishing mark of civilization, and forms the main support of a people. It early occupied the time of the Latins, and was their chief pursuit. In the earliest ages arable land was cultivated in common, and was not distributed among the people as their special property, but in the time of Servius there was a distribution. Attention was chiefly given to cereals, but roots and vegetables were also diligently cultivated. Vineyards were introduced before the Greeks made settlements in Italy, but the olive was brought to Italy by the Greeks. The fig-tree is a native of Italy. The plow was drawn by oxen, while horses, asses, and mules were used as beasts of burden. The farm was stocked with swine and poultry, especially geese. The plow was a rude instrument, but no field was reckoned perfectly tilled unless the furrows were so close that harrowing was deemed unnecessary. Farming on a large scale was not usual, and the proprietor of land worked on the soil with his sons. The use of slaves was a later custom, when large estates arose.

Fruits and cereals.

Trades.

Trades scarcely kept pace with agriculture, although in the time of Numa eight guilds of craftsmen were numbered among the institutions of Rome—flute-blowers, goldsmiths, coppersmiths, carpenters, fullers, dyers, potters, and shoemakers. There was no yield for workers in iron, which shows that iron was a later introduction than copper.

Commerce was limited to the mutual dealings of the Italians themselves. Fairs are of great antiquity, distinguished from ordinary markets, and barter and traffic were carried on in them, especially that of Soracte, being before Greek or Phœnicians entered from the sea. Oxen and sheep, grain and slaves, were the common mediums of exchange. Latium was, however, deficient of articles of export, and was pre-eminently an agricultural country.

Commerce.

The use of measures and weights was earlier than the art of writing, although the latter is of high antiquity. Latin poetry began in the lyrical form. Dancing was a common trade, and this was accompanied with pipers, and religious litanies were sung from the remotest antiquity. Comic songs were sung in Saturnian metre, accompanied by the pipe. The art of dancing was a public care, and a powerful impulse was early given by Hellenic games. But in all the arts of music and poetry there was not the easy development as in Greece. Architecture owed its first impulse to the Etruscans, who borrowed from the Greeks, and was not of much account till the reigns of the Tuscan kings.

Measures and weights.

CHAPTER XXVII.

THE ROMAN REPUBLIC TILL THE INVASION OF THE GAULS.

Heroic period of Roman history.

THE Tarquins being expelled, political power fell into the hands of the patricians, under whose government the city slowly increased in wealth and population. But it was the heroic period of Roman history, and the legends of patriotic bravery are of great interest.

The consuls.

The despotism of Tarquinius Superbus inflamed all classes with detestation of the very name of king—the wealthy classes, because they were deprived of their ancient powers; the poorer classes, because they were oppressed with burdens. The executive power of the State was transferred to two men, called consuls, annually elected from the patrician ranks. But they ruled with restricted powers, and were shorn of the trappings of royalty. They could not nominate priests, and they were amenable to the laws after their term of office expired. They were elected by the Comitia Centuriata, in which the patrician power predominated. They convened the Senate, introduced embassadors, and commanded the armies. In public, they were attended by lictors, and wore, as a badge of authority, a purple border on the toga.

The Senate.

The Senate, a great power, still retained its dignity. The members were elected for life, and were the advisers of the consuls. They were elected by the consuls; but, as the consuls were practically chosen by the wealthy classes, men were chosen to the Senate who belonged to powerful families. The Senate was a judicial and legislative body, and numbered three hundred men. All men who had held curule magistracies became members. Their decisions, called Senatus Consulta, became laws—*leges.*

The Roman government at this time was purely oligarchic. The aristocratical element prevailed. Nobles virtually controlled the State.

Brutus, on the overthrow of the monarchy, was elected the first consul, B. C. 507, with L. Tarquinius Collatinus; but the latter was not allowed to possess his office, from hatred of his family, and he withdrew peaceably to Lavinium, and Publius Valerius was elected consul in his stead—a harsh measure, prompted by necessity.

Brutus the first consul.

The history of Rome at this period is legendary. The story goes that Tarquin, at the head of the armies of Veii and Tarquinii, seeking to recover his throne, marched against Rome, and that for thirteen years he struggled with various success, assisted by Porsenna, king of Etruria. The legends say Horatius Cocles defended a bridge, single-handed, against the whole Etrurian army—that Mamillus, the ruler of Tuscalum, fought a battle at Lake Regillus, in which the cause of Tarquin was lost—the subject of the most beautiful of Macaulay's lays—and that Mutius Scævola attempted to assassinate Porsenna, and, as a proof of his fortitude, held his hand in the fire until it was consumed, which act converted Porsenna into a friend. Another interesting legend is related in reference to Brutus, who slew his own sons for their sympathy with, and treasonable aid, to the banished king. These stories are not history, but still shed light on the spirit of the time. It is probable that Tarquin made desperate efforts to recover his dominion, aided by the Etruscans, and that the first wars of the republic were against them.

The legends of ancient Rome.

Tarquin attempts to recover his throne.

The Etruscans were then in the height of their power, and were in close alliance with the Carthaginians. Etruria was a larger State than Latium, from which it was separated by the Tiber. It was bounded on the west by the Tyrrhenian Sea, on the north by the Appenines, and the east by Umbria. Among the cities were Veii and

Etruria.

Tarquinii, the latter the birthplace of Tarquinius Priscus, and the former the powerful rival of Rome.

War with the Etruscans.

In the war with the Etruscans, the Romans were worsted, and they lost all their territory on the right bank of the Tiber, won by the kings, and were thrown back on their original limits. But the Etruscans were driven back, by the aid of the Latin cities, beyond the Tiber. It took Rome one hundred and fifty years to recover what she had lost.

Dictators.

It was in these wars with the Etruscans that we first read of dictators, extraordinary magistrates, appointed in great political exigencies. The dictator, or commander, was chosen by one of the consuls, and his authority was supreme, but lasted only for six months. He had all the powers of the ancient kings.

Oppression and miseries of the plebeians.

The misfortunes of the Romans, in the contest with the Etruscans, led to other political changes, and internal troubles. The strife between the patricians and the plebeians now began, and lasted two centuries before the latter were admitted to a full equality of civil rights. The cause of the conflict, it would appear, was the unequal and burdensome taxation to which the plebeians were subjected, and especially vexations from the devastations which war produced. They were small land-owners, and their little farms were overrun by the enemy, and they were in no condition to bear the burdens imposed upon them: and this inequality of taxation was the more oppressive, since they had no political power. They necessarily incurred debts, which were rigorously exacted, and they thus became the property of their creditors.

Their rebellion.

In their despair, they broke out in open rebellion, in the fifteenth year of the republic, during the consulship of Publius Servilius and Appius Claudius—the latter a proud Sabine nobleman, who had lately settled in Rome. They took position on a hill between the Anio and Tiber, commanding the most fertile part of the Roman territory. The patrician and wealthy classes, abandoned by the farmers, who tilled the lands, were compelled to treat, in spite of the opposition of Appius Claudius. And the result was, that the plebeians gained a remission of their debts, and the appointment of two magistrates, as protectors, under the name of tribunes.

This new office introduced the first great change in the condition of the plebeians. The tribunes had the power of putting a stop to the execution of the law which condemned debtors to imprisonment or a military levy. Their jurisdiction extended over every citizen, even over the consul. There was no appeal from their decisions, except in the Comitia Tributa, where the plebeian interest predominated—an assembly representing the thirty Roman tribes, according to the Servian constitution, but which, at first, had insignificant powers. The persons of the tribunes were inviolable, but their power was negative. They could not originate laws; they could insure the equitable administration of the laws, and prevent wrongs. They had a constitutional veto, of great use at the time, but which ended in a series of dangerous encroachments.

The Tribunes.

Comitia Tributa.

The office of ædiles followed that of tribunes. There were at first two, selected from plebeians, whose duty it was to guard the law creating tribunes, which was deposited in the temple of Vesta. They were afterward the keepers of the resolutions of the Senate as well as of the plebs, and had the care of public buildings, and the sanitary police of the city, the distribution of corn, and of the public lands, the superintendence of markets and measures, the ordering of festivals, and the duty to see that no new deities or rites were introduced.

Ædiles.

One year after the victory of the plebeians, a distinguished man appeared, who was their bitter enemy. This was Caius Marcius, called Coriolanus, from his bravery at the capture of a Volscian town, Corioli. When a famine pressed the city, a supply of corn was sent by a Sicilian prince, but the proud patrician proposed to the Senate to withhold it from the plebeians until they surren-

Coriolanus.

dered their privileges. The rage of the plebeians was intense, and he was impeached by the tribunes, and condemned by the popular assembly to exile. He went over, in indignation, to the Volscians, became their general, defeated the Romans, and marched against their city. In this emergency, the city was saved by the intercession of his mother, Volumnia, who went to seek him in his camp, accompanied by other Roman matrons.

Spurius Cassius.

A greater man than he, was Spurius Cassius, who rendered public services of the greatest magnitude, yet a man whose illustrious deeds no poet sang. He lived in a great crisis, when the Etruscan war had destroyed the Roman dominions on the right bank of the Tiber, and where the Volscians and Acquians were advancing with superior forces. Rome was in danger of being conquered, and not only conquered, but reduced to servitude. But he concluded a league with the Latins, and also with the Hernicians—a Sabine people, who dwelt in one of the valleys of the Appenines, by which the power of Rome was threatened. He is also known as the first who proposed an agrarian

Agrarian law.

law. It seems that the patricians had occupied the public lands to the exclusion of the plebeians. Spurius Cassius proposed to the Comitia Centuriata that the public domain—land obtained by conquest—should be measured, and a part reserved for the use of the State, and another portion distributed among the needy citizens—a just proposition, since no property held by individuals was meddled with. This popular measure was carried against violent opposition, but when the term of office of Cassius as consul expired, he was accused before the curiæ, who assumed the right to judge a patrician, and he lost his life. He was accused of seeking to usurp regal power, because he had sought to protect the commons against his own order. "His law was buried with him, but its spectre haunted the rich, and again and again it arose from its tomb, till the conflicts to which it led destroyed the commonwealth."

The following seven years was a period of incessant war

with the Acquians and Veientines, as well as dissensions in the city, during which the great house of the Fabii arose to power for Fabius was chosen consul seven successive years, and even proposed the execution of the agrarian law of Cassius, for which he was scorned by the patricians, and left Rome in disgust, with his family, and all were afterward massacred by the Veientines. But one of the tribunes accused the consuls for their opposition of the tribunes for the execution of the agrarian law. He was assassinated. This violation of the sacred person of a tribune created great indignation among the commons, and Volero, a tribune, proposed the celebrated "Publilian Law," that the tribunes henceforth, as well as the plebeian ædiles, should be elected by the plebeians themselves in the Comitia Tributa. Great disorders followed, but the commons prevailed, and the Senate adopted the plebiscitum, and proposed it to the Comitia Curiata, and it became a law. This step raised the authority of the tribunes, and added to Roman liberties.

Fabius.

Increased power of plebeians.

The critical condition of Rome, from the renewed assaults of the Acquians and Volscians, led to the appointment of another very remarkable man to the dictatorship—L. Quintius Cincinnatus, a patrician, who maintained the virtues of better days. He cultivated a little farm of four jugera with his own hands, and lived with great simplicity. He summoned every man of military age to meet him in the Campus Martius, and these were provided with rations for five days. He then marched against the triumphant enemy, surrounded them, and compelled them to surrender. He made no use of his political power, and after sixteen days, laid down the dictatorship, and retired to his farm, B. C. 458. All subsequent ages and nations have embalmed the memory of this true patriot, who preferred the quiet labors of his small farm of three and a half acres to the enjoyment of absolute power.

The dictatorship of Cincinnatus.

But his victory was not decisive, and the Romans continued to be harassed by the neighboring nations, and they, moreover, suffered all the evils of pestilence. It was at this time, in the three hundredth year of the city, that they sought to make improvements in their laws—at least, to embody laws in a written form. Greece was then in the height of her glory, in the interval between the Persian and Peloponnesian wars, and thither a commission was sent to examine her laws, especially those of Solon, at Athens. On the return of the three commissioners, a new commission of ten was appointed to draw up a new code, composed wholly of patricians, at the head of which was Appius Claudius, consul elect, a man of commanding influence and talents, but ill-regulated passions and unscrupulous ambition. The new code was engraved upon ten tables, and subsequently two more tables were added, and these twelve tables are the foundation of the Roman jurisprudence, that branch of science which the Romans carried to considerable perfection, and for which they are most celebrated. The jurisprudence of Rome has survived all her conquests, and is the most valuable contribution to civilization which she ever made.

The decemvirs—those who codified the laws—came into supreme power, and suspended the other great magistracies, and ruled, under the direction of Appius Claudius, in an arbitrary and tyrannical manner. Their power came to an end in a signal manner, and the history of their fall is identified with one of the most beautiful legends of this heroic age, which is also the subject of one of Macaulay's lays.

The decemvirs.—Appius Claudius.

Appius Claudius, who perhaps aspired to regal power, became enamored of the daughter of a centurion, L. Virginius. In order to gratify his passions, Claudius suborned a false accuser, one of his clients, who was to pretend that the mother of Virginia had been his slave. Appius sat in judgment, and against his own laws, and also the entreaties of the people, declared her to be the slave of the accuser. Her father returned from the army, and in his indignation plunged a dagger in her breast, preferring her

His injustice and punishment.

death to shame. The people and soldiers rallied around the courageous soldier, took the capitol, and compelled the decemvirs to lay down their office. The result of this insurrection was the creation of ten tribunes instead of the old number, and ten continued to be the regular number of tribunes till the fall of the republic. It was further decreed that the votes of the plebs, passed in the Comitia Tributa, should be binding on the whole people, provided they were confirmed by the Senate and the assemblies of the curiæ and centuries. The persons of the tribunes were declared to be inviolable, under the sanctions of religion, and they, moreover, were admitted to the deliberations of the Senate, though without a vote. Thus did the commons ascend another step in political influence, B. C. 449. The next movement of the commons was to take vengeance on Appius Claudius, who ended his life in prison.

Intermarriage of plebeians and patricians.

The plebs, now strengthened by the plebeian nobles, who sought power through the tribunate, insisted on the abrogation of the law which prevented the marriage of plebeians with patricians. This was effected four years later, B. C. 445. These then attempted to secure the higher magistracies, but this was prevented for a time, although they acquired the right of plebeians to become military tribunes, or chief officer of the legions, but none of the plebeians arose to that rank for several years.

Censors.

A new office of great dignity was now created, that of censors, who were chosen from men who had been consuls, and therefore had higher rank than they. It was their duty to superintend the public morals, take the census, and administer the finances. They could brand with ignominy the highest officers of the State, could elect to the Senate, and control, with the ædiles, the public buildings and works. There were two elected to this high office, and were chosen from the patrician ranks till the year B. C. 421, when plebeians were admitted. They were even held in great reverence, and enjoyed a larger term of office than the consuls, even of five years.

The commons gained additional importance by the opening of the quæstorship to the plebeians, which took place about this time. The quæstors virtually had charge of the public money, and were the paymasters of the army. As these were curule officers, they had, by their office, admission to the Senate. Another great increase of power among the plebeians, about twenty years after the decemviral legislature, was the right, transferred from the curiæ to the centuries, of determining peace and war.

Quæstors.

While these internal changes were in progress, the State was in almost constant war with the Volscians and Acquians, and also with the Etruscans. The former were kept at bay by the aid of the Latin and Hernican allies. The latter were more formidable foes, and especially the inhabitants of Veii —a powerful city in the plain of Southern Etruria, and the largest of the confederated Etruscan cities, equal in size to Athens, defended by a strong citadel on a hill. The Veientines, not willing to contend with the Romans in the field, shut themselves up in their strong city, to which the Romans laid siege. They drew around it a double line of circumvallation, the inner one to prevent egress from the city, the outer one to defend themselves against external attacks. The siege lasted ten years, as long as that of Troy, but was finally taken by the great Camillus, by means of a mine under the citadel. The fall of this strong place was followed by the submission of all the Etruscan cities south of the Ciminian forest, and the lands of the people of Veii were distributed among the whole Roman people, at the rate of seven jugera to each landholder, B. C. 396.

The siege and fall of Veii.

But this event was soon followed by a great calamity to Rome—the greatest she had ever suffered. The city fell into the hands of the Gauls—a Celtic race. They were rather pastoral than agricultural, and reared great numbers of swine. They had little attachment to the soil, like the Italians and Germans, and delighted in towns. Their chief qualities were personal bravery, an impetuous temper, boundless vanity, and want of perse-

Invasion of the Gauls.

Habits and manners of the Gauls.

verance. They were good soldiers and bad citizens. They were fond of a roving life, and given to pillage. They loved ornaments and splendid dresses, and wore a gold collar round the neck. After an expedition, they abandoned themselves to carousals. They sprung from the same cradle as the Hellenic, Italian, and German people. Their first great migration flowed past the Alps, and we find them in Gaul, Britain, and Spain. From these settlements, they proceeded westward across the Alps. In successive waves they invaded Italy. It was at the height of Etruscan power, that they assumed a hostile attitude. From Etruria they proceeded to the Roman territories.

Disastrous battle with the Gauls.

The first battle with these terrible foes resulted disastrously to the Romans, who regarded them as half-disciplined barbarians, and underrated their strength. Their defeat was complete, and their losses immense. The flower of the Roman youth perished, B. C. 390.

The fall of Rome.

The victors entered Rome without resistance, while the Romans retreated to their citadel, such as were capable of bearing arms. The rest of the population dispersed. The fathers of the city, aged citizens, and priests, seated themselves in the porches of their patrician houses, and awaited the enemy. At first, they were mistaken for gods, so venerable and calm their appearance; but the profanation of the sacred person of Papirius dissolved the charm, and they were massacred.

M. Manlius.

The Gauls then attempted to assault the capitol, but failed. But a youth, Pontius Cominius, having climbed the hill in the night with safety, and opened communication with the Romans at Veii, the marks of his passage suggested to the Gauls the means of taking the citadel. In the dead of the following night a party of Gauls scaled the cliff, and were about to surprise the citadel, when some geese, sacred to Juno, cried out and flapped their wings, which noise awakened M. Manlius, who rushed to the cliff and overpowered the foremost Gaul. A panic seized the rest, and the capitol was saved. At length, when the siege had lasted seven months, and famine pressed, the invaders were bought off by a ransom of one thousand pounds weight of gold. "The iron of the barbarians had conquered; but they sold their victory, and by selling, lost it." They were subsequently defeated by Camillus, and Manlius, surnamed Torquatus, from the gold collar he took from a gigantic Gaul, and also by other generals.

The destruction of Rome was not a permanent calamity; it was a misfortune. The period which followed was one of distress, but the energy of Camillus reorganized the military force, and new alliances were made with the Latin cities. Etruria, humbled and restricted within narrower limits, and moreover enervated by luxury, was in no condition to oppose a people inured to danger and sobered by adversity.

His services and fall.

The subsequent fate of Manlius, who saved the city, suggests the fickleness and ingratitude of a republican State. The distress of the lower classes, in consequence of the Gaulish invasion, became intolerable. They became involved in debt, and thus were in the power of their creditors. Manlius undertook to be their defender, but the envy of the patricians caused him to be accused of aspiring to the supreme power, and he was, in spite of his great services, sentenced to death and hurled from the Tarpeian rock. His error was in premature reform. But, in the year 367 B. C., the tribunes Licinius and L. Sextius secured the passage of three memorable laws in the Curiata Tributa—the abolition of the military tribunate, which had increased the power of the patricians, and the restoration of the consulate, on the condition that one of the consuls should be a plebeian; the second, that no citizen should possess more than five hundred jugera of the public lands; and the third, that all interest thus paid on loans should be deducted from the principal. These were called the *Licinian Rogations*.

The Licinian rogation.

But a new curule magistracy was created, as a sort of compensation to the patricians, that of prætors, to be held by them exclusively. These political changes were made peaceably, and with them the old gentile aristocracy ceased to be a political institution. The remaining patrician offices were not long withheld from the plebeians. But these political changes did not much ameliorate the social condition of the poorer classes. The strictness of the Licinian laws, the oppression of the rich, the high rate of interest, and the existence of slavery, made the poor poorer, and the rich richer, and prevented the expansion of industry. The plebeians had gained political privileges, but not till great plebeian families had arisen. Power was virtually in the hands of nobles, whether patrician or plebeian, and aristocratic distinctions still remained. The plebeian noble sympathized with patricians rather than with the poorer classes. Debt, usury, and slavery began to bear fruits before the conquest of Italy.

CHAPTER XXVIII.

THE CONQUEST OF ITALY.

HITHERTO, the Romans, after the expulsion of the kings, were involved in wars with their immediate neighbors, and exposed to great calamities. All they could do for one hundred and fifty years was to recover the possessions they had lost. During this period great prodigies of valor were performed, and great virtues were generated. It was the heroic period of their history, when adversity taught them patience, endurance, and public virtue.

But a new period opens, when the plebeians had obtained political power, and the immediate enemies were subdued. This was a period of conquest over the various Italian States. The period is still heroic, but historical. Great men arose, of talent and patriotism. The ambition of the Romans now prominently appears. They had been struggling for existence—they now fought for conquest. "The great achievement of the regal period was the establishment," says Mommsen, "of the sovereignty of Rome over Latium." That was shaken by the expulsion of Tarquin, but was re-established in the wars which subsequently followed. After the fall of Veii, all the Latin cities became subject to the Romans. On the overthrow of the Volscians, the Roman armies reached the Samnite territory.

The period of conquest begins.

The next memorable struggle of Rome was with Samnium, for the supremacy of Italy. Samnium was a hilly country on the east of the Volscians, and its people were brave and hardy. The Samnites had, at the fall of Veii, an ascendency over Lower Italy, with the exception of the Grecian colonies. Tarentum, Croton, Metapontum,

Samnium.

Heraclea, Neapolis, and other Grecian cities, maintained a precarious independence, but were weakened by the successes of the Samnites. Capua, the capital of Campania, where the Etruscan influence predominated, was taken by them, and Cumæ was wrested from the Greeks.

But in the year B. C. 343, the Samnites came in collision with Rome, from an application of Capua to Rome for assistance against them. The victories of Valerius Corvus, and Cornelius Cossus gave Campania to the Romans.

In the mean time the Latins had recovered strength, and determined to shake off the Roman yoke, and the Romans made peace with the Samnites and formed a close alliance, B. C. 341. The Romans and Samnites were ranged against the Latins and Campanians. The hostile forces came in sight of each other before Capua, and the first great battle was fought at the foot of Mount Vesuvius. It was here that Titus Manlius, the son of the consul, was beheaded by him for disobedience of orders, for the consuls issued strict injunctions against all skirmishing, and Manlius, disregarding them, slew an enemy in single combat. "The consul's cruelty was execrated, but the discipline of the army was saved."

The Latins throw off the Roman yoke.

This engagement furnishes another legend of the heroic and patriotic self-devotion of those early Romans. The consuls, before the battle, dreamed that the general on the one side should fall, and the army on the other side should be beaten. Decius, the plebeian consul, when he found his troops wavering, called the chief pontiff, and after invoking the gods to assist his cause, rushed into the thickest of the Latin armies, and was slain. The other consul, Torquatus, by a masterly use of his reserve, gained the battle. Three-fourths of the Latin army were slain. The Latin cities, after this decisive victory, lost their independence, and the Latin confederacy was dissolved, and Latin nationality was fused into one powerful State, and all Latium became Roman. Roman citizens settled on the forfeited lands of the conquered cities.

Reconquest of the Latin cities.

The subjugation of Latium and the progress of Rome in Campania filled the Samnites with jealousy, and it is surprising that they should have formed an alliance with Rome, when Rome was conquering Campania. They were the most considerable power in Italy, next to Rome, and to them fell the burden of maintaining the independence of the Italian States against the encroachments of the Romans.

Jealousy of the Samnites.

The Greek cities of Palæapolis and Neapolis, the only communities in Campania not yet reduced by the Romans, gave occasion to the outbreak of the inevitable war between the Samnites and Romans. The Tarentines and Samnites, informed of the intention of the Romans to seize these cities, anticipated the seizure, upon which the Romans declared war, and commenced the siege of Palæapolis, which soon submitted, on the offer of favorable terms. An alliance of the Romans with the Lucanians, left the Samnites unsupported, except by tribes on the eastern mountain district. The Romans invaded the Samnite territories, pillaging and destroying as far as Apulia, on which the Samnites sent back the Roman prisoners and sought for peace. But peace was refused by the inexorable enemy, and the Samnites prepared for desperate resistance. They posted themselves in ambush at an important pass in the mountains, and shut up the Romans, who offered to capitulate. Instead of accepting the capitulation and making prisoners of the whole army, the Samnite general, Gaius Pontius, granted an equitable peace. But the Roman Senate, regardless of the oaths of their generals, and regardless of the six hundred equites who were left as hostages, canceled the agreement, and the war was renewed with increased exasperation on the part of the Samnites, who, however, were sufficiently magnanimous not to sacrifice the hostages they held. Rome sent a new army, under Lucius Papirius Cursor, and laid siege to Lucania, where the Roman equites lay in captivity. The city surrendered, and Papirius liberated his comrades, and

The war.

The Samnite war.

Siege of Lucania.

retaliated on the Samnite garrison. The war continued, like all wars at that period between people of equal courage and resources, with various success—sometimes gained by one party and sometimes by another, until, in the fifteenth year of the war, the Romans established themselves in Apulia, on one sea, and Campania, on the other.

The people of Northern and Central Italy, perceiving that the Romans aimed at the complete subjugation of the whole peninsula, now turned to the assistance of the Samnites. The Etruscans joined their coalition, but were at length subdued by Papirius Cursor. The Samnites found allies in the Umbrians of Northern, and the Marsi and Pæligni of Central Italy. But these people were easily subdued, and a peace was made with Samnium, after twenty-two years' war, when Bovianum, its strongest city, was taken by storm, B. C. 298.

The defeated nations would not, however, submit to Rome without one more final struggle, and the third Samnite war was renewed the following year, for which the Samnites called to their aid the Gauls. This war lasted nine years, and was virtually closed by the great victory of Seutinum—a fiercely contested battle, where the Romans, though victorious, lost nine thousand men. Umbria submitted, the Gauls dispersed, and the Etruscans made a truce for four hundred months. The Samnites still made desperate resistance, but were finally subdued in a decisive battle, where twenty thousand were slain, and their great general, Pontius, was taken prisoner, with four thousand Samnites. This misfortune closed the war, but the Samnites were not subjected to humiliating terms. The Romans, however, sullied their victories by the execution of C. Pontius, the Samnite general, who had once spared the lives of two Roman armies, B. C. 291. Rome now became the ruling State of Italy, but there were still two great nations unsubdued—the Etruscans in the north, and the Lucanians in the south.

Victory of Sentinum.

A new coalition arose against Rome, soon after the Samnites were subdued, composed of Etruscans, Bruttians, and Lucanians. The war began in Etruria, B. C. 283, and continued with alternate successes, until the decisive victory at the Vadimonian Lake, gained by G. Domitius Calvinus, destroyed forever the power of the Etruscans. The attention of Rome was now given to Tarentum, a Greek city, at the bottom of the gulf of that name, adjacent to the fertile plain of Lucania. This city, which was pre-eminent among the States of Magna Grecia, had grown rich by commerce, and was sufficiently powerful to defend herself against the Etruscans and the Syracusans. It was a Dorian colony, but had abandoned the Lacedæmonian simplicity, and was given over to pleasure and luxury; but, luxurious as it was, it was the only obstacle to the supremacy of Rome over Italy.

New coalition against Rome.

Tarentum.

This thoughtless and enervated, but great city, ruled by demagogues, had insulted Rome—burning and destroying some of her ships. It was a reckless insult which Rome could not forget, prompted by fear as well as hatred. When the Samnite war closed, the Tarentines, fearing the vengeance of the most powerful State in Italy, sent to Pyrrhus, king of Epirus, a soldier of fortune, for aid. They offered the supreme command of their forces, with the right to keep a garrison in their city, till the independence of Italy was secured.

Pyrrhus.

Pyrrhus, who was compared with Alexander of Macedon, aspired to found an Hellenic empire in the West, as Alexander did in the East, and responded to the call of the Tarentines. Rome was not now to contend with barbarians, but with Hellenes—with phalanxes and cohorts instead of a militia—with a military monarchy and sustained by military science. He landed, B. C. 281, on the Italian shores, with an army of twenty thousand veterans in phalanx, two thousand archers, three thousand cavalry, and twenty elephants. The Tarentine allies promised three hundred and fifty thousand infantry and twenty thousand cavalry to support him. The Romans strained every

Marches to the assistance of the Tarentines.

nerve to meet him before these forces could be collected and organized. They marched with a force of fifty thousand men, larger than a consular army, under Lævinius and Æmilius. They met the enemy on the plain of Heraclea. Seven times did the legion and phalanx drive one or the other back. But the reserves of Pyrrhus, with his elephants, to which the Romans were unaccustomed, decided the battle. Seven thousand Romans were left dead on the field, and an immense number were wounded or taken prisoners. But the battle cost Pyrrhus four thousand of his veterans, which led him to say that another such victory would be his ruin. The Romans retreated into Apulia, but the whole south of Italy, Lucania, Samnium, the Bruttii, and the Greek cities were the prizes which the conqueror won.

Battle of Heraclea.

Pyrrhus then offered peace, since he only aimed to establish a Greek power in Southern Italy. The Senate was disposed to accept it, but the old and blind Appius Claudius was carried in his litter through the crowded forum—as Chatham, in after times, bowed with infirmities and age, was carried to the parliament—and in a vehement speech denounced the peace, and infused a new spirit into the Senate. The Romans refused to treat with a foreign enemy on the soil of Italy. The embassador of Pyrrhus, the orator Cineas, returned to tell the conqueror that to fight the Romans was to fight a hydra—that their city was a temple, and their senators were kings.

Pyrrhus offers peace.

Two new legions were forthwith raised to re-enforce Lævinius, while Pyrrhus marched direct to Rome. But when he arrived within eighteen miles, he found an enemy in his front, while Lævinius harassed his rear. He was obliged to retreat, and retired to Tarentum with an immense booty. The next year he opened the campaign in Apulia; but he found an enemy of seventy thousand infantry and eight thousand horse—a force equal to his own. The first battle was lost by the Romans, who could not penetrate the Grecian phalanx, and were trodden down by the elephants. But he could not prosecute his vic-

Retreat of Pyrrhus.

tory, his troops melted away, and he again retired to Tarentum for winter quarters.

Like a military adventurer, he then, for two years, turned his forces against the Carthaginians, and relieved Syracuse. But he did not avail himself of his victories, being led by a generous nature into political mistakes. He then returned to Italy to renew his warfare with the Romans. The battle of Beneventum, gained by Curius, the Roman general, decided the fate of Pyrrhus. The flower of his Epirot troops was destroyed, and his camp fell, with all its riches, into the hands of the Romans. The king of Epirus retired to his own country, and was assassinated by a woman at Argos, after he had wrested the crown of Macedonia from Antigonus, B. C. 272. He had left, however, to garrison, under Milo, at Tarentum. The city fell into the hands of the Romans the year that Pyrrhus died.

Battle of Beneventum.

With the fall of Tarentum, the conquest of Italy was complete. The Romans found no longer any enemies to resist them on the peninsula. A great State was organized for the future subjection of the world. The conquest of Italy greatly enriched the Romans. Both rich and poor became possessed of large grants of land from the conquered territories. The conquered cities were incorporated with the Roman State, and their inhabitants became Roman citizens or allies. The growth of great plebeian families re-enforced the aristocracy, which was based on wealth. Italy became Latinized, and Rome was now acknowledged as one of the great powers of the world.

Complete subjugation of Italy.

The great man at Rome during the period of the Samnite wars was Appius Claudius—great grandson of the decemvir, and the proudest aristocrat that had yet appeared. He enjoyed all the great offices of State. To him we date many improvements in the city, also the highway which bears his name. He was the patron of art, of eloquence, and poetry. But, at this period, all individual greatness was lost in the State.

Appius Claudius.

CHAPTER XXIX.

THE FIRST PUNIC WAR.

A CONTEST greater than with Pyrrhus and the Greek cities, more memorable in its incidents, and more important in its consequences, now awaited the Romans. This was with Carthage, the greatest power, next to Rome, in the world at that time—a commercial State which had been gradually aggrandized for three hundred years. It was a rich and powerful city at the close of the Persian wars. It had succeeded Tyre as the mistress of the sea.

We have seen, in the second book, how the Carthaginians were involved in wars with Syracuse, when that city had reached the acme of its power under Dionysius. We have also alluded to the early history and power of Carthage. At the time Pyrrhus landed in Sicily, it contained nearly a million of people, and controlled the northern coast of Africa, and the western part of the Mediterranean. Carthage was strictly a naval power, although her colonies were numerous, and her dependencies large. The land forces were not proportionate to the naval; but large armies were necessary to protect her dependencies in the constant wars in which she was engaged. These armies were chiefly mercenaries, and their main strength consisted in light cavalry.

Causes of the Punic war.

The territories of Carthage lay chiefly in the islands which were protected by her navy and enriched by her commerce. Among these insular possessions, Sardinia was the largest and most important, and was the commercial depot of Southern Europe. A part of Sicily, also, as we have seen (Book ii., chap. 24), was colonized and held by

Territories of Carthage.

her, and she aimed at the sovereignty of the whole island. Hence the various wars with Syracuse. The Carthaginians and Greeks were the rivals for the sovereignty of this fruitful island, the centre of the oil and wine trade, the store-house for all sorts of cereals. Had Carthage possessed the whole of Sicily, her fleets would have controlled the Mediterranean.

Sicilian affairs.

The embroilment of Carthage with the Grecian States on this island was the occasion of the first rupture with Rome. Messina, the seat of the pirate republic of the Mamertines, was in close alliance with Rhegium, a city which had grown into importance during the war with Pyrrhus. Rhegium, situated on the Italian side of the strait, solicited the protection of Rome, and a body of Campanian troops was sent to its assistance. These troops expelled or massacred the citizens for whose protection they had been sent, and established a tumultuary government. On the fall of Tarentum, the Romans sought to punish this outrage, and also to embrace the opportunity to possess a town which would facilitate a passage to Sicily, for Sicily as truly belonged to Italy as the Peloponnesus to Greece, being separated only by a narrow strait. A Roman army was accordingly sent to take possession of Rhegium, but the defenders made a desperate resistance. It was finally taken by storm, and the original citizens obtained repossession, as dependents and allies of Rome. The fall of Rhegium robbed the pirate city of Messina of the only ally on which it could count, and subjected it to the vengeance of both the Carthaginians and the Syracusans. The latter were then under the sway of Hiero, who, for fifty years, had reigned without despotism, and had quietly developed both the resources and the freedom of the city. He collected an army of citizens, devoted to him, who expelled the Mamertines from many of their towns, and gained a decisive victory over them, not far from Messina.

Rhegium.

The Mamertines, in danger of subjection by the Syracusans, then looked for foreign aid. One party looked to Carthage, and another to Rome. The Carthaginian party prevailed on the Mamertines to receive a Punic garrison. The Romans, seeking a pretext for a war with Carthage, sent an army ostensibly to protect Messina against Hiero. But the strait which afforded a passage to Sicily was barred by a Carthaginian fleet. The Romans, unaccustomed to the sea, were defeated. Not discouraged, however, they finally succeeded in landing at Messina, and although Carthage and Rome were at peace, seized Hanno, the Carthaginian general, who had the weakness to command the evacuation of the citadel as a ransom for his person.

The Mamertines.

On this violation of international law, Hiero, who feared the Romans more than the Carthaginians, made an alliance with Carthage, and the combined forces of Syracuse and Carthage marched to the liberation of Messina. The Romans, under Appius, the consul, then made overtures of peace to the Carthaginians, and bent their energies against Hiero. But Hiero, suspecting the Carthaginians of treachery, for their whole course with the Syracusans for centuries had been treacherous, retired to Syracuse. Upon which the Romans attacked the Carthaginians singly, and routed them, and spread devastation over the whole island.

Hiero.

This was the commencement of the first Punic war, in which the Romans were plainly the aggressors. Two consular armies now threatened Syracuse, when Hiero sought peace, which was accepted on condition of provisioning the Roman armies, and paying one hundred talents to liberate prisoners.

The first Punic war began B. C. 264, and lasted twenty-four years. Before we present the leading events of that memorable struggle, let us glance at the power of Carthage—the formidable rival of Rome.

As has been narrated, Carthage was founded upon a peninsula, or rocky promontory, sixty-five years before the foundation of Rome. The inhabitants of Carthage, descendants of Phœnicians, were therefore of Semi-

Wealth and population of Carthage.

tic origin. The African farmer was a Canaanite, and all the Canaanites lacked the instinct of political life. The Phœnicians thought of commerce and wealth, and not political aggrandizement. With half their power, the Hellenic cities achieved their independence. Carthage was a colony of Phœnicians, and had their ideas. It lived to traffic and get rich. It was washed on all sides, except the west, by the sea, and above the city, on the western heights, was the citadel Byrsa, called so from the word *βύρσα*, a hide, according to the legend that Dido, when she came to Africa, bought of the inhabitants as much land as could be encompassed by a bull's hide, which she cut into thongs, and inclosed the territory on which she built the citadel. The city grew to be twenty-three miles in circuit, and contained seven hundred thousand people. It had two harbors, an outer and inner, the latter being surrounded by a lofty wall. A triple wall was erected across the peninsula, to protect it from the west, three miles long, and between the walls were stables for three hundred elephants, four thousand horses, and barracks for two thousand infantry, with magazines and stores. In the centre of the inner harbor was an island, called Cothon, the shores of which were lined with quays and docks for two hundred and twenty ships. The citadel, Byrsa, was two miles in circuit, and when it finally surrendered to the Romans, fifty thousand people marched out of it. On its summit was the famous temple of Æsculapius. At the northwestern angle of the city were twenty immense reservoirs, each four hundred feet by twenty-eight, filled with water, brought by an aqueduct at a distance of fifty-two miles. The suburb Megara, beyond the city walls, but within those that defended the peninsula, was the site of magnificent gardens and villas, which were adorned with every kind of Grecian art, for the Carthaginians were rich before Rome had conquered even Latium. This great city controlled the other Phœnician cities, part of Sicily, Numidia, Mauritania, Lybia—in short, the northern part of Africa, and colonies in Spain and the islands of the

Power of Carthage.

western part of the Mediterranean. The city alone could furnish in an exigency forty thousand heavy infantry, one thousand cavalry, and twenty thousand war chariots. The garrison of the city amounted to twenty thousand foot and four thousand horse, and the total force which the city could command was more than one hundred thousand men. The navy was the largest in the world, for, in the sea-fight with Regulus, it numbered three hundred and fifty ships, carrying one hundred and fifty thousand men.

Such was this great power against which the Romans were resolved to contend. It would seem that Carthage was willing that Rome should have the sovereignty of Italy, provided it had itself the possession of Sicily. But this was what the Romans were determined to prevent. The object of contention, then, between these two rivals, the one all-powerful by land and the other by sea, was the possession of Sicily.

Creation of a Roman fleet.

During the first three years of the war, the Romans made themselves masters of all the island, except the maritime fortresses at its western extremity, Eryx and Panormus. Meanwhile the Carthaginians ravaged the coasts of Italy, and destroyed its commerce. The Romans then saw that Sicily could not be held without a navy as powerful as that of their rivals, and it was resolved to build at once one hundred and twenty ships. A Carthaginian quinquereme, wrecked on the Bruttian shore, furnished the model, the forests of Silo the timber, and the maritime cities of Italy and Greece, the sailors. In sixty days a fleet of one hundred and twenty ships was built and ready for sea. The superior seamanship of the Carthaginians was neutralized by converting the decks into a battle-field for soldiers. Each ship was provided with a long boarding-bridge, hinged up against the mast, to be let down on the prow, and fixed to the hostile deck by a long spike, which projected from its end. The bridge was wide enough for two soldiers to pass abreast, and its sides were protected by bulwarks.

The first encounter of the Romans with the Carthaginians

resulted in the capture of the whole force, a squadron of seventeen ships. The second encounter ended in the capture of more ships than the Roman admiral, Cn. Scipio, had lost. The next battle, that of Mylæ, in which the whole Roman fleet was engaged, again turned in favor of the Romans, whose bad seamanship provoked the contempt of their foes, and led to self-confidence. The battle was gained by grappling the enemy's ships one by one. The Carthaginians lost fourteen ships, and only saved the rest by inglorious flight.

Naval battle of Mylæ.

For six years no decided victories were won by either side, but in the year B. C. 256, nine years from the commencement of hostilities, M. Atilius Regulus, a noble of the same class and habits as Cincinnatus and Fabricius, with a fleet of three hundred and thirty ships, manned by one hundred thousand sailors, encountered the Carthaginian fleet of three hundred and fifty ships on the southern coast of Sicily, and gained a memorable victory. It was gained on the same principle as Epaminondas and Alexander won their battles, by concentrating all the forces upon a single point, and breaking the line. The Romans advanced in the shape of a wedge, with the two consuls' ships at the apex. The Carthaginian admirals allowed the centre to give way before the advancing squadron. The right wing made a circuit out in the open sea, and took the Roman reserve in the rear, while the left wing attacked the vessels that were towing the horse transports, and forced them to the shore. But the Carthaginian centre, being thus left weak, was no match for the best ships of the Romans, and the consuls, victorious in the centre, turned to the relief of the two rear divisions. The Carthaginians lost sixty-four ships, which were taken, besides twenty-four which were sunk, and retreated with the remainder to the Gulf of Carthage, to defend the shores against the anticipated attack.

Great victory of Regulus.

The Romans, however, made for another point, and landed in the harbor of Aspis, intrenched a camp to protect their ships, and ravaged the country. Twenty

Other victories of Regulus.

thousand captives were sent to Rome and sold as slaves, besides an immense booty—a number equal to a fifth part of the free population of the city. A footing in Africa was thus made, and so secure were the Romans, that a large part of the army was recalled, leaving Regulus with only forty ships, fifteen thousand infantry, and five hundred cavalry. Yet with this small army he defeated the Carthaginians, and became master of the country to within ten miles of Carthage. The Carthaginians, shut up in the city, sued for peace; but it was granted only on condition of the cession of Sicily and Sardinia, the surrender of the fleet, and the reduction of Carthage to the condition of a dependent city. Such a proposal was rejected, and despair gave courage to the defeated Carthaginians.

Hamilcar.

They made one grand effort while Regulus lay inactive in winter quarters. The return of Hamilcar from Sicily with veteran troops, which furnished a nucleus for a new army, inspired the Carthaginians with hope, and assisted by a Lacedæmonian general, Xanthippus, with a band of Greek mercenaries, the Carthaginians marched unexpectedly upon Regulus, and so signally defeated him at Tunis, that only two thousand Romans escaped. Regulus, with five hundred of the legionary force, was taken captive and carried to Carthage.

Hasdrubal.

The Carthaginians now assumed the offensive, and Sicily became the battle-field. Hasdrubal, son of Hanno, landed on the island with one hundred and forty elephants, while the Roman fleet of three hundred ships suffered a great disaster off the Lucanian promontory. A storm arose, which wrecked one hundred and fifty ships—a disaster equal to the one which it suffered two years before, when two-thirds of the large fleet which was sent to relieve the two thousand troops at Clupea was destroyed by a similar storm. In spite of these calamities, the Romans took Panormus and Thermæ, and gained a victory under the walls of the former city which cost the Carthaginians twenty thousand men and the capture of one hundred and twenty elephants. This success, gained by Metellus, was the greatest yet obtained in Sicily, and the victorious general adorned his triumph with thirteen captured generals and one hundred and four elephants.

The two maritime fortresses which still held out at the west of the island, Drepanum and Lilybæum, were now invested, and the Carthaginians, shut up in these fortresses, sent an embassy to Rome to ask an exchange of prisoners, and sue for peace. Regulus, now five years a prisoner, was allowed to accompany the embassy, on his promise to return if the mission was unsuccessful. As his condition was now that of a Carthaginian slave, he was reluctant to enter the city, and still more the Senate, of which he was no longer a member. But when this reluctance was overcome, he denounced both the peace and the exchange of prisoners. The Romans wished to retain this noble patriot, but he was true to his oath, and returned voluntarily to Carthage, after having defeated the object of the embassadors, knowing that a cruel death awaited him. The Carthaginians, indignant and filled with revenge, it is said, exposed the hero to a burning sun, with his eyelids cut off, and rolled him in a barrel lined with iron spikes.

Imprisonment of Regulus.

Death of Regulus.

The embassy having thus failed, the attack on the fortresses, which alone linked Africa with Sicily, was renewed. The siege of Lilybæum lasted till the end of the war, which, from the mutual exhaustion of the parties, now languished for six years. The Romans had lost four great fleets, three of which had arms on board, and the census of the city, in the seventeenth year, showed a decrease of forty thousand citizens. During this interval of stagnation, when petty warfare alone existed, Hamilcar Barca was appointed general of Carthage, and in the same year his son Hannibal was born, B. C. 247.

Hamilcar Barca.

The Romans, disgusted with the apathy of the government, fitted out a fleet of privateers of two hundred ships, manned by sixty thousand sailors, and this fleet gained a victory over the Carthaginians, unprepared for such a force, so that fifty ships were sunk, and seventy more were carried by the victors into port. This victory gave Sicily to the Romans, and ended the war. The Roman prisoners were surrendered by Hamilcar, who had full powers for peace, and Carthage engaged to pay three thousand two hundred talents for the expenses of the war.

Conquest of Sicily.

The Romans were gainers by this war. They acquired the richest island in the world, fertile in all the fruits of the earth, with splendid harbors, cities, and a great accumulation of wealth. The long war of twenty-four years, nearly a whole generation, was not conducted on such a scale as essentially to impoverish the contending parties. There were no debts contracted for future generations to pay. It was the most absorbing object of public interest, indeed; but many other events and subjects must also have occupied the Roman mind. It was a foreign war, the first that Rome had waged. It was a war of ambition, the commencement of those unscrupulous and aggressive measures that finally resulted in the political annihilation of all the other great powers of the world.

Acquisition of Sicily.

But this war, compared with those foreign wars which Rome subsequently conducted, was carried on without science and skill. It was carried on in the transition period of Roman warfare, when tactics were more highly prized than strategy. It was by a militia, and agricultural generals, and tactics, and personal bravery, that the various Italian nations were subdued, when war had not ripened into a science, such as was conducted even by the Greeks. There was no skill or experience in the conduct of sieges. The navy was managed by Greek mercenaries.

The great improvement in the science of war which this first contest with a foreign power led to, was the creation of a navy, and the necessity of employing veteran troops, led by experienced generals. A deliberative assembly, like the Senate, it was found could not conduct a foreign war. It was left to generals, who were to learn marches and countermarches, sieges, and a strategical sys-

Creation of a Roman naval power.

tem. The withdrawal of half the army of Regulus by the Senate proved nearly fatal. Carthage could not be subdued by that rustic warfare which had sufficed for the conquest of Etruria or Samnium. The new system of war demanded generals who had military training and a military eye, and not citizen admirals. The final success was owing to the errors of the Carthaginians rather than military science.

CHAPTER XXX.

THE SECOND PUNIC OR HANNIBALIC WAR.

THE peace between the Carthaginians and Romans was a mere truce. Though it lasted twenty-one years, new sources of quarrel were accumulating, and forces were being prepared for a more decisive encounter.

Before we trace the progress of this still more memorable war, let us glance at the events which transpired in the interval between it and the first contest.

Condition of Carthage after the war.

That interval is memorable for the military career of Hamilcar, and his great ascendency at Carthage. That city paid dearly for the peace it had secured, for the tribute of Sicily flowed into the treasury of the Romans. Its commercial policy was broken up, and the commerce of Italy flowed in new channels. This change was bitterly felt by the Phœnician city, and a party was soon organized for the further prosecution of hostilities. There was also a strong peace party, made up of the indolent and cowardly money-worshipers of that mercantile State. The war party was headed by Hamilcar, the peace party by Hanno, which at first had the ascendency. It drove the army into mutiny by haggling about pay. The Libyan mercenaries joined the revolt, and Carthage found herself alone in the midst of anarchies. In this emergency the government solicited Hamilcar to save it from the effect of its blunders and selfishness.

This government, as at Rome, was oligarchic, but the nobles were merely mercantile grandees, without ability—jealous, exclusive, and selfish. The great body of the people whom they ruled were poor and dependent. In intrusting power to Hamilcar, the government of wealthy citizens only gave him military control. The army which he commanded was not a citizen militia, it was made up of mercenaries. Hamilcar was obliged to construct a force from these, to whom the State looked for its salvation.

Hamilcar.

He was a young man, a little over thirty, and foreboding that he would not live to complete his plans, enjoined his son Hannibal, nine years of age, when he was about to leave Carthage, to swear at the altar of the Eternal God hatred of the Roman name.

Hasdrubal.

He left Carthage for Spain, taking with him his sons, to be reared in the camp. He marched along the coast, accompanied by the fleet, which was commanded by Hasdrubal. He crossed the sea at the Pillars of Hercules, with the view of organizing a Spanish kingdom to assist the Carthaginians in their future warfare. But he died prematurely, B. C. 229, leaving his son-in-law, Hasdrubal, to carry out his designs, and the southern and eastern provinces of Spain became Carthaginian provinces. Carthagena arose as the capital of this new Spanish kingdom, in the territory of the Contestana. Here agriculture flourished, and still more, mining, from the silver mines, which produced, a century afterward, thirty-six millions of sesterces—nearly two million dollars—yearly. Carthage thus acquired in Spain a market for its commerce and manufactures, and the New Carthage ruled as far as the Ebro. But the greatest advantage of this new acquisition to Carthage was the new class of mercenary soldiers which were incorporated with the army. At first, the Romans were not alarmed by the rise of this new Spanish power, and saw only a compensation for the tribute and traffic which Carthage had lost in Sicily. And while the Carthaginians were creating armies in Spain, the Romans were engaged in conquering Cisalpine Gaul, and consolidating the Italian conquests.

Hannibal.

Hasdrubal was assassinated after eight years of successful administration, and Hannibal was hailed as his successor by the army, and the choice was confirmed by the Carthaginians, B. C. 221. He was now twenty-nine, trained to all the fatigue and dangers of the camp, and with a native genius for war, which made him, according to the estimation of modern critics, the greatest general of antiquity. He combined courage with discretion, and prudence with energy. He had an inventive craftiness, which led him to take unexpected routes. He profoundly studied the character of antagonists, and kept himself informed of the projects of his enemies. He had his spies at Rome, and was frequently seen in disguises in order to get important information.

This crafty and able general resolved, on his nomination, to make war at once upon the Romans, whom he regarded as the deadly foe of his country. His first great exploit was the reduction of Saguntum, an Iberian city on the coast, in alliance with the Romans. It defended itself with desperate energy for eight months, and its siege is memorable. The inhabitants were treated with savage cruelty, and the spoil was sent to Carthage.

Fall of Saguntum.

This act of Hannibal was the occasion, though not the cause, of the second Punic war. The Romans, indignant, demanded of Carthage the surrender of the general who had broken the peace. On the fall of Saguntum, Hannibal retired to Carthagena for winter quarters, and to make preparations for the invasion of Italy. He collected an army of one hundred and twenty thousand infantry, sixteen thousand cavalry, and fifty-eight elephants, assisted by a naval force. But the whole of this great army was not designed for the Italian expedition. A part of it was sent for the protection of Carthage, and a part was reserved for the protection of Spain, the government of which he intrusted to his brother Hasdrubal.

Hannibal retires to Carthagena.

The nations of the earth, two thousand years ago, would scarcely appreciate the magnitude of the events which were to follow from the invasion of Italy, and the war which followed—perhaps "the most memorable of all the wars ever waged," certainly one of the most memorable in human annals. The question at issue was, whether the world was to be governed by a commercial oligarchy, with all the superstitions of the East, or by the laws of a free and patriotic State. It was a war waged between the genius of a mighty general and the resources of the Roman people, for Hannibal did not look for aid so much to his own State, as to those hardy Spaniards who followed his standard.

He prepares for vigorous war.

In the spring, B. C. 218, Hannibal set out from New Carthage with an army of ninety thousand infantry and twelve thousand cavalry. He encountered at the Ebro the first serious resistance, but this was from the natives, and not the Romans. It took four months to surmount their resistance, during which he lost one-fourth of his army. As it was his great object to gain time before the Romans could occupy the passes of the Alps, he made this sacrifice of his men. When he reached the Pyrenees, he sent home a part of his army, and crossed those mountains with only fifty thousand infantry and nine thousand cavalry; but these were veteran troops. He took the coast route by Narbonne and Nimes, through the Celtic territory, and encountered no serious resistance till he reached the Rhone, opposite to Avignon, about the end of July. The passage was disputed by Scipio, assisted by friendly Gauls, but Hannibal outflanked his enemies by sending a detachment across the river, on rafts, two days' march higher up, and thus easily forced the passage, and was three days' march beyond the river before Scipio was aware that he had crossed. Scipio then sailed back to Pisa, and aided his colleague to meet the invader in Cisalpine Gaul.

Crosses the Ebro.

Hannibal, now on Celtic territory on the Roman side of the Rhone, could not be prevented from reaching the Alps. Two passes then led from the lower Rhone across the Alps—the one by the Cottian Alps (Mount Geneva); and the other, the higher pass of the Grain Alps (Mount St. Bernard), and this was selected by Hannibal. The task of transporting a large army over even this easier pass

Hannibal crosses the Alps.

was a work of great difficulty, with baggage, cavalry, and elephants, when the autumn snows were falling, resisted by the mountaineers, against whom they had to fight to the very summit of the pass. The descent, though free from enemies, was still more dangerous, and it required, at one place, three days' labor to make the road practicable for the elephants. The army arrived, the middle of September, in the plain of Ivrea, where his exhausted troops were quartered in friendly villages. Had the Romans met him near Turin with only thirty thousand men, and at once forced a battle, the prospects of Hannibal would have been doubtful. But no army appeared; the object was attained, but with the loss of half his troops, and the rest so demoralized by fatigue, that a long rest was required.

Scipio.

The great talents by which Scipio atoned for his previous errors now extricated his army from destruction. He retreated across the Ticinio and the Po, refusing a pitched battle on the plains, and fell back upon a strong position on the hills. The united consular armies, forty thousand men, were so posted as to compel Hannibal to attack in front with inferior force, or go into winter quarters, trusting to the doubtful fidelity of the Gauls.

Battle of the Trasimene Lake.

It has been well said, "that it was the misfortune of Rome's double magistracy when both consuls were present on the field." Owing to a wound which Scipio had received, the command devolved upon Sempronius, who, eager for distinction, could not resist the provocations of Hannibal to bring on a battle. In one of the skirmishes the Roman cavalry and light infantry were enticed by the flying Numidians across a swollen stream, and suddenly found themselves before the entire Punic army. The whole Roman force hurried across the stream to support the vanguard. A battle took place on the Trasimene Lake, in which the Romans were sorely beaten, but ten thousand infantry cut their way through the masses of the enemy, and reached the fortess of Placentia, where they were joined by other bands. After this success, which gave Hannibal all of

Northern Italy, his army, suffering from fatigue and disease, retired into winter quarters. He now had lost all his elephants but one. The remains of the Roman army passed the winter in the fortresses of Placentia and Cremona.

The next spring, the Romans, under Flaminius, took the field, with four legions, to command the great northern and eastern roads, and the passes of the Appenines. But Hannibal, knowing that Rome was only vulnerable at the heart, rapidly changed his base, crossed the Appenines at an undefended pass, and advanced, by the lower Arno, into Etruria, while Flaminius was watching by the upper course of that stream. Flaminius was a mere party leader and demagogue, and was not the man for such a crisis, for Hannibal was allowed to pass by him, and reach Fæsulæ unobstructed. The Romans prepared themselves for the worst, broke down the bridges over the Tiber, and nominated Quintus Fabius Maximus dictator.

Hannibal in Italy.

Pyrrhus would have marched direct upon Rome, but Hannibal was more far-sighted. His army needed a new organization, and rest, and recruits, so he marched unexpectedly through Umbria, devastated the country, and halted on the shores of the Adriatic. Here he rested, reorganized his Libyan cavalry, and resumed his communication with Carthage. He then broke up his camp, and marched into Southern Italy, hoping to break up the confederacy. But not a single Italian town entered into alliance with the Carthaginians.

Hannibal marches to the Adriatic.

Fabius, the dictator, a man of great prudence, advanced in years, and a tactitian of the old Roman school, determined to avoid a pitched battle, and starve or weary out his enemy. Hannibal adjusted his plans in accordance with the character of the man he opposed. So he passed the Roman army, crossed the Appenines, took Telesia, and turned against Capua, the most important of all the Italian dependent cities, hoping for a revolt among the Campanian towns. Here again he was disappointed. So, retracing his steps, he took the road to Apulia, the dictator follow-

Fabius.

ing him along the heights. So the summer was consumed by marchings and countermarchings, the lands of the Hispanians, Campanians, Samnites, Pælignians, and other provinces, being successively devastated. But no important battle was fought. He selected then the rich lands of Apulia for winter quarters, and intrenched his camp at Gerenium. The Romans formed a camp in the territory of the Larinates, and harassed the enemy's foragers. This defensive policy of Fabius wounded the Roman pride, and the dictator became unpopular. The Senate resolved to depart from a policy which was slowly but surely ruining the State, and an army was equipped larger than Rome ever before sent into the field, composed of eight legions, under the command of the two consuls, L. Æmilius Paulus, and M. Terentius Varro. The former, a patrician, had conducted successfully the Illyrian war; the latter, the popular candidate, incapable, conceited, and presumptuous.

Efforts of the Romans.

As soon as the season allowed him to leave his winter-quarters, Hannibal, assuming the offensive, marched out of Gerenium, passed Luceria, crossed the Aufidus, and took the citadel of Cannæ, which commanded the plain of Canusium. The Roman consuls arrived in Apulia in the beginning of the summer, with eighty thousand infantry and six thousand cavalry. Hannibal's force was forty thousand infantry and ten thousand cavalry, inured to regular warfare. The Romans made up their minds to fight, and confronted the Carthaginians on the right bank of the Aufidus. According to a foolish custom, the command devolved on one of the consuls every other day, and Varro determined to avail himself of the first opportunity for a battle. The forces met on the plain west of Cannæ, more favorable to the Carthaginians than the Romans, on account of the superiority of the cavalry. It is difficult, without a long description, to give clear conceptions of this famous battle. Hannibal, it would seem, like Epaminondas and Alexander, brought to bear his heavy cavalry, under Hasdrubal, upon the weakest point of the enemy, after the conflict had continued awhile without

Battle of Cannæ.

decisive results. The weaker right of the Roman army, led by Paulus, after bravely fighting, were cut down and driven across the river. Paulus, wounded, then rode to the centre, composed of infantry in close lines, which had gained an advantage over the Spanish and Gaulish troops that encountered them. In order to follow up this advantage, the legions pressed forward in the form of a wedge. In this position the Libyan infantry, wheeling upon them right and left, warmly assailed both sides of the Roman infantry, which checked its advance. By this double flank attack the Roman infantry became crowded, and were not free. Meanwhile, Hasdrubal, after defeating the right wing, which had been led by Paulus, led his cavalry behind the Roman centre and attacked the left wing, led by Varro.

Its great consequences.

The cavalry of Varro, opposed by the Numidian cavalry, was in no condition to meet this double attack, and was scattered. Hasdrubal again rallied his cavalry, and led it to the rear of the Roman centre, already in close fight with the Spanish and Gaulish infantry. This last charge decided the battle. Flight was impossible, for the river was in the rear, and in front was a victorious enemy. No quarter was given. Seventy thousand Romans were slain, including the consul Paulus and eighty men of senatorial rank. Varro was saved by the speed of his horse. The Carthaginians lost not quite six thousand.

Varro.

This immense disaster was the signal for the revolt of the allies, which Hannibal, before in vain had sought to procure. Capua opened her gates to the conqueror. Nearly all the people of Southern Italy rose against Rome. But the Greek cities of the coast were held by Roman garrisons, as well as the fortresses in Apulia, Campania, and Samnium. The news of the battle of Cannæ, B.C. 216, induced the Macedonian king to promise aid to Hannibal. The death of Hiero at Syracuse made Sicily an enemy to Rome, while Carthage, now elated, sent considerable re-enforcements.

Revolt of allies.

Many critics have expressed surprise that Hannibal, after

this great victory, did not at once march upon Rome. Had he conquered, as Alexander did, a Persian, Oriental, effeminate people, this might have been his true policy. But Rome was still capable of a strong defense, and would not have succumbed under any pressure of adverse circumstances, and she also was still strong in allies. And more, Hannibal had not perfected his political combinations. He was not ready to strike the final blow. He had to keep his eye on Macedonia, Africa, Sicily, and Spain. Alexander did not march to Babylon, until he had subdued Phœnicia and Egypt. Even the capture of Rome would not prevent a long war with the States of Italy.

Wisdom of Hannibal.

Nor did the Romans lose courage when they learned the greatest calamity which had ever befallen them. They made new and immense preparations. All the reserve forces were called out—all men capable of bearing arms—young or old. Even the slaves were armed, after being purchased by the State, and made soldiers. Spoils were taken down from the temples. The Latin cities sent in contingents, and the Senate refused to receive even the envoy of the conqueror.

Fortitude of the Romans.

Such courage and fortitude and energy were not without effect, while the enervating influence of Capua, the following winter, demoralized the Carthaginians. The turning point of the war was the winter which followed the defeat at Cannæ. The great aim of Hannibal, in his expedition to Italy, had been to break up the Italian confederacy. After three campaigns, that object was only imperfectly accomplished, in spite of his victories, and he had a great frontier to protect. With only forty thousand men, he could not leave it uncovered, and advance to Rome. The Romans, too, learning wisdom, now appointed only generals of experience, and continued them in command.

The crisis.

The animating soul of the new warfare was Marcus Claudius Marcellus, a man fifty years of age, who had received a severe military training, and performed acts of signal heroism. He was not a general to be a mere

Marcellus.

spectator of the movements of the enemy from the hills, but to take his position in fortified camps under the walls of fortresses. With the two legions saved from Cannæ, and the troops raised from Rome and Ostia, he followed Hannibal to Campania, while other Roman armies were posted in other quarters.

Hannibal now saw that without great re-enforcements from Carthage, Spain, Macedonia, and Syracuse, he would be obliged to fight on the defensive. But the Carthaginians sent only congratulations; the king of Macedonia failed in courage; while the Romans intercepted supplies from Syracuse and Spain. Hannibal was left to his own resources.

Scipio. Scipio, meanwhile, in Spain, attacked the real base of Hannibal, overran the country of the Ebro, secured the passes of the Pyrenees, and defeated Hasdrubal while attempting to lead succor to his brother. The capture of Saguntum gave the Romans a strong fortress between the Ebro and Carthagena. Scipio even meditated an attack on Africa, and induced Syphax, king of one of the Numidian nations, to desert Carthage, which caused the recall of Hasdrubal from Spain. His departure left Scipio master of the peninsula; but Hasdrubal, after punishing the disaffected Numidians, returned to Spain, and with overwhelming numbers regained their ascendency, and Scipio was slain, as well as his brother, and their army routed.

Revolt of Syracuse. It has been mentioned that on the death of Hiero, who had been the long-tried friend of Rome, Syracuse threw her influence in favor of Carthage, being ruled by factions. Against this revolted city the consul Marcellus now advanced, and invested the city by land and sea. He was foiled by the celebrated mathematician Archimedes, who constructed engines which destroyed the Roman ships. This very great man advanced the science of geometry, and made discoveries which rank him among the lights of the ancient world. His theory of the lever was the foundation of statics till the time of New-

Archimedes.

ton. His discovery of the method of determining specific gravities by immersion in a fluid was equally memorable. He was not only the greatest mathematician of the old world, but he applied science to practical affairs, and compelled Marcellus to convert the siege of Syracuse into a blockade. He is said to have launched a ship by the pressure of the screw, which, reversed in its operation, has revolutionized naval and commercial marines.

The time gained by this eminent engineer, as well as geometer, enabled the Carthaginians to send an army to relieve Syracuse. The situation of Marcellus was critical, when, by a fortunate escalade of the walls, left unguarded at a festival, the Romans were enabled to take possession of a strong position within the walls. A pestilence carried off most of the African army encamped in the valley of Anapus, with the general Himilco. Bomilcar, the Carthaginian admiral, retreated, rather than fight the Roman fleet. Marcellus obtained, by the treachery of a Sicilian captain, possession of the island of Ortygia, where Dionysius had once intrenched himself, the key to the port and the city, and Syracuse fell. The city was given up to plunder and massacre, and Archimedes was one of the victims. Marcellus honored the illustrious defender with a stately funeral, and he was buried outside the gate of Acradina. One hundred and fifty years later, the Syracusans had forgotten even where he was buried, and his tomb was discovered by Cicero.

Siege of Syracuse.

Death of Archimedes.

While these events took place in Spain and Sicily, Hannibal bent his efforts to capture Tarentum, and the Romans were equally resolved to recover Capua. The fall of Tarentum enabled Hannibal to break up the siege of Capua, and foiled in his attempts to bring on a decisive battle before that city, he advanced to Rome, and encamped within five miles of the city, after having led his troops with consummate skill between the armies and fortresses of the enemy. But Rome was well defended by two legions, under Fabius, who refused to fight a pitched battle. Hannibal was, therefore, compelled to retreat in order to save Capua, which, however, in his absence, had surrendered to the Romans, after a two years' siege, and was savagely punished for its defection from the Roman cause. The fall of Capua gave a renewed confidence to the Roman government, which sent re-enforcements to Spain. But it imprudently reduced its other forces, so that Marcellus was left to face Hannibal with an inadequate army. The war was now carried on with alternate successes, in the course of which Tarentum again fell into Roman hands. Thirty thousand Tarentines were sold as slaves, B. C. 209.

Fall of Capua.

This great war had now lasted ten years, and both parties were sinking from exhaustion. In this posture of affairs the Romans were startled with the intelligence that Hasdrubal had crossed the Pyrenees, and was advancing to join his brother in Italy. The Romans, in this exigency, made prodigious exertions. Twenty-three legions were enrolled; but before preparations were completed, Hasdrubal crossed the Alps, re-enforced by eight thousand Ligurian mercenaries. It was the aim of the two Carthaginian generals to form a juncture of their forces, and of the Romans to prevent it. Gaining intelligence of the intended movements of Hannibal and Hasdrubal by an intercepted dispatch, the Roman consul, Nero, advanced to meet Hasdrubal, and encountered him on the banks of the Metaurus. Here a battle ensued, in which the Carthaginians were defeated and Hasdrubal slain. Hannibal was waiting in suspense for the dispatch of his brother in his Apulian camp, when the victor returned from his march of five hundred miles, and threw the head of Hasdrubal within his outposts. On the sight of his brother's head, he exclaimed; "I recognize the doom of Carthage." Abandoning Apulia and Lucania, he retired to the Bruttian peninsula, and the victor of Cannæ retained only a few posts to reembark for Africa.

Battle of Metaurus.

Reverses of Hannibal.

And yet this great general was able to keep the field four years longer, nor could the superiority of his opponents compel him to shut himself up in a fortress or re-embark, a proof of his strategic talents.

In the mean time a brilliant career was opened in Spain to the young Publius Scipio, known as the elder Africanus. He was only twenty-four when selected to lead the armies of Rome in Spain; for it was necessary to subdue that country in order to foil the Carthaginians in Italy. Publius Scipio was an enthusiast, who won the hearts of soldiers and women. He was kingly in his bearing, confident of his greatness, graceful in his manners, and eloquent in his speech—popular with all classes, and inspiring the enthusiasm which he felt.

Scipio.

He landed in Spain with an army of thirty thousand, and at once marched to New Carthage, before the distant armies of the Carthaginians could come to its relief. In a single day the schemes of Hamilcar and his sons were dissolved, and this great capital fell into the hands of the youthful general, not yet eligible for a single curule magistracy. Ten thousand captives were taken and six hundred talents, with great stores of corn and munitions of war. Spain seemed to be an easy conquest; but the following year the Carthaginians made a desperate effort, and sent to Spain a new army of seventy thousand infantry, four thousand horse, and thirty-two elephants. Yet this great force, united with that which remained under Hasdrubal and Mago, was signally defeated by Scipio. This grand victory, which made Scipio master of Spain, left him free to carry the war into Africa itself, assisted by his ally Masinassa. Gades alone remained to the Carthaginians, the original colony of the Phœnicians, and even this last tie was severed when Mago was recalled to assist Hannibal.

His successes in Spain.

Scipio, ambitious to finish the war, and seeking to employ the whole resources of the empire, returned to Italy and offered himself for the consulship, B. C. 205, and was unanimously chosen by the centuries, though not of legal age. His colleague was the chief pontiff P. Licinius Crassus, whose office prevented him from leaving

Scipio consul.

Italy, and he was thus left unobstructed in the sole conduct of the war. Sicily was assigned to him as his province, where he was to build a fleet and make preparations for passing over to Africa, although a party, headed by old Fabius Maximus, wished him to remain in Italy to drive away Hannibal. The Senate withheld the usual power of the consul to make a new levy, but permitted Scipio to enroll volunteers throughout Italy. In the state of disorganization and demoralization which ever attend a long war, this enrollment was easily effected, and money was raised by contributions on disaffected States.

He invades Africa.

Hannibal was still pent up among the Bruttii, unwilling to let go his last hold on Italy. Mago, in cisalpine Gaul, was too far off to render aid. The defense of Africa depended on him alone, and he was recalled. He would probably have anticipated the order. Rome breathed more freely when the "Libyan Lion" had departed. For fifteen years he had been an incubus or a terror, and the Romans, in various conflicts, had lost three hundred thousand men. Two of the Scipios, Paulus Gracchus and Marcellus, had yielded up their lives in battle. Only Fabius, among the experienced generals at the beginning of the war, was alive, and he, at the age of ninety, was now crowned with a chaplet of the grass of Italy, as the most honorable reward which could be given him.

Hannibal evacuates Italy.

Hannibal now sought a conference with Scipio, for both parties were anxious for peace, but was unable to obtain any better terms than the cession of Spain, as well as the Mediterranean islands, the surrender of the Carthaginian fleet, the payment of four thousand talents, and the confirmation of Masinissa in the kingdom of Syphax. Such terms could not be accepted, and both parties prepared for one more decisive conflict.

Hannibal seeks for peace.

The battle was fought at Zama. "Hannibal arranged his infantry in three lines. The first division contained the Carthaginian mercenaries; the second, the African allies, and the militia of Carthage; the third, the

The battle of Zama.

veterans who followed him from Italy. In the front of the lines were stationed eighty elephants; the cavalry was placed on the wings. Scipio likewise disposed the legions in three divisions. The infantry fought hand to hand in the first division, and both parties falling into confusion, sought aid in the second division. The Romans were supported, but the Carthaginian militia was wavering. Upon seeing this, Hannibal hastily withdrew what remained of the two first lines to the flanks, and pushed forward his choice Italian troops along the whole line. Scipio gathered together in the centre all that were able to fight of the first line, and made the second and third divisions close up on the right and left of the first. Once again the conflict was renewed with more desperate fighting, till the cavalry of the Romans and of Masinassa, returning from pursuit of the beaten cavalry of the enemy, surrounded them on all sides. This movement annihilated the Punic army. All was lost, and Hannibal was only able to escape with a handful of men."

Scipio gives peace to Carthage.

It was now in the power of Scipio to march upon Carthage and lay siege to the city, neither protected nor provisioned. But he made no extravagant use of his victory. He granted peace on the terms previously rejected, with the addition of an annual tribute of two hundred talents for fifty years. He had no object to destroy a city after its political power was annihilated, and wickedly overthrow the primitive seat of commerce, which was still one of the main pillars of civilization. He was too great and wise a statesman to take such a revenge as the Romans sought fifty years afterward. He was contented to end the war gloriously, and see Carthage, the old rival, a tributary and broken power, with no possibility of reviving its former schemes, B. C. 201.

Close of the war.

This ended the Hannibalic war, which had lasted seventeen years, and which gave to Rome the undisputed sovereignty of Italy, the conversion of Spain into two Roman provinces, the union of Syracuse with the Roman province of Sicily, the establishment of a Roman protectorate over the Numidian chiefs, and the reduction of Carthage to a defenseless mercantile city. The hegemony of Rome was established over the western region of the Mediterranean. These results were great, but were obtained by the loss of one quarter of the burgesses of Rome, the ruin of four hundred towns, the waste of the accumulated capital of years, and the general demoralization of the people. It might seem that the Romans could have lived side by side with other nations in amity, as modern nations do. But, in ancient times, "it was necessary to be either anvil or hammer." Either Rome or Carthage was to become the great power of the world.

CHAPTER XXXI.

THE MACEDONIAN AND ASIATIC WARS.

SCARCELY was Rome left to recover from the exhaustion of the long and desperate war with Hannibal, before she was involved in a new war with Macedonia, which led to very important consequences.

The Greeks had retained the sovereignty which Alexander had won, and their civilization extended rapidly into the East. There were three great monarchies which arose, however, from the dismemberment of the empire which Alexander had founded—Macedonia, Asia, and Egypt—and each of them, in turn, was destined to become provinces of Rome.

Macedonia was then ruled by Philip V., and was much such a monarchy as the first Philip had consolidated. The Macedonian rule embraced Greece and Thessaly, and strong garrisons were maintained at Demetrias in Magnesia, Calchis in the island of Eubœa, and in Corinth, "the three fetters of the Hellenes." But the strength of the kingdom lay in Macedonia. In Greece proper all moral and political energy had fled, and the degenerate, but still intellectual inhabitants spent their time in bacchanalian pleasures, in fencing, and in study of the midnight lamp. The Greeks, diffused over the East, disseminated their culture, but were only in sufficient numbers to supply officers, statesmen, and schoolmasters. All the real warlike vigor remained among the nations of the North, where Philip reigned, a genuine king, proud of his purple, and proud of his accomplishments, lawless and ungodly, indifferent to the lives and sufferings of others, stubborn and tyrannical. He saw with regret the subjugation of Carthage, but

Macedonia.

Philip.

did not come to her relief when his aid might have turned the scale, ten years before. His eyes were turned to another quarter, to possess himself of part of the territories of Egypt, assisted by Antiochus of Asia. In this attempt he arrayed against himself all the Greek mercantile cities whose interests were identified with Alexandria, now, on the fall of Carthage, the greatest commercial city of the world. He was opposed by Pergamus and the Rhodian league, while the Romans gave serious attention to their Eastern complications, not so much with a view of conquering the East, as to protect their newly-acquired possessions. A Macedonian war, then, became inevitable, but was entered into reluctantly, and was one of the most righteous, according to Mommsen, which Rome ever waged.

Makes war with the Romans.

The pretext for war—the *casus belli*—was furnished by an attack on Athens by the Macedonian general, to avenge the murder of two Arcanians for intruding upon the Eleusinan Mysteries, B. C. 201. Athens was an ally of Rome. Two legions, under Publius Sulpicius Galba, embarked at Brundusium for Macedonia, with one thousand Numidian cavalry and a number of elephants. Nothing was accomplished this year of any historical importance. The next spring Galba led his troops into Macedonia, and encountered the enemy, under Philip, on a marshy plain on the northwest frontier. But the Macedonians avoided battle, and after repeated skirmishes and marches the Romans returned to Apollonia. Philip did not disturb the army in its retreat, but turned against the Ætolians, who had joined the league against him. At the end of the campaign the Romans stood as they were in the spring, but would have been routed had not the Ætolians interposed. The successes of Philip filled him with arrogance and self-confidence, and the following spring he assumed the offensive. The Romans, meantime, had been re-enforced by new troops, under the command of Flaminius, who attacked Philip in his intrenched camp. The Macedonian king lost his camp and two thousand men, and retreated to the Pass of Tempe, the gate of Macedonia proper, deserted by many of his allies. The Achæans entered into alliance with Rome. The winter came on, and Philip sought terms of peace. All he could obtain from Flaminius was an armistice of two months. The Roman Senate refused all terms unless Philip would renounce all Greece, especially Corinth, Chalcis, and Demetrias. These were rejected, and Philip strained all his energies to meet his enemy in a pitched battle. He brought into the field twenty-six thousand men, an equal force to the Romans, and encountered them at Cynocephalæ. The Romans were victorious, and a great number of prisoners fell into their hands. Philip escaped to Larissa, burned his papers, evacuated Thessaly, and returned home. He was completely vanquished, and was obliged to accept such a peace as the Romans were disposed to grant. But the Romans did not abuse their power, but treated Philip with respect, and granted to him such terms as had been given to Carthage. He lost all his foreign possessions in Asia Minor, Thrace, Greece, and the islands of the Ægean, but retained Macedonia. He was also bound not to conclude foreign alliances without the consent of the Romans, nor send garrisons abroad, nor maintain an army of over five thousand men, nor possess a navy beyond five ships of war. He was also required to pay a contribution of one thousand talents. He was thus left in possession only of as much power as was necessary to guard the frontiers of Hellas against the barbarians. All the States of Greece were declared free, and most of them were incorporated with the Achæan League, a confederation of the old cities, which were famous before the Dorian migration, to resist the Macedonian domination. This famous league was the last struggle of Greece for federation to resist overpowering foes. As the Achæan cities were the dominant States of Greece at the Trojan war, so the expiring fires of Grecian liberty went out the last among that ancient race.

Battle of Cynocephalæ.

The Achæan League.

The liberator of Greece, as Flaminius may be called, assembled the deputies of all the Greek communities at Corinth, exhorted them to use the freedom which he had conferred upon them with moderation, and requested, as the sole return for the kindness which the Romans had shown, that they would send back all the Italian captives sold in Greece during the war with Hannibal, and then he evacuated the last fortresses which he held, and returned to Rome with his troops and liberated captives. Rome really desired the liberation and independence of Greece, now that all fears of her political power were removed, and that glorious liberty which is associated with the struggles of the Greeks with the Persians might have been secured, had not the Hellenic nations been completely demoralized. There was left among them no foundation and no material for liberty, and nothing but the magic charm of the Hellenic name could have prevented Flaminius from establishing a Roman government in that degenerate land. It was an injudicious generosity which animated the Romans, but for which the war with Antiochus might not have arisen.

The liberties of Greece secured.

Flaminius.

Antiochus III., the great-great-grandson of the general of Alexander who founded the dynasty of the Seleucidæ, then reigned in Asia. On the fall of Philip, who was his ally, he took possession of those districts in Asia Minor that formerly belonged to Egypt, but had fallen to Philip. He also sought to recover the Greek cities of Asia Minor as a part of his empire. This enterprise embroiled him with the Romans, who claimed a protectorate over all the Hellenic cities. And he was further complicated by the arrival at Ephesus, his capital, of Hannibal, to whom he gave an honorable reception. A rupture with Rome could not be avoided.

Antiochus.

To strengthen himself in Asia for the approaching conflict, Antiochus married one of his daughters to Ptolemy, king of Egypt, another to the king of Cappadocia, a third to the king of Pergamus, while the Grecian cities were amused by promises and presents. He was also assured of the aid of the Ætolians, who intrigued against the Romans as soon as Flaminius had left. Then was seen the

Power of Antiochus.

error of that general for withdrawing garrisons from Greece, which was to be the theatre of the war.

Antiochus collected an army and started for Greece, hoping to be joined by Philip, who, however, placed all his forces at the disposal of the Romans. The Achæan League also was firm to the Roman cause. The Roman armies sent against him, commanded by Maninius Acilius Glabrio, numbered forty thousand men. Instead of retiring before this superior force, Antiochus intrenched himself in Thermopylæ, but his army was dispersed, and he fled to Chalcis, and there embarked for Ephesus. The war was now to be carried to Asia.

His preparations for war.

Both parties, during the winter, vigorously prepared for the next campaign, and the conqueror of Zama was selected by Rome to conduct her armies in Asia. It was a long and weary march for the Roman armies to the Hellespont, which was crossed, however, without serious obstacles, from the mismanagement of Antiochus, who offered terms of peace when the army had safely landed in Asia. He offered to pay half the expenses of the war and the cession of his European possessions, as well as of the Greek cities of Asia Minor that had gone over to the Romans. But Scipio demanded the whole cost of the war and the cession of Asia Minor. These terms were rejected, and the Syrian king hastened to decide the fate of Asia by a pitched battle.

Scipio in Asia.

This fight was fought at Magnesia, B. C. 190, not far from Smyrna, in the valley of the Hermus. The forces of Antiochus were eighty thousand, including twelve thousand cavalry, but were undisciplined and unwieldy. Those of Scipio were about half as numerous. The Romans were completely successful, losing only twenty-four horsemen and three hundred infantry, whereas the loss of Antiochus was fifty thousand—a victory as brilliant as that of Alexander at Issus. Asia Minor was surrendered to the Romans, and Antiochus was compelled to pay three thousand talents (little more than three million dollars) at once, and the same contribution for twelve years, so that

Defeat of Antiochus.

he retained nothing but Cilicia. His power was broken utterly, and he was prohibited from making aggressive war against the States of the West, or from navigating the sea west of the mouth of the Calycadnus, in Cilicia, with armed ships, or from taming elephants, or even receiving political fugitives. The province of Syria never again made a second appeal to the decision of arms—a proof of the feeble organization of the kingdom of the Seleucidæ.

Syria a Roman province.

The king of Cappadocia escaped with a fine of six hundred talents. All the Greek cities which had joined the Romans had their liberties confirmed. The Ætolians lost all cities and territories which were in the hands of their adversaries. But Philip and the Achæans were disgusted with the small share of the spoil granted to them.

Subjection of the Greek cities.

Thus the protectorate of Rome now embraced all the States from the eastern to the western end of the Mediterranean. And Rome, about this time, was delivered of the last enemy whom she feared—the homeless and fugitive Carthaginian, who lived long enough to see the West subdued, as well as the armies of the East overpowered. At the age of seventy-six he took poison, on seeing his house beset with assassins. For fifty years he kept the oath he had sworn as a boy. About the same time that he killed himself in Bithynia, Scipio, on whom fortune had lavished all her honors and successes—who had added Spain, Africa, and Asia to the empire, died in voluntary banishment, little over fifty years of age, leaving orders not to bury his remains in the city for which he had lived, and where his ancestors reposed. He died in bitter vexation from the false charges made against him of corruption and embezzlement, with hardly any other fault than that overweening arrogance which usually attends unprecedented success, and which corrodes the heart when the *éclat* of prosperity is dimmed by time. The career and death of both these great men—the greatest of their age—shows impressively the vanity of all worldly greatness, and is an additional confirmation of the fact that the latter years of illustrious men are generally

Death of Hannibal.

sad and gloomy, and certain to be so when their lives are not animated by a greater sentiment than that of ambition.

Philip of Macedon died, B. C. 179, in the fifty-ninth year of his age and the forty-second of his reign, and his son Perseus succeeded to his throne at the age of thirty-one. Macedonia had been humbled rather than weakened by the Romans, and after eighteen years of peace, had renewed her resources. This kingdom chafed against the foreign power of Rome, as did the whole Hellenic world. A profound sentiment of discontent existed in both Asia and Europe. Perseus made alliances with the discontented cities —with the Byzantines, the Ætolians, and the Bœotians. But so prudently did he conduct his intrigues, that it was not till the seventh year of his reign that Rome declared war against him.

Perseus.

The resources of Macedonia were still considerable. The army consisted of thirty thousand men, without considering mercenaries or contingents, and great quantities of military stores had been collected in the magazines. And Perseus himself was a monarch of great ability, trained and disciplined to war. He collected an army of forty-three thousand men, while the whole Roman force in Greece was scarcely more. Crassus conducted the Roman army, and in the first engagement at Ossa, was decidedly beaten. Perseus then sought peace, but the Romans never made peace after a defeat. The war continued, but the military result of two campaigns was null, while the political result was a disgrace to the Romans. The third campaign, conducted by Quintus Marcius Philippus, was equally undecisive, and had Perseus been willing to part with his money, he could have obtained the aid of twenty thousand Celts who would have given much trouble. At last, in the fourth year of the war, the Romans sent to Macedonia Lucius Æmilius Paulus, son of the consul that fell at Cannæ—an excellent general and incorruptible; a man sixty years of age, cultivated in Hellenic literature and art. Soon after his arrival at the camp at Heracleum, he brought about the battle of

Makes war on Rome.

Pydna, which settled the fate of Macedonia. The overthrow of the Macedonians was fearful. Twenty thousand were killed and eleven thousand made prisoners. All Macedonia submitted in two days, and the king fled with his gold, some six thousand talents he had hoarded, to Samothrace, accompanied with only a few followers. The Persian monarch might have presented a more effectual resistance to Alexander had he scattered his treasures among the mercenary Greeks. So Perseus could have prolonged his contest had he employed the Celts. When a man is struggling desperately for his life or his crown, his treasures are of secondary importance. Perseus was soon after taken prisoner by the Romans, with all his treasures, and died a few years later at Alba.

Battle of Pydna.

"Thus perished the empire of Alexander, which had subdued and Hellenized the East, one hundred and forty-four years from his death." The kingdom of Macedonia was stricken out of the list of States, and the whole land was disarmed, and the fortress of Demetrias was razed. Illyria was treated in a similar way, and became a Roman province. All the Hellenic States were reduced to dependence upon Rome. Pergamus was humiliated. Rhodes was deprived of all possessions on the main land, although the Rhodians had not offended. Egypt voluntarily submitted to the Roman protectorate, and the whole empire of Alexander the Great fell to the Roman commonwealth. The universal empire of the Romans dates from the battle of Pydna—"the last battle in which a civilized State confronted Rome in the field on the footing of equality as a great power." All subsequent struggles were with barbarians. Mithridates, of Pontus, made subsequently a desperate effort to rid the Oriental world of the dominion of Rome, but the battle of Pydna marks the real supremacy of the Romans in the civilized world. Mommsen asserts that it is a superficial view which sees in the wars of the Romans with tribes, cities, and kings, an insatiable longing after dominion and riches, and that it was

Its decisive results.

Supremacy of the Romans in the civilized world.

only a desire to secure the complete sovereignty of Italy, unmolested by enemies, which prompted, to this period, the Roman wars—that the Romans earnestly opposed the introduction of Africa, Greece, and Asia into the pale of protectorship, till circumstances compelled the extension of that pale —that, in fact, they were driven to all their great wars, with the exception of that concerning Sicily, even those with Hannibal and Antiochus, either by direct aggression or disturbance of settled political relations. "The policy of Rome was that of a narrow-minded but very able deliberate assembly, which had far too little power of grand combination, and far too much instinctive desire for the preservation of its own commonwealth, to devise projects in the spirit of a Cæsar or a Napoleon." Nor did the ancient world know of a balance of power among nations, and hence every nation strove to subdue its neighbors, or render them powerless, like the Grecian States. Had the Greeks combined for a great political unity, they might have defied even the Roman power, or had they been willing to see the growth of equal States without envy, like the modern nations of Europe, without destructive conflicts, the States of Sparta, Corinth, and Athens might have grown simultaneously, and united, would have been too powerful to be subdued. But they did not understand the balance of power, and they were inflamed with rival animosities, and thus destroyed each other.

CHAPTER XXXII.

THE THIRD PUNIC WAR.

THE peace between Carthage and Rome, after the second Punic war, lasted fifty years, during which the Carthaginians gave the Romans no cause of complaint. Carthage, in the enjoyment of peace, devoted itself to commerce and industrial arts, and grew very rich and populous. The government alone was weak, from the anarchical ascendency of the people, who were lawless and extravagant.

Causes of the third Punic war.

Their renewed miseries can be traced to Masinissa, who was in close alliance with the Romans. The Carthaginians endured every thing rather than provoke the hostility of Rome, which watched the first opportunity to effect their ruin. Having resigned themselves to political degradation, general cowardice and demoralization were the result.

Masinissa.

Masinissa, king of Numidia, made insolent claims on those Phœnician settlements on the coast of Byzacene, which the Carthaginians possessed from the earliest times. Scipio was sent to Carthage, to arrange the difficulty, as arbitrator, and the circumstances were so aggravated that he could not, with any justice, decide in favor of the king, but declined to pronounce a verdict, so that Masinissa and Carthage should remain on terms of hostility. And as Masinissa reigned for fifty years after the peace, Carthage was subjected to continual vexations. At last a war broke out between them. Masinissa was stronger than Carthage, but the city raised a considerable army, and placed it under the conduct of Hasdrubal, who marched against the perfidious enemy with fifty thousand mercenaries. The battle was not decisive, but Hasdrubal retreated without securing his communication with Carthage. His army was cut off, and he sought terms of peace, which were haughtily rejected, and he then gave hostages for keeping the peace, and agreed to pay five thousand talents within fifty years, and acknowledge Masinissa's usurpation. The Romans, instead of settling the difficulties, instigated secretly Masinissa. And the Roman commissioners sent to the Senate exaggerated accounts of the resources of Carthage. The Romans compelled the Carthaginians to destroy their timber and the materials they had in abundance for building a new fleet. Still the Senate, having the control of the foreign relations, and having become a mere assembly of kings, with the great power which the government of provinces gave to it, was filled with renewed jealousy. Cato never made a speech without closing with these words: "*Carthago est delenda.*" A blind hatred animated that vindictive and narrow old patrician, who headed a party with the avowed object of the destruction of Carthage. And it was finally determined to destroy the city.

Usurpation of Masinissa.

The Romans took the Carthaginians to account for the war with Masinissa, and not contented with the humiliation of their old rival, aimed at her absolute ruin, though she had broken no treaties. The Carthaginians, broken-hearted, sent embassy after embassy, imploring the Senate to preserve peace, to whom the senators gave equivocal answers. The situation of Carthage was hopeless and miserable—stripped by Masinissa of the rich towns of Emporia, and on the eve of another conflict with the mistress of the world.

Carthage called to account.

Had the city been animated by the spirit which Hannibal had sought to infuse, she was still capable of a noble defense. She ruled over three hundred Libyan cities, and had a population of seven hundred thousand. She had accumulated two hundred thousand stand of arms, and two thousand catapults. And she had the

Power of Carthage.

means to manufacture a still greater amount. But she had, unfortunately, on the first demand of the Romans, surrendered these means of defense.

War declared.

At last Rome declared war, B. C. 149—the wickedest war in which she ever engaged—and Cato had the satisfaction of seeing, at the age of eighty-five, his policy indorsed against every principle of justice and honor. A Roman army landed in Africa unopposed, and the Carthaginians were weak enough to surrender, not only three hundred hostages from the noblest families, but the arms already enumerated. Nothing but infatuation can account for this miserable concession of weakness to strength, all from a blind confidence in the tender mercies of an unpitying and unscrupulous foe. Then, when the city was defenseless, the hostages in the hands of the Romans, and they almost at the gates, it was coolly announced that it was the will of the Senate that the city should be destroyed.

Despair of the Carthaginians.

Too late, the doomed city prepared to make a last stand against an inexorable enemy. The most violent feelings of hatred and rage, added to those of despair, at last animated the people of Carthage. It was the same passion which arrayed Tyre against Alexander, and Jerusalem against Titus. It was a wild patriotic frenzy which knew no bounds, inspired by the instinct of self-preservation, and aside from all calculation of success or failure. As the fall of the city was inevitable, wisdom might have counseled an unreserved submission. Resistance should have been thought of before. In fact, Carthage should not have yielded to the first Africanus. And when she had again become rich and populous, she should have defied the Romans when their spirit was perceived—should have made a more gallant defense against Masinissa, and concentrated all her energies for a last stand upon her own territories. But why should we thus speculate? The doom of Carthage had been pronounced by the decrees of fate. The fall has all the mystery and solemnity of a providential event, like the fall of all empires, like the defeat of Darius by Alexander, like the ruin of Jerusalem, like the melting away of North American Indians, like the final overthrow of the "Eternal City" itself.

The desperation of the city in her last conflict proves, however, that, with proper foresight and patriotism, her fall might have been delayed, for it took the Romans three years to subdue her. The disarmed city withstood the attack of the Romans for a period five times as long as it required Vespasian and Titus to capture Jerusalem. The city resounded day and night with the labors of men and women on arms and catapults. One hundred and forty shields, three hundred swords, five hundred spears, and one thousand missiles were manufactured daily, and even a fleet of one hundred and fifty ships was built during the siege. The land side of the city was protected by a triple wall, and the rocks of Cape Camast and Cape Carthage sheltered it from all attacks by sea, except one side protected by fortified harbors and quays. Hasdrubal, with the remnant of his army, was still in the field, and took up his station at Nephesis, on the opposite side of the lake of Tunis, to harass the besiegers. Masinissa died at the age of ninety, soon after hostilities began.

The city makes desperate efforts.

Hasdrubal.

The first attack on Carthage was a failure, and the army of the Consuls Censorinus and Manius Manilius would have been cut to pieces, had it not been for the reserve led by Scipio Æmilianus, a grandson of Africanus, who was then serving as military tribune. He also performed many gallant actions when Censorinus retired to Rome, leaving the army in the hands of his incompetent colleague.

Failure of the Romans.

The second campaign was equally unsuccessful, under L. Calpurnius Piso and L. Mancinus. The slow progress of the war excited astonishment throughout the world. The suspense of the campaign was intolerable to the proud spirit of the Romans, who had never dreamed of such resistance. The eyes of the Romans were then turned

Rome disgusted.

to the young hero who alone had thus far distinguished himself. Although he had not reached the proper age, he was chosen consul, and the province of Africa was assigned to him. He sailed with his friends Polybius and Lælius. He was by no means equal to the elder Scipio, although he was an able general and an accomplished man. He was ostentatious, envious, and proud, and had cultivation rather than genius.

Mistake of Mancinus.

When he arrived at Utica, he found the campaign of B. C. 147 opened in such a way that his arrival saved a great disaster. The admiral Mancinus had attempted an attack on an undefended quarter, but a desperate sally of the besieged had exposed him to imminent danger, and he was only relieved by the timely arrival of Scipio.

Siege of Carthage.

The new general then continued the siege with new vigor. His headquarters were fixed on an isthmus uniting the peninsula of Carthage with the main-land, from which he attacked the suburb called Megara, and took it, and shut up the Carthaginians in the old town and ports. The garrison of the suburb and the army of Hasdrubal retreated within the fortifications of the city. The Carthaginian leader, to cut off all retreat, inflicted inhuman barbarities and tortures on all the Roman prisoners they took. Scipio, meanwhile, intrenched and fortified in the suburb, cut off all communication between the city and main-land by parallel trenches, three miles in length, drawn across the whole isthmus. The communication with the sea being still open, from which the besieged received supplies, the port was blocked up by a mole of stone ninety-six feet wide. The besieged worked night and day, and cut a new channel to the sea, and, had they known how to improve their opportunity, might, with the new fleet they had constructed, have destroyed that of their enemies, unprepared for action.

Scipio master of the ports.

Scipio now resolved to make himself master of the ports, which were separated from the sea by quays and a weak wall. His battering-rams were at once destroyed by the Carthaginians. He then built a wall or rampart upon the quay, to the height of the city wall, and placed upon it four thousand men to harass the besieged. As the winter rains then set in, making his camp unhealthy, and the city was now closely invested by sea and land, he turned his attention to the fortified camp of the enemy at Nephesis, which was taken by storm, and seventy thousand persons put to the sword. The Carthaginian army was annihilated.

Meanwhile famine pressed within the besieged city, and Hasdrubal would not surrender. An attack, led by Lælius, on the market-place, gave the Romans a foothold within the city, and a great quantity of spoil. One thousand talents were taken from the temple of Apollo. Preparations were then made for the attack of the citadel, and for six days there was a hand-to-hand fight between the combatants amid the narrow streets which led to the Byrsa. The tall Oriental houses were only taken one by one and burned, and the streets were cumbered with the dead. The miserable people, crowded within the citadel, certain now of destruction, then sent a deputation to Scipio to beg the lives of those who had sought a retreat in the Byrsa. The request was granted to all but Roman deserters. But out of the great population of seven hundred thousand, only thirty thousand men and twenty-five thousand women marched from the burning ruins. Hasdrubal and the three hundred Roman deserters, certain of no mercy, retired to the temple of Æsculapius, the heart of the citadel. But the Carthaginian, uniting pusillanimity with cruelty, no sooner found the temple on fire, than he rushed out in Scipio's presence, with an olive-branch in his hands, and abjectly begged for his life, which Scipio granted, after he had prostrated himself at his feet in sight of his followers, who loaded him with the bitterest execrations. The wife of Hasdrubal, deserted by the abject wretch, called down the curses of the gods on the man who had betrayed his country and deserted at last his family. She then cut the throats of her children and threw them into the flames, and then leaped into them

Attack of the citadel.

Capture and destruction of Carthage.

herself. The Roman deserters in the same manner perished. The city was given up to plunder, the inhabitants whose lives were spared were sold as slaves, and the gold and works of art were carried to Rome and deposited in the temples.

Her awful fate.

Such was the fate of Carthage—a doom so awful, that we can not but feel that it was sent as a chastisement for crimes which had long cried to Heaven for vengeance. Carthage always was supremely a wicked city. All the luxurious and wealthy capitals of ancient times were wicked, especially Oriental cities, as Carthage properly, though not technically, was—founded by Phœnicians, and a worshiper of the gods of Tyre and Sidon. The Roman Senate decreed that not only the city, but even the villas of the nobles in the suburb of Megara, should be leveled with the ground, and the plowshare driven over the soil devoted to perpetual desolation, and a curse to the man who should dare to cultivate it or build upon it. For fourteen days, the fires raged in this once populous and wealthy city, and the destruction was complete, B. C. 146. So deep-seated was the Roman hatred of rivals, or States that had been rivals; so dreadful was the punishment of a wicked city, of which Scipio was made the instrument, not merely of the Romans, but of Divine providence.

Carthage utterly destroyed.

The fate of great commercial capitals.

All the great cities of antiquity, which had been seats of luxury and pride, had now been utterly destroyed—Nineveh, Babylon, Tyre, and Carthage. Corinth was already sacked by Mummius, and Jerusalem was to be by Titus, and Rome herself was finally to receive a still direr chastisement at the hands of Goths and Vandals. So Providence moves on in his mysterious power to bring to naught the grandeur and power of rebellious nations—rebellious to those mighty moral laws which are as inexorable as the laws of nature.

The territory on the coast of Zeugitana and Byzantium, which formed the last possession of Carthage, was erected into the province of Africa, and the rich plain of that fertile province became more important to Rome for supplies of corn than even Sicily, which had been the granary of Rome.

Scipio returned to Rome, and enjoyed a triumph more gorgeous than the great Africanus. He also lived to enjoy another triumph for brilliant successes in Spain, yet to be enumerated, but was also doomed to lose his popularity, and to perish by the dagger of assassins.

Scipio triumphs.

Rome had now acquired the undisputed dominion of the civilized world, and with it, the vices of the nations she subdued. A great decline in Roman morals succeeded these brilliant conquests. Great internal changes took place. The old distinction of patricians and plebeians had vanished, and a new nobility had arisen, composed of rich men and of those whose ancestors had enjoyed curule magistracies. They possessed the Senate, and had control of the Comitia Centuriata, by the prerogative vote of the equestrian centuries. A base rabble had grown up, fed with corn and oil, by the government, and amused by games and spectacles. The old republican aristocracy was supplanted by a family oligarchy. The vast wealth which poured into Rome from the conquered countries created disproportionate fortunes. The votes of the people were bought by the rich candidates for popular favor. The superstitions of the East were transferred to the capitol of the world, and the decay in faith was as marked as the decay in virtue. Chaldæan astrologers were scattered over Italy, and the gods of all the conquered peoples of the earth were worshiped at Rome. The bonds of society were loosed, and a state was prepared for the civil wars which proved even more destructive than the foreign.

Change in Roman manners.

CHAPTER XXXIII

ROMAN CONQUESTS FROM THE FALL OF CARTHAGE TO THE TIMES OF THE GRACCHI.

ALTHOUGH the Roman domination now extended in some form or other over most of the countries around the Mediterranean, still several States remained to be subdued, in the East and in the West.

The subjugation of Spain first deserves attention, commenced before the close of the third Punic war, and which I have omitted to notice for the sake of clearness of connection.

After the Hannibalic war, we have seen how Rome planted her armies in Spain, and added two provinces to her empire. But the various tribes were far from being subdued, and Spain was inhabited by different races.

This great peninsula, bounded on the north by the ocean Cantabricus, now called the Bay of Biscay, and the Pyrenees, on the east and south by the Mediterranean, and on the west by the Atlantic Ocean, was called Iberia, by the Greeks, from the river Iberus, or Ebro. The term Hispania was derived from the Phœnicians, who planted colonies on the southern shores. The Carthaginians invaded it next, and founded several cities, the chief of which was New Carthage. At the end of the second Punic war, it was wrested from them by the Romans, who divided it into two provinces, Citerior and Ulterior. In the time of Augustus, Ulterior Spain was divided into two provinces, called Lusitania and Bætica, while the Citerior province, by far the larger, occupying the whole northern country from the Atlantic to the Mediterranean, was called Tanagona. It included three-fifths of the peninsula, or about one hun-

The Spanish peninsula.

dred and seven thousand three hundred square miles. It embraced the modern provinces of Catalonia, Aragon, Navarre, Biscay, Asturias, Galicia, Northern Leon, old and new Castile, Murcia, and Valentia, and a part of Portugal. Bætica nearly corresponded with Andalusia, and embraced Granada, Jaen, Cordova, Seville, and half of Spanish Estremadura. Lusitania corresponds nearly with Portugal.

The Tanaconneusis was inhabited by numerous tribes, and the chief ancient cities were Barcelona, Tanagona the metropolis, Pampeluna, Oporto, Numantia, Saguntum, Saragossa, and Cartagena. In Bætica were Cordova, Castile, Gades, and Seville. In Lusitania were Olisipo (Lisbon), and Salamanca.

Geography of Spain.

Among the inhabitants of these various provinces were Iberians, Celts, Phœnicians, and Hellenes. In the year 154 B. C., the Lusitanians, under a chieftain called Punicus, invaded the Roman territory which the elder Scipio had conquered, and defeated two Roman governors. The Romans then sent a consular army, under Q. Fulvius Nobilior, which was ultimately defeated by the Lusitanians under Cæsarus. This success kindled the flames of war far and near, and the Celtiberians joined in the warfare against the Roman invaders. Again the Romans were defeated with heavy loss. The Senate then sent considerable reenforcements, under Claudius Marcellus, who soon changed the aspect of affairs. The nation of the Arevacæ surrendered to the Romans—a people living on the branches of the Durius, near Numantia—and their western neighbors, the Vaccæi, were also subdued, and barbarously dealt with. On the outbreak of the third Punic war the affairs of Spain were left to the ordinary governors, and a new insurrection of the Lusitanians took place. Viriathus, a Spanish chieftain, signally defeated the Romans, and was recognized as king of all the Lusitanians. He was distinguished, not only for bravery, but for temperance and art, and was a sort of Homeric hero, whose name and exploits were sounded

War with the Spaniards.

throughout the peninsula. He gained great victories over the Roman generals, and destroyed their armies. General after general was successively defeated. For five years this gallant Spaniard kept the whole Roman power at bay, and he was only destroyed by treachery.

While the Lusitanians at the South were thus prevailing over the Roman armies on the banks of the Tagus, another war broke out in the North among the Celtiberian natives. Against these people Quintus Cæcilius Metellus, the consul, was sent. He showed great ability, and in two years reduced the whole northern province, except the two cities of Termantia and Numantia. These cities, wearied at last with war, agreed to submit to the Romans, and delivered up hostages and deserters, with a sum of money. But the Senate, with its usual policy, refused to confirm the treaty of its general, which perfectly aroused the Numantines to resentment and despair. These brave people obtained successes against the Roman general Lænas and his successors, Mancinus and M. Æmilius Lepides, as well as Philus and Piso.

Inglorious war.

The Romans, aroused at last to this inglorious war, which had lasted nearly ten years, resolved to take the city of the Numantines at any cost, and intrusted the work to Scipio Æmilianus, their best general. He spent the summer (B. C. 134) in extensive preparations, and it was not till winter that he drew his army round the walls of Numantia, defended by only eight thousand citizens. Scipio even declined a battle, and fought with mattock and spade. A double wall of circumvallation, surmounted with towers, was built around the city, and closed the access to it by the Douro, by which the besieged relied upon for provisions. The city sustained a memorable siege of nearly a year, and was only reduced by famine. The inhabitants were sold as slaves, and the city was leveled with the ground. The fall of this fortress struck at the root of opposition to Rome, and a senatorial commission was sent to Spain, in order to organize with Scipio the newly-won terri-

Scipio.

tories, and became henceforth the best-regulated country of all the provinces of Rome.

But a graver difficulty existed with the African, Greek, and Asiatic States that had been brought under the influence of the Roman hegemony, which was neither formal sovereignty nor actual subjection. The client States had neither independence nor peace. The Senate, nevertheless, perpetually interfered with the course of African, Hellenic, Asiatic, and Egyptian affairs. Commissioners were constantly going to Alexandria, to the Achæan diet, and to the courts of the Asiatic princes, and the government of Rome deprived the nations of the blessings of freedom and the blessings of order.

Difficulties in Asiatic provinces.

It was time to put a stop to this state of things, and the only way to do so was to convert the client States into Roman provinces. After the destruction of Carthage, the children of Masinissa retained in substance their former territories, but were not allowed to make Carthage their capital. Her territories became a Roman province, whose capital was Utica.

Province of Africa.

Macedonia also disappeared, like Carthage, from the ranks of nations. But the four small States into which the kingdom was parceled could not live in peace. Neither Roman commissioners nor foreign arbiters could restore order. At this crisis a young man appeared in Thrace, who called himself the son of Perseus. This pseudo-Philip, for such was his name, strikingly resembled the son of Perseus. Unable to obtain recognition in his native country, he went to Demetrius Sotor, king of Syria. By him he was sent to Rome. The Senate attached so little importance to the man that he was left, imperfectly guarded, in an Italian town, and fled to Miletus. Again arrested, and again contriving to escape, he went to Thrace, and obtained a recognition from Teres, the chief of the Thracian barbarians. With his support he invaded Macedonia, and obtained several successes over the Macedonian militia. The Roman commissioner Nasica, without troops, was obliged to call to his

The Macedonian war.

aid the Achæan and Pergamene soldiers, until defended by a Roman legion under the prætor Juventius. Juventius was slain by the pretender, and his army cut to pieces. And it was not until a stronger Roman army, under Quintus Cæcilius Metellus, appeared, that he was subdued. The four States into which Macedonia had been divided were now converted into a Roman province, B. C. 148, and Macedonia became, not a united kingdom, but a united province, with nearly the former limits.

The defense of the Hellenic civilization now devolved on the Romans, but was not conducted with adequate forces or befitting energy, and the petty States were therefore exposed to social disorganization, and the Greeks evidently sought to pick a quarrel with Rome.

Fall of Corinth.

Hence the Achæan war, B. C. 149. It is not of much historical importance. It was commenced under Metellus, and continued under Mummius, who reduced the noisy belligerents to terms, and entered Corinth, the seat of rebellion, and the first commercial city of Greece. By order of the Senate, the Corinthian citizens were sold into slavery, the fortifications of the city leveled with the ground, and the city itself was sacked. The mock sovereignty of leagues was abolished, and all remains of Grecian liberty fled.

Asia Minor.

In Asia Minor, after the Seleucidæ were driven away, Pergamus became the first power. But even this State did not escape the jealousy of the Romans, and with Attalus III. the house of Attalids became extinct.

He, however, had bequeathed his kingdom to the Romans, and his testament kindled a civil war. Aristonicus, a natural son of Eumenes II., made his appearance at Lecuæ, a small sea-port near Smyrna, as a pretender to the crown. He was defeated by the Ephesians, who saw the necessity of the protection and friendship of the Roman government. But he again appeared with new troops, and the struggle was serious, since there were no Roman troops in Asia. But, B. C. 131, a Roman army was sent under the consul Publius Licinius

Crassus Mucianus, one of the wealthiest men of Rome, distinguished as an orator and jurist. This distinguished general was about to lay siege to Leucæ, when he was surprised and taken captive, and put to death. His successor, Marcus Perpenna, was fortunate in his warfare, and the pretender was taken prisoner, and executed at Rome. The remaining cities yielded to the conqueror, and Asia Minor became a Roman province.

War in Asia.

In other States the Romans set up kings as they chose. In Syria, Antiochus Eupater was recognized over the claims of Demetrius Sotor, then a hostage in Rome. But he contrived to escape, and seized the government of his ancestral kingdom. But it would seem that the Romans, at this period, did not take a very lively interest in the affairs of remote Asiatic States, and the decrees of the Senate were often disregarded with impunity. A great reaction of the East took place against the West, and, under Mithridates, a renewed struggle again gave dignity to the Eastern kingdoms, which had not raised their heads since the conquests of Alexander. That memorable struggle will be alluded to in the proper place. It was a difficult problem which Rome undertook when she undertook to govern the Asiatic world. It was easy to conquer; it was difficult to rule, when degeneracy and luxury became the vices of the Romans themselves. We are now to trace those domestic dissensions and civil wars which indicate the decline of the Roman republic. But before we describe those wars, we will take a brief survey of the social and political changes in Rome at this period.

Syria.

CHAPTER XXXIV.

ROMAN CIVILIZATION AT THE CLOSE OF THE THIRD PUNIC WAR, AND THE FALL OF GREECE.

Dominion of Rome.

ROME was now the unrivaled mistress of the world. She had conquered all the civilized States around the Mediterranean, or had established a protectorate over them. She had no fears of foreign enemies. Her empire was established.

Before we proceed to present subsequent conquests or domestic revolutions, it would be well to glance at the political and social structure of the State, as it was two hundred years before the Christian era, and also at the progress which had been made in literature and art.

The rise of a new nobility.

One of the most noticeable features of the Roman State at this period was the rise of a new nobility. The patricians, when they lost the exclusive control of the government, did not cease to be a powerful aristocracy. But another class of nobles arose in the fifth century of the city, and shared their power—those who had held curule offices and were members of the Senate. Their descendants, plebeian as well as patrician, had the privilege of placing the wax images, of their ancestors in the family hall, and to have them carried in funeral processions. They also wore a stripe of purple on the tunic, and a gold ring on the finger. These were trifling insignia of rank, still they were emblems and signs by which the nobility were distinguished. The plebeian families, ennobled by their curule ancestors, were united into one body with the patrician families, and became a sort of hereditary nobility. This body of exclusive families really possessed the political power of the

Roman nobility.

State. The Senate was made up from their members, and was the mainstay of Roman nobility. The equites, or equestrian order, was also composed of the patricians and wealthy plebeians. Noble youths gradually withdrew from serving in the infantry, and the legionary cavalry became a close aristocratic corps. Not only were the nobles the possessors of senatorial privileges, and enrolled among the equites, but they had separate seats from the people at the games and at the theatres. The censorship also became a prop to the stability of the aristocratic class.

Leading families.

We have some idea of the influence of the aristocracy from the families which furnished the higher offices of the State. For three centuries the consuls were chiefly chosen from powerful families. The Cornelii gentes furnished fifteen consuls in one hundred and twelve years, and the Valerii, ten. And, what is more remarkable, for the following one hundred and fifty years these two families furnished nearly the same number. In one hundred and twelve years fifteen families gave seventy consuls to the State: the Cornelii, fifteen; the Valerii, ten; the Claudii, four; the Æmilii, nine; the Fabii, six; the Manilii, four; the Postumii, two; the Servilii, three; the Sulpicii, six; and also about the same number the following one hundred and fifty years, thereby showing that old families, whether patrician or plebeian, were long kept in sight, and monopolized political power. This was also seen in the elevation of young men of these ranks to high office before they had reached the lawful age. M. Valerius Corvus was consul at twenty-three, Scipio at thirty, and Flaminius at twenty-nine.

Provincial governors.

The control of Rome over conquered provinces introduced a new class of magistrates, selected by the Senate, and chosen from the aristocratic circles. These were the provincial governors or prætors, who had great power, and who sometimes appeared in all the pomp of kings. They resided in the ancient palaces of the kings, and had great opportunities for accumulating fortunes. Nor could the governors be called to account, until after their term of office expired, which rarely happened. The governors were, virtually, sovereigns while they continued in office—were satraps, who conducted a legalized tyranny abroad, and returned home arrogant and accustomed to adulation—a class of men who proved dangerous to the old institutions, those which recognized equality within the aristocracy and the subordination of power to the senatorial college.

The burgesses, or citizens, before this period, were a very respectable body, patriotic and sagacious. They occupied chiefly Latium, a part of Campania, and the maritime colonies. But gradually, a rabble of clients grew up on footing equality with these independent burgesses. These clients, as the aristocracy increased in wealth and power, became parasites and beggars, and undermined the burgess class, and controlled the Comitia. This class rapidly increased, and were clamorous for games, festivals, and cheap bread, for corn was distributed to them by those who wished to gain their favor at elections, at less than cost. Hence, festivals and popular amusements became rapidly a great feature of the times. For five hundred years the people had been contented with one festival in a year, and one circus. Flaminius added another festival, and another circus. In the year 550 of the city, there were five festivals. The candidates for the consulship spent large sums on these games, the splendor of which became the standard by which the electoral body measured the fitness of candidates. A gladiatorial show cost seven hundred and twenty thousand sesterces, or thirty-six thousand dollars.

Decline of the burgesses.

Public amusements.

And corruption extended to the army. The old burgess militia were contented to return home with some trifling gift as a memorial of victory, but the troops of Scipio, and the veterans of the Macedonian and Asiatic wars, came back enriched with spoils. A decay of a warlike spirit was observable from the time the burgesses converted war into a traffic in plunder. A great passion also arose for titles and insignia, which appeared under different

Decay of military spirit.

forms, especially for the honors of a triumph, originally granted only to the supreme magistrate who had signally augmented the power of the State. Statues and monuments were often erected at the expense of the person whom they purported to honor. And finally, the ring, the robe, and the amulet case distinguished not only the burgesses from the foreigners and slaves, but also the person who was born free from one who had been a slave, the son of the free-born from the son of the manumitted, the son of a knight from a common burgess, the descendant of a curule house from the common senators. These distinctions in rank kept pace with the extension of conquests, until, at last, there was as complete a net work of aristocratic distinctions as in England at the present day.

Distinctions in society.

All these distinctions and changes were bitterly deplored by Marcus Portius Cato—the last great statesman of the older school—a genuine Roman of the antique stamp. He was also averse to schemes of universal empire. He was a patrician, brought up at the plow, and in love with his Sabine farm. Yet he rose to the consulship, and even the censorship. He served in war under Marcellus, Fabius, and Scipio, and showed great ability as a soldier. He was as distinguished in the forum as in the camp and battle-field, having a bold address, pungent wit, and great knowledge of the Roman laws. He was the most influential political orator of his day. He was narrow in his political ideas, conservative, austere, and upright; an enemy to all corruption and villainy, also to genius, and culture, and innovation. He was the protector of the Roman farmer, plain, homely in person, disdained by the ruling nobles, but fearless in exposing corruption from any quarter, and irreconcilably at war with aristocratic coteries, like the Scipios and Flaminii. He was publicly accused twenty-four times, but he was always backed by the farmers, notwithstanding the opposition of the nobles. He erased, while censor, the name of the brother of Flaminius from the roll of senators, and the brother of Scipio from that of the equites. He

Cato.

attempted a vigorous reform, but the current of corruption could only be stemmed for awhile. The effect of the sumptuary laws, which were passed through his influence, was temporary and unsatisfactory. No legislation has proved of avail against a deep-seated corruption of morals, for the laws will be avoided, even if they are not defied. In vain was the eloquence of the hard, arbitrary, narrow, worldly wise, but patriotic and stern old censor. The age of Grecian culture, of wealth, of banquets, of palaces, of games, of effeminate manners, had set in with the conquest of Greece and Asia. The divisions of society widened, and the seeds of luxury and pride were to produce violence and decay.

Political changes. Still some political changes were effected at this time. The Comitia Centuriata was remodeled. The equites no longer voted first. The five classes obtained an equal number of votes, and the freedmen were placed on an equal footing with free-born. Thus terminated the long conflict between patricians and plebeians. But although the right of precedence in voting was withdrawn from the equites, still the patrician order was powerful enough to fill, frequently, the second consulship and the second censorship, which were open to patricians and plebeians alike, with men of their own order. At this time the office of dictator went into abeyance, and was practically abolished; the priests were elected by the whole community; the public assemblies interfered with the administration of the public property—the exclusive prerogative of the Senate in former times—and thus transferred the public domains to their own pockets. These were changes which showed the disorganization of the government rather than healthy reform. To this period we date **Rise of demagogues.** the rise of demagogues, for a minority in the Senate had the right to appeal to the Comitia, which opened the way for wealthy or popular men to thwart the wisest actions and select incompetent magistrates and generals. Even Publius Scipio was not more distinguished for his arrogance and title-hunting than for the army of clients he supported, and for the favor which he courted, of both legions and people, by his largesses of grain.

At this period, agriculture had reached considerable perfection, but Cato declared that his fancy farm was not profitable. Figs, apples, pears were cultivated, as well as olives and grapes—also shade-trees. The rearing of cattle was not of much account, as the people lived chiefly on vegetables, and fruits and corn. Large cattle were kept only for tillage. Considerable use was made of poultry and pigeons—kept in the farm-yard. Fish-ponds and hare-preserves were also common. The labor of the fields was performed by oxen, and asses for carriage and the turning of mills. The human labor on farms was done by slaves. Vineyards required more expenditure of labor than ordinary tillage. An estate of one hundred jugera, with vine plantations, required one plowman, eleven slaves, and two herdsmen. The slaves were not bred on the estate, but were purchased. They lived in the farm-buildings, among cattle and produce. A separate house was erected for the master. A steward had the care of the slaves. The stewardess attended to the baking and cooking, and all had the same fare, delivered from the produce of the farm on which they lived. Great unscrupulousness pervaded the management of these estates. Slaves and cattle were placed on the same level, and both were fed as long as they could work, and sold when they were incapacitated by age or sickness. A slave had no recreations or holidays. His time was spent between working and sleeping. And when we remember that these slaves were white as well as black, and had once been free, their condition was hard and inhuman. No negro slavery ever was so cruel as slavery among the Romans. Great labors and responsibilities were imposed upon the steward. He was the first to rise in the morning, and the last to go to bed at night; but he was not doomed to constant labor, like the slaves whom he superintended. He also had few pleasures, and was obsequious to the landlord, who performed no work, except in the earlier ages. The

Agriculture.

The slaves.

small farmer worked himself with the slaves and his children. He more frequently cultivated flowers and vegetables for the market of Rome. Pastoral husbandry was practiced on a great scale, and at least eight hundred jugera were required. On such estates, horses, oxen, mules, and asses were raised, also herds of swine and goats. The breeding of sheep was an object of great attention and interest, since all clothing was made of wool. The shepherd-slaves lived in the open air, remote from human habitations, under sheds and sheep-folds.

Small farmers.

The prices of all produce were very small in comparison with present rates, and this was owing, in part, to the immense quantities of corn and other produce delivered by provincials to the Roman government, sometimes gratuitously. The armies were supported by transmarine corn. The government regulated prices. In the time of Scipio, African wheat was sold as low as twelve ases for six *modii* —(one and a half bushel)—about sixpence. At one time two hundred and forty thousand bushels of Sicilian grain were distributed at this price. The rise of demagogism promoted these distributions, which kept prices down, so that the farmers received but a small reward for labors, which made, of course, the condition of laborers but little above that of brutes: when the people of the capital paid but sixpence sterling for a bushel and a half of wheat, or one hundred and eighty pounds of dried figs, or sixty pounds of oil, or seventy-two pounds of meat, or four and a half gallons of wine sold only for fivepence, or three-fifths of a denarius. In the time of Polybius, the traveler was charged for victuals and lodgings at an inn only about two farthings a day, and a bushel of wheat sold for fourpence. At such prices there was very little market for the farmer. Sicily and Sardinia were the real granaries of Rome. Thus were all the best interests of the country sacrificed to the unproductive population of the city. Such was the golden age of the republic—a state of utter misery and hardship among the productive classes, and idleness among the Roman

Decline of agriculture.

The farmers sacrificed to the city population.

people—a state of society which could but lead to ruin. The farmers, without substantial returns, lost energy and spirit, and dwindled away. Their estates fell into the hands of great proprietors, who owned great numbers of slaves. They themselves were ruined, and sunk into an ignoble class. The cultivation of grain in Italy was gradually neglected, and attention was given chiefly to vines, and olives, and wool. The rearing of cattle became more profitable than tillage, and small farms were absorbed in great estates.

The monetary transactions of the Romans were preeminently conspicuous. No branch of commercial industry was prosecuted with more zeal than money-lending. The bankers of Rome were a great class, and were generally rich. They speculated in corn and all articles of produce. Usury was not disdained even by the nobles. Money-lending became a great system, and all the laws operated in favor of capitalists.

Money.

Industrial art did not keep pace with usurious calculations, and trades were concentrated in the capital. Mechanical skill was neglected in all the rural districts.

Business operations were usually conducted by slaves. Even money-lenders and bankers made use of them. Every one who took contracts for building, bought architect slaves. Every one who provided spectacles purchased a band of serfs expert in the art of fighting. The merchants imported wares in vessels managed by slaves. Mines were worked by slaves. Manufactories were conducted by slaves. Everywhere were slaves.

Business operations.

While the farmer obtained only fourpence a bushel for his wheat, a penny a gallon for his wine, and fivepence for sixty pounds of oil, the capitalists, centered in Rome, possessed fortunes which were vastly disproportionate to those which are seen in modern capitals. Paulus was not reckoned wealthy for a senator, but his estate was valued at sixty talents, nearly £15,000, or $75,000. In other words, the daily interest of his capital was fifteen dollars, enough to purchase one hundred and eighty bushels of

Great fortunes.

wheat—as much as a farmer could raise in a year on eight jugera—a farm as large as that of Cincinnatus. Each of the daughters of Scipio received as a dowry fifty talents, or $60,000. The value of this sum, in our money, when measured by the scale of wheat, or oil, or wine—allowing wheat now to be worth five shillings sterling a bushel—against fivepence in those times, would make gold twelve times more valuable then than now. And hence, Scipio left each of his daughters a sum equal to $720,000 of our money. In estimating the fortune of a Roman, by the prices charged at an inn per day, a penny would go further then than a dollar would now. But I think that gold and silver, in the time of Scipio, were about the same value as in England at the time of Henry VII., about twenty times our present standard.

Every law at Rome tended in its operation to the benefit of the creditor, and to vast accumulations of property; for the government being in the hands of the rich, as in England a century since, and in France before the Revolution, favored the rich at the expense of the poor. It became disgraceful at Rome to perform manual labor, and a wall separated the laboring classes from the capitalists, which could not be passed. Industrial art took the lowest place in the scale of labor, and was in the hands of slaves. The traffic in money, and the farming of the revenue formed the mainstay and stronghold of the Roman economy. The free population of Italy declined, while the city of Rome increased. The loss was supplied by slaves. In the year 502 of the city, the Roman burgesses in Italy numbered two hundred and ninety-eight thousand men capable of bearing arms. Fifty years later, the number was only two hundred and fourteen thousand. The nation visibly diminished, and the community was resolved into masters and slaves. And this decline of citizens and increase of slaves were beheld with indifference, for pride, and cruelty, and heartlessness were the characteristics of the higher classes.

The rich favored.

With the progress of luxury, and the decline of the rural

population, and the growth of disproportionate fortunes, residence in the capital became more and more coveted, and more and more costly. Rents rose to an unexampled height. Extravagant prices were paid for luxuries. When a bushel of corn sold for fivepence, a barrel of anchovies from the Black Sea cost £14, and a beautiful boy twenty-four thousand sesterces (£246), more than a farmer's homestead. Money came to be prized as the end of life, and all kinds of shifts and devices were made to secure it. Marriage, on both sides, became an object of mercantile speculation.

Extravagant prices for luxuries.

In regard to education, there was a higher development than is usually supposed, and literature and art were cultivated, even while the nation declined in real virtue and strength. By means of the Greek slaves, the Greek language and literature reached even the lower ranks, to a certain extent. "The comedies indicate that the humblest classes were familiar with a sort of Latin, which could no more be understood without a knowledge of Greek, than Wieland's German without a knowledge of French." Greek was undoubtedly spoken by the higher classes, as French is spoken in all the courts of Europe. In the rudiments of education, the lowest people were instructed, and even slaves were schoolmasters. At the close of the Punic wars, both comedy and tragedy were among the great amusements of the Romans, and great writers arose, who wrote, however, from the Greek models. Livius translated Homer, and Nævius popularized the Greek drama. Plautus, it is said, wrote one hundred and thirty plays. The tragedies of Ennius were recited to the latter days of the empire. The Romans did not, indeed, make such advance in literature as the Greeks, at a comparatively early period of their history, but their attainments were respectable when Carthage was destroyed.

Education.

CHAPTER XXXV.

THE REFORM MOVEMENT OF THE GRACCHI.

A NEW era in the history of Rome now commences, a period of glory and shame, when a great change took place in the internal structure of the State, now corrupted by the introduction of Greek and Asiatic refinements, and the vast wealth which rolled into the capital of the world.

"For a whole generation after the battle of Pydna, the Roman State enjoyed a profound calm, scarcely varied by a ripple here and there upon the surface. Its dominion extended over three continents; all eyes rested on Italy; all talents and all riches flowed thither; it seemed as if a golden age of peaceful prosperity and intellectual enjoyment of life had begun. The Orientals of this period told each other with astonishment of the mighty republic of the West. And such was the glory of the Romans, that no one usurped the crown, and no one glittered in purple dress; but they obeyed whomsoever from year to year they made their master, and there was among them neither envy nor discord."

Rome after the battle of Pydna.

So things seemed at a distance. But this splendid external was deceptive. The government of the aristocracy was hastening to its ruin. There was a profound meaning, says Mommsen, in the question of Cato: "What was to become of Rome when she should no longer have any State to fear?" All her neighbors were now politically annihilated, and the single thought of the aristocracy was how they should perpetuate their privileges. A government of aristocratic nobodies was now inaugurated, which kept new men of merit from doing any thing, for fear they should

The inefficiency of the government.

belong to their exclusive ranks. Even an aristocratic conqueror was inconvenient.

Still opposition existed to this aristocratic régime, and some reforms had been carried out. The administration of justice was improved. The senatorial commissions to the provinces were found inadequate. An effort was made to emancipate the Comitia from the prepondering influence of the aristocracy. The senators were compelled to renounce their public horse on admission to the Senate, and also the privilege of voting in the eighteen equestrian centuries. But there was the semblance of increased democratic power rather than the reality. All the great questions of the day turned upon the election of the curule magistracies, and there was sufficient influence among the nobles to secure these offices. Young men from noble families crowded into the political arena, and claimed what once was the reward of distinguished merit. Powerful connections were indispensable for the enjoyment of political power, as in England at the time of Burke. A large body of clients waited on their patron early every morning, and the candidates for office used all those arts which are customary when votes were to be bought. The government no longer disposed of the property of burgesses for the public good, nor favored the idea among them that they were exempted from taxes. Political corruption reached through all grades and classes. Capitalists absorbed the small farms, and great fortunes were the scandal of the times. Capital was more valued than labor. Italian farms depreciated from the conversion of tillage into pasture lands and parks, as in England at the present day. Slavery inordinately increased from the captives taken in war. Western Asia furnished the greatest number of this miserable population, and Cretan and Cilician slave-hunters were found on all the coasts of Syria and Greece. Delos was the great slave-market of the world, where the slave-dealers of Asia Minor disposed of their wares to Italian speculators. In one day as many as ten thousand slaves were

Opposition to the ruling classes.

Capitalists.

Slaves.

disembarked and sold. Farms, and trades, and mines were alike carried on by these slaves from Asia, and their sufferings and hardships were vastly greater than ever endured by negroes on the South Carolinian and Cuban plantations. But they were of a different race—men who had seen better days, and accustomed to civilization—and hence they often rose upon their masters. Servile wars were of common occurrence. Sicily at one time had seventy thousand slaves in arms, and when consular armies were sent to suppress the revolt, the most outrageous cruelties were inflicted. Twenty thousand men, at one time, were crucified in Sicily by Publius Rupilius.

At this crisis, when disproportionate wealth and slavery were the great social evils, Tiberius Gracchus arose—a young man of high rank, chivalrous, noble, and eloquent. His mother, Cornelia, was the daughter of Scipio Africanus, and therefore belonged to the most exclusive of the aristocratic circles. Tiberius Gracchus was therefore the cousin of Scipio Æmilianus, under whom he served with distinction in Africa. He was seconded in his views of reform by some stern old patriots and aristocrats, who had not utterly forgotten the interests of the State, now being undermined. Appius Claudius, his father-in-law, who had been both consul and censor; Publius Mucius Scævola, the great lawyer and founder of scientific jurisprudence; his brother, Publius Crassus Mucianus; the Pontifex Maximus; Quintus Metellus, the conqueror of Macedonia—all men of the highest rank and universally respected, entered into his schemes of reform.

Tiberius Gracchus.

This patriotic patrician was elected tribune B. C. 134, at a time when political mismanagement, moral decay, the decline of burgesses, and the increase of slaves, were most apparent. So Gracchus, after entering upon his office, proposed the enaction of an agrarian law, by which all State lands, occupied by the possessors without remuneration, should revert to the State, except five hundred jugera for himself, and two hundred and fifty for each son. The domain land thus resumed was to be divided into lots of thirty jugera, and these distributed to burgesses and Italian allies, not as free property, but inalienable leaseholds, for which they paid rent to the State. This was a declaration of war upon the great landholders. The proposal of Gracchus was paralyzed by the vote of his colleague, Marcus Octavius. Gracchus then, in his turn, suspended the business of the State and the administration of justice, and placed his seal on the public chest. The government was obliged to acquiesce. Gracchus, also, as the year was drawing to a close, brought his law to the vote a second time. Again it was vetoed by Octavius. Gracchus then, at the invitation of the consuls, discussed the matter in the Senate; but the Senate, composed of great proprietors, would not yield. All constitutional means were now exhausted, and Gracchus must renounce his reform or begin a revolution.

His reforms.

He chose the latter. Before the assembled people he demanded that his colleague should be deposed, which was against all the customs, and laws, and precedents of the past. The assembly, composed chiefly of the proletarians who had come from the country—the Comitia Tributa—voted according to his proposal, and Octavius was removed by the lictors from the tribune bench, and then the agrarian law was passed by acclamation. The commissioners chosen to confiscate and redistribute the lands were Tiberius Gracchus, his brother Gaius, and his father-in-law Appius Claudius, which family selection vastly increased the indignation of the Senate, who threw every obstacle in the way.

His unlawful movements.

The author of the law, fearing for his personal safety, no longer appeared in the forum without a retinue of three or four thousand men, another cause of bitter hatred on the part of the aristocracy. He also sought to be re-elected tribune, but the Assembly broke up without a choice. The next day the election terminated in the same manner, and it was rumored in the city that Tiberius had deposed all the tribunes, and was resolved to continue in office without re-election. A tumult, originating with the Senate, was the result. A mob of senators rushed through the streets, with fury in their eyes and clubs in their hands. The people gave way, and Gracchus was slain on the slope of the capitol. The Senate officially sanctioned the outrage, on the ground that Tiberius meditated the usurpation of supreme power.

His death.

In regard to the author of this agrarian law, there is no doubt he was patriotic in his intentions, was public-spirited, and wished to revive the older and better days of the republic. I do not believe he contemplated the usurpation of supreme power. I doubt if he was ambitious, as Cæsar was. But he did not comprehend the issues at stake, and the shock he was giving to the constitution of his country. He was like Mirabeau, that other aristocratic reformer, who voted for the spoliation of the church property of France, on the ground, which that leveling sentimentalist Rousseau had advanced, that the church property belonged to the nation. But this plea, in both cases, was sophistical. It was, doubtless, a great evil that the property of the State had fallen into the hands of wealthy proprietors, as it was an evil that half the landed property of France was in possession of the clergy. But, in both cases, this property had been enjoyed uninterruptedly for centuries by the possessors, and, to all intents and purposes, was *private* property. And this law of confiscation was therefore an encroachment on the rights of property, in all its practical bearings. It appeared to the jurists of that age to be an ejection of the great landholders for the benefit of the proletarians. The measure itself was therefore not without injustice, desirable as a division of property might be. But the mode to effect this division was incompatible with civilization itself. It was an appeal to revolutionary forces. It was setting aside all constitutional checks and usages. It was a defiance of the Senate, the great ruling body of the State. It was an appeal to the people to overturn the laws. It was like assem-

Character of Gracchus.

Nature of his reform.

bling the citizens of London to override the Parliament. It was like the French revolution, when the Assembly was dictated to by the clubs. Robespierre may have been sincere and patriotic, but he was a fanatic, fierce and uncompromising. So was Gracchus. In setting aside his colleagues, to accomplish what he deemed a good end, he did evil. When, this rich patrician collected the proletarian burgesses to decree against the veto of the tribune that the public property should be distributed among them, he struck a vital blow on the constitution of his country, and made a step toward monarchy, for monarchy was only reached through the democracy—was only brought about by powerful demagogues. And hence the verdict of the wise and judicious will be precisely that of the leading men of Rome at the time, even that of Cornelia herself: "Shall then our house have no end of madness? Have we not enough to be ashamed of in the disorganization of the State?"

The law of Tiberius Gracchus survived its author. The Senate had not power to annul it, though it might slay its author. The work of redistribution continued, even as the National Assembly of France sanctioned the legislation of preceding revolutionists. And in consequence of the law, there was, in six years, an increase of burgesses capable of bearing arms, of seventy-six thousand. But so many evils attended the confiscation and redistribution of the public domain—so many acts of injustice were perpetrated—there was such gross mismanagement, that the consul Scipio Æmilianus intervened, and by a decree of the people, through his influence, the commission was withdrawn, and the matter was left to the consuls to adjudicate, which was virtually the suspension of the law itself. For this intervention Scipio lost his popularity, unbounded as it had been, even as Daniel Webster lost his prestige and influence when he made his 7th of March speech—the fate of all great men, however great, when they oppose popular feelings and interests, whether they are right or wrong. Scipio, the hero of three wars, not only lost his popularity, but his

The death of Scipio.

life. He was found murdered in his bed at the age of fifty-six. "Scipio's assassination was the democratic reply to the aristocratic massacre of Tiberius Gracchus." The greatest general of the age, a man of unspotted moral purity, and political unselfishness, and generous patriotism, could not escape the vengeance of a baffled populace, B. C. 129.

The distribution of land ceased, but the revolution did not stop. The soul of Tiberius Gracchus "was marching on." A new hero appeared in his brother, Gaius Gracchus, nine years younger—a man who had no relish for vulgar pleasures,—brave, cultivated, talented, energetic, vehement. A master of eloquence, he drew the people; consumed with a passion for revenge, he led them on to revolutionary measures. He was elected tribune in the year 123, and at once declared war on the aristocratic party, to which by birth he belonged.

Gaius Gracchus.

He inaugurated revolutionary measures, by proposing to the people a law which should allow the tribune to solicit a re-election. He then, to gain the people and secure material power, enacted that every burgess should be allowed, monthly, a definite quantity of corn from the public stores at about half the average price. And he caused a law to be passed that the existing order of voting in the Comitia Centuriata, according to which the five property classes voted first, should be done away with, and that all the centuries should vote in the order to be determined by lot. He also caused a law to be passed that no citizen should enlist in the army till seventeen, nor be compelled to serve in the army more than twenty years. These measures all had the effect to elevate the democracy.

He also sought to depress the aristocracy, by dividing its ranks. The old aristocracy embraced chiefly the governing class, and were the chief possessors of landed property. But a new aristocracy of the rich had grown up, composed of speculators, who managed the mercantile transactions of the Roman world. The old senatorial aristocracy were debarred by the Claudian ordinance

He makes war on the aristocracy.

from mercantile pursuits, and were merely sleeping partners in the great companies, managed by the speculators But the new aristocracy, under the name of the equestrian order, began at this time to have political influence. Originally, the equestrians were a burgess cavalry; but gradually all who possessed estates of four hundred thousand sesterces were liable to cavalry service, and became enrolled in the order, which thus comprehended the whole senatorial and non-senatorial noble society of Rome. In process of time, the senators were exempted from cavalry service, and were thus marked off from the list of those liable to do cavalry service. The equestrian order then, at last, comprehended the aristocracy of rich men, in contradistinction from the Senate. And a natural antipathy accordingly grew up between the old senatorial aristocracy and the men to whom money had given rank. The ruling lords stood aloof from the speculators; and were better friends of the people than the new moneyed aristocrats, since they, brought directly in contact with the people, oppressed them, and their greediness and injustice were not usually countenanced by the Senate. The two classes of nobles had united to put down Tiberius Gracchus; but a deep gulf still yawned between them, for no class of aristocrats was ever more exclusive than the governing class at Rome, confined chiefly to the Senate. The Roman Senate was like the House of Peers in England, when the peers had a preponderating political power, and whose property lay in landed estates.

The Equestrian order.

Gracchus raised the power of the equestrians by a law which provided that the farming of the taxes raised in the provinces should be sold at auction at Rome. A gold mine was thus opened for the speculators. He also caused a law to be passed which required the judges of civil and criminal cases to be taken from the equestrians, a privilege before enjoyed by the Senate. And thus a senator, impeached for his conduct as provincial governor, was now tried, not as before, by his peers, but by merchants and bankers.

The speculators.

Gracchus, by the aid of the proletarians and the mercantile class, then proceeded to the overthrow of the ruling aristocracy, especially in the functions of legislation, which had belonged to the Senate. By means of comitial laws and tribunician dictation, he restricted the business of the Senate. He meddled with the public chest by distributing corn at half its value; he meddled with the domains by sending colonies by decrees of the people; he meddled with provincial administration by overturning the regulations which had been made by the Senate. He also sought to re-enforce the Senate by three hundred new members from the equestrians elected by the comitia, a creation of peers which would have reduced the Senate to dependence on the chief of the State. But this he did not succeed in effecting.

The power of the Senate curtailed.

It is singular that he could have carried these measures during his term of office, two years, for he was re-elected, with so little opposition—a proof of the power of the moneyed classes, such, perhaps, as are now represented by the Commons of England. The great change he sought to effect was the re-election of magistrates—an unlimited tribuneship, which was truly Napoleonic. And he knew what he was doing. He was not a fanatic, but a statesman of great ability, seeking to break the oligarchy, and transfer its powers to the tribunes of the people. He desired a firm administration, but resting on continuous individual usurpations. He was a political incendiary, like Mirabeau. He was the true founder of that terrible civic proletariate, which, flattered by the classes above it, led to the usurpations of Sulla and Cæsar. He is the author of the great change, which in one hundred years was effected, of transferring power from the Senate to an emperor. He furnished the tactics for all succeeding demagogues.

Radical reforms.

Great revolutionists are doomed to experience the loss of popularity, and Gracchus lost his by an attempt to extend the Roman franchise to the people of the provinces. The Senate and the mob here united to pre-

Gracchus loses his popularity.

vent what was ultimately effected. The Senate seized the advantage by inciting a rival demagogue, in the person of Marcus Livius Drusus, to propose laws which gave still greater privileges to the equestrians. The Senate bid for popularity, as English prime ministers have retained place, by granting more to the people than their rivals would have granted. The Livian laws, which released the proletarians from paying rent for their lands, were ratified by the people as readily as the Sempronian laws had been. The foundation of the despotism of Gracchus was thus assailed by the Senate uniting with the proletarians. An opportunity was only wanted to effect his complete overthrow.

On the expiration of two years, Gracchus ceased to be tribune, and his enemy, Lucius Opimius, a stanch aristocrat, entered upon his office. The attack on the ex-tribune was made by prohibiting the restoration of Carthage, which Gracchus had sought to effect, and which was a popular measure. On the day when the burgesses assembled with a view to reject the measure which Gracchus had previously secured, he appeared with a large body of adherents. An attendant on the consul demanded their dispersion, on which he was cut down by a zealous Gracchian. On this, a tumult arose. Gracchus in vain sought to be heard, and even interrupted a tribune in the act of speaking, which was against an obsolete law. This offense furnished a pretense for the Senate and the citizens to arm. Gracchus retired to the temple of Castor, and passed the night, while the capitol was filled with armed men. The next day, he fled beyond the Tiber, but the Senate placed a price upon his head, and he was overtaken and slain. Three thousand of his adherents were strangled in prison, and the memory of the Gracchi remained officially proscribed. But Cornelia put on mourning for her last son, and his name became embalmed in the hearts of the democracy.

Gracchus assassinated.

Thus perished Gaius Gracchus, a wiser man than his brother —a man who attempted greater changes, and did not defy the constitutional forms. He was, undoubt-

His character.

edly, patriotic in his intentions, but the reforms which he projected were radical, and would have changed the whole structure of government. It was the consummation of the war against the patrician oligarchy. Whether wise or foolish, it is not for me to give an opinion, since such an opinion is of no account, and would imply equally a judgment as to the relative value of an aristocratical or democratic form of government, in a corrupt age of Roman society. This is a mooted point, and I am not capable of settling it. The efforts of the Gracchi to weaken the power of the ruling noble houses formed a precedent for subsequent reforms, or usurpations, as they are differently regarded, and led the way to the rule of demagogues, to be supplanted in time by that of emperors, with unbounded military authority.

CHAPTER XXXVI.

THE WARS WITH JUGURTHA AND THE CIMBRI.—MARIUS.

The fall of the Gracchi restored Rome to the rule of the oligarchy. The government of the Senate was resumed, and a war of prosecution was carried on against the followers of Gracchus. His measures were allowed to drop. The claims of the Italian allies were disregarded, the noblest of all the schemes of the late tribune, that of securing legal equality between the Roman burgesses and their Italian allies. The restoration of Carthage was set aside. Italian colonies were broken up. The allotment commission was abolished, and a fixed rent was imposed on the occupants of the public domains, but the proletariate of the capital continued to have a distribution of corn, and jurymen or judges (*judices*) were still selected from the mercantile classes. The Senate continued to be composed of effeminated nobles, and insignificant persons were raised to the highest offices.

The administration, under the restoration, was feeble and unpopular. Social evils spread with alarming rapidity. Both slavery and great fortunes increased. The provinces were miserably governed, while pirates and robbers pillaged the countries around the Mediterranean. There was a great revolt of slaves in Sicily, who gained, for a time, the mastery of the island.

The Numidian war.

While public affairs were thus disgracefully managed, a war broke out between Numidia and Rome. That African kingdom extended from the river Molochath to the great Syrtis on the one hand, and to Cyrene and Egypt on the other, and included the greatest part of the ancient Carthaginian territories. Numidia, next to Egypt, was the most important of the Roman client States. On the fall of Carthage, it was ruled by the eldest son of Masinassa, Micipsa, a feeble old man, who devoted himself to the study of philosophy, rather than affairs of State. The government was really in the hands of his nephew, Jugurtha, courageous, sagacious, and able. He was adopted by Micipsa, to rule in conjunction with his two sons, Adherbal and Hiempsal. In the year B. C. 118 Micipsa died, and a collision arose, as was to be expected, among his heirs. Hiempsal was assassinated, and the struggle for the Numidian crown lay between Adherbal and Jugurtha. The latter seized the whole territory, and Adherbal escaped to Rome, and laid his complaint before the Senate. Jugurtha's envoys also appeared, and the Senate decreed that the two heirs should have the kingdom equally divided between them, but Jugurtha obtained the more fertile western half.

Jugurtha.

Then war arose between the two kings, and Adherbal was defeated, and retired to his capital, Aita, where he was besieged by Jugurtha. Adherbal made his complaints to Rome, and a commission of aristocratic but inexperienced young men came to the camp of Jugurtha to arrange the difficulties. Jugurtha rejected their demands, and the young men returned home. Adherbal sent again messengers to Rome, being closely pressed, demanding intervention. The Senate then sent Marcus Scaurus, who held endless debates with Jugurtha, at Utica, to which place he was summoned. These were not attended with any results. Scaurus returned to Rome, and Jugurtha pressed the siege of Aita, which soon capitulated. Adherbal was executed with cruel torture, and the adult population was put to the sword.

A cry of indignation arose in Italy. The envoys of Jugurtha were summarily dismissed, and Scaurus was sent to Africa with an army, but a peace with Rome was purchased by the African prince through the bribery of the generals. The legal validity of the peace was violently assailed in the Senate, and Massiva, a grandson of Masinissa, then in Rome, laid claim to the Numidian throne. But this prince was assassinated by one of the confidants of Jugurtha, which outrage, perpetrated under the eyes of the Roman government, led to a renewed declaration of war, and Spurius Albinus was intrusted with the command of an army. But Jugurtha bribed the Roman general into inaction, and captured the Roman camp. This resulted in the evacuation of Numidia, and a second treaty of peace.

Such an ignoble war created intense dissatisfaction at Rome, and the Senate was obliged to cancel the treaty, and renewed the war in earnest, intrusting the conduct of it to Quintus Metellus, an aristocrat, of course, but a man of great ability. Selecting for his lieutenants able generals, he led over his army to Africa. Jugurtha made proposals of peace, which were refused, and he prepared for a desperate defense. Intrenched on a ridge of hills in the wide plain of Muthul, he awaited the attack of his enemies, but was signally defeated by Metellus, assisted by Marius, a brave plebeian, who had arisen from a common soldiers. After this battle Jugurtha contented himself with a guerrilla warfare, while his kingdom was occupied by the conquerors. Metellus even intrigued to secure the assassination of the king.

Metellus.

The war continued to be prosecuted without decisive results, as is so frequently the case when civilized nations fight with barbarians. Like the war of Charlemagne against the Saxons, victories were easily obtained, but the victors gained unsubstantial advantages. Jugurtha retired to inaccessible deserts with his children, his treasures, and his best troops, to await better times. Numidia was seemingly reduced, but its king remained in arms.

Difficulties of the war.

It was then, in the third year of the renewed war, that Metellus was recalled, and Marius, chosen consul, was left with the supreme command. But even he did not find it easy, with a conquering army, to seize Jugurtha, and he was restricted to a desultory war. At last Bocchus, king of Mauritania, slighted by the Romans, but in alliance with Jugurtha, effected by treachery what could

Marius.

not be gained by arms. He entered into negotiations with Marius to deliver up the king of Numidia, who had married his daughter, and had sought his protection. Marius sent Sulla to consummate the treachery. Jugurtha, the traitor, was thus in turn sacrificed, and became a Roman prisoner.

Close of the war.

This miserable war lasted seven years, and its successful termination secured to Marius a splendid triumph, at which the conquered king, with his two sons, appeared in chains before the triumphal car, and was then executed in the subterranean prison on the Capitoline Hill.

Results of the war.

Numidia was not converted into a Roman province, but into a client State, because the country could not be held without an army on the frontiers. The Jugurthan war was important in its consequences, since it brought to light the venality of the governing lords, and made it evident that Rome must be governed by a degenerate and selfish oligarchy, or by a tyrant, whether in the form of a demagogue, like Gracchus, or a military chieftain, like Marius.

The Cimbri.

But a more difficult war than that waged against the barbarians of the African deserts was now to be conducted against the barbarians of European forests. The war with the Cimbri was also more important in its political results. There had been several encounters with the northern nations of Spain, Gaul, and Italy, under different names, with different successes, which it would be tedious to describe. But the contest with the Cimbri has a great and historic interest, since they were the first of the Germanic tribes with which the Romans contended. Mommsen thinks these barbarians were Teutonic, although, among older historians, they were supposed to be Celts. The Cimbri were a migratory people, who left their northern homes with their wives and children, goods and chattels, to seek more congenial settlements than they had found in the Scandinavian forests. The wagon was their house. They were tall, fair-haired, with bright blue eyes. They were well armed with sword, spear, shield, and helmet.

They were brave warriors, careless of danger, and willing to die. They were accompanied by priestesses, whose warnings were regarded as voices from heaven.

This homeless people of the Cimbri, prevented from advancing south on the Danube by the barrier raised by the Celts, advanced to the passes of the Carnian Alps, B. C. 113, protected by Gnæus Papirius Carbo, not far from Aquileia. An engagement took place not far from the modern Corinthia, where Carbo was defeated. Some years after, they proceeded westward to the left bank of the Rhine, and over the Jura, and again threatened the Roman territory. Again was a Roman army defeated under Silanus in Southern Gaul, and the Cimbri sent envoys to Rome, with the request that they might be allowed peaceful settlements. The Helvetii, stimulated by the successes of the Cimbri, also sought more fertile settlements in Western Gaul, and formed an alliance with the Cimbri. They crossed the Jura, the western barrier of Switzerland, succeeded in decoying the Roman army under Longinus into an ambush, and gained a victory.

War with the Cimbri.

In the year B. C., 105 the Cimbrians, under their king Boiorix, advanced to the invasion of Italy. They were opposed on the right bank of the Rhone by the proconsul Cæpio, and on the left by the consul Gnæus Mallius Maximus, and the consular Marcus Aurelius Scaurus. The first attack fell on the latter general, who was taken prisoner and his corps routed. Maximus then ordered his colleague to bring his army across the Rhone, where the Roman force stood confronting the whole Cimbrian army, but Cæpio refused. The mutual jealousy of these generals, and refusal to co-operate, led to one of the most disastrous defeats which the Romans ever suffered. No less than eighty thousand soldiers, and half as many more camp followers, perished. The battle of Aransio (Orange) filled Rome with alarm and fear, and had the Cimbrians immediately advanced through the passes of the Alps to Italy, overwhelming disasters might have ensued.

Invasion of Italy.

Marius called to command.

In this crisis, Marius was called to the supreme command, hated as he was by the aristocracy, which still ruled, and in defiance of the law which prohibited the holding of the consulship more than once. He was accompanied by a still greater man, Lucius Sulla, destined to acquire great distinction. Marius maintained a strictly defensive attitude within the Roman territories, training and disciplining his troops for the contest which was yet to come with the most formidable antagonists the Romans had ever encountered, and who were destined in after times to subvert the empire.

The Cimbri formed a confederation with the Helvetii and the Teutons, and after an unsuccessful attempt to sweep away the Belgæ, who resisted them, concluded to invade Italy, through Roman Gaul and the Western passes of the Alps. They crossed the Rhone without difficulty, and resumed the struggle with the Romans. Marius awaited them in a well-chosen camp, well fortified and provisioned, at the confluence of the Rhone and the Isère, by which he intercepted the passage of the barbarians, either over the Little St. Bernard—the route Hannibal had taken—or along the coast. The barbarians attacked the camp, but were repulsed. They then resolved to pass the camp, leaving an enemy in the rear, and march to Italy. Marius, for six days, permitted them to defile with their immense baggage, and when their march was over, followed in the steps of the enemy, who took the coast road. At Aquæ Sextiæ the contending parties came into collision, and the barbarians were signally defeated; the whole horde was scattered, killed, or taken prisoners. It would seem that these barbarians were Teutons or Germans; but on the south side of the Alps, the Cimbri and Helvetii crossed the Alps by the Brenner Pass, and descended upon the plains of Italy. The passes had been left unguarded, and the Roman army, under Catulus, on the banks of the Adige, suffered a defeat, and retreated to the right bank of the Po. The whole plain between the Po and the Alps was in the hands

Battle of Aquæ Sextiæ.

of the barbarians, who did not press forward, as they should have done, but retired into winter quarters, where they became demoralized by the warm baths and abundant stores of that fertile and lovely region. Thus the Romans gained time, and the victorious Marius, relinquishing all attempts at the conquest of Gaul, conducted his army to the banks of the Po, and formed a junction with Catulus.

Battle of Vercillæ.

The two armies met at Vercillæ, not far from the place where Hannibal had fought his first battle on the Italian soil. The day of the battle was fixed beforehand by the barbaric general and Marius, on the 30th of June, B. C. 101. A complete victory was gained by the Romans, and the Cimbri were annihilated. The victory of the rough plebeian farmer was not merely over the barbarians, but over the aristocracy. He became, in consequence, the leading man in Rome. He had fought his way from the ranks to the consulship, and had distinguished himself in all the campaigns in which he fought. In Spain, he had arisen to the grade of an officer. In the Numantine war he attracted, at twenty-three, the notice of Scipio. On his return to Rome, with his honorable scars and military *éclat*, he married a lady of the great patrician house of the Julii. At forty, he obtained the prætorship; at forty-eight, he was made consul, and terminated the African war, and his victories over the Cimbri and Teutons enabled him to secure his re-election five consecutive years, which was unexampled in the history of the republic. As consul he administered justice impartially, organized the military system, and maintained in the army the strictest discipline. He had but little culture; his voice was harsh, and his look wild. But he was simple, economical, and incorruptible. He stood aloof from society and from political parties, exposed to the sarcasms of the aristocrats into whose ranks he had entered.

Reforms of Marius.

He made great military reforms, changing the burgess levy into a system of enlistments, and allowing every free-born citizen to enlist. He abolished the aristocratic classification, reduced the infantry of the line to a level, and raised the number of the legion from four thousand two hundred to six thousand, to which he gave a new standard—the silver eagle, which proclaims the advent of emperors. The army was changed from a militia to a band of mercenaries.

After effecting these military changes, he sought political supremacy by taking upon himself the constitutional magistracies. In effecting this he was supported by the popular, or democratic party, which now regained its political importance. He, therefore, obtained the consulship for the sixth time, while his friends among the popular party were made tribunes and prætors. He was also supported at the election by his old soldiers who had been discharged.

But the whole aristocracy rallied, and Marius was not sufficiently a politician to cope with experienced demagogues. He made numerous blunders, and lost his political influence. But he accepted his position, and waited for his time. Not in the field of politics was he to arise to power, but in the strife and din of arms. An opportunity was soon afforded in the convulsions which arose from the revolt of the Roman allies in Italy, soon followed by civil wars. It is these wars which next claim our notice.

CHAPTER XXXVII.

THE REVOLT OF ITALY, AND THE SOCIAL WAR.—MARIUS AND SULLA.

GREAT discontent had long existed among the Italian subjects of Rome. They were not only oppressed, but they enjoyed no political privileges. They did not belong to the class of burgesses.

With the view of extending the Roman franchise, a movement was made by the tribune, M. Livius Drusus, an aristocrat of great wealth and popular sympathies. He had, also, projected other reforms, which made him obnoxious to all parties; but this was peculiarly offensive to the order to which he belonged, and he lost his life while attempting to effect the same reforms which were fatal to Gracchus.

On his assassination, the allies, who outnumbered the Roman burgesses, and who had vainly been seeking citizenship, found that they must continue without political rights, or fight, and they made accordingly vast preparations for war. Had all the Italian States been united, they would, probably, have obtained their desire without a conflict in the field, but in those parts where the moneyed classes preponderated, the people remained loyal to Rome. But the insurgents embraced most of the people in Central and Southern Italy, who were chiefly farmers.

The insurrection broke out in Asculum in Picenum, and spread rapidly through Samnium, Apulia, and Lucania. All Southern and Central Italy was soon in arms against Rome. The Etruscans and Umbrians remained in allegiance as they had before taken part with the equestrians, now a most powerful body, against Drusus. Italy was divided into two great military camps. The insurgents sent envoys to Rome, with the proposal to lay down their arms if citizenship were granted them, but this was refused. Both sides now made extensive preparations, and the forces were nearly balanced. One hundred thousand men were in arms, in two divisions, on either side, the Romans commanded by the consul, Publius Rutilius Lupus, and the Italians by Quintus Silo and Gaius Papius Mutilus. Gaius Marius served as a lieutenant-commander. The war was carried on with various successes, for "Greek met Greek." The first campaign proved, on the whole, to the disadvantage of the Romans, who suffered several defeats. In a political point of view, also, the insurgents were the gainers. Great despondency reigned in the capital, for the war had become serious. At length, it was resolved to grant the political franchise to such Italians as had remained faithful, or who had submitted. This concession, great as it was, did not include the actual insurgents, but it operated in strengthening wavering communities on the side of Rome. Etruria and Umbria were tranquilized.

Indecisive war.

The second campaign, B. C. 89, was opened in Bicenum. Marius was not in the field. His conduct in the previous campaign, was not satisfactory, and the conqueror of the Cimbri, at sixty-six, was thought to be in his dotage. Asculum was besieged and taken by the Romans, who had seventy-five thousand troops under the walls. The Sabellians and Marsians were next subjugated, and all Campania was lost to the insurgents, as far as Nola. The Southern army was under the command of the consul, Lucius Sulla, whose great career had commenced in Africa, under Marius. Sulla advanced into the Samnite country and took its capital, Bovianum. Under his able generalship, the position of affairs greatly changed. At the close of the campaign, most of the insurgent regions were subdued. The Samnites were almost the only people which held out.

Sulla.

It was fortunate for Rome that the rebellion was so far suppressed when the flames of war were rekindled in the

East. A great reaction against the Roman domination had taken place, and the eastern nations seemed determined to rally once more for independent dominion. This was the last great Asiatic rising till the fall of the Roman empire. The potentate under whom the Oriental forces rallied, was Mithridates, king of Pontus.

Asiatic rising.

The army of Sulla, in Campania, was destined to embark for Asia as soon as the state of things in Southern Italy should allow his departure. So the third campaign of the Social war, as it is called, began favorably for Rome, when events transpired in the capital which gave fresh life to the almost extinguished insurrection. The attack of Drusus on the equestrian courts, and his sudden downfall, had sown the bitterest discord between the aristocracy and the burgess class. The Italian communities, received into Roman citizenship, were fettered by restrictions which had an odious stigma, which led to great irritation, for the aristocracy had conferred the franchise grudgingly. And this franchise was moreover withheld from the insurgent communities which had again submitted. A deep indignation also settled in the breast of Marius, on his return from the first campaign, to find himself neglected and forgotten. To these discontents were added the distress of debtors, who, amid the financial troubles of the war, were unable to pay the interest on their debts, and were yet inexorably pressed by creditors.

Disgust of Marius.

It was then, in this state of fermentation and demoralization, that the tribune Publius Sulpicius Rufus proposed that every senator who owed more than two thousand denarii (£82) should forfeit his seat in the Senate; that burgesses condemned by non-free jury courts should have liberty to return home; and that the new burgesses should be distributed among all the tribes, in which the freed men should also have the privilege of voting. These proposals, although made by a patrician, met with the greatest opposition from the Senate, but were passed amid riots and tumults. Sulla was on the best terms with the Senate,

The Sulpician laws.

and Sulpicius feared that he might return from his camp at Nola, and take vengeance for these popular measures. The tribune, therefore, conceived the plan of taking the command from Sulla, who was then consul, and transfer it upon Marius, who was also to conduct the war against Mithridates, in Asia.

The Sullan legislation.

Sulla disobeyed the mandate, and marched to Rome with his army—little more than a body of mercenaries devoted to him. In his eyes, the sovereign Roman citizens were a rabble, and Rome itself a city without a garrison. Sulla had an army of thirty-five thousand men, and before the Romans could organize resistance he appeared at the gate, and crossed the sacred boundary which the law had forbidden war to enter. In a few hours Sulla was the absolute master of Rome. Marius and Sulpicius fled. It was the conservative party which exchanged the bludgeon for the sword. Sulla at once made null the Sulpician laws, punished their author and his adherents, as Sulpicius had feared. The gray-haired conqueror of the Cimbri fled, and found his way to the coast and embarked on a trading-vessel, but the timid mariners put him ashore, and Marius stole along the beach with his pursuers in the rear. He was found in a marsh concealed in reeds and mud, seized and imprisoned by the people of Minturnæ, and a Cimbrian slave was sent to put him to death. The ax, however, fell from his hands when the old hero demanded in a stern voice if he dared to kill Gaius Marius. The magistrates of the town, ashamed, then loosed his fetters, gave him a vessel, and sent him to Ænaria (Ischia). There, in those waters, the proscribed met, and escaped to Numidia, and Sulla was spared the odium of putting to death his old commander, who had delivered Rome from the Cimbrians.

Sullan constitution.

Sulla, master of Rome, did not destroy her liberties. He suggested a new series of legislative enactments in the interests of the aristocracy. He created three hundred new senators, and brought back the old Servian rule of voting in the Comitia Centuriata. The poorer classes were thus virtually again disfranchised. He also abolished the power of the tribune to propose laws to the people, and the initiatory of legislation was submitted to the Senate. The absurd custom by which a consul, prætor, or tribune, could propose to the burgesses any measure he pleased, and carry it without debate, was in itself enough to overturn any constitution.

Having settled these difficulties, and made way with his enemies, Sulla, still consul, embarked with his legion for the East, where the presence of a Roman army was imperatively needed. But before he left, he extorted a solemn oath from Cinna, consul elect, that he would attempt no alteration in the recent changes which had been made. Cinna took the oath, but Sulla had scarcely left before he created new disturbances.

CHAPTER XXXVIII.

THE MITHRIDATIC AND CIVIL WARS.—MARIUS AND SULLA.

THERE reigned at this time in Pontus, the northeastern State of Asia Minor, bordered on the south by Cappadocia, on the east by Armenia, and the north by the Euxine, a powerful prince, Mithridates VI., surnamed Eupator, who traced an unbroken lineage to Darius, the son of the Hystaspes, and also to the Seleucidæ. He was a great eastern hero, whose deeds excited the admiration of his age. He could, on foot, overtake the swiftest deer; he accomplished journeys on horseback of one hundred and twenty miles a day; he drove sixteen horses in hand at the chariot races; he never missed his aim in hunting; he drank his boon companions under the table; he had as many mistresses as Solomon; he was fond of music and poetry; he collected precious works of art; he had philosophers and poets in his train; he was the greatest jester and wit of his court. His activity was boundless; he learned the antidotes for all poisons; he administered justice in twenty-two languages; and yet he was coarse, tyrannical, cruel, superstitious, and unscrupulous. Such was this extraordinary man who led the great reaction of the Asiatics against the Occidentals.

Mithridates.

The resources of this Oriental king were immense, since he bore rule over the shores of the Euxine to the interior of Asia Minor. His field for recruits to his armies stretched from the mouth of the Danube to the Caspian Sea. Thracians, Scythians, Colchians, Iberians, crowded under his banners. When he marched into Cappadocia, he had six hundred scythed chariots, ten thousand horse, and eighty thousand foot. A series of aggressions and conquests made this monarch the greatest and most formidable Eastern foe the Romans ever encountered. The Romans, engrossed with the war with the Cimbri and the insurrection of their Italian subjects, allowed his empire to be silently aggrandized.

The Roman Senate, at last, disturbed and jealous, sent Lucius Sulla to Cappadocia with a handful of troops to defend its interests. On his return, Mithridates continued his aggressions, and formed an alliance with his father-in-law, Tigranes, king of Armenia, but avoided a direct encounter with the great Occidental power which had conquered the world. Things continued for awhile between war and peace, but, at last, it was evident that only war could prevent the aggrandizement of Mithridates, and it was resolved upon by the Romans.

Tigranes.

The king of Pontus made immense preparations to resist his powerful enemies. He strengthened his alliance with Tigranes. He made overtures to the Greek cities. He attempted to excite a revolt in Thrace, in Numidia, and in Syria. He encouraged pirates on the Mediterranean. He organized a foreign corps after the Roman fashion, and took the field with two hundred and fifty thousand infantry and forty thousand cavalry—the largest army seen since the Persian wars. He then occupied Asia Minor, and the Roman generals retreated as he advanced. He made Ephesus his head-quarters, and issued orders to all the governors dependent upon him to massacre, on the same day, all Italians, free or enslaved—men, women, and children, found in their cities. One hundred and fifty thousand were thus barbarously slaughtered in one day. The States of Cappadocia, Sinope, Phrygia, and Bithynia were organized as Pontic satrapies. The confiscation of the property of the murdered Italians replenished his treasury, as well as the contributions of Asia Minor. He not only occupied the Asiatic provinces of the Romans, but meditated the invasion of Europe. Thrace and Macedonia were occupied by his armies, and his fleet appeared in the Ægean

Preparations of Mithridates.

Power of Mithridates.

Sea. Delos, the emporium of Roman commerce, was taken, and twenty thousand Italians massacred. Most of the small free States of Greece entered into alliance with him—the Achæans, Laconians, and Bœotians. So commanding was his position, that an embassy of Italian insurgents invited him to land in Italy.

The position of the Roman government was critical. Asia Minor, Hellas, and Macedonia were in the hands of Mithridates, while his fleet sailed without a rival. The Italian insurrection was not subdued, and political parties divided the capital.

Sulla lands in Epirus.

At this crisis Sulla landed on the coast of Epirus, but with an army of only thirty thousand men, and without a single vessel of war. He landed with an empty military chest. But he was a second Alexander—the greatest general that Rome had yet produced. He soon made himself master of Greece, with the exception of the fortresses of Athens and the Piræus, into which the generals of Mithridates had thrown themselves. He intrenched himself at Eleusis and Megara, from which he commanded Greece and the Peloponnesus, and commenced the siege of Athens. This was attended with great difficulties, and the city only fell, after a protracted defense, when provisions were exhausted. The conqueror, after allowing his soldiers to pillage the city, gave back her liberties, in honor of her illustrious dead.

Siege of Athens.

Sulla deposed.

But a year was wasted, and without ships it was impossible for Sulla to secure his communications. He sent one of his best officers, Lucullus, to Alexandria, to raise a fleet, but the Egyptian court evaded the request. To add to his embarrassments, the Roman general was without money, although he had rifled the treasures which still remained in the Grecian temples. Moreover, what was still more serious, a revolution at Rome overturned his work, and he had been deposed, and his Asiatic command given to M. Valerius Flaccus.

Sulla was unexpectedly relieved by the resolution of

Mithridates to carry on the offensive in Greece. Taxiles, one of the lieutenants of the Pontic king, was sent to combat Sulla with an army of one hundred thousand infantry and ten thousand cavalry.

Battle of Chæronea.

Then was fought the battle of Chæronea, B. C. 86, against the advice of Archelaus, in which the Romans were the victors. But Sulla could not reap the fruits of victory without a fleet, since the sea was covered with Pontic ships. In the following year a second army was sent into Greece by Mithridates, and the Romans and Asiatics met once more in the plain of the Cephissus, near Orchomenus. The Romans were the victors, who speedily cleared the European continent of its eastern invaders. At the end of the third year of the war, Sulla took up his winter quarters in Thessaly, and commenced to build ships.

Revolt of Asia against Mithridates.

Meanwhile a reaction against Mithridates took place in Asia Minor. His rule was found to be more oppressive than that of the Romans. The great mercantile cities of Smyrna, Colophon, Ephesus, and Sardis were in revolt, and closed their gates against his governors. The Hellenic cities of Asia Minor had hoped to gain civil independence and a remission of taxes, and were disappointed. And those cities which were supposed to be secretly in favor of the Romans were heavily fined. The Chians were compelled to pay two thousand talents. Great cruelties were also added to fines and confiscations. Lucullus, unable to obtain the help of an Alexandrian fleet, was more fortunate in the Syrian ports, and soon was able to commence offensive operations. Flaccus, too, had arrived with a Roman army, but this incapable general was put to death by a mob-orator, Fimbria, more able than he, who defeated a Pontic army at Miletopolis. The situation of Mithridates then became perilous. Europe was lost; Asia Minor was in rebellion; and Roman armies were pressing upon him.

He therefore negotiated for peace. Sulla required the restoration of all the conquests he had made: Cappadocia,

Paphlagonia, Galatia, Bithynia, the Hellenic cities, the islands of the sea, and a contribution of three thousand talents. These conditions were not accepted, and Sulla proceeded to Asia, upon which Mithridates reluctantly acceded to his terms.

Negotiations for peace.

Sulla then turned against Fimbria, who commanded the Roman army sent to supplant him, which, as was to be expected, deserted to his standard. Fimbria fled to Pergamus, and fell on his own sword. Sulla intrusted the two legions which had been sent from Rome under Flaccus to the command of his best officer, Murena, and turned his attention to arrange the affairs of Asia. He levied contributions to the amount of twenty thousand talents, reduced Mithridates to the rank of a client king, richly compensated his soldiers, and embarked for Italy, leaving Lucullus behind to collect the contributions.

Sulla returns to Italy.

Thus was the Mithridatic war ended by the genius of a Roman general, who had no equal in Roman history, with the exception of Pompey and Julius Cæsar. He had distinguished himself in Africa, in Spain, in Italy, and in Greece. He had defeated the barbarians of the West, the old Italian foes of Rome, and the armies of the most powerful Oriental monarch since the fall of Persia. He had triumphed over Roman factions, and supplanted the great Marius himself. He was now to contend with one more able foe, Lucius Cornelius Cinna, who represented the revolutionary forces which had rallied under the Gracchi and Marius—the democratic elements of Roman society.

His greatness.

Cinna.

When Sulla embarked for the Mithridatic war, Cinna, supported by a majority of the College of Tribunes, concerted a reaction against the rule which Sulla had re-established—the rule of the aristocracy. But Cinna, a mere tool of the revolutionary party,—a man without ability,—was driven out of the city by the aristocratic party, and outlawed, and L. Cornelia Mesula was made consul in his stead. The outlaws fled to the camp before Nola. The Campanian army, democratic and revolutionary, recognized Cinna as the leader of the republic. Gaius Marius, then an exile in Numidia, brought six thousand men, whom he had rallied to his standard, to the disposal of the consul, and was placed by Cinna in supreme command at Etruria. A storm gathered around the capitol. Cinna was overshadowed by the greatness of that plebeian general who had defeated the Cimbrians, and who was bent upon revenge for the mortification and insults he had received from the Roman aristocracy. Famine and desertion soon made the city indefensible, and Rome capitulated to an army of her own citizens.

Marius, now master of Rome, entered the city, and a reign of terror commenced. The gates were closed, and the slaughter of the aristocratic party commenced. The consul Octavius was the first victim, and with him the most illustrious of his party. The executioners of Marius fulfilled his orders, and his revenge was complete. He entered upon a new consulate, execrated by all the leading citizens. But in the midst of his victories he was seized with a burning fever, and died in agonies, at the age of seventy, in the full possession of honor and power. Cinna succeeded him in the consulship, and Rome was under the government of a detested tyrant. For four years his reign was absolute, and was a reign of terror, during which the senators were struck down, as the French nobles were in the time of Robespierre. Cinna, like Robespierre, reigned with the mightiest plenitude of power, united with incapacity.

Civil war.

Success of Cinna.

In this state of anarchy Sulla's wife and children escaped with difficulty, and Sulla himself was deprived of his command against Mithridates. But Cinna, B. C. 84, was killed in a mutiny, and the command of the revolutionists devolved on Carbo. The situation of Sulla was critical, even at the head of his veteran forces. In the spring of the year following the death of Cinna, he landed in Brundusium, where he was re-enforced by partisans and deserters. The Senate made advances to Sulla, and many patricians joined his ranks, including Cneius Pompeius, then twenty-three years of age.

Civil war was now inaugurated between Sulla and the revolutionary party, at the head of which were now the consul Carbo and the younger Marius. Carbo was charged with Upper Italy, while Marius guarded Rome at the fortress of Præneste. At Sacriportus Sulla defeated Marius, and entered Rome. But the insurgent Italians united with the revolutionary forces of Rome, and seventy thousand Samnites and Lucanians approached the capital. At the Colline gate a battle was fought, in which Sulla was victorious. This ended the Social war, and the subjugation of the revolutionists soon followed.

Sulla ends the war.

Sulla was now made dictator, and the ten years of revolution and insurrection were at an end in both West and East. The first use which Sulla made of his absolute power was to outlaw all his enemies. Lists of the proscribed were posted at Rome and in the Italian cities. It was a fearful visitation. A second reign of terror took place, more fearful and systematic than that of Marius. Four thousand seven hundred persons were slaughtered, among whom were forty senators, and one thousand six hundred equites.

Absolute power of Sulla.

The next year Sulla celebrated his magnificent triumph over Mithridates, and was saluted by the name of Felix. The despotism at which the Gracchi were accused of aiming was introduced by a military conqueror, aided by the aristocracy.

His triumphs.

Sulla then devoted himself to the reorganization of the State. He conferred citizenship upon all the Italians but freedmen, and bestowed the sequestered estates of those who had taken side against him or his soldiers. The office of judices was restored to the Senate, and the equites were deprived of their separate seats at festivals. The Senate was restored to its ancient dignity and power, and three hundred new members appointed. The number of prætors was increased to eight. The government still rested

He reforms.

on the basis of popular election, but was made more aristocratic than before. The Comitia Centuriata was left in possession of the nominal power of legislation, but it could only be exercised upon the initiation of a decree of the Senate. The Comitia Tributa was stripped of the powers by which it had so long controlled the Senate and the State. Tribunes of the people were selected from the Senate. The College of Pontiffs was no longer filled by popular election, but by the choice of their own members. A new criminal code was made, and the several courts were presided over by the prætors. Such, in substance, were the Cornelian laws to restore the old powers of the aristocracy.

The reforms of Sulla.

Having effected this labor, Sulla, in the plenitude of power, retired into private life. He retired, not like Charles V., wearied of the toils of war, and disgusted with the vanity of glory and fame, nor like Washington, from lofty patriotic motives, but to bury himself in epicurean pleasures. In the luxury of his Cumænon villa he divided his time between hunting and fishing, and the enjoyments of literature, until, worn out with sensuality, he died in his sixtieth year, B. C. 78. A grand procession of the Senate he had saved, the equites, the magistrates, the vestal virgins, and his disbanded soldiers, bore his body to the funeral pyre, and his ashes were deposited beside the tombs of the kings. A splendid monument was raised to his memory, on which was inscribed his own epitaph, that no friend ever did him a kindness, and no enemy a wrong, without receiving a full requital.

His retirement.

CHAPTER XXXIX.

ROME FROM THE DEATH OF SULLA TO THE GREAT CIVIL WARS OF CÆSAR AND POMPEY.—CICERO, POMPEY, AND CÆSAR.

On the death of Sulla, the Roman government was once more in the hands of the aristocracy, and for several years the consuls were elected from the great ruling families. But, in spite of all the conquests of Sulla and all his laws, the State was tumbling into anarchy, and was convulsed with fresh wars.

Reaction in favor of the aristocracy.

Sulla was alive when M. Lepidus came forward as the leader of the democratic party against C. Lutatius Catulus—a man without character or ability, who had deserted from the optimates to the popular party, to escape prosecution for the plunder of Sicily. The fortune he acquired in his government of that province enabled Lepidus to secure his election as consul, B. C. 78, and he even attempted to deprive Sulla of his funeral honors. A conspiracy was organized in Etruria, where the Sullan confiscation had been most severe. Lepidus came forward as an avenger of the old Romans whose fortunes had been ruined. The Senate, fearing convulsions, made Lepidus and Catulus, the consuls, swear not to take up arms against each other; but at the expiration of the consulship of Lepidus, went, as was usual, to the province assigned to him. This was Gaul, and here the war first broke out. An attempt on Rome was frustrated by Catulus, who defeated Lepidus, and the latter soon died in Sardinia, whither he had retired.

Sertorius was then in command of the army in Spain,—a

man who had risen from an obscure position, but who possessed the hardy virtues of the old Sabine farmers. He served under Marius in Gaul, and was prætor when Sulla returned to Italy. When the cause of Marius was lost in Africa, he organized a resistance to Sulla in Spain. His army was re-enforced by Marian refugees, and he was aided by the Iberian tribes, among whom he was a favorite. For eight years this celebrated hero baffled the armies which Rome, under the lead of the aristocracy, sent against him, for he undertook to restore the cause of the democracy.

Sertorius.

Against Sertorius was sent the man who, next to Cæsar, was destined to play the most important part in the history of those times—Cn. Pompeius, born the same year as Cicero, B. C. 106, who had enlisted in the cause of Sulla, and early distinguished himself against the generals of Marius. He gained great successes in Sicily and Africa, and was, on his return to Rome, saluted by the dictator Sulla himself with the name of *Magnus*, which title he ever afterward bore. He was then a simple equestrian, and had not risen to the rank of quæstor, or prætor, or consul. Yet he had, at the early age of twenty-four, without enjoying any curule office, the honor of a triumph, even against the opposition of Sulla.

Pompey.

Pompey was sent to Spain with the title of proconsul, and with an army of thirty thousand men. He crossed the Alps between the sources of the Rhone and Po, and advanced to the southern coast of Spain. Here he was met by Sertorius, and at first was worsted. I need not detail the varied events of this war in Spain. The Spaniards at length grew weary of a contest which was not to their benefit, but which was carried on in behalf of rival factions at the capital. Dissensions broke out among the officers of Sertorius, and he was killed at a banquet by Perpenna, his lieutenant. On the death of the only man capable of resisting the aristocracy of Rome, and whose virtues were worthy of the ancient heroes, the progress of Pompey was easy. Per-

Death of Sertorius.

penna was taken prisoner and his army was dispersed, and Spain was reduced to obedience.

Servile war.

In the mean time, while Pompey was fighting Sertorius in Spain, a servile war broke out in Italy, produced in part by the immense demand of slaves for the gladiatorial shows. One of these slaves, Spartacus, once a Thracian captain of banditti, escaped with seventy comrades to the crater of Vesuvius, and organized an insurrection, and he was soon at the head of one hundred thousand of those wretched captives whose condition was unendurable. Italy was ravaged from the Alps to the Straits of Messina. No Roman general, then in Italy, was equal to the task of subduing them. But, in the second year of the war, Crassus, who was a great proprietor of slaves, and who had ably served under Sulla, undertook the task of subduing the insurrectionary slaves. With six legions he drove them to the extremity of the Bruttian peninsula, and shut them up in Rhegium by strong lines of circumvallation. Spartacus was killed, after having broken through the lines, and most of his followers were destroyed; but six thousand escaped into Cisalpine Gaul, as the northern part of Italy was then called, and met Pompey on his victorious return from Spain, by whom they were utterly annihilated. Pompey claimed the merit of ending the servile war, and sought the honor of the consulship, although ineligible. Crassus, also ineligible, also demanded the consulship, and both these lieutenants of Sulla obtained their ends. But both, in order to obtain the consulship, made great promises. Pompey, in particular, promised to restore the tribunitian power. Pompey now broke with the aristocracy, whose champion he had been, and even carried another law by which the judices were taken from the equites as well as the Senate. Thus was the constitution of Sulla subverted within ten years. In this movement Pompey was supported by Julius Cæsar, who was a young man of thirty years of age.

Pompey.

On the expiration of his consulship, Pompey remained

inactive, refusing a province, until the troubles with the Mediterranean pirates again called him into active military service. These pirates swarmed on every coast, plundering cities, and cutting off communication between Rome and the provinces. They especially attacked the corn vessels, so that the price of provisions rose inordinately. The people, in distress, turned their eyes to Pompey; but he was not willing to accept any ordinary command, and through his intrigues, his tool, the tribune Gabinius, proposed that the people should elect a man for this service of consular rank, who should have absolute power for three years over the whole of the Mediterranean, and to a distance of fifty miles inward from the coast, and who should command a fleet of two hundred ships. He did not name Pompey, but everybody knew who was meant. The people, furious at the price of corn, and full of admiration for the victories of Pompey, were ready to appoint him; the Senate, alarmed and jealous, was equally determined to prevent his appointment. Tumults and riots were the consequence. Pompey affected to desire some other person for the command but himself; but the law passed, in spite of the opposition of the Senate, and Pompey was commissioned to prepare five hundred ships, enlist one hundred and twenty thousand sailors and soldiers, and also to take from the public treasury whatever sum he needed.

The pirates.

Great power given to Pompey.

In the following spring his preparations were made, and in forty days he cleared the western half of the Mediterranean from the pirates, and drove them to the Cilician coast. Here he gained a great victory over their united fleets, and took twenty thousand prisoners, whom he settled at various points on the coasts, and returned home in forty-nine days after he had sailed from Brundusium. In less than three months he had ended the war.

This great success led to his command against Mithridates, who had again rallied his forces for one more decisive and desperate struggle with the Romans. Asia rallied against Europe, as Europe rallied against Asia

Renewal of hostilities in the East.

in the crusades. Mithridates, after his defeat by Sulla, had retired to Armenia to the court of his son-in-law, Tigranes, whose power was greater than that of any other Oriental potentate. Tigranes was not at first inclined to break with Rome, but (B. C. 70) he consented to the war, which continued for seven years without decisive results. The Romans were commanded by Lucullus, the old lieutenant of Sulla, and although his labors were not appreciated at Rome, he broke really the power of Mithridates. But, through the intrigues of Pompey and his friends, he was recalled, and Pompey was commissioned, with the extraordinary power of unlimited control of the Eastern army and fleet, and the rights of proconsul over the whole of Asia. He already had the dominion of the Mediterranean. The Senate opposed this dangerous precedent, but it was carried by the people, who could not heap too many honors on their favorite. Cicero, then forty years of age, with Cæsar, supported the measure, which was opposed by Hortensius and Catulus.

Lucullus.

Lucullus retired to his luxurious villa to squander the riches he had accumulated in Asia, and to study the academic philosophy, while Pompey pursued his conquests in the East over foes already broken and humiliated. He showed considerable ability, and drove Mithridates from post to post in the heart of his dominion. The Eastern monarch made overtures of peace, which were rejected. Nothing but unconditional surrender would be accepted. His army was finally cut to pieces, and the old man escaped only with a few horsemen. Rejected by Tigranes, he made his way to the Cimmerian Bosphorus, which was his last retreat. Pompey then turned his attention to Armenia, and Tigranes threw himself upon his mercy, at the cost of all his territories but Armenia Proper. Pompey then resumed the pursuit of Mithridates, fighting his way through the mountains of Iberia and Albania, but he did not pursue his foe over the Caucasus. Mithridates, secure in the Crimea, then planned a daring attempt on Rome herself, which was to march round the Euxine and

His victories.

Defeat of Mithridates.

up the Danube, collecting in his train the Sarmatians, Gætæ, and other barbarians, cross the Alps, and descend upon Italy. *His* kingdom of Pontus was already lost, and had been made a Roman province. His followers, however, became disaffected, his son Pharnaces rebelled, and he had no other remedy than suicide to escape capture. He died B. C. 63, after a reign of fifty-three years, in the sixty-ninth year of his age—the greatest Eastern prince since Cyrus. Racine has painted him in one of his dramas as one of the most heroic men of the world. But it was his misfortune to contend with Rome in the plenitude of her power.

His death.

Pompey, before the death of Mithridates, went to Syria to regulate its affairs, it being ceded to Rome by Tigranes. After the defeat of Tigranes by Lucullus, that kingdom, however, had been recovered by Antiochus XIII., the last of the Seleucidæ, who held a doubtful sovereignty. He was, however, reduced by a legate of Pompey, and Syria became a Roman province. The next year, Pompey advanced south, and established the Roman supremacy in Phœnicia and Palestine, the latter country being the seat of civil war between Hyrcanus and Aristobulus. It was then that Jerusalem was taken by the Roman general, after a siege of three months, and the conqueror entered the most sacred precincts of the temple, to the horror of the priesthood. He established Hyrcanus as high priest, as has been already related, and then retired to Pontus, settled its affairs, and departed with his army for Italy, having won a succession of victories never equaled in the East, except by Alexander. And never did victories receive such great éclat, which, however, were easily won, as those of Alexander had been. No Asiatic foe was a match for either Greeks or Romans in the field. The real difficulties were in marches, in penetrating mountain passes, in crossing arid plains.

Pompey in Syria.

His victories.

But before the conqueror of Asia received the reward of his great services to the State—the most splendid triumph which had as yet been seen on the Via

His triumph.

Sacra—Rome was brought to the verge of ruin by the conspiracy of Catiline. The departure of Pompey to punish the pirates of the Mediterranean and conquer Mithridates, left the field clear to the two greatest men of their age, Cicero and Cæsar. It was while Cicero was consul that the conspiracy was detected.

Cicero.

Marcus Tullius Cicero, the most accomplished man, on the whole, in Roman annals, and as immortal as Cæsar himself, was born B. C. 106, near Arpinum, of an equestrian, but not senatorial family. He received a good education, received the manly gown at sixteen, and entered the forum to hear the debates, but pursued his studies with great assiduity. He was intrusted by his wealthy father to the care of the augur, Q. Mucius Scævola, an old lawyer deeply read in the constitution of his country and the principles of jurisprudence. At eighteen he served his first and only campaign under the father of the great Pompey, in the social war. He was twenty-four before he made a figure in the eye of the public, keeping aloof from the fierce struggles of Marius and Sulla, identifying himself with neither party, and devoted only to the cultivation of his mind, studying philosophy and rhetoric as well as law, traveling over Sicily and Greece, and preparing himself for a forensic orator. At twenty-five he appeared in the forum as a public pleader, and boldly defended the oppressed and injured, and even braved the anger of Sulla, then all-powerful as dictator. At twenty-seven he again repaired to Athens for greater culture, and extensively traveled in Asia Minor, holding converse with the most eminent scholars and philosophers in the Grecian cities. At twenty-nine he returned to Rome, improved in health as well as in those arts which contributed to his unrivaled fame as an orator—a rival with Hortensius and Cotta, the leaders of the Roman bar. At thirty he was elected quæstor, not, as was usually the case, by family interest, but from his great reputation as a lawyer. The duties of his office called him to Sicily, under the prætor of Lilybæum, which he admirably discharged, showing not only executive ability, but rare virtue and impartiality. The vanity which dimmed the lustre of his glorious name, and which he never exorcised, received a severe wound on his return to Italy. He imagined he was the observed of all observers, but soon discovered that his gay and fashionable friends were ignorant, not only of what he had done in Sicily but of his administration at all.

For the next four years he was absorbed in private studies, and in the courts of law, at the end of which he became ædile, the year that Verres was impeached for misgovernment in Sicily. This was the most celebrated State trial for impeachment on record, with the exception, perhaps, of that of Warren Hastings. But Cicero, who was the public accuser and prosecutor, was more fortunate than Burke. He collected such an overwhelming mass of evidence against this corrupt governor, that he went into exile without making a defense, although defended by Hortensius, consul elect. The speech which the orator *was to have* made at the trial was subsequently published by Cicero, and is one of the most eloquent tirades against public corruption ever composed or uttered.

Verres.

Nothing of especial interest marked the career of this great man for three more years, until B. C. 67 he was elected first prætor, or supreme judge, an office for which he was supremely qualified. But it was not merely civic cases which he decided. He appeared as a political speaker, and delivered from the rostrum his celebrated speech on the Manilian laws, maintaining the cause of Pompey when he departed from the policy of the aristocracy. He had now gained by pure merit, in a corrupt age, without family influence, the highest offices of the State, even as Burke became the leader of the House of Commons without aristocratic connections, and now naturally aspired to the consulship,—the great prize which every ambitious man sought, but which, in the aristocratic age of Roman history, was rarely conferred except on members of the ruling houses, or very eminent success in war. By the friendship of Pompey, and also

Public career of Cicero.

from the general admiration which his splendid talents and attainments commanded, this great prize was also secured. He had six illustrious competitors, among whom were Antonius and Catiline, who were assisted by Crassus and Cæsar. As consul, all the energies of his mind and character were absorbed in baffling the treason of this eminent patrician demagogue. L. Sergius Catiline was one of those wicked, unscrupulous, intriguing, popular, abandoned and intellectual scoundrels that a corrupt age and patrician misrule brought to the surface of society, aided by the degenerate nobles to whose class he belonged. In the bitterness of his political disappointments, headed off by Cicero at every turn, he meditated the complete overthrow of the Roman constitution, and his own elevation as chief of the State, and absolutely inaugurated rebellion. Cicero, who was in danger of assassination, boldly laid the conspiracy before the Senate, and secured the arrest of many of his chief confederates. Catiline fled and assembled his followers, which numbered twelve thousand desperate men, and fought with the courage of despair, but was defeated and slain.

Cicero as consul.

Catiline.

Had it not been for the vigilance, energy, and patriotism of Cicero, it is possible this atrocious conspiracy would have succeeded. The state of society was completely demoralized; the disbanded soldiers of the Eastern wars had spent their money and wanted spoils; the Senate was timid and inefficient, and an unscrupulous and able leader, at the head of discontented factions, on the assassination of the consuls and the virtuous men who remained in power, might have bid defiance to any force which could then, in the absence of Pompey in the East, have been marshaled against him.

But the State was saved, and saved by a patriotic statesman, who had arisen by force of genius and character to the supreme power. The gratitude of the people was unbounded. Men of all ranks hailed him as the savior of his country; thanksgivings to the gods were voted in his name, and all Italy joined in enthusiastic praises.

Cicero's services.

But he had now reached the culminating height of his political greatness, and his subsequent career was one of sorrow and disappointment. Intoxicated by his elevation,—for it was unprecedented at Rome, in his day, for a man to rise so high by mere force of eloquence and learning, without fortune, or family, or military exploits,—he became conceited and vain. In the civil troubles which succeeded the return of Pompey, he was banished from the country he had saved, and there is nothing more pitiful than his lamentations and miseries while in exile. His fall was natural. He had opposed the demoralizing current which swept every thing before it. When his office of consul was ended, he was exposed to the hatred of the senators whom he had humiliated, of the equites whose unreasonable demands he had opposed, of the people whom he disdained to flatter, and of the triumvirs whose usurpation he detested. No one was powerful enough to screen him from these combined hostilities, except the very men who aimed at the subversion of Roman liberties, and who wished him out of the way; his friend Pompey showed a mean, pusillanimous, and calculating selfishness, and neither Crassus nor Cæsar liked him. But in his latter days, part of which were passed in exile, and all without political consideration, he found time to compose those eloquent treatises on almost every subject, for which his memory will be held in reverence. Unlike Bacon, he committed no crime against the laws; yet, like him, fell from his high estate in the convulsions of a revolutionary age, and as Bacon soothed his declining years with the charms of literature and philosophy, so did Cicero display in his writings the result of long years of study, and unfold for remotest generations the treasures of Greek and Roman wisdom, ornamented, too, by that exquisite style, which, of itself, would have given him immortality as one of the great artists of the world. He lived to see the utter wreck of Roman liberties, and was ultimately executed by order of Antonius, in revenge for those bitter philippics which the orator had launched against him before

His fall.

Accomplishments and character of Cicero.

34

the descending sun of his political glory had finally disappeared in the gloom and darkness of revolutionary miseries.

But we resume the thread of political history in those tangled times. Cicero was at the highest of his fame and power when Pompey returned from his Asiatic conquests, the great hero of his age, on whom all eyes were fixed, and to whom all bent the knee of homage and admiration. His triumph, at the age of forty-five, was the grandest ever seen. It lasted two days. Three hundred and twenty-four captive princes walked before his triumphal car, followed by spoils and emblems of a war which saw the reduction of one thousand fortresses. The enormous sum of twenty thousand talents was added to the public treasury.

Pompey.

Pompey was, however, greater in war than in peace. Had he known how to make use of his prestige and his advantages, he might have henceforth reigned without a rival. He was not sufficiently noble and generous to live without making grave mistakes and alienating some of his greatest friends, nor was he sufficiently bad and unscrupulous to abuse his military supremacy. He pursued a middle course, envious of all talent, absorbed in his own greatness, vain, pompous, and vacillating. His quarrels with Crassus and Lucullus severed him from the aristocratic party, whose leader he properly was. His haughtiness and coldness alienated the affections of the people, through whom he could only advance to supreme dominion. He had neither the arts of a demagogue, nor the magnanimity of a conqueror.

His policy.

It was at this crisis that Cæsar returned from Spain as the conqueror of the Lusitanians. Caius Julius Cæsar belonged to the ancient patrician family of the Julii, and was born B. C. 100, and was six years younger than Pompey and Cicero. But he was closely connected with the popular party by the marriage of his aunt Julia with the great Marius, and his marriage with Cornelia, the daughter of Cinna, one of the chief opponents of Sulla. He early served in the army of the East, but devoted his earliest

Cæsar.

years to the art of oratory. His affable manners and unbounded liberality made him popular with the people. He obtained the quæstorship at thirty-two, the year he lost his wife, and went as quæstor to Antistius Vetus, into the province of Further Spain. On his return, the following year, he married Pompeia, the granddaughter of Sulla, of the Cornelia gens, and formed a union with Pompey. By his family connections he obtained the curule ædileship at the age of thirty-five, and surpassed his predecessors in the extravagance of his shows and entertainments, the money for which he borrowed. At thirty-seven he was elected Pontifex Maximus, so great was his popularity, and the following year he obtained the prætorship, B. C. 62, and on the expiration of his office he obtained the province of Further Spain. His debts were so enormous that he applied for aid to Crassus, the richest man in Rome, and readily obtained the loan he sought. In Spain, with an army at his command, he gained brilliant victories over the Lusitanians, and returned to Rome enriched, and sought the consulship. To obtain this, he relinquished the customary triumph, and, with the aid of Pompey, secured his election, and entered into that close alliance with Pompey and Crassus which historians call the first triumvirate. It was merely a private agreement between the three most powerful men of Rome to support each other, and not a distinct magistracy.

The consulship of Cæsar.

As consul, Cæsar threw his influence against the aristocracy, to whose ranks he belonged, both by birth and office, and caused an agrarian law to be passed, against the fiercest opposition of the Senate, by which the rich Campanian lands were divided for the benefit of the poorest citizens—a good measure, perhaps, but which brought him forward as the champion of the people. He next gained over the equites, by relieving them, by a law which he caused to be passed, of one-third of the sum they had agreed to pay for the farming of the taxes of Asia. He secured the favor of Pompey by causing all his acts in the East to be confirmed. At the expiration of his consulship he obtained the province of Gaul, as the fullest field for the development of his military talents, and the surest way to climb to subsequent greatness. At this period Cicero went into exile without waiting for his trial—that miserable period made memorable for aristocratic broils and intrigues, and when Clodius, a reckless young noble, entered into the house of the Pontifex Maximum, disguised as a woman, in pursuit of a vile intrigue with Cæsar's wife.

The succeeding nine years of Cæsar's life were occupied by the subjugation of Gaul. In the first campaign he subdued the Helvetii, and conquered Ariovistus, a powerful German chieftain. In the second campaign he opposed a confederation of Belgic tribes—the most warlike of all the Gauls, who had collected a force of three hundred thousand men, and signally defeated them, for which victories the Senate decreed a public thanksgiving of fifteen days. That given in Pompey's honor, after the Mithridatic war, had lasted but ten. At this time he made a renewed compact with Pompey and Crassus, by which Pompey was to have the two Spains for his province, Crassus that of Syria, and he himself should have a prolonged government in Gaul for five years more. The combined influence of these men was enough to secure the elections, and the year following Crassus and Pompey were made consuls. Cæsar had to resist powerful confederations of the Gauls, and in order to strike terror among them, in the fourth year of the war, invaded Britain. But I can not describe the various campaigns of Cæsar in Gaul and Britain without going into details hard to be understood—his brilliant victories over enemies of vastly greater numbers, his marchings and countermarchings, his difficulties and dangers, his inventive genius, his strategic talents, his boundless resources, his command over his soldiers and their idolatry, until, after nine years, Gaul was subdued and added to the Roman provinces. During his long absence from Rome his interests were guarded by the tribune Curio, and Marcus Antonius, the future triumvir. During this time Crassus had inglori-

Cæsar in Gaul.

ously conducted a distant war in Parthia, in quest of fame and riches, and was killed by an unknown hand after a disgraceful defeat. This avaricious patrician must not be confounded with the celebrated orator, of a preceding age, who was so celebrated for his elegance and luxury.

Affairs at Rome had also taken a turn which indicated a rupture with Cæsar and Pompey, now left, by the death of Crassus, at the head of the State. The brilliant victories of the former in Gaul were in everybody's mouth, and the fame of the latter was being eclipsed. A serious rivalry between these great generals began to show itself. The disturbances which also broke out on the death of Clodius led to the appointment of Pompey as sole consul, and all his acts as consul tended to consolidate his power. His government in Spain was prolonged for five years more; he entered into closer connections with the aristocracy, and prepared for a rupture with his great rival, which had now become inevitable, as both grasped supreme power. That struggle is now to be presented in the following chapter.

CHAPTER XL.

THE CIVIL WARS BETWEEN CÆSAR AND POMPEY.

Power of Cæsar and Pompey.

THE condition of Rome when Cæsar returned, crowned with glory, from his Gallic campaign, in which he had displayed the most consummate ability, was miserable enough. The constitution had been assailed by all the leading chieftains, and even Cicero could only give vent to his despair and indignation in impotent lamentations. The cause of liberty was already lost. Cæsar had obtained the province of Gaul for ten years, against all former precedent, and Pompey had obtained the extension of his imperium for five additional years. Both these generals thus had armies and an independent command for a period which might be called indefinite—that is, as long as they could maintain their authority in a period of anarchy. Rome was disgraced by tumults and assassinations; worthless people secured the highest offices, and were the tools of the two great generals, who divided between them the empire of the world. All family ties between these two generals were destroyed by the death of Julia. The feud between Clodius and Milo, the one a candidate for the prætorship, and the other for the consulship, was most disgraceful, in the course of which Clodius was slain. Each wanted an office as the means of defraying enormous debts. Pompey, called upon by the Senate to relieve the State from anarchy, was made sole consul—another unprecedented thing. The trial of Milo showed that Pompey was the absolute master at Rome, and it was his study to maintain his position against Cæsar.

It was plain that the world could not have two absolute

masters, for both Pompey and Cæsar aspired to universal sovereignty. One must succumb to the other—be either anvil or hammer. Neither would have been safe without their armies and their armed followers. And if both were destroyed, the State would still be convulsed with factions. All true constitutional liberty was at an end, for both generals and demagogues could get such laws passed as they pleased, with sufficient money to bribe those who controlled the elections. It was a time of universal corruption and venality. Money was the mainspring of society. Public virtue had passed away,—all elevated sentiment,—all patriotism,—all self-sacrifice. The people cared but little who ruled, if they were supplied with corn and wine at nominal prices. Patrician nobles had become demagogues, and demagogues had power in proportion to their ability or inclination to please the people. Cicero despaired of the State, and devoted himself to literature. There yet remained the aristocratic party, which had wealth and prestige and power, and the popular party, which aimed to take these privileges away, but which was ruled by demagogues more unprincipled than the old nobility. Pompey represented the one, and Cæsar the other, though both were nobles.

Rivalship between Cæsar and Pompey.

Deplorable state of public affairs.

Both these generals had rendered great services. Pompey had subdued the East, and Cæsar the West. Pompey had more prestige, Cæsar more genius. Pompey was a greater tactician, Cæsar a greater strategist. Pompey was proud, pompous, jealous, patronizing, self-sufficient, disdainful. Cæsar was politic, intriguing, patient, lavish, unenvious, easily approached, forgiving, with great urbanity and most genial manners. Both were ambitious, unscrupulous, and selfish. Cicero distrusted both, flattered each by turns, but inclined to the side of Pompey as more conservative, and less dangerous. The Senate took the side of Pompey, the people that of Cæsar. Both Cæsar and Pompey had enjoyed power so long, that neither would have been contented with private life.

In the year B. C. 49, Cæsar's proconsular imperium was to terminate one year after the close of the Gallic war. He wished to be re-elected consul, and also secure his triumph. But he could not, according to law, have the triumph without disbanding the army, and without an army he would not be safe at Rome, with so many enemies. Neither could he be elected consul, according to the forms, while he enjoyed his imperium, for it had long been the custom that no one could sue for the consulship at the head of an army. He, therefore, could neither be consul nor enjoy a triumph, legitimately, without disbanding his army. Moreover, the party of Pompey, being then in the ascendant at Rome, demanded that Cæsar should lay down his imperium. The tribunes, in the interests of Cæsar, opposed the decree of the Senate; the reigning consuls threatened the tribunes, and they fled to Cæsar's camp in Cisalpine Gaul. It should, however, be mentioned, that when the consul Marcellus, an enemy of Cæsar, proposed in the Senate that he should lay down his command, Curio, the tribune, whose debts Cæsar had paid, moved that Pompey should do the same; which he refused to do, since the election of Cæsar to the consulship would place the whole power of the republic in his hands. Cæsar made a last effort to avoid the inevitable war, by proposing to the Senate to lay down his command, if Pompey would also; but Pompey prevaricated, and the compromise came to nothing. Both generals distrusted each other, and both were disloyal to the State. The Senate then appointed a successor to Cæsar in Gaul, ordered a general levy of troops throughout Italy, and voted money and men to Pompey. Cæsar had already crossed the Rubicon, which was high treason, before his last proposal to compromise, and he was on his way to Rome. No one resisted him, for the people had but little interest in the success of either party. Pompey, exaggerating his popularity, thought he had only to stamp the ground, and an army would appear, and when he discovered that his rival was advancing on the Flaminican way,

The Senate demands the abdication of Cæsar.

Cæsar seeks a compromise.

Rejected by Pompey.

fled hastily from Rome with most of the senators, and went to Brundusium. Cæsar did not at once seize the capital, but followed Pompey, and so vigorously attacked him, that he quit the town and crossed over to Illyricum. Cæsar had no troops to pursue him, and, therefore retraced his steps, and entered Rome, after an absence of ten years, at the head of a victorious army, undisputed master of Italy.

Cæsar pursues Pompey.

But Pompey still controlled his proconsular province of Spain, where seven legions were under his lieutenants, and Africa also was occupied by his party. Cæsar, after arranging the affairs of Italy, marched through Gaul into Spain to fight the generals of Pompey. That campaign was ended in forty days, and he became master of Spain. While in Spain he was elected to his second consulship, and also made dictator. He returned to Rome as rapidly as he had marched into Spain, and enacted some wholesome laws, among others that by which the inhabitants of Cisalpine Gaul, the northern part of Italy, obtained citizenship. After settling the general affairs of Italy, he laid down the dictatorship, and went to Brundusium, and collected his forces from various parts for a decisive conflict with Pompey, who had remained, meanwhile, in Macedonia, organizing his army. He collected nine legions, with auxiliary forces, while his fleet commanded the sea. He also secured vast magazines of corn in Thessaly, Asia, Egypt, Crete, and Cyrene.

Cæsar in Spain.

Cæsar was able to cross the sea with scarcely more than fifteen thousand men, on account of the insufficiency of his fleet, and he was thrown upon a hostile shore, cut off from supplies, and in presence of a vastly superior force. But his troops were veterans, and his cause was strengthened by the capture of Apollonia. He then advanced north to seize Dyrhachium, where Pompey's stores were deposited, but Pompey reached the town before him, and both armies encamped on the banks of the river Apsus, the one on the left and the other on the right bank. There Cæsar was joined by the remainder of his troops, brought over with

Military preparations.

great difficulty from Brundusium by Marcus Antonius, his most able lieutenant and devoted friend. Pompey was also re-enforced by two legions from Syria, led by his father-in-law, Scipio. Both parties abstained from attacking each other while these re-enforcements were being brought forward, and Cæsar even made a last effort at compromise, while the troops on each side exchanged mutual courtesies.

Battle of Dyrhachium.

Pompey avoided a pitched battle, and intrenched himself on a hill near Dyrhachium. Cæsar surrounded him with lines of circumvallation. Pompey broke through them, and compelled Cæsar to retire, with considerable loss. He retreated to Thessaly, followed by Pompey, who, had he known how to pursue his advantage, might, after this last success—the last he ever had—have defeated Cæsar. He had wisely avoided a pitched battle until his troops should become inured to service, or until he should wear out his adversary; but now, puffed up with victory and self-confidence, and unduly influenced by his officers, he concluded to risk a battle. Cæsar was encamped on the plain of Pharsalia, and Pompey on a hill about four miles distant. The steep bank of the river Enipeus covered the right of Pompey's line and the left of Cæsar's. The infantry of the former numbered forty-five thousand; that of the latter, twenty-two thousand, but they were veterans. Pompey was also superior in cavalry, having seven thousand, while Cæsar had only one thousand. With these, which formed the strength of Pompey's force, he proposed to outflank the right of Cæsar, extended on the plain. To guard against this movement, Cæsar withdrew six cohorts from his third line, and formed them into a fourth in the rear of his cavalry on the right. The battle commenced by a furious assault on the lines of Pompey by Cæsar's veterans, who were received with courage. Meanwhile Pompey's cavalry swept away that of Cæsar, and was advancing to attack the rear, when they received, unexpectedly, the charge of the cohorts which Cæsar had posted there. The cavalry broke, and fled to the mountains. The six cohorts then turned upon the slingers

Battle of Pharsalia.

and archers, who had covered the attack of the cavalry, defeated them, and fell upon the rear of Pompey's left. Cæsar then brought up his third line, and decided the battle. Pompey had fled when he saw the defeat of his cavalry. His camp was taken and sacked, and his troops, so confident of victory, were scattered, surrounded, and taken prisoners. Cæsar, with his usual clemency, spared their lives, nor had he any object to destroy them. Among those who surrendered after this decisive battle was Junius Brutus, who was not only pardoned, but admitted to the closest friendship.

Pompey, on his defeat, fled to Larissa, embarked with his generals, and sailed to Mitylene. As he had still the province of Africa and a large fleet, it was his policy to go there; but he had a silly notion that his true field of glory was the East, and he saw no place of refuge but Egypt. That kingdom was then governed by the children of Ptolemy Auletes, Cleopatra and Ptolemy, neither of whom were adults, and who, moreover, were quarreling with each other for the undivided sovereignty of Egypt. At this juncture, Pompey appeared on the coast, on which Ptolemy was encamped. He sent a messenger to the king, with the request that he might be sheltered in Alexandria. To grant it would compromise Ptolemy with Cæsar; to refuse it would send Pompey to the camp of Cleopatra in Syria. He was invited to a conference, and his minister Achillus was sent out in a boat to bring him on shore. Pompey, infatuated, imprudently trusted himself in the boat, in which he recognized an old comrade, Septimius, who, however, did not return his salutation. On landing, he was stabbed by Septimius, who had persuaded Ptolemy to take his life, in order to propitiate Cæsar and gain the Egyptian crown. Thus ingloriously fell the conqueror of Asia, and the second man in the empire, by treachery.

Flight of Pompey to Egypt.

Pompey assassinated.

On the flight of Pompey from the fatal battle-field, Cæsar pressed in pursuit, with only one legion and a troop of cavalry. Fearing a new war in Asia, Cæsar waited to collect his forces, and then embarked for Egypt.

Cæsar in Egypt.

He arrived at Alexandria only a few days after the murder of his rival, and was met by an officer bearing his head. He ordered it to be burned with costly spices, and placed the ashes in a shrine, dedicated to Nemesis. He then demanded ten million drachmas, promised by the late king, and summoned the contending sovereigns to his camp. Cleopatra captivated him, and he decided that both should share the throne, but that the ministers of Ptolemy should be deposed, which was reducing the king to a cipher. But the fanaticism of the Alexandrians being excited, and a collision having taken place between them and his troops, Cæsar burned the Egyptian fleet, and fortified himself at Pharos, awaiting re-enforcements. Ptolemy, however, turned against him, when he had obtained his release, and perished in an action on the banks of the Nile. Cleopatra was restored to the throne, under the protection of Rome.

Eastern conquests.

Pharnaces, son of Mithridates, rewarded by Pompey with the throne of the Bosphorus for the desertion of his father, now made war against Rome. Galvinus, sent against him, sustained a defeat, and Cæsar rapidly marched to Asia to restore affairs. It was then he wrote to the Senate that brief, but vaunting letter: "*Veni, vidi, vici.*" He already meditated those conquests in the East which had inflamed the ambition of his rival. He caught the spirit of Oriental despotism. He was not proof against the flatteries of the Asiatics. But his love for Cleopatra worked a still greater change in his character, even as it undermined the respect of his countrymen. History brands with infamy that unfortunate connection, which led to ostentation, arrogance, harshness, impatience, and contempt of mankind—the same qualities which characterized Napoleon on his return from Egypt.

Pharnaces.

In September, B. C. 47, Cæsar returned to Italy, having been already named dictator by a defeated and obsequious Senate. Cicero was among the first to meet him, and was graciously pardoned. The only severe measure which he would allow was the confiscation of the

Dictatorship of Cæsar.

property of Pompey and his sons, whose statues, however, he replaced. He now ruled absolutely, but under the old forms, and was made tribune for life. The Senate nominated him consul for five years, and he was also named dictator.

The only foes who now seriously stood out against him were the adherents of Pompey, who had time, during his absence in the East, to reorganize their forces, and it was in Africa that the last conflict was to be fought. The Pompeians were commanded by Scipio, who fixed his head-quarters at Hadrumentum, with an army of ten legions, a large force of Numidian cavalry, and one hundred and twenty elephants. But Cæsar defeated this large army with a vastly inferior force, and the rout was complete. Scipio took ship for Spain, but was driven back, as Marius had been on the Italian coasts when pursued by the generals of Sulla, and ended his life by suicide. Cato, the noblest Roman of his day, whose march across the African desert was one of the great feats of his age, might have escaped, and would probably have been pardoned: but the lofty stoic could not endure the sight of the prostration of Roman liberties, and, fortifying his courage with the *Phœdon* of Plato, also fell upon his sword. The Roman republic ended with his death.

Cato.

After reducing Numidia to a Roman province, Cæsar returned to Italy with immense treasures, and was everywhere received with unexampled honors. At Rome he celebrated a fourfold triumph—for victories in Gaul, Egypt, Africa, and the East—and the Senate decreed that his image in ivory should be carried in procession with those of the gods. His bronze statue was set upon a globe in the capitol, as the emblem of universal sovereignty. All the extravagant enthusiasm which marked the French people for the victories of Napoleon, and all the servility which unbounded power everywhere commands, were bestowed upon the greatest conqueror the ancient world ever saw. A thanksgiving was decreed for forty days; the number of the lictors was doubled; he was made dictator for ten years, with the command of all the armies of the State,

Triumph of Cæsar.

The vast power of Cæsar.

and the presidency of the public festivals. He also was made censor for three years, by which he regulated the Senate according to his sovereign will. His triumphs were followed by profuse largesses to the soldiers and people, and he also instituted magnificent games under an awning of silk, at the close of which the *Forum Julium* was dedicated.

Such were his unparalleled honors and powers. All the great offices of the State were invested and united in him, and nothing was wanted to complete his aggrandizement but the name of emperor. But we turn from these, the usual rewards of conquerors, to glance at the services he rendered to civilization, which constitute his truest claim to immortality. One of the greatest was the reform of the calendar, for the Roman year was ninety days in advance of the true meaning of that word. The old year had been determined by lunar months rather than by the apparent path of the sun among the fixed stars which had been determined by the ancient astronomers, and was one of the greatest discoveries of ancient science. The Roman year consisted of three hundred and fifty-five days, so that January was an autumn month. Cæsar inserted the regular intercalary month of twenty-three days, and two additional ones of sixty-seven days. These were added to the three hundred and sixty-five days, making a year of transition of four hundred and forty-five days, by which January was brought back to the first month of the year, after the winter solstace. And to prevent the repetition of the error, he directed that in future the year should consist of three hundred and sixty-five days and one quarter of a day, which he effected by adding one day to the months of April, June, September, and November, and two days to the months of January, Sextilis, and December, making an addition of ten days to the old year of three hundred and fifty-five, and he provided for a uniform intercalation of one day in every fourth year. Cæsar was a student of astronomy, and always found time for its contemplation. He even wrote an essay on the motion of the stars, assisted in his observation by Sosigenes, an Alex

The Julian calendar.

andrian astronomer. He took astronomy out of the hands of priests, and made it a matter of civil legislation. He was drawn away from legislation to draw the sword once more against the relics of the Pompeian party, which had been collected in Spain. On the field of Munda was fought his last great battle, contested with unusual fury, and attended with savage cruelties. Thirty thousand of his opponents fell in this battle, and Sextus Pompey alone, of all the marked men, escaped to the mountains, and defied pursuit. On this victory he celebrated his last triumph, and the supple Senate decreed to him the title of Imperator. He was made consul for ten years, dictator for life, his person was decreed inviolable, and he was surrounded by a guard of nobles and senators. He also received the insignia of royalty, a golden chair and a diadem set with gems, and was allowed to wear the triumphal robe of purple whenever he appeared in public. The coins were stamped with his image, his statue was placed in the temples, and his friends obtained all the offices of the State. He adopted Octavius, his nephew, for his heir, and paved the way for an absolute despotism under his successors. The measure of his glory and ambition was full. He was the undisputed master of the world.

Last battle of Cæsar.

He then continued his reforms and improvements, as Napoleon did after his coronation as emperor. He gave the Roman franchise to various States and cities out of Italy, and colonized new cities. He excluded *judices* from all ranks but those of senators and knights, and enacted new laws for the security of persons and property. He gave unbounded religious toleration, and meditated a complete codification of the Roman law. He founded a magnificent public library, appointed commissioners to make a map of the whole empire, and contemplated the draining of the Pontine marshes.

After these works of legislation and public improvement, he prepared for an expedition to Parthia, in which he hoped to surpass the conquests of Alexander in the East. But his career was suddenly cut off by his premature death. The nobles whom he humiliated, and the Oriental despotism he contemplated, caused a secret hostility which he did not suspect amid the universal subserviency to his will. Above all, the title of king, the symbol of legitimate sovereignty, to which he aspired, sharpened the daggers of the few remaining friends of the liberty which had passed away for ever. All the old party of the State concocted the conspiracy, some eighty nobles, at the head of which were Brutus and Cassius.

Death of Cæsar.

On the fifteenth day of March, B. C. 44, the Ides of March, the day for which the Senate was convened for his final departure for the East, he was stabbed in the senate-house, and he fell, pierced with wounds, at the foot of Pompey's statue, in his fifty-sixth year, and anarchy, and new wars again commenced.

The concurrent voices of all historians and critics unite to give Cæsar the most august name of all antiquity. He was great in every thing,—as orator, as historian, as statesman, as general, and as lawgiver. He had genius, understanding, memory, taste, industry, and energy. He could write, read, and dictate at the same time. He united the bravery of Alexander with the military resources of Hannibal. He had a marvelous faculty of winning both friends and enemies. He was generous, magnanimous, and courteous. Not even his love for Cleopatra impaired the energies of his mind and body. He was not cruel or sanguinary, except when urged by reasons of State. He pardoned Cicero, and received Brutus into intimate friendship. His successes were transcendent, and his fortune never failed him. He reached the utmost limit of human ambition, and was only hurled from his pedestal of power by the secret daggers of fanatics, who saw in his elevation the utter extinction of Roman liberty. But liberty had already fled, and a degenerate age could only be ruled by a despot. It might have been better for Rome had his life been prolonged when all constitutional freedom had become impossible. But he took the sword, and Nemesis demanded that he should perish by it, as a warning to all future usurpers who would accomplish even good ends by infamous means. Vulgar pity compassionates

Character of Cæsar.

the sad fate of the great Julius; but we can not forget that it was he who gave the last blow to the constitution and liberties of his country. The greatness of his gifts and services pale before the gigantic crime of which he stands accused at the bar of all the ages, and the understanding of the world is mocked when his usurpation is justified.

CHAPTER XLI.

THE CIVIL WARS FOLLOWING THE DEATH OF CÆSAR.—ANTONIUS.—AUGUSTUS.

THE assassination of Cæsar was not immediately followed with the convulsions which we should naturally expect. The people were weary of war, and sighed for repose, and, moreover, were comparatively indifferent on whom the government fell, since their liberties were hopelessly prostrated. Only one thing was certain, that power would be usurped by some one, and most probably by the great chieftains who represented Cæsar's interests.

Great men of Rome at this time.

The most powerful men in Rome at this time, were Marcus Antonius, the most able of Cæsar's lieutenants, the most constant of his friends, and the nearest of his relatives, although a man utterly unprincipled; Octavius, grandson of Julius, whom Cæsar adopted as his heir, a young man of nineteen; Lepidus, colleague consul with Cæsar, the head of the ancient family of the Lepidi, thirteen of whom had been honored with curule magistracies; Sextus Pompeius, son of Pompey; Brutus and Cassius, chief conspirators; Dolabella, a man of consular rank, and one of the profligate nobles of his time; Hirtia and Pansa, consuls; Piso, father-in-law of Cæsar, of a powerful family, which boasted of several consuls; and Cicero—still influential from his great weight of character. All these men were great nobles, and had filled the highest offices.

The man who, to all appearance, had the fairest chance for supreme command in those troubled times, was Antony, whose mother was Julia, Cæsar's sister. He was grandson to the great orator M. Antonius, who flourished during the civil wars between Marius and Sulla, and was distinguished for every vice, folly, and extravagance which characterized the Roman nobles. But he was a man of consummate ability as a general, was master of the horse, and was consul with Cæsar, when he was killed, B. C. 44. He was also eloquent, and pronounced the funeral oration of the murdered Imperator, as nearest of kin. He had possession of Cæsar's papers, and was the governor of Cisalpine Gaul. He formed a union with Lepidus, to whom he offered the office of Pontifex Maximus, the second office in the State. As consul, he could unlock the public treasury, which he rifled to the extent of seven hundred million of sesterces—the vast sum left by Cæsar. One of his brothers was prætor, and another, a tribune. He convened the Senate, and employed, by the treasure he had at command, the people to overawe the Senate, as the Jacobin clubs of the French revolution overawed the Assembly. He urged the Senate to ratify Cæsar's acts and confirm his appointments, and in this was supported by Cicero and a majority of the members. Now that the deed was done, he wished to have the past forgotten. This act of amnesty confirmed his fearful pre-eminence, and the inheritance of the mighty dead seemingly devolved upon him. The conspirators came to terms with him, and were even entertained by him, and received the provinces which he assigned to them. Brutus received Macedonia; Cassius, Syria; Trebonius, Asia; Cimber, Bythinia; and Decimus, Cisalpine Gaul. Dolabella was his colleague in the consulship,—a personal enemy, yet committed to his policy.

Antonius takes the lead at Rome.

Cæsar had left three hundred sesterces to every citizen, (about £3,) and his gardens beyond the Tiber to the use of the people. Such gifts operated in producing an intense gratitude for the memory of a man who had proved so great a benefactor, and his public funeral was of unprecedented splendor. Antony, as his nearest heir, and the first magistrate, pronounced the oration, which was a consummate piece of dramatic art, in which he inflamed the passions of the people, and stimulated them to frenzy, so that they turned upon the assassins with fury. But he assured the Senate of his moderation, abolished the dictatorship forever, and secured his own personal safety by a body-guard.

Octavius.

He had, however, a powerful rival in the young Octavius, who had been declared by Cæsar's will his principal heir, then absent in Apollonia. He resolved to return at once and claim his inheritance, and was warmly received at Brundusium by the veteran troops, and especially by Cicero, who saw in him a rival to Antony. Octavius flattered the old orator, and ingratiated himself in the favor of everybody by his unassuming manners, and his specious language. He entered Rome under favorable omens, paid his court to the senators, and promised to fulfill his uncle's requests. He was received by Antony in the gardens of Pompeius, and claimed at once his inheritance. Antony replied that it was not private property but the public treasure, and was, moreover, spent. Octavius was not to be put off, and boldly declared that he would and could pay the legacies, and contrived to borrow the money. Such an act secured unrivaled popularity. He gave magnificent shows, and then claimed that the jeweled crown of Cæsar should be exhibited on the festival which he instituted to Venus, and to whose honor Cæsar had vowed to build a temple, on the morning of his victory at Pharsalia. The tribunes, instigated by Antonius, refused to sanction this mark of honor, but fortune favored Octavius, and, in the enthusiasm of the festival, which lasted eleven days, the month Quintilus was changed to Julius—the first demigod whom the Senate had translated to Olympus.

Brutus and Cassius.

Meanwhile Brutus and Cassius retired from public affairs, lingering in the neighborhood of Rome, and the provinces promised to them were lost. At Antium they had an interview with Cicero, who advised them to keep quiet, and not venture to the capital, where the people were inflamed against them. Their only encouragement was the successes of Sextus Pompeius in Spain, who had six legions at his command. Cicero foresaw that another civil war was at hand, and had the gloomiest forebodings, for one or the other of the two great chieftains of the partisans of Cæsar was sure of ultimately obtaining the supreme power. The humiliating conviction that the murder of Cæsar was a mistake, was now deeply impressed upon his mind, since it would necessarily inaugurate another bloody war. Self-banished from Rome, this great and true patriot wandered from place to place to divert his mind. But neither the fascinations of literature, nor the attractions of Tusculum, Puteoli, Pompeii, and Neapolis, where he had luxurious villas, could soothe his anxious and troubled soul. Religious, old, and experienced, he could only ponder on the coming and final prostration of that cause of constitutional liberty to which he was devoted.

Antonius, also aware of the struggle which was impending, sought to obtain the government of Cisalpine Gaul, and of the six legions destined for the Parthian war. But he was baffled by the Senate, and by the intrigues of Octavius, who sheltered himself behind the august name of the man by whom he had been adopted. He therefore made a hollow reconciliation with Octavius, and by his means, obtained the Gaulish provinces. Cicero, now only desirous to die honorably, returned to Rome to accept whatever fate was in store for him, and defend to the last his broken cause. It was then, in the Senate, that he launched forth those indignant philippics against Antonius, as a public enemy, which are among his greatest efforts, and which most triumphantly attest his moral courage.

Cicero.

The hollow reconciliation between Antonius and Octavius was not of long duration, and the former, as consul, repaired to Brundusium to assume command of the legions stationed there, and Octavius collected his forces in Campania. Both parties complained of each other, and both invoked the name of Cæsar. Cicero detested the one, and was blinded as to the other.

The term of office as consul, which Antonius held, had now

expired, and Hirtius, one of the new consuls, marched into Cisalpine Gaul, and Octavius placed himself under his command. The Senate declared a state of public danger. The philippics of Cicero had taken effect, and the Senate and the government were now opposed to Antonius, as the creator of a new revolution. The consuls crossed swords with Antonius at Forum Gallorum, and the consul Pansa fell, but success was with the government. Another success at Mutina favored the government party, which Octavius had joined. On the news of this victory, Cicero delivered his fourteenth and last philippic against Antonius, who now withdrew from Cisalpine Gaul, and formed a junction with Lepidus beyond the Alps. Octavius declined to pursue him, and Plancus hesitated to attack him, although joined by Decimus, one of the murderers of Cæsar, with ten legions. Octavius now held aloof from the government army, from which it was obvious that he had ambitious views of his own to further, and was denounced by Plancus to Cicero. The veteran statesman, at last, perceived that Octavius, having deserted Decimus (who, of all the generals, was the only one on whose fidelity the State could securely lean), was not to be further relied upon, and cast his eyes to Macedonia and Syria, to which provinces Brutus and Cassius had retired. The Senate, too, now distrusted Octavius, and treated him with contumely; but supported by veteran soldiers, he demanded the consulship, and even secretly corresponded with Antonius, and assured him of his readiness to combine with him and Lepidus, and invited them to follow him to Rome. He marched at the head of eight legions, pretending all the while to be coerced by them. The Senate, overawed, allowed him, at twenty years of age, to assume the consulship, with Pedius, grand-nephew of Cæsar, for his colleague. Since Hirtius and Pansa had both fallen, Octavius, then leaving the city in the hands of a zealous colleague, opened negotiations with Antonius and Lepidus, perceiving that it was only in conjunction with them that his usurpation could be maintained. They met

Prospects of civil war.

Situation of Roman affairs.

for negotiations at Bononia, and agreed to share the empire between them. They declared themselves triumvirs for the settlement of the commonwealth, and after a conference of three days, divided between themselves the provinces and legions. They then concerted a general proscription of their enemies. The number whom they thus doomed to destruction was three hundred senators and two thousand knights, from the noblest families of Rome, among whom were brothers, uncles, and favorite officers. The possession of riches was fatal to some, and of beautiful villas to others. Cicero was among this number, as was to be expected, for he had exhausted the Latin language in vituperations of Antonius, whom he hated beyond all other mortals, and which hatred was itself a passion. He spoke of Cæsar with awe, of Pompey with mortification, of Crassus with dislike, and of Antony with bitter detestation and unsparing malice. It was impossible that he could escape, even had he fled to the ends of the earth. The vacillation of his last hours, his deep distress, and mournful agonies are painted by Plutarch. He fell a martyr to the cause of truth, and public virtue, and exalted patriotism, although his life was sullied by weakness and infirmities, such as vanity, ambition, and jealousy. In the dark and wicked period which he adorned by his transcendent talents and matchless services, he lived and died in faith —the most amiable and the most noble of all his contemporaries.

The triumvirate of Antonius, Octavius, and Lepidus.

They proscribe their enemies.

The triumvirs had now gratified their vengeance by a series of murders never surpassed in the worst ages of religious and political fanaticism. And all these horrible crimes were perpetrated in the name of that great and august character who had won the world by his sword. The prestige of that mighty name sanctioned their atrocities and upheld their power. Cæsar still lived, although assassinated, and the triumvirs reigned as his heirs or avengers, even as Louis Napoleon grasped the sceptre of his uncle, not from any services *he* had rendered, but as the heir of his conquests.

The Romans loved Cæsar as the French loved Napoleon, and submitted to the rule of the triumvirs, as the French submitted to the usurpations of the proscribed prisoner of Ham. And in the anarchy which succeeded the assassination of the greatest man of antiquity, it must need be that the strongest would seize the reins, since all liberty and exalted patriotism had fled.

Cassius and Brutus rally the aristocracy.

But these usurpers did not secure their power without one more last struggle of the decimated and ruined aristocracy. They rallied under the standards of Brutus and Cassius in Macedonia and Syria. The one was at the head of eight legions, and the other of eleven, a still formidable force. Sextus Pompeius also still lived, and had intrenched himself in Sicily. A battle had still to be fought before the republic gave its last sigh. Cicero ought to have joined these forces, and might have done so, but for his vacillation. So Lepidus, as consul, took control of Rome and the interests of Italy, while Antonius marched against Brutus and Cassius in the East, and Octavius assailed Sextus in Sicily; unable, however, to attack him without ships, he joined his confederate. Their united forces were concentrated in Philippi, in Thrace, and there was fought the last decisive battle between the republicans, if the senatorial and aristocratic party under Brutus and Cassius can be called republicans, and the liberators, as they called themselves, or the adherents of Cæsar. The republicans had a force of eighty thousand infantry and twenty thousand cavalry, while the triumvirs commanded a still superior force. The numbers engaged in this great conflict exceeded all former experience, and the battle of Philippi was the most memorable in Roman annals, since all the available forces of the empire were now arrayed against each other. The question at issue was, whether power should remain with the old constitutional party, or with the party of usurpation which Cæsar had headed and led to victory. It was whether Rome should be governed by the old forms, or by an imperator with absolute authority.

Battle of Philippi.

The forces arrayed on that fatal battle-field—the last conflict for liberty ever fought at Rome—were three times as great as fought at Pharsalia. On that memorable battle-field the republic perished. The battle was fairly and bravely fought on both sides, but victory inclined to the Cæsarians, in two distinct actions, after an interval of twenty days, B. C. 42. Both Cassius and Brutus fell on their own swords, and their self-destruction, in utter despair of their cause, effectually broke up their party.

The empire was now in the hands of the triumvirs. The last contest was decisive. Future struggles were worse than useless. Destiny had proclaimed the extinction of Roman liberties for ever. It was vice and faction which had prepared the way for violence, and the last appeal to the sword had settled the fate of the empire, henceforth to be governed by a despot.

Roman liberty extinguished.

But there being now three despots among the partisans of Cæsar, who sought to grasp his sceptre, Which should prevail? Antonius was the greatest general; Octavius was the greatest man; Lepidus was the tool of both. The real rivalry was between Octavius and Antonius. But they did not at once quarrel. Antonius undertook the subjugation of the eastern provinces, and Octavius repaired to Rome. The former sought, before the great encounter with his rival, to gain military *éclat* from new victories; the latter to control factions and parties in the capital. They first got rid of Lepidus, now that their more powerful enemies were subdued, and compelled him to surrender the command in Italy and content himself with the government of Africa. Antonius, commanding no less than twenty-eight legions, which, with auxiliaries, numbered one hundred and seventy thousand, had perhaps the best chance. His exactions were awful; but he squandered his treasures, and gave vent to his passions.

The real cause of his overthrow was Cleopatra, for had he not been led aside by his inordinate passion for this woman, and had he exercised his vast power with the wisdom and ability which he had previously shown,

Cleopatra and Antonius.

the most able of all of Cæsar's generals, he probably would have triumphed over every foe. On his passage through Cilicia, he was met by Cleopatra, in all the pomp and luxury of an Oriental sovereign. She came to deprecate his wrath, ostensibly, and ascended the Cydnus in a bark with gilded stern and purple sails, rowed with silver oars, to the sound of pipes and flutes. She reclined, the most voluptuous of ancient beauties, under a spangled canopy, attended by Graces and Cupids, while the air was scented with the perfumes of Olympus. She soon fascinated the most powerful man in the empire, who, forgetting his ambition, resigned himself to love. Octavius, master of himself, and of Italy, confiscated lands for the benefit of the soldiers, and prepared for future contingencies. Though Antonius married Octavia, the sister of Octavius, he was full of intrigues against him; and Octavius, on his part, proved more than a match in duplicity and concealed hostilities. They, however, pretended to be friends; and the treaty of Brundusium, celebrated by Virgil, would seem to indicate that the world was now to enjoy the peace it craved. After a debauch, Antonius left Rome for the East, and Octavius for Gaul, each with a view of military conquests. Antonius, with his new wife, had seemingly forgotten Cleopatra, and devoted himself to the duties of the camp with an assiduity worthy of Cæsar himself. Octavius has a naval conflict with Sextus, and is defeated, but Sextus fails to profit from his victory, and Octavius, with the help of his able lieutenants, and re-enforced by Antonius, again attacks Sextus, and is again defeated. In a third conflict he is victorious, and Sextus escapes to the East. Lepidus, ousted and cheated by both Antonius and Octavius, now combines with Sextus and the Pompeians, and makes head against Octavius; but is deserted by his soldiers, and falls into the hands of his enemy, who spares his life in contempt. He had owed his elevation to his family influence, and not to his own abilities. Sextus, at last, was taken and slain.

War between Octavius and Sextus.

At this juncture Octavius was at the head of the Cæsarian

party. He had won the respect and friendship of the Romans by his clemency and munificence. He was not a great general, but he was served by a great general, Agrippa, and by another minister of equal talents, Mecænas. He controlled even more forces than Antonius, no less than forty-five legions of infantry, and twenty-five thousand cavalry, and thirty-seven thousand light-armed auxiliaries. Antonius, on the other hand, had forfeited the esteem of the Romans by his prodigalities, by his Oriental affectations, and by his slavery to Cleopatra.

This artful and accomplished woman again met Antonius in Asia, and resumed her sway. The general of one hundred battles became effeminated by his voluptuous dalliance, so that his Parthian campaign was a failure, even though he led an army of one hundred thousand men. He was obliged to retreat, and his retreat was disastrous. It was while he was planning another campaign that Octavia, his wife, and the sister of his rival,—a woman who held the most dignified situation in the world,—brought to his camp both money and troops, and hoped to allay the jealousies of her husband, and secure peace between him and her brother. But Antonius heartlessly refused to see this noble-minded woman, while he gave provinces to Cleopatra. At Alexandria this abandoned profligate plunged, with his paramour, into every excess of extravagant debauchery, while she who enslaved him only dreamed of empire and domination. She may have loved him, but she loved power more than she did debauchery. Her intellectual accomplishments were equal to her personal fascinations, and while she beguiled the sensual Roman with costly banquets, her eye was steadily directed to the establishment of her Egyptian throne.

The rupture which Octavia sought to prevent between her brother and her husband—for, with the rarest magnanimity she still adhered to him in spite of his infatuated love for Cleopatra—at last took place, when Octavius was triumphant over Sextus, and Antonius was unsuccessful in the distant East. Octavius declared war against the queen of Egypt, and Antonius divorced Octavia. Throughout the winter of B. C. 31, both parties prepared for the inevitable conflict, for Rome now could have but one master. The fate of the empire was to be settled, not by land forces, but a naval battle, and that was fought at Actium, not now with equal forces, for those of Antonius had been weakened by desertions. Moreover, he rejected the advice of his ablest generals, and put himself under the guidance of his mistress, while Octavius listened to the counsels of Agrippa.

The battle had scarcely begun before Cleopatra fled, followed by Antonius. The destruction of the Antonian fleet was the consequence. This battle, B. C. 31, gave the empire of the world to Octavius, and Antonius fled to Alexandria with the woman who had ruined him. And it was well that the empire fell into the hands of a politic and profound statesman, who sought to consolidate it and preserve its peace, rather than into those of a debauched general, with insatiable passions and blood-thirsty vengeance. The victor landed in Egypt, while the lovers abandoned themselves to despair. Antonius, on the rumor of Cleopatra's death, gave himself a mortal wound, but died in the arms of her for whom he had sacrificed fame, fortune, and life. Cleopatra, in the interview which Octavius sought at Alexandria, attempted to fascinate him by those arts by which she had led astray both Cæsar and Antonius, but the cold and politic conqueror was unmoved, and coldly demanded the justification of her political career, and reserved her to grace his future triumph. She eluded his vigilance, and destroyed herself, as is supposed, by the bite of asps, since her dead body showed none of the ordinary spots of poison. She died, B. C. 30, in the fortieth year of her age, and was buried as a queen by the side of her lover. Her son Cæsarion, by Julius Cæsar, was also put to death, and then the master of the world "wiped his blood-stained sword, and thrust it into the scabbard." No more victims were needed. No rivalship was henceforth to be dreaded, and all opposition to his will had ceased.

Octavius reduced Egypt to the form of a Roman province,

and after adjusting the affairs of the East, among which was the confirmation of Herod as sovereign of Judea, he returned to Rome to receive his new honors, and secure his undivided sovereignty. Peace was given to the world at last. The imperator dedicated temples to the gods, and gave games and spectacles to the people. The riches of all previous conquests were his to dispose and enjoy—the extent of which may be conjectured from the fact that Cæsar alone had seized an amount equal to one hundred and seventy million pounds, not reckoning the relative value to gold in these times. Divine honors were rendered to Octavius as the heir of Cæsar. He assumed the prænomen of imperator, but combined in himself all the great offices of the republic which had been overturned. As censor, he purged and controlled the Senate, of which he was appointed *princeps*, or chief. As consul he had the control of the armies of the State; as perpetual proconsul over all the provinces of the empire, he controlled their revenues, their laws, their internal reforms, and all foreign relations. As tribune for life, he initiated legal measures before the Comitia of the tribes; as Pontifex Maximus, he had the regulation of all religious ceremonials. All these great offices were voted him by a subservient people. The only prerogative which remained to them was the making of laws, but even this great and supreme power he controlled, by assuming the initiation of all laws and measures,—that which Louis Napoleon has claimed in the Corps Législatif. He had also resorted to edicts, which had the force of laws, and ultimately composed no small part of the Roman jurisprudence. Finally, he assumed the name of Cæsar, as he had of Augustus, and consummated the reality of despotism by the imposing title of imperator, or emperor.

CHAPTER XLII.

THE ROMAN EMPIRE ON THE ACCESSION OF AUGUSTUS.

OCTAVIUS, now master of the world, is generally called Augustus Cæsar—the name he assumed. He was the first of that great line of potentates whom we call emperors. Let us, before tracing the history of the empire, take a brief survey of its extent, resources, population, institutions, state of society, and that development of art, science, and literature, which we call civilization, in the period which immediately preceded the birth of Christ, when the nations were subdued, submissive to the one central power, and at peace with each other.

Prosperity of the empire.

The empire was not so large as it subsequently became, nor was it at that height of power and prosperity which followed a century of peace, when uninterrupted dominion had reconciled the world to the rule of the Cæsars. But it was the golden age of imperial domination, when arts, science, and literature flourished, and when the world rested from incessant wars. It was not an age of highest glory to man, since all struggles for liberty had ceased; but it was an age of good government, when its machinery was perfected, and the great mass of mankind felt secure, and all classes abandoned themselves to pleasure, or gain, or uninterrupted toils. It was the first time in the history of the world, when there was only *one* central authority, and when the experiment was to be tried, not of liberty and self-government, but of universal empire, growing up from universal rivalries and wars—wielded by one central and irresistible will. The spectacle of the civilized world obedient to *one* master has sublimity, and moral grandeur, and suggests principles of grave interest. The last of the great monarchies which revelation had foretold, and the greatest of all—the iron monarchy which Daniel saw in prophetic vision, reveals lessons of profound significance.

The empire then embraced all the countries bordering on the Mediterranean—that great inland sea upon whose shores the most famous cities of antiquity flourished, and toward which the tide of Assyrian and Persian conquests had rolled, and then retreated for ever. The boundaries of this mighty empire were great mountains, and deserts, and oceans, and impenetrable forests. On the east lay the Parthian empire, separated from the Roman by the Tigris and Euphrates, and the Armenian Mountains, beyond which were other great empires not known to the Greeks, like the Indian and the Chinese monarchies, with a different civilization. On the south were the African deserts, not penetrated even by travelers. On the west was the ocean; and on the north were barbaric tribes of different names and races—Slavonic, Germanic, and Celtic. The empire extended over a territory of one million six hundred thousand square miles, and among its provinces were Spain, Gaul, Sicily, Africa, Egypt, Syria, Asia Minor, Achaia, Macedonia, and Illyricum—all tributary to Italy, whose capital was Rome. The central province numbered four millions who were free, and could furnish, if need be, seven hundred thousand foot, and seventy thousand horse for the armies of the republic. It was dotted with cities, and villages, and villas, and filled with statues, temples, and works of art, brought from remotest provinces—the spoil of three hundred years of conquest. In all the provinces were great cities, once famous and independent—centres of luxury and wealth—Corinth, Athens, Syracuse, Carthage, Alexandria, Antioch, Ephesus, Damascus, and Jerusalem, with their dependent cities, all connected with each other and the capital by granite roads, all favored by commerce, all rejoicing in a uniform government. Rome, the great mistress who ruled over one hundred and twenty millions, contained an immense popula-

Extent of the empire.

Cities of the empire.

tion, variously estimated, in which were centred whatever wealth or power had craved. This capital had become rapidly ornamented with palaces, and temples, and works of art, with the subjugation of Greece and Asia Minor, although it did not reach the climax of magnificence until the time of Hadrian. In the time of Augustus, the most imposing buildings were the capitol, restored by Sulla and Cæsar, whose gilded roof alone cost $15,000,000. The theatre of Pompey could accommodate eighty thousand spectators, behind which was a portico of one hundred pillars. Cæsar built the Forum Julium, three hundred and forty feet long, and two hundred wide, and commenced the still greater structures known as the Basilica Julia and Curia Julia. The Forum Romanum was seven hundred feet by four hundred and seventy, surrounded with basilica, halls, porticoes, temples, and shops—the centre of architectural splendor, as well as of life and business and pleasure. Augustus restored the Capitoline Temple, finished the Forum and Basilica Julia, built the Curia Julia, and founded the imperial palace on the Palatine, and erected many temples, the most beautiful of which was that of Apollo, with columns of African marble, and gates of ivory finely sculptured. He also erected the Forum Augusti, the theatre of Marcellus, capable of holding twenty thousand spectators, and that mausoleum which contained the ashes of the imperial family to the time of Hadrian, at the entrance of which were two Egyptian obelisks. It was the boast of this emperor, that he found the city of brick and left her of marble. But great and beautiful as Rome was in the Augustan era, enriched not only by his own munificence, but by the palaces and baths which were erected by his ministers and courtiers,—the Pantheon, the Baths of Agrippa, the Gardens of Mæcenas,—it was not until other emperors erected the Imperial Palace, the Flavian Amphitheatre, the Forum Trajanun, the Basilica Ulpia, the Temple of Venus and Rome, the Baths of Caracalla, the Arches of Septimius Severus and Trajan, and other wonders, that the city became so astonishing a wonder, with its pal-

Magnificence of Rome.

aces, theatres, amphitheatres, baths, fountains, bronze statues of emperors and generals, so numerous and so grand, that we are warranted in believing its glories, like its population, surpassed those of both Paris and London combined.

The imperial master.

And this capital and this empire seemed to be the domain of one man, so vast his power, so august his dignity, absolute master of the lives and property of one hundred and twenty millions, for the people were now deprived of the election of magistrates and the creation of laws. How could the greatest nobles otherwise than cringe to the supreme captain of the armies, the prince of the Senate, and the high-priest of the national divinities—himself, the recipient of honors only paid to gods! But Augustus kept up the forms of the old republic—all the old offices, the old dignities, the old festivals, the old associations. The Senate, prostrate and powerless, still had external dignity, like the British House of Peers. There were six hundred senators, each of whom possessed more than one million two hundred thousand sesterces—about $50,000, when that sum must have represented an amount equal to a million of dollars in gold, at the present time, and some of whom had an income of one thousand pounds a day, the spoil of the provinces they had administered.

Roman Senate.

The Roman Senate, so august under the republic, still continued, with crippled legislative powers, to wield important functions, since the ordinary official business was performed by them. The provinces were governed by men selected from senatorial ranks. They wore the badges of distinction; they had the best places in the circus and theatre; they banqueted in the capitol at the public charge; they claimed the right to elect emperors.

The equestrians.

The equestrian order also continued to farm the revenues of the provinces, and to furnish judges. The knights retained external decorations, were required to possess property equal to one-third of the senators, and formed an aristocratic class.

The consuls, too, ruled, but with delegated powers from the

emperor. They were his eyes, and ears, and voice, and hands; but neither political experience nor military services were required as qualifications of the office. They wore the wreath of laurel on their brow, the striped robe of white and purple, and were attended with lictors. All citizens made way for them, and dismounted when they passed, and rose in their presence. The prætors, too, continued to be the supreme judges, and the quæstors regulated the treasury. The tribunes existed also, but without their former independence. The prefect of the city was a new office, and overshadowed all other offices—appointed by the emperor as his lieutenant, his most efficient executive minister, his deputy in his absence from the city.

The consuls.

A standing army, ever the mark of despotism, became an imperial institution. At the head of this army were the prætorian guards, who protected the person of the emperor, and had double pay over that of the ordinary legionaries. They had a regular camp outside the city, and were always on hand to suppress tumults. Twenty-five legions were regarded as sufficient to defend the empire, and each legion was composed of six thousand one hundred foot and seven hundred and twenty-six horse. They were recruited with soldiers from the countries beyond Italy. Auxiliary troops were equal to the legions, and all together numbered three hundred and forty thousand—the standing army of the empire, stationed in the different provinces. Naval armaments were also established in the different seas and in great frontier rivers.

The army.

The revenue for this great force, and the general expenses of the government, were derived from the public domains, from direct taxes, from mines and quarries, from salt works, fisheries and forests, from customs and excise, from the succession to property, from enfranchisement of slaves.

The monarchy instituted by Augustus, in all but the name, was a political necessity. Pompey would have ruled as the instrument of the aristocracy, but he would only have been *primus inter pares;* Cæsar recognized

Policy of Augustus.

the people as the basis of sovereignty; Augustus based his power on an organized military establishment, of which he was the permanent head. All the soldiers swore personal fealty to him—all the officers were appointed by him, directly or indirectly. But he paid respect to ancient traditions, forms, and magistracies, especially to the dignity of the Senate, and thus vested his military power, which was his true power, under the forms of an aristocracy, which was the governing power before the constitution was subverted.

It need scarcely be said that the great mass of the people were indifferent to these political changes. The horrors of the Marian and Sullan revolutions, the struggles of Cæsar and Pompey, and the awful massacres of the triumvirs had alarmed and disgusted all classes, and they sought repose, security, and peace. Any government which would repress anarchy was, to them, the best. They wished to be spared from executions and confiscations. The great enfranchisement of foreign slaves, also, degraded the people, and made them indifferent to the masters who should rule over them. All races were mingled with Roman citizens. The spoliation of estates in the civil wars cast a blight on agriculture, and the population had declined from war and misery.

Institutions of Augustus.

Augustus, intrenched by military power, sought to revive not merely patrician caste, but religious customs, which had declined. Temples were erected, and the shrines of gods were restored. Marriage was encouraged, and the morals of the people were regulated by sumptuary laws. Severe penalties were enacted against celibacy, to which the people had been led by the increasing profligacy of the times, and the expenses of living. Restrictions were placed on the manumission of slaves. The personal habits of the imperator were simple, but dignified. His mansion on the Palatine was moderate in size. His dress was that of a senator, and woven by the hands of Livia and her maidens. He was courteous, sober, decorous, and abstemious. His guests were chosen for their social qualities. Virgil and Horace, plebeian poets, were received at his table, as well as

Pollio and Messala. He sought to guard morals, and revive ancient traditions. He was jealous only of those who would not flatter him. He freely spent money for games and festivals, and secured peace and plenty within the capital, where he reigned supreme. The people felicitated themselves on the appearance of unbounded prosperity, and servile poets sung the praises of the emperor as if he were a god.

Roman commerce.

And, to all appearance, Rome was the most favored spot upon the globe. Vast fleets brought corn from Gaul, Spain, Sicily, Sardinia, Africa, and Egypt, to feed the four millions of people who possessed the world. The capital was the emporium of all the luxuries of distant provinces. Spices from the East, ivory, cotton, silk, pearls, diamonds, gums thither flowed, as well as corn, oil, and wine. A vast commerce gave unity to the empire, and brought all the great cities into communication with each other and with Rome—the mighty mistress of lands and continents, the directress of armies, the builder of roads, the civilizer and conservator of all the countries which she ruled with her iron hand. There was general security to commerce, as well as property. There were order and law, wherever proconsular power extended. The great highways, built originally for military purposes, extending to every part of the empire, and crossing mountains and deserts, and forests and marshes, and studded with pillars and post-houses, contributed vastly to the civilization of the world.

Residences of the nobility.

At this time, Rome herself, though not so large and splendid as in subsequent periods, was the most attractive place on earth. Seven aqueducts already brought water to the city, some over stone arches, and some by subterranean pipes. The sepulchres of twenty generations lined the great roads which extended from the capital to the provinces. As these roads approached the city, they became streets, and the houses were dense and continuous. The seven original hills were covered with palaces and temples, while the valleys were centres of a great population, in which were the forums, the suburra, the quarter of the shops the circus, and the velabrum. The Palatine, especially, was occupied by the higher nobility. Here were the famous mansions of Drusus, of Crassus, of Cicero, of Clodius, of Scaurus, and of Augustus, together with the temples of Cybele, of Juno Sospita, of Luna, of Febris, of Fortune, of Mars, and Vesta. On the Capitoline were the Arx, or citadel, and the temple of Jupiter. On the Pincian Hill were villas and gardens, including those of Lucullus and Sallust. Every available inch of ground in the suburra and velabrum was filled with dwellings, rising to great altitudes, even to the level of the Capitoline summit. The temples were all constructed after the Grecian models. The houses of the great were of immense size. The suburbs were of extraordinary extent. The population exceeded that of all modern cities, although it has been, perhaps, exaggerated. It was computed by Lipsius to reach the enormous number of four millions. Nothing could be more crowded than the streets, whose incessant din was intolerable to those who sought repose. And they were filled with idlers, as well as trades-people, and artisans and slaves. All classes sought the excitement of the theater and circus—all repaired to the public baths. The amphitheatres collected, also, unnumbered thousands within their walls to witness the combats of beasts with man, and man with man. The gladiatorial sports were the most exciting exhibitions ever known in ancient or modern times, and were the most striking features of Roman society. The baths, too, resounded with shouts and laughter, with the music of singers and of instruments, and even by the recitations of poets and lecturers. The luxurious Roman rose with the light of day, and received, at his levee, a crowd of clients and retainers. He then repaired to the forum, or was carried through the crowds on a litter. Here he presided as a judge, or appeared as a witness or advocate, or transacted his business affairs. At twelve, the work of the day ceased, and he retired for his midday siesta. When this had ended, he recreated himself with the sports of the Field of Mars, and then repaired to the baths, after which was the supper, or

Amusements of the aristocracy.

principal meal, in which he indulged in the coarsest luxuries, valued more for the cost than the elegance. He reclined at table, on a luxurious couch, and was served by slaves, who carved for him, and filled his cup, and poured water into his hand after every remove. He ate without knives or forks, with his fingers only. The feast was beguiled by lively conversation, or music and dancing.

Roman literature.

At this period, the literature of Rome reached its highest purity and terseness. Livy, the historian, secured the friendship of Augustus, and his reputation was so high that an enthusiastic Spaniard traveled from Cadiz on purpose to see him, and having gratified his curiosity, immediately returned home. He took the dry chronicles of his country, drew forth from them the poetry of the old traditions, and incited a patriotic spirit. A friend of the old oligarchy, an aristocrat in all his prejudices and habits, he heaped scorn on tribunes and demagogues, and veiled the despotism of his imperial master. Virgil also inflamed the patriotism of his countrymen, while he flattered the tyrant in whose sunshine he basked. Patronized by Mæcenas, countenanced by Octavius, he sung the praises of law, of order, and of tradition, and attempted to revive an age of faith, a love of agricultural life, a taste for the simplicities of better days, and a veneration of the martial virtues of heroic times. Horace ridiculed and rebuked the vices of his age, and yet obtained both riches and honors. His matchless wit and transcendent elegance of style have been admired by every scholar for nearly two thousand years. Propertius and Tibullus, and Ovid, also adorned this age, never afterward equaled by the labors of men of genius. Literature and morals went hand in hand as corruption accomplished its work. The age of Augustus saw the highest triumph in literature that Rome was destined to behold. Imperial tyranny was fatal to that independence of spirit without which all literature languishes and dies. But the limit of this work will not permit an extended notice of Roman civilization. This has been attempted by the author in another work.

CHAPTER XLIII.

THE SIX CÆSARS OF THE JULIAN LINE.

We have alluded to the centralization of political power in the person of Octavius. He simply retained all the great offices of State, and ruled, not so much by a new title, as he did as consul, tribune, censor, pontifex maximus, and chief of the Senate. But these offices were not at once bestowed.

His reign may be said to have commenced on the final defeat of his rivals, B. C. 29. Two years later, he received the title of Augustus, by which he is best known in history, although he was ordinarily called Cæsar. That proud name never lost its pre-eminence.

The first part of the reign was memorable for the organization of the State, and especially of the army; and also for the means he used to consolidate his empire. Augustus had no son, and but one daughter, although married three times. His first wife was Clodia, daughter of Clodius; his second was Scribonia, sister-in-law of Sextus Pompey; and the third was Livia Drusilla. The second wife was the mother of his daughter, Julia. This daughter was married to M. Claudius Marcellus, son of Marcellus and Octavia, the divorced wife of Antonius, and sister of Octavius. M. Claudius Marcellus thus married his cousin, but died two years afterward. It was to his honor that Augustus built the theatre of Marcellus.

The wives of Augustus.

On the death of Marcellus, Augustus married his daughter Julia to Agrippa, his prime minister and principal lieutenant. The issue of this marriage were three sons and two daughters. The sons died early. The youngest daughter, Agrippina, married Germanicus, and was the

The family of Augustus.

mother of the emperor Caligula. The marriage of Agrippina with Germanicus united the lines of Julia and Livia, the two last wives of Augustus, for Germanicus was the son of Drusus, the younger son of Livia by her first husband, Tiberius Claudius Nero. The eldest son of Livia, by Tiberius Claudius Nero, was the emperor Tiberius Nero, adopted by Augustus. Drusus married Antonia, the daughter of Antonius the triumvir, and was the father, not only of Germanicus, but of Claudius Drusus Cæsar, the fifth emperor. Another daughter of Antonius, also called Antonia, married L. Domitius Ahenobardus, whose son married Agrippina, the mother of Nero. Thus the descendants of Octavia and Antony became emperors, and were intertwined with the lines of Julia and Livia. The four successors of Augustus were all, in the male line, sprung from Livia's first husband, and all, except Tiberius, traced their descent from the defeated triumvir. Only the first six of the twelve Cæsars had relationship with the Julian house.

I mention this genealogy to show the descent of the first six emperors from Julia, the sister of Julius Cæsar, and grandmother of Augustus. Although the first six emperors were elected, they all belonged to the Julian house, and were the heirs of the great Cæsar.

Mæcenas and Agrippa.

When the government was organized, Augustus left the care of his capital to Mæcenas, his minister of civil affairs, and departed for Gaul, to restore order in that province, and build a series of fortifications to the Danube, to check the encroachments of barbarians. The region between the Danube and the Alps was peopled by various tribes, of different names, who gave perpetual trouble to the Romans; but they were now apparently subdued, and the waves of barbaric conquest were stayed for three hundred years. Vindelicea and Rhætia were added to the empire, in a single campaign, by Tiberius and Drusus, the sons of Livia—the emperor's beloved wife. Agrippa returned shortly after from a successful war in the East, but sickened and died B. C. 12. By his death Julia was again a widow, and was given in marriage to Tiberius, whom Augustus afterward adopted as his successor. Drusus, his brother, remained in Gaul, to complete the subjugation of the Celtic tribes, and to check the incursions of the Germans, who, from that time, were the most formidable enemies of Rome.

What interest is attached to those Teutonic races who ultimately became the conquerors of the empire! They were more warlike, persevering, and hardy, than the Celts, who had been incorporated with the empire. Tacitus has painted their simple manners, their passionate love of independence, and their religious tendency of mind. They occupied those vast plains and forests which lay between the Rhine, the Danube, the Vistula, and the German Ocean. Under different names they invaded the Roman world—the Suevi, the Franks, the Alemanni, the Burgundians, the Lombards, the Goths, the Vandals; but had not, at the time of Augustus, made those vast combinations which threatened immediate danger. They were a pastoral people, with blue eyes, ruddy hair, and large stature, trained to cold, to heat, to exposure, and to fatigue. Their strength lay in their infantry, which was well armed, and their usual order of battle was in the form of a wedge. They were accompanied even in war with their wives and children, and their women had peculiar virtue and influence. They inspired that reverence which never passed away from the Germanic nations, producing in the Middle Ages the graces of chivalry. All these various tribes had the same peculiarities, among which reverence was one of the most marked. They were not idol worshipers, but worshiped God in the form of the sun, moon, and stars, and in the silence of their majestic groves. Odin was their great traditional hero, whom they made an object of idolatry. War was their great occupation, and the chase was their principal recreation and pleasure. Tacitus enumerates as many as fifty tribes of these brave warriors, who feared not death, and even gloried in their losses. The most powerful of these tribes, in the time of Augustus was the confederation of the

The Teutonic races.

Suevi, occupying half of Germany, from the Danube to the Baltic. Of this confederation the Cauci were the most powerful, living on the banks of the Elbe, and obtaining a precarious living. In close connection with them were the Saxons and Longobardi (Long-beards). On the shores of the Baltic, between the Oder and the Vistula, were the Goths.

The arms of Cæsar and Augustus had as yet been only felt by the smaller tribes on the right bank of the Rhine, and these were assailed by Drusus, but only to secure his flank during the greater enterprise of sailing down the Rhine, to attack the people of the maritime plains. Great feats were performed by this able step-son of Augustus, who advanced as far as the Elbe, but was mortally injured by a fall from his horse. He lingered a month, and died, to the universal regret of the Romans, for he was the ablest general sent against the barbarians since Julius Cæsar, B. C. 9. The effect of his various campaigns was to check the inroads of the Germans for a century. It was at this time that the banks of the Rhine were studded by the forts which subsequently became those picturesque towns which now command the admiration of travelers.

Drusus.

After the death of Drusus, to whose memory a beautiful triumphal arch was erected, Tiberius was sent against the Germans, and after successful warfare, at the age of forty, obtained the permission of Augustus to retire to Rhodes, in order to improve his mind by the study of philosophy, or, as it is supposed by many historians, from jealousy of Caius and Lucius Cæsar, the children of Julia and Agrippa—those young princes to whom the throne of the world was apparently destined. At Rhodes, Tiberius, now the ablest man in the empire, for both Agrippa and Mæcenas were dead, lived in simple retirement for seven years. But the levities of Julia, to which Augustus could not be blind, compelled him to banish her—his only daughter—to the Campanian coast, where she died neglected and impoverished. The emperor was so indignant in view

Banishment of Julia.

of her disgraceful conduct, that he excluded her from any inheritance. The premature death of her sons nearly broke the heart of their grandfather, bereft of the wise councils and pleasant society of his great ministers, and bending under the weight of the vast empire which he, as the heir of Cæsar, had received. The loss of his grandsons compelled the emperor to provide for his succession, and he turned his eyes to Tiberius, his step-son, who was then at Rhodes. He adopted him as his successor, and invested him with the tribunitian power. But, while he selected him as his heir, he also required him to adopt Germanicus, the son of his brother Drusus.

Another great man now appeared upon the stage, L. Domitius Ahenobardus, the son-in-law of Octavia and Antony, who was intrusted with the war against the Germanic tribes, and who was the first Roman general to cross the Elbe. He was the grandfather of Nero. But Tiberius was sent to supersede him, and following the plan of his brother Drusus, he sent a flotilla down the Rhine, with orders to ascend the Elbe, and meet his army at an appointed rendezvous, which was then regarded as a great military feat, in the face of such foes as the future conquerors of Rome. After this Tiberius was occupied in reconquering the wide region between the Adriatic and the Danube, known as Illyricum, which occupied him three years, A. D. 7–9. In this war he was assisted by his nephew and adopted son, Germanicus, whose brilliant career revived the hope which had centred in Drusus.

Domitius Aheno-bardus.

Meanwhile Augustus, wearied with the cares of State, provoked by the scandals which his daughter occasioned, and irritated by plots against his life, began to relax his attention to business, and to grow morose. It was then that he banished Ovid, whose *Tristia* made a greater sensation than his immortal *Metamorphoses*. The disaster which befel Varus with a Roman army, in the forest of Teutoburg, near the river Lippe, when thirty thousand men were cut to pieces by the Germans under Arminius (Hermann), completed

Disaster of Varus.

the humiliation of Augustus, for, in this defeat, he must have foreseen the future victories of the barbarians. All ideas of extending the empire beyond the Rhine were now visionary, and that river was henceforth to remain its boundary on the north. New levies were indeed dispatched to the Rhine, and Tiberius and Germanicus led the forces. But the princes returned to Rome without effecting important results.

Soon after, in the year A. D. 14, Augustus, died in his seventy-seventh year, after a reign of forty-four years from the battle of Actium, and fifty from the triumvirate—one of the longest reigns in history, and one of the most successful. From his nineteenth year he was prominent on the stage of Roman public life. Under his auspices the empire reached the Elbe, and Egypt was added to its provinces. He planted colonies in every province, and received from the Parthians the captured standards of Crassus. His fleets navigated the Northern Ocean; his armies reduced the Pannonians and Illyrians. He added to the material glories of his capital, and sought to secure peace throughout the world. He was both munificent and magnificent, and held the reins of government with a firm hand. He was cultivated, unostentatious, and genial; but ambitious, and versed in all the arts of dissimulation and kingcraft. But he was a great monarch, and ruled with signal ability. After the battle of Actium, his wars were chiefly with the barbarians, and his greatest generals were members of the imperial family. That he could have reigned so long, in such an age, with so many enemies, is a proof of his wisdom and moderation, as well as of his good fortune. That he should have triumphed over such generals as Brutus, and Antonius, and Sextus—representing the old parties of the republic, is unquestionable evidence of transcendent ability. But his great merit was his capacity to rule, to organize, and to civilize. He is one of the best types of a sovereign ruler that the world has seen. It is nothing against him, that, in his latter years, there were popular discontents. Such generally happen at the close of all long reigns, as in the case of

Death of Augustus.

Character of Augustus.

Solomon and Louis XIV. And yet, the closing years of his reign were melancholy, like those of the French monarch, in view of the extinction of literary glories, and the passing away of the great lights of the age, without the appearance of new stars to take their place. But this was not the fault of Augustus, whose intellect expanded with his fortunes, and whose magnanimity grew with his intellect—a man who comprehended his awful mission, and who discharged his trusts with dignity and self-reliance.

Tiberius Cæsar, the third of the Roman emperors, found no opposition to his elevation on the death of Augustus. He ascended the throne of the Roman world at the mature age of fifty-six, after having won great reputation both as a statesman and a general. He was probably the most capable man in the empire, and in spite of all his faults, the empire was never better administered than by him. His great misfortune and fault was the suspicion of his nature, which made him the saddest of mankind, and finally, a monster of cruelty.

Like Augustus, he veiled his power as emperor by assuming the old offices of the republic. A subservient Senate and people favored the consolidation of the new despotism to which the world was now accustomed, and with which it cheerfully acquiesced as the best government for the times. The last remnant of popular elections was abolished, and the Comitia was transferred from the Campus Martius to the Senate, who elected the candidate proposed by the emperor.

Tiberius veils his power.

The first year of the accession of Tiberius was marked by mutinies in the legions, which were quelled by his nephew Germanicus, whose popularity was boundless, even as his feats had been heroic. This young prince, on whom the hopes of the empire rested, had married Agrippina, the daughter of Julia and Agrippa, and traced through his mother Antonia, and grandmother Octavia, a direct descent from Julia, the sister of the dictator. The blood of Antony also ran in his veins, as well as that of Livia. His

Germanicus.

wife was worthy of him, and was devotedly attached to him. By this marriage the lines of Julia and Livia were united; and by his descent from Antony the great parties of the revolution were silenced. He was equally the heir of Augustus and of Antonius, of Julia and of Livia; and of all the chiefs of Roman history no one has been painted in fairer colors. In natural ability, in military heroism, in the virtues of the heart, in exalted rank, he had no equal. As consul, general, and governor, he called forth universal admiration. His mind was also highly cultivated, and he excelled in Greek and Latin verse, while his condescending and courteous manners won both soldiers and citizens.

Of such a man, twenty-nine years of age, Tiberius was naturally jealous, especially since, through his wife, Germanicus was allied with the Octavian family, and through his mother, with the sister of the great Julius; and, therefore, had higher claims than he, on the principle of legitimacy. He was only the adopted son of Octavius, but Germanicus, through his mother Antonia, had the same ancestry as Octavius himself. Moreover, the cries of the legionaries, "Cæsar Germanicus will not endure to be a subject," added to the fears of the emperor, that he would be supplanted. So he determined to send his nephew on distant and dangerous expeditions, against those barbarians who had defeated Varus.

Jealousy of Tiberius.

Germanicus, no sooner than he had quelled the sedition in his camp, set out for Germany with eight legions and an equal number of auxiliaries. With this large force he crossed the Rhine, revisited the scene of the slaughter of Varus, and paid funeral honors to the remains of the fallen Romans. But the campaigns were barren of results, although attended with great expenses. No fortresses were erected to check the return of the barbarians from the places where they had been dislodged, and no roads were made to expedite future expeditions. Germanicus carried on war in savage and barbarous tracts, amid innumerable obstacles, which tasked his resources to the utmost. Tibe-

The campaign of Germanicus.

rius was dissatisfied with these results, and vented his ill-humor in murmurs against his nephew. The Roman people were offended at this jealousy, and clamored for his recall. Germanicus, however, embarked on a third campaign, A. D. 15, with renewed forces, and confronted the Germans on the Weser, and crossed the river in the face of the enemy. There the Romans obtained a great victory over Arminius, leader of the barbaric hosts, who retreated beyond the Elbe. The great German confederacy was, for a time, dispersed. Germanicus himself retired to the banks of the Rhine—which became the final boundary of the empire on the side of Germany. The hero who had persevered against innumerable obstacles, in overcoming which the discipline and force of the Roman legions were never more apparent, not even under Julius Cæsar, was now recalled to Rome, and a triumph was given him, amid the wildest enthusiasm of the Roman people. The young hero was the great object of attraction, as he was borne along in his triumphal chariot, surrounded by the five male descendants of his union with Agrippina—his faithful and heroic wife. Tiberius, in the name of his adopted son, bestowed three hundred sesterces apiece upon all the citizens, and the Senate chose the popular favorite as consul for the ensuing year, in conjunction with the emperor himself.

Triumph of Germanicus.

Troubles in the East induced Tiberius to send Germanicus to Asia Minor, while Drusus was sent to Illyricum. This prince was the son of Tiberius by his first wife, Vipsania, and was the cousin of Germanicus. He was disgraced by the vices of debauchery and cruelty, and was finally poisoned by his wife, Livilla, at the instance of Sejanus. So long as Germanicus lived, the court was divided between the parties of Drusus and Germanicus, and Tiberius artfully held the balance of favor between them, taking care not to declare which should be his successor. But Drusus was, probably, the favorite of the emperor, although greatly inferior to the elder prince in every noble quality. Tiberius, in sending him to Illyricum, wished to remove him from the

Drusus.

dissipations of the capital, and also, to place a man in that important post who should be loyal to his authority.

In appointing Germanicus to the chief command of the provinces beyond the Ægean, Tiberius also gave the province of Syria to Cnæus Piso, of the illustrious Calpurnian house, one of the proudest and most powerful of the Roman nobles. His wife, Plancina, was the favorite of Livia,—the empress-mother,—and he believed himself appointed to the government of Syria for the purpose of checking the ambitious designs which were imputed to Germanicus, while his wife was instructed to set up herself as a rival to Agrippina. The moment Piso quitted Italy, he began to thwart his superior, and to bring his authority into contempt. Yet he was treated by Germanicus with marked kindness. After visiting the famous cities of Greece, Germanicus marched to the frontiers of Armenia to settle its affairs with the empire—the direct object of his mission. He crowned a prince, called Zeno, as monarch of that country, reduced Cappadocia, and visited Egypt, apparently to examine the political affairs of the province, but really to study its antiquities, even as Scipio had visited Sicily in the heat of the Punic war. For thus going out of his way, he was rebuked by the emperor. He then retraced his steps, and shaped his course to Syria, where he found his regulations and appointments had been overruled by Piso, between whom and himself bitter altercations ensued. While in Syria, he fell sick and died, and his illness was attributed to poison administered by Piso, although there was little evidence to support the charge.

Cnæus Piso.

Death of Germanicus.

The death of Germanicus was received with great grief by the Roman people, and the general sorrow of the Roman world, and his praises were pronounced in every quarter. He was even fondly compared to Alexander the Great. His character was embellished by the greatest master of pathos among the Roman authors, and invested with a gleam of mournful splendor. His remains were brought to Rome by his devoted wife, and the most splendid

Funeral of Germanicus.

funeral honors were accorded to him. Drusus, with the younger brother and children of Germanicus, went forth to meet the remains, and the consuls, the Senate, and a large concourse of people, swelled the procession, as it neared the city. The precious ashes were deposited in the Cæsarian mausoleum, and the memory of the departed prince was cherished in the hearts of the people. Whether he would have realized the expectations formed of him, had he lived to succeed Tiberius, can not be known. He, doubtless, had most amiable traits of character, while his talents were undoubted. But he might have succumbed to the temptations incident to the most august situation in the world, or have been borne down by its pressing cares, or have shown less talent for administration than men disgraced by private vices. Had Tiberius died before Augustus, his character would have appeared in the most favorable light, for he was a man of great abilities, and was devoted to the interests of the empire. He became moody, suspicious, and cruel, and yielded to the pleasures so lavishly given to the master of the world. When we remember the atmosphere of lies in which he lived,—as is the case with all absolute monarchs, especially in venal and corrupt times,—the unbounded temptations, the servile and sycophantic attentions of his courtiers, the perpetual vexations and cares incident to such overgrown and unlimited powers, and the disgust, satiety, and contempt which his experiences engendered, we can not wonder that his character should change for the worse. And when we see a man rendered uninteresting and unamiable by cares, temptations, and bursts of passion or folly, yet who still governs vigilantly and ably, our indignation should be modified, when the lower propensities are indulged. It is not pleasant to palliate injustices, tyrannies, and lusts. But human nature, at the best, is weak. Of all men, absolute princes claim a charitable judgment, and our eyes should be directed to their services, rather than to their defects. These remarks not only pertain to Tiberius, but to Augustus, and many other emperors who have been

Able administration of Tiberius.

harshly estimated, but whose general ability and devotion to the interests of the empire are undoubted. How few monarchs have been free from the stains of occasional excesses, and that arbitrary and tyrannical character which unlimited powers develop! Even the crimes of monsters, whom we execrate, are to be traced to madness and intoxication, more than to natural fierceness and wickedness. But when monarchs *do* reign in justice, and conquer the temptations incident to their station, like the Antonines, then our reverence becomes profound. "Heavy is the head that wears a crown." Kings are objects of our sympathy, as well as of our envy. Their burdens are as heavy as their temptations are great; and frivolous or wicked princes are almost certain to yield, like Nero or Caligula, to the evils with which they are peculiarly surrounded.

Excellence of the imperial rule.

But to return to our narrative of the leading events connected with the reign of Tiberius, one of the ablest of all the emperors, so far as administrative talents are concerned. After the death of Germanicus, which was probably natural, the vengeance of the people and the court was directed to his supposed murderer, Piso. He was arraigned and tried by the Senate, not only for the crime of which he was accused by the family of Germanicus, who thought himself poisoned, but for exceeding his powers as governor of Syria, which province he continued unwisely to claim. Tiberius abstained from all interference with the great tribunal which sat in judgment. He even checked the flow of popular feeling. Cold and hard, he allowed the trial to take its course, without betraying sympathy or aversion, and acted with great impartiality. Piso found no favor from the Senate or the emperor, and killed himself when his condemnation was certain.

Tiberius becomes a tyrant.

Relieved by the death of Germanicus and Piso, Tiberius began to reign more despotically, and incurred the hatred of the people, to which he was apparently insensible. He was greatly influenced by his mother, Livia, an artful and ambitious princess, and by Sejanus, his favorite, a man of rare energy and ability, who was prefect of the prætorian guards. This office, unknown to the republic, became the most important and influential under the emperors. The prefect was virtually the vizier, or prime minister, since it was his care to watch over the personal safety of a monarch whose power rested on the military. The instruments of his government, however, were the Senate, which he controlled especially by his power as censor, and the law of *majestas*, which was virtually a great system of espionage and public accusation, which the emperor encouraged. But his general administration was marked by prudence, equity, and mildness. Under him the Roman dominion was greatly consolidated, and it was his policy to guard rather than extend the limits of the empire. The legions were stationed in those provinces which were most likely to be assailed by external dangers, especially on the banks of the Rhine, in Illyricum, and Dalmatia. But they were scattered in all the provinces. The city of Rome was kept in order by the prætorian guards. Their discipline was strenuously maintained. Governors of provinces were kept several years in office, which policy was justified by the apologue he was accustomed to use, founded on the same principle as that which is recognized in all corrupt times by great administrators, whether of States, or factories, or railroads. "A number of flies had settled on a soldier's wound, and a compassionate passer-by was about to scare them away. The sufferer begged him to refrain. 'These flies,' he said, 'have nearly sucked their full, and are beginning to be tolerable; if you drive them away, they will be immediately succeeded by fresh-comers with keener appetites.'" The emperor saw the abuses which existed, but despaired to remedy them, since he distrusted human nature. But there is no doubt that the government of the provinces was improved under this prince, and the governors were made responsible. The emperor also was assiduous to free Italy from robbers and banditti, and in stimulating the diligence of the police, so that riots seldom occurred, and

Instruments of tyranny.

Provincial governors.

were severely punished. There was greater security of life and property throughout the empire, and the laws were wise and effective. Tiberius limited the number of the gladiators, expelled the soothsayers from Italy, and suppressed the Egyptian rites. The habits of the people, even among the higher classes, were so generally disgraceful and immoral,—the dissipation was so widely spread, that Tiberius despaired to check it by sumptuary laws, but he restrained it all in his power. He was indefatigable in his vigilance. For several years he did not quit the din and dust of the city for a single day, and he lived with great simplicity, apparently anxious to exhibit the ancient ideal of a Roman statesman. He took no pleasure in the sports of the circus or theatre, and was absorbed in the cares of office, as Augustus had been before him. Augustus, however, was a man of genius, while he was only a man of ability, and his great defect was jealousy of the family of Germanicus, and the favor he lavished on Sejanus, who even demanded the hand of Livilla, the widow of Drusus,—a suit which Tiberius rejected.

Reforms of Tiberius.

Weariness of the cares of State, and the desire of repose, at last induced Tiberius to retire from the city. He had neither happiness nor rest. He quarreled with Agrippina, the widow of Germanicus, and his temper was exasperated by the imputations and slanders from which no monarch can escape. His enemies, however, declared that he had no higher wish than to exercise in secret the cruelty and libidinousness to which he was abandoned. For eleven years he ruled in the retirement of his guarded fortress, and never again re-entered the city he had left in disgust. But in this retirement, he did not relax his vigilance in the administration of affairs, although his government was exceedingly unpopular, and was doubtless stained by many acts of cruelty. At Capreæ, a small island near Naples, barren and desolate, but beautiful in climate and scenery, the master of the world spent his latter years, surrounded with literary men and soothsayers. I do not

Tiberius secludes himself in Capreæ.

believe the calumnies which have been heaped on this imperial misanthrope. And yet, the eleven years he spent in his retreat were marked by great complaints against him, and by many revolting crimes and needless cruelties. He persecuted the family of Germanicus, banished Agrippina, and imprisoned her son, Drusus. Sejanus, however, instigated these proceedings, and worked upon the jealousy of the emperor. This favorite was affianced to Livilla, the widow of Drusus, and was made consul conjointly with Tiberius.

Sejanus.

Tiberius penetrated, at last, the character of this ambitious officer, and circumvented his ruin with that profound dissimulation which was one of his most marked traits. Sejanus conspired against his life, but the emperor shrank from openly denouncing him to the Senate. He used consummate craft in securing his arrest and execution, the instrument of which was Macro, an officer of his body-guard, and his death was followed by the ruin of his accomplices and friends.

His conspiracy and death.

Shortly after the execution of Sejanus, Drusus, the son of Agrippina, was starved to death in prison, and many cruelties were inflicted on the friends of Sejanus. Tiberius now began to show signs of insanity, and his life henceforth was that of a miserable tyrant. His career began to draw to a close, and he found himself, in his fits of despair and wretchedness, supported by only three surviving members of the lineage of Cæsar: Tiberius Claudius Drusus, the last of the sons of Drusus, and nephew of the emperor, infirm in health and weak in mind, and had been excluded from public affairs; Caius, the younger son of Germanicus, and Tiberius, the son of the second Drusus, —the one, grand-nephew, and the other, grandson, of the emperor. Both were young; one twenty-five, the other eighteen. The failing old man failed to designate either as his successor, but the voice of the public pointed out the son of Germanicus, nicknamed Caligula. At the age of seventy-eight, the tyrant died, unable in his last sickness to restrain

Death of Drusus.

his appetite. He died at Misenum, on his way to Capreæ, which he had quitted for a time, to the joy of the whole empire; for his reign, in his latter years, was one of terror, which caused a deep gloom to settle upon the face of the higher society at Rome, A. D. 37. The body was carried to Rome with great pomp, and its ashes were deposited in the mausoleum of the Cæsars. Caius was recognized as his successor without opposition, and he commenced his reign by issuing a general pardon to all State prisoners, and scattering, with promiscuous munificence, the vast treasures which Tiberius had accumulated. He assumed the collective honors of the empire with modesty, and great expectations were formed of a peaceful and honorable reign.

Death of Tiberius.

His funeral.

Caligula was the heir of the Drusi, grandson of Julia and Agrippa, great-grandson of Octavius, of Livia, and of Antony. In him the lines of Julia and Livia were united. His defects and vices were unknown to the people, and he made grand promises to the Senate. He commenced his reign by assiduous labors, and equitable measures, and professed to restore the golden age of Augustus. His popularity with the people was unbounded, from his lavish expenditure for shows and festivals, by the consecration of temples, and the distribution of corn and wine.

Caligula.

But it was not long before he abandoned himself to the most extravagant debauchery. His brain reeled on the giddy eminence to which he had been elevated without previous training and experience. Augustus fought his own way to power, and Tiberius had spent the best years of his life in the public service before his elevation. Yet even he, with all his experience and ability, could not resist the blandishments of power. How, then, could a giddy and weak young man, without redeeming qualities? He fell into the vortex of pleasures, and reeling in the madness which excesses caused, was soon guilty of the wildest caprices, and the most cruel atrocities. He was corrupted by flattery as well as pleasure. He even de-

His infamous pleasures.

scended into the arena of the circus as a charioteer, and the races became a State institution. In a few months he squandered the savings of the previous reign, swept away the wholesome restraints which Augustus and Tiberius had imposed upon gladiators, and carried on the sports of the amphitheatre with utter disregard of human life. His extravagance and his necessities led to the most wanton murders of senators and nobles whose crime was their wealth. The most redeeming features of the first year of his reign were his grief at the death of his sister, his friendship with Herod Agrippa, to whom he gave a sovereignty in Palestine, and the activity he displayed in the management of his vast inheritance. He had a great passion for building, and completed the temple of Augustus, projected the grandest of the Roman aqueducts, enlarged the imperial palace, and carried a viaduct from the Palatine to the Capitoline over the lofty houses of the Velabrum. But his prodigalities led to a most oppressive taxation, which soon alienated the people, while his senseless debaucheries, especially his costly banquets, disgusted the more contemplative of the nobles. He was also disgraced by needless cruelties, and it was his exclamation: "Would that the people of Rome had but one neck!" His vanity was preposterous. He fancied himself divine, and insisted on divine honors being rendered to him. He systematically persecuted the nobles, and exacted contributions. He fancied himself, at one time an orator, and at another a general; and absolutely led an army to the Rhine, when there was no enemy to attack. He married several wives, but divorced them with the most fickle inconstancy.

Cruelty of Caligula.

It is needless to repeat the wanton follies of this young man who so outrageously disgraced the imperial station. The most charitable construction to be placed upon acts which made his name infamous among the ancients is that his brain was turned by his elevation to a dignity for which he was not trained or disciplined—that unbounded power, united with the most extravagant aban-

His madness and folly.

donment to sensual pleasures, undermined his intellect. His caprices and extravagance can only be explained by partial madness. He had reigned but four years, and all expectations of good government were dispelled. The majesty of the empire was insulted, and assassination, the only way by which he could be removed, freed the world from a madman, if not a monster.

His assassination.

There was great confusion after the assassination of Caius Cæsar, and ill-concerted efforts to recover a freedom which had fled forever, ending, as was to be expected, by military power. The consuls convened the Senate for deliberation (for the forms of the republic were still kept up), but no settled principles prevailed. Various forms of government were proposed and rejected. While the Senate deliberated, the prætorian guards acted.

Among the inmates of the palace, in that hour of fear, among slaves and freedmen, half hidden behind a curtain in an obscure corner, was a timid old man, who was dragged forth with brutal violence. He was no less a personage than Claudius, the neglected uncle of the emperor, the son of Drusus and Antonia, and nephew of Tiberius, and brother of Germanicus. Instead of slaying the old man, the soldiers, respecting the family of Cæsar, hailed him, partly in jest, as imperator, and carried him to their camp. Claudius, heretofore thought to be imbecile, and therefore despised, was not unwilling to accept the dignity, and promised the prætorians, if they would swear allegiance to him, a donation of fifteen thousand sesterces apiece. The Senate, at the dictation of the prætorians, accepted Claudius as emperor.

Claudius.

He commenced his reign, A. D. 41, by proclaiming a general amnesty. He restored confiscated estates, recalled the wretched sisters of Caius, sent back to Greece and Asia the plundered statues of temples which Caius had transported to Rome, and inaugurated a *régime* of moderation and justice. His life had been one of sickness, neglect, and obscurity, but he was suffered to live because he

His efforts at reform.

was harmless. His mother was ashamed of him, and his grandmother, Livia, despised him, and his sister, Livilla, ridiculed him. He was withheld from public life, and he devoted himself to literary pursuits, and even wrote a history of Roman affairs from the battle of Actium, but it gained him no consideration. Tiberius treated him with contumely, and his friends deserted him. All this neglect and contempt were the effects of a weak constitution, a paralytic gait, and an imperfect utterance.

Claudius took Augustus as his model, and at once a great change in the administration was observable. There was a renewed activity of the armies on the frontiers, and great generals arose who were destined to be future emperors. The colonies were strengthened and protected, and foreign affairs were conducted with ability. Herod Agrippa, the favorite of Caius, was confirmed in his government of Galilee, and received in addition the dominions of Samaria and Judæa. Antiochus was restored to the throne of Commagene, and Mithridates received a district of Cilicia. The members of the Senate were made responsible for the discharge of their magistracies, and vacancies to this still august body were filled up from the wealthy and powerful families. He opened an honorable career to the Gauls, revised the lists of the knights, and took an accurate census of Roman citizens. He conserved the national religion, and regulated holidays and festivals. His industry and patience were unwearied, and the administration of justice extorted universal admiration. His person was accessible to all petitioners, and he relieved distress wherever he found it. He relinquished the most grievous exactions of his predecessors, and tenderly guarded neglected slaves. He also constructed great architectural works, especially those of utility, completed the vast aqueduct which Caius commenced, and provided the city with provisions. He built the port of Ostia, to facilitate commerce, and drained marshes and lakes. The draining of the Lake Fucinus occupied thirty thousand men for eleven years.

The able administration of Claudius.

While he executed vast engineering works to supply the city with water, he also amused the people with gladiatorial shows. In all things he showed the force of the old Roman character, in spite of bodily feebleness.

Conquest of Britain.

The most memorable act of his administration was the conquest of South Britain. By birth a Gaul, being born at Lugdunum, he cast his eyes across the British channel and resolved to secure the island beyond as the extreme frontier of his dominions, then under the dominion of the Druids—a body of Celtic priests whom the Romans ever detested, and whose rites all preceding emperors had proscribed. Julius Cæsar had pretended to impose a tribute on the chiefs of Southern Britain, but it was never exacted. Both Augustus and Tiberius felt but little interest in the political affairs of that distant island, but the rapid progress of civilization in Gaul, and the growing cities on the banks of the Rhine, elicited a spirit of friendly intercourse. Londinium, a city which escaped the notice of Cæsar, was a great emporium of trade in the time of Claudius. But the southern chieftains were hostile, and jealous of their independence. So Claudius sent four legions to Britain, under Plautius, and his lieutenant, Vespasianus, to oppose the forces under Caractacus. He even entered Britain in person, and subdued the Trinobantes. But for nine years Caractacus maintained an independent position. He was finally overthrown in battle, and betrayed to the Romans, and exhibited at Rome. The insurrection was suppressed, or rather, a foothold was secured in the island, which continued henceforth under the Roman rule.

Messalina.

The feeble old man, always nursed by women, had the misfortune to marry, for his third wife, the most infamous woman in Roman annals (Valeria Messalina), under whose influence the reign, at first beneficent, became disgraceful. Claudius was entirely ruled by her. She amassed fortunes, sold offices, confiscated estates, and indulged in guilty loves. She ruled like a Madame de Pompadour, and degraded the throne which she ought to have exalted. The influence of women generally was bad in those corrupt times, but her influence was scandalous and degrading.

Claudius also was governed by his favorites, generally men of low birth—freedmen who usurped the place of statesmen. Narcissus and Pallus were the most confidential of the emperor's advisers, who, in consequence, became enormously rich, for favors flowed through them, and received the great offices of State. The court became a scene of cabals and crimes, disgraced by the wanton shamelessness of the empress and the venality of courtiers. Appius Silamus, one of the best and greatest of the nobles, was murdered through the intrigues of Messalina, to whose progress in wickedness history furnishes no parallel, and Valerius Asiaticus, another great noble, also suffered the penalty of offending her, and was destroyed; and his magnificent gardens, which she coveted, were bestowed upon her.

Agrippina.

But Messalina was rivaled in iniquity by another princess, between whom and herself there existed the deadliest animosity. This was Agrippina, the daughter of Germanicus, who had been married to Cn. Domitius Ahenobardus, grandson of Octavia, and whose issue was the future emperor Nero. The niece of Claudius occupied the second place in the imperial household, and it became her aim to poison the mind of her uncle against the woman she detested, and who returned her hatred. She now leagued with the freedmen of the palace to destroy her rival. An opportunity to gratify her vengeance soon occurred. Messalina, according to Tacitus, was guilty of the inconceivable madness of marrying Silanus, one of her paramours, while her husband lived, and that husband an emperor, which story can not be believed without also supposing that Claudius was a perfect idiot. Such a defiance of law, of religion, and of the feelings of mankind, to say nothing of its folly, is not to be supposed. Yet such was the scandal, and it filled the imperial household with consternation. Callistus, Pallas, and Narcissus—the favorites who ruled Claudius—

united with Agrippina to secure her ruin. The emperor, then absent in Ostia, was informed of the shamelessness of his wife. It was difficult for him to believe such a fact, but it was attested by the trusted members of his household. His fears were excited, as well as his indignation, and he hastened to Rome for vengeance and punishment. Messalina had retired to her magnificent gardens on the Pincian, which had once belonged to Lucullus, the price of the blood of the murdered Asiaticus; but, on the approach of the emperor, of which she was informed, she advanced boldly to confront him, with every appearance of misery and distress, with her children Britannicus and Octavia. Claudius vacillated, and Messalina retired to her gardens, hoping to convince her husband of her innocence on the interview which he promised the following day. But Narcissus, knowing her influence, caused her to be assassinated, and the emperor drowned his grief, or affection, or anger, in wine and music, and seemingly forgot her. That Messalina was a wicked and abandoned woman is most probable; that she was as bad as history represents her, may be doubted, especially when we remember she was calumniated by a rival, who succeeded in taking her place as wife. It is easier to believe she was the victim of Agrippina and the freedmen, who feared as well as hated her, than to accept the authority of Tacitus and Juvenal. On the death of Messalina, Agrippina married her uncle, and the Senate sanctioned the union, which was incest by the Roman laws.

Assassination of Messalina.

Marriage of Claudius with Agrippina.

The fourth wife of the emperor transcended the third in intrigue and ambition, and her marriage, at the age of thirty-three, was soon followed by the betrothal of her son, L. Domitius, a boy of twelve, with Octavia, the daughter of Claudius and Messalina. He was adopted by the emperor, and assumed the name of Nero. Henceforth she labored for the advancement of her son only. She courted the army and the favor of the people, and founded the city on the Rhine which we call Cologne. But she outraged the notions and sentiments of the people more by her unfeminine usurpation of public honors, than by her cruelty or her dissoluteness. She seated herself by the side of the emperor in military festivals. She sat by him at a sea-fight on the Lucrine Lake, clothed in a soldier's cloak. She took her station in front of the Roman standard, when Caractacus, the conquered British chief, was brought in chains to the emperor's tribunal. She caused the dismissal of the imperial officers who incurred her displeasure. She exercised a paramount sway over her husband, and virtually ruled the empire. She distracted the palace with discords, cabals, and jealousies.

Infamy of Agrippina.

How the bad influence of these women over the mind of Claudius can be reconciled with the vigilance, and the labors, and the beneficent measures of the emperor, as generally admitted, history does not narrate. But it was during the ascendency of both Messalina and Agrippina, that Claudius presided at the tribunals of justice with zeal and intelligence, that he interested himself in works of great public utility, and that he carried on successful war in Britain.

In the year A. D. 54, and in the fourteenth of his reign, Claudius, exhausted by the affairs of State, and also, it is said, by intemperance, fell sick at Rome, and sought the medicinal waters of Sinuessa. It was there that Agrippina contrived to poison him, by the aid of Locusta, a professed poisoner, and Xenophon, a physician, while she affected an excess of grief. She held his son Britannicus in her arms, and detained him and his sisters in the palace, while every preparation was made to secure the accession of her own son, Nero. She was probably prompted to this act from fear that she would be supplanted and punished, for Claudius had said, when wine had unloosed his secret thoughts, "that it was his fate to suffer the crim of his wives, but at last to punish them." She also was eager to elevate her own son to the throne, which, of right, belonged to Britannicus, and whose rights might have been subsequently acknowledged by the emperor, for his eyes

Death of Claudius.

could not be much longer blinded to the character of his wife.

Claudius must not be classed with either wicked or imbecile princes, in spite of his bodily infirmities, or the slanders with which his name is associated. It is probable he indulged to excess in the pleasures of the table, like the generality of Roman nobles, but we are to remember that he ever sought to imitate Augustus in his wisest measures; that he ever respected letters when literature was falling into contempt; that his administration was vigorous and successful, fertile in victories and generals; that he exceeded all his ministers in assiduous labors, and that he partially restored the dignity and authority of the Senate. His great weakness was in being ruled by favorites and women; but his favorites were men of ability, and his women were his wives.

Character of Claudius.

Nero, the son of Agrippina and Cn. Domitius Ahenobardus, by the assistance of the prætorian guards, was now proclaimed imperator, A. D. 54, directly descended, both on his paternal and maternal side, from Antonia Major, the granddaughter of Antony and Domitius Ahenobardus. Through Octavia, his grandmother, he traced his descent from the family of Cæsar. The Domitii—the paternal ancestors of Nero—had been illustrious for several hundred years, and no one was more distinguished than Lucius Domitius, called Ahenobardus, or Red-Beard, in the early days of the republic. The father of Nero, who married Agrippina, was as infamous for crimes as he was exalted for rank. But he died when his son Nero was three years of age. He was left to the care of his father's sister, Domitia Lepida, the mother of Messalina, and was by her neglected. His first tutors were a dancer and a barber. On the return of his mother from exile his education was more in accordance with his rank, as a prince of the blood, though not in the line of succession. He was docile and affectionate as a child, and was intrusted to the care of Seneca, by whom he was taught rhetoric and moral phi-

Ascension of Nero.

His early character.

losophy, and who connived at his taste for singing, piping, and dancing, the only accomplishments of which, as emperor, he was afterward proud. He was surrounded with perils, in so wicked an age, as were other nobles, and, by his adoption, was admitted a member of the imperial family —the sacred stock of the Claudii and Julii. He was under the influence of his mother—the woman who subverted Messalina, and murdered Claudius,—who used every art and intrigue to secure his accession.

When he mounted the throne of the Cæsars, he gave promise of a benignant reign. His first speech to the Senate made a good impression, and his first acts were beneficent. But he ruled only through his mother, who aspired to play the empress, a woman who gave answers to ambassadors, and sent dispatches to foreign courts. Burrhus, the prefect of the imperial guard, and Seneca, tutor and minister, through whose aid the claims of Nero had been preferred over those of Britannicus, the son of the late emperor, opposed her usurpations, and attempted to counteract her influence.

He gives promise of reigning wisely.

The early promises of Nero were not fulfilled. He soon gave vent to every vice, which was disguised by his ministers. One of the first acts was to disgrace the freedman, Pallas,—the prime minister of Claudius,—and to destroy Britannicus by poison, which crimes were palliated, if not suggested, by Seneca.

New developments in the character of Nero.

The influence which Seneca and Burrhus had over the young emperor, who screened his vices from the eyes of the people and Senate, necessarily led to a division between Nero and Agrippina. He withdrew her guard of honor, and paid her only formal visits, which conduct led to the desertion of her friends, and the open hostility of her enemies. The wretched woman defended herself against the charges they brought, with spirit, and for a time she escaped. The influence of Seneca, at this period, was paramount, and was exerted for the good of the empire, so that the Senate acquiesced in the public measures of Nero, and no notice was

His ministers.

taken of his private irregularities. The empress mother apparently yielded to the ascendency of the ministers, and provoked no further trial of strength.

Thus five years passed, until Nero was twenty-two, when Poppæa Sabina, the fairest woman of her time, appeared upon the stage. Among the dissolute women of imperial Rome, she was pre-eminent. Introduced to the intimacy of Nero, she aspired to still higher elevation, and this was favored by the detestation with which Agrippina was generally viewed, and the continued decline of her influence, since she had ruled by fear rather than love. Poppæa was now found intriguing against her, and induced Nero to murder his own mother, to whose arts and wickedness he owed his own elevation. The murder was effected in her villa, on the Lucrine Lake, under circumstances of utter brutality. Nero came to examine her mangled body, and coolly praised the beauty of her form. Nor were her ashes even placed in the mausoleum of Augustus. This wicked Jezebel, who had poisoned her husband, and was accused of every crime revolting to our nature, paid the penalty of her varied infamies, and her name has descended to all subsequent ages as the worst woman of antiquity.

Poppæa Sabina.

Her vile character.

With the murder of Agrippina, the madness and atrocities of Nero gained new force. He now appears as a monster, and was only tolerated for the amusements with which he appeased the Roman people. He disgraced the imperial dignity by descending upon the stage, which was always infamous; he instituted demoralizing games; he was utterly insensible to national sentiments and feelings; he exceeded all his predecessors in extravagance and follies; he was suspected of poisoning Burrhus, by whom he was advanced to power; he executed men of the highest rank, whose crime was their riches; he destroyed the members of the imperial family; he murdered Doryphorus and Pallas, because they were averse to his marriage with Poppæa; he drove his chariot in the Circus Maximus, pleased with the acclamations of two hundred thousand spectators;

The infamies of Nero.

he gave banquets in which the utmost excesses of bacchanalian debauchery were openly displayed; he is said to have kindled the conflagration of his own capital; he levied oppressive taxes to build his golden palace, and support his varied extravagance; he even destroyed his tutor and minister, Seneca, that he might be free from his expostulations, and take possession of the vast fortune which this philosopher had accumulated in his service; and he finally kicked his wife so savagely that she died from the violence he inflicted. If it were possible to add to his enormities, his persecution of the Christians swelled the measure of his infamies—the first to which they had been subjected in Rome, and in which Paul himself was a victim. But his government was supported by the cruelty and voluptuousness of the age, and which has never been painted in more vivid colors than by St. Paul himself. The corrupt morality of the age tolerated all these crimes, and excesses, and follies—an age which saw no great writers except Seneca, Lucan, Perseus, and Martial, two of whom were murdered by the emperor.

Conspiracies against him.

But the hour of retribution was at hand. The provinces were discontented, and the city filled with cabals and conspiracies. Though one of them, instigated by Piso, was unsuccessful, and its authors punished, a revolt in Gaul, headed by Galba—an old veteran of seventy-two, and assisted by Vindex and Virginius, was fatal to Nero. The Senate and the prætorian guards favored the revolution. The emperor was no longer safe in his capital. Terrified by dreams, and stung by desertion, the wretched tyrant fled to the Servilian Gardens, and from thence to the villa of one of his freedmen, near which he committed suicide, at the age of thirty-six, and in the fourteenth year of his inglorious reign, during which there are scarcely other events to chronicle than his own personal infamies. "In him perished the last scion of the stock of the Julii, refreshed in vain by grafts from the Octavii, the Claudii, and the Domitii." Though the first of the emperors had married four wives, the second three, the third two,

Flight of Nero.

Death of Nero.

38

the fourth three, the fifth six, and the sixth three, yet Nero was the last of the Cæsars. None of the five successors of Julius were truly his natural heirs. They trace their lineage to his sister Julia, but the three last had in their veins the blood of Antony as well as Octavia, and thus the descendants of the triumvir reigned at Rome as well as those of his rival Octavius. We have only to remark that it is strange that the Julian line should have been extinguished in the sixth generation, with so many marriages.

GENEALOGICAL TABLE OF THE FIRST SIX CÆSARS.

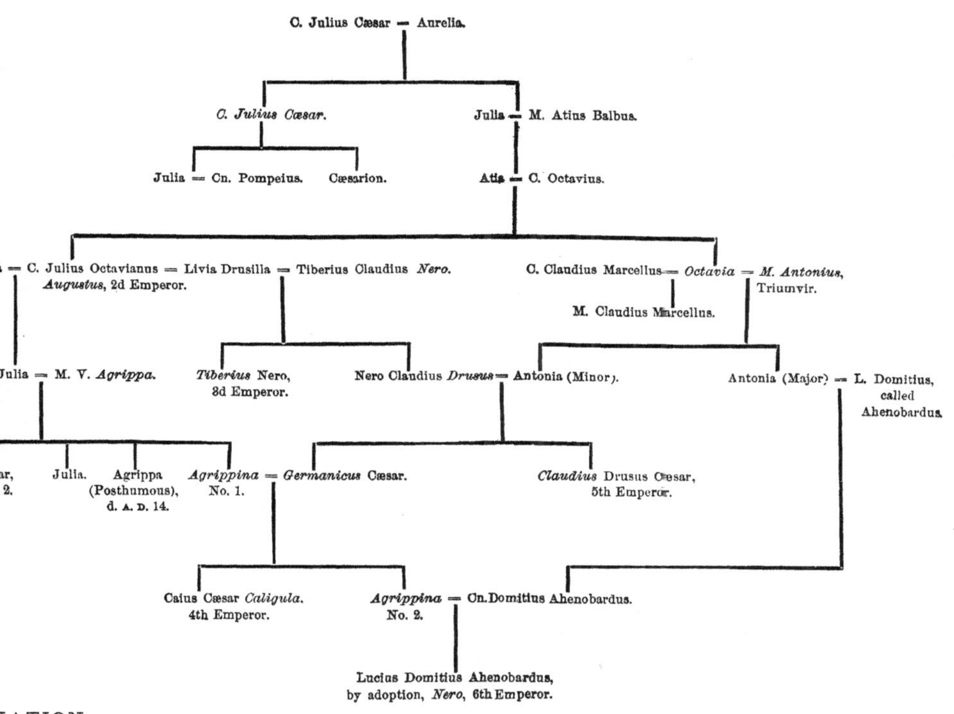

NATION:

-nephew of Julius Cæsar, and son by adoption.
on of Augustus, and son by adoption, son of Livia and T. C. Nero.
son of Agrippina and Germanicus—grandson of Julia and Agrippa, also of Drusus and Antonia—great-grandson of Augustus and Antony.
s, son of Nero Claudius Drusus and Antonia Minor—grandson of Livia and Tiberius Claudius Nero, also of Octavia and Antony.
s Ahenobardus, and *Nero* by adoption, son of Agrippina No. 2 and Cn. Domitius Ahenobardus, grandson of Agrippina No. 1 and Germanicus, also of
L. Domitius Ahenobardus, great-grandson of Octavia and Antony, and great-great-grandson of Augustus.

CHAPTER XLIV.

THE CLIMAX OF THE ROMAN EMPIRE.

On the extinction of the Julian line, a new class of emperors succeeded, by whom the prosperity of the empire was greatly advanced. We have now to fall back on Niebuhr, Gibbon, and the Roman historians, and also make more use of Smith's digest of these authors. But so much ground still remains to go over, that we can only allude to salient points, and our notice of succeeding emperors must be brief.

The empire was now to be the prize of successful soldiers, and Galba, at the age of seventy-three, was saluted imperator by the legions before the death of Nero, A. D. 68, and acknowledged by the Senate soon after. There is nothing memorable in his short reign of a few months, and he was succeeded by Otho, who only reigned three months, and he was succeded by Vitellius, who was removed by violent death, like Galba and Otho. These three emperors left no mark, and were gluttons and sensualists, who excited nothing but contempt; soldiers of fortune—only respectable in inferior rank. Galba.

On the first of July, A. D. 69, Titus Flavius Vespasianus, of humble family, arose, as general, to the highest honors of the State, and was first proclaimed emperor at Alexandria, at the close of the Jewish war, which he conducted to a successful issue. A brief contest with Vitellius secured his recognition by the Senate, and the first of the Flavian line began to reign—a man of great talents and virtues. On the fall of Jerusalem, his son Titus returned to Rome, and celebrated a joint triumph with his father, and the gates of the temple of Janus were shut,—the Vespasian proclaimed emperor.

first time since Augustus,—and universal peace was proclaimed.

One of the first acts of the new emperor was to purify the Senate, reduced to two hundred members, soon followed by the restoration of the finances. He rebuilt the capitol, erected the temple of Peace, the new forum, the baths of Titus, and the Coliseum. He extended a generous patronage to letters, and under his reign Quintilian, the great rhetorician, and Pliny, the naturalist, flourished. It was in the ninth year of his reign that an eruption of Vesuvius occurred, when Herculaneum and Pompeii were destroyed, to witness which Pliny lost his life. Vespasian had associated with himself his son Titus in the government, and died, after a reign of ten years, exhausted by the cares of empire; and Titus quietly succeeded him, but reigned only for two years and a quarter, and was succeeded by his brother, Domitian, a man of some ability, but cruel, like Nero. He was ten years younger than Titus, and was thirty years of age when proclaimed emperor by the prætorians, and accepted by the Senate, A. D. 81. At first he was a reformer, but soon was stained by the most odious vices. He continued the vast architectural works of his father and brother, and patronized learning.

His first acts.

Titus.

It was during the reign of Domitian that Britain was finally conquered by Agricola, who was recalled by the jealousy of the emperor, after a series of successes which gave him immortality. The reduction of this island did not seriously commence until the reign of Claudius. By Nero, Suetonius Paulinus was sent to Britain, and under him Agricola took his first lessons of soldiership. Under Vespasian he commanded the twentieth legion in Britain, and was the twelfth Roman general sent to the island. On his return to Rome he was made consul, and Britain was assigned to him as his province, where he remained seven years, until he had extended his conquests to the Grampian Hills. He taught the Britons the arts and luxuries of civilized life, to settle in towns, and to

Domitian.

Conquest of Britain.

build houses and temples. Among the foes he encountered, the most celebrated was Boadicea, queen of the Iceni, on the eastern coast, who led the incredible number of two hundred and forty thousand against the Roman legions, but was defeated, with the loss of eighty thousand,—some atonement for the seventy thousand Romans, and their allies, who had been slain at Londinium, when Suetonius Paulinus commanded.

The year of Agricola's recall, A. D. 84, forms the epoch of the undisguised tyranny which Domitian subsequently exercised. The reign of informers and proscriptions recommenced, and many illustrious men were executed for insufficient reasons. The Christians were persecuted, and the philosophers were banished, and yet he received the most fulsome flattery from the poet Martial. The tyrant lived in seclusion, in his Alban villa, and was finally assassinated, after a reign of fifteen years, A. D. 96.

Persecution of Christians.

On his death a new era of prosperity and glory was inaugurated, by the election of Nerva, and for five successive reigns the Roman world was governed with virtue and ability. It is the golden era of Roman history, praised by Gibbon and admired by all historians, during which the eyes of contemporaries saw nothing but to panegyrize.

Nerva.

Marcus Cocceius Nerva was the great-grandson of a minister of Octavius, and was born in Umbria. He was consul with Vespasian, A. D. 71, and with Domitian, in A. D. 90, and was far advanced in life when chosen by the Senate. The public events of his short but beneficent reign are unimportant. He relieved poverty, diminished the expenses of the State, and set, in his own life, an example of republican simplicity. But he did not reign long enough to have his character tested. He died in sixteen months after his elevation to the purple. His chief work was to create a title for his successor, for he assumed the right of adoption, and made choice of Trajan, without

Death of Nerva.

regard to his own kin, then at the head of the armies of Germany.

Trajan

The new emperor, one of the most illustrious that ever reigned at Rome, was born in Spain, A. D. 52, and had spent his life in the camp. He had a tall and commanding form, was social and genial in his habits, and inspired universal respect. No better choice could have been made. He entered his capital without pomp, unattended by guards, distinguished only for the dignity of his bearing, allowing free access to his person, and paying vows to the gods of his country. His wife, Plotina, bore herself as the spouse of a simple senator, and his sister, Marciana, exhibited a demeanor equally commendable.

The Dacian war.

The great external event of his reign was the war against the Dacians, and their country was the last which the Romans subdued in Europe. They belonged to the Thracian group of nations, and were identical with the Getæ. They inhabited the country which was bordered on the south by the Danube and Mœsia. They were engaged in frequent wars with the Romans, and obtained a decided advantage, in the reign of Domitian, under their king Decebalus. The honor of the empire was so far tarnished as to pay a tribute to Dacia, but Trajan resolved to wipe away the disgrace, and headed himself an expedition into this distant country, A. D. 101, with eighty thousand veterans, subdued Decebalus, and added Dacia to the provinces of the empire. He built a bridge over the Danube, on solid stone piers, about two hundred and twenty miles below the modern Belgrade, which was a remarkable architectural work, four thousand five hundred and seventy feet in length. Enough treasures were secured by the conquest of Dacia to defray the expenses of the war, and of the celebrated triumph which commemorated his victories. At the games instituted in honor of this conquest, eleven thousand beasts were slain, and ten thousand gladiators fought in the Flavian Amphitheatre. The column on which his victories were represented still remains to perpetuate his magnificence, with its

Gladiatorial sports.

two thousand five hundred figures in bas-relief, winding in a spiral band around it from the base to the summit—one of the most interesting relics of antiquity. Near this column were erected the Forum Trajanum and the Basilica Ulpia, the former one thousand one hundred feet long, and the basilica connected with it, surrounded with colonnades, and filled with colossal statues. This enormous structure covered more ground than the Flavian Amphitheatre, and was built by the celebrated Apollodorus, of Damascus. It filled the whole space between the Capitoline and the Quirinal. The double colonnade which surrounded it was one of the most beautiful works of art in the world.

The Forum Trajanum.

On the conquest of Dacia, Trajan devoted himself to the internal administration of his vast empire. He maintained the dignity of the Senate, and allowed the laws to take their course. He was untiring in his efforts to provide for the material wants of his subjects, and in developing the resources of the empire, nor did he rule by oppressive exactions.

After seven years of wise administration, he again was called into the field to extend the eastern frontier of the empire. His efforts were directed against Armenia and Parthia. He reduced the former to a Roman province, and advanced into those Caucasian regions where no Roman imperator had preceded him, except Pompey, receiving the submission of Iberians and Albanians. To overthrow Parthia was now his object, and he advanced across the Tigris to Ctesiphon. In the Parthian capital he was saluted as imperator; but, oppressed with gloom and enfeebled by sickness, he did not presume to reach, as he had aspired, the limits of the Macedonian conquest. He was too old for such work. He returned to Antioch, sickened, and died in Cilicia, August, A. D. 117, after a prosperous and even glorious reign of nineteen and a half years. But he had the satisfaction of having raised the empire to a state of unparalleled prosperity, and of having extended its limits on the east and on the west to the farthest point it ever reached.

The Parthian expedition.

Death of Trajan.

Publius Ælius Hadrian succeeded this great emperor, and was born in Rome A. D. 76, and was a son of the first cousin of Trajan. He made extraordinary attainments as a youth, and served honorably in the armies of his country, especially during the Dacian wars. At twenty-five he was quæstor, at thirty-one he was prætor, and in the following year was made consul, for the forms of the old republic were maintained under the emperors. He was adopted by Trajan, and left at the head of the army at Antioch at the age of forty-two, when Trajan died on his way to Rome. He was at once proclaimed emperor by the army, and its choice was confirmed by the Senate.

Hadrian.

He entered upon his reign with matured knowledge and experience, and sought the development of the empire rather than its extension beyond the Euphrates. He therefore withdrew his armies from Armenia, Mesopotamia, and Parthia, and returned to Rome to celebrate, in Trajan's name, a magnificent triumph, and by employing the spoils of war in largesses and remission of taxes. Averse to the extension of the empire, he still aimed to secure its limits from hostile inroads, and was thus led to repel invasions in Dacia and Britain. He marched at the head of his legions, bareheaded and on foot, as far as Mœsia, and in another compaign through Gaul to the Rhine, and then crossed over to Britain, and secured the northern frontier, by a wall sixty-eight and a half miles in length, against the Caledonians. He then returned to Gaul, passed through Spain, crossed the straits to Mauritania, threatened by the Moors, restored tranquillity, and then advanced to the frontiers of Parthia. He then returned through Asia Minor, and across the Ægean to Athens, and commenced the splendid works with which he adorned the intellectual capital of the empire. Before returning to Rome, he visited Carthage and Sicily.

His warlike expeditions.

Five years later, he made a second progress through the empire, which lasted ten years, with some intervals, spent in his capital, residing chiefly at Athens, constructing great architectural works, and holding converse with philosophers and scholars. During this period he visited Alexandria, whose schools were rivaled only by those of Athens, studying the fantastic philosophy of the Gnostics, and probably examining the Christian system. He ascended the Nile as far as Thebes, and then repaired to Antioch, and returned to Rome through Asia Minor. In his progress, he not merely informed himself of the condition of the empire, but corrected abuses, and made the Roman rule tolerable.

Hadrian visits the provinces.

His remaining years were spent at Rome, diligently administrating the affairs of his vast government, founding libraries and schools, and decorating his capital with magnificent structures. His temple of Venus at Rome was the largest ever erected in the city, and his mausoleum, stripped of its ornaments, now forms the Castle of St. Angelo. Next to the Coliseum, it was the grandest architectural monument in Rome. He also built a villa at Tivoli, whose remains are among the most interesting which seventeen centuries have preserved.

His public works.

This good emperor made a noble choice for his successor, Titus Aurelius Antonius, and soon after died childless, A. D. 138, after a peaceful reign of twenty-one years, in which, says Merivale, "he reconciled, with eminent success, things hitherto found irreconcilable: a contented army and a peaceful frontier; an abundant treasury with lavish expenditure; a free Senate and stable monarchy; and all this without the lustre of a great military reputation, the foil of an odious predecessor, or disgust at recent civil commotions. He recognized, in theory, both conquerors and conquered as one people, and greeted in person every race among his subjects." He had personal defects of character, but his reign is one of the best of the imperial series, and marked the crowning age of Roman civilization.

Antonius Pius, his successor, had less ability, but a still more faultless character. He sprung from the ranks of the nobility; was consul in the third

Antonius Pius.

year of Hadrian, and was prefect of Asia until his adoption, when he took up his residence in Rome, and never left its neighborhood during the remainder of his life. His peaceful reign is barren of external events, but fruitful in the peace and security of his subjects, and the only drawback in his happiness was the licentious character of his wife, who bore him two sons and two daughters. The sons died before his elevation, but one of his daughters married M. Annius Verus, whom he adopted as his successor, and associated with him in the government of the empire. He died after a reign of twenty-three years, and was buried in the mausoleum of Hadrian, which he completed. His character is thus drawn by his son-in-law and successor, Marcus Aurelius: "In my father, I noticed mildness of manner with firmness of resolution, contempt of vainglory, industry in business, and accessibility of person. He knew how to relax, as well as when to labor. From him I learned to acquiesce in every fortune, to exercise foresight in public affairs, to rise superior to vulgar praises, to worship the gods without superstition, to serve mankind without ambition, to be sober and steadfast, to be content with little, to be no sophist or dreaming bookworm, to be practical and active, to be neat and cheerful, to be temperate, modest in dress, and indifferent to the beauty of slaves and furniture, not to be led away by novelties, yet to render honor to true philosophers." What a picture of a heathen emperor, drawn by a pagan philosopher!—the single purpose of ruling for the happiness of their subjects, and realizing the idea of a paternal government, and this in one of the most corrupt periods of Roman society.

Death of Antonius.

His eulogy.

Marcus Aurelius, like Trajan and Hadrian, derived his origin from Spain, but was born in Italy. His features are the most conspicuously preserved in the repositories of ancient art, as his name is the most honorably enshrined on the pages of history—the noblest and most august type of the ancient rulers of the world, far transcending any Jewish king in the severity of his virtues, and

Marcus Aurelius.

the elevation of his soul. His life was modeled on the strictest discipline of the stoical philosophy, of which he was the brightest ornament. He was nearly forty years of age on the death of his father-in-law, although for twenty-three years he had sat side by side with him on the tribunals of the State. His reign, therefore, was virtually a long one, and he was devoted to all the duties which his station imposed. He was great as ruler, as he was profound as a philosopher.

It was under his illustrious reign that the barbarians formed a general union for the invasion of the Roman world, and struck the first of those fatal blows under which the empire finally succumbed. We have but little information of the long contest with Germans, Sarmatians, Marcomanni, Quadi, and Alani, on the banks of the Danube, who were pressed forward by the Scythian tribes. They were repelled, indeed, but they soon after advanced, with renovated forces, when the empire was weakened by the miserable emperors who succeeded Aurelius. And although this great prince commemorated his victory over the barbarians by a column similar to that of Trajan, still they were far from being subdued, and a disgraceful peace, which followed his death, shows that they were exceedingly formidable. He died at Sirmium, or Vindobona (Vienna), exhausted by incessant wars and the cares of State, A. D. 180, in the fifty-ninth year of his age, and twentieth of his reign. The concurrent testimony of historians represents this emperor as the loftiest character that ever wielded a sceptre among the nations of antiquity, although we can not forget that he was a persecutor of the Christians.

Invasion of the empire.

Death of Aurelius.

His son, Commodus, succeeded him, and the thirteen years of his inglorious reign are summed up in conflicts with the Moors, Dacians, and Germans. Skillful generals, by their successes, warded off the attacks of barbarians, but the character and rule of the emperor resembled that of Nero and Domitian. He was weak, cruel, pleasure-seeking, and dissolute. His time was divided between pri-

Commodus.

vate vices and disgraceful public exhibitions. He fought as a gladiator more than seven hundred times, and against antagonists whose only weapons were tin and lead. He also laid claim to divinity, and was addicted to debasing superstitions. He destroyed the old ministers of his father, and decimated the Senate. All who excited his jealousy, or his covetousness, were put out of the way. He was poisoned by his favorite mistress, Marcia, and the Senate set the brand of infamy on his name. Thus perished the last of the line of the Antonines, even as the Julian line was ended by the assassination of Nero, and the Flavian by that of Domitian, and the empire became once again the prize of the soldier, A. D. 192.

CHAPTER XLV.

THE DECLINE OF THE EMPIRE.

Apparent prosperity.

Able or virtuous princes had now ruled the Roman world, with a few exceptions, from Julius Cæsar to Commodus, a period of more than two hundred years. Among these were some odious tyrants, or madmen, who were removed by assassination. But some of these very tyrants governed with ability, and such was the general prosperity, such the wonderful mechanism of government for which the Romans had a genius, that the general condition of the world was better than at any preceding period. All that government could do to preserve and extend civilization was done, on the whole. Despotism was not signally oppressive, and the *régime* of Augustus, of Vespasian, and Hadrian was generally maintained. The Roman governors, appointed by the emperors, ruled more wisely and beneficently than in the time of the republic. Peace, security, and law reigned, and, in consequence, the population increased, civilization advanced, and wealth was accumulated. The whole empire rejoiced in populous cities, in works of art, in literary culture, and in genial manners. Society was pagan, but attractive, and Rome herself was the resort of travelers, the centre of fashion and glory, the joy and the pride of the whole earth. There were no destructive wars, except on the frontiers; all classes were secure, the face of nature was cultivated and beautiful, and poets sung the praises of civilization such as never existed but in isolated cities and countries.

But now we observe the commencement of a great and melancholy change. Prosperity had led to vice, false security, and pride. All classes had become corrupt. Disproportionate fortunes, slavery, and luxury undermined the moral health, and destroyed not only elevation of sentiment but martial virtues. Literature declined in spirit and taste, and was directed to frivolous subjects. Christianity had not become a power sufficiently strong to change or modify the corrupt institutions controlled by the powerful classes. The expensive luxury of the nobles was almost incredible. The most distant provinces were ransacked for game, fish, and fowl for the tables of the great. Usury was practiced at a ruinous rate. Every thing was measured by the money standard. Art was prostituted to please degraded tastes. There was no dignity of character; women were degraded; only passing vanities made any impression on egotistical classes; games and festivals were multiplied; gladiatorial sports outraged humanity; the descendants of the proudest families prided themselves chiefly on their puerile frivolities; the worst rites of paganism were practiced; slaves performed the most important functions; the circus and the theatre were engrossing pleasures; the baths were the resort of the idle and the luxurious, who almost lived in them, and were scenes of disgraceful orgies; great extravagance in dress and ornaments was universal; the pleasures of the table degenerated to riotous excesses; cooks, buffoons, and dancers received more consideration than scholars and philosophers; everybody worshiped the shrine of mammon; all science was directed to utilities that demoralized; sensualism reigned triumphant, and the people lived as if there were no God.

Great moral changes.

Such a state must prepare the way for violence, and when external dangers came there were not sufficient virtues to meet them. But the decline was gradual, and dangers were still at a distance. Both nature and art were the objects of perpetual panegyric, and the worldly and sensual Romans dreamed only of a millennium of protracted joys.

Preparations for violence.

The last experiment of a constitutional empire was succeeded by undisguised military despotism, and no one now desired or expected the restoration of the republic. The Senate was servile and submissive, the people had no voice in public affairs, and the prefects of the imperial guard were the recognized lieutenants and often masters of the emperors.

Pertinax and Julianus.

Pertinax succeeded to the sceptre of Commodus, a wise and good man, and great hopes were entertained of a beneficent reign, when they were suddenly blasted by a sedition of the prætorians, only eighty-six days after the death of Commodus, and these guards publicly sold the empire to Didius Julianus, a wealthy senator, at the price of one thousand dollars to each soldier. Such a bargain disgusted the capital, and raised the legions in the provinces to revolt. Each of the three principal armies set up their own candidate, but L. Septimius Severus, who commanded in Illyricum, was the fortunate one, and was confirmed by the Senate. Didius Julianus was murdered after a brief reign of sixty-six days, and the prætorians who had created the scandal were disbanded.

Severus.

The reign of this general was able and fortunate, although he was cruel and superstitious. His vigor prevented the separation of the empire for a century; but he had powerful rivals in Clodius Albinus, in Britain, and Pescennius Niger, in Syria, both of whom he subdued. At Lyons it is said that one hundred and fifty thousand Romans fought on both sides, when Albinus was killed. The fall of Niger at the Hellespont insured the submission of the East, and the victorious emperor penetrated as far as Ctesiphon, and received the submission of Mesopotamia and Arabia. The triumphal arch erected by him celebrated those military successes.

Vigorous rule of Severus.

Having bestowed peace, and restored the dignity of the empire, this martial prince established an undisguised military despotism, and threw aside all deference to the Senate. He created a new guard of prætorian soldiers four times as numerous as the old, which were recruited from the ranks of the barbarians, who thus began to overawe the capital. The commander of this great force was no less a man than the celebrated jurist, Papianus, and he was the prime minister of the emperor. It was during his reign that a violent persecution of the Christians took place, A. D. 200, which called out the famous apology of Tertullian. Severus died in Britain, to which he was summoned by an irruption of Caledonians, A. D. 211, having reigned nineteen years, and with a vigor worthy of Trajan.

Caracalla and Geta.

He left two sons, who are best known by the names of Caracalla and Geta, and both of whom, in their father's lifetime, had been raised to the dignity of Augustus. The oldest son succeeded to the empire, and the year after his elevation murdered his brother in his mother's arms. He also executed Papinian, the prætorian prefect, because he refused to justify the fratricide, together with twenty thousand persons who were the friends of Geta. After this wholesale murder he left his capital, and never returned to it, spending his time in different provinces, which were alternately the scene of his cruelty and rapine, a victim of the foulest superstitions of the East, and arrogant and vainglorious as he was savage. His tyranny became unendurable, and he was murdered by an agent of the prætorian prefect, A. D. 217, Opilius Macrinus, who became the next emperor.

Macrinus.

Macrinus was only elevated to the purple by promising rich donations to the soldiers, for his rank was only that of a knight. He undertook to restore discipline in the army, and the licentious soldiery found a new candidate for the empire in the person of Avitus, of the family of Severus, a beautiful boy of seventeen, who officiated as priest of the sun in Syria, and whose name in history, from the god he served, is called Elagabalus, or Heliogabalus. But Macrinus was at the head of a formidable force, and fought his rival with bravery, but without success. The battle was decided against him, and he was overtaken in flight and put to death, A. D. 218.

With Elagabalus is associated the most repulsive and loathsome reign of all the emperors. He was guilty of the most shameless obscenities, and the most degrading superstitions. He painted and dressed himself like an Oriental prince; he banqueted in halls hung with cloth of gold, and enriched with jewels; he slept on mattresses stuffed with down found only under the wings of partridges; he dined from tables of pure gold; he danced in public, arrayed in the garb of a Syrian priest; and he collected in his capital all the forms of idolatry and all the hideous abominations which even Grecian paganism despised. This wretch, who insulted every consecrated sentiment, was murdered after a reign of little more than three years, A. D. 222, and his body was thrown into the Tiber, and his memory branded with infamy by the Senate.

Elagabalus.

His luxury.

The prætorians, who now controlled the State, offered the purple to his cousin, Alexander Severus, grand-nephew of Septimius Severus, an emperor who adorned those degenerate times, and who resembled the great Aurelius in the severity of his virtues. His prime minister—the prefect of the prætorian guards—was the celebrated Ulpian, the greatest of Roman jurists, and next to him in dignity and power was the historian, Dion Cassius, consul, governor in Africa, and legate in Dalmatia.

Alexander Severus.

The great labors of Alexander Severus were to quell the mutinous spirit of the prætorian guards, who reveled in the spoil of the empire; to subdue the Persians; and to repel barbarian inroads on the western frontiers. It was while he was in Thrace that a young barbarian of gigantic stature solicited permission to contend for the prize of wrestling. Sixteen of the stoutest Roman soldiers he successively overthrew, and he was permitted to enlist among the troops. The next day he attracted the notice of the emperor, and again contended successfully with seven of the Roman champions, and received, at the hand of the emperor, a gold collar and a place in the body-guard. He rose, step

His labors.

by step, till appointed to discipline the recruits of the army of the Rhine. He became the favorite of the army, and was saluted as imperator. Severus fled to his tent, and was assassinated, A. D. 235.

Maximin.

The savage, Maximin, who now governed the empire, ruled like a barbarian, as he was, disdaining all culture, and hostile to all refinements. Confiscations, exile, or death awaited the few illustrious men who adorned the age. Only brute force was recognized as a claim to imperial favor. The sole object of Maximin was to secure the favor of the soldiers, barbarians like himself, whom he propitiated with exorbitant donations, extorted by fines and confiscations, and derived from the sack of temples. He lived in the camp, and knew nothing of the cities he ruled.

His cruelties.

Gordianus.

Such outrages of course provoked rebellion, and M. Antonius Gordianus, the proconsul of Africa, a descendant of the Gracchi and of Trajan, distinguished for wealth and culture, was proclaimed emperor, at the age of eighty, who associated with him, in the government, his son. The Senate confirmed the Gordians, who fixed their court at Carthage, but Maximin suppressed the insurrection, and proceeded to Rome to satisfy his vengeance. The Senate, in despair, conferred the purple on two members of their own body, Maximus, an able soldier, and Balbinus, a poet and orator. The prætorians supported their claims, and Maximin was assassinated in his tent, A. D. 238. But the new emperors had scarcely given promise of a wise administration, before they in turn were assassinated by the prætorians, and Gordian, a grandson of the first of that name, was elevated to the imperial dignity. He, again, was soon murdered in a mutiny of the soldiers, who elected Philip as his successor, A. D. 244. This emperor, whose reign was marked by the celebration of the secular games with unwonted magnificence, to commemorate the one thousand years since Rome was founded, was put to death by the prætorian guards the

Death of Maximin.

Philip.

following year, and the dignity of Augustus was conferred on Decius.

His reign is memorable for a savage persecution of the Christians, and the victories of the Goths, who, in the preceding reign, had penetrated to Dacia, and conquered Mœsia. The next twenty years were mournful and disgraceful. The emperor marched against these barbarians in person, but was defeated by them in Thrace, and lost his life at a place called Abrutum, A. D. 251. The Goths continued their ravages along the coasts of the Euxine, and made themselves masters of the Crimea. They then sailed, with a large fleet, to the northern parts of the Euxine, took Pityus and Trapezus, attacked the wealthy cities of the Thracian Bosphorus, conquered Chalcedon, Nicomedia, and Nice, and retreated laden with spoil. The next year, with five hundred boats, they pursued their destructive navigation, destroyed Cyzicus, crossed the Ægean, landed at Athens, plundered Thebes, Argos, Corinth and Sparta, advanced to the coasts of Epirus, and devastated the whole Illyrian peninsula. In their ravages they destroyed the famous temple of Ephesus, and, wearied with plunder, returned through Mœsia to their own settlements beyond the Danube.

Persecution of the Christians.

Ravages of the Goths.

During this raid, the son of Decius, Hostilianus, reigned in conjunction with Gallus, one of the generals of Decius, but were put to death by Æmilianus, governor of Pannonia and Mœsia, who had succeeded in gaining a victory over the new and terrible enemy. He was in turn overthrown by Valerianus—a nobleman of great distinction, who signalized himself by considerable military ability, and who associated with himself in the empire his son, Gallienus, A. D. 253, whose frivolities were an offset to the virtues of his father. Valerian was taken prisoner by Sapor, king of Persia, and shortly after died, and the Roman world relapsed under the sway of his son, and at a time of great calamity, memorable for the successes of the Goths, and the direst pestilence which had ever visited the empire. Galli-

Successive emperors.

enus—not without accomplishments, but utterly unfit to govern an empire in the stormy times which witnessed the fierce irruptions of the Goths—was slain by a conspiracy of his officers, A. D. 268.

Gallienus.

The empire was now threatened by barbarians, and wasted by pestilence, and distracted by rebellions and riots. It was on the verge of ruin; but the ruin was averted for one hundred years by a succession of great princes, who traced their origin to the martial province of Illyricum. The first of these emperors was Claudius, one of the generals of Gallienus, and was fifty-four years of age when invested with the purple. He led the armies of the waning empire against the Alemanni, who had invaded Italy, and drove them beyond the Alps. But a fiercer tribe of Germanic barbarians remained to be subdued or repelled—those who had devastated Greece—the Goths. They again appeared upon the Euxine with a fleet, variously estimated from two thousand to six thousand vessels, carrying three hundred and twenty thousand men. A division of this vast, but undisciplined force, invaded Crete and Cyprus, but the main body ravaged Macedonia, and undertook the siege of Thessalonica. Claudius advanced to meet them, and gained at Naissus a complete victory, where fifty thousand of the barbarians perished. A desultory war followed in Thrace, Macedonia, and Mœsia, which resulted in the destruction of the Gothic fleet, and an immense booty in captives and cattle.

Gothic invasions.

Defeat of the barbarians.

Claudius survived this great, but not decisive victory, but two years, and was carried off by pestilence, at Sirmiun, A. D. 270; but not until he had designated for his successor a still greater man—the celebrated Aurelian, whose father had been a peasant. Every day of his short reign was filled with wonders. He put an end to the Gothic war, chastised the Germans who invaded Italy, recovered Gaul, Britain, and Spain, defeated the Alemanni, who devastated the empire from the Po to the Danube, destroyed the proud monarchy which Zenobia had

Aurelian.

Zenobia.

built up in the deserts of the East, took the queen captive, and carried her to Rome, where he celebrated the most magnificent triumph which the world had seen since the days of Pompey and Cæsar. This celebrated woman, equaling Cleopatra in beauty, and Boadicea in valor, and blending the popular manners of the Roman princes with the stately pomp of Oriental kings, had retired, on her defeat, to the beautiful city which Solomon had built, shaded with palms, and ornamented with palaces. There, in that Tadmor of the wilderness, Palmyra, the capital of her empire, which embraced a large part of Asia Minor, Syria, and Egypt, she had cultivated the learning of the Greeks, and the Oriental tongues of the countries she ruled, excelling equally in the chase and in war, the most truly accomplished woman of antiquity,—sprung, like Cleopatra, from the Greek kings of Egypt. Among her counselors was the celebrated Longinus—the most conspicuous ornament of the last age of Greek classic literature, and a philosopher who taught the wisdom of Plato. When Palmyra was taken by Aurelian, this great man, who had stimulated Zenobia in her rebellion, was executed, without uttering a word of complaint, together with the people of the city, with remorseless barbarity, and the city of Solomon became an inconsiderable Arab town. The queen, who had fled, was pursued and taken, and graced the magnificent triumph of the martial emperor. The captive queen was made to precede the triumphal chariot, on foot, loaded with fetters of gold, and arrayed in the most gorgeous dress of her former empire. She was not executed, but permitted to reside in the capital in the state of princes.

Palmyra.

Zenobia taken captive.

This great and brilliant triumph—one of the last glories of the setting sun of Roman greatness—seemed to augur the restoration of the empire. The emperor was sanguine, and boasted that all external danger had passed away. But in a few months he was summoned to meet new enemies in the East, and he was murdered by a conspiracy of his officers, probably in revenge for the cruel-

Triumph of Aurelian.

ties and massacres he had inflicted at Rome. In one of his reforms a sedition arose, and was quelled inexorably by the slaughter of seven thousand of the soldiers, besides a large number of the leading nobles.

Tacitus.

His sceptre descended to Tacitus, A. D. 275, a descendant of the great historian; a man, says Niebuhr, "who was great in every thing that could distinguish a senator; he possessed immense property, of which he made a brilliant use; he was a man of unblemished character; he possessed the knowledge of a statesman, and had, in his youth, shown great military skill." Scarcely was he inaugurated as emperor before he marched against the Alans, a Scythian tribe, who had ravaged Pontus, Cappadocia, Cilicia, and Galatea. He, however, lost his life amid the hardships of his first campaign, at the age of seventy-five, and after a brief reign of six months.

Probus.

The veteran general, M. Aurelius Probus, the commander of the Eastern provinces, was proclaimed emperor by the legions, although originally of peasant rank. He was forty-five years of age, and united the military greatness of Aurelian with political prudence, in all respects the best choice which could have been made, and one of the best and greatest of all the emperors. His six years of administration were marked by uninterrupted successes, and he won a fame equal to that of the ancient heroes. He restored peace and order in all the provinces; he broke the power of the Sarmatians; he secured the alliance of the Goths; he drove the Isaurians to their strongholds among their inaccessible mountains; he chastised the rebellious cities of Egypt; he delivered Gaul from the Germanic barbarians; he drove the Franks to their morasses at the mouth of the Rhine; he vanquished the Burgundians who had wandered in quest of booty from the banks of the Oder; he defeated the Lygii, a fierce tribe on the borders of Silesia; he extended his victories to the Elbe, and erected a wall, two hundred miles in length, from the Danube to the Rhine; so that "there was not left," says Gibbon, "in all the

His warlike career.

provinces, a hostile barbarian, or tyrant, or even a robber." After having destroyed four hundred thousand of the barbarians, he returned to his capital to celebrate a triumph, which equaled in splendor that of Aurelian. He, too, fancied that all external enemies were subdued forever, and that Rome should henceforth rejoice in eternal peace. But scarcely had the pæans of victory been sung by a triumphant and infatuated people, when he was assassinated in a mutiny of his own troops, whom he had compelled to labor in draining the marshes around Sirmium, A. D. 282.

The soldiers, repenting the act as soon as it was done, conferred the purple on the prætorian prefect, and *notified* the Senate of its choice. And the choice was a good one; and the new emperor, Carus, at sixty years of age, conferring the title of Cæsar upon his two sons, Carinus and Numerianus, whom he left to govern the West, hastened against the Sarmatians, who had overrun Illyricum. Successful in his objects, he advanced, in the depth of winter, through Thrace and Asia Minor to the confines of Persia. The Persian king, wishing to avert the storm, sent his embassadors to the imperial camp, and found the emperor seated on the grass, dining from peas and bacon, in all the simplicity of the early successors of Mohammed. But before he could advance beyond the Tigris, his tent was struck by lightning, and he was killed, on Christmas day, A. D. 283.

Carus.

Carinus and Numerian succeeded to the vacant throne. The former, at Rome, disgraced his trust by indolence and shameless vices; while the latter, in the camp, was unfit, though virtuous, to control the turbulent soldiers, and was found murdered in his bed the very day that Carinus celebrated the games with unusual magnificence.

Carinus.

The army raised C. Valerius Diocletianus to the vacant dignity, and his first act was to execute the murderer of Numerian. His next was to encounter Carinus in battle, who was slain, A. D. 285, and Diocletian—perhaps the greatest emperor after Augustus—reigned alone.

Diocletian. Diocletian is, however, rendered infamous in ecclesiastical history, as the most bitter of all the persecutors of the Christians, now a large and growing body; but he was a man of the most distinguished abilities, though of obscure birth, in a little Dalmatian town. He commenced his illustrious reign at the age of thirty-nine, and reigned twenty years,—more as a statesman than warrior,—politic, judicious, indefatigable in business, and steady in his purposes.

Important political changes. This emperor inaugurated a new era, and a new policy of government. The cares of State in a disordered age, when the empire was threatened on every side by hostile barbarians, and disgraced by insurrections and tumults, induced Diocletian to associate with himself three colleagues, who had won fame in the wars of Aurelian and Carus. Maximian, Galerius, and Constantius—one of whom had the dignity of Augustus, and two that of Cæsar.

Maximian, associated with Diocletian, with the rank of Augustus, had been also an Illyrian peasant, and was assigned to the government of the western provinces, while Diocletian retained that of the eastern. Maximian established the seat of his government at Milan, giving a deathblow to the Senate, which, though still mentioned honorably by name, was henceforth severed from the imperial court. The empire had been ruled by soldiers ever since pressing dangers had made it apparent that only men of martial virtues could preserve it from the barbarians. But now the most undisguised *military* rule, uninfluenced by old constitutional form, was the only recognized authority, and the warlike emperors, bred in the camp, had a disdain of the ancient capital, as well as great repugnance to the enervated prætorian soldiers, who made and unmade emperors, whose privileges were abolished forever. Milan was selected for the seat of imperial government, from its proximity to the frontier, perpetually menaced by the barbarians; and this city, before a mere military post, now assumed the splendor of an imperial city, and was defended by a double wall.

Diocletian made choice, at first, of Nicomedia, the old capital of the Bithynian kings, as the seat of his Eastern government, equally distant from the Danube and the Euphrates. He assumed the manner and state of an Oriental monarch. He wore a diadem set with pearls, and a robe of silk and gold instead of the simple toga with its purple stripe. His shoes were studded with precious stones, and his court was marked by Oriental ceremonials. His person was difficult of access, and the avenues to his palace were guarded by various classes of officers. No one could approach him without falling prostrate in adoration, and he was addressed as "My lord the emperor." But he did not live in Oriental seclusion, and was perpetually called away by pressing dangers.

New seat of government.

Oriental pomp of Diocletian.

The Cæsars Galerius and Constantius were sent to govern the provinces on the frontiers; the former, from his capital, Sirmium, in Illyricum, watched the whole frontier of the Danube; the latter spent his time in Britain. Galerius was adopted by Diocletian, and received his daughter Valeria in marriage; while Constantius was adopted by Maximian, and married his daughter Theodora.

Galerius and Constantius.

The division of the empire under these four princes nearly corresponded with the prefectures which Constantine subsequently established, and which were deemed necessary to preserve the empire from dissolution—a dissolution inevitable, had it not been for the great emperors whom the necessities of the empire had raised up, but whose ruin was only for a time averted. Not even able generals and good emperors could save the corrupted empire. It was doomed. Vice had prepared the way for violence. The four emperors, who now labored to prevent a catastrophe, were engaged in perpetual conflicts, and through their united efforts peace was restored throughout the empire, and the last triumph that Rome ever saw was celebrated by them.

Only one more enemy, to the eye of Diocletian, remained to be subdued, and this was Christianity. But this enemy was unconquerable. Silently, surely, without pomp, and without art, the new religion had made its way, against all opposition, prejudice, and hatred, from Jews and pagans alike, and was now a power in the empire. The followers of the hated sect were, however, from the humble classes, and but few great men had arisen among them, and even these were unimportant to the view of philosophers and rulers. The believers formed an esoteric circle, and were lofty, stern, and hostile to all the existing institutions of society. They formed an *imperium in imperio*, but did not aim, at this time, to reach political power. They were scattered throughout the great cities of the empire, and were ruled by their bishops and ministers. They did not make war on men, but on their ideas and habits and customs. They avoided all external conflicts, and contended with devils and passions. But government distrusted and disliked them, and sought at different times to exterminate them. There had already been nine signal persecutions from the time of Nero, and yet they had constantly increased in numbers and influence. But now a more serious attack was to be made upon them by the emperors, provoked, probably, by the refusal of some Christians to take the military oath, and serve in the armies, on conscientious principles; but interpreted by those in authority as disloyalty in a great national crisis. The mind of the emperor was alienated; and both Galerius and Diocletian resolved that a religion which seemed hostile to the political relations of the empire, should be suppressed. A decree was issued to destroy all the Christian churches, to confiscate their property, to burn the sacred writings, to deprive Christians of their civil rights, and even to doom them to death. The decree which was publicly exhibited in Nicomedia, was torn down by a Christian, who expressed the bitterest detestation of the tyrannical governors. The fires which broke out in the palace were ascribed to the Christians, and the command was finally issued to imprison all the ministers of religion, and punish those who protected them. A persecution which has had no parallel in history, was extended to all parts of the

Persecution of Christians.

The reason of their persecution.

empire. The whole civil power, goaded by the old priests of paganism, was employed in searching out victims, and all classes of Christians were virtually tormented and murdered. The earth groaned for ten years under the sad calamity, and there was apparently no hope. But whether scourged, or lacerated, or imprisoned, or burned, the martyrs showed patience, faith, and moral heroism, and invoked death to show its sting, and the grave its victory.

The persecution of the Christians—this attempt to suppress religion thought to be hostile to the imperial authority, and not without some plausibility, since many Christians refused to be enrolled in the armies, and suffered death sooner than enlist—was the last great act of Diocletian. Whether wearied with the cares of State, or disgusted with his duties, or ill, or craving rest and repose, he took the extraordinary resolution of abdicating his throne, at the very summit of his power, and at the age of fifty-nine. He influenced Maximian to do the same, and the two Augusti gave place to the two Cæsars. The double act of resignation was performed at Nicomedia and Milan, on the same day, May 1, A. D. 305. Diocletian took a graceful farewell of his soldiers, and withdrew to a retreat near his native city of Salonæ, on the coast of the Adriatic. He withdrew to a magnificent palace, which he had built on a square of six hundred feet, in a lovely and fertile spot, in sight of the sea, and the mountains, and luxurious plains. He there devoted himself to the pleasures of agriculture, and planted cabbages with his own hand, and refused all solicitations to resume his power. But his repose was alloyed by the sight of increasing troubles, and the failure of the system he had inaugurated. If the empire could not be governed by one master, it could not be governed by four, with their different policies and rivalries. He lived but nine years in retirement; but long enough to see his religious policy reversed, by the edict of Milan, which confirmed the Christian religion, and the whole imperial fabric which he had framed reversed by Constantine.

Retirement of Diocletian.

Confusion followed his abdication. Civil wars instead of barbaric wasted the empire. The ancient heart of the empire had no longer the presence of an Augustus, and a new partition virtually took place, by which Italy and Africa became dependencies of the East. Galerius—now Augustus—assumed the right to nominate the two new Cæsars, one of whom was his sister's son, who assumed the name of Galerius Valerius Maximinus, to whom were assigned Syria and Egypt, and the other was his faithful servant, Severus, who was placed over Italy and Africa. According to the forms of the constitution, he was subordinate to Constantius, but he was devoted to Galerius. The emperor Constantius, then in Boulogne, was dying, and his son, Constantine, was at the court of Galerius. Though summoned to the bedside of his father, Galerius sought to retain him, but Constantine abruptly left Nicomedia, evaded Severus, traversed Europe, and reached his father, who was just setting out for Britain, to repel an invasion of the Caledonians. He reached York only to die, A. D. 306, and with his last breath transmitted his empire to his son, and commended him to the soldiers. Galerius was transported with rage, but was compelled to submit, and named Constantine Cæsar over the western provinces, who was not elevated to the dignity of Augustus till two years later.

The evils which flowed from it.

Death of Constantius.

The elevation of Severus to supreme power in Italy by Galerius, filled the abdicated emperor Maximian with indignation, and humiliated the Roman people. The prætorians rose against the party of Severus, who retired to Ravenna, and soon after committed suicide. The Senate assumed their old prerogative, and conferred the purple on Maxentius, the son of Maximilian. Galerius again assumed the power of nominating an Augustus, and bestowed the purple, made vacant by the death of Severus, on an old comrade, Licinius, originally a Dacian peasant.

Thus, there were six emperors at a time; Constantine, in Britain; Maximian, who resumed the purple; Maxentius, his son; Licinius Galerius, in the East; and Maximin, his nephew. Maximian crossed the Alps in person, won over Constantine to his party, and gave him his daughter, Fausta, in marriage, and conferred upon him the rank of Augustus; so, in the West, Maxentius and Constantine affected to be subordinate to Maximian; while, in the East, Licinius and Maximin obeyed the orders of their benefactor, Galerius. The sovereigns of the East and West were hostile to each other, but their mutual fears produced an apparent tranquillity, and a feigned reconciliation.

Six emperors.

The first actual warfare, however, broke out between Maximian and his son. Maxentius insisted on the renewed abdication of his father, and had the support of the prætorian guards. Driven into exile, he returned to Gaul, and took refuge with his son and daughter, who received him kindly; but in the absence of Constantine, he seized the treasure to bribe his troops, and was holding communication with Maxentius when Constantine returned from the Rhine. The old intriguer had only time to throw himself into Marseilles, where he strangled himself, when the city was hard pressed by Constantine, A. D. 310.

Civil wars.

In a year after, Galerius died, like Herod Agrippa, a prey to loathsome vermin—*morbus pediculosus*, and his dominions were divided between Maximin and Licinius, each of whom formed secret alliances with Maxentius and Constantine, between whom was war.

Death of Galerius.

The tyranny of Maxentius led his subjects to look to Constantine as a deliverer, who marched to the relief of the Senate and Roman people. He crossed the Alps with forty thousand men. Maxentius collected a force of one hundred and seventy thousand, to maintain which he had the wealth of Italy, Africa, and Sicily. Constantine first encountered the lieutenants of Maxentius in the plains of Turin, and gained a complete victory, the prize of which was Milan, the new capital of Italy. He was advancing to Rome on the Flaminian way, before Maxentius was aroused to his danger, being absorbed in pleasures. A

Elevation of Constantine.

few miles from Rome was fought the battle of Saxa Rubra, A. D. 312, between the rival emperors, at which Maxentius perished, and Constantine was greeted by the Senate as the first of the three surviving Augusti. The victory of Constantine was commemorated by a triumphal arch, which still remains, and which was only a copy of the arch of Trajan.

Successes of Constantine. The ensuing winter was spent in Rome, during which Constantine abolished forever the prætorian guards, which had given so many emperors to the world. In the spring Constantine gave his daughter Constantia in marriage to Licinius, but was soon called away to the Rhine by an irruption of Franks, while Licinius marched against Maximin, and defeated him under the walls of Heraclea. Maximin retreated to Nicomedia, and was about to renew the war, when he died at Tarsus, and Licinius became master of the Eastern provinces.

Conversion of Constantine. There were now but two emperors, one in the East, and the other in the West. Constantine celebrated the restoration of tranquillity by promulgating at Milan an edict in favor of universal religious toleration, and the persecution of the Christians by the pagans was ended forever, in Europe. About this time Constantine himself was converted to the new religion. In his march against Maxentius, it is declared by Eusebius, that he saw at noonday a cross in the heavens, inscribed with the words, "By this conquer." It is also asserted that the vision of the cross was seen by the whole army, and the cross henceforth became the standard of the Christian emperors. It was called the *Labarum*, and is still seen on the coins of Constantine, and was intrusted to a chosen guard of fifty men. It undoubtedly excited enthusiasm in the army, now inclined to accept the new faith, and Constantine himself joined the progressive party, and made Christianity the established religion of the

Establishment of Christianity. empire. Henceforth the protection of the Christian religion became one of the cherished objects of his soul, and although his life was stained by superstitions and many acts of cruelty and wickedness, Constantine stands out in history as the first Christian emperor. For this chiefly he is famous, and a favorite with ecclesiastical writers. The edict of Milan is an era in the world's progress. But he was also a great sovereign, and a great general.

The harmony between so ambitious a man and Licinius was not of long duration. Rival interests and different sympathies soon led to the breaking out of hostilities, and Licinius was defeated in two great battles, and resigned to Constantine all his European possessions, except Thrace. The nine successive years were spent by Licinius in slothful and vicious pleasures, while Constantine devoted his energies to the suppression of barbarians, and the enactment of important laws. He repulsed the Gothic and Sarmatian hordes, who had again crossed the Danube, and pursued them into Dacia; nor did the Goths secure peace until they had furnished forty thousand recruits to the Roman armies. This recruiting of the imperial armies from the barbarians was one of the most melancholy signs of decaying strength, and indicated approaching ruin.

Renewed wars.

In the year 323 a new civil war broke out between Constantine and Licinius. The aged and slothful Eastern emperor roused himself to a grand effort and marshalled an army of one hundred and fifty thousand foot and fifteen thousand horse on the plains of Hadrianople, while his fleet of three hundred and fifty triremes commanded the Hellespont. Constantine collected an army of one hundred and twenty thousand men at Thessalonica, and advanced to attack his foe, intrenched in a strong position. The battle was decided in favor of Constantine, who slew thirty-four thousand of his enemies, and took the fortified camp of Licinius, who fled to Byzantium, July, A. D. 323.

Victory of Constantine over Licinius.

The fleet of Licinius still remained, and with his superior naval force he might have baffled his rival. But fortune, or valor, again decided in favor of the Western emperor, and after a fight of two days the admiral of Licinius retired to Byzantium. The siege of this city was now pressed with valor by Constantine, and Licinius fled with his treasures to Chalcedon, and succeeded in raising another army of fifty thousand men. These raw levies were, however, powerless against the veterans of Constantine, whom he led in person. The decisive battle was fought at Chrysopolis, and Licinius retired to Nicomedia, but soon after abdicated, and was banished to Thessalonica. There he was not long permitted to remain, being executed by order of Constantine, one of the foul blots on his memory and character.

Death of Licinius.

The empire was now reunited under a single man, at the cost of vast treasures and lives. The policy of Diocletian had only inaugurated civil war. There is no empire so vast which can not be more easily governed by one man than by two or four. It may be well for empires to be subdivided, like that of Charlemagne, but it is impossible to prevent civil wars when the power is shared equally by jealous rivals. It was better for the Roman world to be united under Octavius, than divided between him and Antony.

Constantine reigns alone.

On the fall of Byzantium, Constantine was so struck with its natural advantages, that he resolved to make it the capital of the empire. Placed on the inner of two straits which connect the Euxine and the Ægean with the Mediterranean, on the frontiers of both Europe and Asia, it seemed to be the true centre of political power, while its position could be itself rendered impregnable against any external enemy that threatened the Roman world. The wisdom of the choice of Constantine, and his unrivaled sagacity, were proved by the fact, that while Rome was successively taken and sacked by Goths and Vandals, Constantinople remained the capital of the eastern Roman empire for eleven continuous centuries.

Foundation of Constantinople.

The reign of Constantine as sole emperor was marked by another event, A. D. 325, which had a great influence on the subsequent condition of the world in a moral and religious point of view, and this was the famous

Council of Nice.

Council of Nicæa, which assembled to settle points of faith and discipline in the new religion which was now established throughout the empire. It is called the first Ecumenical, or General Council, and was attended by three hundred and eighteen bishops, with double the number of presbyters, assembled from all parts of the Christian world. Here the church and the empire met face to face. In this council the emperor left the cares of State, and the command of armies, to preside over discussions on the doctrine of the Trinity, as expounded by two great rival parties,—one headed by Athanasius, then archdeacon, afterward archbishop of Alexandria—the greatest theologian that had as yet appeared in the church,—and the other by Arius, a simple presbyter of Alexandria, but a man of subtle and commanding intellect. Arius maintained that the Son, the second person of the Trinity, derived his being from the Father within the limits of time, and was secondary to him in power and glory. Athanasius maintained that the Son was co-eternal with the Father, and the same in substance with the Father. This theological question had long been discussed, and the church was divided between the two parties, each of which exhibited extreme acrimony. Constantine leaned to the orthodox side, although his most influential adviser, Eusebius, bishop of Cæsarea, the historian, inclined to the Arian view. But the emperor was more desirous to secure peace and unity, than the ascendency of any dogma, and the doctrine of Athanasius became the standard of faith, and has since remained the creed of the church.

Athanasius.

Theological discussion on the Trinity.

After the settlement of the faith of the church, now becoming the great power of the world, the reign of Constantine was disgraced by a domestic tragedy seldom paralleled in history. His son, Crispus, by a low-born woman, conspicuous for talents and virtues, either inflamed the jealousy of his father, or provoked him by a secret conspiracy. It has never been satisfactorily settled whether he was a rival or a conspirator, but he was accused,

Assassination of Crispus.

tried, and put to death, in the twentieth year of the reign, while Constantine was celebrating at Rome the festival of his *vicennalia.* After this bloody tragedy, for which he is generally reproached, he took his final departure from Rome, and four years after, the old capital was degraded to the rank of a secondary city, and Constantinople was dedicated as the new capital of the empire. From the eastern promontory to the Golden Horn, the extreme length of Constantinople was three Roman miles, and the circumference measured ten, inclosing an area of two thousand acres, besides the suburbs. The new city was divided into fourteen wards, and was ornamented with palaces, fora, and churches. The church of St. Sophia was built on the site of an old temple, and was in the form of a Greek cross, surmounted by a beautiful and lofty dome. In a century afterward, Constantinople rivaled Rome in magnificence. It had a capitol, a circus, two theatres, eight public baths, fifty-two porticoes, eight aqueducts, four halls, and fourteen churches, and four thousand three hundred and eighty-three large palatial residences.

The new capital.

After the building of this new and beautiful city, Constantine devoted himself to the internal regulation of the empire, which he divided into four prefectures, subdivided into thirteen dioceses, each governed by vicars or vice-prefects, who were styled counts and dukes. The provinces were subdivided to the number of one hundred and sixteen. Three of these were governed by proconsuls, thirty-seven by consuls, five by correctors, and seventy-one by presidents, chosen from the legal profession, and called *clarissimi.* The prefecture of the East embraced the Asiatic provinces, together with Egypt, Thrace, and the lower Mœsia; that of Illyricum contained the countries between the Danube, the Ægean, and the Adriatic; that of Italy extended over the Alps to the Danube; and that of the Gauls embraced the western provinces beyond the Rhine and the Alps.

New divisions of the empire.

The military power was separated from the civil. There

were two master-generals, one of infantry, and the other of cavalry, afterward increased to eight, under whom were thirty-five commanders, ten of whom were counts, and twenty dukes. The legions were reduced from six thousand to fifteen hundred men. Their number was one hundred and thirty-two, and the complete force of the empire was six hundred and forty-five thousand, holding five hundred and eighty-three permanent stations.

Changes in the army.

The ministers of the palace, who exercised different functions about the presence of the emperor, were seven in number: the prefect of the bed-chamber; a eunuch, who waited on the emperor; the master of offices—the supreme magistrate of the palace; the quæstor—at the head of the judicial administration, and who composed the orations and edicts of the emperor; the treasurer, and two counts of domestics, who commanded the body-guard.

The ministers.

The bishopric nearly corresponded with the civil divisions of the empire, and the bishops had different ranks. We now observe archbishops and metropolitans.

The bishoprics.

The new divisions complicated the machinery of government, and led to the institution of many new offices, which greatly added to the expense of government, for which taxation became more rigorous and oppressive. The old constitution was completely subverted, and the emperor became an Oriental monarch.

Constantine was called away from his labors of organization to resist the ambition of Sapor II., when he died, at the age of sixty-four, at his palace near Nicomedia, A. D. 337, after a memorable but tumultuous reign—memorable for the recognition of Christianity as a State religion; tumultuous, from civil wars and contests with barbarians. Constantinople, not Rome, became the future capital of the empire.

Death of Constantine.

CHAPTER XLVI.

THE FALL OF THE EMPIRE.

After the death of Constantine, the decline was rapid, and new dangers multiplied. Warlike emperors had staved off the barbarians, and done all that man could do to avert ruin. But the seeds of ruin were planted, and must bear their wretched fruit. The seat of empire was removed to a new city, more able, from its position, to withstand the shock which was to come. In the strife between new and hardy races, and the old corrupt population, the issue could not be doubtful. The empire had fulfilled its mission. Christianity was born, protected, and rendered triumphant. Nothing more was wanted than the conversion of the barbarians to the new faith before desolation should overspread the world—and a State prepared for new ideas, passions, and interests.

The heirs of Constantine.

Constantine left three sons and two daughters, by Fausta, the daughter of Maximian,—Constantinus, Constantius, Constans, Constantina, and Helena. The imperial dignity was enjoyed by the sons, and the youngest daughter, Helena, married the emperor Julian, grandson of Constantius Chlorus. The three sons of Constantine divided the empire between them. The oldest, at the age of twenty-one, retained the prefecture of Gaul; Constantius, aged twenty, kept Thrace and the East; while Constans, the youngest, at the age of seventeen, added the Italian prefecture with Greece.

Constantius.

The ablest of these princes was Constantius, on whom fell the burden of the Persian war, and which ultimately ended on the defeat of Julian, in Sapor wresting from the emperor all the countries beyond the Euphrates.

Constantine II. was dissatisfied with his share of the empire, and compelled Constans to yield up Africa, but was slain in an expedition beyond the Julian Alps, A. D. 340.

Constans.

Constans held the empire of the West for ten years, during which he carried on war with the Franks, upon the Rhine, and with the Scots and Picts. His vices were so disgraceful that a rebellion took place, under Magnentius, who slew Constans, A. D. 350, and reigned in his stead, the seat of his government being Treves.

War with Magnentius.

Constantius II. made war on the usurper, Magnentius, a rough barbarian, and finally defeated him on the banks of the Danube, where fifty-four thousand men perished in battle, soon after which the usurper killed himself.

Death of Athanasius.

Constantius, by the death of his brother, and overthrow of Magnentius, was now sole master of the empire, and through his permission Athanasius was restored to the archbishopric of Alexandria, but was again removed, the emperor being an Arian. This second removal raised a tumult in Alexandria, and he was allowed to return to his see, where he lived in peace until he died, A. D. 372—the great defender of the orthodox creed, which finally was established by councils and the emperors.

Wars of Constantius.

The emperor Constantius was engaged in successive wars with the barbarians,—with the Persians on the East, the Sarmatians on the Danube, and the Franks and Alemanni, on the Rhine. During these wars, his brother-in-law, Julian, was sent to the West with the title of Cæsar, where he restored order, and showed signal ability. On the death of Constantius, he was recognized as emperor without opposition, A. D. 361.

Julian.

Julian is generally called the Apostate, since he proclaimed a change in the established religion, but tolerated Christianity. He was a Platonic philosopher—a man of great virtue and ability, whose life was unstained by vices. But his attempt to restore paganism was senseless and ineffectual. As a popular belief, paganism had expired. His character is warmly praised by Gibbon, and commended by other historians. He struggled against the spirit of his age, and was unsuccessful. He was worthy of the best ages of the empire in the exercise of all pagan virtues—the true successor of Hadrian and the Antonines.

Death of Julian.

He was also a great general, and sought to crush the power of the Persian kings and make Babylonia a Roman province. Here, too, he failed, although he gained signal successes. He was mortally wounded while effecting a retreat from the Tigris, after a short reign of twenty months. With him ended the house of Constantine. The empire was conferred by the troops on Flavius Claudius Jovianus, chief of the imperial household, A. D. 363 —a man of moderate talents and good intentions, but unfit for such stormy times. He restored Christianity, which henceforth was the national religion. He died the following year, and was succeeded by Flavius Valentinianus, the son of Count Gratian, a general who had arisen from obscurity in Pannonia, to the command of Africa and Britain.

Jovian.

Valentinian.

Valentinian was forty-four years of age when he began to reign, A. D. 364, a man of noble character and person, and in a month associated his brother Flavius Valens with him in the government of the empire. Valentinian kept the West, and conferred the East on Valens. Thus was the empire again formally divided, and was not reunited until the reign of Theodosius. Valentinian chose the post of danger, rather than of pleasure and luxury, for the West was now invaded by various tribes of the Germanic race. The Alemanni were powerful on the Rhine; the Saxons were invading Britain; the Burgundians were commencing their ravages in Gaul; and the Goths were preparing for another inroad. The emperor, whose seat of power was Milan, was engaged in perpetual, but indecisive conflicts. He reigned with vigor, and repressed the barbarians. He bestowed the title of Augustus on his

Barbaric invasions.

son Gratian, and died in a storm of wrath by the bursting of a blood-vessel, while reviling the embassadors of the Quadi, A. D. 375.

The emperor Valens, at Constantinople, was exposed to no less dangers, without the force to meet them. The great nation of the Goths, who had been at peace with the empire for a generation, resumed their hostilities upon the Danube. Hermanneric, the first historic name among these fierce people, had won a series of brilliant victories over other barbarians, after he was eighty years of age. His dominions extended from the Danube to the Baltic, and embraced the greater part of Germany and Scythia.

Valens.

But the Goths were invaded by a fierce race of barbarians, more savage than themselves, from the banks of the Don, called Scythians, or Huns, of Sclavonic origin. Pressed by this new enemy, they sought shelter in the Roman territory. Instead of receiving them as allies, the emperor treated them as enemies. Hostages from the flower of their youth were scattered through the cities of Asia Minor, while the corrupt governors of Thrace annoyed them by insults and grievances. The aged Hermanneric, exasperated by misfortune, made preparations for a general war, while Sarmatians, Alans, and Huns united with them. After three indecisive campaigns, the emperor Valens advanced to attack their camp near Hadrianople, defended by Fritagern. Under the walls of this city was fought the most bloody and disastrous battle which Rome ever lost, A. D. 378. Two-thirds of the imperial army was destroyed, the emperor was slain, and the remainder fled in consternation. Sixty thousand infantry and six thousand cavalry lay dead upon the fatal field. The victors, intoxicated with their success, invested Hadrianople, but were unequal to the task, being inexperienced in sieges. Laden with spoil, they retired to the western boundaries of Thrace. From the shores of the Bosphorus to the Julian Alps, nothing was seen but conflagration, murder, and devastation. So

Gothic invasion.

Death of Valens.

great were the misfortunes of the Illyrian provinces, that they never afterward recovered. Churches were turned into stables, palaces were burned, works of art were destroyed, the relics of martyrs were desecrated, the population decimated, and the provinces were overrun.

Ravages of the Goths.

In this day of calamity a hero and deliverer was needed. The feeble Gratian, who ruled in the West, cast his eyes upon an exile, whose father, an eminent general, had been unjustly murdered by the emperor Valentinian. This man was Theodosius, then living in modest retirement on his farm near Valladolid, in Spain, as unambitious as David among his sheep, as contented as Cincinnatus at the plow. Even Gibbon does not sneer at this great Christian emperor, who revived for a while the falling empire. He accepted the sceptre of Valens, A. D. 379, and the conduct of the Gothic war, being but thirty-three years of age. One of the greatest of all the emperors, and the last great man who swayed the sceptre of Trajan, his ancestor, he has not too warmly been praised by the Church, whose defender he was—the last flickering light of an expiring monarchy,—although his character has been assailed by modern critics of great respectability.

Theodosius.

As soon as he was invested with the purple, he took up his residence in Thessalonica, and devoted his energies to the task assigned him by the necessities of the empire. He succeeded in putting a stop to the progress of the Goths, disarmed them by treaties, and allowed them to settle on the right bank of the Danube, within the limits of the empire. He invited the aged Athanaric to his capital and table, who was astonished by his riches and glory. Peace was favored by the death of Fritagern, and forty thousand Goths were received as soldiers of the empire,—an impolitic act.

Successes over the Goths.

At this period the Goths settled in Mœsia were visited by Uphilas, a Christian missionary and Arian bishop, who translated the Bible, and had great success in the conversion of the barbarians to a nominal faith. This is

Uphilas.

the earliest instance of the reception of the new faith by the Germanic races.

While Theodosius was restoring the eastern empire, Gratian relapsed into indolent pleasures at Milan, which provoked a revolution. Maximus was proclaimed emperor by the legions in Britain, and invaded Gaul. Gratian fled, with a retinue of three hundred horse, and was overtaken and slain. Theodosius recognized the claims of the usurper, unwilling to waste the blood of the enfeebled soldiers in a new civil war, provided that Italy and Africa were secured to Valentinian II., the younger brother of Gratian. The young emperor made himself unpopular by espousing Arianism, and for being governed by his mother Justina, and four years after was obliged to flee to Thessalonica, on an invasion of Italy by Maximus, and invoke the aid of Theodosius, who responded to his call, won by the charms of the princess Galla, whom he married. Maximus was defeated, put to death, and Valentinian II. was replaced upon his throne.

Gratian.

Valentinian II.

It was when Maximus was triumphant in Gaul that the celebrated Ambrose, archbishop of Milan, was sent to the usurper's camp to demand the dead body of the murdered Gratian. But this intrepid prelate made himself still more famous for his defense of orthodoxy against the whole power of Valentinian II. and his mother. He is also immortalized for the chastisement he inflicted upon Theodosius himself for the slaughter of Thessalonica. The emperor was in Milan when intelligence arrived of a sedition in the city, caused by factions of the circus, during which Boderic, the commander of the imperial troops, was killed. This outrage was revenged by the wanton massacre of seven thousand people. The news of this barbarity filled Ambrose with horror, and he wrote a letter to the emperor, which led to his repentance; but as he was about to enter the basilica, the prelate met him at the door, and refused admission until he had expiated his crime by a rigorous penance, and the emperor submitted to the humiliation—an

Ambrose.

Penance of Theodosius.

act of submission to the Church which was much admired—an act of ecclesiastical authority which formed a precedent for the heroism of Hildebrand.

Under the influence of the clergy, now a great power, Theodosius the same year promulgated an edict for the suppression of all acts of pagan worship, private and public, under heavy penalties, and the Church, in turn, became persecuting. At this time the corruption of the Church made rapid progress. Pretended miracles, pious frauds, the worship of saints, veneration for relics, ascetic severities, monastic superstitions, the pomp of bishops, and a secular spirit marked the triumph of Christianity over paganism. The Church was united to the State, and the profession of the new faith was made a necessary qualification for the enjoyment of civil rights. But the Church was now distinguished for great men, who held high rank, theologians, and bishops, like Augustine, Ambrose, Chrysostom, Gregory, Nazianzin, Basil, Eusebius, and Martin of Tours.

Theodosius defends the church.

Theodosius died in Milan, in the arms of Ambrose, A. D. 395, and with him the genius of Rome expired, and the real drama of the fall of the empire began. He was succeeded by his two sons, Arcadius and Honorius, the one in the East and the other in the West, the former being under the tutelage of Rufinus, the latter under the care of Stilicho, master-general of the armies. Both emperors were unworthy or unequal to maintain their inheritances. The barbarians gained fresh courage from the death of Theodosius, and recommenced their ravages. The soldiers of the empire were dispirited and enervated, and threw away their defensive armor. They even were not able to bear the weight of the cuirass and helmet, and the heavy weapons of their ancestors were exchanged for the bow. Thus they were exposed to the deadly missiles of their enemies, and fled upon the approach of danger. Gainas the Goth, who commanded the legions, slew Rufinus in the presence of Arcadius, who abandoned himself at Constantinople to the influence of the eunuch Eutropius, most

Death of Theodosius.

Arcadius and Honorius.

celebrated for introducing Chrysostom to the court. The eunuch minister soon after was murdered in a tumult, and Arcadius was then governed by his wife Eudoxia, who secured the banishment of Chrysostom.

The empire was now finally divided. A long succession of feeble princes reigned in the East, ruled by favorites and women, at whose courts the manners and customs of Oriental kings were introduced. The Eastern empire now assumes the character of an Eastern monarchy, and henceforth goes by the name of the Greek empire, at first, embracing those countries bounded by the Adriatic and Tigris, but gradually narrowed to the precincts of Constantinople. It lasted for one thousand years longer, before it was finally subdued by the Turks. The history of the Greek empire properly belongs to the mediæval ages. It is our object to trace the final fall of the Western empire.

Final division of the empire.

Under Honorius, the Visigoths, ruled by Alaric, appear in history as a great and warlike people. Stilicho, the general of Honorius, encountered them unsuccessfully in two campaigns, in Macedonia and Thessaly, and the degenerate cities of Greece purchased their preservation at an enormous ransom. In the year 402, Alaric crossed the Alps, and Honorius fled to the marshes of Ravenna, where, protected by the shallow sea, the Western emperors a long time resided. Stilicho gained, however, a great victory over the Goths at Pollentia, near Turin, and arrested the march of Alaric upon Rome. The defeated Goth rose, however, superior to this defeat, celebrated by the poet Claudian, as the greatest victory which Rome had ever achieved. He escaped with the main body of his cavalry, broke through the passes of the Apennines, spread devastation on the fruitful fields of Tuscany, resolved to risk another battle for the great prize he aimed to secure, even imperial Rome. But Stilicho purchased the retreat of the Goths by a present of forty thousand pounds of gold. The departure of Alaric from Italy, which he had ravaged, was regarded by the Roman people as a

Alaric.

Defeat of the Goths.

Stilicho.

complete and final deliverance, and they abandoned themselves to absurd rejoicings and gladiatoral shows.

But scarcely was Italy delivered from the Goths before an irruption of Vandals, Suevi, and Burgundians, under the command of Rodogast, or Rhadagast, two hundred thousand in number, issued from the coast of the Baltic, crossed the Vistula, the Alps, and the Apennines, ravaged the northern cities of Italy, and laid siege to Florence. The victor of Pollentia appeared for the rescue with the last army which the empire could raise, surrounded the enemy with strong intrenchments, and forced them to retire. Stilicho again delivered Italy, but one hundred thousand barbarians remained in arms between the Alps and the Apennines, who crossed into Gaul, then the most cultivated of the Western provinces, and completely devastated its fields, and villas, and cities. Mentz was destroyed; Worms fell, after an obstinate siege; Strasburg, Spires, Rheims, Tournay, Arras, and Amiens, all fell under the German yoke, and Gaul was finally separated from the empire. The Vandals, Sueves, and Alans, passed into Spain, while the Burgundians remained behind, masters of the mountainous regions of Eastern Gaul, to which was given the name of Burgundy, A. D. 409.

Successive barbaric irruptions.

Loss of Gaul to the empire.

The troubles of the empire led to the final withdrawal of the legions from Britain about the time that Gaul was lost, and about forty years before the conquest of the island by the Saxons.

Italy, for a time delivered, forgot the services of Stilicho, the only man capable of defending her. The jealousy of the timid emperor he served, and the frivolous Senate which he saved, removed for ever the last hope of Rome. This able general was assassinated at Ravenna, A. D. 408.

The Gothic king, in his distant camp, beheld with joy the intrigues and factions which deprived the emperor of his best and last defender, and prepared for a new invasion of Italy. He descended like an avalanche upon the plains of Italy, and captured the cities of Aquileia,

Alaric advances to Rome.

Concordia, and Cremona. He then ravaged the coasts of the Adriatic, and following the Flaminian way, crossed the Appennines, devastated Umbria, and reached, without obstruction, the city which for six hundred years had not seen a foreign enemy at her gates. Rome still contained within her walls, twenty-three miles in circuit, a vast population, but she had no warriors. She could boast of a long line of senatorial families, one thousand seven hundred and eighty palaces, and two million of people, together with the spoil of the ancient world, immense riches, and innumerable works of art; but where were her defenders? It is a sad proof of the degeneracy of the people that they were incapable of defense.

Alaric made no effort to storm the city, but quietly sat down, and inclosed the wretched inhabitants with a cordon through which nothing could force its way. He cut off all communication with the country and the sea, and commanded the gates. Famine, added to pestilence, did the work of soldiers. Despair seized the haughty and effeminate citizens, who invoked the clemency of the barbarians. He derided the embassadors, and insulted them with rude and sarcastic jokes. "The thicker the hay, the easier it is mowed," replied he, when warned not to drive the people to despair. He condescended to spare the lives of the people on condition that they gave up *all* their gold and silver, *all* their precious movables, and *all* their slaves of barbaric birth. More moderate terms were afterward granted, but the victor did not retreat until he had loaded his wagons with precious spoil. He retired to the fertile fields of Tuscany, to make negotiations with Honorius, intrenched at Ravenna; and it was only on the condition of being appointed master-general of the imperial army, with an annual subsidy of corn and money, and the free possession of Dalmatia, Noricum, and Venetia, that he consented to peace with the emperor. These terms were disregarded, and the indignant barbarian once again turned his face to the city he had spared. He took

Siege of Rome.

Heavy tribute imposed on Rome.

Alaric master-general.

possession of Ostia, and Rome was at his mercy, since her magazines were in his hands. Again the Senate, fearful of famine, consented to the demands of the conqueror. He nominated Atticus, prefect of the city, as emperor, and from him received the commission of master-general of the armies of the West.

Atticus, after a brief reign, was degraded, and negotiations were opened with Honorius. Repelled by fresh insults, which can not be comprehended other than from that infatuation which is sent upon the doomed, Alaric, vindictive and indignant, once more set out for Rome, resolved on plunder and revenge. In vain did the nobles organize a defense. Cowardice or treachery opened the Salarian gate. In the dead of night the Goths entered the city, which now was the prey of soldiers. For five days and five nights the "Eternal City" was exposed to every barbarity and license, and only the treasures accumulated and deposited in the churches of St. Paul and St. Peter were saved. A cruel slaughter of the citizens added to the miseries of a sack. Forty thousand slaves were let loose upon the people. The matrons and women of Rome were exposed to every indignity. The city was given up to pillage. The daughters and wives of senatorial families were made slaves. Italian fugitives thronged the shores of Africa and Syria, begging daily bread. The whole world was filled with consternation. The news of the capture of Rome made the tongue of St. Jerome cleave to the roof of his mouth, in his cell at Bethlehem. Sorrow, misery, desolation, and despair, were everywhere. The end of the world was supposed to be at hand, and the great churchmen of the age found consolation only in the doctrine of the second coming of our Lord amid the clouds of heaven, A. D. 410.

Sack of Rome.

After six days the Goths evacuated the city, and advanced on the Appian way, to the southern provinces of Italy, destroying ruthlessly all who opposed their march, and laden with the spoil of Rome. The beautiful villas of the Campanian coast, where the masters of the

Evacuation of Rome.

world had luxuriated for centuries, were destroyed or plundered, and the rude Goths gave themselves up to all the license of barbaric soldiers.

At length, gorged with wine and plunder, they prepared to invade Sicily, when Alaric sickened and died in Bruttium, and was buried beneath the bed of a river, that the place of his sepulchre should never be found out. He was succeeded by his brother-in-law, Adolphus, with whom Honorius concluded peace, and whom he created a general of his armies. As such, he led his forces into Gaul, and the southern part of the country became the seat of their permanent settlement, with Toulouse for a capital. The Visigoths extended their conquests on both sides of the Pyrenees; Vandalusia was conquered by his son, Wallia, A. D. 418, on whom the emperor bestowed Aquitania. His son, Theodoric, was the first king of the Goths.

Death of Alaric.

The same year that saw the establishment of this new Gothic kingdom, also witnessed the foundation of the kingdom of the Franks, by Pharamund, and the final loss of Britain. Thus province after province was wrested away from the emperor, who died, A. D. 423, and was succeeded by Constantius, who had married his sister. He died the same year, leaving an infant, called Valentinian. The chief secretary of the late emperor, John, was proclaimed emperor; but he was dethroned two years after, and Valentinian III. six years of age, reigned in his stead, favored by the services of two able generals, Boniface and Aetius, who arrested by their talents the incursions of the barbarians. But they quarreled, and their discord led to the loss of Africa, invaded by the Vandals.

Kingdom of the Franks.

Discords between Boniface and Aetius.

These barbarians also belonged to the great Teutonic race, and their settlements were on the Elbe and the Vistula. In the time of Marcus Aurelius they had invaded the empire, but were signally defeated. One hundred years later, they settled in Pannonia, where they had a bitter contest with the Goths. Defeated by them, they sought the protection of Rome, and enlisted in her armies. In 406 they invaded Gaul, and advanced to the Pyrenees, inflicting every atrocity. They then crossed into Spain, and settled in Andalusia, A. D. 409, and resumed the agricultural life they had led in Pannonia. The Roman governor of Spain intrigued with their old enemies, the Goths, then settled in Gaul, to make an attack upon them, under Wallia. Worried and incensed, the Vandals turned against the Romans, and routed them, and got possession of the peninsula.

The Vandals.

It was then that Aetius, the general of Valentinian III., persuaded the emperor,—or rather his mother, Placidia, the real ruler,—to recall Boniface from the government of Africa. He refused the summons, revolted, and called to his aid the Vandals, who had possession of Spain. They were commanded by Genseric, one of those hideous monsters, who combined great military talents with every vice. He responded to the call of Boniface, and invaded Africa, rich in farms and cities, whose capital, Carthage, was once more the rival of Rome, and had even outgrown Alexandria as a commercial city. With fifty thousand warriors, Genseric devastated the country, and Boniface, too late repenting of his error, turned against the common foe, but was defeated, and obliged to cede to the barbarians three important provinces, A. D. 432.

The Vandals in Africa.

Peace was not of long duration, and the Vandals renewed the war, on the retreat of Boniface to Italy, where he was killed in a duel, by Aetius. All Africa was overrun, and Carthage was taken and plundered, and met a doom as awful as Tyre and Jerusalem, for her iniquities were flagrant, and called to heaven for vengeance. In the sack of the city, the writings of Augustine, bishop of Hippo, were fortunately preserved as a thesaurus of Christian theological literature, the influence of which can hardly be overrated in the dark period which succeeded, A. D. 439.

Fall of Carthage.

The Vandals then turned their eyes to Rome, and landed on the Italian coast. The last hope of the imperial city, now threatened by an overwhelming force,

Vandals in Italy.

was her Christian bishop—the great Leo, who hastened to the barbarians' camp, and in his pontifical robes, sought the mercy of the unrelenting and savage foe. But he could secure no better terms, than that the unresisting should be spared, the buildings protected from fire, and the captives from torture. But this promise was only partially fulfilled. The pillage lasted fourteen days and fourteen nights, and all that the Goths had spared was transported to the ships of Genseric. The statues of the old pagan gods, which adorned the capitol, the holy vessels of the Jewish temple, which Titus had brought from Jerusalem, the shrines and altars of the Christian churches, the costly ornaments of the imperial palace, the sideboards of massive silver from senatorial mansions,—the gold, the silver, the brass, the precious marbles,—were all transported to the ships. The Empress Eudoxia, herself, stripped of her jewels, was carried away captive, with her two daughters, the sole survivors of the family of Theodosius.

Sack of Rome by the Vandals.

Such was the doom of Rome, A. D. 455, forty-five years after the Gothic invasion. The haughty city met the fate which she had inflicted on her rivals, and nothing remained but desolation and recollections.

The fall of Rome.

While the Vandals were plundering Rome, the Huns—a Sclavonic race, hideous and revolting barbarians, under Attila, called the scourge of God, were ravaging the remaining provinces of the empire. Never since the days of Xerxes was there such a gathering of nations as now inundated the Roman world—some five hundred thousand warriors, chiefly Asiatic, armed with long quivers and heavy lances, cuirasses of plaited hair, scythes, round bucklers, and short swords. This host, composed of Huns, Alans, Gepidæ, and other tribes, German as well as Asiatic, from the plains of Sarmatia, and the banks of the Vistula and Niemen, extended from Bash to the mouth of the Rhine. The great object of attack was Orleans—an important strategic position.

The Huns.

The leader of the imperial forces was Aetius, banished for

the death of Boniface, composed of Britains, Franks, Burgundians, Sueves, Saxons, and Visigoths. It was not now the Romans against barbarians, but Europe against Asia. The contending forces met on the plains of Champagne, and at Chalons was fought the decisive battle by which Europe was delivered from Asia, and the Gothic nations from the Mongol races, A. D. 451. Attila was beaten, and Gaul was saved from Sclavonic invaders. It is said that three hundred thousand of the barbarians, on both sides, were slain.

Battle of Chalons.

The discomfited king of the Huns led back his forces to the Rhine, ravaging the country through which he passed The following year he invaded Italy.

Aetius had won one of the greatest victories of ancient times, and alone remained to stem the barbaric hosts. But he was mistrusted by the emperor at Ravenna, whose daughter he had solicited in marriage for his son, and was left without sufficient force. Aquileia, the most important city in Northern Italy, fell into the hands of Attila. He then resolved to cross the Apennines and give a last blow to Rome. Leo, the intrepid bishop, sought his camp, as he had once before entreated Genseric. The Hun consented to leave Italy for an annual tribute, and the hand of the princess Honoria, sister of the Emperor Valentinian. He retired to the Danube by the passes of the Alps, and spent the winter in bacchanalian orgies, but was cut off in his career by the poisoned dagger of a Burgundian princess, whose relations he had slain.

Attila in Italy.

The retreat of the Huns did not deliver the wasted provinces of a now fallen empire from renewed ravages. For twenty years longer, Italy was subject to incessant depredations. Valentinian, the last emperor of the family of Theodosius, was assassinated A. D. 455, at the instigation of Maximus—a senator of the Anician family, whose wife had been violated by the emperor. The successive reigns of Maximus, Avitus, Majorian, Severus, Anthemius, Olybrius, Glycerius, Nepos, and Augus-

Retreat of the Huns.

The last emperors.

tulus—nine emperors in twenty-one years, suggest nothing but ignominy and misfortune. They were shut up in their palaces, within the walls of Ravenna, and were unable to arrest the ruin. Again, during this period, was Rome sacked by the Vandals. The great men of the period were Theodoric—king of the Ostrogoths, who ruled both sides of the Alps, and supported the crumbling empire, and Count Ricimer, a Sueve, and generalissimo of the Roman armies. It was at this disastrous epoch that fugitives from the Venetian territory sought a refuge among the islands which skirt the northern coast of the Adriatic—the haunts of fishermen and sea-birds. There Venice was born—to revive the glory of the West, and write her history upon the waves for one thousand years.

The last emperor was the son of Orestes—a Pannonian, who was christened Romulus. When elevated by the soldiers upon a shield and saluted Augustus, he was too small to wear the purple robe, and they called him Augustulus!—a bitter mockery, recalling the foundation and the imperial greatness of Rome. This prince, feeble and powerless, was dethroned by Odoacer—chief of the Heruli, and one of the unscrupulous mercenaries whose aid the last emperor had invoked. The throne of the Cæsars was now hopelessly subverted, and Odoacer portioned out the lands of Italy among his greedy followers, but allowed Augustulus to live as a pensioner in a Campanian villa, which had once belonged to Sulla, A. D. 476. Odoacer, however, reigned but fourteen years, and was supplanted by Theodoric, king of the Ostrogoths, A. D. 490. The barbarians were now fairly settled in the lands they had invaded, and the Western empire was completely dismembered.

Odoacer.

Theodoric.

In Italy were the Ostrogoths, who established a powerful kingdom, afterward assailed by Belisarius and Narses, the generals of Justinian, the Eastern emperor, and also by the Lombards, under Alboin, who secured a footing in the north of Italy. Gaul was divided among

Gothic kingdom of Italy.

the Franks, Burgundians, and Visigoths, among whom were perpetual wars. Britain was possessed by the Saxons. Spain became the inheritance of Vandals, Suevi, and Visigoths. The Vandals retained Africa. The Eastern empire, with the exception of Constantinople, finally fell into the hands of the Saracens.

Division of the empire among barbarians.

It would be interesting to trace the various fortunes of the Teutonic nations in their new settlements, but this belongs to mediæval history. The real drama of the fall of Rome was ended when Alaric gained possession of the imperial city. "The empire fell," says Guizot, "because no one would belong to it." At the period of barbaric invasion it had lost all real vigor, and was kept together by mechanism—the mechanism of government which had been one thousand years perfecting. It was energy, patriotism, patience, and a genius for government which built up the empire. But prosperity led to luxury, self-exaggeration, and enervating vices. Society was steeped in sensuality, frivolity, and selfishness. The empire was rotten to the core, and must become the prey of barbarians, who had courage and vitality. Three centuries earlier, the empire might have withstood the shock of external enemies, and the barbarians might have been annihilated. But they invaded the provinces when central power was weak, when public virtue had fled, when the middle classes were extinct, when slavery, demoralizing pleasures, and disproportionate fortunes destroyed elevation of sentiment, and all manly energies. A noble line of martial emperors for a time arrested ruin, but ruin was inevitable. Natural law asserted its dignity. The penalty of sin must be paid. Nothing could save the empire. No conservative influences were sufficiently strong—neither literature, nor art, nor science, nor philosophy, nor even Christianity. Society retrograded as the new religion triumphed, a mysterious fact, but easily understood when we remember that vices were universal before a remedy could be applied. The victories of Christianity came not too late for the human race, but too late for the salvation of a worn-out empire.

Reflections on the fall of the empire.

The barbarians were advancing when Constantine was converted. The salvation of the race was through these barbarians themselves, for, though they desolated, they reconstructed; and, when converted to the new faith, established new institutions on a better basis. The glimmering life-sparks of a declining and miserable world disappeared, but new ideas, new passions, new interests arose, and on the ruins of the pagan civilization new Christian empires were founded, which have been gaining power for one thousand five hundred years, and which may not pass away till civilization itself shall be pronounced a failure in the present dispensations of the Moral Governor of the World.

THE END.